DEEDS OF VALOR

How America's Civil War Heroes
Won The
Congressional Medal
of Honor

Edited by
W.F. Beyer and O.F. Keydel

Illustrated

SMITHMARK

This edition published in 2000 by SMITHMARK Publishers, a division of U.S. Media Holdings, Inc., 115 West 18th Street, New York, NY 10011.

SMITHMARK books are available for bulk purchase for sales promotion and premium use. For details write or call the manager of special sales, SMITHMARK Publishers, 115 West 18th Street, New York, NY 10011.

Published by special arrangement with Platinum Press

Library of Congress Cataloging-in-Publication Data

Deeds of valor: how America's Civil War heroes won the Congressional Medal of Honor / edited by W.F. Beyer and O.F. Keydel.
       p. cm.
      Originally published: Stamford, CT : Longmeadow Press, 1994.
      ISBN 0-7651-1769-X
      1. United States--History, Military--To 1900--Anecdotes.
2. United States--History, Naval--To 1900--Anecdotes. 3. United States--Armed Forces--Biography. 4. Medal of Honor. 5. Military decorations--United States. 6. United States--History--Civil War, 1861-1865--Sources. 7. United States--History--Civil War, 1861-1865--Personal narratives. I. Beyer, Walter F. II. Keydel, Oscar F. (Oscar Frederick), b. 1871.

E181 .D385 2000
973.7'6--dc21   99-087289

Printed in the United States of America

10 9 8 7 6 5 4 3 2 1

The Congressional
MEDAL OF HONOR

THE ARMY

EXTRACT FROM REGULATIONS RELATIVE TO THE MEDAL OF HONOR.

B Y DIRECTION of the President, the following regulations are promulgated respecting the award of Medals of Honor:

Medals of Honor authorized by the Act of Congress approved March 3, 1863, are awarded to officers and enlisted men, in the name of the Congress, for particular deeds of most distinguished gallantry in action.

In order that the Congressional Medal of Honor may be deserved, service must have been performed in action of such a conspicuous character as to clearly distinguish the man for gallantry and intrepidity above his comrades — service that involved extreme jeopardy of life or the performance of extraordinarily hazardous duty. Recommendations for the decoration will be judged by this standard of extraordinary merit, and incontestible proof of performance of the service will be exacted.

Soldiers of the Union have ever displayed bravery in battle, else victories could not have been gained; but as courage and self-sacrifice are the characteristics of every true soldier, such a badge of distinction as the

THE NAVY

Congressional Medal is not to be expected as the reward of conduct that does not clearly distinguish the soldier above other men, whose bravery and gallantry have been proved in battle. * * *

Recommendations for medals on account of service rendered subsequent to January 1, 1890, will be made by the commanding officer at the time of the action or by an officer or soldier having personal cognizance of the act for which the badge of honor is claimed, and the recommendation will embrace a detailed recital of all the facts and circumstances. Certificates of officers or the affidavits of enlisted men who were eyewitnesses of the act will also be submitted if practicable.

In cases that may arise for service performed hereafter, recommendations for award of medals must be forwarded within one year after the performance of the act for which the award is claimed. Commanding officers will thoroughly investigate all cases of recommendations for Congressional Medals arising in their commands, and indorse their opinion upon the papers, which will be forwarded to the Adjutant-General of the Army through regular channels.

INTRODUCTION

During the progress of the War of Rebellion, in July, 1862, and March, 1863, Congress provided by joint resolution for Medals of Honor for most distinguished gallantry in action. Under the regulations of the War Department pursuant to these joint resolutions it is provided that every soldier and sailor in the service of the United States who, outside of the strict line of his duty and beyond the order of his superiors, performed an act of conspicuous bravery of advantage to the service, should be rewarded by receiving a "Medal of Honor," specially struck for that purpose, on satisfactory proof being presented of the circumstances of the act. From the beginning of the War of the Rebellion to the opening of the war with Spain, only about 1,400 of these medals were granted, including all those given for services in the Indians Wars which intervened. For services in the Spanish War, only 26 medals were awarded. When it is considered that nearly two million men served in these wars, and that their course was marked with innumerable gallant actions, the signal merit of these actions which earned the medals and the care with which the proof was scrutinized, may be better appreciated. Mere recklessness of danger, when duty is to be performed or orders obeyed, is a common attribute of all American soldiers, and those who received the Medal of Honor were doubtless, in many cases, more fortunate in opportunity rather than braver of heart than their comrades; yet the fact that less than 1,400 out of two millions wear this badge of heroism marks the wearers as soldiers of extraordinary merit and heroism.

The official record of these stories of heroic deeds in the service of the Republic is of the most meager character, a mere line, with the name of the individual, his company and regiment, and a brief phrase designating the character of his achievement, without any of the details which would give it life and dramatic interest. It scarcely rises above the form of a tabular statement. As time passed, the heroes of these deeds were rapidly disappearing from the stage of life, and soon all recollection of the essential features of their achievements, would be buried in the graves of those who performed and witnessed them. The design of this work was to gather these details together, verified by the medal bearers, their superior officers, or other witnesses, and present them to the American public in a form worthy of the subject.

The work has been by no means an easy one. It involved several years of arduous pursuit by the compilers, voluminous correspondence and exhaustive search; but it has been accomplished with a degree of completeness which was hardly to be expected. The compilers have had the advantage of the zealous assistance of every officer of the army to whom they applied, access to the official reports of the War Department, and written reports of the incidents from the medal holders themselves. So far therefore, as historical accuracy is concerned, there is little apology to be made for the work. As to its literary merit, it may be said that much of it is in the simple and modest language of the heroes themselves, who have minimized their own merits, and taken from their narratives much of the dramatic interest which a disinterested witness would have found in the deeds they performed. Many of the incidents, on the other hand, have been related by officers who were witnesses of the deeds of their subordinates, and who had the literary skill to mark and describe them in the manner they deserved, but without exaggeration for embellishment.

The editing of the work was committed to competent hands, whose chief purpose was to eliminate crudities, and to avoid extravagant expressions to which such a work was easily liable. Whatsoever may be its demerits, its publishers may at least fairly claim that it is a truthful and modest narration of the most heroic personal achievements of our soldiers during the past half century, verified by competent officers, and sustained by proofs which have been accepted by the Government of the United States as evidence of the facts which deserved the distinguishing acknowledgment of the Medal of Honor.

Henry M. Duffield

Brigadier-General, U.S. Volunteers

COMPILERS' PREFACE

The pages of our country's history abound with instances of the most lofty courage, which thrill the pulse and kindle the spirit of every true patriot. Congress itself has singled out many of these instances and given them special recognition. It has provided for a medal, known as the "Medal of Honor." It is the nation's grateful acknowledgment of a great and heroic deed, a reward for such gallant services in action as make him who renders them conspicuous among his comrades.

The heart beats faster and the blood courses through the veins more rapidly, as one reads these simple stories published in the heroes' own modest words. These narrations speak for themselves. Editorial embellishment could only detract from their value.

To the contributors of these narrations, and all who have assisted in this task, and especially to General Lewellyn G. Estes and Captain James R. Durham, Washington, D.C., and His Excellency, Hazen S. Pingree, Governor of the State of Michigan, the compilers feel themselves deeply indebted.

The compilers submit this work for the approval of the American people, hoping that their effort to preserve these heroic episodes in a permanent and worthy form, before all recollection of them has passed away, will not have been in vain, and that the result will be a monument to remind generation after generation of Americans of the heroism of their fathers.

THE WAR OF SECESSION

PRELIMINARY EVENTS

IF it is conceded that the question of slavery constituted the main point at issue which led to the tremendous struggle now known as the War of Secession or the Civil War, then the very beginnings of this great commonwealth show us clearly the presence of two antagonistic principles that made the coming of this struggle eventually inevitable. Those principles were represented in the cargoes of two ships which entered the American waters at the end of the second decade of the seventeenth century within the short time-space of nineteen months, the first, a Dutch vessel, unshipping a load of African negroes on the banks of the James river in 1619, the second, the Mayflower, landing her company of white liberty-seekers in Plymouth Bay in the following year.

In the wording of the Constitution of the United States of America the term "slave" was carefully avoided, three provisions in it, though, relating to slaves. By the time of the Declaration of Independence, however, the necessity and righteousness of slavery had become a creed in the South, which grew in intensity as the years passed on and the demand of the English mills for Southern cotton increased. In the meanwhile the territory of the United States grew at the astonishing rate so well known to recent history, and in the same proportion grew the anti-slavery feeling in the North. So when the important question arose whether or not to allow slavery in the newly developed territories the first heavy clash occurred between the two opposing principles. At last the breech reached its climax with Abraham Lincoln's election as president by the Republican party, on a platform declaring that Congress forbid slavery in the Territories.

South Carolina, the most pronounced opponent to any anti-slavery movement, called a convention which, on the 20th of December, 1860, unanimously passed an ordinance declaring that the union between South Carolina and the other States was thereby dissolved. Within two months Mississippi, Florida, Alabama, Georgia, Louisiana and Texas passed similar ordinances. These were quickly followed by seizures of the United States forts, arsenals and custom houses within the seceding states, and by the establishment of a Confederate Government, with its capital at Montgomery, Alabama, in February, 1861, with Jefferson Davis as provisional President and Alexander H. Stephens Vice-President.

Although there were still eight slave-holding states out of the Confederacy there was no apprehension on the part of the latter's government as to their ultimate joining, but the great prize to capture now was Virginia, both because of her own power and resources, and because her accession to the Confederacy would necessarily bring North Carolina also. But at an election of delegates to a convention to consider the question of secession, the Unionist majority was no less than sixty thousand, and on the fourth of April, when President Lincoln had been in office for a month, that convention refused, by a vote of 89 to 45, to pass an ordinance of secession. Now in the Confederate Constitution there was a provision that empowered Congress to "prohibit the introduction of slaves from any State or territory not belonging to the Confederacy." Yet it was in this very line of trade that proud Virginia held great possessions. Her export of slaves into the cotton States, especially the new territory of Texas, was enormous, amounting to about 50 percent of the whole trade ; Virginia's share in 1835 for instance being computed at 40,000 slaves valued at $24,000,000.

Under the circumstances the Confederate constitutional clause mentioned above meant nothing less than economic disaster for this State ; the ordinance of secession was taken up again and on April 17th the Virginian convention passed it in secret session by a vote of 88 to 55. Governor Letcher, without awaiting the date it was to take effect, six weeks distant, immediately turned over the entire military force and equipment of the State to the Confederate authorities, and the seat of the Confederate Government was transferred from Montgomery to Richmond. Arkansas and North Carolina followed the example of Virginia during May. In Tennessee the struggle over the two principles lasted until June when the Confederates literally captured this State. Maryland, West Virginia, Kentucky, and Missouri went finally with the Union after more or less desperate struggles, about which more anon.

An incident that hastened the catastrophy was the attack on Fort Sumter, in Charleston Harbor, on April 12th. The history of this now famous event is interwoven with rumors and intrigues. This much seems certain that Lieutenant-Colonel J. L. Gardner, who commanded the place in 1860, was relieved by the War Department on account of his having asked for reinforcements during November of this year. The new Commander, Major Robert Anderson, a Kentuckian, was beyond any reasonable doubt believed to sympathize with the Confederates, but Secretary of War J. B. Floyd learned soon that in this respect he was entirely mistaken. Anderson reported immediately after his arrival that in his conviction the people of South Carolina would by force of arms capture all the forts in the harbor as soon as their ordinance of secession be voted through. At that time of the three forts in Charleston Harbor: Sumter, Castle Pinckney and Moultrie, only the latter had a garrison ; Anderson requested immediate reinforcements and garrisons for all the forts, " if the government determines to keep command of the harbor."

It was a much less determined letter which had caused the recall of Col. Gardner, but Major Anderson's demand found a most energetic supporter, much to the discomfiture, undoubtedly, of the Secretary of War, in the person of the Secretary of State, the venerable Mr. Lewis Cass. In spite of this the Southern faction in the War-Department succeeded in frustrating completely all attempts to secure reinforcements. In consequence General Cass resigned his office as Secretary of State on the 17th of December. A delegation from South Carolina was in the meanwhile " negotiating " with the President about maintaining the " Relative Military Status " in Charleston Harbor. The members of the Delegation found fault with Anderson, who had moved his garrison from Fort Moultrie to Fort Sumter on December 26th. In face of the aspect of an imminent outbreak the Major had thought it best to occupy the latter fort after spiking the guns and destroying the gun-carriages in Moultrie. The North was delighted at this " audacious " move, unnecessarily though, since the people were under the wrong impression that the War-Department or the President had caused this move. However, the general outburst of patriotic sentiment in the Northern States compelled the President to approve Anderson's move. Major Anderson was not only in a difficult, but also extremely delicate and morally desperate position. Imagine his feelings at reading a letter from the Secretary of War which, among other things, contained the following passages : " Under these instructions "—referring to the verbal instructions received by Major Buell and requesting the Commander in case of an attack to resist the attackers to the last extremity—" you might infer that you are required to make a vain and useless sacrifice of your own life and the life of the men under your command, upon a mere point of honor. This is far from the President's intentions . . . . It is neither expected nor desired that you should expose your own life or that of your men in a hopeless conflict in defense of these forts. If they are invested or attacked by a force so superior that resistance would, in your judgment, be a useless waste of life, it will be your duty to yield to necessity, and make the best terms in your power.

This will be the conduct of an honorable, brave and humane officer, and you will be fully justified in such action. These orders are strictly confidential ,and not to be communicated even to the officers under your command without close necessity."

By the trend of public opinion in the North, President Buchanan was forced furthermore to announce in a message to Congress, on the 8th of January, 1861, that he felt it an imperative duty to hold the Charleston forts as public property. On December 29th Secretary of the War Floyd deemed it timely to hand in his resignation.

In the meantime the South Carolina militia had taken possession of the abandoned forts Moultrie and Castle Pinckney, and on the 30th of December the militia-men seized the United States arsenal in Charleston. Batteries were begun to be built by the South Carolinaians about Sumter the day after its occupation by the little National force of nine officers and seventy-three men.

On the 9th of January, 1861, the merchant steamer "Star of the West" tried to make the entrance of the harbor, with a relief-force of 200 men under Lieutenant Wood; but, one of the newly erected land batteries opening fire at her, the vessel turned back to sea.

On the 11th of January the Commander at Fort Sumter received the peremptory demand of the Governor of South Carolina to surrender the fort. The intrigues planned during the following weeks to cause the National garrison to be withdrawn are so many that there is not space enough here to narrate them in detail. They all failed. According to Lieut.-Col. Thomas A. Anderson, who certainly for good reasons must be considered the main authority on this subject, Major Robert Anderson himself was of the opinion that "all three forts or none should have been held." As to the Commander's reluctance to take the initiative in opening fire upon the seceded and aggressive Carolinians it must be said that had he done so Kentucky, his native State, would beyond all doubt have been lost for the Union, not to mention several other difficult complications that would have considerably increased the already heavily embarassed situation for the North.

On the same day the "Star of the West" started south on her resultless relief-trip, the 5th of January, there was a secret caucus held in Washington by the Southern leaders in which the first real plain for the rebellion was laid out and sanctioned by four resolutions which it is not deemed necessary to reproduce here.

On the 4th of March, 1861, Mr. Lincoln was inaugurated as President and four weeks later he gave orders to send a relief-squadron to Fort Sumter. Thereupon the Southern General Beauregard demanded again the surrender of the fort and, this being refused by Anderson, opened fire on April the 12th. After a defense of thirty-four hours until, according to Major Anderson's official report, "the quarters were entirely burned, the main gates destroyed by fire, the gorge walls seriously injured, the magazine surrounded by flames, its door closed from the effects of the heat, four barrels and three carriages of powder only being available, and no provisions remaining but pork," the Union Commander accepted the terms of evacuation offered by the Southern General. On Sunday, the 14th of April, the small Union force marched out of the fort, with colors flying and drums beating; the dies were cast, the inevitable must now take its course.

On that same Sunday President Lincoln wrote down his proclamation, issued on the 15th, in which he called for 75,000 militia for three months, stating "that the laws of the United States have been for some time past, and now are, opposed, and the execution thereof obstructed in the States ... (follow the names of the seven original secession States), by combinations too powerful to be suppressed by the ordinary course of judicial proceedings or by the powers vested in the marshals by law." A special session of Congress was called for July the 4th.

The result of this proclamation must have been astounding to even the most fervent and enthusiastic patriot in the Union; the Confederates were certainly very disagreeably shaken by it; for the whole vast North moved forward as one man; it was as if one single, huge, irresistible wave of the most thrilling enthusiasm had seized the twenty millions of the North. As if by magic recruiting stations appeared everywhere, from every public or suitable private building the Stars and Stripes were wafting, the inspiring guide-mark for the eager and ubiquitous volunteer seeking where to enlist.

But the real magnitude of the step taken by the South, and of the task for whose final solution both sides were clamoring now, with the certainty of utter ruin as a result for at least one of them, was then in no way comprehended or felt by those who now prepared to grapple with it. Not until after the four fearful years did people begin to realize what it had meant and what had to be met to save the Union and secure its future growth and prosperity.

There was no military or naval preparedness then whatever in the vast country. The North had the crude advantage of numbers, as two to one. in the raw material; the South could pride itself of having gained for its cause the ablest trained naval and military leaders from the "Old Service." In the Old Navy it was one of its characteristics that while the seamen came almost exclusively from the North the overwhelming majority of the line-officers were Southerners; and at the first sign of the impending war over forty percent of all the naval officers went with the South. So much greater the honor then to the most famous of our sea-heroes, Old Farragut, who was stationed in Virginia at that critical period and at the time when Robert E. Lee cast his fate with that of his State, refused to be "dragooned out of the Union with Virginia." — Another feature that counted much more to the advantage of the South than the one just mentioned was the colossal system of espionage established by the friends of Confederacy at Washington. During the greater part of the war no important measure was taken or order issued by the Federal authorities without the Confederate headquarters being immediately and promptly informed of their full contents and reach. Never before or after had an attacker been enabled to observe and report so openly and fully the ways and means his opponent was trying to prepare for defense. And so peculiar were the circumstances that no remedy was found against this all-pervading evil.

JOHN C. HESSE,

Corporal, Co. A. 8th U.S. Infantry.

While the raw regiments of the Union, pouring into the Capitol as fast as they could be gotten together, were equipped and drilled in over-haste in order to secure the defense of Washington, the struggle in Missouri, Kentucky and Maryland for deciding their preference in the question became more and more intense, and the formation of West-Virginia as a separate and anti-slavery State was realizing.

The first bloodshed occurred on the 19th of April, 1861, at Baltimore, when, two days after the President's proclamation, the Sixth Massachusetts Infantry arrived there on its way to Washington. On that day the mob attacked a battalion of this regiment which had to march across the city to reach its railroad station. The mob, calling the soldiers "nigger-thieves" and similar names, finally fired into the battalion which returned the fire. Several of the rioters were killed and also three infantry men. Their bodies were sent back for burial to their native State—they were the first of an alas! almost endless list of "victims of the war" to follow. The excitement in Maryland was aroused by this incident to such intensity in favor of the South that many Unionists believed this State then lost for their cause.

On the 23rd of April happened a deed which secured for its performers the first "Medals of Honor" Congress issued a year later. Among those United States troops which were surrendered to the Government of the seceding States shortly after the latter had declared their secession, was the small military post at San Antonio, Texas, held by a detachment of the Eighth U. S. Infantry. The secessionist Colonel Van Doorn seized the post, and the few officers and men forming the garrison were made prisoners, but paroled at once and permitted to go north the best they could. At the suggestion of an officer, Lieutenant Hartz, two non-commissioned officers, Sergeant-Major Joseph K. Wilson and Corporal John C. Hesse, secured in the former headquarters-office the flag which the regiment had carried through the

Mexican War, took the torn colors from the staff, and Hesse concealed it by winding it around his bare body. They passed unmolested through the dense line of Secessionist sentinels and left San Antonio the next day for the North. On the 20th of May they turned the flag over to the regiment at Washington, D. C. Both Wilson and Hesse were awarded the Medal of Honor for fearlessness and loyalty, and thus their names are heading the distinguished list of heroes to which almost every subsequent battle in this great war furnished new additions.

On the 24th of May occurred the killing of Colonel Ellsworth, the commander of the New York Fire Zouaves. On that night this regiment, being one of four detached to occupy the Arlington Heights in protection of Washington, reached Alexandria where a Confederate flag had been long observed flying from the staff of a hotel. Ellsworth himself tore it down. While he was coming down the stairs the proprietor murdered him by firing a shotgun into him. One of the accompanying soldiers shot the murderer dead immediately, and Ellsworth's name became a by-word of great power at the time being.

In Missouri meanwhile the crisis had attained its climax. Governor Claiborne F. Jackson with, Southern sympathies, called out the State militia to go into a camp of instruction near St. Louis during the first week of May. As the 20,000 stand of arms in the Government arsenal there had been removed in time by the officer in charge, Captain Lyon, to Springfield, Ill, Jackson asked for and obtained the necessary supply of arms and cannon from the Confederate authorities. General John Fremont having pointed out to the President the utmost importance of the possession of the immediate Mississippi Valley, and consequently, the State of Missouri, the Federal authorities sent a small reinforcement placed under the command of the fearless Captain Lyon mentioned above. Lyon had gathered a force, mostly consisting of Germans, at St. Louis and from the neighboring counties, armed it in haste and, marching it out to the State Camp, surrounded the latter and caused the State forces, about six hundred and thirty men, to surrender. A great crowd had by this time gathered witnessing the spectacle, and as their sympathies were with the South, the clash was inevitable and came quick. As the mob insulted Lyon's troops and even fired into them one of Lyon's German regiments fired back killing twenty-eight of the rioters, men, women and children. The prisoners were paroled twenty-four hours later. But the capture of this camp and the accompanying bloodshed had greatly increased the antipathy among the State populace against the North, and the indefatigable Lyon saw himself compelled to resort to arms again. On the 17th of June he dispersed a force of State militia at Boonville and caused the Governor to flee. However, in spite of his energy, the outcome of the First Bull Run nourished the flame of Southern enthusiasm anew, and it was only after Fremont had taken possession of the State with an overwhelming Federal force that its adherence to the Unity was finally secured. Lyon fell fighting the Missourians and Arkansans at Wilson's Creek near Springfield, on the 10th of August. This extraordinary man, a bachelor, left all his property, at the value of about $30,000, to the Federal Government for war purposes.

Kentucky intended from the beginning to remain neutral although the greater part of the populace sympathized with the South. Neutrality proved, of course, to be impossible as soon as the war began raging all around. While a great number of individual Kentuckians took service with the South the Union Government succeeded, though, in saving the State as such for the Union which became an acknowledged fact during the fall of '61.

Maryland's adherence to the cause of the North was secured during May although this State furnished many champions for the Confederacy on the numerous battlefields.

While thus the haze was slowly or rapidly raised from over the doubtful border slave-states the first regular encounter of the great war, the "First Battle of Bull Run," came to pass on the 21st of July, 1861.

THE FIRST BATTLE OF BULL RUN

CONSIDERATIONS other than strictly military compelled the Federal authorities to inaugurate a campaign toward Richmond as early as the beginning of July although the army in and around Washington, under command of General Irwin McDowell, was yet in no way trained and fitted for such a task. But the northern populace, impatient, although ignorant of the circumstances of war, was crying incessantly their "on to Richmond," and it became imperative to do something to smother this growing restlessness.

On the natural line of defense formed by the Bull Run the Confederate General G. T. Beauregard was known to hold a position with over 20,000 troops to cover Manassas Junction, then the railroad centre of Northern Virginia, with General Joseph E. Johnston and about 10,000 men in the Shenandoah Valley as a possible support. McDowell was to offer battle to Beauregard while General Patterson was sent with a force to prevent Johnston from joining the Confederate main force. McDowell's army of five divisions, these under Generals Hunter, Heintzelman, Tyler, Miles and Runyon, reached the neighborhood of the Bull Run on July 18th. On this day the outposts of the opposing forces came together in a skirmish at Blackburn's Ford. In this engagement Private Chas. F. Rand, of the Twelfth New York Infantry, gained the Medal of Honor by distinguished bravery. The enemy's overwhelming fire having driven all of his battalion to the rear he held his ground until the Southerners, impressed with such uncommon loyalty and courage, would not fire at this single, brave man. After his ammunition had been spent he succeeded in working his way back unhurt and reached his command.

On the 21st the main forces of the opposing armies came together at Sudley's Ford and here the real battle of the "First Bull Run" commenced.

Tyler's demonstration at the Stone Bridge, which was to have enabled Burnside's flanking column to fall upon the enemy's rear, was feeble, and the flank movement was discovered, and met by Evans with a detachment. The rebels were repulsed, and the center of the action was transferred to the Henry House plateau, where the Confederates were re-enforced and the Union Army was at length entirely routed, falling back to Washington in utter confusion. The Union Army lost in killed, wounded, and missing 2,952 men, while the Confederates lost 1,782 men. The first severe battle was lost for the Union, still there were cases of individual distinction which brought the Medal of Honor to several men on the Union side.

One of the men thus distinguished was Lieutenant Adelbert Ames, of the famous Griffin Battery, the D Battery of the Fifth U. S. Artillery, which went into the battle with Porter's, the first brigade of the second division. When the fatal moment came where the two batteries, Griffin and Ricketts, were exposed to the tremendous close range fire of the enemy on the plateau near Henry House, and their infantry supports failed them completely, Ames who commanded a section, was struck down by a shot shattering his thigh. Sitting on the limber he continued to direct the fire of his section in the midst of the terrible fracas of shot and shell until a wheel of the gun carriage was smashed and the gun disabled. Under the galling fire of the enemy Corporal McGough and the remaining men of the decimated gun crews fixed up a spare wheel as directed by Ames, and succeeded to bring this gun away, the other five and those of Ricketts' battery were lost.

Another heroic act was performed by Sergeant John G. Merritt, Company K, First Minnesota Infantry. Just before the battle he obtained permission to take four men and attempt the capture of a Confederate flag. He selected Sergeant Dudley, Privates Duffee and Grimm and a man whose name remains unknown.

When Ricketts' battery sent grape and cannister into the enemy's lines Merritt thought his opportunity come ; he and his companions rushed upon a Confederate color-bearer. They knocked the man down, Merritt seized the flag, and they tried to make their way back. But the Confederates pursued them firing furious volleys which killed Grimm, the unknown man and Duffee and wounded Merritt in the leg. Still he held on to his prize until a Confederate, overtaking the wounded man, struck him down with the butt of his musket and recovered the flag. Merritt, assisted by Dudley, finally managed to reach his own regiment.

A DARING ESCAPE FROM LIBBY PRISON

CHARLES J. MURPHY,

1st. Lieut., 38th N. Y. Vols.
Highest rank attained: Colonel.
Born in Stockport, England, June 3, 1832.

" AT BULL RUN, VA., July 21, 1861, this officer, then a first lieutenant, and R. Q. M., Thirty-eighth New York Volunteers, took a rifle and fought with his regiment in ranks. When the regiment was forced back, he voluntarily remained on the field with the wounded, was taken prisoner, confined in Libby Prison, thence escaped, and after great suffering and privation, made his way into the Union lines and rejoined his regiment."

The above is the brief, official record of a feat of gallantry and an experience of hardship and suffering which is deserving of more detailed description.

After the battle, when his position was at the rear with his wagon trains, Lieutenant Murphy was repeatedly urged to leave the field with the routed army, but steadfastly refused, on the ground that not one man could be spared from care of the wounded, and chose rather to risk death or capture than leave the men to die uncared for.

His zealous and efficient aid to the surgeons won him the sobriquet of "Doctor," which clung to him at Manassas and Richmond prisons, where he was sent after his capture. He says: "After reaching Manassas, the rebels, believing me to be a doctor, offered me parole, but when I found that a sufficient number of surgeons was to return to attend the wounded, I peremptorily refused to accept it, and was taken prisoner to Richmond, from which place, with two companions, Captain J. R. Hurd and Colonel Wm. H. Raynor, I effected an escape, after the most unheard of sufferings and privations."

There was a large number of prisoners, sick or wounded crowded together in the buildings, and the suffering was so terrible that several Union surgeons, who were prisoners, were permitted to assist in caring for them. Upon giving their parole, they were provided with red rosettes, and allowed to pass from one prison to another, and also to go about the city. Among these was Lieutenant Murphy, though not on parole, and, when not on hospital duty, always accompanied by an armed guard.

Captain Hurd, Colonel Raynor, and Lieutenant Murphy planned to escape, by passing the guards, wearing red rosettes cut from Captain Hurd's red flannel shirt. They succeeded in getting out of the city, and started on their painful and hazardous journey north, traveling as rapidly as possible through the night, and hiding in the thickets by day, never moving forward by daylight, unless under cover of the dense forest, and never free from apprehension of pursuit and discovery. Though unarmed they had resolved to fight against any odds, and to sell their lives as dearly as possible rather than submit to recapture.

They suffered terribly from sore feet, and even more from thirst, but, undiscouraged, pressed on. For eleven days they struggled on over rough country roads, through underbrush and dense woods, enduring hunger and thirst, pain and fatigue, chased by rebel sympathizers, passing themselves off as rebel soldiers, encountering every kind of obstacle, hardship, and suffering. but still undismayed, and determined to reach their goal.

When they reached Lower Cedar Point it seemed that their troubles must be over, for a Union Revenue Cutter was anchored in the river, but the captain made no response to their hail, and soon weighed anchor and sailed down the river. This disappointment was a terrible blow to the poor fugitives, who, like shipwrecked sailors, had been elated to the highest pitch in hope of relief, by a sail on the horizon, only to be cast into greater despair than ever by its disappearance. They passed the night in anxiety and discouragement, surrounded by the rebels, and tormented by reflection on their past suffering and present situation.

In the morning. however, the Cutter returned, and the captain decided to take the risk of coming closer and taking them aboard. The neighborhood was dangerous, and he had thought their signal in the night a decoy of the enemy to get his men ashore.

The three were sent to Washington on a tug, and when they stepped ashore Captain Hurd said: "Boys, I have lived twenty-seven days in the Rocky Mountains on mule's meat, with the snow four feet deep, but that was nothing to the hardships we have just gone through."

AT LIBBY PRISON.

A HERO OF THREE BRAVE DEEDS

WALTER JAMIESON,
Sergeant, 189th N. Y. S. V.
Highest rank attained:
Lieutenant.
Born at Boulogne, France, 1842.

IN JUNE, 1861, Lieutenant, then Sergeant Jamieson, first distinguished himself as a soldier. It was at Arlington Heights, Va., and in reference to the deed he says: "We had a drove of forty head of cattle in camp, and the rebels managed to get them away one night. The officers and men were furious at the loss, because beef was needed to properly prepare the men for the work in the trenches. A detail was ordered out from each regiment of cavalry and infantry present. I was one of the detail of the Twenty-eighth. We marched past Bailey's crossroads on the Fairfax Courthouse road, deploying and scattering through the woods in search of the missing cattle, but without success. Late in the afternoon we were recalled and ordered to return to camp.

"I made up my mind to find those cattle, so I stole away alone, expecting to return to camp during the night. About sundown I found the missing cattle hidden in a ravine, and started to drive them to camp. A man who had charge of them came rushing up. Seeing my gray militia uniform, he mistook me for a Confederate and yelled out: 'You damn fool, don't you know that the Yankee cavalry is out after these cattle? Keep 'em here until night.' By this time he had come up to me, so I brought my rifle down on him, and told him I was one of those 'Damned Yankees': that I was sorry to have come across him, but as the affair stood he would have to help me drive the cattle into camp. The arguments I used were strong and convincing and he agreed.

"The two of us brought the cattle in before daybreak, but at one time my success looked dubious in the extreme. I stumbled over a stump, had a bad fall and my gun landed several feet away from me. The rebel got to it first, but I was upon him before he could straighten up. We had a little tussle, during which my early training in boxing served me well, and I frightened him so that he tried no more tricks on me during the remainder of the trip. We reached Bailey's crossroads and the outside pickets before daybreak in safety. The sight of the cattle was countersign enough, and we passed all the pickets. I took the rebel to the guardhouse and reached my own tent just as reveille sounded at headquarters."

From June 1 to July 20, 1861, there were frequent skirmishes and engagements in Virginia, West Virginia, Maryland, and Missouri, in which the advantage was in favor of the Federals. At none of the engagements during this period did the opposing forces exceed 4,000.

LIEUTENANT JAMIESON'S second conspicuous act of bravery is related as follows: "On the 29th of July, 1864, we occupied the entrenchments on the right of the line of works in front of Petersburg, Va., our brigade resting on the bank of the Appomattox River. The fighting during the night had been severe and the intense heat of the previous day had not abated when morning came.

RECAPTURING A DROVE OF CATTLE

"After swallowing my coffee and hard-tack, I took my rifle and went to my lookout hole to see how the field appeared by daylight. It looked far worse than the day before, most of the wounded had died. The body of the captain that I had so often looked at regretfully was nowhere to be seen. What could have happened to him, I wondered. I was sure he could not have been carried away, for we had watched the field too closely by the musketry flashes for that to be accomplished. During the forenoon some of our men made him out, over near the other side, and, sure enough, he was alive, lying on his back, fanning himself with a rebel hat—a black one with a very broad rim. Some rebels had gotten to him during the night and swapped hats.

"The heat was terrible, but the firing on both sides never ceased. Towards evening it was reported that we were to be relieved as soon it grew dark. As I gazed at the poor captain, my feelings got the better of me, and I made up my mind not to let the poor fellow die there in agony. As the evening closed in, my resolution to save him grew more fixed. I wanted it to be just dusk, but not so dark that the men could not see the loopholes of the enemy and make it dangerous for any one to look through.

"So I studied the gloaming. I got an empty cracker box, stood it on end against the breastworks and, climbing upon it, told the men to throw it over after me. Then out I sprang, headforemost, with such force that I landed away out on the abatis among the dead, where I tried to appear as one whose last fight is fought. I kept quiet for some minutes, and saw that my comrades, whom I had left, were getting to work in earnest and firing rapidly, which would keep the enemy from the loopholes. This gave me fresh courage, and I started to crawl along the ground, pushing the dead bodies so as to cover my movements on my return.

"When I reached the spot where the captain lay, I could feel the concussion of the rebel guns upon my face. I lay alongside of him and whispered to him to roll upon my back. With my load I started to crawl towards our lines, making a few inches with each effort, until I reached the abatis. I could not pull him through, and asked some one to lend me a hand. The orderly sergeant of Company C, of our regiment, jumped over to me. It was now getting dark, so we lifted him over the sticks and threw him into the arms of our comrades. I found a stretcher, and with the aid of some men carried him to the Ninth Corps Hospital."

AGAIN at Fort Harrison, Lieutenant Jamieson and Sergeant Wolff captured the fort entirely unaided.

"Fort Harrison was one of the many forts upon the main line of the defenses of Richmond, built to resist General McClellan in 1862. The works were large and substantial and mounted sixteen heavy guns. To capture this fort it would be necessary for some one to lead on the boys, who, though brave enough, could not face the withering fire of the protected enemy. Giving my gun to Wolff and telling him to follow me, I seized our flag and started to try to plant it on the enemy's fortifications. With a rush we reached a place beneath their walls, and then, with his aid, I crawled to the top, letting down the flagstaff for him to crawl up the side. Then another scramble, and we stood at the top of their earthworks. At the sight of the flag the Confederates, thinking we were followed by large numbers, turned and fled, all but a few who surrendered.

"Thereupon I waved the flag around my head and planted it on the top of the defense. Our men now came up and took possession of the fort, which we held against all efforts of the rebels to retake it."

ONLY SEVEN

ABIATHER J. KNOWLES,
Private, Co. D, 2d Maine Infantry.
Born at La Grange, Maine, March 15, 1830.

ACCORDING to the official report, Private A. J. Knowles was honored for "removing dead and wounded under heavy fire." He relates his experience briefly.

"On the 21st of July, after a des perate charge on a hill held by the rebels, the Second Maine Infantry, of which I was a member, was ordered to fall back. The colonel, seeing that a number of the men were left where they had fallen, asked for volunteers to go with him to bring them within the lines. When the colonel called for volunteers seven of us stepped forward and signified our willingness to go with him.

"The colonel then addressed the regiment, saying: 'Are these seven men the only ones of the Second Maine who will follow their colonel to pick up the wounded?'

"Not another man advanced, and, led by the colonel, we proceeded, under a withering fire, to pick up our wounded and bring them within our lines."

AN EXCITING CHASE

A FEW days prior to the 10th of August, 1861, the term of service of the First Iowa Infantry had expired, and they were asked whether they would take their discharges or remain in service until after the expected battle at Wilson's Creek. The men, with one accord, decided to remain in service, all of them

Wilson's Creek.—In the month of August, 1861, General Lyon, with a force of 5,500, was at Springfield, Mo., confronting 12,000 of the enemy under McCullough and Price.

After a skirmish at Dug Springs on the 1st, the Union force retreated to Springfield.

On the 9th, General Lyon moved against the enemy, sending General Sigel, with 1,200 men and six guns to gain his rear by the right.

The frontal attack, led by General Lyon, was energetic and effective, but the flanking party was overwhelmed, losing five guns and more than half of its men.

General Lyon was killed at the head of his column, and, the news of Sigel's disaster reaching the main division, the troops fell back to Springfield. The Union loss was 1,236: the Confederate, 1,095.

being eager for action. Private Nicholas Bouquet, a member of Company D of this regiment, describes his experience in the battle as follows:

"We all wanted to have a whack at the Rebels before going home, and, as luck would have it, Company D, to which I belonged, along with Company E, were detailed by Lieutenant-Colonel Merritt to support Totten's Battery. This order brought us into a hand-to-hand contest with the enemy, and, although we were engaging a superior force, we four times repulsed them.

"When the retreat of our forces was ordered, after General Lyon had fallen, one of the guns of Totten's Battery had been left behind, because one of its horses had been killed.

NICHOLAS BOUQUET,
Private, Co. D, 1st Iowa Infantry.
Born in Bavaria, Germany, Nov. 14, 1842.

"Being this time on the skirmish line, I was called by the gunner of the piece to help catch a riderless horse which was galloping about the field between the lines. To catch this horse was to save the gun from falling into the enemy's hands — a most important factor in battle.

"The enemy were closing in upon us, but, with the thought of saving the gun, not heeding the rain of bullets from both lines, we started after the horse, and in a short time had him. Leading him with all possible haste to the abandoned gun, we soon had him hitched to it, and away we went, following the retreating regiment, and in a short time had it safely within the lines of our army."

The first important movement after Bull Run, though skirmishes and minor actions were of almost daily occurrence, was the capture of **Fort Henry,** on the Tennessee River, on the 6th of February, 1862, followed on the 16th by the surrender of **Fort Donelson** and 15,000 Confederate troops. The operations were conducted by General Grant in co-operation with Commodore Foote and resulted in breaking the Confederate lines at the west, giving control of the Mississippi River above Vicksburg to the Federal Government.

New Berne, N. C.— Burnside's attack on New Berne, N. C., was a feature of his Roanoke Expedition, in January, 1862, in which he was supported by the fleet in command of Flag Officer Goldsborough. The force consisted of 31 gunboats, 11,500 troops, and a fleet of small vessels for transportation.

On the 14th of March he attacked New Berne.

The place was taken, together with 46 heavy guns, 3 batteries of light artillery, and a supply of stores, while Burnside's loss was 90 killed and 466 wounded.

RESCUED 1,000 ROUNDS OF AMMUNITION AND A WOUNDED COMRADE

ELWOOD N. WILLIAMS,
Private, Co. A, 28th Illinois Infantry.
Born in Philadelphia, Pa., Nov. 11, 1842.

"AFTER two hours of hard fighting at the battle of Shiloh," says Private Elwood N. Williams, "we were ordered to beat a retreat, with the Thirty-second Alabama Infantry close at our heels. Our force, though inadequate, fought unflinchingly, and for a time maintained a successful resistance.

"In the heat of the action a box containing a thousand rounds of ammunition was inadvertently left between the lines. Colonel Johnson was informed of the fact and immediately called for volunteers to recover the box. W. P. Price a former schoolmate of mine, and I volunteered to do this.

"The box lay about one thousand yards from our lines, and in order to reach it under the heavy fire of both sides, we were compelled to crawl on our hands and knees. We reached the box in safety, but while we were returning with it, Price fell mortally wounded.

"I then shouldered the box and started off for our lines, expecting momentarily to meet the fate of Price. Luckily, however, I succeeded in safely delivering the box, and was greeted by my fellow soldiers with cheers.

"Having safely delivered the box, it was now my duty to look after my wounded comrade, and I immediately returned and brought him within the lines. I turned him over to the care of the hospital corps, where twelve days later he died from the effects of his wounds."

Shiloh.—In March, 1862, a force was posted at Shiloh, or Pittsburg Landing, on the Tennessee River, to watch the operations of the enemy gathering at Corinth. The force was gradually increased to a strength of about 32,000, consisting of the divisions of McClernand, Prentiss, Hurlbut, Lew Wallace, and Sherman, under command of General U. S. Grant.

On the 6th of April the troops were engaged in action, which lasted two days. On the evening of the 16th, when fortune seemed against the Federals, they were re-enforced by General Buell with three divisions, aggregating 18,000 men. The next day they assumed the offensive and swept the enemy from the field.

The Confederate Army, commanded by General Albert Sidney Johnston, was 45,000 strong, and suffered a loss of 10,694.

The Union killed and wounded amounted to 9,195 with 3,122 taken prisoners.

THE MITCHELL RAIDERS

(1) MARK WOOD,
   Private, Co. C, 21st Ohio Inf.

(2) W. J. KNIGHT,
   Private, Co. E, 21st Ohio Inf.

(3) DAN'L. A. DORSEY,
   Corp., Co. H, 33d Ohio Inf.

(4) ROBT. BUFFUM,
   Private, Co. H, 21st Ohio Inf.

(5) *J. A. WILSON,
   Private, Co. C, 21st Ohio Inf.

JAMES SMITH

(6) WM. BENSINGER,
   Private, Co. G, 21st Ohio Inf.

(7) WM. REDDICK,
   Corp., Co. B, 33d Ohio Inf.

(8) JOHN WOLLAM,
   Private, Co. C, 33d Ohio Inf.

(9) W. A. FULLER.

(10) W. W. BROWN,
   Private, Co. F, 21st Ohio Inf.

*SAM'L. ROBERTSON

(11) *SAM'L. SLAVENS,
   Private, Co. E, 33d Ohio Inf.

(12) E. H. MASON,
   Serg't., Co. K, 21st Ohio Inf.

(13) M. J. HAWKINS,
   Corp., Co. A, 33 Ohio Inf.

(14) *MARIAN A. ROSS,
   Serg't-Maj., 2d Ohio Inf.

(15) JOHN R. PORTER,
   Private, Co. G, 21st Ohio Inf.

*WM. CAMPBELL

(16) JACOB PARROTT,
   Private, Co. K, 33d Ohio Inf.

(17) *JOHN M. SCOTT,
   Serg't., Co. F, 21st Ohio Inf.

(18) ANDREW MURPHY.

(19) WM. PITTINGER,
   Serg't-Maj., 21st Ohio Inf.

*J. J. ANDREWS

*PERRY SHADRACK

NOTE.—*Hanged at Atlanta, Ga., as spies.

THE MITCHELL RAID

ONE of the most interesting and thrilling incidents of the early campaigns of 1862, as an exploit of reckless daring, if not of successful strategy, was this celebrated railroad raid, organized with the purpose of destroying the rebel line of communication with Chattanooga, and placing that important stronghold at the mercy of General Mitchell's forces.

The raid was led by James J. Andrews of Kentucky, who had previously acted as a spy for General Buell. The expedition consisted of twenty men of the Second, Twenty-first, and Thirty-third Ohio regiments, who volunteered for the service, and two civilians.

Wearing citizens' clothes, and carrying only side-arms, they proceeded from General Mitchell's camp at Shelbyville, Tenn., to Chattanooga, in detachments of three or four, representing themselves to be Kentuckians on their way to join the Confederate Army. From Chattanooga they made their way to Marietta, Ga., which was to be the starting point for the raid.

On the morning of the 12th of April they boarded a train loaded with rebel troops and ammunition, and rode to Big Shanty (now Kenesaw Station), having bought tickets to different stations along the line to disarm suspicion. At Big Shanty the train stopped, and the conductor, engineer, and many of the passengers went out to breakfast, leaving the train unguarded

The little band immediately took possession, uncoupled a section of the train, consisting of three empty box-cars, the locomotive and tender, and started at full speed on their wild ride through the enemy's country to Chattanooga.

The plan was, by cutting the telegraph wires and tearing up the track, to destroy all means of communication east and south, preventing the re-enforcement of the garrison at Chattanooga, and leaving the way clear for General Mitchell, who, with a detachment from his division, was at this very moment moving on the town by rail from Huntsville, Ala., one hundred miles to the west.

The train was run at a furious rate of speed, stopping occasionally to enable the men to tear up the rails and cut the wires. At the stations where he was compelled to stop, Andrews replied to all inquiries that he was running an impressed powder train through to General Beauregard.

The only difficulties ahead were the extra trains flying south from General Mitchell's forces, whose approach had stampeded the enemy. The danger was all in the rear, where another engine in charge of Anthony Murphy, master-mechanic and superintendent of the road, assisted by the conductor and engineer of the captured train, was gradually gaining on them in spite of the obstacles in its way. The pursuers had started on a hand car, which had run off the track at one of the breaks in the road, had been obliged to proceed on foot for some distance, and had finally pressed into service a locomotive and a company of soldiers.

Delayed by the south-bound trains as well as by the necessary work of destruction, the Union men lost valuable time, while the Confederates seemed able to surmount all obstacles. The chase was as desperate as the flight, the issue almost equally vital to pursuer and pursued.

At Kingston the Federals were only four minutes ahead, and, at their next halt, the whistle of the enemy's engine was heard while they were pulling up the rails. The rebels saw the obstruction in time to avoid a wreck, but had to leave their engine and start again on foot. The relief to the fugitives, however, was slight, for, before going far the rebels stopped and reversed a south-bound train, and continued the chase.

From Calhoun there was a clear track to Chattanooga, but the pursuers were gaining rapidly. The fugitives dropped a car which was taken up and pushed ahead by the engine in the rear. The Federals broke out the end of their last box-car, and dropped cross-ties on the track, checking slightly the progress of the rebels, and gaining enough time to get in wood and water at two stations. Several times they stopped, and almost succeeded in lifting a rail, but each time the Confederates, coming within rifle range, compelled them to give up the attempt. As a final desperate effort they set fire to their third and last car, and as they passed over a long, covered bridge at Oostenaula, uncoupled it and left it in the center of the bridge. The Confederates were upon the bridge before the fire had gained much headway, and the pursuing engine, dashing through the flame and smoke, drove the car before it to the next side-track. Every effort had failed that ingenuity could devise and reckless courage execute, and, on the very threshold of success, it was plain that escape was impossible. Fuel was now very low, and, though the locomotive was urged to its greatest speed, swaying and trembling from its tremendous impulse, it was a question of very few minutes before it would have to be abandoned.

As it began to slow down the signal was given for a general *sauve-qui-peut*, but the little band was at once overpowered. They were taken to Atlanta, where the leader and seven of his men were tried by court-martial, condemned, and executed.

The others were kept in prison until the following October, when, agreeing among themselves that death by a bullet would be preferable to the scaffold, they planned an escape, a venture quite as desperate as that upon which they had embarked in the spring, but, fortunately, more successful. By a concerted attack upon the guards they managed to escape, but only eight of them reached home, after a most terrible experience, thus described by one of the survivors:

"In just forty-eight days and nights, for the nights should be counted, since under cover of darkness we made most progress, we reached the Federal lines, footsore and worn to skeletons. We were forced to wade streams, swim swift-running rivers, scale mountains, and at the same time be constantly on the alert against the enemy, who were always around us. The thought that capture meant certain death alone kept us on the march. No person can describe our sufferings—God only knows what we were forced to endure.

"To gain rest in sleep was impossible. To close our eyes in unconsciousness was only to dream of pursuit by bloodhounds, of the huge scaffold on the outskirts of Atlanta, where our friends had been hanged, and where, it was said, we should share the same fate; or of a sudden attack in which a bullet would have been more merciful than man."

A PLUCKY CHARGE

SAMUEL E. PINGREE,
Captain, Co. F, 3d Vermont Infantry.
Born at Salisbury, N. H., Aug. 2, 1832.

"ON THE 16th of April, 1862," Captain Pingree, who led the charge at Lee's Mills, Va., narrates "General McClellan confronted the enemy, entrenched along the Warwick and south of Yorktown. No attempt to force the line had been made, although cannonading at long range and musketry firing at close quarters had been brisk.

"About the middle of the afternoon two companies of my regiment, supported by two others were selected to attack the enemy's line on the other side of the creek, and to capture and hold a crescent battery and the lines of rifle pits protecting it. My company, which headed the assault, was deployed quite closely. Unclasping their waist-belts, each held high his cartridge-box in the left hand and his rifle in the right. As soon as the batteries on the slope in the rear ceased firing, both companies started for the creek. The enemy at the same time opened fire from the rifle-pits across the stream.

"The water was breast high in the narrow channel, but shallower on both sides of it, about two hundred feet wide, mostly artificial flowage for a line of defense, and was further obstructed with felled trees.

"In spite of the deadly fire of the enemy, the two companies pushed on, and, without a halt on the other shore, dashed straight for the rifle-pits and battery, driving the enemy into the woods. Shouts of triumph went up and signals of success were waved back to our lines. The two supporting companies followed us up and joined in holding the captured works. The line of the Warwick was broken. We anxiously waited for the arrival of the head of the division which was to follow us if we found the crossing possible, but no assistance came.

"The enemy rallied from their panic, and with several regiments hastened to attack our little party of less than two hundred rifles. `

"We had lost heavily while fording the stream, and now the men were falling fast as the enemy rallied against us in overwhelming force. Messengers were sent back twice, explaining the situation and asking for re-enforcements or orders to fall back.

"As we rushed for the rifle-pits, I received a wound below the left hip, which for a few moments prostrated me and benumbed my left leg so that I could not rise, but I soon recovered, and, finding no bones broken, continued to lead the men on, as our orders were to capture and hold the works till re-enforcements came. It was a critical moment when the Fifteenth North Carolina came charging down upon us at a run, but the well-directed fire of the brave Vermonters checked and hurled them back, extending their confusion to the two Georgia regiments on their right.

"It was at this stage of the fight that my right hand was disabled by a shot which tore away my right thumb. While these attacking regiments were reorganizing for an assault on our position, the order came to fall back across the river, which we did, helping our wounded along.

"The fight had lasted forty minutes. Out of the fifty-two officers and men of my company, twenty-seven were killed or wounded, and of the three hundred and ninety-two men engaged, forty-five per cent were killed or wounded."

A GALLANT DRUMMER BOY

DRUMMER LANGBEIN was the smallest member of the drum corps in his regiment, and his face and figure was so plump and girlish, that he was known to all his comrades as "Jennie," a nickname given to him by a soldier of the regiment who said that the lad looked just like his sweetheart at home in the North.

The battle of Camden, or South Mills, N. C., known to the Confederates as the battle of Sawyer's Lane, though not one of the most famous in the War of the Rebellion, was a hotly contested engagement nevertheless. It occurred during the expedition sent to destroy the Culpeper Lock at the southern end of the Dismal Swamp Canal, in the rear of the city of Norfolk, Va. One ot its notable features was a charge by the Hawkins' "Zous," not so disastrous as the one at Antietam, but quite as daring. It was during this mad dash that Adjutant Thomas L. Bartholomew, who had promised "Jennie's" mother to keep special watch over her boy, and between whom and the boy the closest comradeship existed, was struck by a fragment of an exploding shell, which made a frightful wound in his neck. He did not fall at once, but in the delirium of pain staggered outside the ranks, and in a moment was between the hostile lines. In time of action, it is the duty of the musicians to act as an ambulance corps; to look after the wounded and to carry them on stretchers to the rear. Yet it is not part of the drummer's work to unnecessarily expose himself; indeed, it is expected that he will shelter himself as much as possible, since, if the members of the ambulance corps are killed, fighting men must leave the ranks to take their places. Little "Jennie" Langbein, however, had no notion of looking out for his own safety. When the order was given to charge he went with his regiment, with a sharp eye for disabled comrades, and especially for Adjutant Bartholomew.

JULIUS C. J. LANGBEIN,

Drummer, Co. B, 9th N. Y. Volunteers
(Hawkins' Zouaves).
Born, Sept. 29, 1846, in Germany.

Seeing his friend's terrible position, the boy rushed up to him through the rain of bullets, and screaming shot and shell, caught him as he was wandering deliriously and aimlessly about, and managed to pilot him to a comparatively quiet place to the rear towards the hospital field.

The wounded man was pronounced by the regimental surgeon "nearly dead" and "not worth while to remove," but young Langbein would not abandon his friend. Securing the assistance of a stronger comrade, he managed to carry the unconscious man to a house near by.

Later in the day the Confederates were re-enforced, and the Federals had to retreat in such haste, that there was no question of taking care of the wounded. The adjutant would have been abandoned had it not been for the continued devotion of his little friend, who managed to get him into the army wagon, and stayed by him till he was safe in the Federal hospital at Roanoke.

"WHAT IN H--L ARE WE HERE FOR?"

MICHAEL A. DILLON,
Private, Co. G, 2d New Hampshire Infantry.
Born at Chelmsford, Mass., Sept. 29, 1839.

ABOUT four o'clock on the morning of May 5, 1862, Hooker's division, after a night march through a drenching rain, over muddy roads, with but two hours of rest, came upon the enemy before Fort Magruder, near Williamsburg, Va. A hotly contested battle ensued between Hooker's forces, about nine thousand men, and a vastly superior number. The Union skirmish line was advanced through a mass of fallen timber on the right of Williamsburg road, close to Fort Magruder, and kept up a severe fire at short range. Longstreet, who commanded the Confederates' rear, had passed beyond Williamsburg, but turned back with re-enforcements to crush, if possible, Heintzelman's corps. Charge after charge was made from the fort, but could not release the grip with which Hooker's men held the enemy's left. The battle raged until four o'clock in the afternoon in a heavy rain. Hooker's ammunition was nearly exhausted, and he had vainly appealed for re-enforcements.

Sumner, coming upon the field, relieved Heintzelman, who hastened to the field where Hooker was engaged. He gathered drummers, fifers, buglers, and other musicians to the number of a hundred or more pieces, and directed them to play. "Play anything, 'Yankee Doodle,' 'Hail Columbia,' anything," he ordered. As the music swelled above the din of the fight with increased volume and resonance, the failing courage of the wearied men was revived, and the cry went up: "Hold on, boys, re-enforcements are coming!" Stubbornly and hopefully they continued the contest, until Kearney's arrival afforded Hooker's tired, but not dispirited men the relief which they sorely needed.

During one of the charges of the enemy it had been found impossible to withdraw one of our batteries, and four guns fell into the enemy's hands as our lines were being pressed back. Then occurred the incident which displayed the courage of young Dillon, and won for him the Medal of Honor awarded by Con-

---

Williamsburg, Va.—After the evacuation of Yorktown by General Magruder, May 4, 1862, the rebels were pursued by our forces under Hooker. At Williamsburg, on the 5th, the enemy made a stand, and the attack was made by Hooker, who was checked by the heavy firing from Fort Magruder. He was re-enforced by General Kearney, and the enemy was compelled to retire at night.

The Union loss was 2,200; the Confederate, 1,000.

gress for conspicuous bravery. Seeing the pieces in the hands of the enemy, he sprang to his feet and rushed forward, begging his comrades to follow and re-take the guns. His lieutenant, seeing him thus exposed to the enemy's fire, and fearing it might be concentrated upon the position which they occupied, shouted to him: "Get down, Dillon, you are drawing the enemy's fire."

Dillon exclaimed: "What in hell are we here for? Come on, boys, come on! We mustn't let them take that battery." And, with arms raised high in air pleading for men to follow him, he rallied a gallant group, all boys like himself,

PRIVATE DILLON AT FORT MAGRUDER

rushed into the thickest of the fight, repulsed and drove back the enemy, and rescued Battery H, First United States Artillery.

Dillon received a bad check shot before success. He was struck in the leg by a ball, which felled him; but a moment before the recapture he was venting his wrath in forcible language at the loss of his musket, which was wrenched from his grasp by an exploding shell and shattered into fragments. Staunching the flow of blood, and picking up the musket of a fallen comrade, he pluckily resumed his place and continued the fight until he had the satisfaction of wit-nessing the final repulse of the enemy.

On the 18th of June. just prior to the battle of Oak Grove. General Hooker called for volunteers to take a redoubt of the enemy on the right of the Williamsburg road. Young Dillon was among the first to report by stepping to the front. His lieutenant ordered him to fall back, remarking: "We cannot spare you; there is going to be desperate work to-day, and we need you with us." Dillon, who was aching to get another whack at the enemy, replied: "So does General Hooker need desperate work done, and has called for volunteers, and I am going." He seized his musket. said good-bye to his lieutenant. and joined what seemed like a forlorn hope. Away they started and were soon charging across an open field in the face of a deadly fire from artillery and musketry, leaving many comrades dead and wounded, as they advanced upon the run. The redoubt was reached, the parapet gained, and Dillon was among the first in the short, sharp, and deadly conflict, in which he and his comrades were victorious. They took many prisoners and held the fort until Hooker advanced his lines.

Another brave deed mentioned in his Medal of Honor award was performed by Private Dillon on hands and knees. At the battle of the 25th of June, or the first of the seven days' desperate fighting in front of Richmond, during a lull in front of the Second New Hampshire Volunteers, Dillon performed an act that displayed his coolness as well as his disregard of the ι .. o which he voluntarily exposed himself. He crawled on his hands and knees through the grass and among the bushes, in advance of the line, into the enemy's camp, overheard the details of Longstreet's plans, returned safely, and communicated the information to General Hooker, thereby enabling the general to rearrange his forces in such a manner as to repulse the enemy.

At the battle of Groveton, on the 29th of August, 1862, in which the Federal brigade of John Gibbon and part of Abner Doubleday's were engaged, Dillon again distinguished himself, but was badly wounded. It was while the Second New Hampshire were doggedly retreating step by step from the ground gained before, and attempting to form a new line, that the enemy in turn made a charge upon them. Sergeant Marshall, who was with Dillon, said: "Come, Dillon, we have got to go, they are charging us." Dillon answered: "Not before that color-bearer is downed." He discharged his gun, and lowered both colors and bearer of the Forty-ninth Georgia, but at the same moment he himself dropped, shot through the lungs, the bullet passing through his body and breaking three ribs. In spite of his desperate wound, after partly recovering and receiving his discharge. he returned to the army and served throughout the war.

JOHN N. COYNE,

Sergeant, Co. B, 70th New York Infantry.
Born in New York City, Nov. 14, 1839.
Highest rank attained: Lieutenant-Colonel.

"LET'S CAPTURE THEIR COLORS, BOYS!"

WHEN the enemy were overtaken at Williamsburg the Third Excelsior, of the Seventieth New York Volunteers, was in advance. It was a dark, rainy morning. A heavy vapor covered the field, and the smoke of the battle obscured the scene. As the supporting regiment approached, the enemy, who were concealed in the thick woods, sent up the cry: "Show your colors!" The color-bearer waved the flag, and, as its folds spread out and showed the stars and stripes, the rebels advanced from the woods and opened fire. The fire was returned so effectively that they were driven back. Another advance, with re-enforcements, was also repulsed by the valiant Excelsiors.

After several hours of conflict the ammunition became exhausted, and the New Yorkers were ordered to fall back by companies. Sergeant Coyne's company, which during the latter part of the battle was under his command, the captain and lieutenant having been disabled, became separated, and a number of them, missing their way, found themselves with their leader confronted by a party of the enemy surrounding their color-bearer.

"Let's capture their colors, boys!" shouted Coyne, and, with a ringing cheer, the little band made a dash for the enemy. Coyne singled out the color-bearer and rushed upon him. The rebel was too strong to be conquered by such an assault, and defended his flag bravely until a bullet, shattering his right hand, forced him to loosen his hold and enabled Coyne to drag the trophy from him. Tearing the flag from the staff and tying it around his body, he turned to offer battle to any one who should attempt to retake it; but the survivors of

the enemy were hurriedly leaving the field before a rescuing party sent by General Heintzelman. Of the brave band who had supported their leader but few remained standing, and Sergeant Cook, Corporal Beekman, and Privates Howard and Lynch were killed outright.

Sergeant Coyne received the commission of second lieutenant to date from the battle. He was mentioned for bravery in general orders by General Heintzelman, and was advanced to the rank of lieutenant-colonel for several other acts of gallantry during the war.

THREE DEEDS OF VALOR

"AT WILLIAMSBURG I performed one of the deeds for which Congress awarded me a Medal of Honor. I was out on the skirmish line with our company at the time, and after holding our position for some time, the firing of the enemy was so severe that we were compelled to retreat. This we did slowly, paying back shot for shot.

JOHN H. HAIGHT,
Sergeant, Co. G, 72d New York Infantry.
Born at Westfield, N. Y., July 1, 1841.

"We had retreated to a place of comparative safety, when I noticed that my comrade, R. B. Wilson, was missing, having been wounded or killed in the retreat. My captain called for some one to volunteer to assist him in bringing Wilson off the field. I volunteered, and we started for the late scene of action.

"Not knowing exactly where he had fallen, we spent some time in searching for him. At last we found him and started with him for our lines. While we had been looking for him the enemy had completely surrounded us and cut off our escape. I tried to attract their attention so that the captain could manage to escape, and in so doing was shot in the left groin, received a pretty severe scratch across both legs, and a buckshot wound in the belt.

"I fell, and was immediately taken prisoner, but the next day, when they found I was unable to walk I was let out on parole. I managed to return to my company, then at Harrison's Landing."

"ON AUGUST 27, 1862, at the battle of Bristow Station, I was suffering greatly from a severe carbuncle on my neck. On this account I was ordered to the rear before the battle commenced. From my dreary position I could hear the distant rattle of musketry, and longed to be with my comrades. Soon I began to formulate schemes whereby I could rejoin my regiment. I gave this up and decided simply to forget my orders and join my company. Here I fought until the battle was over, when I fainted and had to be carried from the field."

SERGEANT JOHN H. HAIGHT, who relates the above two stories, also participated in the second battle of Bull Run, or Manassas, on the 29th of August, 1863. The company, to which he belonged, was flanked and compelled to fall back upon the main body of the brigade. When the retreat had been completed the captain called for volunteers to rescue any wounded that would otherwise fall into the hands of the Confederates. Sergeant Haight and two others immediately volunteered for the service. They advanced towards the enemy's lines under a heavy fire, and succeeded in bringing out Private Plumb and several others whose names are not known.

A BOLD STROKE

MAY 5, 1862, Captain George W. Mindil, of Company C, Sixty-first Pennsylvania Infantry, distinguished himself for conspicuous gallantry while aide on General Kearney's staff. His heroism was also rewarded with a colonelcy, he being at the time only nineteen years old.

At Williamsburg Captain Mindil's position as aide gave him considerable freedom of action, and realizing that a bold stroke was necessary, he organized and led a desperate charge, with a battalion of the Fortieth New York.

In the face of a terrific fire from the enemy's infantry and artillery, which was doing great destruction in the Federal ranks, this young officer led his men into the very midst of the rebel force, pierced their center, silenced some of their guns, and, getting in their rear, forced them to abandon their position.

FIRED THE BRIDGE

WILLIAM TAYLOR'S military career is distinguished by two most daring deeds. The first of these was the burning of a bridge at Front Royal, Va., May 23, 1862, where a detachment of Stonewall Jackson's force fell upon and routed a body of General Banks', with a loss of 904 men. Taylor, in company with another man, volunteered to rush forward, in the face of a deadly fire from the enemy, and destroy this bridge to prevent the rebels from crossing. The rush was made in safety, although shot flew all around them, until they neared the place where they were to fire the bridge. Here Taylor's companion was killed, and he himself severely wounded in the right hand. Nevertheless he succeeded in firing the bridge and so prevented an attack by the Confederates.

WILLIAM TAYLOR,
Sergeant, Co. H, 1st Maryland Infantry.
Highest rank attained: Captain.

His second notable adventure took place at the Weldon Railroad, Va., August 19, 1864, after he had been promoted a lieutenant. About this Captain Taylor says:

"On the evening of August 19, during a heavy rain, the rebels charged with a yell. Our brigade was on the extreme left, with the brigade of regulars on our right, who broke and ran. A little later the rebels retreated, and we held the ground until the regulars were brought back.

"That night a regiment of our brigade was sent out on picket line, which they left and came into camp, through some misunderstanding. It was reported to General Warren, who sent an order to Acting Brigadier-General Dushain to send an officer and a few men to find connections of the rebel picket line. I volunteered and took two men with me.

"It was a dark, rainy night. On the way we ran foul of two men whom we mistook for rebels, and made prisoners. They turned out to be officers of our division.

"We found the picket line and came back, and finding Colonel Wilson about to start with the regiment, I took the right and made connections with the picket line. I was then detailed, with Captain McClellan of General Ayres' staff, with sixteen men and a sergeant, to reconnoiter the enemy's position. Leaving the men inside our lines, Captain McClellan, the sergeant and I got through the enemy's lines, and close to a house, where Heath, the rebel general, had his headquarters. The captain and I started to return to our men, leaving the sergeant behind, but were captured on the way, the sergeant being taken shortly after.

DESTROYING THE BRIDGE AT FRONT ROYAL, VA.

"We were sent to Petersburg the next day, and from there to Richmond, and remained in Libby Prison about two months, until Fort Harrison, some four miles below, was taken. Later on I managed to escape in company with two other officers. The hardships that we had to undergo to reach our freedom would be interesting enough, but they do not belong to the incidents for which I received my Medal of Honor."

WITH AN EMPTY GUN

Private Delano J. Morey, Co. B, 82d Ohio Infantry, a native of Licking Co., Ohio, gives the following interesting account of his capture of two rebel sharpshooters:

"When our regiment left Moorefield, Va., where we had been encamped all winter, and was ordered to re-enforce General Milroy, a detail of fifty men, of which I was a member, was sent out to look for bushwhackers, who infested the woods. After traveling over fifty miles of the roughest roads, we re-joined our regiment at McDowell on the 8th of May, 1862, hungry as wolves, but supplied with a few choice specimens of poultry, which we had incidentally taken prisoners of war. These some of us were eating with all the ardor of hungry men, when the report of the pickets' guns aroused us, and as this was to be our first battle our chickens were left behind in our anxiety to have a brush with the enemy. But oh! had we known the strength and numbers of the enemy, we should have been reluctant to attack them; but, eager for a fight, we advanced on Bull Pasture Mountain. We engaged them at this point, and in the midst of the roar of battle came the erroneous order to fix bayonets and charge them. About 150 of us, on the extreme right of the line, from which the order emanated, fixed our bayonets and charged the enemy down in the valley. Down the mountain side we went, to within about a hundred yards from them, when they opened fire on us which was too high, and not a man was touched. We in turn emptied a volley into them, when we found to our surprise that our 150 men were charging about 4,000 of the enemy. No sooner were we aware of this fact than a hasty retreat was made up the mountain side, but I, noting two of the enemy some little distance from me, left the retreating men and made for the two sharpshooters with the intention of capturing them. When they saw me coming on the full run they hastened to load their guns, but I was a little too quick for them. I leveled my empty gun at them and ordered them to surrender, which they promptly did, and I led the captives to my captain. I was sixteen years old, and each of my prisoners was old enough to be my father."

A YOUNGSTER'S HEROISM

"I LEFT home without money or a warning to my parents," writes William Horsfall "and in company with three other boys, stealthily boarded the steamer 'Annie Laurie,' moored at the Cincinnati wharf at Newport and billed for the Kanawha River that evening, about the 20th of December, 1861. When the bell rang for the departure of the boat, my boy companions, having a change of heart, ran ashore before the plank was hauled aboard, and wanted me to do the same. I kept in hiding until the boat was well under way and then made bold enough to venture on deck. I was accosted

WM. H. HORSFALL,

Drummer, Co. G, 1st Kentucky Vol. Inf. Born in Campbell Co., Ky., March 3, 1848.

by the captain of the boat as to my destination, etc., and telling him the old orphan-boy story, I was treated very kindly, given something to eat, and allowed very liberal privileges.

"I arrived at Cincinnati without further incident, and enlisted as a drummer-boy.

"In the fighting before Corinth, Miss., May 21, 1862 — Nelson's Brigade engaged — my position was to the right of the First Kentucky, as an independent sharp-shooter. The regiment had just made a desperate charge across the ravine. Captain Williamson was wounded in the charge, and, in subsequent reversing of positions, was left between the lines. Lieutenant Hocke, approaching me, said: 'Horsfall, Captain Williamson is in a serious predicament; rescue him if possible.' So I placed my gun against a tree, and, in a stooping run, gained his side and dragged him to the stretcher bearers, who took him to the rear."

Drummer Horsfall was on all the subsequent marches of his regiment. During the famous charge at Stone River he presently found himself hemmed in by rebel horsemen and hostile infantry. Even the rebels took pity on his youth and one of them shouted: "Don't shoot the damned little Yank! I want him for a cage." The plucky little drummer made a run for his life and safely got back to his regiment.

During the **Siege of Corinth** a Union force 30,000 strong, under General Pope, occupied Hamburg Landing five miles above Pittsburg, where General Halleck was in full command. The movement against Corinth was made on the 30th of April. There was little or no active engagement. Beauregard evacuated the town on the 26th of May and the Union Army took possession on the 30th.

AGAINST A SUPERIOR FORCE

RUFUS SAXTON,
Brigadier-General, U. S. V.
Highest rank attained: Bvt. Maj-Gen., U.S.V.
Born at Greenfield, Mass., Oct. 19, 1824.

BRIGADIER-GENERAL RUFUS SAXTON reports, regarding the action of his brigade between May 26 and 30, 1862, at Harper's Ferry, Va.:

"I assumed command of the forces at Harper's Ferry, May 26, 1862, occupying Bolivar Heights with my troops, and Maryland Heights with the naval battery. On the same evening I sent two companies of the First Maryland regiment, under Major Steiner, to make reconnoissance of London Heights, where, it was reported, the enemy were in position.

"They were fired upon while ascending, between nine and ten o'clock in the morning, by dismounted rebel cavalry concealed in the bushes on both sides of the road. The fire was returned, but with what effect is not known.

"On Wednesday I shelled the Heights, compelling the enemy to retire, as was proved by subsequent reconnoissance. Our cavalry drove the enemy out of Charleston, but they were almost immediately re-enforced, and, opening fire from a battery of nine guns, compelled our force to retire. A body of the enemy's cavalry was seen occasionally emerging from a point of the woods about two miles distant. Our guns shelled the woods in front, but the enemy made no response, and seemed from their movements, desirous of drawing us from our position.

"On the morning of the 29th the Fiftieth New York Cavalry was sent out to reconnoiter, and was fired upon by the enemy's infantry and artillery. A body was seen stationed in the woods in a position to cover the battery. Having accomplished their object, our cavalry returned.

"About midnight General Cooper's Brigade was set in motion, and, by daylight, had succeeded in crossing the river and occupying the banks on the Maryland side. General Clough's Brigade at the same time fell back to a new position on Camp Hill, and when morning dawned, our batteries, supported by a heavy force of infantry, were in a position to command all the approaches on our front and flanks.

"On Friday morning Major Gardner, with the Fifty-fifth New York Cavalry, was sent to the front to feel the enemy's position and watch his movements. He was later in the day re-enforced by a piece of artillery and two hundred sharpshooters. The enemy opened fire on him with scattering volleys of musketry along his whole front. The first discharge of grape from one piece caused the enemy's skirmishers to fall back in disorder.

AT HARPER'S FERRY

"About dark Friday evening, in a heavy storm, General Clough opened upon the enemy, who was advancing upon Camp Hill with three batteries. The scene at this time was very impressive. The night was intensely dark, the hills around were alive with the signal lights of the enemy; the rain descended in torrents, vivid flashes of lightning illumined at intervals the magnificent scenery, while the crash of thunder, echoing among the mountains, drowned into comparative insignificance the roar of artillery. After an action of an hour's duration the enemy retired. He made another unsuccessful attack at midnight with regiments of Mississippi and Louisiana Infantry, and, after a short engagement disappeared. Signal lights continued to be seen in every direction. On Saturday morning I sent out a reconnoissance and found that the whole rebel force, estimated at 20,000 or 25,000 strong, had retired, and that we had successfully held our position and repulsed his several attacks with less than 7,000 effective men."

HE WAVED HIS SHATTERED ARM

THE fiercest fighting at the battle of Fair Oaks occurred on June 1 — a Sunday. It was a fight which taxed the bravery of every Union officer and soldier. Many a deed of bravery and daring can be recorded from that memorable struggle, but none more noteworthy, than that which will ever connect the name of General O. O. Howard with the history of that battle. His conduct distinguished itself above that of all others and will always furnish an illustrious example of American bravery.

OLIVER O. HOWARD,

Brigadier-General, U. S. A. Highest rank attained: Major-General, U. S. A. Born at Leeds, Me., Nov. 8, 1830.

The battle began at seven o'clock in the morning. The rebels with undaunted courage withstood the deadly charge of the Federal troops. General Howard, who commanded a brigade, led four of his regiments on the right wing of the Union Army, one regiment in the first line, the remaining three in the second line. Assisted by eighteen pieces of Meagher's Artillery, he advanced and was met by the superior numbers of the enemy. The clash was fearful. For an hour and a half a tremendous struggle for supremacy ensued. The general was omnipresent. He was in the thickest of the battle. Wherever the danger was greatest, there he was, inspiring and animating his men.

Twice his horse was shot from under him. Finally a bullet struck and shattered his right arm. Waving the fractured limb high above him, he aroused his soldiers to still greater ardor and enthusiasm. Such heroic fighting the enemy could not withstand. They fled. General Howard was carried to the rear by his admiring soldiers. The brave leader's arm was amputated; but he again went to the front, as soon as he had recovered from the operation and continued on his career of undying fame.

THOUGH WOUNDED, REMAINED AT HIS POST

"I WAS engaged with the pioneers of the brigade on the 31st of May, 1862, in constructing a bridge across the Chickahominy River. An attack of the Confederates on our extreme left, on the Virginia side of the Chickahominy, caused the Second Corps to be thrown across the river immediately after twelve o'clock noon, and the battle of Fair Oaks began soon after.

"As my services were not necessary at the bridge, I took half of my command of forty-five men, and proceeded to the head of the brigade, reaching it just as it was about to engage the enemy. I was directed by General Dana to proceed across an open field in front of an advancing rebel regiment, which I did, arriving at the point designated with only four out of a party of twenty-two men, eighteen having been killed or wounded within a couple of minutes.

WM. R. SHAFTER,
1st Lieutenant, Co. I, 7th Michigan Infantry.
Highest rank attained: Major-General, U. S. A.
Born at Galesburg, Mich., Oct. 16, 1835.

"The adjutant of the regiment to which I belonged, the Seventh Michigan Infantry, was, about this time, dangerously wounded and incapacitated for

Fair Oaks.— On the 30th of May, 1862, the right wing of the Union Army rested near New Bridge, on the west bank of the Chickahominy, the center at Seven Pines, and the left on the White Oak Swamp. General Sumner's Corps remained on the east side of the river. The force was under command of General McClellan.

The efforts of General Johnston, the Confederate commander, were directed chiefly against the left wing, where Heintzelman's and Keyes' Divisions were placed. The Union position was supported at this point by General Kearney, Berry's Brigade, and an Irish Battalion, and was held in spite of repeated assaults in force. The arrival of General Sumner's Corps decided the day in favor of the Federals.

Fighting was resumed on the following day on the left bank of the river, and ceased about midday with the retreat of the enemy.

The Union loss was 5,739; the Confederate, 7,997.

It was in this battle that General Johnston, the Confederate commander, was disabled, and relieved by General Lee.

further service, whereupon I was directed by Major Richardson, who commanded the regiment that afternoon, to assume the duties of regimental adjutant, which I did.

"Just at the close of the battle, about half an hour later, my horse was shot from under me and I was wounded, a severe flesh wound, but as no bones were hit, my injuries were not considered dangerous. I was perfectly able to remain in the field, and did so during the fight of the next day. In order to escape being sent north with the wounded, I went to the rear of the command and remained there for two or three days until the wounded had all been sent

IN FRONT OF AN ADVANCING REBEL REGIMENT

away, and I then returned to my regiment. I was unable to ride a horse, and was confined to my couch and there performed the duties of adjutant, so far as the office part of the work was concerned.

"At the change of base I had the choice of being left in the hands of the enemy or mounting my horse and going with our troops, and although riding horseback in my then wounded condition was very painful, I adopted the latter alternative, and was with the regiment in all of the seven days' battles subsequent."

General Shafter, who gives this account of his services at Fair Oaks, voluntarily went with half of his little band into the battle, when his pioneer work gave him a satisfactory reason for remaining at the grapevine bridge, instead of engaging in the gallant charge of his regiment, and remained in action for twenty-four hours after receiving a bullet wound. His intelligent energy and activity during the battle, and his example of soldierly heroism, had an effect on the men, to which a great share of their success may be credited.

HEROIC RESCUE OF TWO FLAGS

THE One hundred and fourth Pennsylvania Infantry had been under fire for an hour and a half at the battle of Fair Oaks, and a large number of the men had fallen. The fighting line had been maintained unusually well, and the men fought more like veterans of a hundred battles than recruits under fire for almost the first time. The enemy was pressing them in front and flank, and his fire had become so warm as to endanger the battery they were supporting. He approached within a short distance of the right. At this crisis, a charge was ordered in the hope of checking his advance. The One hundred and fourth had no expectation of crossing bayonets with the rebels, but hoped

W. H. PURCELL,
Sergeant, Co. G, 104th Penn. Infantry.
Born at Upper Black Eddy, Buck Co., Pa.,
Aug. 1, 1837.

to gain time. The men were ordered to cease firing and fix bayonets, which was done with great promptness, considering their excited condition. The command was given: "Charge bayonets, forward, double-quick, march!" and the men sprang toward the enemy with a tremendous yell.

They advanced about a hundred yards over a piece of ground covered with dwarf bushes. In the way was an old worn fence that had not been observed before, which cut the old line of battle at an angle of about thirty degrees. The men sprang over this obstacle into the clearing where the enemy stood, and immediately began to reform and open fire. Both flags were carried over the fence by the bearers. This movement had the desired effect. It was foolhardy under the circumstances, but it staggered the enemy, and the heavy fire checked him at once. It soon became apparent that the regiment must relinquish the ground unless re-enforced, and Lieutenant Ashenfelder was dispatched across to the Williamsburg road to request General Casey to send support. The general sent word to hold out a few minutes longer, when re-enforcements would be sent.

It must be understood that, at this time, the One hundred and fourth Pennsylvania was engaged single-handed, in front of the line of the army, with a greatly superior force. Three hours had now elapsed since the regiment had gone into action, and more than one-third of the men had fallen. The promised re-enforcements did not arrive, and they could hold out no longer. There was no order given to retire, but they were literally pushed back by the superior force of the enemy pressing against them. Individual soldiers on either side came almost near enough to strike each other with the musket. The regiment retired slowly and sullenly, not an officer or man running.

In the excitement and confusion of retiring, one flag was left on the other side of the fence, the staff sticking in the ground, and the enemy made a bold

THE FLAG WAS LEFT ON THE OTHER SIDE OF THE FENCE

effort to capture it. Color-Sergeant Purcell had already secured his own standard, and, with it in his hands, he jumped over the fence and seized the other. The enemy saw the movement, and five of their men rushed forward at the same time, still keeping up their fire. Purcell reached it first, seized the staff, and sprang for the fence with both flags in his hands. As he mounted the fence he was struck by a bullet in the left thigh and fell, carrying the colors with him. Getting to his feet again he ran about 500 yards, handed one flag to Sergeant Myers, and started for the rear with the other, but, becoming faint from the loss of blood, he gave it to Corporal Mitchner and fell exhausted on the field, having received two slight wounds in the arm and neck. He was rescued by General Casey's bugler, Israel Stidinger, who took him on his horse to Savage Station.

The flags were brought off the field in safety, and delivered to the regiment after the battle.

AT THE RISK OF HIS LIFE

JOHN C. HUNTERSON,
Private, Co. B, 3d Pa. Cavalry.

Aʙᴏᴜᴛ June 5, 1862, a few days after the battle of Fair Oaks, John C. Hunterson, then a private in Co. B, Third Pennsylvania Cavalry, on duty as one of the escort of two to an engineer officer, accompanied him on an reconnoissance between the lines of the two armies for the purpose of ascertaining the best available position for earthworks. This party was discovered and fired upon by the enemy.

The horse of the engineer officer was killed, and the second person in escort hurriedly returned to our lines. This placed the officer in a most exasperating position. Here he had, at great personal peril, approached the enemy's lines, surveyed the topography of the battle-field, made valuable sketches and drawings, and now, at the very last moment, found himself deprived of the means to carry the information obtained to his superior officers! Hunterson keenly appreciated the situation. He realized that the engineer's life was of the greatest value to his army and his noble impulse quickly made him reach a conclusion. He voluntarily gave up his mount to the officer, enabling him to escape with the important plans and drawings which were upon his person.

Hunterson effected his escape, and at once reported to General Dickinson, then the assistant adjutant-general of Hooker's Division, who investigated and verified the incident. The act is worthy of special note as an exhibition of exceptional daring and devotion to duty. In giving up his horse in a desperate emergency, Hunterson reduced his own chance of escape to a minimum, entirely losing sight of his own welfare in his zeal for the safety of his superior officer and the interests of his country.

MUD BATHS FOR FUTURE GOOD HEALTH

DEWITT C. LEWIS,

Captain, Co. F, 97th Penn. Inf.
Highest rank attained: Bvt.
Lieutenant-Colonel, U. S. V.
Born at West Chester, Chester
Co., Penn., July 30, 1822.

"ON JUNE 15, 1862, the enemy, having secured the range of our camps from Fort Lamar, opened on them with shell, making it quite lively for us. General Benham, then in command of the Union troops, resolved to make an assault on the fort on the morning of the 16th, at daybreak. The attack was made by General Stevens' Division, which was repulsed with a loss of about 600 men. Our brigade commander, Colonel Robert Williams of the First Massachusetts Cavalry, was ordered to advance two of his regiments, the Ninety-seventh Pennsylvania and the Third New Hampshire, to support the assault.

"It was low tide and we forced our way through a thicket, or hedge, finding ourselves in a swamp, and under fire from the fort. But we drove the enemy's advance back to the fort, and located ourselves along the embankment about 200 yards from the enemy's works. We were able, at that distance, to effectually keep them from using their guns on two sides of the works.

"About 10 o'clock A. M., re-enforcements for the enemy commenced to arrive by way of the Charleston and Savannah Railroad. Their artillery went into position on the ridge and rendered our position untenable by enfilading our line. The order was given to retire, and we commenced falling back towards the swamp we had crossed at daylight. As soon as we left the embankment the field artillery and fort opened on us with canister at about 250 yards' range. When we reached the swamp the tide was well up and the place was a slimy, oozy mass of mud, which the "Johnnies" were stirring up with canister and round shot for all they were worth, and making it unfit to swim in or to drink. After a severe struggle I landed on the far side from the enemy, as a matter of choice and necessity, assisting a number of comrades,

In June, 1862, General Benham attempted to reach Charleston by the Stono River. The Union force crossed over to James Island on the 9th. Assaults were made upon a fort which the Confederates had erected at **Secessionville** during the week following. The attack on June 16 was a dismal failure, the Federals being compelled to fall back losing 500 men killed and wounded.

whose heads were covered with mud, when their feet reached the bottom. I suppose they were dodging the canister. We were very good at that.

"I landed, tired, disgusted, and dreadfully covered with mud, and was trying to find out where I was located in the mass of filth, when I heard a faint call that sounded thick and muddy. Looking back over the ground and water, I saw a head pop up above the sticky mass about one-third of the way back, and I felt satisfied that some poor fellow was having trouble and was in need of prompt assistance. The prospect was not inviting, with the shot flying

RETURNING TO RESCUE A COMRADE

about, but there was no time to think, so I drew off my accoutrements, plunged in and got him to the shore, both of us thoroughly exhausted, and found him to be one of my own men."

Colonel Lewis, who writes this account of his adventure at Fort Lamar, was present at the Mine Explosion at Petersburg, Va. When the attack was made upon the rebels, after the explosion, he was directly behind the major of the Forty-eighth New York, whose head was blown off, the bloody fragments striking him in the face. Soon after, his bravery and kindheartedness were again called forth by the misfortune of one of the men of his company who was wounded on the retreat. In the face of an awful storm of bullets, Colonel Lewis returned to the wounded man and carried him off the field to a place of safety.

FOUR CHARGES WITH A SHATTERED ARM

FREDERICK R.
JACKSON,
1st Serg't., Co. F.,
7th Conn. Inf.
Highest rank attained: Major, U. S. V.
Born at New Haven, Conn.

WHEN the Seventh Connecticut Infantry was storming Fort Lamar, James Island, S. C., at daybreak June 16, 1862, Sergeant Jackson was in command of Company F. He was struck above the elbow with a canister shot from an eight-inch columbiad, and his left arm was shattered. With his right hand Jackson seized his splintered arm, pressed it tightly to prevent, as much as possible, the flow of blood, and dashed forward with his men. The regiment retired, rallied again, and went forward on the second charge, only to be again repulsed. Once more the regiment rallied, and in this charge, Sergeant Jackson fell, fainting from the loss of blood.

He lay on the field from five o'clock in the morning until half-past ten at night, only a hundred feet from the fort, neither Federals nor Confederates daring to succor their wounded, so fierce was the firing. During more than seventeen hours he remained unable to move, all the while exposed to the fire from the Union forces, but too near the fort to be in range of the enemy's missiles.

Referring to this part of his experience, he writes:

"Of the fourteen comrades who came under the Confederate surgeon's knife as prisoners, only myself and one other lived to reach home. I was put under the influence of chloroform, and, when I became conscious again, discovered two surgeon's knives and another instrument lying across my breast. Among those in the room were General Gist, commanding the Confederates, and the colonel in charge of the fort. On regaining consciousness some one asked me:

"'How many troops have your forces got?'

"'Go over and count them,' I replied.

"'We will go over and we shall get them all,' said he.

"The surgeon was Doctor Bellinger, the son of one of the most famous surgeons in the South at that time. He said to me:

"'The Southern Confederacy is not abundantly supplied with chloroform, and will not throw any away on you.'

"Before beginning to amputate my arm, they divided some of my clothing among themselves. The first thing taken was a pair of new boots which had been sent from home by my father. My uniform was also disposed of, and they gave me a shabby suit of clothes in case I should ever need any more. Then the surgeon proceeded to cut off my arm, and, true to his word, he did not waste any of the Southern Confederacy's chloroform on me.

"I was made acquainted with six of the Southern prisons, and was graduated from Libby October 14, 1862."

TWO GALLANT OFFICERS

THE following story, describing an important movement in the action at Gaines Mills, Va., June 27, 1862, is written by a captain of the Eighty-third Pennsylvania Infantry, who testifies warmly to the gallant conduct and able leadership of General Daniel Butterfield and Major Ernst Von Vegesack, and the inspiriting influence upon the men of their fine example.

DANIEL BUTTERFIELD,
Brigadier-General, U. S. Volunteers.
Highest rank attained: Maj-Gen., U. S. V.
Born in Oneida Co., N. Y., Oct. 31, 1831.

"The Twelfth and Forty-fourth New York Volunteers, who were deployed in the rear and on the heights in the woods above us, opening fire upon the enemy, the fire was returned, and the right wing of the Eighty-third, being more on a level and in view of the enemy, commenced also a heavy fire. The enemy still approached in column of brigade, covered by a regiment in line of battle, but discovering, when too late, the position our regiment held, precipitately fled back with a heavy loss in killed and wounded.

"At this moment Brigadier-General Butterfield, amidst a gallant fire from his line of support in the rear, and that of the enemy in front, came coolly down the knoll, and, sword in hand, seized the colors, waving them repeatedly aloft, encouraging the valor of our regiment and stimulating with new vigor our thinned ranks. 'My boys,' he shouted, 'Your ammunition is never expended while you have your bayonets, and use them to the socket!'

"The battle at this juncture raged furiously. The trees were lopped and the leaves fell as thick as snowflakes, while the balls flew like a hailstorm, the solid shot, grape, canister, and shrapnel scattering destruction in all directions. It was intimated that the regiments on our right had been repulsed and had given way under the destructive fire of the enemy, who also threatened our right flank and were at that moment gradually gaining the rear. In this situation one regiment was ordered to face by the rear rank and wheel obliquely by a quarter on the proper right, and then become the left. This manœuvre was rapidly executed, but during its performance, our commander, Colonel McLane, was killed, and Major Nagel mortally wounded.

"The enemy, being fairly driven from the woods, as a last resort made their final stand on their own chosen ground. Major Von Vegesack, who was serving voluntarily as aide, came galloping along our lines, and, in a voice never to be forgotten, ordered the Eighty-third to face by the right flank, advance, half to the left, thereby still keeping the rear rank in front, deep on the center, and again face the foe. This cool and determined move on the part of Major Von Vegesack, which cannot be too warmly appreciated by the Eighty-third, so astounded the enemy, who were drawn up in line at about a hundred yards' distance, that they remained perfectly motionless for several minutes. They waved signals, which we did not understand, and finally sent forward a flag of truce, the Eighty-third sending out an officer to receive their communications, which were to the effect that they considered themselves so powerful that we had better surrender.

"This proposition, I need hardly say, caused some indignant mirth among us, and before the officers of the Eighty-third, who bore our flag of truce, returned to the ranks, the rebels, contrary to the rules of civilized warfare, poured a deadly volley into the ranks of our regiment. We fell flat on the ground, then rising to our knees, returned the fire, which was kept up in the bravest and most determined manner against overwhelming numbers, keeping the enemy at bay until dark, when the total expenditure of our cartridges caused us to retreat across the Chickahominy River."

The "Seven Days'" Battle before Richmond commenced with the battle of Oak Grove, on the 25th of June, when General Lee's attack on the right wing was made without decisive results. In an engagement at Mechanicsville on the 26th, General Hill, of the Confederate Army, was repulsed, with considerable loss, by the Sixth Corps under Porter.

DISTINGUISHED CONDUCT IN ACTION

CHARLES F. HOPKINS touches briefly upon his rescue of a wounded comrade in his description on the action at Gaines Mills, Va., but he was reported and highly praised for this act.

"Our regiment, the First New Jersey Volunteers, was ordered from the south side of the Chickahominy River to support Fitz John Porter, who was attacked at that place, by 'Stonewall' Jackson and Longstreet, determined to crush our right wing. We reached the field about 1 P. M., and were sent in to relieve the Fourteenth Regulars. The First Michigan's right was turned, and they were swept from the field for a short time. This left an opening by which the Fourth New

CHAS. F. HOPKINS,
Private, Co. I, 1st New Jersey Vols.
Born at Hope, New Jersey,
May 16, 1842.

York Volunteers were taken prisoners, only about ninety escaping, our regiment being compelled to retire its right. A similar movement was taking place on the left, leaving our company in the apex of the angle, thus made.

On the 27th of June the Fifth Corps, with about 25,000 men, was attacked by a rebel force of 70,000, on **Gaines Mills Heights**, and made a firm stand until the cavalry was repulsed, falling back in disorder on the lines. The enemy, pursuing their advantage, had almost accomplished the destruction of the corps when darkness enabled the Federals to cross the river.

On the 28th the general retreat began, during which occurred the engagements of **Savage Station, Glendale** (Charles City Cross Roads), **Peach Orchard, Chickahominy, White Oak Swamp,** and **Malvern Hill.**

At the last-named place, on July 1, the Second, Third, and Sixth Corps occupied a strong position, protected by gunboats on the river. The enemy's attack was defeated and the rebel force rendered incapable of further pursuit. The Union loss during the Seven Days' Battle is estimated at 15,249; the Confederate at 17,583.

"The order to retire, keeping up the fire, was given by our captain. Not hearing the order, or unconscious of the dangerous position, the company did not retire promptly, and the enemy poured a terrific fire on us from every point but our immediate rear, and even that was not exempt until we reached a point parallel with the line of battle.

"A comrade and myself were laggards in retiring, but were keeping up the fire. Having been twice wounded, I was looking for shelter to cover by backward movement, and, while moving from one place to another among the bushes, came across Sergeant Richard Donnelly of our company, who was badly wounded in the right leg. I told him I would take him out, and we could both chance the awful fire from all quarters. I got him on my back, and through that gauntlet of flame and bullets, made my way to the rear in safety.

"I was badly wounded in the hand twenty minutes after leaving him, and was left for dead on the field, but recovered, and was taken prisoner the next morning, being released five hours later with a large number of wounded who were able to walk."

THE DRUMMER-BOY OF THE CHICKAHOMINY

GEORGE D. SIDMAN,
Private, Co. C, 16th Michigan Infantry.
Born at Rochester, N. Y., Nov. 25, 1844.

GEORGE DALLAS SIDMAN, "The Drummer-Boy of the Chickahominy," as he was called, was but little over sixteen years of age when he enlisted in 1862. At the battle of Gaines Mills, Va., the second of the Seven Days' Battle before Richmond, and during his subsequent experience with the army, his great pluck and nerve, his presence of mind and fortitude, established for him a record which is barely suggested by the official description, "distinguished bravery in battle."

From early morning of that memorable day, the enemy had been concentrating in front of Porter's Corps, believing that the whole of McClellan's force was before them. Several times they had charged the Union lines in force, but had been repulsed each time with great loss.

General Butterfield's Brigade, composed of the Twelfth, Seventeenth, and Forty-fourth New York Infantry, Eighty-third Pennsylvania Infantry, and Sixteenth Michigan Infantry, occupied the extreme left of the line, resting on the

Chickahominy Swamp, not far from Bottom's Bridge, which with a corduroy road across the swamp, offered the only means of retreat to the left flank in case of defeat.

The sun was low on the horizon when the enemy advanced, four columns deep, to charge the Union center by an enfilading movement. They broke through the weakened lines and forced the left flank back into the swamp, where, for a time, it looked as if the entire corps had been caught like rats in a trap. The

SEIZED ONE OF THE GUIDONS OF HIS REGIMENT

stampede was so complete that a part of the brigade, under Butterfield, was forced back almost into the swamp. At this juncture General Butterfield and a part of his staff rode into the lines, calling upon his men to rally and save the day.

Young George Sidman, caught by the enthusiasm of the moment, seized one of the guidons of his regiment, and, rushing to the side of the general, called upon his comrades to rally there. His action, with the calls of the officer, had the effect of rallying a remnant of the brigade, and, in less time than it takes to tell the story, this handful of men formed a "forlorn hope" that charged back, and almost crossed bayonets with the enemy, then in full posses-sion of the field. The rebels, not knowing the strength of the force charging them, fell back a short distance, and night set in before they discovered that "Stonewall" Jackson's army had been whipped by less than a thousand

Yankees. There is little doubt that this "forlorn hope" rally, incited, in a measure, by the heroic example of George Sidman, was the means of saving the Fifth Corps from almost total destruction.

Sidman was severely wounded by a minie ball through the left hip, in the charge back upon the enemy, and lay upon the field until the firing ceased, when he clubbed his musket over a stump, to destroy its usefulness to the enemy, and threw his accoutrements into a ditch of water near by. He crawled off the field and through Chickahominy Swamp on his hands and knees, being unable to walk, or even stand, on his wounded leg. The next morning he was picked up by an ambulance and taken to Savage Station, where, two days later, he was taken prisoner with 3,000 other sick and wounded, left by McClellan to the tender mercies of the enemy.

He celebrated the 4th of July by a ride to Richmond on a flat car, exposed all day to the hot sun, without food or water, weak and helpless. He was confined in Libby Prison, Castle Thunder, and finally at Belle Isle. While at the last-named place gangrene formed in his wound, and, without medical attention he would have died, as thousands of others did from the same cause, had he not cured it himself by the most heroic treatment. He had with him a little "house-wife," containing, among other things, a small package of capsicum, which he deliberately poured into the open wound. The remedy was nearly as bad as the disease, but Sidman declares that it removed the gangrene and saved his life.

He was exchanged in August and sent to the hospital at Point Lookout, Md., but the place was so isolated and lonesome that he begged to be sent north. This request being refused, he took passage one night in the stoke-hole of a steamboat going up the Potomac River, and arrived the following morning in Washington, where he reported at the War Department and requested to be sent to his regiment, then campaigning in Virginia. The spectacle of a soldier on crutches, of very uninviting appearance, reporting at the headquarters of the army and requesting to be sent to his regiment for duty, was such a novelty that the officers regarded him as a lunatic.

The hospitals being crowded at this time with the wounded from the second battle of Bull Run, he was sent to Convalescent Camp, near Alexandria, Va., where he remained until he could move about with the aid of a stick, when, hearing that his regiment was encamped not far away, he took "French Leave," and joined his company much to the amazement of his comrades. The surgeon of the regiment would not certify him for duty, because his wound was not yet healed, and as it was evident that he could not march, he was ordered to return to the hospital, which he refused to do. The following day the army started on the Maryland Campaign, and his regiment marched away, leaving him behind to shift for himself. Nothing daunted, he begged a ride across the river to Georgetown, and succeeded in reaching his regiment that night, nearly worn out. The next morning he found a condemned horse by the roadside, and, with a bridle made of knapsack straps, and a pile of blankets to soften the protruding bones of his fiery steed, he rode into camp that night. The colonel of his regiment, admiring his pluck, ordered that Sidman be permitted to remain with the command and that he be allowed rations. He followed his regiment to Antietam, mounted on his condemned horse, and participated in the battle that resulted in driving General Lee out of Maryland.

JAMES QUINLAN,
Major, 88th N. Y. Infantry.
Highest rank attained: Colonel.
Born at Tipperary, Ireland, Sept. 13, 1833.

MOST BRAVE AND INTREPID ON THE FIELD

"ON THE morning after the battle of Gaines Mills, Va., the colonel and lieutenant-colonel of my regiment, the Eighty-eighth New York (Meagher's Irish Brigade), of which I was major, reported sick and went to the rear, the command devolving on me.

"The afternoon of that day we took up our march for our new base, which, we were informed, would be Harrison's Landing, Va. Harassed all the way by the enemy, fighting each day and marching at night, Sunday morning, June 29, we arrived at a place called Savage Station, Va., and were ordered to halt and make ourselves as comfortable as possible. Early that day the enemy appeared in force at Tyler's and Nelson's farms. My regiment and the Twenty-ninth Massachusetts, under Colonel Pierce, were ordered into action at both places. The fighting was pretty severe, but the enemy were repulsed, and we were ordered back to our original position.

"The army under General McClellan was crossing the White Oak Swamp on its retreat. Our turn came to move, as the corps of General E. V. Sumner, to which we were attached, had the rear of the whole army. As we neared White Oak Swamp a Confederate Battery of six guns, supported by a large column of infantry under Generals Magruder and Huger, opened a terrific fire, which caused Sumner's Corps to halt. General W. W. Burns, U. S. A., with his brigade, was sent to silence the Battery, and being unsuccessful called for re-enforcements. Several regiments were sent to his assistance, notably, the First Minnesota, under the gallant Sully, but still the fire of the battery kept up. General Sumner sent for the Eighty-eighth Regiment, and when I reported to him he said: 'Quinlan, what formation have you?' I answered: 'Double on the center.' 'Good he said, I know your regiment well, and they can deploy at the double-quick.' He ordered me to report to General Burns, who ordered me forward at double-quick to charge the battery. As we started, the enemy's guns ceased firing, and when we got within the range that suited them best, their six guns were discharged simultaneously. But the Eighty-eighth did not falter. They pushed on and silenced the battery."

In addition to Major Quinlan's account of the charge, the official statement of one of his superior officers is as follows:

"The conduct of Major Quinlan on that occasion was that of a self-sacrificing soldier. He dashed into the very face of death, so far as he could know, thereby relieving the troops massed in a *cul de sac* from the battery's devastating fire, and probably discouraging the enemy for the day, for the fighting was not renewed after the silencing of their guns until past nightfall. Major Quinlan deserves the badge of gallantry to be awarded to the most brave and intrepid on the field."

RESCUED AN ABANDONED BATTERY

GEORGE UHRY,
5th U. S. Artillery.
Born in Baden, Germany, Oct. 31, 1838.

"ON THE 30th of June, 1862, after the battle of White Oak Swamp, the Fifth United States Artillery, of which I was a member, was stationed on the road leading to Richmond, Va. About four o'clock that afternoon we received orders to move to a new position and, while our regiment was preparing to make this move, I saw that Captain Mott's Battery, of the First New York Artillery, had been abandoned and was in danger of being captured by the advancing enemy.

"I at once went to Captain Ayres of our battery and told him that if he would let me have two men I would recover some, if not all, of the abandoned battery. Permission was granted, and with my two companions I started back.

"We soon reached the battery, and, after much hard work, in constant danger of losing our lives, we succeeded in recovering two guns, two limbers, and caissons, which we delivered to Captain Ayres."

The service which George Uhry performed and here describes, deserves notice, not only for the bravery of the act, but for its importance in preventing a possible advantage to the enemy.

UNDER CONSTANT FIRE FOR SEVENTEEN HOURS

L IEUTENANT KING gives this account of the trying position maintained by the battery under his command at White Oak Swamp:

"During the retreat of the Army of the Potomac, commanded by General George B. McClellan, from in front of Richmond to Harrison's Landing, Va., the batteries to which I belonged — A and C, Fourth United States Artillery, commanded by Captain George Hazard, a veteran of the Mexican War,—was detailed as part of the rear guard, which was composed of Richardson's Division of Sumner's Corps, covering the retreat from Savage Station to White Oak Swamp. After three days of constant

RUFUS KING,
1st Lieutenant, 4th U. S. Artillery.
Highest rank attained: Colonel.
Born in New York City, March 21, 1838.

fighting we reached White Oak Swamp, and there had a narrow escape from capture.

"On the morning of June 30, about nine o'clock, arriving at the swamp, and discovering that the bridge had been burned by the retreating army, we made the crossing at the place where the bridge had been, to the intense astonishment of our army, congregated on the other side watching the perilous experiment. The Confederates were striving with all their skill to build a new bridge, and, on the defeat of this attempt, depended the safety of our army. On the heights opposite the Confederates were piled enormous quantities of our transportation, accumulated there in our hasty retreat from Richmond. Sumner's Corps still occupied the post of honor on the rear guard, and Batteries A and C were ordered into position on the brow of the hill with instructions to prevent the enemy from crossing, and to hold the ground at any cost. About ten minutes after our taking position, Captain Hazard was mortally wounded and carried from the field, the command then devolving upon me, the senior lieutenant present for duty.

"Our battery was made the object of attack by some thirty pieces of artillery concentrated by the enemy in an endeavor to dislodge us from our position. The fire from the guns was frightful, and there was not a portion of the battery that did not get its share of it. Our fire was so accurate that it was impossible for the enemy's engineers and bridge builders to accomplish their work while we were pouring our spherical case and solid shot into their midst, but the strain on us was tremendous. Our battery, consisting of eight guns and about one hundred and seventy-five men, was depended upon to reply to a concentrated attack by thirty guns that had our range accurately, and whose efforts to dislodge us were most persistent. The fire from Jackson's Artillery was so heavy that cannoneers and drivers were shot down and horses killed in such numbers that some of the non-commissioned officers took it upon themselves to withdraw one of the guns. I went after them and succeeded in having the gun brought back to its old position.

"The demands on our diminished numbers to serve the guns efficiently were most exhausting, and it required my constant presence in all parts of the battery, encouraging and cheering the men, assisting them to serve the pieces, and praising them, to give them the confidence necessary to enable our battery to accomplish the desired result.

"We remained in position from 9 A. M. until 2 A. M. the next day, under constant fire all the time, losing a great many men and horses from the fire of the enemy, but succeeded in preventing them from building the bridge and crossing the swamp before our army had reached a place of safety."

BENJAMIN B. LEVY,
Drummer, 1st New York Vols.
Born in New York City, Feb. 22, 1845.

BETTER WORK WITHOUT THE DRUM

ON THAT memorable retreat from Richmond, June 30, 1862, the First New York Volunteers, in which Benjamin Levy was the drummer, had been on picket duty the night before, and it consequently fell to their lot to cover the retreat. In this position they were considerably harassed by sharpshooters and guerrillas who lay in wait for those who fell by the wayside. Levy, who was little over sixteen years old, was marching with his tent-mate who was sick with malaria, and in his feeble condition could make but slow progress. He was about to lie down, when Levy broke his drum and cast it aside, took the accoutrements and gun of his sick comrade, and encouraged him to keep up so as to avoid capture.

This regiment became engaged that afternoon in the battle of Charles City Cross Roads, Va. (or Glendale). Levy, being a drummer, was not obliged to go into action. He reported, however, to his superior officer and bravely volunteered to shoulder a rifle and participate in the action on the firing line. His brave offer being accepted he proceeded to the front with his regiment and thus became actively engaged in the fighting.

There were four colors in this engagement belonging to the regiment. All but two of the color-bearers and corporals were killed or wounded. Immediately he threw away his gun, which he still carried in one hand, grasped the other flag and, with a stand of colors on each shoulder beat a hasty retreat, during which he received a slight flesh wound.

On emerging from the woods with the two colors, he met General Phil. Kearney, who was in command of his division at that time. The general inquired what regiment he belonged to, and on being informed, directed him to the point where the remnant of the regiment was stationed. For his gallantry in rescuing the two colors he was then and there promoted by General Kearney to be color-sergeant.

The day after, at the battle of Malvern Hill, the regiment had been marching, and the men were so covered with dust, that their uniforms looked more gray than blue. While obeying an order to cross an open field, they were fired upon by one of the Union batteries stationed

ROLLED OVER AND OVER

on a hill, the gunners mistaking them for Confederates. The colonel, Garret Dyckman, seeing the danger of his regiment, ordered the men to lie down, and directed Levy to unfurl his flag, advance down the center of the field, and wave the colors until the firing should cease. Levy promptly obeyed and, when the firing stopped, was about to return to the regiment, when a volley from the enemy's pickets or sharpshooters, lined along the edge of the woods, opened upon him. The staff of the colors was struck, and a ball pierced the tin cup attached to his haversack. He lay down, tore his handkerchief into strips, with which he tied his colors up, and then rolled over and over back to the regiment, arriving safe amid the laughter and applause of his comrades.

RETALIATION

IT was at Charles City Cross Roads that Corporal Shambaugh captured a Confederate flag. During the battle his eye was caught by the stars and bars of a Georgia regiment waving defiantly amid the hail of shot and shell not far away. He remarked to Sergeant Howard, who stood near him, that, as the Confederates had taken some of their battle flags at Gaines Mills, and had captured at the same time, nine companies of the Eleventh Pennsylvania Reserves, it would be a good idea to retaliate.

The two men took up a position considerably in advance of the Federal line of battle, and, when the rebels charged, Shambaugh dashed forward, in the face of almost certain death, and grappled with the color-bearer for his flag. A very short tussle ensued, and Shambaugh succeeded in wresting the color from the bearer. Upon gaining the colors he turned and ran, and managed, in the Federal countercharge, to get back to the ranks unhurt. Howard was separated from Shambaugh at the beginning of the charge, and had no hand in the capture.

SEVEN WOUNDS IN SEVEN DAYS

PETER F. RAFFERTY,
Private, Co. B, 69th N. Y. Vol. Inf.
Highest rank attained: Captain.
Born in New York City, June 12, 1845.

CAPTAIN RAFFERTY's story as he tells it, shows, besides an extraordinary degree of nerve and pluck, that love of fighting which seems to have been characteristic of the members of the Irish Brigade. He writes:

"I was seventeen years old when I enlisted as a private in the Sixty-ninth New York Volunteers. This was not the Sixty-ninth Militia, which, in the volunteers, had another number. Both regiments, however, were enlisted in New York City, and ninety-five per cent of our regiment were Irishmen. We were in the Irish Brigade, and were called into action at Malvern Hill, Va., late in the afternoon of the first day of July, 1862, the last day of the fight before Richmond. The Sixty-ninth, Colonel Robert Nugent, and the Eighty-eighth New York attempted to check the advance of a powerful column of rebels. We were in the lead, and as soon as we had exhausted our sixty rounds of cartridges, the Eighty-eighth took our place until we could get a fresh supply of ammunition and go into the fight again.

"We had scarcely gotten well warmed up before Colonel Nugent saw that a detachment of the enemy had mounted the foothills and was bearing down upon our flank. Nugent charged with both regiments, and we had a hand-to-hand encounter with the famed Louisiana Tigers. The 'Terriers' wiped the 'Tigers' off the field, but we were pretty well used up ourselves.

"It was in this part of the fight that I felt a stinging sensation in my right thigh and realized that I was hit. It made me limp, but I concluded to stay in the ring—in fact there wouldn't have been anywhere else to go—until there should

"I'LL STAY AND FIGHT IT OUT"

have been a lull in the fighting. After we had repulsed the 'Tigers,' our company (B) took stock of the dead and wounded. Captain Thomas Leddy told several of us who had been hit, to go to the rear, but there was nothing at the rear that could do us any good—no surgeons, no ambulances. We would be among strangers, and, if our army shifted its position, it might leave us in the hands of the enemy.

"'I don't want to go to the rear, captain,' said I, 'I'm all right. I'll stay and fight it out with the boys.' So after some arguing, the captain let all of us come back to the company who were able to get around.

"But the 'Tigers' hadn't had enough, and, at about half-past eight, they came up to the assault again. There were a thousand men on each side in full view of each other, and for ten minutes shooting was good. Then Colonel Nugent ordered a charge, and that was the end of the 'Tigers.' Their colonel was captured and with him a good many men.

"I didn't come out of this second fight in as good condition as the first. I got two bullets in the mouth and the lower part of the jaw, which smashed the bones and carried away part of my tongue. Besides this another went through my foot entering at the top and coming out at the sole.

"I was left on the field for a long time, and two days later was captured and sent to Libby, reaching there on the Fourth of July. In those last seven days of fighting I had received just seven wounds but as I was rated a good shot in my company, and could hit anything I fired at, it is very likely that I did not have the worst of the bargain.

"I was exchanged later, and was discharged in March, 1863, on account of my wounds, having served a year and a half. In 1864 I had recovered sufficiently to re-enlist in the Sixth District of Columbia Volunteers, in which I was lieutenant."

CAPTURED TWO REBELS

JOHN C. CURTIS,
Born at Bridgeport, Conn.

IT WAS at the battle of Baton Rouge, La., on the 5th of August, 1862, that John C. Curtis, then a second lieutenant, performed an act of military daring, which won the plaudits of his comrades, the commendation of officers, and the official recognition of his Government.

Twenty-five hundred Federals faced a foe of twice this strength. For eight hours the struggle continued with varying success until the Union gunboats Essex, Sumter, and Kineo came to the support of the troops and rendered most valuable assistance.

General Williams, who in a brilliant charge led the Yankees to victory, was shot in the chest and killed during this engagement. Under ordinary circumstances the death of the commander might have caused a panic among the troops. The presence of mind of the various officers, however, prevented any such disastrous effect. One of these was Second Lieutenant Curtis. His undaunted courage animated and inspired the men. He was always in the lead, once even approaching the enemy so closely as to be within their own rank. With great coolness and nerve he captured two rebel soldiers and at the point of the bayonet marched them to the regimental headquarters.

A DANGEROUS MISSION

JOHN L. YUNKER,
Private, Co. A, 12th U. S. Infantry.
Born in Würtemberg, Germany, November 16, 1836.

"At the battle of Cedar Mountain," writes Private Yunker, "our command was flanked by the enemy on the right, and we came under a heavy cross-fire from our own guns in the rear, while we were, at the same time, under a severe fire, at close range, from the Confederate batteries. Our men fell dead and wounded almost by companies. Captain Anderson called for a volunteer to carry an order back to our artillery, to cease firing on us, and noticing that the men were hesitating, I stepped forward, took the order and safely delivered it to the captain of the battery.

"On my quarter-of-a-mile trip, shot and shell and missiles of every description flew around me like hail, but I reached the officer unharmed, and on my return received only a slight wound in the left arm."

It requires but slight powers of reading between the lines, to discern, in this brief and modest recital, a deed of the utmost bravery. It appears, that the enemy, perceiving the mission of the daring volunteer, made him the objective point of their concentrated fire during his trip to and from the battery, so that his escape alive was a very narrow one. Although wounded in the performance of this service, he returned to his company and resumed his place in the fighting line.

Cedar Mountain.— On the 9th of August, General Pope in command of the Army of Virginia, with about 32,000 men, came in contact with a rebel force, under Jackson, of between 18,000 and 20,000, at a little stream called Cedar Run, near Gordonsville, Va.

The cannonading on both sides was heavy, and the battle was of short duration, fortune seeming, at first, in favor of the Union men; but a brilliant rally, led by Jackson himself, changed the conditions, and the rebels drove our troops from the field. The loss to Pope's command amounted to about 1,400; the Confederate loss being 1,307.

A TIMELY WARNING

JAMES W. WEBB,
Private, Co. F, 5th N. Y. Infantry.
Highest rank attained: Brevet Captain.
Born at Brooklyn, N. Y., Sept. 20, 1844.

ONE of the most conspicuous individual incidents of the second battle of Bull Run was the exploit of James Webb, who relates the circumstances and partly describes the fight.

"We went into action with the Nineteenth New York Infantry, and while waiting for orders, with the Tenth on our left, we were permitted to make coffee. We had not been long at this, when Colonel G. R. Warren rode up, and, after a consultation with General Reynolds, gave the order, 'Forward, guide center,' and away we went, carrying our kilters of coffee with us. We continued the march until within about ten paces from the edge of the woods, where Longstreet's Army, under Hood and Evans, was concealed. Six companies of the Tenth were deployed to the front as skirmishers, but in a few minutes they came back helter-skelter, having found the enemy in the woods.

"The rebels came out directly behind them, so that we were unable to fire, lest we fire into our own men, and we therefore opened our ranks to let the skirmishers through. The enemy's fire was too much for us, and we were swept off the field as if mown down by a scythe. When we got beyond the creek we halted, and what was left of us reformed.

"Though we had been through the Peninsular Campaign under General McClellan, we were dodging bullets like raw recruits. While thus engaged, I saw that Hazlett's Battery (D), Fifth U. S. Artillery, was still in position at the edge of the woods, firing away as if victory were ours, and wholly unaware of the fact that our forces had drawn back. There was the battery, without support of any kind, and Evans' Brigade preparing to charge it. I wondered what that battery was doing out there all alone, and, in my excitement I called out that they would be captured. I said:

"'I am going over there and tell them of their danger,' and with that I started across the field.

At the **Second Battle of Bull Run,** which occurred on the 30th of August, 1862, General Pope was in command of a force near Groveton, consisting of two of Heintzelman's divisions, under Hooker and Kearney, on the right, and Reno and Sigel, on the left. He was opposed by Lee's entire army.

The attack was made on the enemy's left, with disastrous result to the Union force. On the following day the attack was renewed on the left, which at first retired, as Lee's plan was also to attack Pope on his left. Porter's Corps, in pursuit of a supposed flying foe, received a severe check from the rebels concealed in the woods, and was repulsed with great loss.

Our troops retreated across Bull Run under cover of darkness, unpursued by the enemy.

The Union loss in this engagement amounted to 14,462; the rebels lost 9,197.

"At this time the firing had ceased, but I was no more than about fifty feet from our lines when the enemy, evidently surmising my intention, opened fire upon me. The bullets whistled all around me, but I kept on, for I was in a place where I could not stop.

"AS WE WERE HURRYING BACK"

"I finally reached the battery, which was about 600 feet away from us, and managed to say to Lieutenant Hazlett:

"'The Rebs are on your front and rear!'

"He looked around, and, seeing his danger, at once ordered the battery to limber up to the rear, and away we went to the Warrenton Turnpike.

"Just as we started, a bullet struck me in the side and went through me. As we were hurrying back, each man for himself, there was no one to assist me, and, after falling down three or four times, I finally reached the turnpike, where I dropped.

"After lying there some time a surgeon came along, and, seeing that I was pretty badly wounded, ordered me taken to the rear, a fit subject for the hospital. This I did not want done, and, with the assistance of some of the boys, I made my way to Centreville, about eight miles distant. After my wound was dressed, I joined my company and fought with it through the Maryland campaign."

"SURRENDER—SURRENDER"

NERVE and pluck are essential qualifications of a soldier. They were abundantly displayed by the Union men, but here is a sample which earned for Sergeant Mills an official recognition and will awaken the interest of every reader. The sergeant himself narrates:

"I was on the advance guard with some of our men September 4, 1862, when we moved towards Sandy Cross Roads. Some noise and faint cheering gave us our direction. When we came in sight of Sandy Cross Roads, we discovered the rebels. Giving the signal to our troops, we rushed in on the surprised enemy as fast as our horses could carry us. It happened that my horse carried me in the lead. Before I realized it, I was right among the rebels. That I came out of the affair alive, was a surprise to me. At the time, however, I thought of nothing but to capture the enemy before me. Unmindful of all danger I kept yelling to them: 'Surrender—Surrender.'

FRANK W. MILLS,
Sergeant, Co. A, 8th N. Y. City Militia.
Born at Middletown, Orange Co., New York,
August 5, 1845.

"The rebels were completely taken by surprise. They believed the Yankees to be miles away. They were actually paralyzed and did not recover from their surprise, until the captain arrived with the rest of our troops. Then they tried a little resistance — some of them even stood their ground, others ran and got behind anything they could find.

"During the mêlée a rebel aimed his gun at Captain Hamilton, but I had just time enough to spur in on him and cut him down, before he fired.

"We captured about 120 Confederates and nearly 100 horses and mules. While occupied in gathering them in, a most satisfactory job for a soldier, a colored lad came up to me and told me, that two prisoners had got away and gone down the road with a mule and cart. He added:

"'Boss, they may stop at a store four miles down the road.' Here was something for me to do; I took one man and started after them, in the hurry even forgetting to notify the captain.

"We soon came in sight of the store and, sure enough, the mule was tied outside. No one saw us come up, so I dismounted, gave my bridle to my companion, and crept up to the store. The rebels were just relating their experience with the damned Yankees, when I sailed in on them and shouted: 'Surrender'; I fired a shot in order to scare them, and, finding their guns near the door, had little trouble in capturing everything in sight.

"As we hastened the mule and the prisoners back to our lines, we barely escaped being left behind by our command. Captain Hamilton was very glad to

"WE HASTENED THE PRISONERS BACK"

see us return. He had missed us, and was reluctant to go without us, though he knew, that every minute spent on this ground might have brought an attack by the rebels to free their comrades.

"Our prisoners felt greatly mortified to think, that a sergeant and thirty-five Yankee soldiers should have captured them, when it had been within their power to 'do us up,' and let no one go back to tell the story.'"

A HIGHLY HONORED SOLDIER

JOSEPH L. FOLLET,
2d Lieutenant, Co. G, 1st Mo. L. Art.
Highest rank attained: Lieutenant-Colonel.
Born at Newark, N. J., Feb. 16, 1843.

LIEUTENANT JOSEPH L. FOLLET enlisted as a private in Co. G, First Missouri Infantry in 1861. From September of that year he served continuously throughout the war, never absent from his command a single day and, though twice wounded, always in active service. He saw, perhaps, as much real hard fighting, and actual duty, as any other man. He has the distinction of being the youngest officer in command of a battery.

"I was nineteen years old," Lieutenant Follet writes, "when at the battle of Perryville, Ky., I had charge of a battery as first sergeant. Again at the age of twenty-one, as a second lieutenant, I drew and equipped a six-gun battery and reported to General King on Lookout Mountain. I commanded Fort Sheridan, one of the defenses at the right of Chattanooga, which I afterward turned over to my successor. Later I was appointed adjutant of the Artillery District of the Etowah,—General J. B. Steedman commanding,—comprising the defenses of Lookout Mountain, Chattanooga, and Bridgeport."

Lieutenant Follet took part in all the battles and campaigns under Generals Sheridan, Pope, King, and Steedman, who repeatedly selected him to carry orders under the most trying circumstances. He himself says in regard to these services:

"It really looked sometimes as though I would never return. On more than one occasion I had a miraculous escape from death."

That Lieutenant Follet in the pursuit of these missions overcame all dangers and obstacles is evidence of his daring bravery and great presence of mind.

He was wounded at the battle of New Madrid, Mo., March 2, 1862, and at Farmington, Miss., May 9, 1862, yet, as stated before, continued in active service. He received his Medal of Honor for his intrepidity and fine soldierly qualities throughout his military career and was honored by General Sheridan by special mention in several reports of important battles and in the general's personal memoirs.

HEROIC STAND OF A BRAVE YOUNG CORPORAL

WILSON SMITH,
Corporal, Battery H, 3d N. Y. Lt. Art.
Born at Oriskany Falls, N. Y., Sept. 7, 1841.

"BEFORE daylight of September 6, 1862, the men of Battery H, New York Light Artillery of which I was a corporal, were encamped in the streets of Little Washington, N. C. We were ordered to fall in, and an expedition consisting of Battery H, four guns, a detachment of cavalry and infantry and a supply train, started for some point unknown to us.

"The morning was dark and foggy. Several gunboats lay in the stream, the men on board being asleep. After the column had moved six or seven blocks, firing was heard to the left. Then a mounted officer appeared, shouting that the town had been surprised by a large force. A stampede immediately followed this announcement and the column ahead was in complete confusion. The cavalry following maintained discipline. The order of the commanding officer: 'Steady, men' could be plainly heard. The lieutenant in charge of one gun having disappeared in the confusion, I assumed command and proceeded rapidly in the direction of the firing.

"After advancing some blocks we came upon the remainder of the battery unlimbered and ready for action. We continued until we reached River Street, where the gun was unlimbered and loaded with canister. Our piece was unsupported. As the men finished loading, the fog lifted, and a body of men filling the entire street, and numbering about 600, was discovered marching rapidly toward our gun. I hesitated, not knowing who they were. Just then Adjutant Guiero, of the Third New York Cavalry, rode up and said:

"'Young man, why don't you fire?'

"I replied: 'I don't know who they are.'

"'Quite right,' he said. 'I'll soon see.'

"He advanced in the direction of the men, but, in an instant, he wheeled and shouted: 'In God's name fire!'

"Then I gave the order to fire, and in a few minutes fifteen charges of canister were hurled against the advancing men, who first halted, and then retreated rapidly in the direction whence they came. Up to this time not one of my small detachment had been injured except myself, a bullet cutting my ear slightly.

"The gun was then limbered, and we followed the enemy up the street to the next block, where the Tar River Bridge provides an entrance to the town.

Upon arriving at the corner we could see that the retreating Confederates were mixed in confusion with another regiment, which had been following them. The officers were endeavoring to rally and reform their lines. We again attempted to unlimber the gun, but the horses, in making a short turn at the entrance to the bridge, became stalled, and the gun remained fast.

"Just then the Confederates discharged a volley, a portion of which struck the wheel horses, causing them to plunge and wheel. Now our men were enabled to unlimber the gun. Before it could be loaded, however, the Confederates were upon us with their bayonets, and a hand-to-hand fight ensued in front

"WE LOADED THE GUN FOR THE LAST TIME"

of the gun. During this combat John Malone and John McGrehan loaded the gun with canister. We immediately discharged it, and after a few shots the street was rapidly cleared of the enemy. But their rifle fire on the street was terrible. Within a few minutes every man at the gun was killed except John Malone and myself. Two soldiers from Battery G, one named Lincoln, the other Albert Willard, three members from Potter's North Carolina Infantry, and three members of the Third New York Cavalry then joined us and assisted in working the gun.

"A large body of Confederates, in the meantime, had entered the grounds of ex-Governor Grice's residence and was pouring volley after volley into our detachment. The last charge left was a solid shot. All our newly joined comrades had been killed or wounded, and Malone and I loaded the gun for the last time. Just before the shot was inserted into the gun a bullet shattered my knee, and as I fired, Malone received a shot through the body, which completely paralyzed his leg.

"He threw his arms about me and I carried him on my back to the bridge stairs, hobbling along with the aid of my saber. How it was possible to reach the edge of the water alive, is a mystery to me. A cutter then took us both, with the wounded Lincoln, to the gunboat Louisiana. As our gun ceased firing, the Louisiana came into action, her guns covering the position we had abandoned, and soon after the Confederates were in full retreat.

"The next day, September 7, on my twenty-first birthday, my leg was amputated above the knee. While I was lying in the hospital at New Berne, Major-General J. B. Foster, the corps commander, and Colonel J. H. Ladlie, the regimental commander, met at my bedside. The colonel said that the action of my gun detachment had saved Little Washington to the Union forces."

On September 12, 1862, Corporal Wilson Smith was promoted to the rank of sergeant for the gallantry which he describes so graphically.

HELD ON TO THE REBEL CAPTAIN

LEONIDAS H. INSCHO,
Corporal, Co. E, 12th Ohio Infantry.
Born at Chatham, Ohio, July 20, 1840.

CORPORAL L. H. Inscho describes his act of bravery as if it were but a mere incident in the course of his regular duty.

"I was a member of Co. E, Twelfth Ohio Infantry, when, at South Mountain, Md., our regiment, with others, charged the Confederates, who were posted behind a stone wall on the side of the mountain. As we approached the enemy, a rifle-ball struck my gun, wounding my left hand. While I stopped to examine my piece and my hand, the regiments made a flank movement to the left, leaving me alone near the wall.

"A Confederate captain was on the other side, and as he came near me, I caught him by the collar and told him to surrender. He refused, and pointed his revolver at my head, but I caught it by the barrel and turned it up just as he fired. I clung to the revolver and disarmed him, and grabbing him by the shoulders began

"I GOT HIM OVER THE WALL"

to pull him over the wall. He struggled vigorously and struck me in the face several times, but I got him over the wall and knocked him down compelling him to surrender.

"I then turned my attention to some of his men, who were taking refuge behind a clump of trees. I pointed my revolver at them and demanded their surrender. Four of them dropped their guns and came over to the Union side of the wall, but a fifth man came up to me with his gun in his hand and swore he would not give up to a Yankee. He took aim at me as he spoke, and I dropped behind the wall just as he fired.

"He turned to run away and I at once rose from my position and emptied the contents of my revolver into him. I then ordered the captain and his four men to fall in, and marched them over to the colonel of my regiment."

BOLDLY CAPTURED FOURTEEN REBELS

PRIVATE JAMES ALLEN furnishes a fine example of audacity and presence of mind in the following narration:

"On the 14th of September, 1862, our regiment engaged the enemy at South Mountain, Md. A charge brought us to a dense cornfield, separated from the base of the mountain by a stone wall. While we were charging through the corn, the command: 'Right oblique' was given, which a comrade and myself did not hear. We kept straight on toward the wall. When quite near it we were met by a volley which checked us for a moment. My comrade said to me:

"'Hold on, Jim, what shall we do?'

"'We'll charge them from behind that wall,' I replied.

"At our approach the rebels retreated from the

JAMES ALLEN,
Private, Co. F, 16th N. Y. Infantry.
Born in Ireland, May 6, 1843.

breastworks up the steep mountain side. We followed and climbed the wall. A ball struck my brave comrade in the left leg and made him unfit for further

South Mountain.—After the capture of Colonel Miles with 11,583 men, at Harper's Ferry, General Jackson hurried with the greater part of his force to rejoin General Lee.

McClellan learning the Confederate plan, ordered Franklin's Corps to pass through Crampton's Gap of the South Mountain, a continuation of the Blue Ridge, to relieve Harper's Ferry; the corps of Reno and Hooker he moved to Turner's Gap.

McClellan himself arrived at the passes on the 14th of September, but Lee had observed the movement and posted forces at both points.

A bloody all-day battle ensued in which the Union men forced the passage of the mountain.

The loss at Turner's Gap was 1,500 on each side, 1,500 prisoners being taken by the Union troops. At Crampton's Gap, the loss was about 500 on each side, and 400 rebel prisoners were taken.

SCANNING ALLEN'S PRISONERS

action. I found a comfortable place for the poor fellow in a crevice and gave him a drink from my canteen. 'Richards,' said I, 'if I pull through all right, I'll come and take care of you.' I then followed the retreating rebels.

"By this time they had reached a road running up the mountain which was skirted on our side by another wall, over which they had disappeared. The only thing for me to do was to climb also. As I drew myself up, I was met by another volley, but was only slightly wounded.

"Putting on a bold face, and waving my arms, I said to my imaginary company: 'Up, men, up!'

"The rebels, thinking they were cornered, stacked their arms in response to my order to surrender. I made haste to get between them and the guns, and found that I had fourteen prisoners and a flag taken from the color-guard.

"While thus situated I saw our colonel advancing up the road. Just out of gunshot he stopped, and taking his glasses, carefully scanned my party. He then approached, and, learning the details, rode back for a guard, to whom I handed over the prisoners.

"Knowing that the mountain top was the position to be secured by my regiment, I went up in advance, and when they arrived and saw the captured flag they gave three hearty cheers. I spoke to the colonel about my wounded comrade lying far down the mountain side, and a party was sent at once to bring him in.

"The morning following this episode found us on the march to Antietam, where we arrived at three o'clock and went into the fight, charging a battery that was shelling our General Hospital, where the surgeons were at work. We silenced the battery and then lay on the ground, in position, for twenty-four hours."

JOHN COOK, THE BOY GUNNER

"I was fifteen years of age, and was bugler of Battery B, which suffered fearful losses in the field at Antietam where I won my Medal of Honor," writes Bugler John Cook.

"General Gibbon, our commander, had just ordered Lieutenant Stewart to take his section about one hundred yards to the right of the Hagerstown Pike, in front of two straw stacks, when he beckoned me to follow. No sooner had we unlimbered, when a column of Confederate infantry, emerging from the so-called west woods, poured a volley into us, which brought fourteen or seventeen of my brave comrades to the ground. The two straw stacks offered some kind of shelter for our wounded, and it was a sickening sight to see those poor, maimed, and crippled fellows, crowding on top of one another, while several stepping but a few feet away, were hit again or killed.

JOHN COOK,
Bugler, Battery B, 4th U. S. Artillery.
Born in Cincinnati, Ohio, Aug. 10, 1847.

"Just then Captain Campbell unlimbered the other four guns to the left of Stewart, and I reported to him. He had just dismounted, when he was hit twice, and his horse fell dead, with several bullets in its body. I started with the captain to the rear and turned him over to one of the drivers. He ordered me to report to Lieutenant Stewart and tell him to take command of the battery. I reported, and, seeing the cannoneers nearly all down, and one, with a pouch full of

---

Antietam.—After his repulse at South Mountain, General Lee, with his force reduced to about 50,000 crossed Antietam Creek and took up a strong position, with both flanks resting on the Potomac, the creek flowing in front, crossed by three bridges and two fords, all but the north bridge being strongly guarded. In the afternoon of Tuesday, the 16th of September, 1862, General Hooker crossed the Antietam by the upper bridge, and, assisted by Sumner's Corps, attacked Jackson's flank the next morning, when the bloody battle began in earnest.

At one o'clock Burnside carried the ridge commanding Sharpsburg and captured a battery, but a Confederate division, 2,000 strong, coming up, compelled him to abandon it.

About this time the battle ceased without apparent victory to either side and with terrible slaughter on both.

Two-thirds of McClellan's force of 90,000 had been engaged with Lee's entire army. The Union loss was 12,469, of which number 2,010 were killed. The Confederates' total loss was over 25,000.

ammunition, lying dead, I unstrapped the pouch, started for the battery, and worked as a cannoneer. We were then in the very vortex of the battle. The enemy had made three desperate attempts to capture us, the last time coming within ten or fifteen feet of our guns. It was at this time that General Gibbon, seeing the condition of the battery, came to the gun that stood in the pike, and in full uniform of a brigadier-general, worked as a gunner and cannoneer. He was very conspicuous, and it is indeed surprising, that he came away alive. "At this battle we lost forty-four men, killed and wounded, and about forty horses which shows how hard a fight it was."

Bugler John Cook, although but fourteen years of age when he enlisted, showed great courage and daring in every battle in which he participated. At Gettysburg, Captain Stewart was compelled to use the bugler as an orderly because the battery suffered such heavy losses. He carried messages to the left half of the battery, nearly a half mile away, the route being well covered by the enemy's riflemen, who lost no opportunity of firing at him, thus

ASSISTING THE CAPTAIN

making it a most perilous undertaking. At the same battle he assisted in destroying the ammunition of a damaged and abandoned caisson, to prevent its being of use to the enemy, who were closing in on the Union men.

"BOB, I'LL HELP THE DOE-BOYS."

THE Fourth U. S. Artillery being short of men, and unable to get recruits for the regular service, Captain Gibbon obtained permission from the War Department, to fill his battery detaching men from volunteer regiments. One of the men selected from the many who responded to the call was Private William P. Hogarty of the Twenty - third New York Infantry.

He was one of the volunteers who were promoted to the vacancies in the rank of non-commissioned officers, and was made lance corporal.

WILLIAM P. HOGARTY,
Private, Co. D, 23d New York Infantry.
Highest rank attained: Lieutenant, U. S. A., and Captain, U. S. Vols.
Born in New York City, Feb. 16, 1840.

It is necessary to explain here, that detached volunteers cannot hold an actual rank in the regular service. Hence, when Hogarty was promoted lance corporal to fill the vacancy in the rank of non-commissioned officers, the duties and obligations of that rank were exacted of him, though his pay and actual rank were not above that of a private.

Bright and early on the morning of September 17, 1862, made over memorable as the bloodiest one-day battle of the war, General Gibbon gave orders to Lieutenant Stewart, commanding the center section, to go to the front with the utmost speed, and take position in advance of the skirmish line, on an elevated piece of ground to the right of the Hagerstown road, in front of a cluster of wheat stacks, and facing the Dunker Church about a half mile distant. The section came into action, the cannoneers mounted and the horses started on a run. The men had barely time to unlimber the guns, when the charging columns of "Stonewall" Jackson's Infantry were upon them, determined to capture the section and turn the right wing of the army. This furious onslaught was met by a rapid, accurate, and deadly fire from these two Napoleon guns of Stewart's section, triple shotted with canister, which stopped the charge, driving the enemy back with fearful loss. In this charge Stewart's section lost fourteen men out of twenty-four actually engaged at the guns.

While the enemy were reforming their lines preparatory to renewing their attack, the other four guns of the battery under the command of Captain J. B. Campbell came up taking position on the right and left of Stewart's section, the left gun resting on the Hagerstown Pike.

The battery had little opportunity to remove its wounded to a barn in the rear of the wheat stacks, and to replenish its exhausted ammunition, when the re-enforced columns of Jackson's Corps again came madly charging on the battery. At the same time the enemy's artillery, massed on a hill to the right, opened fire on it. This time, however, the charging masses were met by the withering fire of the entire six guns, each double and triple shotted with canister. At this critical juncture the "Iron Brigade" charged the enemy on the right, and a New York brigade, through the cornfield on the left. During the fifteen or twenty minutes that the battle raged around Battery B, it seemed that all the missiles of destruction were flying through the sulphur-laden atmosphere screeching, hissing, howling their discordant song of death.

During this final charge, Corporal Hogarty perceived through the stifling air one of the guns of the battery, at which all the men had been killed or disabled, standing idle on the summit of the slightly elevated ground, in a very commanding position, just in advance of the line of battle. He seized a shrapnel, cut the fuse to explode the shell the moment it left the muzzle of the gun, and alone and unaided fired it into the ranks of the enemy.

With a few remaining men and horses the battery was moved into the cornfield on the left of the Hagerstown Pike, and again unlimbered for action in the rear of a firing line of infantry, which acted as a screen and prevented it from again becoming engaged. While here awaiting orders, Corporal Hogarty picked up a loaded, new Springfield rifle from the side of a dead soldier. The gun was capped and ready for firing. Turning to one of his comrades Hogarty said: "Bob, the supply of ammunition is running mighty low to-day, I think I will take this gun up to the firing line and help the 'Doe-boys.' (Doe-boys was a nickname for infantry soldiers.)

After the battle of Antietam the battery, its ranks depleted marched with the advance of the army through Northern Virginia to Fredericksburg in pursuit of the retreating enemy.

On the evening of December 12, 1862, Battery B, with the advance of the First Corps, crossed the Rappahannock River at the lower pontoon bridge.

The next morning, the 13th, the battery engaged the enemy on the extreme left of the army, driving them from their entrenchments. It then swung up to the Bowling Green road, and immediately became engaged with a couple of the enemy's batteries posted in their front in a commanding position.

The rebels having previously measured the ground closely, marked the distances, opened fire on the battery with deadly accuracy, but "old Battery B" soon silenced them, dismounting their guns and blowing up their caissons. At this critical point, while getting the range for his guns, Corporal Hogarty was wounded by a four-inch solid shot striking him just above the elbow, tearing off his left arm, necessitating subsequent amputation at the shoulder. The force of the blow whirled him around. He fell, landing on his right arm and elbow. He was not, however, rendered unconscious. Three of his comrades seeing him fall came to his assistance, and with a stick twisted a handkerchief around his arm at the shoulder to stop, as much as possible, the flow of blood.

SAMUEL C. WRIGHT,
Sergeant, Co. E, 29th Mass. Infantry.
Born at Plympton, Plymouth Co., Mass.,
Sept. 29, 1842.

AT BLOODY LANE

SERGEANT SAMUEL C. WRIGHT, during his service in the War of the Rebellion, participated in thirty battles. In those engagements he was wounded five times and twice reported dead. On one occasion he was shot directly in the right eye, and still keeps the bullet as an awful souvenir of his closeness to death. In speaking of the taking of the fence at Antietam, he says nothing of his own action but describes the wild rush and retreat of the volunteers for that desperate service.

"September 16, 1862, found our division (Richardson's) in the advance from South Mountain to Antietam, where we came upon the enemy. The shot from the first piece of artillery fired took off the leg of the color-bearer of my regiment. During the afternoon of that day the artillery fight was at times very lively. Early the next morning troops were sent to engage the enemy in our front. The roar of cannon and small arms was deafening. But, while, from where we lay we could only hear the cannonading, we could not see the enemy, as a growth of woods impaired our view. It was, perhaps, as well, that we could not see the carnage wrought.

"Soon an aid-de-camp, whose horse was white with foam, rode up to our position and ordered us to cross to the support of the troops so hotly engaged. We left hurriedly, made a detour to the right and left, and were soon fording Antietam Creek. The stream was so deep, that in crossing, we had only to remove the stoppers of our canteens and they would fill themselves. We held rifles and ammunition above our heads. The opposite bank reached, we removed our shoes, wrung out our stockings, and were then ordered forward, straight toward the 'Sunken Road.' Going up the hill we could see the cause of our sudden call. The hill was strewn with dead and dying; yes, and with those unhurt, for to stand was to be instantly killed by the sharpshooters who filled the 'Sunken Road.' The main army in line was only a few feet to the rear of them.

"Some 200 yards in advance of our position, which we were holding at a terrible cost, was a fence built high and strong. The troops in advance had tried to scale the fence and reform under that hell of fire. They were actually torn in shreds and wedged into the fence.

"The cry came to us for volunteers to pull down the fence. Instantly there sprang from the long line, fast being shortened as the ranks closed up over the dead, seventy-six volunteers. We ran straight for the fence amid a hail of iron and lead, the dead falling all about us, but to reach the fence was our only thought. A part of the force reached it, and, as one would grasp a rail it would be sent flying out of his hands by rifle-shots.

"The fence leveled, we made the attempt to return, and it was as hot for us on the retreat, as it had been on the advance. Few escaped death or wounds. I had almost regained my regiment, when I was hit. The line then successfully pressed on, and the 'Sunken Road,' or 'Bloody Lane,' as it is now known, was within our lines."

Sergeant Wright's intrepidity and fine soldierly qualities were readily conceded by his superior officers and found substantial recognition by two promotions on the field of battle. He was further rewarded by being placed in charge of the prisons at Paris, Ky., and Tazewell, East Tennessee.

"AMID A HAIL OF LEAD"

CARED FOR THE WOUNDED AMIDST A HAIL OF BULLETS

DR. RICHARD CURRAN,
Asst-Surgeon, 33d N. Y. Infantry.
Born in Ireland.

"ON THE morning of September 17, 1862, the command to which I belonged arrived, after a forced march, on the battlefield of Antietam," Assistant-Surgeon Richard Curran writes. "My regiment and brigade were immediately put into action. I was the only medical officer present, and, in the absence of orders how to proceed or where to report, I decided to follow my regiment, a course which brought me at once into the midst of a battle, terrible but brief, as the enemy, after a stubborn resistance, yielded, and fell far to the rear. The loss in killed and wounded sustained by the Third Brigade in this charge, and in the subsequent effort to hold the position, was 313.

"The ground of the battlefield at this point was a shallow valley looking east and west. The elevated land on the south was occupied by the Confederates, while the slight ridge on the north was held by our troops and batteries. From this formation of ground it was impossible for our wounded to reach the field hospital without being exposed to the fire of the enemy. In a battle men will suffer their wounds to go uncared for and undressed for a long time, if in a measurably secure place, rather than expose their lives to obtain surgical attention; and this was the case with our wounded. At this point the injured, Union and Confederate, numbering many hundred, preferred to remain close to the ground, and in shelter of the valley, rather than take the risk of seeking care in the rear. During the severest of the fight, and later on, I was told many times by the officers and men, that if I did not seek a place of safety I would surely be killed. I realized that the danger was great, and the warnings just, for, in the performance of my work I had to be on my feet constantly, with no chance to seek protection. But here were the wounded and suffering of my command, and here I believed was my place of duty, even if it cost my life.

"Close to the lines, and a little to the right, were a number of straw stacks. I visited the place and found that many of the disabled had availed themselves of this protection. Without delay I had the wounded led or carried to the place, and here, with such assistance as I could organize, although exposed to the overhead firing of shot and shell, I worked with all the zeal and strength I could muster, caring for the wounded and dying until far into the night. My only fear then was that my improvised straw-stack hospital would catch fire.

But we were spared this misfortune and the harrowing scene which would have followed. That there was good reason for this fear is illustrated by one of very many similar incidents. While dressing a wound on the leg of a soldier I turned away to get something to be used in the dressing. On my return I found the leg had been shot off by a cannon ball.

"Happily," the doctor concludes, "in no other position could I have rendered

IMPROVISED STRAW-STACK HOSPITAL

equally good service, for I am confident that, by my action, many lives were saved."

In the report of the commanding officers of the brigade, Doctor Curran is mentioned in one place as follows:

"Assistant-Surgeon Richard Curran, of the Thirty-third New York Volunteers, was in charge of our temporary hospital, which unavoidably was under fire. He attended faithfully to his severe duties, and I beg to mention this officer with particular commendation. His example is most unfortunately but too rare."

TO SAVE THE STARS AND STRIPES

"THE First Delaware Infantry," Second Lieutenant Charles B. Tanner writes, " formed the right of Brigadier-General Weber's Brigade. On the morning of the 17th of September, 1862, we forded Antietam Creek and marched in column for a mile and facing to the left, advanced in line of battle. We now formed the first line of General French's Division of General Sumner's Second Army Corps.

CHARLES B. TANNER,
2d Lieutenant, Co. H, 1st Del. Infantry.
Highest rank attained: 1st Lieut. Vols.
Born at Philadelphia, Pa., Nov. 25, 1842.

"Presently the enemy's batteries opened a severe fire of spherical case, shell and solid shot. We advanced steadily through woods and cornfields, driving all before us, and met the Confederates in two lines of battle, posted in a sunken road or ravine, with rudely constructed breastworks of rails, sod, etc., and still a third line of troops in a cornfield forty yards in the rear, where the ground was gradually rising and permitted them to fire at us over the heads of those below. Our right was also exposed to the sudden and terrible fire from the troops who had broken the center division of our formation.

"The cornfield, where we had taken up our position terminated about 100 yards distant from the sunken road, leaving nothing but short grass pastureland between us.

"On coming out of the corn, we were unexpectedly confronted by heavy masses of Confederate infantry, with their muskets resting on the temporary breastwork. We all realized that the slaughter would be great, but not a man flinched, and cheerfully we went to our baptism of fire.

"Our colonel dashed in front with the ringing order: 'Charge!' and charge we did into that leaden hail. Within less than five minutes 286 men out of 635, and eight of ten company commanders, lay wounded or dead on that bloody slope. The colonel's horse had been struck by four bullets; the lieutenant-colonel was wounded and his horse killed, and our dearly loved colors were lying within twenty yards of the frowning lines of muskets, surrounded by the lifeless bodies of nine heroes, who died while trying to plant them in that road of death.

"Those of us who were yet living got back to the edge of the cornfield, and opened such a fire, that, though the enemy charged five times to gain possession of the flag, they were driven back each time with terrible slaughter.

"We had become desperately enraged, thinking, not of life, but how to regain the broad strips of bunting under which we had marched, bivouacked, suffered, and seen our comrades killed. To lose what we had sworn to defend with our blood, would have been, in our minds, a disgrace, and every man of the First Delaware was ready to perish, rather than allow the colors to fall into the hands of the enemy. Two hundred rifles guarded the Stars and Stripes, and, if they were not to be recovered by us, the foe should not have them, while a single member of the regiment remained alive.

"I REACHED THE GOAL"

"Charge after charge was made, and the gallant Fifth Maryland, forming on our left, aided in the defense. The fire from our lines directed to the center of that dense mass of Confederates, was appalling. Over thirteen hundred noble dead were covered with earth in that sunken road by the burying party on the following day.

"When the Maryland boys joined us, Captain Rickets, of Company C, our regiment, called for volunteers to save the colors, and more than thirty brave fellows responded. It seemed as if they had but just started, when at least twenty, including the gallant leader, were killed and those who would have rushed forward, were forced back by the withering fire.

"Maddened, and more desperate than ever, I called for the men to make another effort, and before we marched fifty yards only a scattering few remained able to get back to the friendly corn, in which we sought refuge from the tempest of death.

"Then Major Thomas A. Smyth (afterward Major-General, and killed on the day General Lee surrendered) said he would concentrate twenty-five picked men, whose fire should be directed right over the colors.

"'Do it,' I cried, 'and I will get there!'

"There were hundreds of brave men yet alive on that awful field, and, at my call for assistance, twenty sprang toward me.

"While covering that short distance, it seemed as if a million bees were singing in the air. The shouts and yells from either side sounded like menaces and threats. But I had reached the goal, had caught up the staff which was already splintered by shot, and the colors pierced with many a hole, and stained here and there with the lifeblood of our comrades, when a bullet shattered my arm. Luckily my legs were still serviceable, and, seizing the precious bunting with my left hand, I made the best eighty-yard time on record, receiving two more wounds.

"The colors were landed safely among the men of our regiment just as a large body of Confederate infantry poured in on our flank, compelling us to face in a different direction. We had the flags, however, and the remainder of the First Delaware held them against all comers."

Lieutenant Tanner modestly forgets to mention one fact in his vivid pen-picture, to wit: That he was promoted on the spot and his bravery formed the text of a flattering report.

After recovering from his wounds he participated in several engagements equally as exciting, and one year later was so badly disabled, that he was given his discharge. Nevertheless, three months later the lieutenant again took up the sword and remained in active service until the war had virtually come to an end. Altogether he was wounded three times and has had as many narrow escapes from death as any soldier in the army.

JACOB G. ORTH,
Corporal, Co. D, 28th Pa. Infantry.
Born in Philadelphia. Pa.. Nov. 25, 1837.

A STRUGGLE FOR
THE COLORS

CORPORAL JACOB G. ORTH disposes of his own daring exploit with the following sketch: "Business commenced quite early for the Twenty-eighth Pennsylvania Infantry at Antietam. It was six o'clock in the morning, when we charged and drove the rebels back across the fields to an apple orchard where we encountered a very hard task. No less than three rebel regiments and a battery were our opponents. To secure a victory over them meant hard fighting.

"It fell to my lot to encounter the color-sergeant of the Seventh South Carolina regiment. A hand-to-hand fight ensued. The final result of our short but sharp conflict was, that the Carolinian was minus his flag, and I had secured the trophy. I also had a shot wound through my shoulder. Six other stands of colors were taken by our regiment in this charge."

This description, though brief, is sufficiently clear to indicate a hard, stubborn, and desperate struggle between two men intent on the possession of the same object, and reckless of the consequences to themselves.

WOUNDED WHILE CAPTURING A FLAG

AT THE battle of Antietam, Captain Theodore W. Greig, then a lieutenant in the Sixty-first New York Infantry, captured the battle flag of the Fourth Alabama. The two regiments were close together, firing into each other's ranks, when, with a bravado spirit the Alabama color-bearer planted his flag in the ground a few paces in front of his regiment, as if defying the Federals and daring them to capture it.

Greig saw it, and the thought of capturing it had no sooner entered his mind, than he was off, running like mad across the open space. The flag was in his hands before the Alabamians realized what was happening, but as the young officer started back, a shower of bullets was sent after him. Near his lines he fell, shot in the neck, but, recovering his strength, saved the flag that he had so gallantly captured.

SURROUNDED BY REBELS

DURING the battle at Antietam, Colonel William H. Irwin, finding it necessary to dislodge the enemy's sharpshooters, who were annoying a Union battery of four Napoleon guns, ordered the Seventh Maine out for that purpose. The regiment advanced in front of the skirmishers on the left. Major Hyde also threw out skirmishers and soon drove in those of the enemy from the edge of a cornfield and a hollow in front of timber.

The battalion was ordered forward, and, as the enemy opened fire on it from the front and left flank, a charge was ordered. With fixed bayonets the men rushed forward cheering, led by the gallant major. A body of the enemy in an orchard to the left, being flanked, broke and ran. Those directly in front, behind haystacks and outbuildings, also broke, and, their colors having fallen, the Seventh pushed on up the hill to secure them, when a rebel regiment suddenly rose from behind a stone wall on its right, poured in a volley, and, at the same time, double-quicked around to the left to cut off the retreat. Those in front, seeing the small number of Union troops, had rallied and advanced in force.

Looking back and seeing no chance to escape, Major Hyde marched the regiment by the left flank, formed them on a crest in the orchard, poured a volley into those who were endeavoring to cut off the retreat, and faced those in front. Here the regiment received a severe fire from three directions. A rebel battery opened on it with grape, and it suffered heavy loss, although shielded somewhat by the trees of the orchard.

Having disposed of most of their cartridges, the men retreated through the orchard, gave the rebels, who attempted to follow, another volley, which drove them back, and, closing up on their colors, marched back in good order to their old position on the left of the Third Brigade.

The affair had lasted perhaps thirty minutes. The color-sergeant was killed and all the other guards shot but one, who brought off the regimental flag riddled with bullets. Of the 181 men, who went into action, there were twelve killed, sixty-three wounded, and twenty missing.

THE LAST ON ANTIETAM'S BLOODY BATTLEFIELD

FRANK M. WHITMAN,
Corporal, Co. G, 35th Mass. Infantry.
Born at Woodstock, Oxford Co., Maine, Sept. 30, 1838.

To venture, for the sake of wounded comrades, into a conspicuous and dangerous position is the height of soldierly pluck. Corporal Frank M. Whitman describes it thus:

"At the battle of Antietam, General Burnside, commander of the Ninth Corps, was ordered to take and hold the bridge that crossed a stream of water, on the opposite side of which the Confederates were in large force and well protected by the natural formation of the bank.

"The duty of taking this bridge was given to our brigade by the commander of the corps. The fight was a fierce one, but was soon won by our forces. We then advanced in line of battle up the hill, driving the enemy before us, until we reached a very high stone wall, behind which they made another stand. This stone wall ran along the ascending slope of the next hill beyond the one over which we were advancing. Our forces steadily went up and over the first hill and were part way down the descending slope, when our progress was stopped by the terrible fire of the enemy.

"We were obliged to retire. I and a few others were separated from our comrades and left behind with the dead and wounded on the field. We fired a last volley, receiving one in return which sent death to one of our men.

"Lying low and carefully watching, I discovered the enemy moving to another part of the field a short distance away. Cautiously I looked around among the men, and found that two besides myself were alive and unhurt. Turn which way one would, nothing could be seen or heard but the dead, the dying and the wounded, and the suppressed moans and cries of agony from all directions; here and there cries for a cooling drink of water, or a call for assistance and a helping hand. Mangled bodies of brave men, wherever one turned! A ghastly scene, that will ever be before my eyes!

"We three undertook to relieve the suffering as far as we could and to get the wounded away from the place. This work we continued for several hours, after which we set out to find the regiment. On regaining our lines, at my urgent solicitation, two officers and a number of men were sent with me to remove as many wounded as possible without drawing the fire of the enemy.

"On returning to the field, we found that the enemy had advanced his picket line some distance beyond his own line, and well up to that of ours. Because of this advance our picket would not allow us to go outside of the lines, but I pleaded with him so earnestly, that I was permitted to make the attempt to get a wounded comrade of my own company. This was a very delicate task, for had I attracted the attention of the enemy, an engagement would, without

"I REACHED
MY WOUNDED COMRADE"

doubt, have been precipitated. Stealthily, however, I worked my way to where my comrade lay, within a few feet of the enemy's pickets, and told him in a whisper what I could do for him with his co-operation. My friend, though suffering great pain from a wound in the leg that caused his death three weeks afterward, mutely and thankfully took up the journey to our lines, which, though near, seemed yet so far away. With great difficulty the task was accomplished, and we got within the lines, unobserved by the enemy, or at least without drawing their fire. The two officers and other men were able to remove quite a number of our wounded to a place where they could receive medical care.

"The morning dawned sad and dreary through the falling rain. Company G was astir early, and counting its members, I saw only eight present, with myself the sole surviving company officer. All commissioned and non-commissioned officers who had been in action, except myself, were gone. Nine were killed and thirty-five wounded."

In a later engagement the brave corporal was shot and lost his right leg.

THE FLAG WAS SAVED

WILLIAM H. PAUL,
Sergeant, Co. E, 90th Pa. Infantry.
Born at Philadelphia, Pa., Oct. 3, 1844.

THE usually brief and indifferent official record grows more eloquent when it refers to Sergeant William H. Paul and his inspiring behavior on the field of battle. The sergeant himself, modest as well as brave, tells the following:

"During the battle of Antietam, our corps was being vigorously attacked in a wooded and hilly part of the country, where our forces could not very well cope with an enemy accustomed to bush fighting. Nevertheless, in a hard and deadly struggle we were slowly but surely driving the enemy back, when Color-Sergeant Mason, who was in advance of our lines some four or five yards, cheering us on, was shot.

"A rebel detachment immediately rushed forward to capture the fallen colors. Seeing this, I placed myself at the head of a few men, probably ten in number, and charged out to meet the enemy, and if possible rescue the colors. We clashed with a shock, and a sharp hand-to-hand fight ensued in which two of our men were killed and five so severely wounded, that they were unable to be of any assistance.

"A rebel had already seized the colors, but I grasped them and with one supreme effort wrenched the precious banner from his hold. Waving it high above my head, I carried it throughout the remainder of the battle. In the *mêlée* my comrades managed to kill one of the enemy and capture another.

"I afterwards carried the flag in all the battles in which our regiment participated, until after the battle of Gettysburg, when I was relieved from further duty as color-bearer, because of a wound received during that battle."

PLACED HIS COMRADE'S LIFE
ABOVE HIS OWN

IGNATZ GRESSER,
Corporal, Co. D, 128th Pa. Infantry.
Born in Germany.

A N INCIDENT during the battle of Antietam made a hero of Corporal Ignatz Gresser of the One hundred and twenty-eighth Pennsylvania Infantry and saved the life of a brave Union soldier from an almost certain death. In the heat of the struggle, when the telling fire of both armies brought havoc to Union and Confederate ranks, Gresser saw one of his comrades drop to the ground, struck by the enemy's bullet. To leave him where he had fallen, meant death, almost inevitable; but to get at his side and carry him off, was equally as dangerous. Gresser placed the life of his wounded comrade above his own and undertook the perilous task. He succeeded in carrying on his strong arms the wounded man to the rear, miraculously escaping the deadly hail of balls and bullets. Thus it was, that Corporal Gresser earned his medal.

ATTEMPTED TO SPIKE
AN ABANDONED GUN

W HEN the Union troops fell back across the Potomac, at Shepherdstown Ford, Va., on the 20th of September, 1862, they had to leave a number of fieldpieces to the advancing Confederates. The enemy, however, gained nothing by their capture, as almost every gun had been spiked. As the Second U. S. Infantry was retiring an officer of the regiment presently remembered that one large gun had been overlooked and left unspiked.

"Who is willing to go and spike that gun?" he inquired.

First Sergeant Daniel W. Burke of Company B, at once offered his services. The fire from the enemy was severe, but nothing daunted, he started out on his perilous task and boldly attempted to unfit this gun for further service. After repeated attempts to fulfill his mission, he saw that the task was impossible of accomplishment, and reluctantly returned to his own lines, which he reached in safety. He was thereupon complimented by his superior officers for his display of coolness and courage.

"AIM LOW AND
GIVE THEM H--L!"

"A T Iuka the Eleventh Ohio Battery under my
command made a most desperate fight,
which was not only returned 'full measure,
pressed down and overflowing,' but in
which it lost, in killed and wounded,
over 52 per cent of its entire force and
over 88 per cent of its combatants or
cannoneers—or forty-eight out of fifty-
four men.

"The part taken by this battery in
the field was in violation of orders.
When we reached a point just south of
its battle ground—which was done un-

CYRUS SEARS,
1st Lieutenant, 11th Ohio Artillery.
Highest rank attained: Lieutenant-Colonel.
Born in Delaware Co., N. Y., March 10, 1832.

der pretty heavy fire from the enemy's artillery and infantry—I was ordered
to 'form in battery' at a point designated, and 'await further orders.' These
orders never came, but the enemy did, in force, sneaking up with their pieces at
'charge bayonets,' in plain view and at easy canister range. Though just then there
was a comparative lull in the enemy's firing, their bullets were s-s-z-z-z-ipping
among the battery with very uncomfortable frequency, and occasionally winging a
two or four-footed victim. On the charging masses came, 150 or 200 yards. Still the
battery was waiting 'further orders,' every man at his post, toeing the mark,
with everything 'ready' under fire.

"Of course, this wait was not actually long, though it seemed longer than
the whole fight. Naturally, the boys grew uneasy, and chafed from seeing such
splendid chances for the most beautiful pot-shot going to waste, and gave expression to views on the conduct of the war accordingly.

Iuka.—The battle of Iuka was fought on the 19th of September, 1862. General Grant, commanding
the Union forces entrenched at Corinth on the Tennessee River, sent General Rosecrans with 20,000 men to
Rienzi, and General Ord with another body of troops to Iuka. This plan, if successful, would have caught
the rebels in a triangle. General Price, who led the Confederate troops, evaded the trap and crossed the
country diagonally toward Iuka. Rosecrans followed in close pursuit and overtook the rear guard at Iuka.
That night the hostile armies camped some miles apart and clashed at about 2 P. M. General Hamilton
held the Federal right, Rosecrans commanded the center, and General Stanley the left. The battle lasted
until night. The telling fire of the Federal artillery decided the day in favor of the Union cause. The
rebels were routed and escaped with a loss of 300 prisoners and 500 killed and wounded. The Federal loss
was 350 killed and wounded.

"For example, one sergeant said:

"'By God, I guess we're going to let them gobble the whole damned shooting match before we strike a lick, if we don't mind and quickly too.'

"A corporal replied: 'I guess we are obeying orders.'

"'Damn the orders! To wait for orders in a time like this!' the sergeant retorted.

"This dialogue struck a responsive chord in my mind, and was, perhaps, the last straw that moved me to take a chance and shoulder the responsibility. I

"OUR BATTERY POURED A DEADLY FIRE UPON THE ENEMY"

gave the order: 'With canister, load, aim low, and give them hell as fast as you can!' And so the fight was on.

"Before the end it became evident that the position of the guns of this battery had become so much the bone of contention in that fight, that everything else, both flags, the Union and the Confederacy, and even the 'damned nigger' were forgotten in that all-absorbing, handspike and ramrod, rough-and-tumble, devil-take-the-hindmost fight for those six guns.

"I was wounded, and after the battle was ordered home to Ohio for repairs."

In recalling the fight, Lieutenant Cyrus Sears quotes the following from the report of General Rosecrans:

"The enemy's line of infantry now moved forward on the battery, coming up from the woods on our right on the Fifth Iowa, while a brigade showed itself on our left and attempted to cross the road toward Colonel Puiczel. The battle became furious. Our battery poured a deadly fire upon the enemy's column advancing up the road, while musketry concentrated upon it soon killed or wounded most of the horses. When within one hundred yards they received a volley from our entire line. The enemy penetrated the battery, were repulsed; again returned, were again repulsed, and finally bore down upon it with a column of three regiments, this time carrying the battery.

"Many of the cannoneers were 'knocked out' with ramrods and handspikes in the hands of the batterymen. Sands' Eleventh Ohio Battery, under Lieutenant Sears, was served with unequaled bravery under circumstances of danger and exposure such as rarely, perhaps never, have fallen to the lot of a single battery during the war."

SPLENDID HEROISM
OF A PRIVATE

WM. G. SURLES,
Private, Co. G, 2d Ohio Infantry.
Born at Steubenville, Ohio, Feb. 24, 1845.

IT SEEMS strange and paradoxical even that war with the horrors of the battlefield should serve to bring out the highest virtues and noblest impulses of mankind. The same cannon ball that carries death and injury, that destroys many a hopeful life, arouses at the same time along its swift and fatal course an increased feeling of patriotism, awakens bravery and incites men to the most brilliant deeds of heroism. Amidst the roar of guns and the hail of bullets sentiments of the most tender kind are born. Love, friendship, and sacrifice have found their most fervent manifestations on the battlefield. The love and admiration that a soldier, a mere youth, bore toward his commander forms a highly touching incident of the war. The scene was at the battle of Perryville, Ky, October 8, 1862, the heroes were Private W. G. Surles and Colonel Anson G. McCook.

Colonel McCook, commanding the Second Ohio Infantry had attacked the rebel infantry under General Bragg. The Confederates outnumbered the Union forces almost three to one, but, with noteworthy skill and bravery, the latter inflicted severe losses on the enemy, and retreated in good order.

"Although General Buell with a large force was within sound of our guns" Private Surles says, "he did not come to our assistance and we were forced to fall back. During the retreat Colonel McCook's horse was shot from under him.

Arming himself with a musket taken from a dead soldier, he fought on foot and by his own gallant example, cheered the drooping spirits of his men. The ground we traversed was thickly strewn with the dead and wounded of our own army and presented a ghastly picture.

"We observed with horror that our pursuers, with the cruelty of barbarians, were plunging their bayonets into the prostrate forms of many of our comrades. Colonel McCook himself noticed one of the ghouls, just about to extinguish the

HE SPRANG IN FRONT OF HIS COMMANDER

life of one of our boys with his bayonet. The colonel halted, fired his musket and dropped the fellow, before he could accomplish his dastardly deed.

"The death of the rebel made the enemy still more furious. A Confederate soldier, a veritable giant in appearance, presently sprang from behind a tree close by and took deliberate aim at the colonel. I had observed this fellow's movements and realized the great danger of my beloved commander. How I wished I could with a well-directed shot, end this 'Johnny's' life. But like the colonel himself I had just fired my musket and did not have time to intercept the shot. My blood froze in my veins as I saw the rebel raise his gun and take aim at our brave leader. Presently, on the spur of the moment and moved by the love and admiration I felt toward our commander I sprang directly in front of Colonel McCook, ready to receive the bullet, which was to strike him.

"Happily the rebel giant was a little too slow in firing or hesitated to make sure of his shot; anyway, before he pulled the trigger, he himself was shot through the head and rolled on the ground to die within a few seconds. One of the crack shots of our company had frustrated his plans.

"All of this happened, while shot and shell were flying around us like hail, and within less time than it takes to tell it. I should not forget to mention the conclusion of the episode, for it made me the happiest man in our regiment and has ever been one of the proudest moments of my life.

"When Colonel McCook saw his would-be assassin fall, he took me in his arms and with tears in his eyes kissed me as a father would his son.

"We all" Private Surles ends his narration "fairly idolized our commander and I'm sure, every one in our regiment would have willingly sacrificed his life as I was willing to do. I suppose, the fact, that at the time I was a mere boy, weighing less than 100 pounds and of almost girlish appearance, while the rebel was such a big, burly man, made the incident a trifle more prominent, than it, perhaps, otherwise would have been."

Private Surles served with his regiment throughout the war. At the battle of Chickamauga he and an older brother were fighting side by side. Both were giving a good account of themselves and paying back the enemy shot for shot, when the older brother was struck by a bullet, fell and died before William could grasp him in his arms or bid him a last farewell.

In addition to these two battles Private Surles fought with great distinction in some of the bloodiest battles of the war.

Perryville (or Chaplin Hills), Ky.— In the latter part of 1862, a formidable Confederate force under Generals Bragg and Kirby Smith invaded Kentucky. This invasion not only threatened the permanent occupation of the State, but also exposed the States north of the Ohio River to invasion. Learning that Louisville was to be General Bragg's objective point, General Buell left a sufficient force to protect Nashville, Tenn., which he occupied, and put his army in march for Kentucky, reaching Louisville on the 25th of September, 1862, ahead of Bragg's army.

On the 1st of October General Buell marched his army in three corps to Bardstown, but the enemy's infantry had retired from that place eight hours before the arrival of the Union forces. After a sharp engagement with the enemy's rear guard of cavalry and artillery, the pursuit was continued toward Springfield. Upon discovering that the enemy would concentrate for battle at Perryville, General Buell moved his army to that place; the center (third) corps, under General Rousseau, arriving on the afternoon of the 7th when the battle commenced, and lasted till nightfall. The engagement which terminated at night the previous day, was renewed on the morning of the 8th, the First, Second and Third Corps participating.

The rebels were repulsed with a loss of 2,500 killed and wounded and 4,500 missing. The loss sustained by the Federals was 3,859 killed and wounded and 489 missing.

"THREE CHEERS FOR THE COLOR-BEARER!"

"OUR brigade left Donaldsonville on the 26th of October, 1862, under command of General Godfrey Weitzel," writes Sergeant J. J. Nolan. "After a march of about four or five miles our advance guard had a running fight with the Confederates, which lasted all day.

"Next morning General Weitzel, seeing a number of Confederates on the right bank of the Bayou Lafourche, decided to throw our regiment (the Eighth New Hampshire Volunteer Infantry) across it and pick

JOHN J. NOLAN,
Color-Sergeant, 8th N. H. Vol. Infantry.
Born in Ireland, June 24, 1844.

all we could of them. After crossing the Bayou we advanced about two miles, when we discovered quite a force of Confederate cavalry in front of us.

"Colonel Hawks Fearing, of the Eighth New Hampshire, formed the regiment into a hollow square to resist the cavalry, which was in close pursuit. When we came to an open field the colonel deployed the regiment from square to line of battle. The Confederates formed in line on a road which ran along the woods to the right of the Bayou.

"By this time General Weitzel discovered that, during the night, General Mouton had crossed with his whole brigade from the left to the right of the Bayou, at the same time giving orders to make a pontoon of the boats that he had towed up from Donaldsonville, in order to get re-enforcements to our assistance. He then ordered our regiment to advance, which we did, and after throwing down the last fence between the Confederates and ourselves, the colonel ordered us to charge the enemy. After advancing about half way through the field, the flag staff was shot in two in my hands. I picked up the several pieces and advanced shouting: 'Come on and chase that battery!'

The Lafourche District, La.—During the latter part of October, 1862, an expedition was organized, which consisted of a brigade (five regiments of infantry, two batteries of artillery, and four companies of cavalry) under command of Brigadier-General Godfrey Weitzel, and a fleet of gun-boats, to move upon the western bank of the Mississippi through Western Louisiana, for the purpose of dispersing the forces assembled there under General Mouton.

The expedition arrived at Donaldsonville, La., on the 25th of October, and entered it without opposition. Thence the expedition proceeded to Bayou Lafourche, Thibodeaux, Berwick Bay, Boutte Station, Bayou des Allemands, etc., all of which places were entered. Valuable stores, freight cars, guns, and accoutrements, along with many prisoners were captured. The expedition proved a perfect success and gave undisputed possession of the Lafourche District to the Union Troops.

"FLAUNTED THE STARS AND STRIPES"

"Our hard fight was rewarded with success. We took about 200 prisoners, one piece of artillery, and routed the whole Confederate brigade.

"After the battle the colonel formed line, took the colors out of my hands, and called for three cheers for the color-bearer, and General Weitzel rode up and thanked me in the presence of the regiment."

Colonel O. W. Lull under date of November 16, 1862, furnishes a few more details of the incident, which Sergeant Nolan, who relates the above story, omits. The colonel writes: "Young Nolan was as fine and brave an Irish lad as ever shouldered a gun in the Union Army. At the fight at Georgia Landing he was the color-bearer and moved up and looked straight into the muzzles of the enemy's artillery, as steady and cool as Marshall Ney ever faced a battery. When his colors, struck by a cannon shot, fell forward on the ground, our young friend threw himself prostrate on his face and gathered the colors in his outstretched arms. Two or three of his own company also sprang for the flag, but young Nolan held on to his treasure, and with a 'No you don't' arose, moved on and flaunted the Stars and Stripes where grape and canister fell as thick as hail stones in a northern storm."

LED A GALLANT CHARGE

THE Thirty-seventh Illinois Infantry, commanded by Lieutenant-Colonel John C. Black, participated in the battle of Prairie Grove, Ark., on the 7th of December, 1862. Its position was on the extreme right, supporting Captain Murphy's Battery (F. First Missouri Light Artillery). After some manœuvring the regiment came to a halt, the men were ordered to lie down and being exhausted from marching sixty-six miles in thirty-six hours, most of them fell asleep almost immediately. Firing, however, by the artillery on both sides, commenced within five minutes after the halt was made and was kept up for an hour.

JOHN C. BLACK,
Lieu.-Colonel, 37th Illinois Infantry.
Highest rank attained: Brevet Brig-Gen., U.S.V.
Born at Lexington, Miss., Jan. 27, 1839.

The action from this point on is best told in Colonel Black's own words: "At the end of an hour we were ordered to advance into the open field. A cheer was given and we moved out a short distance, and remained stationary for some fifteen minutes, when I was ordered by Colonel Huston, commanding the Second Division, to advance the regiment down the slope to the support of the batteries of the Third Division. Scarcely had this position been reached, before Colonel Huston again ordered our advance against the hill, on which the center of the enemy was posted in unknown strength, and from which two regiments had first been driven with heavy loss. Throwing out Company A on the right and Company I on the right and left, as skirmishers, I ordered a charge up the hill. It was executed in fine style, the men advancing steadily and swiftly up to the edge The firing of the skirmishers in front announced the enemy close at hand. Clearing the edge, we stood face to face with them, their numbers overwhelming, one column moving by left-oblique upon our left and the right of the Twenty-sixth Indiana, another moving directly upon our right. They moved in column *en masse*, with guns at a ready. The firing began first upon the left and in a few minutes was general along the line. But, pressed by overwhelming numbers, the right of the Twenty-sixth gave way after most gallantly contesting the ground. My skirmishers about the same time reported the enemy's artillery posted on our right. Thus overwhelmed, the only hope from annihilation was the bayonet or retreat. The bayonet could not be used; directly in front of us was a rail fence, and it could not have been passed and we re-formed before the enemy would have been upon us; so, reluctantly, I ordered a retreat. Not a man had moved from his post till that order. Falling back some 300 yards, they reformed in the rear of our batteries.

"In this charge and retreat I was too seriously wounded to retain the command, and so, turning it over to Major H. N. Frisbie, I left the field, not how-ever, until the regiment was reformed and had again commenced its fire."

In his report of the action Colonel Daniel Huston, Jr., who commanded the Second Division of the Army of the Frontier, refers to Colonel Black's gallant regiment as follows:

"Finding on my arrival at the foot of the ridge, that the other regiments had fallen back so far and were so badly cut up, that it was necessary to give them time to reform, I brought up the Twenty-sixth Indiana and the Thirty-seventh Illinois at double-quick and ordered them to move up the hill to as-sault the position of the enemy, strongly posted on the crest of the ridge. Throwing out a company of skirmishers from each to cover their front, both regiments moved steadily and compactly forward till they reached a point 75 to 100 yards beyond the crest of the ridge, when the skirmishers commenced firing upon the enemy, of whom comparatively few could be seen. Suddenly the infantry of the enemy, which had been lying down, concealed by the thick brush and leaves, rose up in one overwhelming number and poured in a deadly, galling fire, which was withstood and returned by our troops with the coolness and firmness of veteran soldiers. The preponderance of numbers on the part of the enemy was so great that the infantry was eventually forced to retire in some little confusion; but they soon reformed in good order, taking a position about 250 yards from the foot of the ridge, which they maintained until the close of the action. The two regiments had lost nearly one-third of their number in killed and wounded in the desperate assault."

THE SINKING CREEK VALLEY RAID

"Our regiment, the Second West Virginia Cavalry," relates Major William H. Powell, "having as we supposed completed its campaign of 1862, was enjoying winter quarters at Camp Piatt, in November 1862, on the bank of the Kanawha River, about twelve miles above Charleston, S. C., when, to the surprise and gratification of the boys, they were ordered into the saddle and en route for Cold Knob Mountain, at which point the command was to be re-enforced by the Eleventh Ohio Volunteer Infantry, Colonel P. H. Lane commanding. From this point we moved against the Fourteenth Virginia Cavalry, then in winter quarters, recruiting, occupying two separate camps, one in the Sinking Creek Valley, the other some two miles west near Williamsburg, both in Greenbriar County, twelve miles west of Lewisburg.

WILLIAM H. POWELL,
Major, 2d W. Va. Cavalry.
Highest rank attained: Brevet Maj-Gen.,U.S.V.
Born in South Wales, G. B., May 10, 1825.

"Leaving the Kanawha River Valley route at Connelton, to avoid suspicion as to the objective point of operation, the column proceeded via the old road to Lewisburg, passing through Summerville, where the command arrived the same evening, having traveled sixty miles that day over rough mountain roads.

"Next morning we pushed forward as rapidly as possible through a blinding snowstorm, the snow being a foot deep on the ground. About noon, while accompanying the advance guard, composed of a lieutenant and eight men, I encountered a squad of rebel scouts consisting also of a lieutenant and eight men. We took them evidently by surprise, and, at the first sight of us, disregarding my polite invitation to halt, they ran into a log cabin but a short distance away from the roadside. Observing that the lieutenant had made his escape into the woods beyond the cabin, I pushed on after him, ordering my lieutenant and guard to surround the cabin. I captured him about a mile away. I have often wondered since, why the fellow did not take a position behind a tree, and, with good aim, stop my advance upon him, especially when he became convinced that I was pursuing him with a determined purpose to run him down. On returning to the cabin I learned that Lieutenant Davidson had captured the entire rebel squad, which result proved a very important factor in the final mission of the raid, as no one escaped to report the movement of the command.

"Resuming the march we pressed forward through snow nearly two feet deep, arriving at noon of the 26th on the summit of Cold Knob Mountain, where we found Colonel Lane awaiting us.

"After a conference between Colonels Paxton and Lane, the latter decided that the condition of his regiment, caused by exposure to the terrible storm and deep snow of the past twenty-four hours, rendered the continuance of the march utterly impracticable, and compelled him, in justice to his men and officers, to return to their winter quarters at Summerville.

"Influenced by the action of Colonel Lane, Colonel Paxton submitted to the officers of the regiment the question of returning to camp with Colonel Lane and the Eleventh Ohio Volunteer Infantry. This proposition met with my decided and unqualified opposition. When General Crook delivered the order to make the raid upon the enemy in the Sinking Creek Valley,—knowing Paxton's failings, and being disposed to throw the mantle of charity over them and allow him to accompany the expedition rather than detain him in camp,—he had confidentially charged me not to return to camp without good results. Influenced by these instructions and the fact that the men in the ranks and many of the company commanders were in full accord with my views favoring a forward movement, I said to the colonel that I would call for volunteers to accompany me in the advance movement upon the enemy's camp. This announcement, fully understood by Colonel Paxton, induced him to change his mind. He gave me orders, as the major of the regiment, to make a detail and move down the mountains as the advance guard.

"I ordered Lieutenant Jeremiah Davidson and twenty men of Company G, to accompany me, and immediately moved out in advance of the regiment. Proceeding about a mile, I met four rebel scouts at a sharp turn of the road. I instantly commanded a halt, and seeing that they preferred attempting their escape to a surrender, fired and charged upon them, wounding one and capturing another. The remaining two made good their escape.

"From our prisoners I hastily obtained valuable information as to the strength, location, and relative position of the two camps. The two scouts who had escaped, having seen but a part of our advance guard, concluded, as we afterwards learned, that as we did not press them closely down the mountain, we were nothing more or less than a squad of Union Home Guards living in the neighborhood.

"On nearing the foot of the mountain we discovered the two escaped scouts in the distance in the valley, moving leisurely towards their camp, the smoke of which was perceptible to me. I halted for a moment until they had passed out of my view around a point in the turn of the valley. Seeing that the coast was clear, and conscious that we had no time to waste, I pushed forward rapidly to the point where the scouts had disappeared, reaching it with my little band unobserved by the enemy.

"I could plainly see that they were in a state of 'innocuous desuetude,' unapprised of our proximity, and therefore unprepared to welcome us. Appreciating the golden opportunity, I decided promptly to charge the camp. Announcing

THE SINKING CREEK VALLEY RAID

the situation and my purpose to my heroic little command of Lieutenant Davidson and his twenty men, they answered:

"'We will follow where you lead!'

"Having not a moment to lose, I wheeled my command into line, facing the camp, and charged my handful of men on a full run of half a mile down the Sinking Creek Valley, into the center of the enemy's camp, 500 strong. We were each armed with a saber and a brace of Colt's 54 caliber navy revolvers, giving us 220 shots, which we held in reserve to avoid alarming the other camp, some two miles away, and to be used only in case of absolute necessity.

"It was soon made evident that the camp was surprised, and that the enemy's firearms were unloaded. During the brief and very exciting hand-to-hand encounter which ensued, some few of their number, in their confusion, ran up to us grasping us by the legs, and claiming us as their prisoners. To such daring and undignified assaults and claims we responded politely by tapping them on the tops of their heads with our revolvers, which we held in our hands, felling several of the rudest of them to the ground and causing them to loosen their grasp. After thus dealing with them for but a moment, I demanded the surrender of the rebels' camp, offering the protection of their lives. These terms Lieutenant-Colonel John A. Gibson promptly accepted, and surrendered the command to me without reservation.

"Thus I captured the camp of the Fourteenth Regiment Virginia Cavalry, 500 strong, in the Sinking Creek Valley, Va., November 26, 1862, without the loss of a life or the firing of a gun or revolver. Colonel Paxton did not reach the camp until after the surrender, at which time the other portion of the rebel regiment, in camp at Williamsburg, came over to a point within respectful distance to look at us. The achievement of the Sinking Creek Valley raid by a mere handful of men, at noonday, far into the heart of the enemy's country, requiring a continuous forced march in the saddle of thirty-six hours, from the Union lines to the enemy's camp, under the most unfavorable conditions of weather and roads, is an example of what a few brave, loyal, and determined men can accomplish."

VOLUNTEER INFANTRYMEN AT THE GUN

WALLACE A. BECKWITH,
Private, Co. F, 21st Conn. Infantry.
Born at New London, Conn.

JOHN G. PALMER,
Corp. Co. F, 21st Conn. Infantry.
Born at Montville, Conn., Oct. 14, 1845.

AN EXAMPLE of dashing bravery and courage, which General Daniel E. Sickles designates "a heroic act," was furnished by Corporal John G. Palmer and Private Wallace A. Beckwith of Company F, Twenty-first Connecticut Infantry. The story is interestingly told by Corporal Palmer:

"At the time of Burnside's great battle of Fredericksburg, I was a boy seventeen years of age and a member of Company F, Twenty-first Connecticut Infantry. We were held in reserve in the streets of the city until the last afternoon of the desperate fight. At 4:30 P. M. we received a hurry order to go to the support of the Second Division. Away we went, glad to take an active part, as we had been under fire more or less for two or three days. As soon as we cleared the streets of the city, we were exposed to a perfect shower of bullets and exploding shells from a general attack which was now taking place all along the front. Amidst this terrible fire we formed and moved rapidly towards the line of battle, our company marching for two or three blocks through the

---

Fredericksburg. — In December, 1862, General Burnside, superseding McClellan as commander-in-chief of the Union Army, directed an attack against Fredericksburg, Va., on the southern bank of the Rappahannock. The town is situated on the steep slopes of one of the three wooded terraces in the narrow valley. The battle took place on the second terrace, while on the third the enemy under Lee had gathered a force of 90,000 men.

Burnside, stationed at Falmouth was occupied from December 11 to 13 in building bridges and throwing across the river the two divisions of Franklin and Sumner. On the 13th, assaults were made by these divisions, which were repulsed with great loss. Hooker, ordered across, had the same experience. The Union troops were gathered at Fredericksburg and withdrawn across the river.

Burnside's losses amounted to 13,000 men, while the Confederate loss was not more than a third of that number.

back yards of houses and dwellings. We had a most lively time pulling up and scaling numerous fences to keep up with that part of the line which was meeting with less obstructions. We advanced to the scene of operations until the right of the regiment reached the railroad at the depot, the line extending to the left

"THE BATTLE GREW MORE FIERCE"

through some brickkilns. A light battery of four pieces, situated on a low ridge in front of the left of the regiment was shelling the enemy, whose fronts were near, as fast as they could fire their guns.

"We were ordered to lie down, which we did in short order, and settled ourselves into the soft clay of the brickyard, which offered some degree of shelter from the iron and lead which were flying so furiously around and dangerously near our heads.

"After a time the fire slackened. Our assault had met with a bloody repulse. Manoeuvres were immediately ordered with a view of making one more grand final charge and ending the battle.

"As the attack ceased and the firing had become desultory I raised up on my elbows; the colors of the regiment brushed my face. Pushing the flag aside

I glanced up and down the line. Our regiment appeared like two rows of dead men, every one except the colonel, with his head face down in the mud as low as possible.

"Presently the captain of a battery came running towards our regiment and hurriedly saluting the colonel, said: 'For God's sake, colonel, give me six men, quick, who know something about firing a gun. I haven't men enough left to work my battery in the coming charge.'

"Our colonel faced the colors and repeated the call. Though I was the youngest member of the company I had heard and seen enough for several days, and especially during the previous hour, to know the seriousness of the situation, to realize the probable consequences of the act, and to compare the exposure on the knoll with the safety of the shelter of the brickkilns.

"It took but a few moments for me to determine what to do. By the time the colonel had pronounced the word 'men,' I stepped from the ranks, closely followed by Comrade Beckwith and four others. We had but a few moments to look over the field and receive instructions from the sergeant, when the captain, reading the signals from the church belfry, gave the order to stand by the guns ready for action.

"The troops that were selected to make the final attack moved forward to the charge.

"Suddenly the enemy opened with every gun and musket that could be brought to bear. As we occupied the only rise of ground on our side and were the only battery in action on our left, we found that several of the enemy's batteries were paying us particular attention and that we had to take their concentrated fire. The battle grew more fierce.

"Twilight came on; twilight passed to darkness. It was a grand and awe-inspiring spectacle — one mighty and thundering roar.

"Around us rained a perfect shower of bullets, which completely riddled a board fence in front of the knoll. They struck the guns and splintered the spokes of the wheels. Shells exploded constantly over and around us and knocked down several of my comrades. Many officers and men were killed, and a great number, including several in my own regiment, were wounded in our immediate rear. We kept our little battery barking. Our commander said that our shells were bursting squarely in the ranks of the enemy, but our army could not accomplish the impossible. The heights were too strong with earthworks, cannon, and men, and the assault ended the battle for the night.

"We lived through the entire attack uninjured. Sunday morning the captain of the battery thanked us heartily for our services and told us to return to our regiment. Our colonel said, as he received us: 'I am proud of my men.'"

"IT SEEMED I GRASPED FOR DEATH"

" I won my medal at the charge upon Marye's Heights," writes Lieutenant John G. B. Adams. "At that time I was second lieutenant of Company I, Nineteenth Massachusetts Infantry. At Falmouth, Va., where we were in camp, the Third Brigade, Second Division, Second Corps, received orders on the 11th of December, to march to the banks of the Rappahannock, where we found an engineer company endeavoring to lay a pontoon bridge across the river. Our enemy, Barksdale's Mississippi Brigade, in the rifle-pits and houses of Fredericksburg on the opposite shore, had prevented our men from completing their work. After several fruitless attempts to continue, the bridge was abandoned, and volunteers were called for to cross in boats. My regiment and the Seventh Michigan responded to the call and undertook the task. History tells of the hard fight we had, trying to take the position of the rebels. Many a brave life was lost while crossing the river, and during the subsequent severe fight clearing the city.

"But these were only part of the hardships which we were to undergo at this place. On the 13th we were ordered up with the rest of the army to charge Marye's Heights, our regiment being on the extreme right. Shots from the batteries ploughed through our ranks as we pressed forward through the streets towards the enemy. Under a steep bank, not far from the rebel works, we took position until the order was given to move forward. The terrible havoc which took place after we had advanced over the embankment will surely stay in the mind of every participant to his last day. As fast as the colors came in sight, the color-bearer fell, and, in less than no time, eight were killed or wounded. The color-sergeant fell and Lieutenant Edgar W. Newcomb grasped the national flag. A moment later he, too, shared the fate of the sergeant. As he went down, I snatched the colors. It seemed as if I grasped for death, expecting every moment to be my last.

"Almost at the same instant the bearer of the state colors at my side was shot and, directed by a sudden instinct, I also took possession of our state emblem. Realizing that it would be sure death, and probably the loss of both colors, if we remained where I was, I rushed across the field to a fence at the left, my men following. Here the regiment was reformed, we changed front, and, by lying close to the ground, had a good opportunity to respond effectively to the fire of the rebel sharpshooters.

"The Nineteenth Massachusetts lost more than half of the men engaged and was finally obliged to retreat across the river and return to camp at Falmouth."

IT SEEMED I GRASPED FOR DEATH "

BOTH ARMS SHOT OFF

THE Twenty-first Massachusetts Infantry crossed the Rappahannock at Fredericksburg on the upper pontoon bridge December 12, and the next morning advanced on the enemy's works. The Second Brigade moved forward most gallantly in double line of battle, across a plain swept by a destructive fire of the enemy. Colonel W. S. Clark, of the Twenty-first Massachusetts, says in his report:

"When about sixty rods from the city, Color-Sergeant Collins of Company A, was shot, and fell to the ground. Sergeant Thomas Plunkett of Company E, seized the colors and carried them proudly forward to the farthest point reached by our troops during the battle. When the regiment had commenced the delivery of its fire, about forty rods from the position of the rebel infantry, a shell was thrown with fatal accuracy at the flag.

"Both arms of the brave Plunkett were shot off and literally carried away, and once more the colors, wet with the bearer's blood, were brought to the ground. Color-Corporal Olney of Company H, immediately raised the flag and defiantly bore it through the remainder of the day. Color-Corporal Barr of Company C, who carried the state colors, was shot, and his post of honor and danger quickly taken by Color-Corporal Wheeler of Company I. Color-Corporal Miller was also wounded."

Plunkett survived his injuries and was awarded the Medal of Honor.

COLONEL COLLIS "PITCHED IN" WITH HIS ZOUAVES

CHAS. H. F. COLLIS,
Colonel, 114th Pa. Infantry.
Highest rank attained: Brevet Maj-Gen., U.S.V.
Born in Ireland, Feb. 4, 1838.

IN THE official report, upon which the Medal of Honor was awarded to Colonel Charles H. F. Collis, it is stated that at the battle of Fredericksburg General John C. Robinson, who commanded a brigade, was thrown off his horse, which was killed by a solid shot. Lying on the ground the general called out to Colonel Collis: "Pitch in, pitch in, colonel!"

Here is the story of how Colonel Collis executed the order and "pitched in." He was commanding the One hundred and fourteenth Pennsylvania Volunteers, called the Collis Zouaves, and was attached to the First Brigade, First Division, Third Corps, which was commanded by General John C. Robinson.

The brigade was brought into action at the critical moment when the Pennsylvania reserves, commanded by General George G. Meade, had been repulsed and were being driven back towards the Rappahannock River. The enemy's infantry were pursuing the reserves, while the rebel batteries on the ridge were keeping up a terrific fire of solid shot and shell. Randolph's and Livingston's Batteries on the Union side were doing their utmost to protect the retreating Federal soldiers, but the enemy had reached Randolph and were about to take possession of his guns, when Robinson's Brigade, led by the Collis Zouaves, came up on the field at double-quick time, in column formation. General Robinson's horse was disemboweled by a solid shot; his adjutant-general was severely wounded, and his bugler killed, while they were all riding at the head of the column. This caused a momentary check to the advance of the Zouaves, who were now engaged in their first fight, though some of the officers, including Colonel Collis, had seen previous service. It was a moment of supreme importance to the Union Army. If the enemy had secured Randolph's and Livingston's Batteries, and turned them upon the Union ranks, the left flank of the

COLONEL COLLIS AT FREDERICKSBURG

Army of the Potomac would have been doubled up, and serious disaster would have been imminent. Colonel Collis, though a young man, only twenty-four years of age, quickly took in the situation, and seizing the colors of his regiment from the color-sergeant, galloped with them to the front, deploying his regiment into line of battle at the same time, and attacking the advancing foe with the bayonet. The charge of the Zouaves was not only brilliant, but picturesque, as they were uniformed in scarlet and blue, their heads being decorated with the red fez and white turban of the French Zouaves d'Afrique.

They came into collision with the enemy in the midst of the guns of Randolph's Battery, but their advance was so impetuous as to be irresistible and the enemy fell back in great confusion, leaving one entire regiment on the field, which was captured by the Zouaves. Robinson's Brigade held the position thus secured until the entire army retired two days later.

AT ANTIETAM AND
FREDERICKSBURG

"FOR distinguished bravery, coolness in action, soldierly conduct and conspicuous gallantry at the battles of Antietam and Fredericksburg." This is the inscription on Private John Johnson's medal. The gallant soldier's narration follows:

"I enlisted in the Second Wisconsin Infantry, but was on detached service in Captain Gibbon's Light Battery, B, Fourth U. S. Artillery.

"At the battle of Antietam the enemy opened fire at break of day, from a battery on a knoll, about halfway between the turnpike and the east wood. Shot and shell whistled over us but we returned the fire and soon silenced the enemy's

JOHN JOHNSON,
Private Co. D, 2d Wis. Infantry.
Born in Norway, March 25, 1842.

guns. Lieutenant Stewart, who commanded the right section of Battery B was ordered to take his section, to which I belonged, and proceed with Gibbon's Brigade. He formed in front of Dr. Miller's barnyard on the right, west side of the pike looking south on a little ridge, close to some buildings and within thirty or forty yards of a fence separating the cornfield from the pasture ground. The cornfield was full of the enemy's skirmishers and sharpshooters. It was here that 'Stonewall' Jackson's troops made three desperate charges to capture the battery at the point of the bayonet, and the last time came within a few rods of our guns before we could stop them. The infantry of General Gibbon and General Patrick's Brigade rallied to its support with equal resolution, the result being as fierce and murderous a combat as ever surged about a six-gun battery. Battery B was the very vortex of the fight. General John Gibbon came up to one of the guns, straddled the trail, sighted the gun, and exclaimed: 'Give them hell, boys!'

"Stewart's section in this position had three men killed and eleven wounded in a few moments. Among the wounded was Sergeant Joe Herzog, who with myself had hold of the handspike of the gun's trail and was trying to change the position of the gun, when he was shot through the lower part of the abdomen. Knowing that the wound was fatal and being in great agony, poor Joe deliberately drew his revolver and shot himself through the right temple. I was a cannoneer during the whole time the section and battery were engaged. We were firing double canister. During this time I filled different positions at the piece, including gunner. The cannoneers had been killed and wounded so rapidly that those remaining had to fill their places as best they could. By this time the other four guns of the battery had come up and commenced firing. This terrific contest resulted in the battery driving the enemy's infantry out of their cover. Our casualties in this action were forty killed and wounded. At my piece there were but two cannoneers left, myself and one other. As near as I can remember, we fired from ten to fifteen rounds of canister, brought to us by teamsters of the extra caissons, after the other cannoneers had been killed or wounded. The battery limbered up and hauled off without the loss of a single gun or caisson. Some of the guns had only two horses left, and the battery went into action again on another part of the field during the day.

"Again, at the battle of Fredericksburg I was a cannoneer in the right section (Stewart's), and filled the different positions at the gun, of cannoneers who had been killed or wounded. While carrying two case shots to the gun, having cut the fuse of one and made it ready to be inserted, I was wounded by a piece of shell, which carried away my right arm at the shoulder, with a portion of the clavicle and scapula. So much of the shoulder was carried away that the cavity of the body was exposed, and the tissue of the lungs made plainly visible. It has been said by comrades who were at that gun as cannoneers that I inserted the shell into the gun after my arm was torn off, before I fell. This, however, I do not remember.

"This same shell played havoc in the section, killing two men outright, Bartly Fagen of the Second Wisconsin, and Patrick Hogan of the regulars, and wounding several. It has been said by survivors of this engagement that the same shell also tore William Hogarty's left arm off. (See page 77 for Hogarty's story.) I served in the same section and at the same gun with him in this battle.

"Naturally this was my last battle."

MATTHEW S. QUAY,
Colonel, 134th Pa. Infantry.
Highest rank attained: Colonel, U. S. V.
Born at Dillsburg, York Co., Pa., Sept. 30, 1833.

"I'D RATHER BE KILLED, THAN CALLED A COWARD"

WHILE Colonel Matthew S. Quay was in command of the One hundred and thirty-fourth Pennsylvania Infantry he contracted typhoid fever at Falmouth, Va., opposite Fredericksburg, in the latter part of 1862. He was so broken down by the disease that his friends urged him to resign his commission and go home to recuperate. Colonel Quay finally applied for his discharge. General Tyler, handing him his papers, told him that he regretted his departure, particularly at this time, as they expected to go into action very soon. On hearing this Colonel Quay refused to accept the papers, and declared his intention of waiting for the battle. General Tyler told him, that he would be foolish to remain, in his broken state of health, and furthermore, that his discharge had been signed and he was a private citizen. The general said that if he went into the battle, he could surely not survive it, and all concurred in the advisability of his going home. Colonel Quay put these kindly suggestions aside with an impatient gesture, and said: "I'll be in this battle, if I have to take a musket and fight as a private, for I would rather be killed in battle and be called a fool, than go home and be called a coward."

General Tyler, seeing that further argument would be useless, gave in, and made him an aide on his staff, in which capacity he fought all day and well into the night in the famous battle of Fredericksburg.

FOUGHT, WHEN HE SHOULD BE AT THE HOSPITAL

CORPORAL MARTIN SCHUBERT, Company E, Twenty-Sixth New York Infantry, writes: "I received my first wound at Antietam, September 17, 1862, and was sent to the Columbia College Hospital, Washington, D. C., for treatment. While there I was given furlough to go home, but, instead of doing so I went back to the regiment, and joined it at Brook Station, Va., December 10, 1862. We crossed the Rappahannock below Fredericksburg on the night of the 12th, and the battle opened about seven o'clock next morning.

"My old wound, not yet healed, still gave me considerable trouble. I went into the battle with the regiment, however, against the protests of my colonel and captain, who insisted that I should use the furlough. I thought the Government needed me on the battlefield rather than at home.

"Within an hour I received another wound, this time in the left side. I still carry the bullet.

"General Burnside knowing of the fact that I had gone into the battle while I had a furlough and should have been in the hospital, promised me then and there a Medal of Honor, which I received in due time."

SEIZED THE COLORS AND TOOK THE LEAD

JACOB G. FRICK,
Colonel, 129th Pa. Vol. Infantry.
Born at Northumberland, Pa., Jan. 23, 1825.

COLONEL JACOB G. FRICK, with the One hundred and twenty-ninth Pennsylvania Infantry took a prominent part in the fighting at Fredericksburg. Charge after charge had been made on the stone wall and other parts of the rebel works, each attempt meeting with a bloody repulse. In spite of these repeated failures and futile efforts, it was deemed expedient to try a further experiment, and Tyler's Brigade of Humphrey's Division was chosen for the purpose of carrying the stone wall, behind which a heavy force of the enemy was strongly entrenched. The brigade was formed ready for the charge. Before the word was given to advance, Generals Hooker, Butterfield, and Humphrey rode up to Colonel Frick, who occupied his proper position in the formation in the rear of the Ninety-first Pennsylvania Volunteers, on the left of the line, and expressed the desire that he should lead the charge with the One hundred and twenty-ninth Infantry, informing him: "that he had a most difficult job before him."

In conformity with the desire of his superior officers, Colonel Frick moved his regiment between the files of the Ninety-first, and, upon orders, led his command boldly up to the very base of the stone wall, where the enemy poured forth a merciless fire of musketry upon him, aided by the fire from numerous batteries posted on Marye's Heights.

The charge was a signal failure. Flesh and blood could not stand the terrible fire which met them from the stone wall enveloping the whole command in a sheet of flame.

Colonel Frick's loss was 143 out of the 500 men of the One hundred and twenty-ninth taken into action. He himself was hit by pieces of shell in the thigh and right ear. A shell from the batteries concentrating their fire on the charging column, struck a horse at his side and literally covered him with the flesh and blood of the slaughtered animal. At the critical point of this charge the color-bearer was shot down, but the colonel quickly seized the colors and took the lead. Shortly afterward the flagstaff was shot off in his hands, close to his head, and the flag fell drooping over his shoulders. But he steadily advanced, leading his men through the terrible fire.

At the battle of Chancellorsville, May 3, 1863, Colonel Frick, with the One hundred and twenty-ninth Pennsylvania Infantry, on the right of the brigade, occupied a conspicuous position, and was brought into action in the midst of the heaviest fighting. French's Division was on his left, but the nature of the ground was such that the colonel felt justified in occupying a more advanced position. Having held this position against superior numbers, until many of his men had fallen, and long after the troops that covered his right and left had retired, he discovered that the enemy had already passed his right flank and was gaining his rear. Then he retired in good order to the rear of the batteries, which had gotten into position, while his steady musketry held the enemy in check.

He had retired none too soon, for the enemy fell upon him, captured his colors and a few prisoners, including his lieutenant-colonel. Colonel Frick quickly rallied his men, and, in a hand-to-hand fight, recaptured comrades and colors and brought to his rear as prisoners the very Confederates who had made the dash.

CAPTURED THREE HUNDRED REBELS

First Lieutenant E. M. Woodward relates a most thrilling adventure, of which perhaps, the most remarkable feature was his escape uninjured:

"At Fredericksburg the Pennsylvania Reserves held the left of our line, and when we charged the rifle-pits, our brigade struck the left of Archer's and passed up the Heights. I saw that the pit was still held by the enemy, and, knowing the danger of leaving an armed foe in our rear, I succeeded in halting

E. M. WOODWARD,
1st Lieutenant, 2d Pa. Reserves.
Highest rank attained: Major.
Born at Philadelphia, Pa., March 11, 1838.

some twenty men, and, with them attacked the pit from high ground in the rear, hoping to hold 'the occupants in position until assistance came. In about twenty minutes the Seventh Reserves advanced, halted some three hundred yards in our front, and opened fire, their balls passing over the enemy into our men.

"Instantly realizing that we should be wiped out if something were not done, I sheathed my sword, and, with my hat in hand, advanced between the lines to the rifle-pits, stopped the fire of my own men and that of the enemy, and demanded and received the surrender of the Nineteenth Georgia regiment. The rebel color-bearer attempted to escape up the heights with his flag, but I headed him off and captured it. I gave it to Charles Uphorn, who was soon afterwards wounded, and it fell into the hands of the Seventh Reserves.

"By this time all but five men of my small party were killed or wounded, and, seeing the impossibility of holding the prisoners with this handful, I crossed the rifle-pits, and, with a Confederate on each side, advanced towards the Seventh, waving my hat and thereby stopping their destructive fire. Returning to the rifle-pits, I got the Johnnies out, and sent them with their arms and accoutrements over to the Seventh. They numbered over three hundred, and were the only prisoners taken in this battle. With the remainder of my men I advanced up the Heights and joined the brigade, which was soon after crushed out and driven over the rifle-pits. During this fight thirteen bullets pierced my clothing and hat, but I felt that my own men could not kill me while I was saving their lives. It was this conviction which gave me courage to step between the firing lines and stop the deadly fusilade."

" STOPPING THEIR FIRE"

SAVED HIS
CAPTAIN'S BROTHER

FRANCIS H. GOODALL,
1st Sergeant, Co. G, 11th N. H. Infantry.
Born at Bath, N. H., January 10, 1838.

"AT THE battle of Fredericksburg, Va.," Sergeant F. H. Goodall writes, "both of the lieutenants being sick, I was directed by Captain George E. Pingree of Company G, Eleventh New Hampshire Volunteers to act as lieutenant during the engagement, and told that the regiment had been ordered to advance from Princess Charlotte Street, Fredericksburg (in the lower part of town), to attack the Confederates at 11:30 A. M. We were the first regiment of our brigade to make the advance, and it was our first real battle.

"We marched out in the rear of the city, under a very heavy fire of shot, shells, and musketry, past some brickkilns, filed to the right, crossed the Fredericksburg and Richmond Railroad, and went up on a little crest or elevation, within twenty-five rods of the famous 'Stone Wall,' at the foot of Marye's Heights, facing McLaw's and Cobb's Confederate troops under General Longstreet, without any breastworks or protection, commenced firing and so continued until all of the ammunition we had was expended — sixty rounds to each man. Our regiment remained there for six long hours under a galling fire, and lost nearly 200 men in killed and wounded. After the battle, there were 620 dead bodies by actual count picked up on the place immediately at and close by the spot where the Eleventh New Hampshire fought.

"Early in the engagement, William L. Pingree, one of the sergeants of Company G, Eleventh New Hampshire Volunteers, and a brother of Captain George E. Pingree of the same company and regiment, was very badly wounded in the head, and Captain Pingree said to me: 'Orderly, if anything happens to me, will you see that my brother Will gets off the field all right?' I replied: 'I will do so.'

"Not long after that, a shell burst close by us, killed two men, and knocked Captain Pingree over, so that we supposed for some little time that he would not regain consciousness. But he revived, although still feeling dazed, and just before dark he retired with his company and the regiment to the city, while I remained to take his brother off the field as I had promised, and selected Chester Simons, another sergeant of our company, to assist me.

"So, when the firing had about ceased and we thought the battle was all over for that day, we started to take the captain's brother off the field. But we had gone only a very short distance before a wild yell broke out on our right and immediately the firing began, faster and more furious than at any time during the day, and we were right out in the open field back of the city, exposed to the whole of it. It was the last desperate charge of General Meagher's Irish Brigade, and the bullets flew like hail; but we managed to escape somehow and finally got back to camp in the city with the regiment, and with the captain's brother, who lived almost three years before he died from the effects of his terrible wound."

TRADED HIS INSTRUMENT FOR A GUN

ONE of the many acts of daring and pluck that occurred during the battle of Fredericksburg, is here described by Sergeant Philip Petty, the hero of the action:

"In August, 1862, I enlisted as a musician in the One hundred and thirty-sixth Pennsylvania Volunteers, but not long after my enlistment, I exchanged places with a private of Company A, and took his gun. I was soon promoted to corporal and sergeant, and in the latter capacity was frequently called upon by our captain to temporarily fill higher positions.

PHILIP PETTY,
Sergeant, Co. A, 136th Pa. Infantry.
Born in Tingewick, England, May 17, 1840.

"In December, 1862, we found ourselves encamped near Bell Plain Landing, Va., and on the morning of the 13th we crossed the river below Fredericksburg, on our way to battle. While at a halt near the bank of the river, we could plainly see the lines of battle to our right, while in front and to our left, for a considerable distance, the ground was covered with tall grass. We were ordered forward and advanced slowly, when suddenly, within a few rods from us, the enemy's line of battle rose from the grass and fired a volley into our ranks. We retaliated, lay down, loaded, rose, and fired, and continued this operation until we reached the railroad slowly driving the rebels back. Comrades were falling all around me and, the color-sergeant being wounded, the colonel at once called for some one to carry the fallen colors. At the time the colonel made this request I was busy taking charge of and marching to the rear the Confederates whom we had captured in the battle, and as no one else responded, I stepped up and told him I would pick up the colors, and carried them in the advance until we were repulsed by a flank movement of the enemy and were ordered to retreat.

"I PLANTED THE FLAGSTAFF IN THE GROUND"

"I had advanced a little beyond the railroad track with the colors when the retreat was ordered, and, as I could not very well retreat with a gun and the colors in my hands, I planted the flagstaff in the ground and fired about thirty rounds into the rebels, then broke my gun by striking it on the rails, and carried the colors safely off the field. The colonel formed what was left of the regiment in a hollow square, and when he told the boys what I had done, they gave me three rousing cheers, after which the colonel promoted me to be color-sergeant."

A CHARGE IN WATER
AND DARKNESS

"ABOUT nine o'clock on December 29, 1862,"
writes Captain Milton T. Russel, "an
orderly came quietly along the line of sleeping
soldiers and in a low tone called my name, and
said that Colonel Streight wanted to see me.
I went a short distance with the orderly and
found the colonel and General Harker standing by their horses in consultation. They had
just returned from a reconnoissance. The colonel said: 'Russel, take your Company A, move
quietly to the front until you come to the river
(which was about 200 yards in our immediate

MILTON T. RUSSEL,
Captain, Co. A, 51st Ind. Vol. Infantry.
Born at North Salem, Ind., Sept. 25, 1836.

front), wade across, form your company on the south bank, and wait for further
orders.' He explained that General Wood, our division commander, was ordered
to cross and attack the enemy at that point at daylight the next morning, and
he wanted to know more about the ford and find whether or not the enemy
were close down on the bank of the river. This move was necessary in order
to fully develop the enemy's position. It required but a moment to return to
my company and form it in line, as the men had rolled up in their blankets
without removing any of their clothing. It was cold and chilly, and all the men
were lying on their arms. Without further ceremony the company moved off.
As we left the regiment, the officers were busy forming the men into line to
support us. We moved down and crossed the river, wading it with the water

---

Stone River.—On the 30th of December, 1862, the Confederate General Bragg had concentrated
his army of 62,000 two miles in front of Murfreesboro, Tenn.

The position of the Union Army 43,000 strong, under the Reserves, was on the west bank of Stone
River. The line ranged north and south three or four miles, the left wing touching the river.

On the 31st Johnson's Union Division was furiously charged and swept away by the enemy's left
under Bragg, who followed up his advantage by driving off Davis, and rushing upon the next division
under Sheridan, who retired after an hour's hard fighting, losing 1,630 of his men.

Rosecrans had massed his artillery on a knoll in the rear, which was assailed by four charges of
the enemy, who were repulsed with great loss.

Bragg then brought up Breckenridge with 7,000 fresh men, but his attacks were also unsuccessful.

On the 1st of January nothing was done. On the 2d, Rosecrans threw a force across the river,
and, with his artillery on the heights almost destroyed Breckenridge's Division, which was ordered to
drive him from the river.

On the 3d Bragg withdrew. His loss was 14,700 men. On the Union side there was a loss of
11,553. More than a third of our artillery and a large portion of our train were taken.

in some places up to our hips. Talk about cold water or a cold bath, it was so cold that our teeth chattered!

"As the company was nearing the opposite shore a terrific volley was fired from behind a rail fence not over forty steps in our front. The enemy, being on higher ground than we, fired too high, their bullets taking effect in the regiment that was standing in line where we left them on the opposite side of the river. There were but two ways out of the trap: one was to recross the river, the other was to advance. There was only a second in which to decide which horn of the dilemma to take. It flashed through my mind that their guns were empty, ours loaded. I gave the

"WE MOVED ACROSS THE RIVER"

command: 'On right into line, double-quick, charge'; and in less time than it takes to tell it, we were over that fence. My boys emptied their guns, fixed bayonets, and went at them. The best troops on earth will not stand with empty guns and receive cold steel. The Johnnies gave way and Company A, Fifty-first Indiana Volunteer Infantry followed right at their heels. Before I could bring the men to a halt the rebel line was driven back 400 yards and the desired information obtained. Had the charge proved a failure I would have been court-martialed for exceeding my orders. As it turned out all right, Uncle Sam has conferred this beautiful medal on me, but no captain ever had the honor of commanding a braver body of troops than I had in that charge."

LIKE AN ANGEL AMONG THE WOUNDED

REV. JOHN M. WHITEHEAD,
Chaplain of the 15th Ind. Infantry.
Born in Wayne Co., Ind., March 6, 1823.

"ON THE night of December 30, 1862, my regiment, the Fifteenth Indiana, was ordered to cross Stone River, at the ford. The command was obeyed, but as we advanced up the hill on the opposite side, we met the enemy in force, and, countermarching, recrossed the river. Here we bivouacked. Early the next morning our colonel passed along the officers' lines and said: 'Get your men up. Our pickets are falling back. The enemy is advancing.' In a second we were all astir, and at the dawn of day the bloody battle of Stone River commenced.

"Our position was between Stone River on our left and the railroad and turnpike on our right, and directly in front of Breckenridge's Corps. The firing from the Confederate batteries was terrible and very destructive.

"Colonel G. A. Wood, who commanded our regiment, was ordered to hold our position on the left, nearest to the river, at all hazards. Three times he charged Jackson's Brigade and three times put the enemy to flight, capturing a greater number of prisoners than there were men in our own command when we went into battle. But this was accomplished only with a fearful loss of life. Of my own regiment every alternate man was either killed or wounded. Though a non-combatant, I was with my regiment during the entire battle, comforting the dying, carrying off the wounded and caring for them.

"During the struggle Captain **Templeton** fell, fatally wounded. I carried him to the rear and remained at his side, until he breathed his last. I copied his last message and sent it to his friends at home. My own next-door neighbor in Westville, Ind., Captain J. N. Forster, dropped mortally wounded into my arms, the same ball killing two other brave soldiers.

"Colonel I. C. B. Surnan, of the Ninth Indiana, was shot twice, one ball severing the artery in the arm, the other penetrating the body and lodging between two ribs, whence I pulled it out.

"One boot was filled with blood and he was bleeding his life away. I dressed his wounds and helped him on his horse and he rode back into the raging battle. John Long, a private, had one leg shot to pieces. He cut the dangling limb off with his pocketknife and hobbled off using his gun for a crutch, until I took him up and carried him to the rear. Calvin Zenner of Company

G, received a fatal wound. I carried him back. A number of soldiers gathered around the dying comrade and I offered a prayer for him. He talked to all of us and then said: 'Now boys, let us all once more sing a song together.' And he struck up the hymn, 'O Sing to Me of Heaven.' Then he said: 'Good-bye boys, I am going home. I am mustered out.' And he closed his eyes and ceased to breathe. After nightfall, when both armies were quiet along the front lines, I helped to bring the wounded to the general hospital, carrying those who could not walk on my shoulder to the ambulance."

Chaplain John M. Whitehead who furnishes the foregoing vivid pen picture from the battlefield with all its horrors, modestly omits to mention that he helped many hundreds of wounded soldiers, brought comfort and solace to a great number of dying and preached at many a hero's grave. Colonel I. C. B. Suman says of him: "I was severely wounded at the battle of Stone River. When Chaplain Whitehead gave me his assistance, he was all besmeared with the blood of the wounded he had cared for. He seemed to be an angel among the wounded, Yankees and Johnnies alike. He thought nothing of the danger he was in, caring for the wounded, looking after the dead, directing and assisting their burial. I came in contact with many chaplains during my long service in the army and can truthfully state, that Rev. John M. Whitehead was the most worthy one that ever came under my notice. In camp, on the march, and on the field of battle, especially that of Stone River, his services were performed admirably, and without the hope of reward or promotion."

BROUGHT IN HIS MAJOR --- DEAD

PRIVATE JOSEPH R. PRENTICE writes: "It was at the battle of Stone River that Major Carpenter was killed. We had been ordered to advance on the enemy, so we formed up, and, marching at ease, we left the wood which had sheltered us up to that time, and started to cross a large, barren field. As soon as we emerged from the cover of the wood, the enemy opened a terrible fusilade on us, and several of our men were killed. The Confederates had a small breastwork or shelter on the other side of the clearing among some cedar trees, about five hundred yards from the position which we occupied. From this shelter they kept up a galling fire on our men. Our brigade was in the middle

JOSEPH R. PRENTICE,
Private, Co. E, 19th U. S. Infantry.
Born at Lancaster, Fairfield Co., Ohio,
Dec. 6, 1838.

of the line of attack, and very soon the rebels slackened their fire on our division and concentrated all their energies upon the two wings of our line.

"It was evident that if the flanks were weakened, the enemy could very easily surround us almost completely and so have us wholly at their mercy. To defeat this plan Major Carpenter ordered us to retreat in good order, and, after we had about faced, he fell in behind, and proceeded to follow us in the rear.

"No sooner did the enemy see us retreating, than they opened fire on us again. I was in the front rank in the advance, now in the rear in the retreat, and could plainly see the awful destruction wrought upon our ranks by the death-dealing work of the enemy. Suddenly, above the din and roar of battle, I heard our major call out: 'Scatter and run, boys!' and was about to join the rest in the rush to a place of safety, when I heard a horse bearing down on me like mad. As I ran, I looked around, and saw that it was Major Carpenter's horse dashing after us, frenzied by several slight bullet wounds. By yelling at him I managed to turn him and head him along our lines. Then I rushed after the boys to tell them of the fate of the major, but did not manage to see any of the commanding officers until we had retreated about a quarter of a mile. Then I gained permission to return and look for him. Back I went at the top of my speed, and as soon as I entered the clearing the enemy's sharpshooters opened a brisk fire on me. Still I was bound to find the major if possible, and,

"I MANAGED TO TURN THE HORSE

knowing about where he fell, rushed to the spot. Bullets ploughed up little puffs of dust at my feet and whistled around my head. A short spurt more and I was at the place. Glancing round I saw him lying face downward upon the dust, and rushed to his assistance. But, poor fellow, he was past need of human assistance! Nevertheless, I picked him up and carried him to the rear, my ears filled with the mournful dirge of the bullets that threatened me at every step."

SAVED A BATTALION

THE regular brigade of the Army of the Cumberland consisting of battalions from the Fifteenth, Sixteenth, Nineteenth, and two of the Eighteenth regiments of infantry and Battery H, Fifth Artillery, marched early on a gray frosty morning, December 31, 1862, from Stewart's Creek, where it had bivouacked during the night, to the battlefield of Stone River or Murfreesboro, Tenn., arriving there at about eight o'clock. After having been drawn up in column for possibly an hour the brigade was ordered into the cedars to the support of the right wing which was obviously being forced back by the enemy.

FREDERICK PHISTERER,
1st Lieutenant, 18th U. S. Infantry.
Highest rank attained: Brevet Brig-Gen., N. Y. N. G.
Born in Germany.

The two battalions of the Eighteenth formed the left wing, the other three battalion the right wing. The position of the battery was between the battalion of the Sixteenth and the Second Battalion of the Eighteenth, the right and left wings.

The infantry marched into the woods and after a march of about fifteen minutes on a wood road, the battalions of the Eighteenth regiment received orders to halt—which order was executed.

After some ten minutes or more had elapsed Major Frederick Townsend, commanding the detachment of the Eighteenth Infantry consisting of his own, the Second and the First Battalions, received orders to return and support the battery of the brigade. This order indicated that the battery was to the rear,—yet, there was a possibility that it might have gone to the front on another road and joined the right wing. In order to make sure that this was not the case, Major Townsend sent an orderly to the rear to find the battery and Lieutenant Frederick Phisterer, his adjutant, volunteered to go to the front, find the remainder of the brigade and ascertain whether or not the battery was with it. After a gallop of about ten minutes along the wood road, which first lead directly toward the approaching enemy and then turned to the right along his front, Lieutenant Phisterer came up with the battalion of the Sixteenth Infantry under Major Slemmer which was engaged with the enemy and under a heavy fire. From the moment that he had come to the turn in the road he had been exposed to musketry fire which increased in force as he came nearer the battalion of the Sixteenth.

He reported to Major Slemmer, inquired if the major had seen anything of the battery, and received the information that Major Slemmer had not seen anything of it and did not know its whereabouts.

This showed conclusively that the battery was not in advance as it was thought possible to be. Lieutenant Phisterer informed Major Slemmer of the orders received by Major Townsend. This was the first intimation Major Slemmer had received of any movement since he had struck the enemy, and as there was no support on his left and any delay might cause the capture of his battalion, Major Slemmer decided to fall back.

Lieutenant Phisterer then returned by the road over which he had come under a very uncomfortable fire, and rejoined his battalion, which he found moving out of the woods into the open field, there to support the brigade battery of whose whereabouts the orderly sent by Major Townsend had brought word.

Lieutenant Phisterer, in voluntarily going to the front and continuing his search for the battery in the face of a heavy fire from the enemy until he found the left battalion of the right wing of the brigade, imparting to its commanding officer the situation and the orders received by the left wing of the brigade, unquestionably saved that battalion at least and probably another battalion to its right from annihilation or capture. The brigade had but barely formed in support of its battery in the new position of the latter, when the enemy came out of the woods and made most determined and repeated efforts to take the battery, which efforts were, however, sturdily defeated by the latter, its regular supports, and additional troops formed to the left and right of the brigade; the determined assault showing that the strength of the enemy greatly exceeded the few hundred men of the right wing of the regular brigade engaging him but half an hour before

SQUIRE E. HOWARD,
1st Sergeant, 8th Vt. Infantry.
Highest rank attained : Captain.
Born in Jamaica, Vt., May 15, 1840.

"FOR GOD'S SAKE, RUN!"---HE RAN

JANUARY 13, 1863, a force of infantry, which included the Eighth Vermont Infantry and four small gun-boats, under General Godfrey Weitzel, attacked an entrenched force of the enemy, supported by the Cotton, a very formidable ironclad gun-boat, at a point on the Bayou Teche, La. The object of the expedition was the destruction of the ironclad, as she was much more powerful than any other of the fleet, and threatened the safety of the camps at Brashear City.

On the morning of the second day of the fight, General Weitzel asked for sixty volunteers from the Eighth Vermont, to act as sharpshooters. They were to be carried on a gun-boat as near as possible to the enemy's iron-clad, and there landed, to steal up near enough to pick off the gunners. Captain H. F. Dutton of Com-

"ESCAPED UNHURT"

pany H, volunteered to lead the party on this dangerous mission, and was at once confronted with the necessity of selecting his sixty men from more than twice that number, who stepped to the front at the call for volunteers. When finally selected, the number included First Sergeant S. E. Howard of Dutton's Company.

The party was carried on the gun-boat Diana, to the point where our three gun-boats were hotly engaged with the enemy, where it was found that the Calhoun, the largest of our boats, and the flagship, carrying Commodore Buchanan, the commanding officer of our fleet, had run hard aground on a bar; that the enemy having foreseen this, had a force in the rifle-pits on the shore near by, had killed Commodore Buchanan and many men on the Calhoun, driving the survivors from the guns, and were getting boats to board and capture her. At this critical moment Dutton arrived on the Diana, and was eagerly hailed by the nearest boat and asked, if he could send a message to Colonel Thomas, commanding the Eighth Vermont, which in the meantime had crossed to the west side of the Bayou, and was about 500 yards distant, entirely unaware of the grave situation of our fleet.

Sergeant Howard volunteered to carry the message, and received this from the naval officer: "Run, for God's sake, and tell Colonel Thomas that if he doesn't take those rifle-pits in five minutes, the Calhoun is lost. She is hard aground, Buchanan is killed, the men are driven from the guns and the enemy are preparing to board her."

Discarding all equipments, Howard was put ashore from a small boat and ran for his life, drawing a heavy fire from the enemy the moment he mounted the bank, but fortunately escaped unhurt, and delivered his message. The regiment was already in line of battle, and a moment later was swooping down on the doomed rifle-pits like a whirlwind.

The force in the pits was so busy trying to capture the Calhoun, that they neglected to watch their flank and rear, and before they knew what had happened, as one of the Union men expressed it, "a regiment of Yankees jumped square on top of them." The pits were taken in a moment, the Calhoun was saved, and was soon afloat, roaring her defiance.

Sergeant Howard received his commission as second lieutenant, immediately, and the medal which was awarded him later was accompanied by this flattering notice from the authorities: "To Captain S. E. Howard, for most distinguished gallantry at the battle of Bayou Teche, La., January 14, 1863."

FORT HUGER TAKEN BY BOLD AND ALMOST RECKLESS BRAVERY

HAZARD STEVENS,
Captain, and A. A. G., U. S. Vols.
Highest rank attained: Brevet Brig-Gen., U. S. V.
Born at Newport, R. I., June 9, 1842.

ON THE 19th of April, 1863, the enemy appeared in heavy force upon the line of the Nansemond River, Va., planting batteries at a number of points, threatening to force a passage, and compelling a few unarmored gun-boats which assisted in the defense, improvised from ferry-boats and the like, to shift their position to avoid destruction. Some five miles below the town the river was narrowed by a salient point on the opposite, or the enemy's side, known as Hill's Point. Here was an old earthwork — Fort Huger — erected by the Confederates during the first year of the war. They occupied this with a battery of five guns, and all efforts to dislodge, or silence them by the fire of the gun-boats and artillery from the opposite bank proved abortive. One gun-boat was almost destroyed, being struck over a hundred times by shot and shell, and the others were repulsed. Five small gun-boats above the fort were cut off from escape by its fire, and their destruction became a question of only a few days, or even hours.

Such was the state of affairs when General Getty, Captain Hazard Stevens,

"STRUGGLED ASHORE WAIST DEEP IN THE WATER"

and Lieutenant R. H. Lamson of the Navy, who commanded the gun-boats, rode to that part of the line opposite Fort Huger to observe it more closely.

Captain Stevens and Lieutenant Lamson climbed a tree near by to obtain a better view, but the more closely it was scanned, the more formidable and un-approachable the fort appeared. Finally, Captain Stevens declared, that the only way to silence the fort was to cross the river and take it. Lieutenant Lamson responded, that he would furnish the boats, if General Getty would furnish the troops, whereupon the gallant fellows hastened to lay the suggestion before the general.

He adopted it at once. As rapidly as possible a detachment of 270 men was embarked on one of the gun-boats, at a landing some two miles above the fort. General Getty went aboard and accompanied the expedition in person. A canvas screen was drawn up all around the deck, effectually concealing the troops.

The boat steamed rapidly down the stream, followed by the other gun-boats, all firing their guns and blowing their whistles. The enemy, observing the leader, and supposing that she was about to try to run past the battery, shotted guns until she should come abreast, and within fifty yards of the fort as the channel ran, all ready to blow her out of the water.

Just above the work, the vessel was run into the bank, but, glancing on a pile, she struck some forty or fifty feet from the shore. At this juncture, Captain Stevens leaped off the deck of the vessel, calling upon the troops to follow him, and struggled ashore, waist deep in mud and water. He was immediately followed by the troops. They waded in, climbed the steep bank, made for the fort, and stormed it on the run, though the enemy opened a hot fire of musketry, and reversed and fired one of their guns on the attacking party.

The capture of five guns, nine officers, and one hundred and thirty men, the rescue of five gun-boats, and the occupation of a point of vital importance, were the results of this achievement, one of the most brilliant of the war, accomplished, too, with a loss of only four killed and ten wounded.

LOVILO H. HOLMES.
Sergt. Co. H, 2nd Minnesota
Infantry.
Highest rank attained: Captain.
Born in Catharangus Co., N. Y.,
Oct. 10th, 1830.

BYRON E. PAY.
Private, Co. H, 2nd Minn.
Infantry.
Born in Le Roy Township, Jef-
ferson Co. N. Y., Oct. 21st,
1844.

MILTON HANNA.
Corp. Co. H, 2nd Minn.
Infantry.
Born in Jefferson Co., N. Y.,
Oct 21st. 1844.

THE "D--D YANKS" DIDN'T BEG FOR MERCY.

A T NOLENSVILLE, TENN., on the 15th of February, 1863, occurred an incident, in which a small body of Union men had an opportunity to call into play all their energies and determination against a party of the enemy, more than seven times their number. This little squad was composed of sixteen men, of which eight received the Medal of Honor after the war. These eight are Joseph Burger, William A. Clark, James Flannigan, Milton Hanna, Lovilo H. Holmes, Byron E. Pay, John Vale and Samuel Wright, members of the Second Minnesota Infantry. Corporal Milton Hanna, one of the members of this little squad, tells the story of the exploit:

"On Sunday morning, February 15th, 1863, after inspection and before breaking ranks, we were ordered to report at regimental headquarters. Here we found Co. C of the Ninth Ohio, commanded by the second lieutenant, awaiting us, with First Lieutenant H. R. Couse, of Co. C, of the Second Minnesota, who, being the ranking officer, had command of both companies.

"We received orders to go to the front to forage for mules, and started with ten teams. We marched south along the turnpike about three miles from camp, on a cross-road known as Concord Church Road. Here a colored man informed us that just over the hill, about a half mile away, near where the turnpike crossed over, the Sixth Alabama Cavalry, 500 strong, had camped the night before. After satisfying ourselves that this was true, we turned to the left on the mud road, and went a mile east to a farmhouse.

"At this point Sergeant Holmes received orders from Lieutenant Couse, to take fourteen men and four wagons, and go in a southwesterly direction to the foot of a hill near where the turnpike crossed over, and where the enemy was supposed to be, while he with the rest of the company should keep on east about three miles to another farmhouse, to load the other six wagons. We could not understand why we were separated, as there was more forage at either place than the ten wagons could hold.

"On reaching the farmhouse, located on a little hill, with a small creek some eight or ten rods away, we came to a lane leading from the house, some 500 yards in length, running east and west, at the head of which were some barns, cribs, etc., arranged in the form of a letter V. The sergeant at once stationed sentinels at different points to prevent surprise, and John Vale, who stood at the foot of the hill, was soon hailed by a colored man coming on the run, and nearly out of breath, yelling : 'See 'em ! See 'em !'

"The enemy were west of the turnpike, and had passed into the timber where we were unable to see them. They aimed to cut us off from our camp and the other foraging party. Sergeant Holmes ordered me to go to the cross-road and see what they were doing, while he returned to the cribs to prepare for defense. I placed myself in a cedar thicket a few rods from where the enemy crossed over the turnpike, and could hear them talk and laugh as the horses' hoofs pattered over the road.

"The captain of the rebel cavalry remarked that he would pick up the squad of fourteen blue-coats and take them prisoners, as they would not offer fight, but throw up their hands and beg for mercy. He would then send them with a small guard, over the hill to the reserve.

"I returned at once and reported, but the enemy had already arrived at the farm. They filed into the field following the same course we had taken, spreading out and making as large a showing as possible, giving us a chance to count them. They numbered 125, all mounted.

"Holmes saw they were coming to us first, and ordered us to get under cover as best we could, and hold our fire until he shot first.

"'We can die' ; said he, 'but we'll never surrender.'

"With these orders we took refuge in the buildings. I took shelter in the lower part of the barn, Holmes with two men in the hay-mow, the others in cribs, hog pens, and other out-buildings between the house and barn. When the enemy reached the head of the lane, they put spurs to their horses, each trying to be first to catch a live Yankee. On they came across the creek, yelling : 'Surrender, you damned Yanks !' Moments seemed hours as we sighted our rifles, and waited for the signal gun.

"The advance was less than two rods from us, when three shots from the hay-mow took down the leading horse, which fell on its rider, and held him down during the fight, after which he was taken prisoner. Other shots quickly followed, killing

"WE WERE HOLDING OUR FIRE"

eight horses and wounding several men. The others quickly dismounted, and running back, took shelter behind the fences. During their confusion we had time to reload our guns, and as some loaded quicker than others, we kept up a continuous fire until the enemy were driven away.

"When the fight had continued for some time, I noticed a man sitting on his horse in a very dignified manner, who, we afterwards learned, was the captain in charge of the command. He was out of my range, but I took careful aim and fired. As he did not heed my salute, I gave him two more charges of powder and ball. Those familiar with the old musket know what this meant at my end of the gun. He had occasion to dismount and lead his horse farther back. I yelled that I had to do something on account of my shoulder. This, of course, was done in jest, and the other boys began yelling and asking why they didn't come and take the 'damned Yanks;' if they wanted us.

"The Confederates finally withdrew, and when the smoke had cleared away, we found two dead rebels, several wounded, and ten dead horses. We took three prisoners, and three horses who broke from their riders and came to us. Jim Flannigan was mounted on one of the captured horses and sent to camp, and Charles Krause, on another, was dispatched to the remainder of the company, which was nowhere to be seen at that time.

"We finished loading our wagons, and prepared to return to camp. Our loss was Sergeant Holmes, Charles Liscomb and Sam Louden, slightly wounded; one mule killed and a wagon-tongue broken. We had three good horses to return to Uncle Sam for the dead mule."

THREE HUNDRED YANKEES AGAINST FOUR REGIMENTS.

ON THE advance to Chancellorsville in the latter part of April, 1863, part of the Sixth New York Cavalry, under the command of Lieutenant-Colonel Duncan McVicar was detailed to the Twelfth Corps and led the right wing of the army, crossing at Kelly's Ford on the Rappahannock on the 29th and the Rapidan River at Germania Ford, reaching Chancellorsville in the afternoon of the 30th, when orders were received from General Slocum to go to Spottsylvania Court House and ascertain the force there. From prisoners taken on the advance Colonel McVicar knew that a large body of Confederate cavalry was in front of us, but calling his officers to him, repeated the orders to them, and the bugle sounded "forward." Passing by a road through the woods, they halted where the crossroad led to Spottsylvania Court House. A scouting party was sent to that point and a guard sent to the rear. The command dismounted and lay by the roadside, holding their horses' bridles and, exhausted by continuous work, rested. In a short time the party sent to the Court House returned and reported a heavy force there, and just then the rear guard was fired on and driven in. It was then about dusk; the men sprang to their feet, some mounting, others leading their horses into an open field in front of the road where they formed in line. A bugle sounded for a parley, when word was sent for the Sixth to surrender, as they were surrounded by Fitz Hugh Lee's Brigade. Colonel McVicar's response was: "Draw sabers and cut your way through to our lines."

W. L. HEERMANCE.

Captain, 6th N. Y. Cavalry.
Highest rank attained: Lieutenant-Colonel.
Born in Kinderhook, N. Y., Feb. 23. 1837.

The bugle sounded the charge, all hesitated for they knew the enemy were massed in the road to meet them. The first squadron was commanded by Captain W. L. Heermance. After a moment's delay he said to his first lieutenant, George W. Goler: "George, some one must make the start," and gave the order: "By fours from the right, forward, charge." They started with a yell, Heermance and Goler leading the first set of fours; Colonel McVicar on the flank of the leading column. As they came from the field into the road McVicar was shot and instantly killed. Goler's horse was shot and the rider fell with him. Heermance was in the lead and alone as they struck the enemy massed in the road, who poured a volley from their carbines on the advancing troops. For a moment he was without assistance, and while engaged with one of the enemy on his right, another placed a pistol to his side on the left and as he wheeled his horse to give a left cut, the man fired and the ball

---

Chancellorsville, Va.—About the middle of April, 1863, General Hooker had massed his troops, an effective force of 130,000, in camp on the south side of the Rappahannock, while General Lee with his 60,000 remained on the north side. On the 30th of April, Hooker marched his corps to the Wilderness, around Chancellorsville, where his army encamped, Lee's army being at Fredericksburg, ten miles away on the same side of the river. Lee, however, knew nothing of Hooker's movement until noon of the 30th.

About noon on the 1st of May, Hooker's advance began, the march being by three different roads,—Sickles' corps was held in reserve,—to Banks Ford, at which point Hooker ordered a return to Chancellorsville.

On the 2d, Hooker prepared for a defensive battle. Lee sent "Stonewall" Jackson to the attack, he driving Howard back to Hooker's center. General Pleasanton with his cavalry and General Sickles' corps kept Lee back, by skirmishing with Jackson's rear guard.

After dark Hooker directed Sedgwick to march towards Chancellorsville, but he was already below Fredericksburg, fighting to gain the road to Chancellorsville. In the vicinity of Banks Ford he was engaged on the 3d with Lee's main army where he fought until dark. He was still contesting his ground on the 4th, when Hooker ordered him to retire across the river.

On the 3d, Lee's army closed in from left to right, assaulting the Union forces and directing their artillery fire at the Chancellor House, Hooker's headquarters. It was at this time that Hooker was temporarily disabled. The Union troops persistently held their ground against the repeated assaults, and after much hard fighting, Hooker ordered them to retire across the river, yielding the roads to Lee.

The Union loss was 12,145 and the Confederate, 12,463

THEY STARTED WITH A YELL

passed through his arm into his stomach, and a blow on the head knocked him from his horse. As he fell his men broke through to where he was and he called on them "to go on, as he was done for," which they did, driving back the Fifth and Third Virginia Cavalry, who came up as reinforcements. The Second Virginia, commanded by Colonel Thomas Munford, came in from Todd's Tavern, after the remainder of the Sixth had reached the forks of the road leading to the Union Army at Chancellorsville and took prisoners the wounded who had been left behind. Colonel Munford told Captain Heermance that the three hundred men of the Sixth had held Stuart's Division of cavalry, numbering four regiments, for six hours, preventing him from joining General Lee and cutting off the Union Army line to the Rapidan, and so materially changing Lee's plan of attack at Chancellorsville. Colonel Heermance was taken to Richmond and Libby Prison, but was soon exchanged. He was in over sixty engagements, severely wounded three times, was with Kilpatrick and Sheridan on their rides around Richmond, and with four companies, after the fight at Yellow Tavern, charged down the Brooks Pike and took his troopers inside the first line of works at Richmond, they being the first Union troops to enter them.

Bugler Wells, who afterwards received the Medal of Honor for the capture of a flag and its guard at Cedar Creek, was chief bugler and sounded the charge at McVicar's order, and was with him when he fell.

AN EXTENDED HAIR CUT.

STEPHEN O'NEILL,
Corporal Co. E, 7th U. S. Inf.
Born in St. John, P. Q., Canada,

CORPORAL STEPHEN O'NEILL tells an amusing story in connection with the incident at Chancellorsville, which earned for him his Medal of Honor. He says:

"Our regiment, the Seventh U. S. Infantry, of which I was a corporal, on the night of April 30th, camped on a highway near Chancellorsville, Va. The enemy was in front of us; we could hear the bands playing. Our pickets were sent out at once and pioneers ordered to chop down all the trees, in order to obstruct a possible attack from the enemy. By daylight we were all on the alert, waiting for the next command. I sat down to get my hair cut. The barber was about half done when the assembly sounded, and we had to fall in. Then came the order to 'double quick' to meet the enemy. Line of battle was formed on a clearing off the road. We soon met the enemy and were but a short time engaged, when the color-bearer who carried the national flag was mortally wounded. I was close at his side when the poor fellow staggered and dropped. Stepping up to where he lay, I quickly picked up the colors and bore them throughout the battle, leading our men to victory. Our own loss in killed and wounded was rather heavy. We were not allowed to maintain the position which we had gained in the struggle, but were ordered to retreat to our original position which we had left in the morning. We had just stacked our arms, the pickets had gone out again and I had just sat down on the same stump to have my haircut finished, when with a bang! bang! bang! the rebels came down on us. We ran for our guns and commenced firing. The enemy found, however, that there was too much climbing over the trees which had been felled the night before and retired under our well directed fire. We were ordered to another position of the line on the next morning, May 2nd, and held it all day, fighting, resting, playing poker, and eating at intervals. At night we retreated to our old camp ground near Falmouth, a sorry and disappointed lot of boys. Then I had the haircut completed."

SOLDIERS AS GOOD SAMARITANS.

A T CHANCELLORSVILLE, four members of Company A, Sixty-sixth Ohio Volunteer Infantry, Wallace W. Cranston, Henry Heller, Thomas Thompson, and Elisha B. Seaman, accomplished a deed, which won the admiration of their comrades, the gratitude of the enemy, and a Medal of Honor from the Government.

This story is told by Private Cranston as follows: " At about nine o'clock in the morning, the Twenty-third North Carolina Infantry came up the plank road, and marched by platoons to within about seventy-five yards of our works. A few charges of grape and canister from a Pennsylvania battery, stationed with our

WALLACE W. CRANSTON.

Private. Co. A. 66th Ohio Vol. Infantry.
Highest rank attained : Captain.
Born near Woodstock, Ohio, Nov. 20th, 1839.

division on the plank road, served to stop their progress.

" In their retreat they left a Confederate soldier on the road. The poor fellow's piteous cries for help attracted the attention of the commanding general, who was passing along the lines. He asked for volunteers to go out and bring him in. 'The roads are full of rebels,' said he, 'but if you go boldly down unarmed, they will know that you are after a wounded man and will surely not be so inhuman as to fire on you who are bringing relief to one of their own men.'

"With three of my companions, I volunteered for the service. We laid off our accoutrements, and, with two army blankets for stretchers, marched to where the man lay, in plain view of the enemy. We succeeded in bringing him back alive, and took him to the Chancellor House, which was then being used as a field hospital.

"After we had disposed of our wounded rebel, we rejoined our regiment, and very soon the battle opened in earnest all along the line. It continued for several hours with the greatest fury until we were driven in disorder from the field.

"The Chancellor House took fire from the rebel shells during the engagement, and burned to the ground, and I suppose this poor rebel soldier, with many of our own wounded must have perished in the flames."

"THE OLD VERMONT BRIGADE."

GENERAL LEWIS A. GRANT describes the efficient service of the brigade under his command in the battle of Salem Heights or Banks Ford, Va., as follows :

"When General Hooker crossed the Rappahannock, and proceeded to Chancellorsville, he left the Sixth Corps, commanded by General Sedgwick, in front of Fredericksburg, which caused a large force of the Confederate Army to remain upon the heights. My command was the Second Brigade, Second Division of the Sixth Corps, consisting of six regiments, and was known as the 'Old Vermont Brigade.'

"On the morning of May 3rd, having already crossed the river, General Sedgwick carried the heights of Fredericksburg. The main part of the corps moved from the town and carried Marye's Heights. My brigade was on the left of Hazel run, outside of the town, and in front of the principal heights. It moved to the attack in two columns, scaled

LEWIS A. GRANT.
Colonel 5th Vermont Infantry.
Highest Rank attained : Brevet
Major-General, U. S. V.
Born in Bennington Co., Vt.,
Jan. 17th, 1829.

these heights, drove the enemy from their position, and captured several guns and a number of prisoners. Later in the day, the brigade started for Chancellorsville, following the division of General Brooks. On the heights near the Salem church, General Brooks met a large force of the Confederate Army coming from Chancellorsville, and became heavily engaged. The enemy were turning Brooks' left, when my brigade deployed on the left, and held the rebels in check. The position was held during the night. In the morning it was found that a large Confederate force

had passed
around our left,
and occupied the
ground between us and
Fredericksburg. A change
of position was necessary, and,
during the first part of the day,
the Confederate Army and the Sixth
Corps manœuvred for position.

"THE ENEMY WAS CHECKED."

"A general and concerted attack was
made by the enemy late in the afternoon.
Long lines of Infantry emerged from the woods
and bore directly down upon us, their batteries
successfully opening fire upon us.

"The position chosen for my brigade was one of advantage. Four of the regiments occupied a swell of ground or crest, with an open field in front. The extreme right regiment occupied an advanced position in support of a battery; the extreme left fronted a ravine and strip of woods and had its left thrown back. As the enemy advanced the right regiment and the battery opened fire vigorously. This volley and the firing from a strong skirmish line caused the enemy to oblique to our left. This regiment, pursuant to orders, abandoned its position when no longer tenable, marched around the right and rear of the brigade and took position on the left. The Union forces in our front were met and scattered by the enemy, and the main attack came directly upon my brigade. The attack was gallant and determined. The enemy evidently supposed our lines to be broken and came upon us with cheers. Our men hugged the crest reserving their fire until the Confederates were within a few yards of our line. One volley was sufficient to check the advance. The enemy was thrown into confusion, and a great number of them were slaughtered. For a few minutes the fire from our line was rapid and continuous, then the right of the line charged down upon the shattered and confused mass in front of us and captured a large number of officers and men. At this part of the line our victory was complete. While engaged in gathering in our prisoners, I received imperative orders to withdraw my command, and place it farther to the rear and left. It seemed that the Confederate lines overlapped ours, and their right had gained a position on our left flank, threatening to cut us off from the river. The movement was urgent and necessarily prompt and rapid, and, in making it, we were obliged to abandon most of our prisoners. Nevertheless we succeeded in taking with us about four hundred, including several officers of rank.

"Our new position, covering the retreat, was taken and held. Darkness came on, and the Sixth Corps began recrossing the river on a pontoon bridge, constructed for that purpose near Bank's Ford. The crossing occupied the greater part of the night. During all this time, my brigade held the front with its picket lines extending from the river on our left, around to the river on our right. After all the rest of the corps had crossed, those of my brigade, not on the picket line went over. Then the picket line was gradually called in, and the greater part of it crossed in boats after the southern end of the bridge had been cut loose and had floated down the river around to the northern shore.

"It has been, I think, generally admitted, that, had not the Vermont Brigade checked and broken the enemy's line, and steadfastly held the front that night, the Sixth Corps would have found it difficult, if not impossible to cross the river. We were attacked by a superior force, flushed with apparent victory at Chancellorsville, which overlapped and flanked us and threatened our line of retreat.

"This was the first engagement in which I had command of the brigade, having assumed command as the ranking colonel, only two and one-half months before."

SCOUTS' PERILOUS PLIGHT.

GOTLIEB LUTY.
Sergeant, Co. A. 74th N. Y. Inf.
Born in Berne, Switzerland, Sept. 29th 1842.

THE Seventy-fourth New York Infantry, Fifth "Excelsior," distinguished itself at Williamsburg, where it fought in an abatis of felled timber, holding its position against the main force of the enemy. Its conduct at Chancellorsville was equally notable. A service performed by four of its members at the latter battle is described by Sergeant Gotlieb Luty, as follows:

"On the afternoon of May 3rd, when the Eleventh Corps was driven back, General Hooker ordered the Second Division, Third Corps, to take its place. We advanced to the position about dark.

"While lying there we heard firing in front, and General Berry, supposing that some of the Eleventh Corps were still in advance, asked Colonel Louisberry, of the

Seventy-fourth New York, if he had one or two men who would volunteer to find out if anyone were there, and to observe the enemy's position. Four of Company A, Felix Brannigan, Joseph Gion, Sergeant-Major Eugene P. Jacobson and myself volunteered to go.

"We divided into two squads, Brannigan and I going together, the others taking a different direction. We had advanced about fifty yards beyond the outposts, and were close to the plank road, when we heard horses coming down.

"We concluded to hide and await developments.

"A party of horsemen rode to within fifteen yards of us and we discovered by listening to their conversation that it was a body of rebels. Suddenly the firing commenced from all sides at once. There was only one round, and just as the firing ceased, we heard them say that 'the General' was shot. The reconnoitering party consisted of General Jackson and staff.

"After the Confederates withdrew, we got up, and concluded to go back to our lines, but lost our way and got among the rebels. They were terribly excited about General Jackson, and in the confusion we quietly withdrew.

"We reached our lines about three o'clock in the morning. Here we heard that General Berry had followed us and been mortally wounded. Before his death he requested, that if any of the scouts should get back, they should be rewarded for their services.

EVEN THE ENEMY CHEERED.

PETER McADAMS.

Corporal, Co. A, 98th Penn. Vol. Inf.
Born in Armagh Co., Ireland, Oct. 8th, 1837.

"At Salem Heights (or Bank's Ford), Va., the Ninety-eighth Pennsylvania Infantry, to which I belonged, were forced back from an advanced position. We had to leave some of our wounded men between the lines. Among them was Private Charles Smith, not only a comrade but also a dear friend of mine. I stepped up to Captain J. W. Beemish, of my company: 'If you'll give me permission, Captain,' I said, 'I'll try to save Charlie.' Permission was granted. On a dead run and under heavy fire, I advanced 250 yards, reached my friend, took him on my shoulders and brought him safely within our lines. A number of rebel soldiers, perhaps twenty, who witnessed the incident from a position behind the fence, cheered as they observed me escape their fire with my burden and gain the lines of my regiment. Our own men returned the cheer."

This is Corporal Peter McAdams' story. It furnishes a noble example of true friendship and soldierly virtue which the Government itself felt bound to honor.

GALLANT SERVICE AT CHAN-CELLORSVILLE.

ST. CLAIR A. MULHOLLAND.

Major, 116th Penn. Inf.
Highest rank attained : Brevet Maj.-Gen.
Born at Lisbon, Ireland, April 1, 1839.

DURING the battle of May 4th, 1863, at Chancellorsville, the Confederates immediately opposed to that part of the line of battle occupied by the Second Corps, tried to burn the abatis and log revetment behind which the Union forces were fighting. A high wind was blowing at the time and the danger was great. Repeatedly had General Hancock ordered that the flames should be extinguished, and each time an effort had been made to accomplish the desired result, but the fire of the Confederate sharpshooters was too deadly.

At last, in the afternoon, when the result of the day's work depended upon putting out the fires, General Hancock asked Major St. Clair A. Mulholland, of the One hundred and sixteenth Pennsylvania Infantry, to take command of the picket line and to extinguish the flames. The work had to be done under heavy fire and in full view of the enemy, but Major Mulholland formed squads of men quickly and assigning each squad to a section of the burning abatis, made a series of attacks. The enemy, seeming to comprehend the meaning of these efforts, at once redoubled their firing apparently, because the volleys were concentrated upon each squad in turn so that the brave Pennsylvania tugged and struggled in the midst and under a perfect torrent of bullets. They succeeded, however, in beating down the flaming logs and at last conquered the scorching enemy, completely disposing of the danger from such a source. It was work quickly accomplished and with but very little injury to the men engaged.

Later on, the same day, Major Mulholland scored another no less brilliant achievement. In order to withdraw the Union Army successfully from the field of Chancellorsville, it was thought necessary to sacrifice some officers and men. General Hancock requested Major Mulholland to remain in command of the picket line, keep up a continuous fire and remain fighting all night if necessary, or until the Union forces had fallen back and safely recrossed the river. The major willingly assented, fully realizing that the execution of the task meant almost certain capture by the enemy. Not only that, but he held the enemy in check on the picket line, until seven o'clock on the morning of the 5th, when, the entire army being safe over the Rappahannock, he was notified to abandon the line. In doing so he succeeded in drawing back nearly all of the pickets, getting them safely over the river. Major Mulholland fortunately was not captured by the enemy, though he was among the last to cross the stream.

THE COLONEL CARRIED THE STANDARD.

ALEXANDER SHALER.
Colonel, 65th N. Y. Vol. Inf.
Highest rank attained: Brevet Major-General.
Born at Haddam, Conn., March 19th, 1827.

ALEXANDER SHALER was colonel of the Sixty-fifth New York Volunteer Infantry, and in the spring of 1863, commanded the First Brigade, Third Division, Sixth Corps, Army of the Potomac. While General Hooker was engaging the enemy at Chancellorsville, the Sixth Corps was on the Rappahannock River below Fredericksburg. On the night of May 2nd, under orders from Hooker to move out on the plank road leading from Fredericksburg to Chancellorsville, and attack Lee's rear, the Sixth Corps entered Fredericksburg, but was unable to advance farther in the darkness and fog, on account of the formidable, defensive works of the enemy on Marye's Heights back of Fredericksburg, through which the plank road passed.

At nine o'clock on the morning of May 3rd, the Corps was formed for an assault. On the right were two columns, ordered to charge over the two roads leading up to Marye's Heights. All the troops to the left of these columns were in deployed lines. The enemy's batteries completely enfiladed the two road-ways which led from the city, over an open plain about a quarter of a mile wide, up the heights. The column on the extreme right was composed of the Sixty-first Pennsylvania Volunteers, Colonel George C. Spear, and the Thirty-first New York, Colonel Baker, supported by the Eighty-second Pennsylvania, Colonel Isaac Bassett, and the Sixty-seventh New York, Colonel Nelson Cross, all formed in the order named. Colonel Shaler was ordered to accompany the two last named regiments which belonged to his brigade.

Upon a given signal the troops advanced. As soon as the head of the right column debouched from the city, it received the fire from the enemy's infantry in the rifle-pits at the base of the hill and from the batteries, one of which was placed in the middle of the road, delivering a terrific hail of grape and canister. This momentarily checked the column's advance, but Colonel Spear, with great gallantry, rallied and carried it to a small bridge about half way across the open ground. Here Colonel Spear fell at the head of his column, mortally wounded, and his two regiments were practically dissolved. The demoralization which ensued, greatly imperiled the success of the movement at that point, as the surging column was threatened with destruction from the severe fire of the infantry and artillery. The Eighty-second Pennsylvania, next in the column, seemed unable to make any head-way. Seeing this, Colonel Shaler caught up the standard of the regiment, rushed forward, calling upon the two regiments of his brigade to follow him, forced the passage, advanced up the hill and captured two guns, one officer and a few men of the

COLONEL SHALER AT CHANCELLORSVILLE.

Washington Battery of artillery, of New Orleans, posted in a redoubt on the right of the road. The other regiments of this brigade, soon after greeted him within the enemy's works with cheers and congratulations. His men had not expected to again see him alive.

Colonel Shaler's bravery was reported to President Lincoln the night of the same day by Doctor Hosmer, the *Herald* correspondent with the Sixth Army Corps, who witnessed the assault and started for Washington immediately thereafter to report the success of the Sixth Corps in capturing all the enemy's works around Fredericksburg. Colonel Shaler was promptly made a Brigadier-General of Volunteers, and subsequently received the Congressional Medal of Honor for this act of bravery.

ON HORSEBACK DOWN A PRECIPITOUS BLUFF.

CHARLES A. CLARK.

Lieutenant, 6th Maine Infantry.
Highest rank attained : Brevet Lieutenant-Colonel.
Born at Sangerville, Maine, Jan. 26th, 1841.

DURING that memorable retreat across the Rappahannock, Lieutenant Charles A. Clark, of the Sixth Maine Infantry, accomplished a feat which saved his regiment from capture or annihilation, at Brooks' Ford on the night of May 4th, 1863, when the Sixth Maine was ordered to protect a single pontoon. "General Sedgwick was withdrawing his troops across the Rappahannock," says Adjutant Clark; "and our position was at the extreme right, on a bluff. The spot was important. A battery of artillery stationed on this bluff would command our pontoon bridge. We had orders to hold the position as long as possible, and then, if cut off from the remainder of the corps, to make our way to the bridge if we could. We all understood this to mean that a desperate enterprise was confided to our hands, and we were not mistaken. We were posted in a belt of timber which screened us from the enemy. The corps was retired from its center, which in time left us detached and upon the right flank without support. About 11 o'clock the enemy moved between us and our picket line, the pickets on our left, towards the center, having been withdrawn, and our pickets were captured without firing a shot. At this time I was adjutant of the regiment. Hearing a confused noise, Lieutenant-Colonel Harris and I rode to the edge of the timber, and we discovered in the moonlight the enemy forming its lines and coming on to attack us. Riding back hastily, the alignment of the regiment was somewhat changed to conform to the direction from which this attack was about to be delivered. This was hardly done before the enemy were upon us. There was a sharp fight of ten or fifteen minutes, and the night was filled with wild outcries and uproar. The result was a complete repulse. We held our position, but the extent of our force having been discovered, and it being demonstrated that we were entirely cut off from the remainder of the corps, our situation was more critical than ever. Riding again to the front to see what was going on, I discovered that the open space in front of us was filled with augmented forces whose lines were drawn around us, and that an immediate renewal of hostilities was to be anticipated. Sewall, of Company A, just then captured a Confederate officer who was attempting to reconnoiter our position. I put him in charge of Private Crockett, of Company A, and told Crockett to take him over the bluff, down to the water's edge, and if he could do so, to make his way to the pontoon bridge and turn his prisoner in to any force he might find there. Crockett started away, but the officer persuaded him that it would be impossible to descend the bluff, as it was too steep, but that to follow the edge of the bluff down towards the pontoons was much easier. Taking this line of march, Crockett in two or three minutes found himself in the Confederate lines which surrounded us and cut us off from the bridge. The tables were turned. He was the prisoner, and his prisoner was now the captor.

"WE WERE IN DEEP SHADOW AS WE PASSED."

"Meanwhile, a further examination showed the enemy in readiness to make an immediate assault. Lieutenant-Colonel Harris in his efforts to ascertain the situation, and if possible to open communications with Colonel Burnham, commanding the Light Division, had been cut off from the regiment by the cordon which was drawn around us. I tried to explain the situation to the senior captain, and to have him take command and withdraw the regiment. He naturally hesitated, thinking the responsibility very great, and that Colonel Harris might reappear at any moment. There was no time to be lost. I rode along the line, cautioned the men to maintain perfect silence and not to rattle their canteens or accoutrements, then left-facing the regiment I led them over the bluff. It was a sheer descent of fifty to sixty feet. I started over on horse-back. When part way down, my horse lost his footing, and I found myself falling with him through the air. I caught in the branches of a tree as we descended, slid down the tree, and on foot made my way to the base of the bluff, with the other men of the regiment. I expected to find a horse with a broken neck, but old "Jim" stood there waiting for me, apparently a good deal dazed and confused, but still ready for faithful service, although strained and sore for days afterwards. The men came on over the bluff helter skelter, but as silent as possible. Directly over our heads, and a few rods down the river towards the bridge, was the Confederate force into which Crockett had been marched by his wily prisoner, and which was waiting to assault us and insure our capture. Fortunately, we were in deep shadow as we passed under the bluff along the water's edge. When directly under the enemy, who reached to the edge of the bluff above us, some of our men became noisy. Just at this time the enemy again advanced upon our now abandoned position, and in the uproar which ensued we passed down the river undiscovered, and made our way in perfect order to our pontoon bridge. On approaching this, masses of troops were visible in the moonlight. Whether Confederate or Union forces it was impossible to tell. Even if Union forces, they might open fire upon us, taking us for the enemy, if we advanced without warning. Riding forward, it was a great relief to find blue uniforms and the stars and stripes. Giving these forces the caution that the Sixth Maine Infantry was coming in, we joined the rear of the Sixth Corps, after it was supposed that every man of us was captured or disabled in battle. When I found Colonel Burnham and told him that the old regiment had come in all right, he cried like a child. We passed over the bridge with the rear guard, and got across just in time, for as we went over the enemy opened fire with a battery from the bluffs above us. Not having the range accurately, the shelling did little harm, and the Sixth Corps reached the left bank of the Rappahannock intact."

"THAT'S THE LAST YOU'LL SEE OF SACRISTE."

LOUIS J. SACRISTE,
2nd Lieut., Co. D, 116th Penn. Inf.
Highest rank attained: Brevet Major.
Born in Delaware, June 15th, 1843.

"I was a second lieutenant commanding Co. D, One hundred and sixteenth Pennsylvania Volunteers, Meagher's Irish Brigade, Hancock's First Division, Second Corps," Lieutenant Louis J. Sacriste relates:

"At Chancellorsville, Saturday night, May 2nd, 1863, our brigade deployed near Scotts Mills and when General 'Stonewall' Jackson charged the Eleventh Corps under Howard, we had orders to prevent a possible stampede, but met with little success. Early the next morning we received orders to move to the front. As we neared the Chancellor House, and before we formed in line of battle, the enemy's shells killed a number of the brigade, because, for some reason, it countermarched while under fire of the enemy's batteries. We then formed in line of battle, my company being on the extreme left of the brigade, at the edge of the clearing around the Chancellor House. As we were forming, the Fifth Maine Battery under Captain Le Peine took up position between our left and the Chancellor House and opened fire at once with excellent effect, which, however, was only temporary.

"General Stuart placed thirty cannon in position and opened upon us with telling result. The man on my right was literally cut in two by a shell; the man on my left, had both legs cut off; the man in my front had a piece of his skull carried away, and the ground was covered with the dead and wounded. Men and horses of our battery were mowed down with such rapidity, that in less than an hour every gun, with one exception, was silenced, and but two noble fellows, Corporal Charles Lebrooke and Private John F. Chase, remained at their posts. Captain LePeine was mortally wounded. After the officers were disabled, a lieutenant of the regular army took command, but in a few minutes he too was fatally wounded.

"So accurate was the enemy's fire, that one of their shells exploded as it struck the mouth of one of our cannon, sending the pieces inside; another shell exploded one of the ammunition chests, the Chancellor House was set on fire, and smoke and dust added to the confusion. The line appeared to melt away and the front to pass out, while soldiers and riderless horses hurried down the road to the rear in something like a panic.

"I was in command of the left company of my regiment and brigade, and, seeing the enemy's infantry advancing, called on my comrades to follow me. I led them through the dust, smoke, and the fire of thirty cannon, into the face of Stuart's men, reached the battery, and brought off the first gun in triumph from the field. My example was followed by others of my regiment and brigade, and every gun and caisson was saved. A few minutes later the enemy had possession of the field.

Of his second exploit at Auburn, Va., which is included in the grounds of award of the Medal of Honor, Lieutenant Sacriste writes:

"On the night of the 13th of October, 1863, during a retrograde movement of the army, I was ordered, with twenty-five picked men from my regiment (One hundred and sixteenth Pennsylvania Volunteers) to report to Colonel James A. Beaver, commanding the picket line of the First Division, Second Corps. Early in the morning of the 14th, while the division and train were crossing Cedar Creek, Ewell's Corps attacked our line with such determination that it was about 11 o'clock A. M. before we forced the position, which we did by turning our flank and securing the ford and road over which our division and train had passed. By this movement the entire line was cut off from the rest of the army, our troops being nearly surrounded, and on the same side of the stream confronting Ewell's Corps. Colonel Beaver, seeing the critical position and danger of capture or destruction of his entire command, and perceiving but one avenue of escape, requested me to proceed along the line, which was heavily engaged and stubbornly contesting the ground, inform the officers of the situation, and direct them as to the route of march, which was to fall back slowly on the same side of the creek with the enemy, cross the stream south of the ford, and then march diagonally across the country to rejoin the division. As we started to obey the order of Colonel Beaver, one of my men remarked to another in my hearing, 'That's the last you'll see of Sacriste.' Colonel Beaver's instructions were carried out to the letter. As we were falling back, however, I discovered that one detail on the extreme right, commanded by a lieutenant of the One hundred and fortieth Pennsylvania Volunteers, had been overlooked in my first instructions. A second time I went in, and succeeded in saving this as well as the rest of the line, the command in the meantime being hard pressed, and closely engaged by cavalry, infantry, and artillery. Considering all the circumstances, the escape of the line was remarkable, and our action and stubborn courage made us the ideal of a rear guard."

THEY STOOD BY THEIR GUNS.

JOHN F. CHASE.
Private, 5th Maine Battery.
Born in Chelsea, Maine, in 1843.

"On Sunday morning, May 3rd," Private John F. Chase narrates, "my battery, the Fifth Maine, was ordered to take position in an apple orchard between the Chancellor House and the woods. The sight which presented itself to our eyes as we came through the woods to our designated position was enough to make the heart of the bravest man falter. Limbs and twigs of trees were falling struck by a storm of iron hail; the very air was laden with these flying missiles of death and it seemed impossible to be in that hell of shot and shell and survive. Into that position of death and annihilation we were ordered, and obeyed. Our battery was ordered to strip for action, a short prayer was offered and the command given: 'Mount battery, forward, gallop,' and as fast as the horses could go, we galloped forward.

"The boys were singing: 'I am going home, to die no more,' and in less than thirty minutes half of our number had gone 'home.' Even before we could get into position our horses and men went down like grass before the scythe. We had to place our guns by hand, and open fire on the enemy's batteries, which were masked on a wooded ridge about 200 yards in our front, and on several regiments of Confederate infantry to the right and left. Our orders were: 'Fight your guns to the death.' Our beloved Captain, George F. Leppien, had his leg shattered, the other officers were soon killed or wounded, and within a short time only two guns out of the six could be worked.

"General Hancock sent Lieutenant Kirby, of the First U. S. Battery, to take charge of us. He had just reached my gun, when a shell exploded, shattering his hip and breaking his horse's leg. I shot the horse to keep him from tramping on the wounded officer, whom I asked whether I should take him from the field. Lieutenant Kirby answered: 'No, not as long as a gun can be fired.' He was lying on the ground near the gun, bleeding from his wound, and liable to be hit again at any moment.

"Only one gun going now, and that short handed! I was number one cannoneer —my duty was to sponge the gun and ram the cartridge home. Beside myself, there was now left only Corporal Lebrooke. We could have gone to the rear and carried honors with us, but we had made up our minds to lie there on the battle field with our dead comrades, and fight the last gun to the death. We loaded several times with canister, and fired at the column of infantry that was charging up to capture our guns. Oh! how we hated to see the guns that we had served through many a hard fought battle, go into the hands of the enemy. At last a rebel shell struck our piece, exploding in the muzzle, and battering it so that we could not get another charge into it. I stepped to the rear of the gun, and reported to Lieutenant Kirby that our last gun was disabled and only two of us left. I also asked him if I could take him off the field. He replied: 'No, not until the guns are taken off.' What a display of courage in that young officer, lying there with his life's blood slowly ebbing away and putting duty before life.

"At this moment the Irish Brigade came charging in to our support. Corporal Lebrooke and I held up the trail of our gun, while the men of the One hundred and sixteenth Pennsylvania, belonging to the Irish Brigade, and led by Colonel St. Claire A. Mulholland, hitched on with the prolong rope and helped us draw it off the field. As soon as I saw that the guns were safe, I returned to Lieutenant Kirby, took him up in my arms and carried him to the rear, where I put him into an ambulance and started him back across the river. I was informed later on that he died before reaching Washington, but before he left, he took the names of myself and my comrade, saying: 'If ever two men have earned a Medal of Honor, you have, and you shall have it.'"

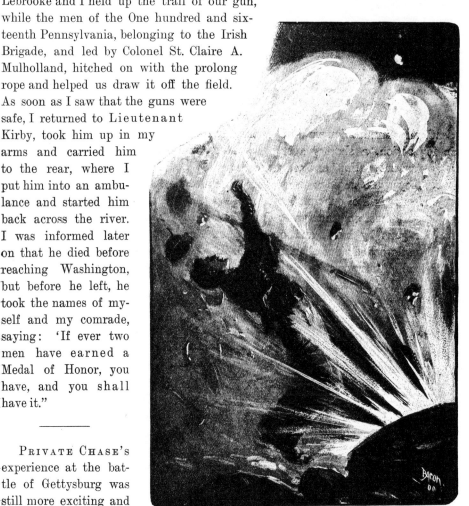

"A SHELL EXPLODED NEAR ME."

PRIVATE CHASE's experience at the battle of Gettysburg was still more exciting and resulted disastrously for the heroic soldier, who at that battle was made a cripple for life. "My battery," he says, "took position on the north side of the Seminary buildings on Seminary Hill, where we fought from 10 o'clock until four on the first day's battle at Gettysburg, July 1st, losing nearly two-thirds of our corps, and being outnumbered five to one. We were forced to fall back through the town of Gettysburg and take position on a knoll between Cemetery and Culps Hills, which position the battery held during the second and third days' battles. It was the time of the historic charges of Early's Division, led by the Louisiana 'Tigers,' on the Union batteries on East Cemetery Hill. My battery was enfilading the charging column as it dashed up the hill. Our shot, shrapnel, and canister was doing such terrible execution that the Confederates opened three or four batteries on us, and made the shot rattle around us pretty lively.

"One of those shrapnel shells exploded near me and forty-eight pieces of it entered my body. My right arm was shattered and my left eye was put out. I was carried a short distance to the rear as dead, and knew nothing more until two days after.

"When I regained consciousness, I was in a wagon with a lot of dead comrades being carted to the trenches to be buried. I moaned and called the attention of the driver, who came to my assistance, pulled me up from among the dead, and gave me a drink of water. He said the first words I uttered, after he gave me the water, were: 'Did we win the battle?'

"Then I was taken to the First Army Corps Hospital. It was a farm owned by Isaac Lightner, three miles from Gettysburg, on the Baltimore Turnpike. They laid me down beside the barn, where I waited three more days before my wounds were dressed. The surgeon let me lie there to 'finish dying,' as they said, while they attended to all the rest of the wounded. No one thought that I could live another hour. I lay on the barn floor several days, and was then taken into the house, where I stopped for a week. From there I was removed to Seminary Hospital.

"After about three weeks I was carried out of the hospital to die again, and was told by the head surgeon that I could not live six hours, but I did not do him the favor. I graduated with honors from that Seminary in about three months, and was sent to West Philadelphia Hospital, where I remained until I was able to return to my home in Augusta, Maine."

ON ERRANDS OF MERCY.

FORRESTER L. TAYLOR.

First Lieutenant Co. H, 23rd N. J. Infantry.
Highest rank attained: Brevet Major.
Born at Philadelphia, Pa., Oct. 30, 1833.

"I WAS detailed to the command of Company H, Twenty-third New Jersey Infantry, and led it at Fredericksburg and Chancellorsville, Va., May 3rd and 4th, 1863," writes Major F. L. Taylor.

"After the retreat was ordered, as I was hurrying down the road, I came to the prostrate form of Second Lieutenant Wilson of my company, who earnestly begged me to save him. Although it looked like suicide, I could not refuse, and stood by him making several unavailing efforts to obtain aid. Finally three of my men who were hurrying by, responded. One of them spread his blanket on the ground; we lifted the lieutenant on it, and, each taking a corner, started to the rear.

"A Union line of battle was formed a quarter of a mile to the rear, made up of men of various regiments, who bade fair to hold their ground. Before we had pursued our toilsome way over half the distance, the line broke under the fierce rebel attack but reformed about 500 yards farther to the rear, and, facing the foe, succeeded in checking his advance.

"As the line broke, I told the wounded lieutenant that our capture or death was now a certainty, and that my duty did not permit me to sacrifice four lives for the bare chance of saving one, so I ordered the men to lower him to the road, took his watch and pocket-book at his request, and left him. Perceiving, however, that the line of battle again formed, I encouraged my men to make another effort to save him. Without a murmur the brave fellows turned back between the fires of the contending forces. We reached Wilson in safety, and, though tired out with our exertion and the heat, staggered on until arrested by shouts. We were so weary that we were not looking where we were going, but with dogged resolution were struggling on, intent only on getting behind the line of the brave fellows who were so fiercely battling against the rebel advance. Looking up I found we were directly in front of a couple of brass field-pieces ready to fire. I hastily ordered my men to spring into the deep gully on the right side of the road, and a charge of grape went hurling over our heads. It was a narrow escape, as the captain of the battery afterwards said, for he could not have held his fire a half minute longer. We scrambled up out of the gully, and, before the guns were reloaded, passed in between them and sank exhausted on the ground. After a very short rest we again picked up our wounded officer and got him back to the field hospital.

"On the way to the rear, I was hailed by one of my corporals, Joel Wainwright, who implored me to save him. I told him that my hands were pretty full just then, but that I would return for him if possible, and cautioned him not on any account, to move from where he was. When I returned for him, it was growing dark, but I had no trouble in finding him, and soon had him in the doctor's hands.

"Shortly after, I heard that my friend, First Lieutenant Charles Sibley, of Company A, had fallen, badly wounded, at a certain place. I went back to my men and asked them to make a third trip, to rescue Sibley. They did not refuse, and, after getting a pass to go outside the lines again, my brave fellows went on their errand

"THREE OF MY MEN RESPONDED."

of mercy. But their effort was in vain. Having reached the described spot and calling his name without response, the rebel pickets began to fire on us, and I thought that discretion was the better part of valor. After covering a half dozen poor fellows with blankets, and giving a dozen or more drinks from our canteens, ordered a return, which was accomplished without injury.

"How we escaped with our lives, while saving Wilson, I cannot tell, unless the rebels, seeing what we were doing, had not the heart to fire on us. The five of us in a bunch were a tempting shot, but there is more good heart shown, even on the battle field, than is generally believed, for the true soldier feels a comradeship even with an enemy, whose conduct shows a spirit not less admirable than his own. As an evidence of this, the cap and shoulder straps of Lieutenant Sibley were sent in to us the next morning, under a flag of truce with a message telling of his death and soldier's burial."

STUCK TO HIS COLORS.

EDWARD BROWNE, Jr.
Corp., Co. G, 62nd N. Y. Inf.
Highest rank attained: Captain, U. S. V.
Born in Ireland, 1842.

CORPORAL EDWARD BROWNE, JR., was reported for gallantry in action at Fredericksburg and Salem Heights. In telling his own experience, he gives an interesting account of the movements of his regiment, the Sixty-second New York Infantry.

"On the morning of May 3rd, General Hooker was at Chancellorsville and General Sedgwick, with the Sixth Corps, crossed to the right bank of the Rappahannock, about three miles below Fredericksburg, and took up his line of march toward that city. The advance, after considerable resistance on the part of the Confederates, entered the city just before daybreak and drove them out. My recollection is that the enemy found refuge behind a stone wall at the base of the heights back of the city. At daylight, six companies of the Sixty-second were thrown in advance to uncover the enemy if behind the wall. I was with the color-guard at the time

"We advanced in line of battle until we came within the rebel works, which formed a circle at the foot of the hill, and uncovered them. But we reached the spot through a murderous fire of small arms at point-blank range, opened upon our front and flanks, and it seemed like going to sure destruction. Our men were literally mowed down. Those of us who were not incapacitated, sought the cover of the city as soon as we could. The color-bearer was injured in the engagement, but my comrades and I brought him back with the colors.

"Upon our return to the city, the remaining companies of the regiment were brought up and the regiment reformed. The colors were entrusted to me. About noon we were in line of battle for the charge, which carried the stone wall and the heights beyond. I was among the first upon the wall with the colors, and kept them flying until we reached the top of the heights and the enemy were routed.

"In the afternoon we pressed forward, after having reformed our columns, to Salem Church or Heights, about four miles to the rear of Marye's Heights, where, in a belt of woods, our advance became engaged with what we supposed to be the rear guard of the enemy. We afterwards learned that it was a part of Lee's forces on their return from Chancellorsville. The Sixty-second Regiment was in the second line of battle, supporting a battery, with its right resting on the road from Fredericksburg. Generals Newton and Wheaton were close by, mounted.

"Suddenly our boys came in hurried retreat from the woods, followed by the enemy in good form. I was at that time in front of the line waving the colors,

"I REMAINED WITH THE COLORS."

when, on turning to the right, I observed a line of the enemy emerging from a belt of woods in that direction, and called the colonel's attention to it. At the same time I was wounded in the side. The colonel noticed that I had been hit, and suggested my retirement to the rear. But the boys were coming across the open field between the woods and our line, and I remained with the colors open so that they might know they had something to rally about, and to show the enemy that we were not in a panic. I remained at my post until the boys had crossed the open and were within our lines, and the enemy had been brought to a halt by our fire. Then the colonel, C. B. Hamilton, commanded me to give up the colors and get to the hospital.

"I transferred the colors to a noble fellow, who afterwards fell under them; and after the enemy's line was broken and they had retired to the woods whence they came, late in the afternoon, I went to the field hospital. On the following day I crossed to the left bank of the river, and from a safe position, in the stone house which served as a hospital, I saw the battle.

"I returned to my regiment as soon as my wound was healed, and was with it in all engagements up to the fight before Washington in '64. I was made sergeant, and a commission was offered me, but I declined the latter through lack of appreciation of its worth. I was brevetted second and first lieutenant and captain in the New York Volunteers."

"SHOOT HIM!—KILL HIM!"

WILLIAM G. TRACY.
Lieut., 122nd N. Y. Infantry.
Highest rank attained: Major.
Born at Syracuse, N. Y., April 7, 1843.

A T the battle of Chancellorsville, Lieutenant William G. Tracy, 122nd U. S. Inf., was an aide-de-camp on the staff of Major-General Henry W. Slocum.

"When the Eleventh Corp was routed by the attack of 'Stonewall' Jackson," Lieutenant Tracy narrates: "I was sent with an order to bring back our troops across the plank road and stop the rebel advance, then about two miles distant. Riding forward, I struck the right brigade of Slocum's command, then under heavy fire, and, informing the brigadier, commanding, of my order, turned to the left and rear and plunged into the thick woods of the wilderness to find General Williams, commanding the division. In my haste and excitement, I soon lost my bearings; the firing in my vicinity ceased and I was completely lost.

"Riding hither and thither wherever I could see an opening, I finally came to a partial clearing of about fifty acres, where the trees had been cut into cord wood and piled up, leaving the stumps still standing. It was on the side of a hill, upon the top of which a piece of artillery was in action. Although it seemed to me to be pointed in a rather singular direction, I breasted the hill in good faith, stopped my horse about twenty feet from the piece and was about to enquire where General Williams was, when suddenly I discovered that the gunners were rebels.

"I was completely taken by surprise; my heart dropped to the bottom of my boots. 'Sent with an important order—lost in the woods and captured!' What a tale for my general! My first thought was to escape. I hastily surveyed my surroundings. An open, narrow road ran down the side of the hill and up another, the valley thus formed being heavily wooded. Upon the crest of the opposite hill was a blue line, which I knew to be our troops.

"In an instant my mind was made up and my heart seemed to come back with a thump to my breast. I resolved to ride down that narrow road to death or freedom. It was entirely open, being commanded by our troops. I walked my horse past the piece of artillery, gazing at the rebels as unconcernedly as I could. Although I was in uniform with shoulder straps, my blouse was covered with dust, and they did not spring for me, apparently not realizing that I was a Union officer. As soon as I passed, I struck into a gallop, not too fast to attract attention, yet ready for a burst of speed. In a moment I passed another piece of artillery and then came down to woods, at the edge of which some horses were tied.

"All this time I was making careful observations and realized that in all probability there was a large force of infantry at the foot of the hill before me—as artillery is never placed in advance of infantry—and the problem now became, how to reach the blue line of friends on the hill. Thus far I had proceeded, apparently without being recognized.

"Suddenly, just as I reached the border of the woods, some one cried out: 'Shoot him!' and I dug the spurs in and rode for my life. And how that brave horse did cover the ground! Down we went along the incline with no sign of a stumble, while I bent low over my pommel and fairly held my breath.

"Instantly, from both sides of the road came volleys of musketry, while all

"FROM BOTH SIDES CAME VOLLEYS."

through the woods the shouts resounded: 'Shoot him! Kill him!' and both forces, aroused by the noise at that point, opened a heavy fire, so that I rode into our line amid a hailstorm of bullets. I was hit once and my right arm was fractured, but I was not thrown from my horse, which was wounded in three places.

"I afterwards learned that I had, in some way, blundered through both lines, and behind a brigade of the enemy, thrown in advance of their line, and that I rode through this brigade and passed the headquarters of the rebel general, A. P. Hill."

"OUR GUN WAS KEPT IN MOTION."

AMOS J. CUMMINGS.

Sergeant-Major, 26th N. J. Volunteers.
Born at Conklin, N. Y., May 15th, 1841.

THE Twenty-sixth New Jersey Infantry, of which Amos J. Cummings was sergeant-major, was part of General Sedgwick's Corps, which was heavily engaged in the ever memorable struggles between Federal and Confederate forces around Chancellorsville. The culmination of the engagements and manœuvrings came with the battle of Salem Church on May 4, 1864. Generals Early, Anderson and McLaws had left Lee's Army at Chancellorsville to drive General Sedgwick's troops into the river. The conflict, which followed, was most obstinate, and lasted all day. Though largely outnumbered, the Northerners bravely repulsed each assault until darkness fell, when they were forced to yield to the superior strength of the enemy, and retreated, in good order, across the Rappahannock. Up to midnight the armies wrestled for supremacy. Both sides displayed bravery and daring, and many were the deeds of heroism performed by friend and foe. The Union soldiers especially were conspicuous for their gallantry. Some incidents occurred which give one a clear conception of the fierceness of the fighting and the heroism of the fighters. In this connection Sergeant-Major Cummings, who earned his medal on that memorable day, furnishes an inspiring narrative in the following:

"At sundown on this fourth of May, the Twenty-sixth New Jersey, Second Brigade, Second Division, lay in line of battle in a depression along a ditch dug by a farmer to drain his land. We were supported by the regular battery occupying a slight elevation in our rear. Our position was about three-fourths of a mile north of Salem Church.

"The Confederates massed and came down on us five lines deep. As they advanced I could hear the officer in charge of the battery behind us giving his commands. He was gauging his fuses by the advance of the enemy.

"'A second and a half' he shouted.

"'Blim! Blim!' responded his guns.

"'A second and a quarter!' he cried.

"'Blim! Blim! Blim!' was the reply.

"'A full second!' he roared.

"'Blim! Blim! Blim!' answered his guns.

"'Three-quarters of a second!' came next.

"'Blim! Blim! Blim!'

"The shrieking of the shells as they swept over our heads was appalling. Suddenly, right in front, there was a flash all along the line. The Confederates were within thirty yards of us and had commenced firing. The rebel yell was still heard, but the column had lost its impetus. As the yell died away our lieutenant-colonel shouted: ''ten-tion!'

"The order was heard by every man of the regiment. In a second everybody was on his feet. The colonel continued: 'Right about face!'

"The regiment obeyed the orders as if on parade.

"Then came, probably, the most singular command ever heard on a battle-field.

"'Regiment, left half wheel!'

"THE ENEMY WERE UPON US."

"The left wing of the regiment on our right had swung back, doing so to take advantage of the natural depression of the field and thus had left a gap between its left and our right.

"Our colonel saw the opening and realized that by left half wheeling he could again cement his line. Hence his singular command. But, when our regiment tried to obey the order, beginning the movement steadily and in perfect form, the result was disastrous. Suddenly there was a waver, then a break and then a rush for the river.

"A few brave men remained, but only a moment, when they began to swear and to coolly walk after their fugitive comrades trying by shouts and curses to rally them. A lieutenant of the battery confronted the demoralized men. He stood straight as an arrow with drawn sword. All of his guns had disappeared but one. It stood unmanned, subject to capture. His amazement knew no bounds. Our men had been acting like veterans and were now running over him like frightened deer. His oaths were terrific. He called them all the names in the vocabulary of indignation. There was a score of our regiment, however, who did not lose their heads.

"'Let us save the gun!' I shouted, at the same time seizing it by a wheel. The enemy were making for the gap, but four of my comrades were with me around the gun. On came the Southerners and our little group was increased by the coming of a few more of our men.

"The piece began to move backward in answer to our efforts, but, suddenly there was a change of scene.

"The enemy had passed through the gap and were upon us. They were holding our gun by the muzzle and then muskets were clubbed, bayonets were used. If the combatants had been personal enemies for years, the cursing and reviling could not have been more bitter. On both sides the wounded fell, uttering oaths and imprecations, but without groans.

"Enough of our men had rallied to the cannon to keep it moving until a Vermont regiment in the woods on our left, a regiment which had stood firm through all, was able to bring an enfilading fire to bear, when the Confederates were quickly dispersed.

"The gun was saved, the medal won."

TRUE COMRADESHIP

FRANK G. BUTTERFIELD.
Lieutenant, Co. A, 6th Vermont Infantry.
Highest rank attained: Brig.-General, U. S. V.
Born at Rochingham, Vt., 1842.

A T THE battle of Salem Heights, the Second Brigade, Second Division, Sixth Army Corps, made a charge on Marye's Heights, near Fredericksburg, when one of the regiments was thrown into confusion, breaking away from the line. This caused a gap in the charging columns and jeopardized the success of the attack, the blame resting entirely with the colonel of the regiment. Repeated efforts to reform the line failed. Finally Lieutenant Frank G. Butterfield, of Company A, Sixth Vermont Infantry, was entrusted with, and assumed the grave responsibility of moving the regiment without the consent of the colonel commanding, bring it back into action in its proper place, in the midst of a fierce battle, and under a galling fire of artillery and infantry. The officer in command of the brigade, General L. A. Grant, thanked and commended the lieutenant, and placed the colonel under arrest.

The day following, May 4th, the Sixth Army Corps was under fire all day. At dusk the lines were shortened and upon a new line being formed near the river at Banks' Ford, General Grant made the startling discovery that the Sixth Vermont Infantry was missing, possibly captured. Lieutenant Butterfield would not believe that his brave Vermonters had been made prisoners, and General Grant sent him to search for the regiment. At last he found his comrades in a strong position several hundred yards in front of the original line of battle. They had repulsed a charge of the enemy, and, charging in return, had been carried far from the original line by their impetuosity and valor. In the meantime, however, the enemy had already attacked the new line. Heavy cannonading sounded from the rear of the Vermont regiment. Colonel Barney, commanding, was loath to retire, but, of course, fell back with his regiment. Lieutenant Butterfield took command of a skirmish line, covered the retreat, and saved the regiment from destruction.

AT Lee's Mills a few weeks before the incident above recorded, Lieutenant Butterfield was forced to fall back over the Warwick Creek with his command while under a fearful fire from the enemy. He and Captain E. F. Reynolds, of Company F, Sixth Vermont Infantry, were the last to retreat. The captain fell, and here it was that Lieutenant Butterfield displayed true comradeship. He assisted the wounded officer across the creek, where in midstream he fainted. But the lieutenant would not desert him. He held his head up above water until he had reached the other bank with his load, only to find that his comrade was dead.

THWARTED THE ENEMY'S ATTACKS

NELSON A. MILES.

Colonel, 61st N. Y. Infantry.

Highest rank attained: Lieut.-Gen., U. S. A.

Born at Westminster, Mass., Aug. 8, 1839.

LIEUTENANT-GENERAL NELSON A. MILES received his Medal of Honor when a colonel during the War of the Rebellion. The proud distinction was given this brilliant American soldier for "distinguished gallantry while holding with his command, an advanced position, against repeated assaults by a strong force of the enemy."

The occurrence took place during the battle of Chancellorsville, May 2 and 3, 1863, and is described by General Miles himself in the following:

"On Friday, May 1, 1863, as the Second Army Corps was advancing from Chancellorsville toward Fredericksburg, Va., my regiment being in advance, I was ordered to move forward and deploy my command as skirmishers on the right of the road. After advancing through the woods some 500 yards, I came to an open field, where I found the enemy, and also a brigade belonging to the Twelfth Army Corps, which was retreating double-quick, without rear guard or flankers. Here I was ordered to halt, and I remained in this position about half an hour, when I was informed by Lieutenant Alvord, of General Caldwell's staff, that the division was falling back, and ordered me to protect the rear. The enemy was then advancing in column with a very strong skirmish line, which was different from any I had ever seen, being much stronger and in four ranks; part filed to the front, keeping up a continued fire. We were also exposed to the fire of their artillery, but without much loss, we fell back until I passed the troops of the Third Corps, when I reformed the line, and was soon ordered forward with the rest of the brigade, taking up a new position on the left of the road, my right connecting with the One hundred and forty-eighth Pennsylvania and my left with that of the Twenty-second Massachusetts Volunteers, General Barnes' Division. I was then ordered by Lieutenant Mitchell, of General Hancock's staff, to take charge of the line of skirmishers in front of the entire division. During the fore part of the night I received instructions from General Hancock that the division was to withdraw to another line some distance to the rear, and ordered me to establish my line on the most favorable ground in its front.

"At 3 A. M. of the 2d, I withdrew the picket line to the rear of an abatis, which had been formed during the night by some regiments of the division. Here I remained during the day. The force on this line consisted of the Fifty-seventh New York Volunteers, Lieutenant-Colonel A. B. Chapman; two companies of the Fifty-second New York, four companies of the Second Delaware, and six companies of the One hundred and forty-eighth Pennsylvania, together with the Eleventh Massachusetts Volunteers, Colonel Blaisdell, which was ordered there by General Carr, for the purpose of feeling the enemy with their sharpshooters.

"We were constantly engaged skirmishing with the enemy during the day, and at about 3 P. M. the enemy commenced massing his troops in two columns, one on each side of the road, flanked by a line of battle about 800 yards in front in the woods. Their orders could be distinctly heard. They soon advanced with a tremendous yell, and were met with a sure and deadly fire of one single line. A very sharp engagement continued for about half an hour after which the enemy fell back in disorder. Their charge was impetuous and determined, advancing within twenty yards of my abatis, but were hurled back with fearful loss, and made no further demonstrations.

"About 9 A. M. of the 3d instant, I received a detachment of 250 men, under command of Lieutenant-Colonel McCreary, of the One hundred and forty-fifth Pennsylvania, as a support. Soon after, my line was vigorously attacked by the enemy on the left, and engaged the entire line. This continued for about half an hour, when I deployed about one-third of my reserve on the left, and was about to order up the remainder when I received a severe wound in the abdomen, and was obliged to leave the field."

Colonel Miles' conduct throughout this campaign was highly commended by his superior officers who in their official reports of this battle lavished their praise upon the young soldier. After the engagement at Chancellorsville, General John C. Cald-well spoke of him in the following flattering terms:

"Colonel Miles, of the Sixty-first New York Volunteers, was placed by General Hancock in command of the picket line of the division, which consisted of six companies of the One hundred and forty-eighth Pennsylvania Volunteers, the Fifty-seventh New York, two companies of the Second Delaware, supported by the Eleventh Massachusetts Volunteers.

"With this force Colonel Miles skirmished all day long with the enemy, and at 3 P. M., repulsed with signal loss, a determined attack of the enemy, made in two columns on each side of the road. I do not doubt, that this repulse of the enemy, which kept them from our main lines, was due principally to the skill and gallantry of Colonel Miles, who, with a single line of skirmishers, deployed at three paces, repelled a determined attack of the enemy made in column, a feat rarely paralleled. * * * * I confess I was somewhat anxious for the One hundred and forty-eighth Pennsylvania Volunteers, it being a new regiment, and, never having been exposed to fire. It behaved, however, throughout with the greatest coolness, vying with

"THEY ADVANCED WITH A TREMENDOUS YELL."

the old troops in steadiness. Colonel Miles speaks in high terms of the six companies that were on picket, and the other four companies fought with the greatest gallantry under my own eye. I have seldom seen a more steady or better-directed fire than was theirs in the woods on Sunday. The Sixty-first New York Volunteers maintained its well earned reputation for steadiness, bravery, and all good soldierly qualities.

"I greatly regret to report that Colonel Miles was severely, if not mortally, wounded on Sunday morning while handling the picket line with masterly ability. I have had occasion heretofore to mention the distinguished conduct of Colonel Miles in every battle in which the brigade has been engaged. His merits as a military man seem to me of the very highest order. I know of no terms of praise too exaggerated to characterize his masterly ability. If ever a soldier earned promotion, he has done so. Providence should spare his life, and I earnestly recommend that he should be promoted and intrusted with a command commensurate with his abilities."

"AMONG THE MOST HEROIC OF THE WAR"

JAMES D. VERNAY.

2d Lieut., Co. B. 77th Ill. Vol. Inf.
Highest rank attained: Brevet Major.
Born at Lacon, Ill., Dec. 24, 1834.

"I REGARD the conduct of the soldiers who manned the transports as among the most heroic of the whole war."

Admiral Porter in expressing this opinion referred to the men who manned the transports Tiger, John F. Cheeseman, Moderator, Henry Clay, Anglo-Saxon, and Horizon, which ferried the Union troops across the Mississippi. This brilliant feat is described by Second Lieutenant James D. Vernay, of the Seventy-seventh Illinois Volunteers, who commanded the Horizon, as follows:

"Some few days before the boats were being prepared for the special service of ferrying the troops across the Mississippi, I overheard Generals Logan's and Grant's quartermasters talking about calling for volunteers to man the boats. The next morning I walked nine miles in the rain and mud down the levee to general headquarters, to put my name down.

"I met Colonel Rawlins, with whom I had a speaking acquaintance, and informed him of my intention. He encouraged me and said, that he thought I would have an opportunity to go. I told him that the whole of Logan's Division would want to volunteer and that I would feel disappointed if my offer were not accepted. He took a slip of paper and wrote my name, rank, and regiment, and said: 'There, will that suit you?' 'Well, that's what I came here for,' I replied.

"I was placed in command of the Horizon, the last one of the six transports. An hour before the time set for our boats to go in under fire, I assembled our men in the cabin. There I gave them some necessary instructions, provided them with pieces of strong cord to tie up a wounded leg or arm, if such emergency should arise, and impressed upon them the importance of our service. They crowded about me, some showing the pictures of their loved ones, wives, children, mothers, and sweethearts, and we finally bade each other goodbye, all hoping for a successful ending, but everyone ready to die in the performance of a sacred duty.

"We worked all night, arriving at New Carthage on the following morning at nine o'clock. On April 23d General Grant, after a consultation, ordered the transports to run the gauntlet of fire. We started at 7 P. M. As we successfully passed the last of the enemy's batteries, our cheers and hurrahs echoed over the water and our joy was boundless. With our six boats, ragged and torn by shot and shell, we had ferried our troops across the Mississippi, and commenced that brilliant campaign, which ended in the capture of General Pemberton and his whole army at Vicksburg."

AN AWFUL BARGE RIDE UNDER FIRE

WILLIAM H. WARD.
Captain, Co. B, 47th Ohio Inf.
Born at Adrian, Mich., Dec. 9, 1840.

ONE of the most desperate feats of the war was the attempt of Captain William H. Ward, of Company B, Forty-seventh Ohio Volunteers, to run the gauntlet of the Confederate batteries at Vicksburg, on the night of May 3, 1863. There were three barges loaded with stores for General Grant's Army, but between them and their destination lay the enemy's batteries, mounting more than one hundred guns, many of them of the heaviest calibre. The Mississippi River makes a double bend at this point, like the letter S, and from the moment the barges entered the first bend, till they emerged on the open river below, they would be under the concentrated fire of the guns every foot of the way, and it seemed impossible that anyone could live under such a terrible fire.

The strength of the position was not unknown to Captain Ward, for he had several times, from a distance watched the batteries in action, when the ironclads were attempting to run the blockade. What he had seen, instead of deterring him, only made him more anxious for a closer acquaintance, and when a call was made for volunteers to take the barge down the stream, he was the first to offer himself. There was no lack of volunteers, and where only thirty-five men were required, ten times that number were willing and anxious to go. One man, Addison J. Hodges, was so eager to go, that he actually offered a comrade a dollar to let him go in his place.

Previous expeditions had run the gauntlet of these batteries with more or less success, but always on the darkest of nights and convoyed by armor-clad gunboats. On this occasion a full moon and a clear sky made the night as light as day, and there were no gunboats to shelter the barges from the enemy's fire. There was only one little tug, the George Sturgis, to tow the barges, and any accident to her would wreck the whole expedition. This did not discourage the gallant little band, and the account of the adventure is entertainingly given by Captain Ward, as follows:

"We cast off from Milliken's Bend, La., about fifteen miles above Vicksburg at ten o'clock P. M, The trip down the river was uneventful until two o'clock in the morning, when a rocket sent up from one of the Confederate batteries, warned the enemy of our approach, and we were soon under a heavy fire. It was a wild ride we had from this time on.

"Battery after battery opened on us as we came within range, until it seemed that the guns were being played upon like the keys of a piano, and to say that the rain of shot and shell was terrific but faintly describes the situation. The scene was indescribably grand and awe-inspiring as we steamed slowly past the city amid the roar of more than a hundred guns, with their death-dealing missiles whistling and shrieking over and around us, and exploding on board, while the patter of bullets from the infantry resembled a fall of hail-stones. The barges were large and unwieldy; and as we could make only about six miles an hour at best, the enemy's gunners were able to get our range accurately. We had been struck many times but not seriously damaged. The little tug seemed to bear a charmed life, for we passed several times within a hundred yards of the heaviest batteries.

"We had now been under fire three-quarters of an hour, and had reached a point below the city where ten minutes more meant safety. The steady 'puff-puff' of the little tug gave assurance that all was right, and we were beginning to indulge in mental congratulations on the success of the expedition, when a roar like the bursting of a volcano, caused the barges to rock as if shaken by an earthquake, and in an instant the air was filled with burning coals, flying timbers, and debris. A plunging shot from a heavy gun, stationed on an eminence far in the rear, had struck the tug and penetrated to the furnaces, where it exploded, blowing the boilers and machinery up through the deck, and completely wrecking the vessel. The blazing coals fell in a shower over both barges, setting fire to the bales of hay in hundreds of places at once. The enemy sent up a cheer upon witnessing our misfortune, and for a few minutes seemingly redoubled their fire. The tug went down like a plummet, while the barges were soon blazing wrecks, drifting with the eddying current of the river. No recourse remained but surrender, and the waving of a handkerchief from a soldier's bayonet caused the firing to cease. The flames compelled the survivors to seek safety by taking to the water, and, having no boats, we floated off on bales of hay and found them surprisingly buoyant. The wounded were first cared for, and then all took passage on the hay-bale line.

"The enemy now hailed us from shore, ordering us to come in and surrender, but, on learning that we had no boats, sent their own to our assistance, capturing all but one of the survivors. That one, Julius C. Conklin by name, was the only man in the party who could not swim. He managed, with the aid of a piece of wreckage, to reach the Louisiana shore unobserved by the enemy, and rejoined his company two days later.

"When all had been rescued and assembled in the moonlight under guard of Confederate bayonets, the roll was called, and just sixteen, less than half our original number, were found to have survived. Some of the scalded men were piteous sights to behold, the flesh hanging in shreds from their faces and bodies, as they ran about in excruciating agony, praying that something be done to relieve their sufferings. These, with the wounded, were speedily sent to a hospital, where some of them died the next day.

"It is not often, even in a soldier's life, that one is compelled to face death in so many forms as beset our little party on that memorable night; shot and shell, fire, water, and a boiler explosion with its attendant horrors. Our captors treated us with marked consideration, affording every courtesy consistent with the rules of war and we were the recipients of many attentions from soldiers and citizens, who seemed to marvel at the temerity of our undertaking. We were held prisoners in Vicksburg for two days, when General Grant, having crossed the river and defeated the enemy near Grand Gulf, Mississippi, began to threaten the city from the rear. We were then paroled, and hurriedly forwarded to Richmond, Va., where, after an eventful journey through the Confederacy, we duly arrived, and were assigned quarters in that famous Confederate hostelry, Libby Prison. Here we remained about six weeks before we were exchanged and we were only able to rejoin the regiment in the trenches before Vicksburg, on the evening before the surrender, just in time to be in at the death.

"Language fails to describe my feelings, when with a few companions I entered the city the next morning, July 4th, immediately after the surrender, under circumstances in such marked contrast with my forced advent of a few weeks before. Now no hostile demonstrations of any kind greeted us. The great guns were still, the hostile flags were furled and 'Old Glory' floated proudly from the public buildings, while our late foes were quietly resting in their camps awaiting the pleasure of the victors."

THE END OF THE JOURNEY.

ROUTED MORGAN'S RAIDERS

BYRON M. CUTCHEON.
Major, 20th Mich. Infantry.
Highest rank attained: Brevet Brig-Gen., U. S. V.
Born at Pembroke, N. H., May 11, 1836.

THE Twentieth Michigan Infantry under the command of Lieutenant W. H. Smith, formed part of a provisional brigade which included three regiments of Kentucky cavalry and the Thirteenth Indiana Independent Battery, and was commanded by Colonel Richard T. Jacob. The gallant regiment from Michigan, was sent with this provisional brigade south of the Cumberland River, to hold the Confederate general, John Morgan, in check. How this was accomplished Major Byron M. Cutcheon describes as follows:

"After some skirmishing at Monticello, Ky., we had fallen back to the Cumberland River on May 9, 1863, and were waiting for a scouting party to come in, to recross, when Morgan's advance attacked our outpost at Horse Shoe Bend, that evening. I hastened back to the Bend to take command of the companies stationed there, while Colonel Smith remained behind to hurry up the rest of the regiment. That night the regiment came up, and on the morning of the 10th we were re-enforced by a small body—a squadron I believe—of the Twelfth Kentucky Cavalry, dismounted, and armed with Henry repeating rifles.

"Before their arrival, Morgan's men made a dash and succeeded in seizing the 'Coffey' house, a large log house on the east side of the road, so called after its owner. We had occupied it as a picket post through the night. The house, outbuildings, and garden were filled with rebel sharpshooters, who, though they harassed us throughout the day, did not attempt to advance.

"About 4 o'clock P. M.,—it was Sunday—Colonel Jacob having been re-enforced by a piece of Captain Sims' battery, resolved to take the aggressive, and to drive the rebels out of the house and grounds. To me was assigned the command of four companies, A and D, on the left of the road in the field, and C and K, in the road and

Morgan's Raid.—In the summer of 1863, General John Morgan conducted his famous raid through Kentucky into Indiana and Ohio. Starting from Sparta, Tennessee, with a force of 3,000 men, he made his way northward to the Ohio at Brandenburg, and crossed into Indiana. He was stopped at various points by local forces, but made his way into Ohio, made a circuit to the north of Cincinnati, and attempted to recross the river. He was driven back by Federal gunboats, and passed on to New Lisbon, where he was captured by the brigade of General Shackleford. He was held a prisoner for four months, then made his escape into Kentucky, and finally reached Richmond.

to the right. At the signal we went forward at our very best pace. I was then just six feet two inches tall, one half of the length in legs, and an expert runner from practice in college. I took a course directly down the road to the south in front of the companies,—one could hardly say 'line', for there was no line; it was a 'go as you please' foot race—with Captain George C. Barnes, an old fireman from Battle Creek, Mich., a good second, a rod behind me. The distance was about 150 yards, and we made it on the jump. There were three steps up to the porch, but I made only one of them. With my sword in my right hand, and a big Colt's navy revolver in my left, I threw myself against the weather-beaten door. A moment later, Captain Barnes came to my side, and the door yielded.

"I THREW MYSELF AGAINST THE WEATHER-BEATEN DOOR."

"Why we were not both shot down then and there, I have never been able to understand. The rebels certainly missed their opportunity. Instead, we saw the Johnnies going out of the back doors and windows, and making for the woods, while the companies coming up right and left of the house, poured volleys into the retreating foe.

"The charge was a complete success, but Lieutenant William Green and two enlisted men were killed, and quite a number wounded."

WIT AND NERVE OF A SOLDIER-CLERGYMAN

JAMES HILL.
1st Lieutenant, Co. I, 21st Iowa Infantry.
Born at Cheddar, Eng., Dec. 6, 1822.

THE matters of food for men, fodder for horses, and horses and mules for the transportation of an army in the enemy's country, are among the most important considerations presented to a commanding officer. Forage duty on the other hand, requires alertness, quick wit and good judgment, and prompt, energetic action on the part of the men detailed on such service. It was while in command of a party of foragers that the acting regimental quartermaster of the Twenty-first Iowa Infantry, won his Medal of Honor at Champion Hills, Miss. This quartermaster, First Lieutenant James Hill, was before the war a clergyman, but he gave up his pastorate and enlisted as a private in the Twenty-first Iowa Volunteer Infantry. He was later promoted to be lieutenant, and was finally assigned to duty as chaplain of his regiment.

Of the episode at Champion Hills, where he captured three Confederate pickets, Lieutenant Hill says:

"On the 16th of May, 1863, while acting as quartermaster of my regiment, I was ordered by my commander, Colonel Samuel Merrill, to select as many soldiers as I needed, and return in the direction of the Raymond and Jackson Cross Roads to forage and collect anything that would serve the regiment on our march to the Big Black River and Vicksburg. I selected a sufficient number of good men, and sent them out to cover part of the country, giving them orders to report to me at Raymond and Jackson Cross Roads with what forage they had gathered in, preparatory to our return to the regiment.

'After getting my men off on their mission, I took a pony belonging to the regiment and rode through some timber and brush in search of food, mules and horses.

Champion Hills—After entering Jackson, Miss., May 13, 1863, and learning that Pemberton was advancing toward the Federals' rear, Grant turned his troops westward so as to be ahead of Pemberton. This move placed McClernand's Corps in the lead, and reaching Champion Hills, Miss., on the 16th, McClernand was forced into an engagement with Pemberton. McPherson came upon the field near noon; a battle of four hours' duration was fought in deadly earnest, and resulted in Pemberton being forced back to Big Black River, where Grant overtook him, and, in a sharp action, routed the enemy. The Federals lost 2,268 in killed and wounded; while the Confederates lost 3,000 in killed and wounded, and 2,000 taken prisoners.

In following a path through the dense timber I unexpectedly rode right into the Confederate lines, and encountered three rebel pickets with their loaded rifles. I realized at once that I had gotten myself into a nasty position. Nevertheless, I did not lose my presence of mind, for as I emerged from the brush, I instantly and in the most natural manner, ordered the Johnnies to 'ground arms!' They obeyed. Then slightly turning my head, I addressed an imaginary guard in the brush, with a hasty order to 'halt'. The under growth and brush were so heavy that the Confederates were prevented from seeing through and thus discovering the deception. I next gave the command: 'Ten paces to the front, eyes to the center.' Seeing my revolver in my hand ready for instant use, the three men complied with my command. I further added that if any of them turned his head to right or left I would shoot him down in his tracks. I frequently gave the order to 'halt' to my imaginary guard, tending to frighten my prisoners into absolute obedience. This done, I deliberately dismounted and gathered up the three rifles, placed them against the neck of the pony, mounted, took the rifles

"SINGLE FILE, MARCH!"

under my arm and then gave the order to my prisoners: 'Single file, march,' and to my imaginary guard: 'Forward, march.' I hurried toward the command at good speed. Before it began to dawn upon my prisoners that I had fooled them, they found themselves within our lines. I turned them and their rifles over to Colonel Merrill who sent them to Major-General McClernand. When the prisoners saw that I had fooled them, their anger was vented in terms more strong than polite, one of them saying to me: 'Lieutenant, you could never have taken us but for that devil of a body-guard we thought you had, from the way you kept halting them.'"

CAPTURES HIS CAPTOR

GEORGE WILHELM.

Captain, Co. F, 56th Ohio Inf.
Highest rank attained: Colonel.
Born in Scioto County, O., April 2, 1830.

DURING the Vicksburg campaign the Fifty-sixth Ohio Infantry was with Colonel J. R. Slack's Second Brigade of the Twelfth Division, Brigadier-General Alvin P. Hovey, of the Thirteenth Army Corps under Major-General John A. McClernand, first, and later, Major-General E. O. C. Ord. On the 16th of May, about noon, the Federal forces attacked the Confederates at Champion Hills. The contest was bitter and stubborn for several hours, but finally General Pemberton ordered his army to fall back towards Vicksburg. Thus closed the last and most strenuous effort of the Confederate general to prevent the complete investment of that city by Grant. The Fifty-sixth Ohio participated in the battle of Champion Hills, and Captain George Wilhelm, of that regiment, tells his experience as follows:

"The country over which we advanced on the enemy was hilly and wooded, with an occasional clearing in which we were raked by a most galling fire from the enemy's sharp-shooters. I was ordered to deploy two companies of infantry as skirmishers. We were to advance across a clearing, and drive the enemy from the woods on the opposite side, where they were ensconced behind trees in large numbers.

"We advanced amid a sweeping fire, and slowly gained on the enemy. During the skirmish I lost a number of men. Unable to maintain the ground I had gained, I turned back and joined my command, the Twelfth Division, Thirteenth Army Corps, in the general engagement.

"The whole brigade charged upon the enemy, but we were not able to strike a decisive blow, although we had inflicted heavy losses on them. Five times a charge was made, and after each attempt we retreated part of the distance we had advanced. During the fifth charge, I received a shot in my left breast, the bullet going through me. I reeled and fell, and was left on the field.

"Some time later, one of the Confederates rushed to the place where I lay, and taking me prisoner, brought me to the rear of their lines. At Baker's Creek I persuaded my guard to stop and allow me to attend to my wound. I managed to stop the flow of blood by bathing the wound, and the cool water revived my energy.

"It was fearfully hot at the time, and I continued to gain new strength, while my guard paid more attention to the fight than to me. When I felt comparatively comfortable, I began to watch for an opportunity to escape. Once my guard turned his back on me; that was his mistake, for no sooner had he turned than I sprang forward, seized his musket and fixed it at his breast. Before he had recovered from his surprise, I ordered him to 'about face' and 'forward, march.' Then I led him by a circuitous route, to the rear of our lines. It wasn't very easy, for I could hardly walk myself. My wound pained me considerably and made breathing very difficult. However, I did not betray my own troubles to my prisoner, and brought him safely to our lines, where I turned him over to the guard. Then I applied for medical aid at the hospital."

"I ORDERED HIM TO 'ABOUT FACE.'"

KENDALL'S TEN FOOT LEAP

On the 17th of May, 1863, the Federal troops under General Lawler, encountered the Confederates at the Big Black River Bridge, Miss., well defended on both sides. A charge was ordered, and notwithstanding the fact that the Federal troops had to wade through a wide ditch in front of the Confederate earthworks, the position was carried, seventeen guns were captured, and several hundred prisoners were taken. Among the troops in this charge was the Forty-ninth Indiana Infantry,

WILLIAM KENDALL.

1st Serg't, Co. A, 49th Indiana Infantry.
Born in Dubois Co., Ind., Aug. 31, 1839.

and almost at the beginning of the charge a majority of the commissioned officers of the regiment were either killed or captured. So it happened that the command of Company A, of the Forty-ninth Indiana, devolved upon First Sergeant William Kendall.

Tall, straight as a gun barrel, athletic, and wholly free from superfluous flesh, Sergeant Kendall had an ideal soldierly appearance, and more than that, he appreciated the responsibility of his position. From both sides the fire was incessant and severe until the advance of his company was suddenly blocked by a ten foot ditch. With a yell and a run he leaped across the opening to a pile of rails, and there, under fire, he personally assisted in laying rails across the ditch that his men might more easily follow him. Then, leading the charge he ordered, he and his men entered the works and captured more prisoners than he had soldiers in his command, the other Confederates beating a hasty retreat.

A BRAVE SACRIFICE

In the woods at Carsville, Va., May 15, 1863, occurred one of the most stubbornly contested engagements experienced by the Seventh Army Corps. Two days prior to this date, about 5,000 infantry, the Eleventh Pennsylvania Cavalry, and two batteries of artillery were tearing up the Roanoke Railroad, while about the same number of Confederates were attempting to drive them away.

In recounting the event, Private Joseph S. G. Sweatt, of the Sixth Massachusetts Infantry, says:

"Skirmishes of more or less importance occurred on the 13th and 14th of May, but on the 15th the two lines of battle faced each other. The company to which I belonged, could muster only twenty-eight men—the remainder being on the sick list. Our company, along with Company I, was thrown forward as skirmishers into the edge of the woods, and at once the firing became furious. In less than fifteen minutes more than one-third of our little company was either killed or wounded. Seeing that the enemy had the advantage, the lieutenant in command ordered us to retreat—but as skirmishers. It was not long before we discovered that our line of battle had fallen back, their retreat being covered by the fire of the Seventh Massachusetts Battery.

"While we were falling back, Comrade Thurston, of Company H, came up to me and enquired about his son, who was a member of our company. Some one said

JOSEPH S. G. SWEATT.

Private Co. C, 6th Massachusetts, Inf.
Born at Boscawen, N. H., Oct. 23, 1843.

that he and George Fox were lying near the edge of the woods, both wounded. His face blanched; that look of despair in his face decided my course. I at once gave my gun to a sergeant and called out for some one to go with me to recover those two wounded boys. Dave Goodhue immediately responded, threw down his gun, and together we started to rescue our comrades. Closely scanning the field after we had started, we could see the two blue spots lying between the lines. The closer we got to them, the thicker the bullets flew. It looked to us as though we would be unable to reach them. We pushed on, however, determined to save our friends, and finally reached them; but as we were lifting Fox from the ground, my companion, Goodhue, was mortally wounded. Immediately after, another shot struck Fox while I was carrying him.

"The Seventh Massachusetts had now ceased firing and our whole line was falling back. The Confederates, heavily re-enforced, charged out of the woods. To reach our retreating lines was now impossible. The enemy were upon us. The Fourth Louisiana 'Tigers' took us prisoners.

"After the engagement the wounded were gathered up and taken to the Hebron Church, which was then being used as a hospital. From there we were shortly after taken to Franklin, Va., where before we left, all our wounded, except Goodhue, had died. I shall never forget the last look on Goodhue's face as we passed up the street. The poor fellow was on his knees looking out of the window,—left, to die among strangers."

Vicksburg—In the beginning of the year 1863, the Union Army, under Generals Grant and McClernand, was collected at Memphis, Tenn., and three months were spent in exploring the vicinity of Vicksburg in the hope of gaining a position in the rear of the town. The expedition was supported by Admiral Porter in command of a flotilla.

Several attempts to open a passage for the gun-boats, by cutting a canal across a bend of the river with the idea of turning the channel, ended in failure.

In April it was decided to run the fleet past the Vicksburg batteries, and on the 16th the passage was effected. General Grant marched his land force down the right or west bank of the Mississippi, formed a junction with the squadron, and, on the 31st defeated the Confederates at Port Gibson. Shortly after, the Union Army took a position in the rear of the city.

On the 14th a decisive battle was fought at Jackson, Miss., in which General Grant's right wing defeated General Johnston's Division and captured the town.

General Pemberton, in command of the Confederate troops in Vicksburg, made a sally with the greater part of his force on the 16th, and was defeated at Champion Hills on Baker's Creek. He had the same experience on the following day at the Black River Bridge, and retired within his defenses.

General Grant ordered assaults on the 19th and 22d, which resulted in repulse with great loss. The loss to his force in these two days was estimated at nearly 3,000. The plan was changed to one of regular siege, assisted by a bombardment by the gun-boats. The Confederates held out until the 4th of July, when Pemberton surrendered with all the defenders of Vicksburg, numbering nearly 30,000, as prisoners of war. His loss in killed and wounded was 31,277. The Union loss during the siege was reported to be 4,536.

"WITHIN A FEW FEET OF THE ENEMY"

PATRICK H. WHITE.
Captain, Chicago Mercantile
Battery, Lt. Art.
Born in Ireland, in 1833.

WILLIAM G. STEPHENS.
Private, Chicago Mercantile
Battery, Lt. Art.
Born in New York, December,
1843.

WHEN Grant, before Vicksburg, realizing that the men of his army were filled with the conviction that they could capture the city by assault, consented to make the last supreme effort in that direction, it was decided to begin the assault on the 22d of May, 1863.

A rush along the entire line of investment was planned, all officers setting their time with that of General Grant so that the attempt might be simultaneous, and when the appointed hour arrived the entire Union Army moved forward. It was during this assault that the following members of the Chicago Mercantile Battery won their Medals of Honor: Captain Patrick H. White, Corporal James Dunne, and Privates Charles Kloth, George Kretsinger, Patrick McGuire and William G. Stephens.

Captain White narrates the occurrence himself in these words:

"The morning of May 22d, at 10 A. M., was set for the grand assault. At 3 o'clock A. M. the cannonading began from the land side. Every available gun was brought to bear on the works. The bombardment this day was the most terrible during the siege and continued without intermission until nearly 11 o'clock, while our sharpshooters kept up such a galling fire that the rebel cannoneers could seldom rise to load their pieces.

"The artillery of McClernand's Thirteenth Corps had succeeded in breaching several points of the enemy's works, silencing five or six guns and exploding four caissons, and at 10 o'clock the column moved to the assault. About twelve o'clock I received a note from General Smith to bring two guns down the ravine, to go up to the breastworks and hammer down a fort. The general concluded his note with: 'We shall be inside the rebel works in half an hour.'

"In order to ascertain the nature of the ground, I went up the gully to the fort and discovered a lunette in their works on the Balding's Ferry Road, with a twenty-four pounder covering that approach. On the top of the fort they had piled cotton bales. In building this fort they covered half of the road with earth, so there was space enough for only one gun. I got a detail from the Eighty-third Indiana Infantry, and with ropes we dragged one gun up to within a few feet of the breast-works by hand, the infantry carrying the ammunition in their arms. We used shrapnel, with fuses cut so close that the shells exploded almost as soon as they left the gun. The first discharge was simultaneous with that of the enemy, striking their gun in the muzzle and scattering death among their gunners. I never saw a gun loaded and fired so fast. Every man was at his best. They did not take much care in sponging, and once or twice the gun was prematurely discharged. We disabled the enemy's gun and set the cotton bales on fire, and they abandoned the fort for twenty minutes, thinking it was undermined. That was the time for our infantry to pass in, but we did not know it then. The rebels returned and threw water on the cotton bales, but our guns blew the latter to pieces. An Irishman of the Eighty-third called out: 'Be gad, captain, there's not a pound of them left. I'll go and get you another load of ammunition.' As he stepped off the road to go down the gully, a shot from the Seventeenth Ohio Battery cut off his right arm.

"The Seventeenth had taken a position in our old place in the road near the First United States Infantry, but the latter stopped them from doing further damage. General Smith told me that Quinby's Brigade was coming to support us, so I told the drivers of the guns and limbers that lay here, to get back to where they came from at full speed, and, should they meet with an accident, not to stop, but keep going. When part way up the hill a shell passed between the swing and wheel drivers, and exploded on the other side of them, throwing the swing driver on his face in the saddle; another shot went under the gun.

"My four guns opened with a terrific fire from their position back on the ridge and

"WE DRAGGED ONE GUN UP."

they saw the troops fall back from the breast-works. Overhead in the ravine the
air was black with projectiles of all descriptions from friend and foe. I thought it
was time to see how the four guns were getting along, and to do this it was necessary to go back over the slope of the ridge. I had not gotten half way to the top
when minnie balls dropped around me as thick as grasshoppers. I retraced my
steps a short distance, and then obliqued around the ridge where it ended abruptly.
When the men saw me they cheered. After dark Sergeant Throop brought the
gun off safely, and it was as hot as a live coal. For a week after the assault we
slept by our guns, occasionally firing through the nights. For two weeks our horses
did not have their harness off."

General Grant sent an account of the operations before Vicksburg to Field-
Marshal Count Von Moltke. The count read it, marked the passage which told of
this incident and sent the description to his chief of ordinance. The latter returned
the book with the remark: "Never was such a brave deed done in all the wars of
Europe."

THE "FORLORN HOPE" AT VICKSBURG

For superb gallantry and reckless indifference to death and danger, there is
nothing in military history to excel the conduct of the "forlorn hope" that led
the general assault on Vicksburg on May 22, 1863. General Grant had encircled the
city on three sides with a line of battle twelve miles long, and on the Mississippi,
which formed the fourth side, were Admiral Porter's warships. The strength of the
enemy had been greatly underestimated, and it was decided to make an attempt
to carry the city by storm, in order to avoid the tedium of a siege. The enemy's
lines ran along the top of a bluff, and the point of attack selected was to the south
of one of the forts. This fort, which was protected by a ditch twelve feet wide and
five or six feet deep, rose about ten feet above the level and sloped up gently
towards the enemy's guns. The face of the fort was perpendicular, the earth
having been tamped, instead of being allowed to adjust itself. The point of attack
was in front of the Second Division of the Fifteenth Army Corps, and on the
afternoon of May 21st, each regimental commander of the division explained the
plan of operations to his men and called for volunteers. One hundred and fifty
men were required for a "forlorn hope" to lead the general assault and prepare the
way for the real attack. As these men would be certain to draw the enemy's fire,
there was little probability of any of them returning alive, and on that account it
was decided not to order any man to go, but to depend entirely on volunteers.
Each regiment was to supply its quota, and in view of the terrible risk to be
incurred, orders were given that none but unmarried men were to be accepted.
The men responded promptly to the call, and in such numbers that twice as many
volunteered as were required, those who had first offered their services being accepted.

The work assigned to the "forlorn hope" was to build a bridge over the ditch which protected the front of the enemy's fort, plant their scaling ladders against the embankment, and it was expected that by the time this was done, the supporting brigades would be ready to carry the works by a grand assault.

On the following morning the storming party was led through a ravine to the Jackson Road, which crossed the enemy's lines at right angles. In this ravine, out of sight of the enemy, was a pile of roughly hewn logs, another of lumber, and a number of scaling ladders. The advance party was to carry the logs, two men to each log, make a dash for the enemy's entrenchments and throw the logs across the ditch to form the ground work of a bridge. The second detachment was to follow close up with the lumber, which was to be thrown across the logs to make sure footing for the stormers. The third detachment was to bring up the scaling ladders, rush across the bridge, and plant them against the enemy's works.

The moment the "forlorn hope" emerged from the ravine, they came within view of the enemy, who opened so heavy a fire on them that their works were covered with clouds of smoke. The gallant little band advanced at a dead run, but in the eighty rods of open ground which lay between them and the fort, about half of them were shot down. When the survivors arrived at the ditch, they found it impossible to build a bridge, as so many of the logs had been dropped by the way, and it was equally impossible to remain where they were, exposed to the enemy's fire. There was nothing for it but to jump into the ditch, and seek shelter. Private Howell G. Trogden, who carried the flag of the storming party, planted it on the parapet of the fort, and dropped back into the ditch, where he kept up a fire on the Confederates whenever they attempted to reach it and take it in.

The other brigades advanced to the support of the stormers, but were driven back by the heavy fire, and all that reached the ditch were thirty men of the Eleventh Missouri with a colonel, major, and two lieutenants. They planted their flag along side that of the storming party, and sought shelter where they could, in the ditch, or in holes dug in the embankment. The Confederates finding it impossible to depress their guns sufficiently to reach them, dropped 12-pounder shells among them, but the fuses were cut too long, and consequently did not explode for about ten seconds. This gave the stormers time not only to get out of the way, but even to toss some of the shells back over the parapet, otherwise not a man would have survived. As it was, the bottom of the ditch was strewn with mangled bodies, with heads and limbs blown off.

The Thirty-seventh Ohio Volunteers, who were advancing to the support, became panic-stricken and broke. The men lay down in the road, and sought shelter behind rocks and inequalities of the ground. They refused to either advance or retire, and lay there for hours, blocking the way of the regiments which were coming up behind, thus compelling them to make a long detour, and deliver their attack on the left of the enemy's position. While making this detour, they were

VOLUNTEER STORMERS.

exposed to the fire of the enemy for nearly the whole distance, and were so weak-ened in consequence, that they failed in their attack.

The assault had now failed at every point, although Admiral Porter's ships had kept up a heavy bombardment, and the Federal troops were obliged to withdraw

VICKSBURG, MAY 22, 1863.

and seek cover, from which they kept up a heavy and well sustained fire. All this time the men in the ditch, unable to either retreat or advance, held their position with the utmost tenacity and weakened the fire of the rebel guns by shooting down the gunners. In order to dislodge them, a gun loaded with grape was dragged to a position where it would enfilade the ditch, but sharpshooters shot down the gunners, before a single round could be fired. Others attempted to take their places, but it was certain death to approach the gun, and it was abandoned.

All day long, from 10 o'clock in the morning until darkness fell, the unequal fight went on ; then the little body of survivors crept out of the ditch, carrying with them their flags, riddled with bullets, and made their way back to their own lines. Of the storming party eighty-five per cent were either killed or dangerously wounded, and few of them escaped without a wound of some kind.

When the storming party withdrew, they left behind them William Archinal, who had been stunned by a fall, and who was afterwards captured by the enemy. Archinal and another man had been carrying a log between them, and had neared the ditch, when his comrade was shot. His sudden fall and the consequent dropping of his end of the log, threw Archinal to the ground, where he struck his head against a stone and he became unconscious. His adventure is best told in his own words ; he says :

"When I came to my senses, I was lying on my face with the log across my body and showers of bullets whistling through the air and dropping all around me. These bullets I found, came from my own division, and to save myself from being shot by my own comrades, I wriggled from under the log, and got it between me and them. It was providential for me that I did so, for I could hear the bullets striking the log in dozens. Sometime during the afternoon one of our cannon balls struck the log close to my head; the log bounded in the air and fell a little way from me, but I crawled up to it again and hugged it close. The firing continued incessantly all day until nightfall, when it gradually slackened, and finally died away altogether. I thought I could make my way back to my regiment, but as I was rising the butt of my gun which was slung on my back, attracted the attention of the enemy above me. Half a dozen rifles were pointed at me, and I was ordered to surrender, which I did, considering discretion the better part of valor.

"When I was taken into the fort, a rebel officer came up to me, slapped me on the shoulder, and said : 'See here, young man, weren't you fellows all drunk when you started this morning ?' I replied: 'No Sir.' 'Well, they gave you some whiskey before you started, didn't they ?' he said, and I answered: 'No Sir, that plan is not practised in our army.'

"'Didn't you know it was certain death,' he asked me again, and I replied: 'Well, I don't know, I am still living.'

"'Yes,' he said, 'You are living, but I can assure you that very few of your comrades are.'

"I was then placed in charge of a guard, taken to the city and put into the yard of the jail where I met some fifty or sixty of our men, taken at different points during the day. The jail yard was enclosed by a high brick wall with large sycamore trees growing inside. I was nearly dead from fatigue, so immediately crawled into one of the tents put up for our accommodation, and was on the point of drop-

"THIS GAVE TIME TO TOSS SOME OF THE SHELLS BACK."

ping off to sleep, when our mortar boats on the Louisiana shore opposite Vicksburg, opened fire on the city, throwing their 450-pound fuse shells promiscuously all over. Of course, there was no sleep for us that night, and just about daylight one of those shells struck the jail, the roof of which was covered with slate. I made a jump for one of the sycamore trees, but before I reached it, a piece of slate from the roof cut the rim of my hat in front of my face as clean as though it had been done by a razor.

"A southern man, suspected of being in sympathy with the Union cause, was located in one of the cells, and when this shell burst in the lower part of the jail, the poor fellow was nearly scared to death. He clung to the iron grating of the window and prayed to God that Grant might come that very minute, and take the God-for-saken city and everybody in it.

"About nine o'clock A. M. an officer came and took our parole, and then with a small detachment of rebel guards, we were marched down to the river in front of the city. The guard intended to escort us to the Louisiana side and deliver us to our own men, but our mortar boats, suspecting this to be merely a ruse of the rebels, and fearing an attack, opened fire on us, dropping big shells all around us into the river. We pushed off in yawls as quickly as possible, and after getting out a little way we did not fear them, as they could not elevate the mortars sufficiently to do us any harm. Thus after many narrow escapes I reached our own lines in safety, a paroled prisoner, having been under fire ten hours and in captivity about twelve."

Uriah H. Brown was one of the section that carried the logs. His captain was shot dead at his side and his lieutenant dangerously wounded, but he kept on till he reached the ditch. He threw his log across, but found it too short to reach to the other side. While considering what he could do he was shot down and tumbled into the ditch. When he came to his senses and found the enemy dropping shells into the ditch among the wounded men, he set to work to drag them into sheltered positions. He had got three of the wounded into a safe place, when one of the officers forbade him to expose himself any longer. He lay quiet for a time, but the longing to get back came over him and he climbed out of the ditch and crawled for fifty yards exposed to the terrible fire, till he found a place of safety behind a little knoll. Two wounded men were lying near by, moaning in pain, and he crept out and dragged them under cover, gave them water and lay down beside them till nightfall, when he assisted them back to their own lines.

Corporal Robert Cox, Company K, Fifty-fifth Illinois Infantry, gives a humorous description of his experience at the assault:

"After Trogden had planted his flag on the parapet, the Confederates tried to capture it by hooking it in with the shanks of their bayonets, but failed, owing to the hot fire kept up by the sharpshooters. Thereupon Trogden asked me for my gun to give the enemy a thrust. This was a very foolish request, for no soldier ever gives up his gun, but I concluded to try it myself. I raised my head again about as high as the safety of the case would permit, and pushed my gun across the intervening space between us and the enemy, gave their bayonets a swipe with mine, and dodged down just in time to escape being riddled. I did not want any more of that kind of amusement, so did not undertake to force the acquaintance any further. After we had been in this predicament about two hours, they sent over a very pressing invitation to 'Come in, you Yanks. Come in and take dinner with us.' We positively declined, however, unless they would come out and give us a chance to see if the invitation were genuine. This they refused to do, but agreed to send a messenger. By and by it arrived in the shape of a shell, which went flying down the hill without, however, doing us any damage."

Jacob Sanford, commissary-sergeant, Fifty-fifth Illinois Infantry, tells that while with the storming party, he came out with no injury more serious than a sprained hip caused by grape shot striking the plank he was carrying. He had been very near death more than once, however, for he had two bullet holes through his hat, nine through his blouse. The bullets in passing through his hat, had carried away locks of hair with them in their course.

The names of the surviving heroes whose courage and bravery was fittingly recognized by a grateful country by the award of the Medal of Honor are as follows:

CHRISTIAN ALBERT,
Private, Co. G, 47th Ohio Inf.

CLINTON L. ARMSTRONG,
Private, Co. D, 83d Ind. Inf.

WILLIAM H. BARRINGER,
Private, Co. F, 4th W. Va. Inf.

THOMAS A. BLASDELL,
Corporal, Co. H, 83d Ind. Inf.

EMMER BOWEN,
Private, Co. C, 127th Ill. Inf.

HENRY G. BUHRMAN,
Private, Co. H, 54th Ohio Inf.

WILLIAM CAMPBELL,
Corporal, Co. I, 30th Ohio Inf.

WILLIAM H. CHISMAN,
Sergeant, Co. I, 83d Ind. Inf.

CARLOS N. COLBY,
Sergeant, Co. G, 97th Ill. Inf.

JAMES S. CUNNINGHAM,
Private, Co. D, 8th Mo. Inf.

MARTIN K. DAVIS,
Sergeant, Co. H, 116th Ill. Inf.

DAVID F. DAY,
Private, Co. D, 57th Ohio Inf.

RICHARD W. DEWITT,
Sergeant, Co. D, 47th Ohio Inf.

DAVID DICKIE,
Sergeant, Co. A, 97th Ill Inf.

JOHN N. ECKES,
Private, Co. E, 47th Ohio Inf.

JOHN H. FISHER,
1st Lieut., Co. B, 55th Ill. Inf.

JAMES E. FLYNN,
Sergeant, Co. G, 6th Mo. Inf.

FRANZ FREY,
Corporal, Co. H, 37th Ohio Inf

NICHOLAS GESCHWIND,
Captain, Co. F, 116th Ill. Inf.

THOMAS GUINN,
Private, Co. D, 47th Ohio Inf.

DAVID H. HELMS,
1st Sergt., Co. B, 83d Ind. Inf.

JAMES HENRY,
Sergeant, Co. B, 113th Ill. Inf.

LEWIS T. HUNT,
Private, Co. H, 6th Mo. Inf.

WILLIAM JOHN,
Private, Co. E, 37th Ohio Inf.

ELISHA JOHNS,
Corporal, Co. B, 113th Ill. Inf.

DAVID JOHNSTON,
Private, Co. K, 8th Mo. Inf.

DAVID JONES,
Lieut., Co. I, 54th Ohio Inf.

JOSEPH S. LABILL,
Private, Co. C, 6th Mo. Inf.

JAMES W. LARRABEE,
Sergeant, Co. I, 55th Ill. Inf.

WILLIAM H. LONGSHORE,
Private, Co. D, 30th Ohio Inf.

JAMES M. MCCLELLAND,
Private, Co. B, 55th Ill. Inf.

ANDREW MCCORMACK,
Sergeant, Co. I, 127th Ill. Inf.

EDWARD MCGINN,
Private, Co. F, 54th Ohio Inf.

WILSON MCGONAGLE,
Private, Co. B, 30th Ohio Inf.

JACOB C. MILLER,
Sergeant, Co. G, 113th Ill. Inf.

JEROME MORFORD,
Private, Co. K, 55th Ill. Inf.

JASPER N. NORTH,
Private, Co. D, 4th W. Va. Inf.

JACOB H. OVERTURF,
Private, Co. K, 83d Ind. Inf.

JOEL PARSONS,
Private, Co. B, 4th W. Va. Inf.

WILLIAM REED,
Private, Co. H, 8th Mo. Inf.

LOUIS RENNIGER,
Private, Co. H, 37th Ohio Inf.

FREDERICK ROCK,
Private, Co. H, 37th Ohio Inf.

BENJAMIN W. SCHENK,
Corporal, Co. D, 116th Ill. Inf.

ANDREW SCHMAUCH,
Private, Co. A, 30th Ohio Inf.

CHRISTIAN SCHNELL,
Corporal, Co. C, 37th Ohio Inf.

REUBEN SMALLEY,
Private, Co. F, 83d Ind. Inf.

WILLIAM STEINMETZ,
Private, Co. G, 83d Ind. Inf.

JAMES C. SUMMERS,
Private, Co. H, 4th W. Va. Inf.

WILLIAM TOOMER,
Sergeant, Co. F, 127th Ill. Inf.

HOWELL G. TROGDEN,
Private, Co. D, 8th Mo. Inf.

JOHN WARDEN,
1st Lieut., Co. E, 55th Ill. Inf

RICHARD H. WOOD,
Captain, Co. A, 97th Ill Inf.

JOSEPH WORTICK,
Private, Co. A, 8th Mo. Inf.

"COME ON, YOU BRAVE YANK"

THOMAS H. HIGGINS.
Private, Co. D. 99th Illinois Infantry.
Born in Franklin Co., New York, June 8, 1831.

T HE assault upon that part of the works of Vicksburg, occupied by the Twenty-Second Texas, was made by the Eighth and Eighteenth Indiana, First United States Regulars and the Thirty-third and Ninety-ninth Illinois, in the order named. Regarding the assault, Captain A. C. Matthews, of the Ninety-ninth Illinois, says: "I was in command of the color company on May 22, 1863. The color bearer had been wounded a few days before and was not on duty that morning. Private Thomas H. Higgins, a big, strong, athletic Irishman, solicited the privilege of carrying the flag for the day. I gave him permission and handed over the standard to him, telling him not to stop until he got into the Confederate works. He obeyed this order literally."

The manner in which Private Higgins carried out the order of his superior officer, cannot be more fittingly recounted and with greater credit to the brave color bearer than by Charles I. Evans, an ex-Confederate soldier of the Second Texas, who says:

"After a most terrific cannonading of two hours, during which the very earth rocked and pulsated like a thing of life, the head of the charging column appeared above the brow of the hill, about 100 yards in front of the breast works, and, as line after line of blue came in sight over the hill, it presented the grandest spectacle the eye of a soldier ever beheld. The Texans were prepared to meet it however, for, in addition to our Springfield rifles, each man was provided with five additional smooth-bore muskets, charged with buck and ball.

"When the first line was within fifty paces of the works, the order to fire ran along the trenches, and was responded to as from one gun. As fast as practiced hands could gather them up, one after another, the muskets were brought to bear. The blue lines vanished amid fearful slaughter. There was a cessation in the firing. And behold, through the pall of smoke which enshrouded the field, a Union flag could be seen approaching.

"As the smoke was slightly lifted by the gentle May breeze, one lone soldier advanced, bravely bearing the flag towards the breast works. At least a hundred men took deliberate aim at him, and fired at point-blank range, but he never faltered. Stumbling over the bodies of his fallen comrades, he continued to advance. **Sud-**

denly, as if with one impulse, every Confederate soldier within sight of the Union color bearer seemed to be seized with the idea that the man ought not to be shot down like a dog. A hundred men dropped their guns at the same time; each of them seized his nearest neighbor by the arm and yelled to him: 'Don't shoot at that man again. He is too brave to be killed that way,' when he instantly discovered that his neighbor was yelling the same thing at him. As soon as they all understood one another, a hundred old hats and caps went up into the air, their wearers yelling at the top of their voices: 'Come on, you brave Yank, come on!'

"ONE
LONE
SOLDIER
ADVANCED."

"He did come, and was taken by the hand and pulled over the breast works, and when it was discovered that he was not even scratched, a hundred Texans wrung his hands and congratulated him upon his miraculous escape from death. That man's name was Thomas J. Higgins, color bearer of the Ninety-ninth Illinois."

Private Higgins was then taken before General Pemberton, the rebel commander, who asked him where General Grant's headquarters were.

"I do not know, as he is moving them every day, but they will be here tomorrow," came the ready response from the quick witted Irishman.

"How many men has your general got?" the rebel leader inquired.

"Oh, not many, only about seventy-five thousand," Higgins replied.

"How far back do his lines extend?"

"As far as Cairo, Illinois, and they are still being formed in the state of Maine."

"Well," General Pemberton observed sarcastically, "we'll have Grant in here as a prisoner tomorrow."

"I know," was the doughty Yankee soldier's reply, "General Grant will come in here tomorrow to ship you and your command to Altona, Illinois, where he has a big boarding house."

At this General Pemberton got angry. "Sergeant," he exclaimed, "take this man away. He is insulting. He is impudent. He is insolent."

Thereupon Private Higgins was led away, a few days later paroled, exchanged, and subsequently he returned to his regiment, where he remained until the end of the war.

His Medal of Honor was awarded him at the request of the very Confederates who captured him at the assault.

MENOMEN O'DONNELL.

1st Lieutenant, Co. A, 11th Missouri Volunteer Infantry.
Highest rank attained: Captain.
Born in Trimborty, Ireland, April 30, 1830.

A STAFF OFFICER'S PLUCK

AT 2 P. M. of the 22d," First Lieutenant Menomen O'Donnell narrates, "orders were given for the second charge on Vicksburg, to be led by the Second Brigade, Third Division, Fifteenth Army Corps, commanded by General Joseph A. Mower. The Eleventh Missouri led the advance. The enemy's guns had been booming for some time, but as soon as the Union advance was seen coming over the bluff, the fire seemed to double its former strength and fury. The ground was covered with the dead and wounded, and, not seeing my colors I felt like one lost in the wilderness. I called out: 'Where is the flag of the Eleventh Missouri?' A captain of an Ohio company answered: 'Lieutenant, your flag is over there!' then pointing still farther to the left he said: 'And the head of your regiment is at the fort.' I soon found the flag, and called all of the Eleventh Missouri, within sound of my voice, to come forward to the colors. Only forty-four appeared. I exhorted the boys to follow me to the fort. The color sergeant refused to carry the flag. Just as I was about to reach for it, brave Corporal Warner stepped forward, grabbed the flag, and to the fort it went with us. It was raised, but soon shot down, only to be again put up and floated on the rebel fort until dark. Twenty-four of the forty-four got to the fort. After arriving there we could do nothing but sit with our backs to the wall until darkness came, when under cover of the night, we finally got out, and safely returned to camp."

Shortly after the fall of Vicksburg, Lieutenant O'Donnell was detailed on General Mower's staff, served with him in his campaign directed against Fort De Russy, La., where he voluntary took a place in the ranks of an assaulting column, and was twice wounded during the engagement. Referring to this action, the lieutenant says: "Returning from a reconnoisance, in which, with a few mounted orderlies, I had taken twenty prisoners, with some supply wagons, I found General Mower with the command, about two miles from the fort. The general said to me: 'Captain, I have received orders to go into camp; what do you say?'

"'General, it is not for me to say what to do,' I answered.

"'I wish you would give me your opinion,' he persisted.

"'General,' I replied, 'if I were in your place, I would capture Fort DeRussy before evening. If we don't, the enemy will be gone before daylight.' 'Just my own opinion,' General Mower said, requesting me to take a brigade, and open fire, which was the signal for a general charge. Subsequently I led the Twenty-fourth Missouri of Colonel Shaw's Brigade against the enemy. There was some hard fighting, but at 6:30 P. M. we were in possession of the fort."

A FLAG THE REBELS DIDN'T GET

ISAAC H. CARMEN.
Corporal, Co. A, 48th Ohio Infantry.
Born in New Jersey, Nov. 17, 1841.

"AT ten o'clock on the morning of May 22d, at Vicksburg, our brigade captured a fort, together with a number of prisoners. The colors of the Forty-eighth Ohio and Seventy-seventh Illinois Infantry, were ordered to be planted on the fort, which was done by Sergeant Dave Vore and one of the Illinois men.

"We were then in a very desperate position, and, in addition to the enemy's fire, received some of the shells of our own batteries, which fell short of their mark. To relieve myself somewhat of this uncomfortable situation, I unfixed my bayonet and dug a little trench near the top of the works, close by our flag. An Illinois man crawled beneath me, into an excavation caused by the explosion of a shell. We arranged that he should reload our guns, while I continued firing at the enemy whenever one of them would come within my sight and range. This lasted several hours, when, the rebels brought a battery to bear on my position, and, for some time the shells were singing their song so dangerously near to my head, that my position became hardly tenable. A little later the enemy began massing troops at this point. I was able to distinctly hear their commands and see their numerous bayonets. Then I thought it high time to notify our officers of the danger our flag was in. I noticed that our men were some distance behind, in the ditch, but determined to rescue the flag, rushed back, and received from Captain Posegate, the permission to get it, if possible. I seized it none too soon, for the terrific assault came sooner than I had expected.

"I reached the top of the bastion and grasped the Ohio flag; the Illinois standard could not be saved. How I got down and paced the hundred feet to our ditch, through all that tremendous fire, I cannot tell. In my great haste I ran right into the bayonet of one of my own company, who was then in charging position, driving its entire length into my leg and thigh. Although I almost dropped into a faint, I had enough presence of mind to run the shaft of the flag into the dust and hang on to it. My comrades pulled me down into their ditch and got the bayonet out of my leg. I was then taken to the rear."

"I SEIZED IT NONE TOO SOON."

Besides the exploit which Corporal Isaac H. Carmen here describes, he also saved the lives of a number of his comrades, by seizing a shell with a burning fuse, and throwing it back to the rebels, whence it came, slaughtering them with their own weapon of death, intended for the Union men.

"LAY HIM IN THE SHADE; HE WON'T LAST LONG"

ON THE morning of May 22, 1863, the Eighth Wisconsin Infantry was sent on a reconnoisance to Chickasaw Bluffs and had proceeded to a point near Mechanicsburg, Miss., when the enemy was discovered in force. It was a time and occasion when every available man was needed, so that Benjamin F. Hilliker, though mustered as a drummer, of Company A, asked for a gun and volunteered to go on the skirmish line. He was known to be a fine shot and brave, therefore his offer was accepted. As to what followed is told by the young drummer himself as follows:

"During the skirmishing near Mechanicsburg, I was still company drummer, but I exchanged my drum for a gun, as I had done on former occasions, and went into the fight with my company. Fear in battle never seemed to unnerve me. I felt better at the front in the heat of the fight than I did at the rear.

BENJAMIN F. HILLIKER,
Drummer, Co. A, 8th Wisconsin Vol. Inf.
Born at Golden, Erie Co., N. Y., May 28, 1843.

"When the fight I mention was becoming interesting, I, with comrade John Horton, advanced about eight rods in front of our line to get a clear view of the Confederate line, and in this we were satisfied, for when we reached the top of a low hill, we were within six or eight rods of the Confederates. My comrade was near my side when we came within this range of the enemy, and we both raised our rifles together to fire. Horton's gun rang out sharply, but mine snapped or missed fire, which placed me in an awkward position. Horton covered himself to the right behind a tree and I jumped into a surface sand pit to the left. While recapping my gun, something occurred that seemed to me like a terrific explosion.

"It proved to be a Minie ball passing through my head. It entered at the base of the mastoid process, tore through my head, and passed out at the left nostril. The first words I heard after that unpleasant incident were: 'Lay him in the shade over there—he won't last long.' But I have lasted, though I have to carry around a bad looking face where good looks might have served me better."

The Eighth Wisconsin, of which Drummer Hilliker was a member, was known throughout the war as the "Live Eagle Regiment." Its mascot was a live bald eagle, famous as "Old Abe," which was carried during all the marches and engagements on a perch, surmounting the Union shield. At the end of the war the eagle was presented to the state of Wisconsin, in the custody of which the historical bird died sixteen years later.

DROPPED THE PEN, SHOULDERED THE MUSKET

OWING to a frail physique, Private Henry T. Johns, after enlisting, was made quartermaster's clerk, hence did not share in a good many of the rougher duties of a soldier. On May 27, 1863, at Port Hudson, however, volunteers were called for, to charge on the enemy's works—a so-called "Forlorn Hope." A genuine forlorn hope it proved to be.

"Ignoring my privilege to keep out of the fight," Private Johns says, "I volunteered as one of a squad of fifty. According to orders we marched towards a rise of ground, from which we were to charge on the enemy's ranks. It was the most peculiar charge that I have ever heard of. There was no sudden rush, no cheering, nor the usual din of a general charge. We were merely following orders without confidence of success, yet determined to do our best. The plan was a failure in conception and execution. We had to charge over three-quarters of a mile of open country, exposed to the fierce fire of the enemy, and then climb the enemy's breastworks. But we never reached it. I ran on, knowing that my comrades were dropping on every side of me. Nevertheless we pressed forward until, seeing that to go farther would be useless and only mean death, we retreated."

Three others, Privates Frederick M. Deland, James W. Strong, and Francis E. Warren, also received the Medal of Honor for participating and distinguishing themselves in this same assault.

FRUSTRATED THE ENEMY'S PLANS.

WILLIAM L. S. TABOR.
Private. Co. K. 15th N. H. Inf.
Born in Methuen, Massachusetts, in 1844.

PRIVATE WILLIAM L. S. TABOR, of Company K, Fifteenth New Hampshire Infantry, in describing the part he played at the siege of Port Hudson, where the Union forces so determinedly, though unsuccessfully, laid siege and assaulted the Confederates, says:

"During the siege of Port Hudson in 1863, it was necessary to undermine the enemy's works, and for this purpose a large number of negroes was set to work digging a trench under the rebel fortifications, and protected by our sharpshooters who were supplied with hand-grenades, to be thrown over the parapets. The sand from the trench was thrown over the breastworks, for there was no place to dispose of it on our side. This exposed our men to the fire of the rebels, and I was one of the men detailed as sharpshooters to prevent the rebels from doing further damage. We were under a scathing fire all this time, as the enemy were enabled to enfilade our ranks, and with their shot and shell did much damage. One of their contrivances for throwing shells amongst our men, was to place short fuse shells into a trough, constructed of planks, lift up one end of it, thus lowering the other end over our works, and drop the shells into our ranks.

"The first time they attempted this they succeeded in killing and wounding 125 men, mostly negroes, who were engaged in shovelling. Just as they were putting a second shell in the trough, I jumped up on the sand bags which formed our breastworks, slipped a noosed rope around the trough, and jerked it into our lines.

"This resulted in throwing the shell the other way, falling among the rebels and exploding there. While slipping the rope around the trough I was necessarily exposed to the full view of the rebel sharpshooters but I did it so quickly and unexpectedly, that for a moment not a shot was fired. Just as I jumped down, the rebels opened up and the air was full of bullets, but just a moment too late to do me any harm."

BRAVE AND RESOURCEFUL

" MARCUS A. HANNA,
Sergeant, Co. B, 50th Mass. Inf.
Born in Franklin Co., Maine, Nov. 3, 1842.

" VOLUNTARILY exposed himself to a heavy fire to get water for comrades in rifle pits." This is the inscription on the Medal of Honor, the proud bearer of which is Marcus A. Hanna, sergeant of Company B, Fiftieth Massachusetts Infantry.

The incident occurred at Port Hudson, on July 4, 1863, and serves not only to illustrate the hero's feeling for his suffering comrades, but his courage and resourcefulness as well. Sergeant Hanna gives a detailed description of the occurrence, as follows:

"While our forces were closely investing Port Hudson, four days before its surrender, the Fiftieth Massachusetts Volunteer Infantry was ordered into the rifle-pits to support a New York battery. It was early in the morning, and we had just been relieved from similar duty, performed during the night. The men went back to the pits without having time to replenish their haversacks or canteens. The day was intensely hot and by noon the men were suffering from thirst. How to get water was a problem, with the enemy on the alert and posted on works but a short distance from and considerably higher than our position.

"At about 2 or 3 o'clock P. M. the thirst of our men had become almost unbearable and Lieutenant William H. Hurd, in command of our company, gave some of us permission to go to the rear for water. Orderly Sergeant Blatchford and myself were the only sergeants present that day. I at once volunteered to go, and asked for a file of men to assist me. No one responded. I decided to try it alone. I took twelve or fifteen canteens—all I could conveniently carry—hung them about my neck, and placed them about my body to afford protection from rebel bullets. A dummy, made by rigging up a musket with a blouse and cap, was prepared, the

---

Port Hudson or Hickey's Landing, situated on a bend of the Mississippi River, twenty-two miles above Baton Rouge, was strongly fortified by the Confederates, and was held in May, 1863, by Colonel Frank Gardner. It was approached by the combined forces of Generals Sherman, Augur and Banks, assisted by the fleet under Admiral Farragut, and the first line of works was abandoned by the rebels on the 25th. An assault by General Weitzel's Brigade, on the 27th, resulted in failure. Bombardment by the fleet continued until the 7th of July, when Colonel Gardner, hearing of the capture of Vicksburg, by the Union Army, surrendered with its force of 6,000 men.

The Union loss during the siege was about 3,000; the Confederate, 7,208, in killed, wounded, and prisoners.

idea being to raise it above our pit and, if possible, draw the fire of the enemy, and then, before they had time to reload, I was to take my chances. Carefully we raised the dummy until the cap only could be seen, then we ducked it out of sight, to hoist it again at once, this time showing the head and body. The deception was a success, for at once there came a heavy volley, and before the smoke had cleared away, I was up and off as rapidly as my light but bulky load

"I SPRANG FROM THE PIT."

would permit. I steered across the level plains for the nearest cover some 500 yards away, but I had not gone far, before I could hear the patter of bullets all around me, and knew that I was within sight and range. Yet, I kept on my course, until about half the distance was covered when I realized that I could not escape being hit, and bethought myself of the ruse of throwing myself prostrate, as if killed or badly wounded. The trick was successful. The firing ceased, and, after lying prone until I was well rested, I sprang to my feet and ran like a deer for the blackberry hedge. In this second race, no further shots were sent after me by the enemy.

"I went about half a mile further to a spring, filled my load of canteens, not one of which, in spite of the firing, had been punctured, and began cautiously to work my way back to my company in the rifle-pits. Instead of making a bee-line for the pit, I made a detour to the left, in order to bring one of our batteries between myself and the enemy. After I had reached the battery I had still some sixty or seventy yards to go to the right, wholly exposed to the enemy's fire. However, I covered this distance unmolested. Lieutenant Hurd and the men warmly congratulated me, and expressed gratitude for the partial relief I had brought them."

SEVERE COST OF SKIRMISHING

O**N** June 14, 1863, the Twelfth West Virginia Infantry left the fortifications at Winchester and were marched to a stone wall on the hills on the opposite side of the Romney Road. They encountered the enemy at the top of the hills, and immediately an order was passed along the line to fall back. The greater part of the regiment obeyed and formed a line some distance back, leaving a number of skirmishers at the wall, where they remained until 4 P. M., when an advance was ordered. At this time, Lieutenant James R. Durham, commanding the skirmishers at the wall, advanced, cleared the wall, and kept on until he was within the lines of the rebels, who were entrenched behind another wall about one hundred and fifty yards distant. The lieutenant says in his account of the action:

"We had been lying behind the stone wall several hours, because to cross it or even show our heads above it, was certain death. Already three of my men had been killed while rising to get a shot. At last, however, we were ordered over the wall. Turning to my boys and shouting a 'Good bye' and 'Come on,' I was the first one over. We advanced about thirty yards, the bullets flying thick and fast on all sides, when I was struck in the right hand. Six or seven of my men were also wounded about the same time. Two advanced too far and fearing to retreat, surrendered.

"I discovered that the line of battle did not intend to advance farther, but instead took shelter behind the stone walls. I therefore ordered my men back, taking our wounded with us. On our retreat two or three others were wounded. After regaining our lines I examined my injuries, and now, for the first time found that my

---

Winchester, Va.—General Ewell's Confederate Army, after entering the Shenandoah Valley, made a forced march to Winchester, reaching that place on the 13th of June, 1863, with the divisions of Jubal, Early, and Edward Johnston. Ewell's lines were extended over one hundred miles of the country. Lee's Army, under Hill and Longstreet, occupied positions at Fredericksburg, and Culpepper Court House.

General Hooker became satisfied that Lee contemplated an invasion and he accordingly withdrew toward Washington, and Ewell prepared to invest Winchester, then held by General Milroy. On the 14th, Milroy was apprised of this movement and after a council of officers, it was decided to retreat toward the Potomac. Johnston met Milroy's force about four miles from Winchester and dispersed the entire body. Milroy's loss was about 4,000 killed, wounded and made prisoners.

right hand and forearm were severely shattered. I reported at the hospital and retreated with the command. The next morning I was obliged to ride forty-five miles on a bare-backed horse to escape capture, while my wound was still bleeding. I was unable to report to my regiment for duty for the next six months."

"I SHOUTED TO MY BOYS: "COME ON!""

A DRAMATIC INCIDENT ON THE BATTLEFIELD

"COLONEL, you are a brave man. You are released from arrest. Here is my own sword. Take it and bring it back to me, red with the enemy's blood."

General Kilpatrick unsheathed his sword and handed it to Colonel Luigi Palma di Cesnola, while a whole regiment in silent reverence witnessed the impressive scene. It was just before the battle of Aldie, June 17, 1863. General Kilpatrick had been sent with his brigade in advance of the main body of the Union troops. The rebels occupied high ground and were behind rails encircling large stacks of hay. Their guns were doing considerable damage to the Union cavalry and the necessity to silence or capture them became urgent.

LUIGI PALMA DI CESNOLA,
Colonel, 4th N. Y. Cavalry
Highest rank attained : Brig-Gen. U. S. V.
Born at Rivarolo, Italy, June 29, 1832.

Colonel di Cesnola's regiment formed part of General Kilpatrick's brigade. On the very morning of the battle an unpleasant episode marred the feeling of comradeship in the Northern ranks. A junior officer had been promoted over Colonel di Cesnola and the latter felt offended. He did not attempt to conceal his injured feelings, but bluntly walked up to General McGregg and protested against the promotion. For this act of indiscretion he was ordered under arrest. In the meantime the general ordered a charge on the enemy's position. Colonel di Cesnola's regiment in a body refused to obey orders. Not a man would stir unless led by his own, dearly beloved commander. For a second the general was nonplussed, but for a second only. Colonel di Cesnola gave him no time to form any conclusion. The honor of his own regiment was now at stake. Without a moment's hesitation Kilpatrick rushed at the head of his men, ordered the charge to be sounded and led his regiment against the rebels. Three times he made an attempt to capture the guns on the crest of the hill. Three times he was forced to retire.

General Kilpatrick could not observe the dashing courage of the brave New Yorkers and their fearless leader and remain unmoved. After the third charge he stepped up to Colonel di Cesnola and addressing him in the language afore mentioned, handed him his own sword.

A fourth charge was made. Though the guns were not captured, the enemy had no desire for further attacks and retreated to a safer position. But the Union troops, too, paid dearly for the advantage gained, and the gallant New Yorkers especially mourned over an almost irreparable loss. Colonel di Cesnola had been severely wounded and taken prisoner. His horse had been killed under him. After nine months confinement at Libby prison he was exchanged, and returned to his colors.

Colonel di Cesnola was a born soldier and a remarkable man. Of noble family— he was a count—he was born in Rivarolo, Italy, June 29, 1832. He entered the Sardinian Army at the age of sixteen, and distinguished himself in the war against Austria. He also participated in the Crimean war, at the conclusion of which he bade the old continent farewell and crossed the ocean to find a new home and serve a new country and a new flag. - He entered the service of the Federal Army in 1861, with the rank of lieutenant-colonel and a year later received his promotion as colonel. He was one of those warriors of whom the poet says that they are : " Every inch a soldier."

"HE WAS FOUND UNDER HIS DEAD HORSE."

NARROW ESCAPE WHILE SAVING A COMRADE,

ELDRIDGE ROBINSON,
Private, Co. C, 122d Ohio Vol. Inf.
Born in Morgan County, Ohio, January 7, 1844.

"THE Romney Pike runs west from Winchester, Virginia, up a ravine with hills rising abruptly to the north and south," Private Eldridge Robinson writes. "In the western outskirts of the city, close to a large walled spring on the north side of the pike, stands the old Mason House, of Mason and Slidell fame. Just south of this, extending from the pike about four hundred yards up the hill, is an old blue-grass field, broken with bushy ravines. Separating this from a clover-field, and about fifty yards before reaching the top of the hill, stands a stone fence. The clover-field extends about four hundred yards on the south side of the hill to a deep woody ravine.

"On Sunday morning, June 14, 1863, the One hundred and twenty-second Ohio Volunteer Infantry occupied a position south of the Romney Road, with several of our companies thrown forward as skirmishers under Lieutenant-Colonel Moses M. Granger. We occupied the crest of the hill till noon.

"On account of a flank movement, we were ordered to fall back to the stone fence and join our commands lying behind it. In falling back, Price Worthington of Co. B, of our regiment, was shot through the body. After we had taken our places in the regiment, I asked several of the boys to go with me and bring Worthington off the field. The drum-major agreed to follow me.

"As soon as I reached the crest of the hill, I came in range of the rebel skirmish line, which opened on me with energy, but hearing Worthington groaning and begging for help, I pushed on to where he was lying, and, in a short time was joined by the drum-major. We picked him up, and, amid a rain of bullets, of which one hit the wounded man in the leg, and many cut holes in our clothes, we reached the top of the hill, when the gunner of a battery about seventy-five yards in the rear of our line, taking us for the enemy, sent a shell so close to our heads that we were both thrown to the ground.

"Although much dazed, we soon regained our feet, and, amidst the applause and congratulations of the officers and comrades of the regiment, placed our wounded comrade in the ambulance."

THE FIRST UNION FLAG IN VICKSBURG

HENRY H. TAYLOR,
Sergeant, Co. C, 45th Ill. Infantry.
Born near Galena, Illinois, July 4, 1841

WHEN Fort Hill, one of the defenses of Vicksburg, was undermined and blown up on the 25th of June, the Forty-fifth Illinois, of which Sergeant Henry H. Taylor was color-bearer, was the first regiment taken into the breach by General M. D. Leggett, and fought there most gallantly until relieved.

According to the statement of General Leggett, the struggle was desperate. The regimental colors were bravely supported by Sergeant Taylor, and the first to be placed on the rebel works, during the siege. In the assault on the 22d of May, a color bearer, further to the left of McClernand's front, had advanced far enough to plant his flag on, or against the enemy's works. This achievement, however, was not regarded as the placing of the Union colors on the rebel works, as they were not held there.

At Fort Hill, the colors of the Forty-fifth remained until the line could be extended to another work further to the right, which was also blown up. Then, as the general saw that he could not hold the position and prevent its reconstruction without remaining in the crater, he withdrew the troops about seventy-five feet from it, and there maintained his position until the surrender of Vicksburg.

This work was done under the orders of Generals Logan and McPherson. The mining was done under the immediate guidance and supervision of General A. Hickenlooper, the corps engineer.

"The Forty-fifth Illinois," says General Leggett, "was the first regiment to march into Vicksburg, receive the surrender, and hoist the flag on the court house. The whole of one division went in on the 4th of July, and no other troops. The Forty-fifth was a part of the first brigade which I had commanded, and it was for its gallantry in breaking the Confederate line as well as for its other services in the campaign, that I gave it the front on that day."

Brigadier-General W. R. Rowley reports, concerning the movements of the Forty-fifth, as follows :

"The honor of leading the entry into the city was accorded to the Forty-fifth Illinois Infantry, by special request of Major-General McPherson, it having been the regiment that first occupied the crater, after the blowing up of Fort Hill, or 'Hell,' as the boys called it. The request was made of General Grant, and I myself saw the flag of the Forty-fifth on the court house, and know the fact to be as I have stated."

"A MORE GALLANT CHARGE WAS NEVER MADE "

ON JUNE 27, 1863, during the operations around Shelbyville, General Sheridan ordered Major Charles C. Davis with 300 troopers of the Seventh Pennsylvania Cavalry to make a charge on the camp of the Fourth Alabama, at Unionville, Tenn. This camp was composed of no less than 1,000 rebels under command of General Russell of General Forrest's Division. Major Davis entered upon the execution of this order with alacrity, made the charge and drove the enemy pell-mell through their own camp and on to Hickory Hill Church, a distance of seven miles, taking Hardee's infantry picket and capturing a wagon train of seventeen six-mule teams. The gallant major then led his men back to the rebel camp, seized everything in sight and subsequently was able to report the complete success of his mission to General Sheridan. The enemy's loss in killed, wounded and captured was 302; the entire camp and garrison equipage fell into the possession of Major Davis' little band and all of the personal effects of the Alabamians were taken, besides $27,000 in Confederate money, which were in keeping of the paymaster. The success of Major Davis' achievement is the more brilliant as it was accomplished with the loss of but two killed and one wounded.

No better idea of this remarkable cavalry charge can be given than by the following account, which Brigadier-General D. S. Stanley gives of it in his report of the engagement. Says General Stanley :

"The right wing of General Rosecrans' army had driven the left of the Confederate Army, a division of cavalry commanded by General Wheeler, into the town of Shelbyville, when Wheeler's force of 3,000 men formed line just at the northern outskirts of the town to defend their stores.

"A battery of four guns pointing north, commanded the principal turnpike, well supported by dismounted cavalry, right and left. It was decided to attack the center

---

Shelbyville, Tenn.—About the middle of June, 1863, General Rosecrans decided to attack Bragg's forces at Shelbyville, and thereby relieve East Tennessee by driving the Confederates into Georgia. The advance began on the 23d of June, when McCook's Corps moved directly upon Shelbyville, where demonstrations were to be made while Crittenden, Thomas and Granger were to move upon the place from different directions. Several severe encounters were had with the enemy, who were in every instance defeated. Granger had been joined by Stanley, and together they proceeded to Guy's Gap, which they took after an hour's engagement. They then moved upon and occupied Shelbyville, which Bragg had abandonded. The Confederate cavalry under Wheeler were driven across Duck River with a loss of about 500 prisoners and a large quantity of stores and provisions.

of this line and ride over the battery. The Seventh Pennsylvania Cavalry was selected for the purpose, supported by the Fourth United States Cavalry. The pike being narrow, the charge was made in column of fours. Major Davis' position would have placed him on the right of the second squadron, but he volunteered to lead the charge and put himself in front of the leading set of fours.

"At the signal of two cannon shots from our guns, the column dashed down the pike, receiving only one round from the hostile battery, rode over the guns, routed the supports, and put the entire force opposed, to precipitate and disastrous flight.

THE ENEMY PUT TO DISASTROUS FLIGHT.

The boldness of the attack insured its success. Only one shell struck the column, killing two men and three horses in the charge. Our captures were 300 prisoners, the battery complete, and a large amount of stores.

"A more gallant charge was never made, and Major Davis rode well in front of the leading sabres, the beau ideal of a trooper."

Major Davis was complimented on the field by General Sheridan. Congress, in bestowing the Medal of Honor upon the gallant major, characterized the charge as "one of the most desperate and successful of the war."

CAPTURED A FLAG AND TWO PRISONERS

THOMAS BURKE,
Sergeant, Co. A, 5th New York Cavalry.
Born in Ireland, in 1842.

FIFTEEN or sixteen miles due east of Gettysburg is the little village of Hanover, Pa. On the morning of June 30, 1863, General Kilpatrick with his Third Division of the Union Cavalry Corps under Major-General Pleasonton, reached Hanover and while passing through the little hamlet, the rear of his column was suddenly surprised by receiving a sharp fire from a Confederate battery posted on a hill. Kilpatrick at once realized that the object for which he had been striving—viz.: to keep his force between Stuart's Confederate cavalry and the Army of the Potomac—had been accomplished and at once accepted Stuart's challenge. The fight continued during the day, resulting in Stuart's falling back toward York.

Sergeant Thomas Burke, of Company A, Fifth New York Cavalry, had a thrilling experience during this fight, of which he says: "We were well worn out by long continued work in the saddle and the attack was almost a complete surprise; but with the first gun my commander, Colonel Hammond, moved us quickly from the street into an open field where we formed in line for a charge. Getting the word we started directly toward the Confederates and we went with such force that the enemy's line in our front broke and we saw men scattering in every direction. As we neared the battery which was still being served, I noticed a Confederate flag and started after it just as Corporal Rickey did the same thing. The colors were in charge of two mounted men and it was a race. Rickey had gone 200 yards perhaps, when his horse was shot and thus I was left to go it alone. Meanwhile the firing was sharp from both sides; but I gained on my prize and closing in on the men, as I used my carbine with good effect, I called on them to surrender.

"My command was almost instantly obeyed and I disarmed each man of carbine, sword and pistol, after which, I rushed them ahead of me as fast as our horses—and they were very tired—would take us back to our lines. It was a precarious ride of course, but we got there, flag and all.

"When I took the prisoners, flag and arms to headquarters, General Kilpatrick complimented me very highly. The colors which I captured were those of the Thirteenth Virginia Regiment."

A GRAVE FOR A PILLOW

JAMES M. RUTTER,
Sergeant, Co. C, 143d Pa. Infantry.
Born at Wilkesbarre, Pa., May 18, 1841.

SERGEANT JAMES M. RUTTER of Company C, One-hundred and forty-third Pennsylvania Infantry, describes his experience on the battlefield of July 1, 1863, thus:

" After being in the great fight at Gettysburg from 11 o'clock in the morning until four in the afternoon, my regiment, the one-hundred and forty-third Pennsylvania Infantry, was ordered to fall back, as we were being surrounded or flanked. The Eleventh Corps had been routed previously, leaving our brigade, with the Sixth Wisconsin, to cover the retreat.

" Lieutenant Kropp of our company called out that it would not do to abandon Captain Reichard, who had been shot during the retreat, and asked for volunteers to take him off the field. No one responded. I could not bear to see the captain left to his fate, so I jumped up—we were all lying down and firing at the rebels in the railroad cut opposite—and started for him, calling back that I would attempt the task. It was on the Chambersburg Pike, about twenty feet in front of the firing line, that Captain Reichard lay.

" When I reached his side, I asked him if he could walk and he answered: 'Yes.' I lifted him up and started back to the company. The Minies sang like bees around our heads. There was a high fence in the rear of our line of battle, which gave me some trouble, but Sergeant Marcy took the butt of his gun and knocked the two top rails down. It seemed as if the rebels had made a target of the captain and myself, and seconds were like hours, as the captain and I finally passed over the fence

---

Gettysburg.—At the end of June, 1863, the command of the Union Army, then gathered in the vicinity of Gettysburg, Pa., was transferred from General Hooker to General George G. Meade. He was confronted by the whole Confederate Army, about 80,000, under Lee, his own force being slightly superior.

The fighting commenced on July 1st, with a struggle for the possession of Seminary Ridge, in which the Union line was driven from its position, and back to the high grounds. Here, a new line was formed during the night, reaching from Round Top around to Cemetery Hill, and there to Wolf Hill. To this position the whole Union force, except Sedgwick's Corps, was hurried forward.

On the morning of July 2d, Longstreet attacked the Union left under Sickles, and after a terrible battle, lasting until six o'clock in the evening, the strong position on Great and Little Round Top remained in the hands of the Federals. In the center, a similar struggle for the possession of Cemetery Hill, also resulted in a Union victory. The Union left was somewhat shattered by the Confederate attack.

On the afternoon of the 3d, there was fierce cannonading for nearly three hours. The Confederate artillery was concentrated against the Union center. A gallant charge, made by the Virginians, under General Pickett, resulted in failure and fearful slaughter.

The victory remained with the Federals, and Lee was obliged to fall back. His loss in this battle was over 30,000, that of the Federals, 23,186.

and along the rear of the firing line. After a few minutes, having gained a little hill, I thought all danger was past, but I was mistaken, for I got in between the fire of the rebel batteries and our own near the seminary. As I walked along with Reichard, a comrade of my company, George Tucker, walked beside me without his hat, the blood running down his face. I asked him where he was hit, but he would not answer and instead turned now and then and started towards the rebels. I would call him back and tell him not to go that way, or he would be captured. Then he would turn and come back to me like a child. I soon saw that a ball had parted his hair in the middle, and that his brain had been affected. "After passing our own batteries, which were being made ready to limber up, I had little trouble in getting into the town, where I left the captain in a private house, and where Tucker disappeared. They both turned up all right, however, and later rejoined the company.

"NO LIBBY PRISON FOR ME."

"After getting Captain Reichard over the fence, near the Chambersburg Pike and McPherson's barn, Lieutenant Kropp immediately detailed George Kindred to help me carry Reichard to the rear. I expected to see an ambulance or stretcher there, but not one was to be found, nor did I see one, until I got into Gettysburg. After leaving Reichard in the private house, I saw one or two of our soldiers running ahead of me. I asked them why they were running so hurriedly and they exclaimed: 'Look back and you'll find out!'

"Sure enough, there were the Johnnies right onto me. 'No Libby Prison for me!' I thought, and I ran a race down an alley, through fields, and at last came up to the old cemetery, where the whole runaway Eleventh Corps was massed. I slept that night in the cemetery, with a grave for a pillow, and never slept sounder. I supposed that I would have trouble finding the balance of the Old First Corps, but a staff officer informed me that they were right down under the hill, and there I found my regiment and answered the roll which was being called.

"Lieutenant Kropp was glad to see me. He had not expected to see the captain or myself alive again."

SAVED A CORPS FROM ANNIHILATION

THOUGH repulsed early during the afternoon of July 1, the Confederates soon rallied and made a most desperate attack upon the Union left, along Willoughby's Run. The Federals were driven back on all sides. The First Corps which had sustained the first shock of the fierce assault of the enemy, formed a new line along Seminary Ridge, and what remained of its artillery was posted as advantageously as possible. This movement left the extreme left of the Eleventh Corps uncovered and when, still later in the afternoon, the Confederates made a second attack upon the Union forces, the enemy broke through the Federal center and threw the entire Union line into disorder. This was the situation of affairs, when, by assuming a responsibility which he was in no way called upon to undertake, Major Alfred J. Sellers, of the Ninetieth Pennsylvania Infantry, saved the Eleventh Army Corps from probable annihilation by repulsing the enemy's attack.

ALFRED J. SELLERS,
Major, 90th Penn., Infantry.
Highest rank attained: Colonel.
Born at Plumsteadville, Bucks County, Penn.

"At the battle of Gettysburg," Major Sellers says, "the Eleventh Corps was being forced back by the rebels, who were coming from the north in overwhelming numbers, and late in the afternoon, July 1, 1863, it gave way, carrying the First Corps along with it as far as Cemetery Hill. This left the Confederates occupying the principal part of the town of Gettysburg. Our brigade was on the crown of Oak Ridge, parallel with Cemetery Ridge, and when the Eleventh Corps gave way, a change of front was ordered under fire. At such a time celerity of motion is of vital importance, as a change of front seemingly indicates a reverse, and it is essential to create confidence in the men as to its object. Although not in command, I rushed to the front, superintended the movement and quickly established the line in its new and more advantageous position. This enabled us to pour an effective fire into the ranks of O Niel's Alabama Brigade of Infantry, repulsing its attempt to turn the right flank of the First Army Corps."

TWO GETTYSBURG HEROES

GEORGE W. ROOSEVELT,

1st Sergeant, Co. K. 26th Pennsylvania Inf.
Highest rank attained : Captain.
Born at Chester, Penn., Feb. 14, 1843.

Sergeant George W. Roosevelt, of Company K, Twenty-sixth Pennsylvania Infantry, distinguished himself at the battle of Gettysburg on July 2, 1863, by capturing a Confederate color-bearer and his flag. In one of the numerous charges which signalized this battle, he came upon the color-bearer, and covering him with his musket, ordered him to surrender. The Confederate handed over his flag and Roosevelt marched him in a prisoner, but before reaching the Northern lines, Roosevelt got a bullet in his leg, which brought him to the ground, and his prisoner escaped. The wound proved a serious one, and his leg had subsequently to be amputated. Roosevelt had previously distinguished himself at the battle of Bull Run in 1862, by recovering the colors of his regiment which had fallen into the hands of the enemy. For these two brave deeds he was rewarded by a Medal of Honor.

Never was there a better instance of presence of mind than that displayed by Sergeant Harvey M. Munsell, of Company A, Ninety-ninth Pennsylvania Infantry, on the second day of the battle of Gettysburg. His regiment was stationed at the Devil's Den, where some of the fiercest fighting took place, and made a series of charges, in the course of which all the color-guard were either killed or wounded with the exception of Munsell, who was the color-bearer.

Another charge was ordered, and Munsell was bearing Old Glory aloft amidst a storm of bullets, when a shell burst directly in front of him, tearing a big hole in the ground, and throwing the earth all around. Munsell tumbled headlong into the hole, and lay there stunned, with the colors under him. His comrades, in the excitement of the battle, did not notice what had taken place, and believed that he had been killed and the colors captured. A cry passed through the ranks, the regiment faltered, came to a stop, and fell back in disorder.

When Munsell came to his senses, he found himself lying close to the enemy's lines, so close that if they made the slightest advance they would see the flag that he was shielding with his body, and nothing could save it from capture. If he got up and tried to make his way back to his regiment, he would assuredly be immediately shot down by the sharpshooters, and the regimental flag would be equally certain to become the prize of the enemy. His best chance lay in remaining where he was, for he knew that his regiment would soon rally and return to the charge, and the probability was that the enemy would not make any advance just then. He was right in his surmise, for the Pennsylvanians, burning at the supposed loss of their colors, came on with a rush that carried them into the enemy's lines. They swept right over Munsell who, immediately they were past, jumped up and rejoined his regiment, waving the colors to the breeze.

A MUSKET BUTT ARGUMENT

EDWARD L. GILLIGAN,
Captain, Co. E, 88th Pa. Vols.
Born in Philadelphia, Apr. 18, 1843.

IT was a gallant feat that entitled Captain Edward L. Gilligan of the Eighty-eighth Pennsylvania Volunteers to a Medal of Honor. He assisted in the capture of the colors of the Twenty-third North Carolina on the first day of the battle of Gettysburg. Gilligan, who was first-sergeant at the time thus describes the affair:

"Iverson's Brigade of North Carolinians had attacked Baxter's Brigade of the First Corps and been repulsed. We got the order to charge the retreating enemy and we struck the Twenty-third North Carolina and captured nearly the entire regiment. Captain Joseph H. Richard, of my company, singled out the color-bearer of the Twenty-third and had a hand-to-hand fight with him. The Confederate pluckily held on to the colors and only gave them up when I reasoned with him with the butt of my musket."

ANOTHER exploit of Captain Gilligan was performed during General Warren's raid to destroy the Weldon railroad in December, 1864. Gilligan was then captain and acting adjutant of the regiment and so was mounted. He says:

"The enemy's cavalry had driven in a squadron of horse which formed our rear guard and annoyed us considerably before they could be driven off. When I saw them coming on again, I rode back and made an effort to rally our cavalry, but was unsuccessful. I found myself alone, facing the rebels who were madly charging after our boys. There was but one way out of it for me. I slipped out of my saddle, threw myself on the ground and allowed them to ride over me. I was covered with mud, but escaped injury. When the rebels once more retired, I rose and made my way back to my command. I was able to report to General Baxter the strength of the enemy and we laid a trap for them.

"The Ninth New York Infantry was left in ambuscade by the side of the road, and when the rebels came on again, gave them such a hot reception, that they fled in confusion and did not trouble us any more."

"THE CONFEDERATE PLUCKILY
HELD ON TO THE COLORS."

FORGOT HE WAS A GENERAL

MAJOR-GENERAL ALEXANDER S. WEBB gained his Medal of Honor at Gettysburg, July 3, 1863, for an act which, as General Meade said when presenting the medal, had not been surpassed by any general in the field. He was brigadier-general of volunteers, and in command of the Second Brigade of the Second Division of the Second Army Corps, but nevertheless spent the whole day on the firing line. He remained with the color guard of the Seventy-second Pennsylvania Volunteers until every man of them had been either killed or wounded.

Noticing a company of rebels led by General Armistead clearing a low stone wall to attack the right of the Sixty-ninth Pennsylvania, General Webb rushed down the line until he reached the threatened regiment, and directed its fire upon the rebels.

General Armistead and General Webb remained in the fire-swept zone between the opposing forces until both were wounded. The fire was so severe that more than half of General Webb's men were either killed or wounded, but inspired by the gallantry of their general, they stood their ground unflinchingly, until they were relieved.

In this engagement General Webb received a bullet in the groin, but in a few weeks he was at the front once more.

CARRIED THE COLORS OF HIS WOUNDED COMRADE

"IT was about seven o'clock in the evening of July 2, 1863," Corporal Harrison Clark writes, "as we moved down into the fight, the sun was sinking low in the west and the heavens were ablaze with its splendor, in marked contrast with the lurid fires of death towards which we were marching. We were halted amid a heavy cloud of smoke in front of a swale and a new growth of trees. Through the smoke covering the field we could dimly see the outlines of men moving about. We commenced to fire, but the word was shouted: 'firing on your own men,' and the command was given to: 'cease firing.' We soon learned our mistake.

"The color-bearer at my right fell, mortally wounded, and before the old flag

HARRISON CLARK,
Corporal, Co. E, 125th N. Y. Vols.
Born at Chatham, N. Y., April 10, 1842.

could touch the ground, I caught it, and on we rushed with loud cries; on, with bullets whizzing by our ears, shells screaming and cannon balls tearing the air, now bursting above and around us, laying many of our comrades either low in death, or bleeding with terrible wounds. Most of our color-guard were killed or wounded.

"The purpose was accomplished. The enemy had failed to break through our lines, and Little Round Top and Cemetery Hill were still ours. On the return march, as we were passing the swale, where over one hundred of our brave men had fallen in the space of half an hour, the regiment was again formed in line of battle, the colonel ordered me to step three paces in front of the regiment, promoted me color-bearer and, by his recommendation to Congress, I was awarded a Medal of Honor."

At the battle of the Wilderness, Color-Sergeant Clark displayed rare bravery and continued fighting, though shot in the leg. He was promoted lieutenant on the battlefield.

"FALL 'OUT' HERE, EVERY D - - D ONE OF YOU!"

JOHN LONERGAN,
Captain Co. A, 13th Vermont
Infantry.
Born in Ireland, April 7, 1839.

THE battle of Gettysburg had been in progress the entire day of July 1st, when early in the evening, the Thirteenth Vermont Infantry, commanded by Colonel Francis V. Randall, reached the battle-field after seven days of steady marching. That night was devoted by the entire Third Brigade, under General Stannard, to much needed rest. On the following day, with the battle renewed, the Vermont boys were called upon for heavy work and they responded bravely all along the line. In the afternoon a body of Confederates was seen dragging off a battery that had just been captured from General Sickles' forces and just at that particular time, batteries were needed. At this juncture General Hancock rode up, and, seemingly addressing the entire regiment, asked: "Can you Vermont men take those guns?" The commander of the regiment, Colonel Randall, replied: "We'll try, General." Then followed the command forming five companies for a charge, then the charge. Company A was in the lead and in command of Captain John Lonergan, who describes the succeeding events as follows:

"My company reached the guns first, and placing my hand upon the nearest gun, I ordered the enemy to surrender. All this time the whole regiment was under severe fire, with men falling all along the entire charge; but we reached the guns comparatively together and in good form. The Confederates obeyed my summons to surrender, after which my men lay down their guns and taking hold of the wheels of the gun carriages, began moving them to a new position where they could be utilized.

"Meanwhile I noticed that we were sustaining much damage from firing that came from the Codories House in our front. And so ordering my command to pick up their guns, we made a charge on the house. We quickly surrounded the building, the men at once covering the windows and doors with their guns, so that no man should escape. Then I stepped to the front door, and knocking it in, I ordered: 'Surrender! Fall out here, every damned one of you!'

"My order was obeyed almost instantly, for the Confederates came tumbling out, led by their commanding officer, until we had eighty-three men as prisoners. The officer in command handed me his sword and each man laid down his gun until I had a considerably larger number of men as prisoners, than I had in my entire command. When all was over for the day General Stannard sent for me, and upon my arrival, he said: 'Captain, you did well to-day, but do you know you violated all military laws in capturing those prisoners in the Codories House?'

COVERED THE WINDOWS AND DOORS WITH THEIR GUNS.

"'How is that, General?' I asked.

"'Why,' replied the general with a smile, 'you know that in forming a company line, the command is, 'fall in!' and at the Codories House you said: 'fall out.'

"I saw the joke and answered: 'Yes, General, but they were already in, and so had to 'fall out.'"

A MOST HEROIC AND HAZARDOUS RIDE AT GETTYSBURG

J. PARKE POSTLES,
Captain, Co. A, 1st Del. Infantry.
Highest rank attained: Inspector-Gen'l,
U. S. V.
Born in Camden, Del., Sept. 28, 1840.

THE delivery of an order in the face of a withering fire from the enemy is told by Captain J. Parke Postles of Co. A, First Delaware Infantry, as follows:

"Right in front of the Federal left center at Gettysburg, just to the left of Ziegler's Grove, and seven hundred yards in front of their lines, stood a farm-house and barn, called the Bliss House. The buildings were just about on the Union advance skirmish line, and parallel to the line of Pickett's charge. Possession of those buildings was important to the Northern troops and also to the enemy, and during the second day of July, many a sharp struggle was had between the Federal advance line and that of the enemy, for their possession, with varying results; sometimes they were in the possession of one, then in that of the other. The troops holding the main and advance line at this point, were the Second Brigade, Third Division Second Army Corps, commanded by General Thomas A. Smyth, consisting of the First Delaware, the Twelfth New Jersey, the Fourteenth Connecticut, and the One-hundred and eighth New York Volunteers. In the afternoon of July 2d, the Federals held the barn, while the enemy held the house, some sixty-five yards distant and on a line with it; and from the cover of the house, the Confederates were greatly annoying the Northern skirmish line, and even the gunners of Woodruff's Battery, in Ziegler's Grove.

"Under these circumstances, General Alexander Hayes, commanding our division, sent word to General Smyth, commanding the brigade, to 'have the men in the barn take that damned white house and hold it all hazards.' General Smyth turned to his staff who were scattered around him and said: 'Gentlemen, you hear, who will take the order?' At the time, I was sitting on a rock a few feet away, with one arm through my bridle and my head in my hands, having been sick for several days and barely able to continue on duty. Not hearing any response to the general's question, I raised my head saying: 'I will take it, sir.' The general replied: 'Well Postles, you need no instructions from me.' I at once threw the rein over my horse's head, mounted and rode off slowly down the lane, passed the little frame building in which the rebels were and crossed the Emmitsburg Road; and on reaching the field beyond, I put my horse into a gentle lope. As soon as I crossed the Emmitsburg Road, the enemy in the house opened fire on me, which grew hotter and hotter as I drew nearer to them, till it was a constant wonder and surprise to me that none of the bullets, which I heard whistling around and so close to me, had hit me. One thinks very fast under such circumstances, and I speedily concluded that the reason that they did not hit me was that I was on horseback and in motion, but that when I should stop at the barn, they would kill me sure. It immediately flashed upon me that my only chance of safety was in keeping my horse in motion,

"I SANK MY SPURS INTO THE HORSE'S SIDES."

not letting him stand. So, as I rode up in front of the barn, I threw my whole weight on the bridle rein and, at the same time raising both heels, sank my spurs deep into the horse's sides, and held them there. The poor brute, his sides torn up by my spurs and his mouth lacerated and bleeding from the cruel curb-bit, reared, kicked and plunged, so that I was as bad a mark as though in full gallop. An officer came to the door of the barn and touched his hat to me for orders. I called out to him at the top of my voice, so that the enemy in the house could hear as well as he could: 'Tell the officer in command here, to take that house with one company of sharpshooters, and hold it at all hazards.' All this time the enemy were firing at me from every door or window of the house in range of me. As soon as the officer in the door of the barn touched his hat again, in token of his receipt of the order, I loosened my bridle rein, still holding my spurs in my horse's sides and the poor brute sped away, almost as though shot out of a gun. When I had gotten about three hundred yards away, beginning to feel quite safe again, I turned in my saddle and, taking off my cap, shook it at them in defiance. They immediately set up the 'rebel yell' and ceased firing at me.

"I rode into our lines, which, as I approached, arose and gave me three cheers. Just inside of our line I saw our corps commander, General W. S. Hancock, sitting on his horse and watching me. He happened to be passing along just then, and seeing the incident under way, not knowing at all who I was, stopped to see the result of it, and as I rode up, he raised his hat, thanked and congratulated me. Our men in the barn on receipt of my order, promptly proceeded to charge, and took the 'damned white house,' capturing forty prisoners.

"When these prisoners were brought in and halted near our headquarters, I stepped over to take a look at them. As I came up, one of them looked up at me— they were seated on the ground—and said:

"'Well sir, I guess your time hain't come yet.' Upon my asking why, he said; 'Well, I had three fair shots at you, and there are plenty more fellows here who had as many.' I had been so close to them when I passed the house and while I stopped in front of the barn that they recognized me as soon as I approached them. It seems almost miraculous that in all that ride, down and back, seven hundred yards each way, under a concentrated fire directed at us, neither myself nor my horse were touched by even a single shot."

A RESOURCEFUL ARTILLERY OFFICER.

"THE noble and gallant conduct of Lieutenant Knox deserves the highest honor that could be conferred on him."

This flattering tribute Captain Patrick Hart pays Lieutenant Edward M. Knox of the Fifteenth Independent New York Light Battery in the official report of the battery's action at the battle of Gettysburg.

On July 2d the battery was ordered to the front and take a position in the line of battle. When this was carried out, General Sickles detailed the battery to go with Major McGilvery and reconnoiter the enemy. Subsequently this order was again modified and the battery ordered to take a position on the left of the Peach Orchard. Here the battery opened and directed a telling fire on one of the enemy's batteries, which was doing heavy execution on the Union line of battle. This artillery duel was of brief duration. The enemy was compelled to withdraw. A heavy column of infantry was now advancing on the brave New Yorkers, who then directed their fire on the advancing columns, repulsing the rebels. A second attack was made and for a second time the enemy was obliged to retreat before the deadly fire of the well served battery. When a third attack was made and frustrated, the battery's ammunition was exhausted and Captain Hart withdrew to a distance of about one mile in good order.

Lieutenant Knox's behavior during these struggles was admirable and highly appreciated by his captain, who pays him the above mentioned tribute. The lieutenant himself says of his experience on that eventful day:

EDWARD M. KNOX,
2d Lieutenant, Fifteenth Ind. N. Y., Lt. Battery.
Born in New York City.

"My battery galloped into Peach Orchard, by order of General Hunt, who, pointing in the direction of the orchard, said: 'Go in there. Rush!' I was junior officer, and with Captain Hart, the only officer there. As we went in, the captain shouted: 'Lieutenant, you fight the right section. I will look out for the left.' My speed had carried me fully 100 yards ahead of the artillery line on the left (the Sixth and Ninth Massachusetts Batteries,) and of my own left section. The Confederates thought they had my guns and made a dash for them. As they came, I let go both pieces with double canister, and as I did so, I yelled to my boys to lay down and pretend that they were done for. And thus, not heeding us, the 'Johnnies' swept through my section to meet a charge from the support in our rear,—the Seventy-second New York Infantry—I think. Then, repulsed and driven back, they came back more rapidly than they came in. After they had again passed over us, we got up and with our prolonges and the assistance of the infantry boys, hauled our guns back.

"I lost seven men and eleven horses; the battery, eight men and thirteen horses. I was myself severely wounded in this action; and the next day, at the time of Pickett's charge on our front, I was shot, a round musket ball passing through both hips. Although the latter wound made me an invalid for the next eighteen months, I received my commission as first lieutenant of the Fifteenth Independent New York Light Battery. I was never physically able, however, to be mustered or serve thereafter."

THE STRUGGLE AT THE "BLOODY ANGLE"

IT was during the repulse of Pickett's charge at Gettysburg, that Sergeant Frederick Fuger of Battery A, Fourth United States Artillery, displayed the gallantry for which he was awarded the Medal of Honor.

The battery, commanded by First Lieutenant A. H. Cushing, was posted behind a stone wall in what afterward became known as the "Bloody Angle."

At 1 o'clock on the afternoon of July 3d, the enemy's artillery, commanded by General Armistead, opened along the whole line, and for an hour and a quarter the artillery brigade of the Federal Second Corps was subjected to a very warm artillery fire.

At first the Union batteries made no reply, till the fire of the enemy became too terrible, when they returned it, till all their ammunition except canister had been expended. Within less than two hours the enemy had silenced the Rhode Island battery and all the guns but one of Cushing's battery. They then followed up this concentrated fire upon the Union lines by an infantry attack.

At three o'clock they left the woods in line of battle and, under a fire from Wheeler's Battery and Cushing's gun, formed in front of the several lines of battle and slowly but surely advanced for the attack. Steadily they approached the stone wall. General Armistead with several hundred of his Virginia troops charged across the stone wall and came directly upon Cushing's battery. Double and triple charges of canister were poured into the ranks of the advancing enemy, making frightful gaps in their lines, and by the time they had reached the battery, there was not much left of them.

The encounter was one of the bloodiest of the war. In the very middle of the battery the fight was continued. Lieutenant Cushing and two officers were instantly killed. Sergeant Fuger, the only remaining officer, was left to conduct the battery's struggle. He bravely held his ground and aided materially to the final defeat of the daring rebels. During the fighting around the guns, General Armistead fell mortally wounded, and almost his whole command was either killed or wounded.

Battery A's loss was forty-five out of ninety-three men killed and wounded and eighty-three out of ninety horses killed. The guns of the battery were turned over to the ordnance department the next day as unserviceable.

Sergeant Fuger's conduct at this engagement was highly praised by his superior officers and found immediate recognition by a promotion to the rank of a second lieutenant.

THE DELAY WAS FATAL

Two gallant actions, one performed at Gettysburg and the other a year later, are thus recalled by Sergeant John M. Pipes of the One hundred and fortieth Pennsylvania Volunteers.

"On the afternoon of July 3, 1863, our brigade charged across a wheat field and engaged the enemy in the woods south of it. Taking advantage of our exposed position far in advance of our line, the enemy, under General Longstreet, poured a deadly fire upon our flank. Our little brigade had lost more than half its men and nearly all its officers, and had begun to waver and fall back before I could fully realize the situation. Standing at the right of my company, a step or two in front, firing as rapidly as I could, I saw that most of our men were getting across the field toward the main line, while the Twenty-fourth Georgia Infantry, crossing from the woods, was close upon us. Lieutenant J. J. Purman, of my company, was standing near me.

JOHN M. PIPES,
Sergeant, Co. A, 140th Penn. Vol.
Highest rank attained: Captain.

"The question confronted us: 'shall we be captured or take the slim chance of crossing that field?' Of course we took the chance. We had hardly started when a wounded comrade pleaded to be taken off the field, as he could not rise. The rebels, who were very close upon us, called: 'Halt, you damned Yankees, halt.' We however, carried this comrade some thirty or forty steps and placed him behind some large boulders where he would have protection from the fire from both sides, and from being trampled upon.

"This occupied but a few moments, but the delay was fatal to our attempt to cross the wheat field. We had just started on a good double-quick, when Lieutenant Purman called out: 'I am hit!' I was then but a few steps from him, and the next moment I received a wound in the leg, and replied: 'I am wounded too.' Realizing that I could not aid the lieutenant, having only one sound leg, I thought 'goodbye comrades,' and, using my gun for a crutch, commenced to hop off the battle-field, but had only gotten a few paces, when to my surprise, I found myself right among the Confederates.

"Our flank was captured, taken to the rear, and put in an old barn, then used by the enemy as a temporary hospital. We remained in their hands until the next morning, when our forces advanced and recaptured us, taking a good number of Confederates at the same time. I was carried on a stretcher to the tents of the Second Corps' hospital, established in the woods, where I found Lieutenant Purman, who had been wounded by my side, and whose leg had been amputated.

"On August 24, 1864, at Ream's Station Virginia, two divisions of Hancock's Corps having torn up and destroyed several miles of railroad, a detail was sent out on picket duty for the night. Being captain and ranking officer, the command devolved upon me," Captain Pipes narrates in describing his second experience. "We were on duty all night, and the next day during the fight the enemy attempted to flank us, causing my command to become uneasy and fear capture. I saw clearly that to remain meant capture with serious loss, so finally assumed responsibility, and moved my men by the left flank back across the railroad, ordering them to lie down there while I reconnoitered.

"I USED MY GUN FOR A CRUTCH."

"I discovered that our forces had left their positions, so I returned and led my command at the double-quick to a depression, where I ordered them to lie down again. I had been there but a few minutes, when a battery of the enemy unlimbered and opened a terrific fire upon us. They soon had the range and would have destroyed us, had not I ordered the command back up the hill at a lively gait. Near the top an officer came galloping up to me and said: 'Captain Pipes, if you will take in your men on the left and help check the enemy in their flank movement, I'll see that you will get credit.'

"Moving some distance I deployed my men as skirmishers and led them in what was supposed to be the direction of the command. Then I ordered them to move forward, taking care to avail themselves of any protection they might find. Shortly afterward the command was given, 'cease firing' to enable us to discover the situation of our men and that of the enemy. While looking out under the smoke, when the fire of the enemy had abated, I received a wound through the right arm, shattering it from near the shoulder down to the elbow. The fight at this time seemed to be nearly over, and with the assistance of two comrades, I was able to lead my command back to the woods, where I ran across my regiment. My ride in an ambulance for ten miles that night was a memorable one. The dangling arm was amputated the next day at City Point, Va."

CAPTURED FOUR REGIMENTAL FLAGS

EDMUND RICE,
Major, 19th Mass. Inf.
Highest rank attained: Lieut.-Col.

THE Nineteenth Massachusetts Infantry was exposed to the full force of Lee's artillery fire during the afternoon of July 3d, at Gettysburg. After the suspension of that fire, it was advanced and obliqued to the left, and placed in part behind the famous "Pile of Rails." When Longstreet's infantry advance had fully developed, the regiment was withdrawn from that position and momentarily held in reserve. About two or three minutes after reaching the reserve position, a break in General Webb's Brigade occurred, and the enemy's battle flags appeared in the gap made by the break. That was the crisis of the battle on that wing of the Union Army. Major Edmund Rice, of the Nineteenth Massachusetts Infantry, fully appreciated the danger of the situation.

"Boys," he shouted to his men, "follow me!" And away he dashed in the direction of the Confederate battle flags. The "boys" did not desert their major, but joined in the race to a man. They were followed by a part of the Seventh Michigan and Forty-second New York Infantry. Major Rice kept the lead and was the first one to come in contact with the surprised enemy. The clash of the two bodies of troops was fierce. Brave Major Rice was among the first ones wounded, which fact however did not prevent him from maintaining his command. The desperate hand-to-hand struggle which his fearless initiative had inaugurated, gave General Webb's Brigade time to rally, expel the enemy from the gap in the Union line, and decide the battle in favor of the Union arms. Major Rice's regiment lost three-fourths of its force during the fight, but the victorious survivors returned with the captured colors of four rebel regiments.

SAW THE REBEL FLAG AND TOOK IT

BENJAMIN H. JELLISON,
Sergeant, Co. C, 19th Massachusetts Infantry.

Sergeant Benjamin H. Jellison of Company C, Nineteenth Massachusetts Infantry has an interesting story to tell of his experience at the battle of Gettysburg. He says:

"We arrived on the field of Gettysburg the night of the first day of July. The next day we were ordered to the left, in the rear of the Third Corps to rally it, as it had been broken and was coming in in bad shape. We were too late, and our charge, made in an attempt to save the battery in front of us, was in vain. The rebels got there first, turned the battery on us, so that we were forced to fall back. As my company was the sixth in line, we were left in charge of the colors. In retreating, I was crowded into the color-guard, and soon found myself in front of the colors. Presently the color-bearer was shot; I picked up the colors and was at once made sergeant.

"On the third day we lay on Cemetery Ridge, and while the officers were eating their dinner in the rear of the colors, the first shell that the rebels fired went into the mess and killed Lieutenant Robertson. The next shell hit one of our gun stacks. Then the colonel ordered to break stacks. The dance now commenced. The Nineteenth Massachusetts was supporting the New York Independent Battery, which by this time had lost all its men except the captain, one lieutenant and one sergeant. The captain came into our regiment bare-headed, with both hands in his hair, and called out: 'For God's sake, men, volunteer to work these guns; don't let this battery be silent.'

"I was lying on the ground, the colors by my side, and Lieutenant Shackly next to me. Shackly said: 'Come, Jellison, let's go and help, we might just as well get killed there as here.'

"'All right,' said I, and so I carried my ammunition from the limber to the guns. The colonel saw me and ordered me back to the colors. The shelling had now stopped, and an old general riding past, called to us: 'Get into line, boys, they are coming.' Upon that, the colonel ordered me on the ridge and gave orders to rally on the colors. We then charged to the fence near by, and some got over.

"Lieutenant Shackly was again at my side. 'Ben,' he remarked this time, 'see the rebel flag? Let's get it.' He pointed to our front, and the next moment I lost him. I rushed forward and succeeded in capturing the flag, and besides assisted in taking quite a number of prisoners. With the Stars and Stripes flying over my head, and carrying the captured flag, I retreated."

A DASHING CHARGE AT GETTYSBURG.

WILLIAM WELLS,

Major, 1st Vermont Cavalry.
Highest rank attained: Bvt.-Maj.-Gen., U. S. V.
Born in Waterbury, Vt., 1838.

DURING the battle of Gettysburg, on the after-noon of July 3d, General Kilpatrick ordered General Farnsworth to charge on the right flank of the enemy in front of both Round Tops, and designated Major William Wells to lead the Second Battalion of the First Vermont Cavalry in the attack.

The charge was made: Major Wells at the head of his brave Vermonters with General Farnsworth riding by his side. At the outset, the Union forces suffered a severe loss. General Farnsworth was struck by a ball and instantly killed. There was no interruption in the attack, however. The death of the gallant general only served to stimulate Major Wells and his men to still more determined action.

With disregard to a most galling fire the major led his batallion over the stone wall against the superior hostile force and drove the foe in all directions. He followed in pursuit, cleared another wall and dashed across a field swept by the rebel batteries, piercing the enemy's second line. A fresh regiment of rebels, sent from the right to intercept some retreating Union troops, was encountered on a little hill. Then there was a desperate fight for the possession of the hill. Major Wells carried it, and took the greater part of the rebel regiment prisoners. It was a wonderful charge, crowned with brilliant success, and showed Major Wells to be a most dashing cavalry officer.

THE CHARGE WAS MADE WITH A MIGHTY SHOUT.

WHEELOCK G. VEAZEY, shortly after his promotion from the Third Vermont to the colonelcy of the Sixteenth Vermont, was carried by the tide of war to the famous Pennsylvania battlefield, where his regiment attained a reputation second to none. This regiment occupied, on the third day of Gettysburg, the front of Stannard's Brigade, in the left center of the Union line. In this advanced position it received the first shock of Pickett's charge. It was a tremendous attack, but the assailants were forced to surge off to the right, and the regiment commanded by Colonel Veazey, wheeled out and attacked them on the flank as they went by with withering effect, and capturing many prisoners

At this moment, while the Sixteenth was partly broken, another column—Wilcox's and Perry's Brigades—came rushing along toward its flank and rear. Colonel Veazey quickly grasped the situation. He explained his plans to General Stannard.

"Veazey," cried the general, "your men will do almost anything, but the men don't live this side of hell, that can be made to charge down there." But in shorter time than it takes to tell it, the regiment had straightened out, reformed, and made another change of front in the very center of the field, where the battle raged in its greatest fury, and men were falling every instant.

"I stepped to the front," says Colonel Veazey, "and called upon the men to follow. With a mighty shout the rush forward was made, and, before the enemy could change his front, we had struck his flank. and swept down the line, and again captured a great number of prisoners. In the two charges my regiment captured three stands of colors. The last charge brought a heavy artillery fire on us, but we lost only 150 out of 400 because the rebels never accurately found our range."

JOHN B. FASSITT,

Captain Co. F, 23d Pennsylvania Infantry
Highest rank attained: Major.
Born in Philadelphia, Pa., Oct. 26, 1836.

USURPED THE GENERAL'S AUTHORITY.

During the battle of Gettysburg many were the exigencies and tremendous responsibilities that confronted the general officers in each army. In most instances, also, they were met and disposed of with all loyalty, patriotism and bravery.

It was on the day before the demonstration known as Pickett's charge, that Captain John B. Fassitt of Company F, Twenty-third Pennsylvania Infantry, displayed his courage, his quick mind, action and willingness to shoulder great responsibility. On the day of the Peach Orchard struggle, shortly after Major-General Daniel E. Sickles had received the wound which later cost him a leg, that Battery I, of the Fifth United States Artillery, was captured by the Confederates. Captain Fassitt, at the time was senior aide to General Birney, who, General Sickles having been carried off the field, was in command of the Third Army Corps. Fassitt had just completed the work of reforming Humphrey's Division on Cemetery Ridge after it had been driven back from Blodensburg Road, and was returning to the left line to report to General Birney, when he saw Lieutenant Samuel Peoples of Battery I, standing on a rock looking to the front. Thereupon Captain Fassitt asked the lieutenant why he was not with his battery, and the lieutenant answered: "Because it has just been captured." And then pointing toward his battery, the lieutenant continued: "And if those Confederates are able to serve my guns, those troops you have just been forming on the ridge, won't stay there a minute."

Captain Fassitt, instantly comprehending the fact that the battery could direct an enfilading fire on Cemetery Ridge, and recognizing that ridge as the key to the Federal position, he rode rapidly to the nearest troops—the Thirty-ninth New York Infantry—and ordered Major Hillebrandt, the commanding officer, to retake the battery.

"By whose orders?" asked the major.

The captain replied: "By order of General Birney."

"I am in General Hancock's Corps," responded the major.

To this the captain said: "Then I order you to take those guns, by order of General Hancock."

"THE CAPTAIN STRUCK UP WITH HIS SABRE."

At this, Major Hillebrandt moved his regiment by flank with superb alacrity, and when opposite the battery, he ordered a charge. Captain Fassitt not only helped to move the regiment by the flank, but, being the only mounted officer, also assisted in the assault. The Confederates were not willing to give up the battery and position without a struggle and the fight was a fierce one. As the Federal line reached the Confederates, one of them seized the bridle of Captain Fassitt's horse while another raised his musket fair into the face of the mounted man. The captain struck up with his sabre just in time to divert the musket ball so that it passed through the visor of his cap, and the next instant a member of the Thirty-ninth ran his bayonet through the man who delivered the shot, while Fassitt shot down the man holding the bridle of his horse. Again free, the captain went on with Major Hillebrandt's troops, until they had secured Cemetery Hill for Hancock's use in repulsing Pickett.

WHERE DISOBEDIENCE WAS A VIRTUE

WILLIAM E. MILLER,

Captain, Troop H, 3rd Penn. Cavalry.

Born at West Hill, Cumberland Co., Penn.

FEDERAL and Confederate cavalry were hotly engaged during the last day's fighting at Gettysburg, July 3d. There were skirmishes, charges, counter-charges from noon till nightfall during that most eventful day. Sometimes it would seem as if the enemy would gain an advantage, when the Union cavalry would rally and with renewed vigor wrest from them the victory which the rebels believed to be already within their grasp. And thus the fighting continued for hours with varying success, until at dark the Confederate cavalry retired to a position behind their artillery, leaving the Federals masters of the contested field.

"Heavy skirmishing," says General Gregg, referring to this cavalry fight, "was maintained by the Third Pennsylvania Cavalry with the enemy and was continued until nightfall. During the engagement a portion of this regiment made a very handsome and successful charge upon one of the enemy's regiments."

General Gregg's flattering mention of the "handsome charge," refers to the gallant feat of Captain William E. Miller of Troop H, who by this deed became the hero of his regiment and the recipient of the precious Medal of Honor.

The captain himself describes the charge as follows:

"Our regiment had been ordered forward, and my squadron was deployed along the edge of the woods, with orders to hold that position. We had nothing to do with the first part of the fight, but when a Virginia regiment approached, we opened fire on them and succeeded in holding them in check. A flank fire also opened on them, and they were obliged to fall back on their main body.

"Suddenly there appeared, moving towards us, a mass of cavalry formed in close column squadrons. They rode with well aligned front and steady reins, their polished sabres glittering in the sun. Shell and shrapnel tore through their ranks, but they closed up the gaps and came on as steadily as ever. As they drew nearer, our artillery-men substituted canister for shrapnel, and horses and men went down by scores. Still they came on, and our cavalry fell into line and prepared for a charge.

"As the columns approached each other, each increased its pace until they came together with a crash like the falling of timber. So violent was the collision that many of the horses were turned over, crushing their riders under them. The clashing of sabres, firing of pistols, and the cries of the combatants filled the air.

"My squadron was still deployed, and I was standing with Lieutenant William Brooke-Rawle on a little rising ground in front. Seeing that the situation was becoming critical, I said to him: 'I have been ordered to hold this position, but I will order a charge if you will back me up in case I am court-martialed for diso-

"WE BROKE THROUGH THE CONFEDERATE COLUMN."

bedience.' The lieutenant enthusiastically promised that he would stand by me. As soon as the line was formed, our men fired a volley from their carbines, drew their sabres, and charged, striking the enemy's left flank about two-thirds down the column.

"We broke through the Confederate column, cut off the rear portion and drove it back; but in the charge my men became somewhat scattered, and were even unable to capture an unsupported rebel battery which was standing only 100 yards away. The flank attack demoralized the Confederate column, and it was driven back to its former position, leaving us in possession of the field."

A SMALL PARTY'S BRAVE DEED

JOHN W. HART,
Sergeant, Co. D, 6th Pa. Reserves.
Born in Germany.

J. L. ROUSH,
Corporal, Co. D, 6th Pa. Reserves.
Born in Woodbury, Pa., Feb. 11, 1838.

GEORGE W. MEARS,
Sergeant, Co. A, 6th Pa. Reserves.
Born in Bloomsburg, Pa.

CHESTER S. FURMAN,
Corporal, Co. A, 6th Pa. Reserves.
Born in Bloomsburg, Pa., Feb. 14, 1842.

THE brunt of the Confederate onslaught, on the second day of the battle of Gettysburg, was directed against General Sickles' extreme left, held by General Ward of General Birney's Division, whose three brigades extended their line from the Round Tops across the Devil's Den to and beyond the Peach Orchard. At first the Federals, after a bitter contest, were forced to yield to the superior strength of the enemy and retreated. Then the Union troops received re-enforcements and made a stand against the advancing Confederates near the Little Round Top. Here a most terrible struggle took place. At all points the ground was contested stubbornly. The odds were against the Federals, but in the face of heavy losses they fought with a bravery rarely equalled. In this contest the Sixth Pennsylvania Reserves was an important factor in General Birney's Division to which it belonged. It not only distinguished itself with the balance of the Union Army during the heat of the battle, but some of its individual members performed deeds of daring and valor which contributed toward the final success of that day as far as the attack on this wing of the Union Army was concerned.

No more conspicuous deed was there, however, than that which was performed by Sergeant John W. Hart of Company D, Sergeant George W. Mears of Company A, Corporals J. Levi Roush and Chester S. Furman, the former of Company D, the latter of Company A, and two others, all members of the aforementioned gallant regiment. The occasion was this: As the battle was raging at its height, the Union troops stationed near Devil's Den, suffered especially from a concentrated and well-directed fire, which was difficult at first to locate. It was finally, however, traced to a small log house nearby. Here a number of sharpshooters had fortified themselves and were pouring their volleys into the Union ranks with deadly accuracy. The necessity to stop this source of destruction became imperative. The colonel of the Sixth Pennsylvania Reserves placed his regiment at the disposal of the commanders to accomplish this task. His offer being accepted, the colonel at once asked for volunteers. Pointing to the log house in the distance he said: "Are any of you men willing to drive those rebels out of that place there ?" He did not have to wait long for a reply. The six men mentioned at once stepped forward and volunteered. The colonel's face beamed with pride and satisfaction as he saw the

DEMANDED THEIR SURRENDER.

brave fellows respond to his call. Subsequently the six made an attack upon the log house. Cautiously and slowly they crept up to the place, but did not get very far, before they were discovered. Then they made a dash, a run, a break for the hut, all the while facing a heavy fire from the rebels. However, they escaped injury and reached the log house unhurt. They knocked down the barricades at the door with the butts of their rifles, and then with levelled guns demanded the surrender of the men on the inside. The Pennsylvanians gave their opponents no time for hesitation or doubt. Determination was written on the face of each of the brave six. The alternative was: immediate surrender or death. The rebels preferred the former and thus became the prisoners of the gallant little band of Union heroes.

A BAYONET CHARGE THE LAST HOPE.

JOSHUA L. CHAMBERLAIN,
Colonel, 20th Maine Infantry.
Highest rank attained: Brig.-Gen., U. S. V.
Born in Brewer, Maine, Sept. 8, 1828.

NEVER had a bayonet charge more effective results than had that of the Twentieth Maine Volunteers, on the slope of Little Round Top, at Gettysburg, July 2, 1863. It not only saved the position of the Union troops, but compelled General Lee to change his whole plan of attack. The incident is thus described by Colonel Joshua L. Chamberlain, commanding the Twentieth Maine:

"My regiment held the extreme left of the Union lines, at Gettysburg. The enemy was shelling the whole crest heavily, and moving a large force to seize this commanding height, while we were rushing up to get the position ourselves. We had scarcely got our troops into something like a line among the rocks of the southern slope, when the enemy's assault struck us. It was a hard hand-to-hand fight, swaying back and forth under successive charges and counter-charges, for an hour. I had been obliged to throw my left wing back at a right-angle or more in order to hold the ground at all.

"As it was a sort of echelon attack, the enemy was constantly coming up on my left, and outflanking me. The losses in my regiment were very heavy. In the center of the apex of the angle, made by throwing back the left wing, the color-guard was shot away, the color-company and that next to it lost nearly half their number, and more than a third of my regiment was disabled. We had, in the lull of the fight, thrown together a low line of loose rocks that were scattered about the ground, and the men were taking such shelter as they could behind these, though they could do this only by lying down and firing over them. This helped us but little; it served chiefly to mark the line we were bound to maintain.

"At last I saw a heavy force that had just come up over the opposite slopes of Great Round Top, coming on to envelop our left. They were close to us, advancing rapidly, and firing as they came. We had expended our last round of cartridges, and had been gathering what we could from the cartridge-boxes of the dead and dying, friend and foe. We met this fresh force with these cartridges, but at the critical moment, when the enemy were within fifty feet of us, our fire fell to nothing. Every round was gone.

"Knowing the supreme importance of holding this ground, which covered the flank of Hazlett's Battery on the summit and gave a clear enfilading and rear fire

"AND INSTANTLY HE SURRENDERED."

upon the whole force holding Little Round Top, I saw no other way to save it, or even ourselves, but to charge with the bayonet. The on-coming force evidently outnumbered us three or four to one, but it was the last resort.

"Giving the order to charge, I placed myself beside the colors at the apex of our formation, sent word to the senior officer on my left to make a right wheel of the charge and endeavor to catch the enemy somewhat in flank on their right. Then we sprang down the rocky slope into the presence of the astonished foe. I came directly upon an officer commanding the center of the opposing line. He attempted to fire a pistol in my face, but my sabre point was at his throat, and instantly he turned the butt of his pistol and the hilt of his sword, and surrendered. His whole line began to throw down their arms likewise. My officers were also in the line with the bayonets.

"This charge was successful beyond all my hopes. We not only cleared our own front, but, by the right wheel, cleared the front of the entire brigade on our right, and also the whole ground between Little and Great Round Top. We took twice as many prisoners as we had men in our ranks, and found 150 of the enemy's dead in our front. These were of the Fifteenth, Forty-seventh and Fourth Alabama, and the Fifth Texas regiments.

"The result of this movement, beyond question, was the saving of Hazlett's Battery, and, in fact, Round Top itself, to our troops. It now appears that it also changed Lee's plans for his attack of the next day which had been intended to be a crushing blow on our left again, but was abandoned for Pickett's charge on the center. The honors belong to my regiment."

THE JOKE WAS ON
THE OTHER FELLOWS.

WILLIAM H. RAYMOND,
Corporal, Co. A, 108th New York Infantry.
Born at Penfield, Monroe Co., N. Y.,
May 30, 1844.

AMONG the comrades of Company A, One-hundred and eighth New York Infantry, Corporal William H. Raymond's physique was the subject of a standing joke. He was so lean and lanky, that it was observed that he was altogether too thin to even cast a shadow or offer sufficient surface for a decent target. These jokes were good-naturedly borne by the corporal, until an incident occurred during the battle of Gettysburg, when Corporal Raymond accomplished a task, where he showed that his physique came in good stead and besides displayed such courage and daring that ever afterward the joke about his being "too thin" was on the other fellow. Corporal Raymond's own words of the incident referred to, follow:

"Early in the morning of July 3d, my regiment, the One-hundred and eighth New York Volunteer Infantry, was sent to the skirmish line in our immediate front. Company A, to which I belonged, had eighteen men present in line for duty.

"The skirmish line, which was entirely destitute of anything in the way of protection, which was also true of the ground between Ziegler's Grove and our line, while the rebel skirmish line was behind and along a rail fence, not more than fifteen or twenty rods in our front, from which we received a very hot fire while going into position. Before reaching it the orderly-sergeant of my company was wounded and Lieutenant Ostrander appointed me orderly-sergeant.

"I ARRIVED UNHURT."

"During the engagement our men were running short of ammunition and I advised them to use the cartridges from the dead and wounded, but these did not last long. I, therefore, reported to Lieutenant Ostrander, who told me to make a detail and send for a fresh supply. This duty was extremely hazardous, and I doubted whether it could be done without the sacrifice of life.

"Under such circumstances I hesitated to make the detail, and suggested a call for volunteers. The lieutenant's reply came: 'I don't care how it is done, as long as you obtain the ammunition.' On calling for volunteers no one responded, whereupon I volunteered to go myself and started for our lines. Here I stated my errand.

"Lieutenant-Colonel Pierce, who had command of the regiment, sent for a supply, and upon its arrival, said. 'Raymond, you have taken your share of risk, let some one else take this down to the skirmish line.' I said that it might as well be myself as anyone else. The chances were talked over rapidly, and appeared poor enough. Nearly every officer present with the regiment, and many of the men bade me good-bye, the opinion being freely expressed, that I could not get back to the skirmish line alive. However, I took a box of ammunition of 1,000 rounds, and carried it down to the line, arriving there unhurt, though I had seven holes shot through my clothing."

WITH BAYONET AND COBBLE STONES.

HENRY D. O'BRIEN,
Corporal, Co. E, 1st Minnesota Infantry.
Born at Colois, Maine, Jan. 21, 1842.

CORPORAL HENRY D. O'BRIEN of Company E, First Minnesota Infantry, received his Medal of Honor for two acts of gallantry at the battle of Gettysburg. On July 2d, 1863, the First Minnesota was ordered by General Hancock to charge the Confederate forces, who were driving in the Third Corps. The regiment numbered 262, officers and men, when it went into that desperate charge, but when it came out, 215 had been killed and wounded. The charge had its due effect, however, for the enemy's line was broken, his advance stopped, and a large number of prisoners taken. While the Minnesota regiment was withdrawing from between the two fires, O'Brien noticed one of his comrades, E. R. Jefferson, drop, shot through the leg. He picked up his wounded comrade on his back, and was carrying him to a place of safety, when a ball struck his cartridge box plate, throwing him to the ground. Undaunted by this, he sprang to his feet, raised the wounded man and carried him to the rear without further injury.

On the following day, when Pickett made his gallant but futile charge, O'Brien had another occasion to display his heroism. The story is well told in the official report of the commanding officer of the First Minnesota: "Corporal Dehn, the last of our color-guard, then carrying our tattered flag, was shot through the hand, and the flagstaff cut in two. Corporal Henry D. O'Brien of Company E, instantly seized the flag by the remnant of the staff. Whether the command to charge was given by any general officer, I do not know. My impression was, that it came as a spontaneous outburst from the men, and instantly the line precipitated itself upon the enemy. O'Brien, who held the broken staff and tatters of our battle flag, with his characteristic bravery and impetuosity sprang with it to the front at the first sound of the word 'charge,' and ran right up to the enemy's line, keeping the flag noticeably in advance of every other color. My feeling, at the instant, blamed his rashness in so risking its capture, but the effect was electrical. Every man of the First Minnesota sprang to protect the flag, and the rest rushed with them upon the enemy. The bayonet was used for a few minutes, and cobble stones, with which the ground was well covered, filled the air, being thrown by those in the rear over the heads of their comrades. The struggle, desperate and deadly while it lasted, was soon over. Corporal O'Brien received two wounds in the final *melee* at the moment of the victory."

In this charge O'Brien was twice wounded in the head and the left hand, but he carried his colors through the fight. In the charge of the previous day, he received a bayonet wound in the side.

CAPTURED THE SHARPSHOOTERS IN THE BARN

THE Third Division of the Eleventh Corps was commanded by General Carl Schurz and known as "Howard's German Army." Attached to it was the Forty-fifth New York Infantry, under command of Colonel George Van Amsberg, composed of soldiers of German blood. This regiment distinguished itself during the initiatory fighting at the battle of Gettysburg, every man displaying great bravery and daring. Captain Francis Irsch, of Company D, especially manifested such skill and intrepidity that a Medal of Honor was awarded him.

The regiment arrived at Gettysburg at 11 A. M., after a double-quick march of several miles, some time in advance of the Eleventh Corps. Captain Irsch was immediately ordered to relieve Buford's Division, which was slowly retiring before General Henry Heth's Confederate forces.

As Captain Irsch, in pursuance of his orders, was cautiously and steadily moving forward, he came in contact with Major Blackford's Alabama sharpshooters and two Confederate batteries planted on Oak and Benness Hills. The enemy's fire did considerable execution and Captain Irsch was forced to seek cover and wait for re-enforcements. When the balance of the regiment and Dilger's Ohio Battery came dashing to his support, the attack on the two rebel batteries was renewed and carried on effectively. General Ewell, however, observed the small number of the Union troops and a large gap in their lines and ordered O'Neil's Alabama and Iverson's North Carolina Brigade to make a dash, break through the Union lines and gain possession of the town of Oak Hill and of the division of the two Union corps. Iverson, however, either misunderstood the order or was belated, and O'Neil's stealthy movement toward the Mummasberg Road along a covered lane at the base of Oak Hill, was discovered by Captain Irsch just in time to advise Captain Dilger's Battery and the other regiments. Dilger's battery poured double shotted shrapnel into the ranks of the advancing Alabamians who, at the same time, were received with a galling fire from the Twelfth and Thirteenth Massachusetts, who, by that time, had faced about to cover the breach and meet the attack. The Alabamians became disordered and staggered back upon the rear regiments of the brigade. Captain Irsch no sooner perceived the predicament of the rebels when he concluded that the time for a bold stroke had come. He ordered a charge and soon drove the Alabamians pell-mell again forward on the Twelfth and Thirteenth Massachusetts. The greater part of three regiments of the rebel brigade surrendered with their battle-flags. Another part had fortified itself in McLean's barn and from there kept up a galling fire. Captain Irsch made a rush for the barn and stormed it, capturing about one hundred more prisoners. Iverson's Brigade of North Carolinians arrived too late and met with a similar fate.

When later in the day General Early turned the right of the Eleventh Corps and was threatening Steinwehr's Second Division on Cemetery Hill, the general break up of the First and Eleventh Corps came. The Union troops poured into the town of Gettysburg, hotly pursued by the Confederates. Baxter's Brigade of the First and Schimmelpfennig's of the Eleventh Corps frequently held the victorious enemy at bay and carried their desperate resistance right into the streets of the town. Gun carriages, ambulances, the wounded and the dead blocked the way and made further resistance impossible. The regiments broke up into small commands, each endeavoring to escape and reach Cemetery Hill as best they could. Captain Irsch's Battalion remained intact till Chambersburg Street was reached, which they cleared to the right and left almost up to Market Square, where a portion of the Forty-fifth with the colors ran through an alley just as the enemy was planting a battery on the square. Captain Irsch already had taken possession of a block of houses from which he and the remainder of his regiment kept up an incessant fire upon the Confederates. Many Union soldiers sought refuge in the same block, so that within a short time there were no less than 600 men barricaded in these houses. The street defense in that section of the town lasted several hours. Toward sundown the Confederates demanded the surrender of the gallant little band. Captain Irsch was permitted to leave the temporary defense under a flag of truce and satisfy himself that no succor was in sight and that further resistance was useless. He was escorted to the outskirts of the town and was soon convinced that nothing could be gained by further bloodshed. After a consultation with the other officers the men were ordered to destroy their arms and ammunition and surrender. Captain Irsch was sent to Libby prison. He made one escape, was recaptured and sent back again behind the walls of this dismal place of confinement.

TEN CAPTURE A FORTIFIED STOCKADE

DURING Rosecrans' campaign against Bragg, in Tennessee, Sergeant George Marsh commanded the "forlorn hope" of ten volunteers, sent to capture the rebel stockade at Elk River, Tenn., July 2, 1863. It had been reported to General John Beatty, commanding the Union troops, that the rebels had burned the bridge over the Elk River and taken position with their artillery and infantry on the bluffs beyond. General Beatty describes the situation as follows:

GEORGE MARSH,
Sergeant, Co. D, 104th Illinois Infantry.
Born at Brookfield, La Salle Co., Ill., 1838.

"Riding forward, I discovered the enemy's cavalry and infantry across the river, and his artillery in position ready to open on us whenever the head of our column should make its appearance in the turn of the road. Seeing that it would be useless to expose my infantry, and that artillery alone would be effectual in dislodging him, I hurried forward Captain Hewett's four guns, and sent back a request for another battery, upon which Captain Schultz' Battery was sent forward. Without exposing my horses and men, so as to draw the enemy's fire, I succeeded in getting ten guns in position, before he was aware of it, and opened fire. The enemy replied vigorously, but so well were the guns of Captains Hewett and Schultz served, that after about forty minutes the enemy retired his artillery double-quick. I then sent forward my regiments to the river, shelled the sharpshooters and cavalry from the hills on the opposite side, sent a few men to occupy a stockade near the bridge, and drive away a few troublesome sharpshooters, who were still concealed in the bluffs." The balance of the interesting story is best told by Sergeant Marsh himself. He says:

"We had skirmished all the morning with a light battery supported by infantry, who were defending their retreating baggage trains. As we advanced we came suddenly to a clearing, on the opposite side of which was a stockade fort plainly visible from our position. A short distance to our right the enemy had crossed the Elk River on a bridge which they burned to prevent our following. Also, in case we should make an attempt to construct a pontoon bridge, they had planted a small battery on the opposite side of the stream, and stationed a squad of infantry to support it.

"Our commanding officer saw, that if we were in possession of the stockade, we could better cope with the advances of the enemy. He asked me to lead a squad to reconnoiter, and if possible, take the stockade. I called out: 'All who are not afraid, fall in!'

"Many offered to go, but I took the first ten who stepped forward, and started for the fortification. We deployed and covered the field at a double-quick under a heavy fire of musketry and artillery from the other side of the Elk River, and at first from the stockade.

"None of us returned the fire until we had forced an entrance into the stockade, then we emptied our rifles into the Confederates, who, upon seeing us enter the fort, climbed the stockade on the opposite side and ran up the bank.   No one who saw

"WE DEPLOYED AND STARTED FOR THE FORTIFICATION."

us go into the fight expected to see us come out alive, but we did, and without the loss of a man."

Of the ten men who followed Sergeant Marsh in this brilliant charge, the names of only six could be obtained.   They were John Shapland, Oscar Slagle, Reuben Smalley, Charles Stacey, Richard J. Gage and Samuel F. Holland.   Each of these was rewarded with a Medal of Honor.   The records state that Sergeant Marsh received his "for having led a small party at Elk River July 2, 1863, captured a stockade and saved the bridge."

A DARE-DEVIL CHARGE.

CHARLES M. HOLTON,
1st Sergeant, Co. A, 7th
Mich. Cavalry.
Born in Potter, Yates Co., N. Y., May 25, 1888.

Sᴇʀɢᴇᴀɴᴛ Cʜᴀʀʟᴇs M. Hᴏʟᴛᴏɴ, Company A, Seventh Michigan Cavalry, won his medal at the battle of Falling Waters, by capturing a flag of the Fifty-fifth Virginia, in one of the most dashing charges in the annals of the war. He thus describes the incident:

"On the morning of July 14, 1863, Custer's Michigan Brigade came face to face with four brigades of rebel infantry strongly entrenched and supported by artillery. This was a division of Lee's army which had failed to cross the Potomac. Although greatly inferior in numbers, the Michigan men formed up and attacked them with great fury. Our skirmish line was rapidly approaching the enemy's battery, where General Kilpatrick ordered a charge by the First Battalion of the Seventh Michigan, which had been left to support Pennington's Battery. The little battalion which comprised only seventy sabres, formed in column of fours, and charged up a lane which was occupied by the right of the Confederate line. They dashed through the enemy and into the field beyond, where the rebel reserve was drawn up. Unheeding the storm of bullets that assailed them, the undaunted little troop dashed into the enemy's ranks and cut its way through.

"Seeing the color-sergeant of the Fifty-fifth Virginia fall wounded, I sprang from my horse and seized the colors. As I remounted, I heard the wounded color-bearer say: 'You Yanks have been after that old flag for a long time, but you never got it before.' While we were forming up to charge them again from their rear, the Confederates threw down their arms, and we marched 400 prisoners from the field.

"General Kilpatrick examined the captured flag, and found on it the names of all the great battles of the Army of the Northern Virginia. The guard ordered me to join his staff with it for the balance of the day, and in the evening Adjutant Briggs wrote an inscription on the margin of the flag, telling how it had been captured by me."

Falling Waters, Va.—The Confederates under Lee drawn up in line of battle on the crest of a hill, one mile and a half from Falling Waters, were attacked July 14, 1863, by Kilpatrick's Third Brigade of the Army of the Potomac, and after two hours' fighting, completely routed. The rebels lost 1,500 men in killed, wounded and prisoners; the Union loss was nominal.

INSUBORDINATION REWARDED

I T is not often that the government of a great nation grants the highest military distinction in its power "for distinguished gallantry," when the conspicuous service rendered was an act committed in direct disobedience of orders.

This was done in the case of Lieutenant Carle A. Woodruff of Battery M, Second U. S. Artillery, and Captain Smith H. Hastings of Troop M, Fifth Michigan Cavalry.

The facts of the interesting occurrence are given in Lieutenant Woodruff's language as follows:

"Early on the morning of July 24th, we marched from Amissville, through Newby's Cross-Roads, and struck the flank of one of the corps of Lee's army marching from Chester Gap towards Culpepper Court House. Our cavalry was at once deployed, and Battery M was brought into action to shell the retreating columns. Some movements on the part of the

CARLE A. WOODRUFF,
Lieutenant, Horse Battery M, 2d U. S. Artillery.
Highest rank attained: Lieut-Col., U. S. A.
Born at Buffalo, N. Y., Aug. 8, 1841.

enemy caused General Custer to hastily withdraw his command, and order a return to Amissville. Colonel George Gray of the Sixth Michigan Cavalry, with two troops of his regiment, two of the Fifth Michigan Cavalry, commanded by Captain S. H. Hastings, and my section, two guns of Horse Battery M, constituted the rear guard. As we retired Colonel Gray led the way with his squadron, and that of Captain Hastings brought up the rear.

S. H. HASTINGS,
Captain, Troop M, 5th Mich. Cavalry.
Highest rank attained: Col. U. S. V.
Born at Quincy, Mich., Dec. 27, 1843.

"The enemy saw a chance to cut off our small command and pushed General Benning's Brigade around a hill and up the bed of a dry stream, which crossed the only road in our rear. Here they concealed themselves waiting for our approach. General Benning thought that the trap laid for the Union soldiers was complete. He felt confident of capturing not only the guns of my battery, but also the two squadrons of cavalry.

"'I now thought' the rebel general wrote to General Longstreet 'we had their cannon and cavalry secured as there was no possible way to Amissville but the road occupied by my brigade, all others being excluded by the mountain and its spur.' General Benning's calculations miscarried, for the trap which he had so carefully planned and set failed of its purpose. As soon as Colonel Gray's squadron came within their range the rebels rushed forth from their place of hiding and fired a volley at point-blank range. The squadron came dashing back upon us, and in the confusion of their flight carried the team of the leading gun with them. The horses turned around so sharply that the gun was almost upset. Colonel Gray called to me: 'Cut your traces, abandon your guns, and follow me.' I replied: 'I will never leave my guns.'

"We unlimbered and opened fire with canister. Just then Captain Hastings came up with his squadron and asked: 'What do you intend to do, Woodruff? How can I help you?' I answered: 'Dismount some of your men, and support me.' Another officer galloped up to me at this moment. 'Colonel Gray,' he said, 'orders you to cut your traces and abandon your guns, and we will try to charge through the enemy's lines.' Again I refused to leave my guns, and turning to my command, said: 'Men, I have received orders to abandon our guns.' They all shouted: 'Never lieutenant, we will stay with you, and we will all go to Richmond together.'

"I kept our gun firing while I moved the other with ten horses and the assistance of dismounted cavalry, over a piece of marshy ground to my left. Then we opened fire with that gun, while we returned with the horses for the other. The pieces were moved alternately to the left, a little at a time, until we got them on the flank of the enemy, and commanding the bed of the stream they occupied. After about two hours of this work, we succeeded in reaching the main body of our command, having held off a whole brigade of the enemy.

"When I reached General Custer, I dismounted, and reported that my men and guns were safe. The general, who was lying down at the time, sprang to his feet and embraced me. He told me he had sent the First Michigan Cavalry and Hamilton's section of Horse Battery M down the road to try and open communication with us. Colonel Gray and his command reported to General Custer after I did, having in his retreat described a much larger circle than we."

Captain Smith H. Hastings of Co. M, Fifth Michigan Cavalry, who shares in a large measure in the success of the engagement and likewise was decorated with the Medal of Honor, has little to add to Lieutenant Woodruff's version:

"I heard Woodruff reply to Colonel Gray," says he, "that he would never abandon his guns, and rode up to him, asking whether I could help him.

"Lieutenant Woodruff ran ahead to assist Sergeant Flood in unlimbering our gun and shouted, that he wished me to dismount my men and help him out. I did not hesitate a moment, but immediately decided to stand by the brave lieutenant."

Success crowned the united efforts of both officers. Speaking of General Custer, to whom Captain Hastings reported, he says: "The general was a mighty pleased soldier that evening, because, by disobeying orders, Lieutenant Woodruff, myself and our brave comrades had preserved intact the record of General Custer's brigade —never to have permitted the enemy to capture from it a single piece of artillery."

"THE FLAG NEVER TOUCHED THE GROUND."

WILLIAM H. CARNEY,
Sergeant, 54th Massachusetts Infantry.
Born at Norfolk, Va.. Feb. 29, 1840.

"ON the 18th of July, about noon," writes Private William H. Carney of the Fifty-fourth Massachusetts Volunteers, "we began to draw near Fort Wagner under a tremendous cannonading from the fleet. When within about a thousand yards of the fort we halted and lay flat on the ground waiting for the order to charge.

"The order came, and we had advanced but a short distance, when we were opened upon with musketry, shell and canister, which mowed down our men right and left. When the color-bearer was disabled, I threw away my gun and seized the colors, making my way to the head of the column, but before I reached there, the line had descended the embankment into the ditch and was advancing upon Fort Wagner itself

"Going down the embankment our column was stanch and full. As we ascended the breastworks the ranks showed dreadful gaps made by the enemy's fire. In less than twenty minutes I found myself alone struggling upon the ramparts, while all around me lay the dead and wounded piled one upon another. As I could not go into the fort alone, I knelt down, still holding the flag in my hands. The musket balls and grape shot were flying all around me, and as they struck, the sand would fly in my face. I knew my position was a critical one and wondered how long I should remain undiscovered.

"Finding at last that our force had renewed the attack farther to the right, and the enemy's attention was drawn thither, I turned to go, when I discovered a battalion coming toward me on the ramparts. As they advanced in front of me I raised my flag and was about to join them, when I noticed that they were enemies.

Fort Wagner, S. C.—The assault upon Fort Wagner, Morris Island, was a feature of the operations against the harbor and islands adjoining Charleston, undertaken by Admiral Dahlgreen with the fleet, co-operating with General Gillmore in charge of the land forces.

On the 9th of July, Morris Island was attacked by Strong's Brigade. The Confederates were driven from all the batteries south of Fort Wagner, and most of the island abandoned to the Union men. On the next day an attack upon the fort was made, which resulted in a repulse. Bombardment by the fleet and the batteries on the adjacent islands commenced on the morning of the 18th, and, in the evening, a storming party, led by Colonel Shaw, (Fifty-fourth Massachusetts) succeeded in carrying the fort, with a loss of 1,500, among whom was the colonel. One hundred and seventy-four of the fort's defenders were killed or wounded.

Instantly winding my colors around the staff, I made my way down the parapet into the ditch, which, when I had first crossed it, had been dry, but was now filled with water that came to my waist.

"All the men who had mounted the ramparts with me, were either killed or wounded, I being the only one left erect and moving.

"Upon rising to determine my course to the rear, I was struck by a bullet, but, as I was not prostrated by the shot, I continued my course. I had not gone very far, however, before I was struck by a second ball.

"I KNELT DOWN, STILL HOLDING THE FLAG IN MY HANDS."

"Soon after I met a member of the One-hundredth New York, who inquired if I was wounded. Upon my replying in the affirmative, he came to my assistance and helped me to the rear. While on our way I was again wounded, this time in the head, and my rescuer then offered to carry the colors for me, but I refused to give them up, saying that no one but a member of my regiment should carry them.

"We passed on until we reached the rear guard, where I was put under charge of the hospital corps, and sent to my regiment. When the men saw me bringing in the colors, they cheered me. and I was able to tell them that the old flag had never touched the ground."

A BRAVE BUGLER

JOSEPH C. HIBSON,
Private, Co. C, 48th New York Infantry.
Born in London, England, August 3, 1843.

Bugler Joseph C. Hibson of Company C, Forty-eighth New York Infantry, was only twenty years old, when he earned his Medal of Honor. It was awarded to him for risking his life to save his comrades from being shot down by their own supports, and afterwards, when his arm had been shattered, saving the regimental colors from falling into the hands of the enemy.

"On the evening of July 18th, after an all-day bombardment by the army and navy, the assault on Fort Wagner was made. We crossed the moat and engaged in a hand-to-hand fight with the Thirty-first North Carolina in their outer works. They soon weakened, and we drove them from the southeast bastion, which we held under a terrible cross fire. Re-enforcements were sent to our support, but by some blunder, they mistook us for the enemy and poured a destructive volley into us. We could not live under the three fires, and something had to be done to stop the fire in our rear. I ran down into the moat and told our men there of the terrible blunder they were making and on this errand was shot in the elbow.

"Having stopped the fire in our rear, I returned to the crest of the fort to find Color-Sergeant George G. Sparks, severely wounded, the color staff shot in two, and all the color-guard either killed or wounded. I picked up the colors with my uninjured hand, but just at that moment the Confederates made a determined assault on us. We managed to repulse the assault, but I received two additional wounds; the bone of my left forearm was completely shattered, and I was wounded in the head by pieces of a shell that burst near me. My scalp was torn and the blood was running into my eyes.

"Lieutenant James Barrett took command of the regiment, all the other officers being killed or wounded, and ordered a retreat. I gave the colors into safe hands, and, my mission ended, went into the hospital."

Hibson recounts another incident which occurred prior to this, on the evening of July 13th. He says:

"During the bombardment of Fort Wagner, I, a musician, was not required to become actively engaged, but went about seeking excitement. I volunteered to take the place of a sick comrade who had been allotted to a vidette. Shortly after midnight some indistinct forms sprang up out of the darkness, and Daniel Kane, my comrade on guard, was stabbed with a bayonet. A voice hissed in my ear the word 'Surrender,' but instead of doing so, I brought my rifle to the 'Shorten arms' and fired without taking aim. The rebel fell at my feet. I rammed another charge of powder into my rifle, but the bullet slipped through my fingers and the other Confederate, who, by this time had risen, charged upon me. I turned and ran for our rifle pits with the Confederate close behind me, until one of my comrades brought him down.

'I PICKED UP THE COLORS WITH MY UNINJURED HAND."

"The following night a volunteer was called for to accompany Lieutenant Edwards on a reconnoitering expedition. I volunteered and was accepted. After we had gone a short distance, I lost the lieutenant, who wandered off in the darkness and strayed back to our lines. I kept on by myself, taking an oblique course. I was constantly falling headlong into shell holes and tripping over obstacles, and I had finally to go down on hands and knees and crawl. Presently I heard some faint voices ahead, and stopping to listen, heard the Confederates shovelling a little ahead of me and to my left. At the same moment I heard in my rear three or four of the enemy's pickets conversing in low tones. I started to crawl back the way I had come and nearly dropped into one of their rifle-pits. I succeeded in avoiding it, and got away without being detected. When I returned to my regiment with my information the men gave three cheers and a tiger for 'The little bugler.'"

ALL FOR HIS MESSMATE

P RIVATE HENRY C. SLUSHER, while a member
of Troop E, of Ringgold's Independent
Volunteer Cavalry, made a desperate attempt
single-handed to rescue a wounded comrade
from a strong party of Mosby's Guerrillas in
the Alleghany Mountains. He tells of his adventure in the following words:

"On September 11, 1863, the rebels, 300
strong, under Captain McNeil, surprised the
Yankee camp of 260 men under Major Stevens,
on Cemetery Hill, at Moorefield, W. Va. At
three A. M., twenty-five men of Company E
were ordered out on the Lost River Road, up to

HENRY C. SLUSHER,
Private, Troop F, 22d Penn. Vol. Cavalry.
Born in Washington Co., Penn., May 10, 1846.

the South Fork of the Potomac. We met the rebels two miles south of Moorefield,
carrying off all the camp equipage and 146 prisoners. We took a position on the

"MY AIM WAS TO
RESCUE MY COMRADE."

west side of the river on a bluff
some thirty feet higher than the
road and the river, dismounted,
and commenced to shoot down
the horses in the ravine, killing
twenty of them, and eight or ten
men of the rebel force. At this
time I caught sight of my mess-
mate, William P. Hagner, who
had been wounded early in the
day, taken prisoner, and placed in
in an ambulance. When we shot
the horses he threw up his hands
as a signal for help. To see him
in such a predicament was too
much for me. I at once crossed
the river. My aim was to rescue
him at all hazards, and I reached
the vehicle under a heavy fire.
In a hand-to-hand fight close by
by the ambulance, I was wounded
and captured and had to share
the fate of my comrade in Libby
Prison."

THIS BUGLER CHECKED A ROUT

W. J. CARSON,
Musician, Co. E, 15th United States Infantry.

BUGLER W. J. CARSON'S story is interesting, because it furnishes a fine example of personal bravery, and in addition, shows to what extent a bugler can become an important factor in battle.

"On September 19, 1863, our brigade consisting of the First Battalion of the Fifteenth and Sixteenth United States Infantry, the three battalions of the Eighteenth United States Infantry, two battalions of the Nineteenth Infantry and Battery H of the Fifth United States Artillery, was ordered to advance to a position one mile east of Kelley's Field, Chickamauga," Bugler Carson narrates. "Just as our battery was getting into position, a battery and two brigades of the enemy opened fire on us. The short, but sharp, engagement resulted in the death of First Lieutenant H. M. Burnham, and twelve men, the capture of thirteen men and the entire battery. In addition, two lieutenants and sixteen men were wounded, while nearly every horse was either killed outright, or fatally injured.

"Our infantry made a grand and noble effort to recapture the battery, but were driven back by the greatly superior force of the enemy. As bugler, I did all in my power to rally and lead the men to the charge, going to the flags and sounding 'to the colors.' The brave fellows rallied, and, with the assistance of the Seventeenth and Ninth Ohio, the battery was retaken.

"On the following morning, our brigade was engaged with Breckenridge's Corps in a most desperate and deadly conflict. Our battalion of 262 men were lying down 100 yards in the rear as reserves. I had picked up a gun, as was always my custom,

---

Chickamauga.—During the summer of 1863, General Rosecrans having succeeded in forcing Bragg into Georgia, took a position at Chattanooga, on the Tennessee. Bragg, strongly re-enforced by Johnston and Longstreet, attacked the Federal Army, September 19, at Chickamauga Creek. The first day's battle was undecisive. On the 20th, the Confederates advanced, Longstreet on the left, Polk on the right, Ewell and Johnston in the center. The Federal left wing was commanded by General Thomas, the center by Crittenden, the right by McCook.

After the fight had lasted several hours, the Union battle-line was opened by General Wood, acting under mistaken orders, and the Confederate general, forcing a column into the gap, cut the army in two and drove the right wing from the field. General Thomas held the left until nightfall, then withdrew to Chattanooga.

The Union losses in these two days amounted to 15,851; the Confederate loss, 17,804.

and was giving the enemy every shot I could, when I saw one of the officers of the Eighteenth skulking back from tree to tree. I went through the rows of our men and sent him back at the point of the bayonet.

"The conflict began, when Beattie's Brigade gave way and was driven back by an overwhelming force of the enemy. The left of our brigade became exposed and likewise gave away. Finally the whole line was coming back in disorder. Try as they would, the officers were powerless to check the rout. I threw down my gun, rushed out some thirty yards to the color-bearer of the Eighteenth and said to him: 'Let us rally these men, or the whole left is gone.' The brave fellow stopped and waived his flag. I sounded 'to the colors.' The men cheered. They rushed into line. Still sounding the rally, I passed back and forth in front of the forming line, and what a few minutes before seemed like a hopeless and disastrous rout, now turned out to be a complete victory. The retreat had been checked and the enemy driven back with awful slaughter. So severe was their repulse, that within a few minutes we were firing towards our rear into the enemy who were pressing Beattie's troops back. I noticed a color-bearer of the Second Ohio running with his men out of the woods on the north side of Kelley's Field. I headed him off and exhorted him to stop, which he promptly did. Then I once more sounded 'to the colors' and many a brave soldier halted, but as the enemy appeared at the edge of the timber and poured a deadly volley into us, all broke and ran like good fellows. We sought shelter at the east of the timber and fired into the enemy from a temporary defense of logs and rails. After two hours of hard fighting and

"I SOUNDED 'TO THE COLORS '"

receiving re-enforcements our lines were once more formed and straightened out. I took an inventory of myself and found ten bullet holes in my clothes; three bullets had pierced my hat and one had struck and slightly wounded my left arm. We held our position until the last cartridge was gone, and at about 6:30 o'clock were taken prisoners."

It was not known till long afterwards that the Fourteenth Corps owed its deliverance from annihilation to Bugler Carson. General Bragg had ordered a charge on the Federal position at 3:30 o'clock in the afternoon, and if it had been delivered at that time the rebels could have broken the left of the defense and got in the rear of General Thomas' men who were holding Snodgrass Hill. The destruction of the Fourteenth Corps would have been inevitable, for both McCook's and Critlander's Corps had been swept from the field. But the rebels were deceived by the bugle calls, and thought they signalled the arrival of heavy re-enforcements, so they delayed the final blow till they had collected all the forces at hand. This took nearly three hours, and by the time the final charge was delivered, and the little defending force crushed by weight of numbers, the Northern Army was well on its way to Chattanooga.

PLANTED THE COLORS AND RALLIED THE REGIMENT

GEORGE S. MYERS,
Sergeant, Co. F, 101st Ohio Infantry.
Born at Lancaster, Ohio, Jan. 26, 1843.

"WHEN General Bragg, the commander of the Confederate Army at Chickamauga, was making a desperate effort to gain possession of the 'State or Lafayette Road,'" Sergeant George S. Myers relates, "the One hundred and first Ohio Regiment, was fighting with its brigade on what was then the right flank of the Union Army, which rested on the Vineyard Farm. An irresistible force of the enemy bore down upon this point, crushing the right of the One hundred and first Ohio, killing and capturing many men of the right companies, and compelling the entire line to fall back in some confusion.

"All of the color-guards were killed, wounded or captured within a few minutes: the color-bearer went down with a bullet through his head, and the colors were thus almost in the hands of the enemy. I sprang back, secured the precious flag, and, instead of continuing the retreat, ran boldly forward and planted the colors on a knoll in the face of the Confederate line. The regiment responded to my initiative and the enemy was temporarily repulsed. I was wounded, however, and, after turning over the colors to Colonel Messer, was taken from the field.

"To illustrate the fierceness of the battle on that part of the line, it may be added that after the engagement, all that was left of Company A, of this regiment, was Captain Bryant and three men. Company F, of which I was a member, had only two men left to answer to the roll call."

Sergeant Myers' gallant act was characterized by his superiors as one of the bravest in their experience.

CAPTURED A CONFEDERATE MAJOR

WILLIAM E. RICHEY,

Sergeant, Co. A, 15th Ohio Inf.
Born in Athens Co., O., June 1, 1841.

SERGEANT WILLIAM E. RICHEY, of Company A, Fifteenth Ohio Infantry, was the hero of a rare occurrence at the battle of Chickamauga, to-wit: the capture of a rebel major on the immediate front of the enemy's lines. The story is told by Sergeant Richey as follows:

"At the beginning of the battle of Chickamauga, General R. W. Johnson's Division was ordered to support General Thomas, whose corps constituted the left of the Union line of battle. The march of Johnson's men to the position of Thomas was a rapid one; the men going almost on a run, their steps being quickened by the sound of artillery and small arms, as the battle had just begun on the left.

"Johnson's men had been marching over mountains, hills and valleys for more than a month, and now, weary, foot-sore and covered with dust, they were hastening to the scene of conflict on the banks of the historic Chickamauga.

"The division went into battle about noon, September 19th, at Kelly's farm, facing toward the east, Willich's Brigade constituting the right of the division.

"Advancing through the woods, the division soon became engaged and furiously assaulting the enemy's lines, drove the rebels about a mile and captured five pieces of artillery which had been doing much damage.

"The division continued to drive the enemy until Willich's Brigade halted near a small field. The division had advanced so far that there was no connection or support on either the right or left. Firing had ceased and the enemy disappeared. It was now late in the afternoon. However, a little before dark, the rebels, largely re-enforced, made another furious attack on Johnson's Division, which met a determined resistance. The air was rent with cannon balls, shells, canister, grape and bullets and the twilight was lurid with the fire of battle. This terrible conflict had

"YOU ARE MY PRISONER."

the effect of throwing the regiments of Willich's Brigade into one solid line, sending death and disorder into the Confederate ranks, where firing soon ceased. For a while then there was a lull in the battle. At this time I was sent to the front with a party of comrades, to observe the enemy and learn, if possible, the exact situation on our front.

"Subsequently I advanced and was soon between the lines of battle of the two armies. Presently I saw an officer on horseback approaching me from the right, only a short distance from me. We were no sooner side by side, than I discovered that we were enemies. As quickly as I could, I said to the man on horseback, in a loud, bold tone: 'You are my prisoner; surrender, or I will blow out your brains.'

"Instantly the officer reached for his pistol, but, pointing my weapon at him, I repeated my demand with increased determination and ordered him to dismount. He complied and became my prisoner.

"He was a rebel major, who had been endeavoring to arrange the Confederate lines of battle. While doing so, he had ridden outside of his lines and come in contact with me, supposing his men to be on the ground which his captor occupied."

Sergeant Richey brought his prisoner to his lines, where he was highly commended for his bold and brave act.

INDISCRETION BROUGHT ARREST—BRAVERY SECURED RELEASE

A. H. REED

1st Sergeant, Co. K, 2nd Minnesota Vol. Infantry.

Born in Hartford, Oxford Co., Me., March 13, 1835.

"SERGEANT REED, you are under arrest!"

With these words a sergeant of the guard approached First Sergeant A. H. Reed, who, with a comrade, was at supper under a "pup-tent" fly. Sergeant Reed at first considered the remark a joke, but the other soon convinced him that he was in earnest by placing him under arrest. It appeared, that, while encamped at Winchester, Tenn., July, 1863, Sergeant Reed had publicly and indiscreetly criticised the food of the Union soldiers. This constituted a breach of discipline and was punished accordingly. Sergeant Reed was arrested. He asked for a speedy trial. Instead, he was deprived of arms and accoutrements, and was marched off with his regiment over the Cumberland Mountains across the Tennessee River to the plains of Chickamauga, where Bragg's Confederate forces were concentrating. An all-night march brought them close to the enemy early Saturday morning, September 19. The regiment unslung knapsacks, put them in a pile and left them under guard with the prisoners, of whom Sergeant Reed was one, while the regiment itself hurried off to meet the enemy.

"Soon the musketry began to rattle and cannons to boom," Sergeant Reed in telling of his interesting experience narrates, "I said to the guard and another soldier under arrest, that I felt as though we ought to be at the front helping the 'boys.' 'If the officers are foolish enough to place me under arrest, I propose to stay where I belong—in the rear,' the other replied. I observed, that, in my opinion, the Government had fed, drilled and paid us for just such an occasion as this, and should not be blamed for the actions of a few foolish officers. At any rate, I intended to take part in the fray. At first I attempted to persuade the guard, an old Prussian soldier, to give me his gun, but he said: 'Oh no, I keep my own gun.' And the old fellow remained firm in his refusal.

"I then started out alone, following the ambulance and sound of guns, until I found my regiment, lying down and under fire. I did not have to wait long before

Bristol Station.—Early in October, General Meade, whose force was about 68,000, formed a plan of attack against Lee, who, with an inferior force, was also preparing for action. On the 14th, Lee advanced from Warrenton, Va., in two columns. Hill, on the left, was ordered to strike the railroad at Bristol Station. When he reached this point, all of Meade's army had passed it, with the exception of Warren's Corps, with which he at once engaged in action. Hill was driven back, with a loss of 450 men, taken prisoners, and five guns.

a man was wounded some distance to my right. I ran up to him, got his gun, and returned to my company. Soon our lieutenant was wounded, which left but one commissioned officer with the company. It now became my duty to act in his place, which I did, but nevertheless I used the musket throughout the two days' fight."

In recognition of this proof of true devotion to duty General Thomas issued a special order releasing him from arrest and restoring him to duty.

AT the storming of Missionary Ridge, November 25, 1863, Sergeant Reed's regiment was placed in the front line covering Van Dever's Brigade, of Baird's Division, Fourteenth Army Corps. In the absence of a commissioned officer, he was placed in command of his company, which was the center and color company of the regiment.

"We were to move forward," Sergeant Reed goes on to tell, "on the first line of the enemy's works at the foot of the ridge, at the signal of the firing of three cannons. This was done and the line of works were carried without much trouble.

"Where the remnant of my company went over the works, two cannons were captured. I ordered the pieces turned on the fleeing enemy, but no ammunition could be found. I dashed off to the left in an oblique course and soon came upon two rebels who had just hitched four iron gray horses to a caisson. I demanded their surrender, but was refused, and aiming at a man on one of the horses, fired. As I was reloading, a Minie ball shattered my arm from elbow to shoulder. I fell and lay within a few rods of where the horses and caisson stood, until firing ceased, and the enemy fled, when I got a wounded soldier to help me put a tourniquet on my arm to stop the flow of blood, and then walked to the foot of the ridge, from where I was taken to a hospital in Chattanooga, Tenn.

AMMUNITION FROM THE DEAD

WILLIAM G. WHITNEY,
Lieutenant, Co. B, 11th Mich. Inf.
Highest rank attained: Captain.
Born in Allen, Hillsdale Co., Mich.,
Dec. 13, 1840.

LIEUTENANT WILLIAM G. WHITNEY, of Company B, Eleventh Michigan Infantry, tells of a unique way of replenishing the empty cartridge pouches of the men of his company as follows:

"Noon of the 20th of September, 1863, found our brigade—Stanley's—Negley's Division, Thomas' Corps, on Snodgrass Hill, a part of Missionary Ridge. We were about 120 yards east of the Snodgrass House. The brigade consisted of the Nineteenth Illinois, Eighteenth Ohio and Eleventh Michigan, about 700 men, placed in line of battle as follows: Nineteenth Illinois on the right, Eleventh Michigan on the left, and the Eighteenth Ohio in reserve. We were expected to repel the assault of Preston's and Kershaw's Divisions of Confederate infantry. Their losses alone during the afternoon were twenty per centum more than the whole number of our brigade. During a lull in the storm of battle we threw up a temporary breastwork of stone, rails and logs. About 5 P. M., after repulsing five successive charges of the enemy, we found ourselves without ammunition. The enemy were about 100 yards in our front, preparing for another charge, and their sharpshooters were firing at every man who showed his head above our light works. Their dead and wounded lay in great numbers, right up to our works. They were

"I HURRIEDLY PASSED ALONG THE FRONT, CUTTING OFF — — — "

armed with Enfield rifles of the same calibre as our Springfield rifles. I don't know what prompted me, but I took my knife from my pocket, stepped over the works, and, while my company cheered and the rebels made a target of me, I hurriedly passed along the front, cutting off the cartridge boxes of the dead and wounded, and threw them over to my company. Thus I secured a few rounds for each of my men. The enemy made one more charge and was again repulsed. Darkness settled down on us, and ended the terrible battle of Chickamauga."

"PICK OFF THE ARTILLERISTS!"

The battle of Wauhatchie, Tenn., on October 28, 1863, was fought by General J. W. Geary, commanding the Second Division of the Twelfth Army Corps, against General Longstreet's Division of General Lee's Army Corps.

General Geary had at his disposal, about 1,500 men, all told.

The presence of the rebels was well known to General Geary, but his position was difficult to ascertain. The first information on this score was furnished by a woman who told one of the officers that the rebels were gathered at the foot of Lookout Mountain. General Geary ordered pickets to be placed and enjoined the utmost vigilance upon the regimental commanders.

Shortly after midnight the Union outposts gave the alarm and the entire command was put under arms at once. A fitful moon cast but a dim light, sufficiently only to see a body of men at a distance of no more than 100 yards, and during the subsequent fierce fight the whereabouts of the combatants could be revealed only by the flashes of the firearms. The Federal position was not a very favorable one. No protection was offered, except a fence, which, was improved under fire, into a rude breastwork. For three hours the contest raged along the whole line.

"Pick off the artillerist!" the rebels exclaimed. Captain C. A. Atwell, who commanded one section of artillery, fell, mortally wounded; Lieutenant E. R. Geary, commander of the other section, son of the general, was killed. The men and horses fell so rapidly that only two guns could be worked after the attack, Still the men refused to yield to the rebel onslaught. General Geary's men stubbornly maintained their ground and held the enemy at bay by a death dealing fire.

Among the most gallant of the leaders was Captain Moses Veale of Company F, One hundred and ninth Pennsylvania Infantry, who was in the thickest of the fight. He and his men fought near one gun of the battery at the most critical period of the battle. General Geary speaks of his coolness, zeal, judgment and courage in the most flattering expressions. The Captain was struck four times by the enemy's bullets, one ball passing through his right shoulder. His horse, too, was shot from under him, but, nevertheless the brave soldier refused to give up or leave his post. He remained at the head of his company, directing its telling fire, until the enemy realizing their numerical strength availed them nothing as against such bravery and valor, retired and left the victors of that bloody night.

MOSES VEALE,
Captain, Co. F. 109th Pennsylvania Vol. Inf.
Highest rank attained : Major.

HE SAVED HIS GUNS

WILLIAM MARLAND,
Lieutenant, 2nd Independent Bat-
tery, Mass, L. A.
Highest rank attained : Brevet-
Major.
Born at Andover, Mass.,
March 11, 1839.

A<small>N INSTANCE</small> where light artillery charged a body of cavalry and mounted infantry, and scored a complete success, occurred at Grand Coteau, La., 1863. The Second Independent Battery, Massachusetts Light Artillery, accomplished this extraordinary feat. How it was done is told by Lieutenant William Marland.

"In obedience to orders," he narrates, "to report to General Burbridge with two pieces of artillery, I harnessed up at 4 A. M. on November 3, 1863 ; remained so for fully seven hours, when I was ordered to unharness ; the pickets firing all the while. About two hours later, at 12:45 P. M. the firing became general. Hearing the cavalry buglers blow 'boots and saddles' I began to harness up on my own responsibility, but was attacked in camp before I could get harnessed. The enemy being within 400 yards of me, I opened on them with canister and percussion shell, which checked their advance and drove them to the right. I limbered to the front and advanced to the fork of the road, which is about 100 yards, went into battery and fired a few shots until all my support had left me. Finding it too warm, I limbered to the rear and moved about 300 yards. Discovering the enemy in my rear and on my right, I fired to the right about fifty shots and was charged upon on three sides. Thus we were completely surrounded. To add to the seriousness of the situation, I discovered that my support had left me and been captured.

"Here we were—a mere handful, surrounded by an overwhelming force of mounted troops! I sent my orderly to see if the enemy held the bridge. He came back and reported that they did. I moved to the edge of the timber and found the enemy drawn up in line. Only one course was now open to us—to cut our way through their lines. My mind was quickly made up. I gave the order: 'Limber to the rear ; caissons to the left of pieces ; cannoneers in line with lead drivers ; draw revolvers and charge !' We made straight for the rebels. Strange to say, they broke right and left. We dashed through the gap thus made and cut our way with only two of our men taken prisoners. The enemy drove us two miles till we reached the commands of Generals Cameron and McGinnis, who were hastening to our support."

Grand Coteau, La.—On the morning of November 3, 1863, the Confederates attacked the Third Division, Thirteenth Army Corps, under command of General Burbridge, in overwhelming force. The impetus of the rebel attack at first drove the Union men back in some confusion. The timely arrival of re-enforcements enabled General Burbridge not only to check the further advance of the enemy, but to drive them off the ground already gained. The Union loss though slight, was somewhat greater than that of the enemy.

No more fitting tribute to the gallantry, vim and determination of Lieutenant Marland can be paid than is expressed by General C. C. Washburn, who, in his official report, reports the incident thus: "The bringing off of the section of Nim's battery, commanded by Lieutenant Marland, after the regiment sent to its support had surrendered, extorted the admiration of every beholder."

"WE DASHED THROUGH THEIR LINES."

A MURDEROUS FIGHT IN THE DARK

CAPTAIN WALTER G. MORRILL of the Twentieth Maine Infantry, won his Medal of Honor at the battle of Rappahannock Station, November 7, 1863.

The Confederate position at that point was skillfully chosen. It was a fortified semi-circle on the north bank of the Rappahannock, just above the point where the old Orange and Alexander Railroad crosses the river. The Confederate right of these entrenchments was at the bank of the river upon a sharp bluff, within a few yards of the railroad itself; thence following the crest of hills along the river these entrenchments swept off up-river until they again reached the bank of the water course a third of a mile further up. In front of the position, and on all sides, the ground was open for three-quarters of a mile, with absolutely nothing to cover the approach of troops. The main body of General Lee's army was immediately south

**WALTER G.
MORRILL,**

Captain, 20th Maine Infantry,
Highest rank attained: Lieut.-
Colonel.
Born at Williamsburg, Me.,
Nov. 13, 1840.

of the Rappahannock; the Third, Fifth and Sixth Corps of Meade's army approached the position from the north and east. Back of the Confederate entrenchments the river was too deep to ford, but the position was reached from the south bank by a pontoon bridge, where Confederate artillery was trained to sweep the approaches to the works, which were held by two brigades of General Jubal A. Early's Division.

The Union forces, across the open ground, were compelled to approach this position cautiously, and with skirmishers only. Over the vast plain down the river and below the railway, came the skirmish line of the Fifth Corps, those nearest the works of the enemy being men from the Twentieth Maine, commanded by Captain Morrill. They approached the right flank of the Confederate position. Directly in front of the works were skirmishers from the Sixth Corps, consisting of five companies of the Sixth Maine who joined their line at the railway. Slowly the Confederate skirmishers were pressed back until they were driven into the works, over a bare and bleak field. A road about 150 yards from the entrenchments was reached by the Sixth Maine, and under the cover of a shallow ditch a long halt was made. Captain Morrill advanced his men and kept in touch with the other troops at the railway. As darkness approached, the skirmish line of the Sixth Maine was doubled with the other five companies, and General D. A. Russell, commanding, sent word along the line thus formed that they were to assault and carry the enemy's works in front. The undertaking was perilous to the last degree, and impossible except in a wild transport of sublime heroism. There were no orders for Captain Morrill's men to join in this assault and share its perils and glory. Though it promised the destruction of all who engaged in it, Captain Morrill could not see his comrades lead such a forlorn hope and not go with them. He explained the situation to his men and called for volunteers to support the "Old Sixth." About fifty responded and he held them in readiness for the advance when it came. In the flank of the enemy's works towards him, just across the railway and next to the river, was an open passage for a road. Captain Morrill with a quick eye and keen judgment, selected this weak point for attack.

When the dusk had deepened so that the real numbers of the assaulting line could not be seen by the Confederates, General Russell set his little force in motion, and with his staff, joined in the terrible charge. The Sixth Maine's double line of skirmishers did not number three hundred, all told. But with a yell and a "tiger" which rent the skies and told of a force fourfold as large, they rushed to the fray. In an instant the works in their front were a sheet of solid flame; the air was hot with the hiss of Minie balls; grape and canister tore and decimated their lines; wilder and fiercer their yells rung upon the night as they rushed upon the foe. They reached the works however, and at points drove out brave men far more numerous than themselves; at other points they seemed swallowed up in the masses of their unfaltering adversaries. Gathering themselves together they kept up the fight in groups, but it seemed as if no human courage and valor could conquer the works they had reached. They began to sweep along the works at last and gained

momentum as they went. Captain Morrill and his little band insured success. Dashing upon the enemy's flank through the open roadway, no storm of lead and iron

THEY RUSHED UPON THE FOE.

could turn them back. The enemy feared that a great force was hammering his flank and rear, and gave way, completing the confusion and defeat. Sweeping along the works he so gallantly helped to empty, Captain Morrill soon joined the "Old Sixth," and the entrenchments beyond the point where the pontoon bridge was laid were wrested from the enemy. This cut off their own retreat and brought new peril to the now greatly reduced Union force which had won unparalled victory. Gathering themselves together in the upper portion of their works the

Confederates by counter attack sought to open a way to the bridge. Minutes were as ages to the little band which repulsed these attacks and still held their ground. The Fifth Wisconsin came up to the support of the Sixth Maine, and then,—then victory was plucked from the "jaws of death and the mouth of hell."

Other forces then advanced and received the surrender of the penned up enemy with little further fighting. There were captured eight battle flags, four pieces of artillery and 1,600 men.

"FORM ON ME"

FREDERICK W. SWIFT,
Lieut-Col., 17th Mich. Infantry.
Highest rank attained: Bvt. Brig-Gen.,
U. S. V.
Mansfield Center, Conn., Jan. 30, 1831.

L IEUTENANT-COLONEL F. W. Swift, of the Seventeenth Michigan Infantry, won his medal by seizing the colors after three color-bearers had been shot down, and rallying the regiment, which had become demoralized and was in imminent danger of capture. The incident occurred on November 16, 1863. General Burnside, who was in command of the Union forces in Eastern Tennessee, was being forced back by General Longstreet, who had from twelve to fifteen thousand men, more than double Burnside's force. Burnside had moved his little army to Huff's Ferry below London, with the intention of preventing Longstreet from crossing the river. The Union Army was ordered to retire towards Knoxville, which it did, closely followed by Longstreet. Before daybreak on the 16th, orders were given to destroy all the army supplies at Lenoir, and more than one hundred wagons and their contents were burned, the animals being used to drag the guns as the roads were very heavy. After the destruction of the stores and ammunition, the Seventeenth Michigan was detached to act as rearguard of the brigade, and Lieutenant-Colonel Comstock was ordered to keep a strong line of skirmishers on the rear and flanks of the regiment. In this order, the Union Army moved back to Turkey Creek, a small stream six or eight miles east of Lenoir Station. The rest of the story is best told by Major Swift. He says:

"Here the advance guard of the enemy came up and opened fire on our line of skirmishers, advancing rapidly with the intention of cutting us off from the rest of the command. Our men began to fall back, and Colonel Comstock, who had been directed to hold the line of the creek as long as practicable to enable the brigade to choose ground for the defense, hung on to his position until the enemy began crossing the creek above and below and enfiladed us. I urged the colonel to move the regiment across the creek and up the slope on the east side, but he understood his orders to mean that he must hold the creek at all hazards. The men became demoralized, and were already crossing the creek without orders.

"Fearing a stampede, I assumed the responsibility of moving the regiment across the creek and up to the top of the hill on the other side. One of the color-guard was killed, another had his eye shot out, and a third was seriously wounded. Seeing the colors fall, I snatched them up and called to the men: 'We have fallen back just far enough; we will form here.'

"Some one asked: 'Who shall we form on?' and I replied: 'Form on me.

"The men obeyed and formed rapidly in order, and were able with a well directed fire to check the advance of the enemy, who had crossed the ravine, and were now advancing at the charge. A counter charge was made by our regiment, and the enemy fled precipitately, after which we resumed our retreat slowly and in good order.

"Sergeant Morgan Dowling, who was taken prisoner in the old distillery, where we had left a party of sharpshooters to check the enemy's advance, told us afterwards that our charge had produced a wonderful result. He said that the enemy had run back in a panic, and did not stop till they had recrossed the creek.

"At the time our charge was delivered, General Longstreet had alighted on the further bank of the creek to question the prisoners and when he saw his men running in confusion, he galloped off and ordered up the reserves. A moment after he had ridden away, a shot from our cannon struck the exact spot where he had been standing."

"WE WILL FORM HERE."

RISKED THE DEATH OF A SPY

CORNELIUS M. HADLEY,
Sergeant. 9th Michigan Cavalry.
Born at Sandy Creek, Oswego Co., N. Y., April 27, 1838.

Sᴇʀɢᴇᴀɴᴛ Cᴏʀɴᴇʟɪᴜs M. Hᴀᴅʟᴇʏ, of the Ninth Michigan Cavalry, earned his Medal of Honor by a bold and venturesome trip into the enemy's country in the disguise of a Confederate to deliver dispatches entrusted to him. Had he been captured in this disguise, his fate would have been that of a spy—hanged at the gallows.

Sergeant Hadley, in recalling the incidents of his journey, says:

"General Wilcox was commanding the forces in and around Cumberland Gap, in November, 1863, when he received a dispatch from General Grant at Chattanooga, to be forwarded to General Burnside, who was besieged at Knoxville, Tenn., with all his communications cut. The dispatch read:

'I shall attack Bragg on the 21st, and if successful, will start immediately to the relief of Knoxville, if you can hold out.
Gʀᴀɴᴛ.'

"General Wilcox instructed Brigadier-General Gerrard to choose two sergeants of the Ninth Michigan Cavalry, and two from the Seventh Ohio, to carry the dispatch into Knoxville. Sergeant Rowe and I were sent for. When we arrived at headquarters, we found the two Ohio sergeants. The general read the dispatch and asked us if we were willing to run the risk of carrying it into Knoxville. We consented, and were sent on our mission without further instructions. A disguise and meeting at the Clinch River was agreed on. My bunkmate, brought me a Confederate uniform that we had captured a few days before, and as I started off in the rain and dark, he said: 'I shall never see you again. What shall I tell your relatives?' I replied: 'Tell them that I never showed the white feather.'

"We met at Clinch River, a mile out of camp, and I was disappointed to see that the Ohio boys were wearing full uniform. They could not get a disguise, and neither could Rowe. We crossed the mountains and Holston River together and then separated, the Ohioans taking one road and Rowe and I another.

"Hard riding had used up my horse at 2 P. M., and I had to borrow another from a stable near by, the owner protesting. At four o'clock we passed New Market, and were now within sound of our artillery, but with two rivers and one range of mountains to cross, and twenty thousand rebels to pass. We succeeded in crossing Bull Mountain and French Broad River, then going south of the city, we reached our lines near Knoxville. Here Sergeant Rowe was taken sick, and I rode alone into the city, reaching General Burnside's headquarters at 9 P. M., after having been continually in the saddle for nineteen hours.

"I expected to remain in Knoxville until the siege was raised, and was surprised when General Burnside asked me to undertake to return with dispatches at four o'clock in the morning. Taking me into a private room, he produced four dispatches written on tissue paper, one to General Wilcox, one to General Grant, one to the Secretary of War, and one to Mrs. Burnside, in Rhode Island, and placing them in my revolver, he said: 'Sergeant Hadley, if captured, be sure to fire off your revolver before surrendering.'

"After passing the last picket, I found Sergeant Rowe better and determined to return with me. I cannot tell how long we manœuvred before we got through the enemy's lines, but all at once, about two o'clock in the morning, as we were descending Clinch Mountain, we discovered the camp fires of some rebels, and had gone out but a few steps when we were ordered to 'Halt.' We turned to retreat, but a volley was fired at us. Our horses being jaded, the rebels gained on us, so we determined to dismount, and foot the rough mountain.

"Rowe thought he could evade the rebels by lying down, but they stumbled over him, and he was captured and sent to Andersonville. As for me, I could take no chances, for I was wearing a Confederate uniform and I knew I would be executed as a spy if I was caught. I kept on around the side of the mountain till I was exhausted and could not go a step farther. I found a big hollow log that had been split open, and I lay down in that with my revolver under my head.

"When I awoke it was daylight and I could hear the rebel pickets talking close by me; they had captured our horses and were looking for me. I was relieved when I heard their officers calling them in. Watching my chance I crept down the mountain, passed between their pickets, and crossed the road about eighty rods from their main camp.

"I came to a house which fortunately was occupied by a Union woman. She told me that her husband was hiding in the mountain, and that the rebels had searched her house for him three times that morning. She pointed out a ravine, by following which I could get across the valley without being seen, and strike the timber. I followed her directions and came to a road at the other end of the timber. While I was considering which direction I should take, a rebel horseman came riding slowly along. I dropped on one knee and drew my revolver on him, but he passed within ten feet of me without seeing me.

"I got to the Clinch River at last and found it too high to swim across. There was no ferry and no one was willing to row me across, as one bank was lined with rebels and the other with Northern troops. Finally I got a man to attempt it, and as we got to the other shore, a squad of Union soldiers came down to meet us. I told them who I was, and they gave me a horse. I rode to General Wilcox's headquarters, where I delivered my dispatches.

"I was completely exhausted, for I had ridden and walked over 100 miles and had tired out two horses, but was thankful to have escaped with my life, and accomplished the purpose of my journey."

THOUGH SICK, BRAVELY LED HIS MEN

JOHN J. TOFFEY,
1st Lieutenant, Co. G, 33d N. J. Inf.
Born at Quaker Hill, N. Y., June 1, 1844.

I T was for an act of superlative bravery, performed altogether outside of the line of his duty, that the Medal of Honor was conferred on Lieutenant John J. Toffey, of Company G, Thirty-third New Jersey Volunteers. At a time when he ought to have been in the hospital, he rushed into almost certain death to lead a storming party, the officers of which had all been shot down. He thus describes his feat:

"For several days prior to the battle of Chattanooga I had been excused from duty on account of illness, and the night before the battle the surgeon of the regiment ordered me into hospital, telling me that I was not able to take part in the engagement that we were expecting. I was determined not to be deprived of my share of the excitement, so I tore up the permit he had given me and marched with the regiment. We were ordered to charge a very strong position on the extreme right of the rebel line. It was well fortified and surrounded by dense woods, while in front there was an open field over which we had to charge.

"Companies I and A, as they emerged into the open, were met with a murderous fire from the entrenched enemy and the swarms of sharpshooters in the woods and buildings that commanded the front of the position. They were directing their attention to the officers, and at the first fire, Captain Waldron, of Company I, was shot down, with a bullet through his head, and Captain Boggs, of Company A, was mortally wounded.

"Seeing their officers fall, the men became demoralized. The line wavered and began to fall back in disorder. As these two companies held the key to our position

---

Chattanooga.—After the battle of Chickamauga, Rosecrans, in a state of siege at Chattanooga, Tenn., was re-enforced by Hooker with two corps, General Sherman with a division, and General Grant, who, at this time in command of the western armies, took the direction of affairs at Chattanooga.

The left wing of the Confederates rested on Lookout Mountain, the right on Missionary Ridge. On the 23d of November, Hooker's Corps gained a position at the mouth of Lookout Creek, facing the mountain, and, on the 24th, the assault was made between eight and nine o'clock in the morning. In two hours, the rebel riflepits were carried. The charge was continued up the mountain in the face of a terrific fire, and, at two o'clock, Hooker held the position on the summit, the Confederates retreating to Missionary Ridge.

The following morning Hooker renewed the battle at the southwestern end of the Ridge, General Sherman gained a lodgement on the northeastern declivity, while General Thomas waited at Orchard Knob. At two o'clock, General Grant gave the order for a general assault. The Union soldiers charged to the summit of Missionary Ridge, and the rebels were completely routed.

Bragg withdrew his force into Georgia, having sustained a loss of nearly 10,000. The Union killed, wounded and missing were 5,616.

and were intended to lead the attack, something had to be done. Colonel George W. Mindil ordered me to hasten to the right and take command of that part of the line, all the officers being killed or wounded.

"I ran across the open field and reached the advance line in time to prevent it from breaking. I reformed the line and we again charged the almost impregnable position in the face of an accurate and deadly fire. Just as we were carrying the position I received a severe wound, which disabled me permanently, and my military career was brought to a close."

Colonel Mindil stated in his report to the Secretary of War, that "the superlatively brave conduct of First Lieutenant John J. Toffey, saved the position, and enabled us on the following morning to press forward the entire line, and to unite the lines of the Army of the Cumberland, with those of General Sherman's Army at the mouth of the Chickamauga."

RISKED HIS LIFE FOR HIS COMRADES

JOHN KIGGINS,
Sergeant, Co. D, 149th N. Y. Inf.

SERGEANT JOHN KIGGINS, Company D, One hundred and forty-ninth New York Volunteers, won his Medal of Honor by risking his life to save his comrades, who were being fired upon by their own batteries, at the battle of Lookout Mountain, Tenn., November 24, 1863. Captain George K. Collins thus describes the incident:

"Our regiment had charged the enemy on the heights above the Craven House, when a Union battery in the valley below, opened a damaging fire upon us, mistaking us for the enemy. Sergeant Kiggins, color-bearer of the regiment, advanced to a point between the two lines, got up on a stump and waved his flag to attract the attention of the artillerymen, thus averting what threatened to be a serious disaster. In accomplishing this brave deed, he drew the enemy's fire upon himself, and nine bullet holes in his clothing, besides one through his cap, which left its mark upon his scalp, and one through his thigh, attested the accuracy of the enemy's fire."

PHILLIP GOETTEL was a corporal of the One hundred and forty-ninth New York Infantry. At the battle of Lookout Mountain, November 24, 1863, his regiment made a charge over fields and fences, through woods and swamps and against a severe fire of the enemy. The Confederates were full of con-fidence and great in strength. They assailed the center of the Union line with almost irresistible fierce-ness, but the onset was met with an unwavering front. A steady, telling fire was poured into the ranks, and the enemy soon gave ground.

In the face of a steady outpouring of grape an canis-ter, Corporal Goettel rushed forward and suc-ceeded in capturing a Confeder-ate flag. This was quite a daring feat, but still more difficult it was to keep the trophy and carry it back to his own lines. The rebels were not willing to lose their colors without making at least a desperate attempt to save them, and thus Cor-poral Goettel became a verit-able human target as he rushed back to his ranks. However, he escaped injury and was at once made the recipient of many congratulations from his comrades and warm praises from his superiors. A week lapsed before Corporal Goettel turned the cap-tured flag over to his quartermaster. In the heat of engagements and fights he had forgotten his own brave act and the importance of his prize.

SIGNALLING TO CEASE FIRING.

AT the same battle another Confederate flag was captured by Private Peter Kappesser, of Company D, of the same regiment. A Confederate camp in a hollow was surprised at breakfast. A brief but extremely sharp struggle ensued. The rebel color-sergeant, with his color-guard, was attempting to retreat under cover of some rocks. Private Kappesser boldly rushed upon them and demanded their surrender. The rebel sergeant and his guard were panic stricken and handed him the colors. Private Kappesser quickly tore the flag off the staff and thrust the bunting under his coat. He then hastened to the rescue of a comrade, who was wounded and writhing in pain, and taking him upon his back, carried comrade and flag to his own ranks. During the intensely cold night the daring soldier wore the Confederate flag as a scarf around his neck, and used it for this purpose until the battle of Missionary Ridge was over, when he gave it to the commanding officer of his regiment.

SIMEON T. JOSSELYN,
Lieutenant, Thirteenth Illinois Infantry.
Highest rank attained: Captain.
Born at Buffalo, N. Y., Jan. 14. 1842.

NINE MEN CAPTURED BY ONE

LIEUTENANT SIMEON T. JOSSELYN performed the extraordinary feat of capturing, single-handed, a rebel battle flag at Missionary Ridge, November 25, 1863, and the whole color-guard with it. He gives this account of the incident:

"We had formed line of battle at the foot of Missionary Ridge, and after waiting a few minutes we received the order to advance at double quick. We crossed an open field and a creek before we came in full view of the rebel lines, near the top of the ridge. With never a chance to regain our breath, we were pushed on under a heavy fire. The order came to my company and another, to advance as skirmishers.

"We had approached within a short distance of the enemy's line when they broke. I caught sight of the rebel colors with the guard, who kept well together, and I determined to have them at any cost. My company was back of me and I knew that, although they were somewhat scattered, the men would follow me. I pushed on and captured a rebel, from whom I took a Springfield musket and cartridges, before ordering him to the rear as a prisoner.

"With the captured musket, I opened fire on the color-guard, and brought down the color-bearer. When the flag came down, the men disappeared in the tall grass and weeds. I reloaded quickly, and rushed to the spot, where I found nine men. I was about to fire upon them again, when they waved their hats and shouted: 'We surrender.'

"I seized the flag, which was that of the Eighteenth Alabama Infantry, and they handed me the belt and socket. Some of my men coming up at this moment, I placed them as a guard over the prisoners. I then pushed forward in the direction of General Bragg's headquarters near the summit of the ridge, carrying the flag with me. The remnant of the rebel army was in full retreat, and our day's work was done. The belt and socket I still have in my possession as a relic."

"THEY WAVED THEIR HATS AND SHOUTED: 'WE SURRENDER.'"

VICTORY CROWNED HIS GALLANTRY

THE effects of the battle of Chattanooga on the 25th of November, 1863, were keenly felt from Nashville to Knoxville and from Chattanooga to Mobile and Savannah; it was a struggle, conducted for the Federal side by General George H. Thomas, commander of the Army of the Cumberland, and handsomely won by him and his brave and gallant troops.

In this battle the Thirtyfifth Ohio Infantry was attached to the Second Brigade of the Third Division of the Fourteenth Corps of the Army of the Cumberland.

The morning of the 25th of November opened clear and bright with General Thomas at his headquarters on Orchard Knob, commanding a full view of the entire field.

The Third Division of the Fourteenth Corps had for two days been in camp three-quarters of a mile in front of Fort Phelps, with its left resting on the Moon Road and its right near Turchin's Brigade. About eight o'clock the Thirty-fifth Ohio, Lieu-

HENRY VAN N. BOYNTON,
Lieutenant-Colonel, 35th Ohio Infantry.
Highest rank attained: Bvt. Brig-Gen.,
U. S. V.
Born at West Stockbridge, Mass.,
July 22, 1835.

tenant-Colonel Henry Van N. Boynton, commander, was deployed along the front and advancing about a mile, strongly opposed. The enemy had drawn in its pickets so that upon the approach of the Ohio men, several small observation parties retired in haste. Shortly after, the regiment rejoined its brigade and moved with the division to a position about half a mile north of the Bald Hill, facing and 1,200 yards distant from Missionary Ridge. Here the Thirty-fifth Ohio was placed in the center of the brigade on the first line. Up to four o'clock in the afternoon this force was engaged in skirmishing with the enemy on the far side of the woods, when an advance was ordered, and under a heavy fire from the enemy's artillery on the ridge and from musketry from the lower works, the brigade dashed forward at double-quick without firing a shot. When within one hundred yards from the rifle pits the Confederates were retreating as rapidly as they could up the precipitous ridge behind them.

Still the Thirty-fifth Ohio, with the other regiments of the brigade, moved on steadily under a very heavy direct and enfilading fire until they were partly under cover of the first line of works. Then the division commander ordered a charge to the crest of the ridge, and with cheers and great energy the Third Division of the Fourteenth Corps began a bloody ascent. The steep surface, the enemy's sharp-shooters in front, a terrific enfilading artillery fire on both flanks did not lessen their eager haste, so that, at last it became practically a race between the first and second lines of the division. After numerous hand-to-hand conflicts the colors of the Second Brigade, Third Division, Fourteenth Army Corps, were planted on the summit of the ridge, such of the Confederates as could do so fleeing precipitately. As the men of the Thirty-fifth Ohio sprang over the works, cannoneers, caught loading their pieces, were driven away, or, refusing to run, were bayoneted before they could fire their pieces. At this point the Thirty-fifth captured three guns, after which they joined in the pursuit of the enemy, who had retreated to the left, for nearly half a mile.

It was during this fight that Lieutenant-Colonel Boynton fell, severely wounded, and because of his day's experience, that officer now wears the Congressional Medal of Honor, "For leading his regiment at Missionary Ridge, Tenn., November 25, 1864, in the face of a severe fire of the enemy, where he was severely wounded."

It had been a fight before the strongest portion of Bragg's army and resulted in a capture of one of the strongest positions in the zone of the battle. Furthermore, it was a vindication of General Thomas and the Army of the Cumberland; and the signal for the immediate relief of Burnside at Knoxville.

CAPTURED BATTLE-FLAGS

ROBERT B. BROWN,

Private, Co. A, 15th Ohio Vet. Vol. Inf.
Born at New Concord, Ohio, Oct. 2d, 1844.

Two incidents occurred at the battle of Missionary Ridge, November 24 and 25, 1863, which stand out prominently among the many gallant deeds of the Union soldiers engaged in that battle. In both instances Ohio men were the heroes, and in both, too, the capture of the Confederate colors was the prize of courage and daring.

Private Robert B. Brown, of Company A, Fifteenth Ohio Infantry, secured the standard of the Ninth Mississippi and took the standard-bearer along with the trophy as his prisoner. Corporal George Green, of Company H, Eleventh Ohio Infantry, was one of the first to scale the enemy's works, and after a fierce hand-to-hand struggle with the rebel color-bearer, likewise carried off the Confederate flag of another rebel regiment. Both incidents are highly dramatic. Private Brown's regiment was part of the Union force, which, on November 24, was ordered to make a demonstration on Missionary Ridge. The line advanced to Orchard Knob and rested there until two o'clock on the next day, when orders were given to take the rifle pits at the foot of the ridge. The troops made the advance, and, without meeting with serious opposition, continued up the ridge. Just as the Fifteenth Ohio reached the crest, Private Brown espied a Confederate color-bearer. His mind was at once set upon the possession of the rebel flag. Not heeding the severe fire, concentrated upon him, he ran up to the color-bearer.

"Surrender!" he shouted with a threatening gesture, which so impressed the rebel, that he hastened to comply. Brown took the flag and the prisoner to his commander, who was proud of the private's achievement.

Private Green's regiment, on November 25, was ordered out on the Rossville Road to support a section of artillery sent to shell the camp of the enemy at the base of Missionary Ridge. Nothing was encountered there and the regiment subsequently returned and rejoined the brigade. Later it moved with the brigade and took a position in front of Fort Wood. Having been formed in double column at half distance, the regiment deployed, and, at a run, moved across the open ground up Missionary Ridge and against a severe fire of musketry and artillery. The breast-

GEORGE GREEN,

Private, Co. H, 11th Ohio Infantry.
Born in Elsham, England, 1840.

works of the enemy on the top of the ridge had to be taken by storm. The Eleventh Ohio made a bold dash for the guns. They met with a most decided resistance and many a brave fellow lost his life in the attempt to be the first one to scale the rebel works. Corporal Green fought with undaunted courage. Though he saw a number of his comrades killed at his side, he bravely approached the works, and—with one daring leap, bounded into the rebel fortifications. He was soon joined by others and then a fierce struggle ensued. Green grappled with the bearer of a Confederate battle-flag and wrenched from him the colors. The fight ended in a complete victory for the Ohioans.

SOONER FIGHT THAN BEAT THE DRUM

JOHN S. KOUNTZ,
Drummer, Co. G, 37th Ohio Inf.
Born in Lucas Co., Ohio, March 25, 1846.

THE WAR DEPARTMENT found Drummer John S. Kountz, of Company G, Thirty-seventh Ohio Infantry, guilty of disobedience to orders in throwing down his drum and joining in the charge at Missionary Ridge, but for his gallantry on this occasion he was awarded the Medal of Honor. When the order was given to advance from the temporary works from which the enemy had been driven that morning, Kountz who was only seventeen years of age, threw aside his drum and joined in the attack, urging and encouraging his comrades. Twice the brigade charged upon the Confederates in their entrenched position, and twice the shattered column was driven back. On the second assault, Kountz was shot through the leg and very dangerously wounded close to the enemy's lines.

When the brigade got back to its old position, Captain Hamm, of Company A, told the boys of Company G, that Kountz was lying in the front severely wounded, and asked: "Who will go and get him out?" Private William Schmidt shouted: "I will," and made for the front, advancing as far as he could under cover of the hill. When he came to the point where cover was no longer available, he made a dash for the spot where Kountz was lying, the enemy pouring a heavy fire upon him. Kountz shouted: "Save yourself. I am a goner anyhow," but Schmidt picked him up on his back and in spite of all protests, carried him back to the Union lines. Kountz' leg was so badly shattered that it had to be amputated the same night. When he was picked up, he was nearer the rebel works than any other man of his regiment.

"NOW YOU HAVE SURRENDERED!"

JAMES C. WALKER,
Private Co. K, 31st Ohio Inf.
Born at Harmony, Clark Co., Ohio.
Nov. 30, 1843.

THE conduct of soldiers like that of Private James C. Walker, of Company K, Thirty-first Ohio Infantry, contributed a large share to the final success of the Union cause. It was at the battle of Missionary Ridge that Private Walker distinguished himself. Though wounded he could not bear to see the colors of his regiment drop and seized them just as the color-bearer, mortally wounded, fell to the ground. Throughout the engagement he carried the stars and stripes, the possession of which inspired him to a degree of courage akin to heroism.

Private Walker himself tells a graphic story of the thrilling events of that day, as far as he was concerned, as follows:

"Turchin's Brigade was drawn up in two lines to attack the Confederate position, but as the second line overlapped the first, our regiment was taken out to form a third line. On arriving at the Confederate breastworks at the foot of the ridge, we found them filled with men of the first and second lines, which left us without protection from the enemy's musketry fire. It was less dangerous to advance than to retreat, and Colonel Lister rode over the breastworks, shouting: 'Forward Thirty-first.' We swarmed over and the whole brigade followed. We made no attempt to keep in line; it was everyone for himself, each striving to be first to gain the top of the ridge. The Thirty-first started up the ravine to the left of the spur known as De Long's Point, but we found that this would lead us into an angle of the rebel line, so we turned to the right and came out on the top of the spur.

"George Wilson, of Company G, and I were among the first to get to this point. We laid down at the foot of the Confederate breastworks, and Sam Wright of Company K, came up and asked us: 'What in hell are you going to do next?' We told him to wait and see. As the other boys came up, they dropped alongside of us until we numbered twenty all told. I then called out: 'Boys are you ready?' and they replied: 'Yes, go ahead.' We climbed to the top of the works and looked down upon the Confederates, formed in two lines, one kneeling in the trench with fixed bayonets, and the other lying down behind them. With a yell we jumped down into the trench on top of them, and a hand-to-hand fight followed, with muskets, bayonets, and even fists. We had broken the Confederate line, and as our men came up to support us, we faced right and left, and kept widening the gap.

"One of the Confederates who had thrown down his musket and held up his hands in token of surrender, fired at us after we had passed and hit one of our boys on the knee. I turned on him with the butt of my gun, but before I could strike, Sam Wright pushed me to one side, and said: 'Let me fix him.' Placing his musket against the man's breast, he fired, literally tearing him to pieces. Looking at the mangled body, he said: 'Now damn you, you have surrendered.'

"As I turned to push on, I was struck in the right breast with a Minie ball which knocked the breath out of me and stunned me, making ten holes through my blanket, blouse and shirt. Our color-bearer, Corporal George W. Franklin, of Company K, had been struck in the arm by a piece of shell as he came over the works, and was on the point of falling from loss of blood when I came to my senses. I jumped up and caught the colors just in time to save them from going down.

DRIVING OFF THE REBEL GUNNERS.

"A rebel battery a short distance to the left, opened a terrible fire of grape and canister upon us. I rushed forward to the first gun of the battery, got in between the piece and the wheel, and with my left hand pulled the fuse out of the gun, just as the cannoneer jerked the lanyard. Sam Wright got in on the other side, rested his musket on the wheel, and shot the officer in command of the battery. As the officer fell, his sword flew out of his hand and came end over end to the feet of Captain A. S. Scott, of the Thirty-first.

"We drove off the rebel gunners, slewed the guns around and poured their contents into their late owners. After capturing the battery, we swept on until the Confederates, being re-enforced, made a desperate charge and drove us over the breastworks. The ridge at this point was so steep that we could fall back no further, and we were compelled to hold our ground. Here we fought for about twenty minutes with the breastworks between us, and the only thing that saved us was that we were on lower ground and the rebels overshot us.

"Our troops attacked the flank and rear of the enemy's line, while we leaped over the breastwork and charged them from the front. I noticed the color-bearer of the Forty-first Alabama, about twenty paces in front of me, endeavoring to rally his regiment. I rushed at him and caught hold of the flag, but in the struggle we fell and the staff was broken. The rebel surrendered and I rolled up his flag and carried it under my left arm till I met Sam Wright and gave it to him. Our own colors I continued to carry throughout the fight and brought them out with eighty-nine bullet holes in them and ten in the staff."

A PRIVATE'S INGENUITY

THE quick wit and action of Private Martin E. Scheibner, of Company G, Ninetieth Pennsylvania Infantry, prevented a disaster at the battle of Mine Run, November 26 and 27, 1863. The fighting in that locality consisted of a series of operations between the forces of General Meade and General Lee with engagements at Racoon Ford, Bartlett's Mills, Robertson's Tavern, Kelley's Ford and New Hope. During these short, but sharp contests, the Federal forces consisted of five corps of infantry and artillery and two divisions of cavalry. The Ninetieth Pennsylvania was part of these troops.

MARTIN E. SCHEIBNER,
Private, Co. G, 90th Pennsylvania Inf.
Born in Russia.

The incident, which furnished Private Scheibner an opportunity to distinguish himself, when Lee took a strong position at Mine Run, shortly after being defeated by General Sedgwick's Corps at Kelley's Ford.

The Confederates were shelling the Union forces and doing considerable damage, so that General Meade decided upon an energetic course of action. Company G of the Pennsylvania regiment was ordered to charge across the Run and up-hill to the fortifications of the rebel army.

Simultaneously with the order, came a shell from the enemy directly in the midst of the infantrymen. The unexploded weapon of death with its rapidly burning fuse caused consternation amounting almost to a panic within the Union ranks. The line formation in the immediate vicinity, where the shell had fallen, was instantly and completely shattered. Some of the men threw themselves flat upon the ground, with eyes shut; some of them running to the nearest shelter, however inadequate the protection offered might be. A panic, the result of which might have been disastrous indeed, was imminent. Private Scheibner glanced at the rapidly burning fuse. He noticed the men running in all directions. One thought flashed through his mind. He decided to take his chances. Quickly removing the stopper from his canteen, he poured the contents, coffee, on the fizzing, burning fuse. The glimmering fire was extiguised and all danger averted. A second or so later and the explosion would have been inevitable. The fuse had just about reached the shell. Many of his comrades had watched him with abated breath and cheered loudly when they perceived his success. The men now came back, reformed and made the charge as ordered. It was the deed of less than a half minute that accomplished this result.

A Medal of Honor was the appropriate reward for this act of presence of mind and courage.

A COLOSSAL BLUFF

JOSEPH S. MANNING,
Private, 29th Massachusetts Vol. Infantry.
Born at Ipswich, Mass., April 13, 1845.

Private Joseph S. Manning of the Twenty-ninth Massachusetts Volunteer Infantry, had the singular good fortune to capture a flag from the midst of two hundred rebels. He gives the following account of it:

"My regiment was with General Burnside at Knoxville, East Tenn., from November 17 till December 5, 1863, and during all that time we were continually under fire from the rifle-pits of the enemy, which were being drawn closer to our earthworks day by day. On the night of November 28th a furious assault was made upon the left of our line, and our pickets were driven in, contesting the ground step by step. My regiment was ordered to the rear of our principal-earthwork, Fort Sanders, where we remained nearly all night. Just before daylight the enemy made a demonstration at the extreme left of our line and my regiment was hurried off to strengthen that point.

"It was a bit- at a fire there, Just then terly cold night, and I had gone to the rear to warm myself and when I came back I found that the regiment had gone. the enemy opened a fierce fire of artillery and musketry on the fort, as a prelude to the assault, so I stayed where I was. The rebel infantry poured in upon us, scaling the parapet and climbing through the embrasures, but as fast as they did so, we shot them down, and they rolled back into the ditch which surrounded the fort. One color-bearer planted his flag upon the parapet, but immediately it was snatched away, and he was shot dead. Never in my life did I experience such a savage feeling. It seemed to me that I could not load and fire fast enough, and although my fingers were numb with cold, I was in a fever of excitement.

"This assault was repulsed, but another was immediately made by fresh troops. Three of the enemy's colors were planted upon the parapet, but were quickly shot away, and a hand-to-hand fight followed, the officers using their swords, the men their bayonets and the butts of their guns. Even the artillery-men took part, using their axes and the rammers of the guns as weapons, the enemy being finally obliged to withdraw, after losing heavily

"WITH MY BAYONET AT HIS BREAST I DEMAND-ED HIS SURRENDER"

"The retreating rebels took a position a short distance from the fort, and for a time kept up a scattering fire, aided by their artillery. General Ferrero, who commanded the fort, called out: 'There are lots of them in the ditch. Go out and get them.' A detail from our regiment was sent to the left, and one from the Second Michigan to the right to sweep the ditch. The first detail entered the ditch from the rifle pits on the left and passed around the salient of the fort. I wanted to go with them but was quite a distance away when they started, and as I saw I could not catch up by following, I adopted another plan.

"Waiting until I thought they had entered the ditch, I jumped upon the parapet, slid down the outside of the fort and landed among the rebels. I was the only Yankee in sight. Hearing the detail from my regiment cheering to the left, I demanded the surrender of those about me, and they threw down their guns. I pushed towards a color-bearer who was attempting to hide his colors and with my bayonet at his breast, I demanded his surrender. He handed over the colors, which were those of the Sixteenth Georgia, and I took him prisoner. Our detail arrived just then, and turning my prisoner over to them, he was marched back along with some 200 others, through the ditch into the works. We also recovered another rebel flag from under the dead body of the color-bearer.

"A wounded rebel in the ditch asked me to take him inside the works as he was in danger of being shot where he lay. I made him climb over the dead and wounded who lay in great numbers at this angle of the fort. I passed up the colors to him and told him to stand where he was till I climbed up. Then I placed the colors and my gun over my left shoulder and supported him with my right arm, thus exposing him to the rebel fire. They seemed to recognize him, for not a shot was fired at us, as we walked a distance of over a hundred yards along the front of the rebel line. When I got the wounded man into our works, I turned and waved the colors to the rebels, who saluted me with a volley, and the bullets whistled about my ears. I did not stop there any longer than was necessary, but got down behind the earthworks.

"On arriving at headquarters, General Burnside received the colors, took me by the hand and complimented me in the most flattering language."

Knoxville.—On the 4th of September, 1863, Burnside with about 12,000 troops entered Knoxville, Tenn., and immediately began to strengthen the defenses around the city, so that by the 17th of November he had shut himself up. He held the city and the surrounding country, though the nearest Union forces were in the vicinity of Missionary Ridge.

Burnside being thus isolated, Bragg sent Longstreet against him with 20,000 troops, and on the 29th of November Longstreet began a terrific artillery fire upon the Union works. Burnside, however, held his fire until four Confederate brigades advanced to charge upon the parapet, when he opened up with his guns with such deadly effect that Longstreet was compelled to withdraw, leaving behind more than 1,000 killed and wounded, while his own loss was less than twenty.

Sherman's army, which had in the meantime been ordered to the relief of Burnside, had forced its marches in order to arrive at Knoxville before it was too late, but was met by an officer of Burnside's staff, who announced that Longstreet had been utterly repulsed.

When Sherman entered the city he was greatly surprised to find that the garrison was not starved and demoralized but that Burnside's army was well supplied with rations, furnished by Union sympathizers in the South.

Burnside's loss during the Knoxville campaign was about 600; Longstreet's was more than 1,000.

BRUNER'S BRAVE RIDE

LOUIS J. BRUNER,
Private, Co. H, 5th Ind. Cav.
Born in Monroe Co., Ind., Oct. 6, 1834.

Oₙₑ of the most precarious and interesting situations in the War of the Rebellion was furnished by the investment of Knoxville, where General Burnside and his army were cooped up for a considerable time, very much to the alarm and anxiety of President Lincoln and his cabinet, as well as that of General Grant. On the other hand Burnside confirmed his previous record as an able soldier by maintaining his position intact, in the face of a bitter siege, conducted by General Longstreet.

With the Chattanooga situation taken well in hand General Grant began the campaign for the relief of General Burnside, and soon General Longstreet was forced to raise the siege in order to turn his attention to the Federal cavalry, who were harrassing his rear.

This brigade consisted of the Fifth Indiana and Fourteenth Illinois Cavalry, the Twenty-first Ohio Battery, the Sixty-fifth, One hundred and sixteenth and One hundred and eighteenth Indiana Volunteers, under command of Colonel Graham. At Walker's Ford on the Clinch River, December 2, 1863, the fifth Indiana Cavalry, under Colonel Thomas H. Butler, was suddenly attacked at daylight, many of the cavalry being still asleep. The Confederates had, during the night, captured the outer picket post at the gap entrance to the mountain, where the Manordsville Road leads toward Walker's Ford and they had done this without discovery. Then, just at dawn, they drove in the reserve pickets and so reached the Indiana men, who occupied the elevated ground north of the Clinch River. The Confederates rested their right a few hundred yards to the southwest, close to an area of timber, where they had been driven by the Indiana cavalry. A hot struggle, lasting five hours, followed, Colonel Butler contesting stubbornly every inch of ground.

The Confederates had just made a spirited attack on the right wing of the cavalry, driving it back, when Private Louis J. Bruner, Company H, and acting orderly of Colonel Butler, was dispatched with orders to Major Mell H. Soper to occupy some timber on the left, extending to the mountain.

Major Soper at once began executing the move, when the Confederates made a spirited attack on the right wing of the cavalry and drove it back for some distance though they failed to break the Union lines. Then by a quick move they extended their lines to the mountains, cutting off the major and his batallion. Curiously enough neither the major nor the rebel commander realized the importance of the situation; Major Soper was ignorant of the danger from capture, the Confederates did not know that they had the Union men at bay. Colonel Butler, however, fully appreciated the seriousness of the situation, and at once consulted with the officers of his staff. "Soper might extricate himself by making for a small ravine in the mountain," he suggested. Just then Bruner rode up to the group of officers. Saluting the colonel, he placed himself at the latter's disposal for any service which might be required to accomplish the rescue of Major Soper. Colonel Butler accepted the offer and without losing time Bruner rode away, toward the lines of enemy, hidden from their view by high banks and bushes. Presently he reached a road leading to the Confederate line and quite close thereto. The distance from the position

DASHING THROUGH THE REBEL LINES.

they occupied to the timber which Bruner desired to reach, was traversed within a few minutes.

So suddenly had Bruner appeared and disappeared that but a few shots were sent after the daring rider. Once among the trees, Bruner made his way to Major Soper, told him of his precarious position and pointed out the ravine as a means of escape. The Major immediately dismounted his batallion and entered the ravine. Bruner, however, returned as he had come to report the Major's escape promptly. He passed the enemy's line close in front of their guns and it is to be called miraculous that his daring return was not brought to a sudden halt.

A SINGULAR PREDICAMENT SKILLFULLY HANDLED

FRANK S. HESSELTINE,
Lieut.-Col., 13th Maine Infantry.
Born at Bangor, Maine, Dec. 10, 1833.

DURING the close of 1863 and the opening of 1864, Major-General C. C. Washburn, in command of the coast expedition with headquarters at Decrow's Point, Texas, ordered Brigadier-General T. E. G. Ransom to order a reconnoissance of the Matagorda Peninsula. Accordingly, General Ransom sent Lieutenant-Colonel Frank S. Hesseltine, commanding the Thirteenth Maine Infantry, at Fort Esperanza, to carry out the mission.

Colonel Hesseltine and 100 members of his regiment embarked on the gunboat Granite City on the evening of December 28, 1863, and during that night proceeded along the shore of the Matagorda Peninsula to a point seven miles distant from its head. In the morning a landing through the surf was effected, the intention being to simply make the reconnoissance ordered. A strong southerly wind rose piling up so strong a surf that all communication with the gunboat was cut off and as far as immediate support was concerned the little band was put upon its own resources.

Meanwhile Lieutenant Hamm, who had been sent with a small force on a scout up the peninsula, returned. Thereupon Colonel Hesseltine deployed a line of skirmishers nearly across the neck of land and moved his force down under convoy of the gunboat, thus driving back and cutting off the Confederate pickets. Because of the numerous bayous, the force had made but seven or eight miles' advance at two o'clock in the afternoon, and Colonel Hesseltine was obliged to shorten his skirmish line. Just then, too, he was warned by the steam whistle of his convoy, of danger in the rear. The colonel, by using his glasses, discovered the van of a body of cavalry (they were two regiments under command of the Confederate Colonel A. Buchel) moving down the peninsula. Under a heavy fire from the thirty-pound Parrott of the Granite City, the enemy moved in until within half an hour their skirmishers were close up to the Maine soldiers. When they were within range, Colonel Hesseltine commanded the rear line to face about and gave Buchel's force a volley, with good effect. Then the Confederates attempted a rapid flank movement, but Colonel Hesseltine quickly assembled his force by countermarching, formed his line face to the foe and in line of battle extending across the narrow neck of land, only two hundred yards wide at this point because of the setting in of a bayou.

The enemy again changed direction, and attempted, by wading the bayou, to gain the rear of the Yankees. At this, Hesseltine ordered a backward movement, quick time, and riding ahead selected a capital defensible position, where he halted his force. Giving the order promptly, his men, as if by magic, and while Buchel was forming his force for attack, threw up a barricade of driftwood, logs and branches, projecting and forming an ugly looking redan, its pan coupé on a sand ridge, its gorge out in the surf. Then the men wheeled in on the beach and were ready. The Confederates, already formed, advanced, hesitated, halted. A small party rode up to reconnoitre and moved back again; then they moved the force obliquely for a fierce charge on the left. They halted and while they were deliberating, darkness came with a heavy mist. Finally they withdrew while the Yankees rang out three cheers and a tiger.

REPULSING THE CHARGE.

Two bonfires at the right and left of Colonel Hesseltine's position, told the gunboat Scioto, coming in from a reconnoissance up the coast, of the whereabouts of the Maine men, and the Granite City went back for re-enforcements. Expecting an attack in the morning, Hesseltine kept his men at work on the barricade all night, but beyond a few shots from the southern pickets, but little trouble was experienced. A foggy morning prevented any serious demonstrations, but at noon the Confederate gunboat J. G. Carr ran down inside and to a point opposite and began shelling the hastily constructed fortification. At 3 P. M., being without food or water and concluding that the enemy had beaten back all re-enforcements sent from Decrow's

Point, Colonel Hesseltine moved his hundred men cautiously and began making his way down the peninsular. At ten o'clock that night the party was struck by the severest norther of the winter and at one o'clock in the morning the bivouac was made. Resuming the march in the morning they plodded along until 2 P. M., when twenty miles from the fort they were discovered by the Scioto and with great difficulty were taken aboard. Not a man or equipment was lost during the entire experience.

CAPTURED GENERAL VANCE

EVERETT W. ANDERSON,
Sergeant, Co. M, 15th Penn. Cav.
Born in Chester Co., Pa., July
12, 1839.

AFTER the battle of Chickamauga, the Fifteenth Pennsylvania Cavalry was sent out to the Sequatchie Valley to forage for the relief of the Army of the Cumberland, penned up at Chattanooga.

On the 14th of January, 1864, while campaigning along the French Broad River, word was received that General Robert B. Vance had captured a wagon train of Union supplies at Sevierville, besides 200 infantrymen and numerous Union citizens, and that he was retreating towards Ashville.

Colonel William I. Palmer, commanding the Fifteenth Pennsylvania Cavalry, started after Vance, whose passage being blocked by large trees thrown across the road by Northern sympathizers, was soon overtaken. Colonel Palmer detailed a party of twenty men to charge through the enemy's rear, which was done successfully, and then the general charge followed, resulting in a total surprise of the enemy and the recapture of all the property. A small squad commanded by Sergeant Everett W. Anderson, of Company M, was looking after the wounded, and thereby became scattered. Thus it happened that Sergeant Anderson, while dismounted and caring for the wounded, had his attention called by a comrade, to the approach of five Confederates. Quickly mounting his horse, Anderson wheeled about and faced General Vance, two aides and two orderlies. Covering the General with his revolver, Anderson demanded their surrender. Seeing that his captor was fingering the trigger of his gun suggestively, General Vance threw his revolver to the ground, at the same time objecting to surrendering to an enlisted man. He said that he would surrender only to a commissioned officer. Anderson thought differently, however, and completed the capture of the five men before his comrades had reached the prisoners and their keeper.

News of a capture brought Colonel Palmer to the scene, and saluting, he extended his hand with: "I am happy to meet you, General Vance." The reply of the prisoner was: "Much more so than I am, under the circumstances."

A REAR GUARD'S HEROIC WORK

THEODORE S. PECK,
First Lieutenant, Co. H, 9th Vermont
Infantry.
Highest rank attained: Bvt. Maj-Gen.
Born at Burlington, Vt., March 22, 1843.

O^N February 2, 1864, at Newport Barracks, North Carolina, the Union troops, comprising some seven hundred and fifty men, with one piece of artillery, were attacked by the Confederates under General Martin, who had about two thousand infantry, fourteen pieces of artillery and four hundred cavalry, and who had outflanked the Federals from the commencement of the engagement. The left of the Union line lay near the river, while the right was in the woods, and commanded by First Lieutenant Theodore S. Peck Company H, Ninth Vermont Infantry.

The line was continually pressed back by the enemy, and made eleven different stands before reaching the Newport River, over which there were two bridges, one a railroad bridge, and the other

JOSIAH C. LIVINGSTONE,
First Lieutenant and Adjutant,
9th Vermont Infantry.
Highest rank attained: Captain
Born at Walden, Vt., Feb. 3, 1837

called the county bridge, located about a quarter of a mile above the former.

The location of the county bridge was at a narrow point of the Newport River, which was very deep just there. The bridge was about forty feet long and with one approach down a hill not very steep, but with bluffs upon either side and woods down the bank. On the opposite side of the river was a marsh full of rushes, dead and dried, and with a level road leading through it from the bridge to the railway crossing.

ERASTUS W. JEWETT,
First Lieutenant, Co. A, 9th Vermont Inf.
Born at St. Albans, Vt., April 1, 1839.

The Confederates pressed so closely that there was barely time to fire the railroad bridge with turpentine and tar. Lieutenant Peck with his men was ordered to fire the county bridge, and was told that he would find on the opposite side of the river, near the bridge head, two companies of cavalry, with plenty of turpentine and tar for his use as soon as he had crossed, but the bridge must be burned at all hazards, and the enemy prevented from crossing, for it was well known throughout the entire command that its salvation depended upon the burning of both these bridges. Should either one be left undestroyed and the enemy permitted to cross, the chances were that what was left of the Union forces would be captured.

Lieutenant Peck had made a desperate fight all the afternoon, and had been the farthest out toward the enemy the entire time, holding them in check until they had broken through the line on his left. At this time the Union troops had mostly crossed the railroad and county bridges, and were rapidly falling back down the county road toward Beaufort, while Lieutenant Peck's rear guard was hotly engaged with the Confederates, who were close at his heels.

He had sent a non-commissioned officer to the bridge to see if everything was in readiness to fire the same after he had crossed it. The sergeant had just reported that there was no tar, no turpentine, and no cavalry; in fact there was nothing—all had fled. Lieutenant Peck, leaving one-half of his men with their officers, fighting the enemy, ran with the other half down the hill to the bridge, determined to destroy the same, if possible. Finding that some of the planks were not spiked down, he had these torn up, and, being fortunate in finding plenty of dry grass in the vicinity, which his men pulled from the ground, he had the same placed in readiness for burning the bridge, then ordered his men, who were fighting, to stop firing and rush across. This order was instantly obeyed, although some were killed and wounded in leaving the enemy, who came forward on the run, increasing their musketry fire.

As soon as the men from the hill had crossed the bridge, they commenced firing upon the enemy, while the others of the party ignited the dead grass. The Confederates brought up a battery and poured in grape and canister.

In the rush, Sergeant Charles F. Branch was wounded and left behind, a fact which, instantly it became known to Peck, caused him to rush back across the now burning bridge, to the sergeant, and half carrying him in his arms, succeeded, in spite of a hot shower of bullets and shell and in momentary danger of death from the flaming bridge, in carrying him safely across to the main body of his forces.

Meanwhile the little band fought the enemy across the river until both ends of the bridge fell, a mass of burning embers, when the retreat was taken up. As the

---

Newport Barracks—On February 2, 1864, a large force of Confederates, under General Martin, made an attack upon the Union lines at **Gales' Creek, N. C.** Though vastly outnumbered, the Federals repulsed the rebels twice, but were finally compelled to fall back. The Confederates then advanced upon **Newport Barracks,** throwing their right flank across the railroad to prevent a retreat. After some severe fighting, the small Union forces retired across the railroad and county bridges toward Newport Village. The bridges were destroyed by the retreating Federals. From Newport, a further retreat was made to **Morehead City,** where the further advance of the Confederates was checked. The losses during the several engagements were small, though those of the Federals were somewhat heavier than the enemy's, because the Union men were mostly raw recruits.

THE RESCUE OF SERGEANT CHARLES F. BRANCH BY LIEUTENANT Γ. S. PECK.

Confederates were obliged to build a new bridge before crossing the river, the Union forces gained an advantage of three hours and so made good their escape.

At the time Lieutenant Peck was holding and burning the county bridge, at Newport Barracks, Lieutenant Erastus W. Jewett was given command of a picket squad of about seventy men, with orders to hold and burn the railroad bridge, which, as stated before, was some three-quarters of a mile below the county bridge. He also was to prevent the enemy, who had a large force on the other side, from crossing and capturing Newport Barracks and its defenders. Relative to this deed Lieutenant Jewett says: "We held the bridge and twice drove the enemy back to the cover of the woods. They then shelled us with a battery at about 600 yards, for fifteen minutes, but as soon as they stopped, we were at them again with our muskets, and succeeded in keeping them back from the bridge till it was burned, so that they could not cross the river. No doubt it was some of the hardest rearguard work ever performed, and my men well deserved all the praise that was bestowed upon them later."

At the outset of the enterprise assigned to Lieutenants Peck and Jewett, Lieutenant Josiah C. Livingstone volunteered his services, which offer was accepted. His was no mean share in the enterprise. He personally supervised the burning of the bridge and was among the last to fall back. In retiring he passed a wounded comrade who was unable to move. Lieutenant Livingstone came to his assistance and helped him to reach the Union lines in safety. It was for such loyal duty that Lieutenant Livingstone's superior officers recommended him for the Medal of Honor.

WITH ELEVEN MEN HELD AN ARMY AT BAY

O^N February 1, 1864, at 3:30 o'clock in the morning, General Pickett, of the Army of Virginia, attacked the outposts of the Union forces at a point where the Neuse Road crosses Batchelder's Creek, about eight miles from New Berne, North Carolina. At that point the Federal force consisted of only eleven men under Lieutenant Abram P. Haring, of Company G, One hundred and thirty-second New York Infantry. The evident purpose of the rebels was the capture of New Berne, which was stocked with ammunition, clothing and general stores in large quantities. General Pickett led his force divided into three columns and chose a most favorable time for his attack, for a fog and a light drizzling rain covered their advance, besides cutting off all Union signal communication. The strength of the Confederates was estimated as high as 11,000.

ABRAM P. HARING,
First Lieutenant, Co. G, 132d New York Inf.
Born in New York in 1838.

"The location of our small reserve," Lieutenant Haring narrates, "was in a naturally strong position. The creek was fifty feet wide in front, with breastworks on either side about fifty feet long. During the preceding night we had taken up the bridge, and with the timbers and planks we constructed a small but strong breastwork, behind which we stationed ourselves.

"About 3:30 o'clock in the morning during a heavy fog, the Confederates attacked us in force, but were unable to dislodge us. I immediately dispatched a messenger to headquarters informing the commanding officer of the situation. In the meantime the enemy, feeling conscious of their strength, made a second attack, which like the first proved futile. We were keeping up a steady fire during this attack, and now our ammunition was pretty well exhausted, but the little we had left we used to good advantage."

Thus did Lieutenant Haring and the eleven men of his command hold the powerful army of the rebel general at bay for several hours. All attempts to dislodge the Spartan band from the bridge and free the way for further advance, failed. Then batteries of artillery were brought up, but still Lieutenant Haring and his men refused to yield. In the meantime the defenders of the bridge were re-enforced by 150 men from the One hundred and thirty-second New York, and the rebels seeing that further attempts to dislodge them were useless changed their plan of attack, constructed a bridge across the creek at a point some distance below, and there attacked Lieutenant Haring's little force from the rear, thus driving them out of their stronghold.

This is the praise which Captain Charles G. Smith, Lieutenant Haring's superior officer, in his official report, bestows upon the hero:

"I feel it my duty to mention several instances of coolness and heroism, particularly that of Lieutenant Haring's brave defense of the Neuse bridge, which is worthy of especial commendation."

Still more flattering is the following official reference to the incident by Colonel Claassen:

"First Lieutenant Abram P. Haring commanded the reserve at the attack at the Neuse bridge and with eleven men heroically held that all-important point for hours, against thousands of the enemy."

CAPTURES HIS CAPTORS AND ESCAPES

ANDREW TRAYNOR,
Corporal, First Michigan Cavalry.
Born at Newark, N. J., Feb. 9, 1843.

DURING the last three months of 1863 and the first three months of 1864, the Army of the Potomac had no great battles, the cavalry being chiefly engaged in raiding under Generals Custer, Smith, Gregg, Merritt and Kilpatrick, while the centers of general interest were Chattanooga and other points on the way to Atlanta. The situation along the Potomac had been extremely unsatisfactory. President Lincoln had just issued a call for 200,000 additional men, which, with the promotion of General Grant to Lieutenant-General in command of the Federal Armies, entirely restored confidence in the north. Meanwhile the several brigades of cavalry in the east had been riding through the entire territory from Harper's Ferry to the James River.

On the 16th of March, 1864, Corporal Andrew Traynor, of the First Michigan Cavalry, was detailed with one private on scout duty in the vicinity of Mason's Hill, Virginia. He says:

"The Confederates were very numerous in the neighborhood, and in fact that whole section of the country was filled with men from both sides, looking for each other. My companion and I were making our way cautiously through a bit of level country covered with pine, in an effort to locate a considerable force of the enemy. We had just wormed our way into a dense thicket and out again, when we were surprised and captured by four heavily armed guerrillas. We were taken a short distance to another spot in the woods, where there was a civilian who, with his team and wagon, had been captured. Leaving two of their companions to guard the captives, the other two guerrillas went back to the woods to return again very shortly with three more prisoners, stragglers from the Union lines. Again leaving the party under guard of two companions, the other two returned to the road for further prizes.

"Here it was that I communicated my intention to escape, telling my companions to watch me closely and keep by my side. Selecting an opportune moment, I sprang at the two guards, and, before they could fire their guns or otherwise give a signal, I

"I SPRANG AT THE TWO GUARDS."

was engaged in a sharp struggle with both. They were able bodied and well armed men, but my attack had been so sudden and well directed that almost in an instant I had both of their guns and had handed one to the civilian, who had kept right at my elbow. Just then the other two guerrillas returned hastily and before they could realize the situation the civilian and I both fired, each one dropping a man. At this moment the two disarmed guerrillas made their escape in one direction, while my five companions and myself made our escape in an opposite direction."

Upon getting clear of the woods, Traynor and his companion separated, while the other soldiers started toward the Union lines. Traynor and his companion resumed their scout, but had gone only a short distance when they were sighted by the escaped guerrillas and a squad of their companions and were pursued for more than two miles. At last, however, they made good their second escape by reaching the Union lines in safety.

CAPTURE OF A BUSHWHACKER OUTPOST

BENJAMIN THAKRAH,
Private, Co. H, 115th New York Infantry.
Born in Scotland in 1845.

JUST after the battle of Olustee, Fla., between the Federal forces commanded by General Seymore, and the Confederates under Generals Finnegan and Gardner—which was engaged in by 5,000 Union and as many more Southern soldiers—the town of Palatka was captured and was placed under provost guard, Company H, One hundred and fifteenth New York Infantry, with Captain S. P. Smith as provost marshal. All through the last week in February and the month of April, 1864, the town and its vicinity were continually harassed by bushwhackers, who raided plantations and dwellings, captured outposts, and stole stock and other property.

Just before sunrise, April 1, 1864, Company H was ordered out for roll call, after which the captain asked for twenty-five volunteers for an expedition up the river, the object being the capture of a Confederate picket known to be stationed about thirty-two miles away. Twenty-five men stepped forward promptly, after which they were ordered to get breakfast and put one day's rations into their haversacks. This was done and as the sun came up over the horizon the volunteers marched to the landing and went aboard a small tug boat in waiting. Among their number was Private Benjamin Thakrah, of Company H, who relates what followed:

"The picket guard we were after were well armed and mounted; thoroughly acquainted with the swamp-ridden country and its people and their habits; and were regularly relieved by details from the large force of cavalry which was in the neighborhood. Indeed, the utmost vigilance and quiet were required during the boat ride in order that the advance might not be discovered and reported in time to put the picket on guard. And so, with our soldiers lying under cover in the engine room, in the tiny cabin and in the wheel-house, the tug boat steamed along to within three miles of our destination, when we were pulled in small boats to a point near where the Confederate picket was stationed.

"On reaching shore, our squad, deployed as skirmishers, were required to proceed alternately through swamps with water to our waists and over little knolls which were fairly baking under the intense heat of the tropical sun, until we reached a house which stood half concealed by a hedge of small bushes and a board fence. Keeping out of sight as well as possible, we extended our line until it surrounded three sides of the place, feeling sure that the Southerners would not attempt to escape by way of the river front, because of alligators.

" WE PROCEEDED THROUGH SWAMPS — — — ".

"Working their way through the underbrush, the twenty-five Union men at last reached the fence, and I straightened up to look over, to find myself in front of and looking into the gun-barrel of a bushwhacker picket. With a quick movement I knocked aside the threatening weapon, my comrades arose around the entire enclosure and the Confederate who had confronted me was on the run for the house.

"Then our twenty-five men, with a yell, dashed over the fence, closed in about the house and demanded a surrender as the thoroughly astonished Confederates came out to capitulate. One of the bushwhackers had an unfinished letter in his hand, the last words written being: 'Everything is quiet along our lines.'

"The entire picket with its arms, horses and supplies was captured without firing a shot, and while doing this, a portion of our little party mounted some of the captured horses and rode out two miles, making prisoners of a sergeant and one man on vidette duty. By prompt use of the small boats all prisoners were placed under guard aboard the tug boat, while the horses were made to swim across the swamp and to the other side of the river. In doing this, two men rowed in each boat, two other men held the horses by the head as they were swimming, and a fifth man stood in the stern with plenty of loaded guns to keep the alligators from attacking them.

"After reaching the other side we made our way for a mile and a half through the swamp, where, as we were afterwards told, no man had ever trodden before.

"At every house on our return we stopped in search for bushwhackers. Our boys on the horses captured a mail carrier with what proved to be valuable letters, and we reached Palatka about sunset.

"While we were swimming the horses across the river, all who could be spared from that work were put on guard, and when the animals were over each told the other to 'come in.' One of the boys, unfortunately, did not hear the summons, and we left him on guard, not knowing until roll call that he was missing. After three days and nights he finally got into camp, having subsisted on wild oranges and berries, during his wearisome march, and was very much weakened by his exertions. He said we had not been away two hours before the Confederate cavalry were as thick in that vicinity as hairs on a dog."

ONE OF "SMITH'S GUERRILLAS"

JOHN H. COOK,
Sergeant, Co. A, 119th Illinois Infantry.
Born at London, England, 1840.

"I ASKED Sherman for 10,000 of his best men and he has sent me 10,000 damned guerrillas."

This severe criticism was expressed by General N. P. Banks, at a review of the troops of General Smith's Division, Sixteenth Army Corps, at Alexandria, in March, 1864.

It was brought on by the apparent lack of discipline, military drill, straggling manner and unsoldierly conduct of the men of this division, and directed especially to the One hundred and nineteenth Illinois Infantry, the colonel of which did not consider "soldierly show business" a necessary qualification of a brave army. However, the general's opinion clung to the division, and ever afterward to the end of the war the One hundred and nineteenth Illinois was designated as "Smith's Guerrillas." If this sobriquet was intended as an expression of contempt, the regiment soon found an opportunity to prove that it had been misjudged, and that its men were as valiant as any in the Union Army. This opportunity presented itself at the fighting at Pleasant Hill, La. After that "Smith's Guerrillas" in the Union ranks became a title of pride.

The Federal troops had captured Fort DeRussy, March 14, 1864, and occupied the surrounding territory. Nevertheless the situation was precarious because the low water, rapid current, frequent eddies and sways of the Red River made the handling of supplies a difficult and hazardous task.

On the morning of April 9, 1864—after fighting all the previous day near Sabine Cross-Roads the Confederates found themselves confronted at Pleasant Hill with the re-enforcement of Smith's Division, in which was the One hundred and nineteenth Illinois posted in the woods on the extreme left. John H. Cook, sergeant of Company A of that regiment, was on that day detailed as clerk at headquarters, and in the following narrates what occurred:

"The thought of being a noncombatant was distasteful, and so, arming myself with a Sharps rifle, I took my place as sergeant in the rear of my company. I was without canteen, haversack or blanket, having only a good big plug of tobacco, my rifle and forty rounds.

"The position assigned my regiment was on the extreme left of the line, my company being posted in advance as skirmishers in the woods. We lay in this position from early in the morning until about three o'clock in the afternoon, witnessing from our commanding position the battle on the right and center. We were ordered to hold our position at all hazards, as a flank movement of the enemy was expected at any moment, which we must stubbornly resist before falling back.

"Our army had a disadvantage as to ground ; the position could be easily turned, we could not occupy it long for want of water. About five o'clock the Confederates, having been heavily re-enforced, made a furious assault on us, hammered in our center, doubled up our right, and fell vigorously on our left, which was the weakest part of General Emory's position. There was nothing left to stop the cyclone now but 'Smith's Guerrillas,' and it seemed that we in the woods were to be flanked and the whole army bagged. A sickening feeling came over me as I took in the situation.

"It was not long after we began to move farther into the galling fire that we could see our division in the center of the field advancing in a gallant charge. The rebels were coming through the woods to flank us. It looked like ten to one against us. Brave Lieutenant 'Jack' Ware took command of our skirmish line, and ordered me to lead the center of the line.

"Advancing under a heavy musketry fire, and rapidly firing, I turned back to cheer

"WAVING MY HAT IN MY LEFT, I RAN FORWARD."

on the boys, when I saw John McIntyre, a brave and sturdy Scotchman (he was the pet and pride of Company A) throw up his left hand and fall forward. I ran back to him and saw that he had been instantly killed. Then I was mad clear through. I ran forward again, rapidly firing my breech-loader. In a moment a musketry fire was focused on me; the bullets whizzed around me thick. One went through my hat, another through my right coat-sleeve, and one so close to my cheek that I could feel it burn. But I cared nothing for life or death—I was in to stay. It seemed to me just then that if our little company did not hold its ground we should be flanked, and our army defeated, and that if I did not do my duty, and cheer our boys, they might not stand. I had fired my 'forty rounds'—my last cartridge was gone. I raised my empty breech-loader in my right hand, and, waving my hat in my left, ran forward, cheering on the boys. I felt a good deal as General Corse ex-expressed himself in his famous dispatch to General Sherman: 'I am out of provisions, I have lost an ear and part of a cheek-bone, but I can whip all hell yet!'

"Well, our boys rallied. It was a sudden rush. We took a number of prisoners and the 'rebs' gave way. Re-enforcements came up, and soon our whole line advanced, and Company A on the skirmish line shared fully in the victory of Pleasant Hill."

A BATTLE BRIEF BUT BLOODY

Two hundred Union men killed and wounded within a few minutes!

This is the record of the engagement at Cane River Crossing, La., than which, considering its brief duration, there was no fiercer or more bloody struggle during the entire war.

The Confederates were in a strongly fortified position; the Union forces had orders to drive them out. The two hostile bodies clashed April 24, 1864.

First Lieutenant William S. Beebe, of the Ordnance Department of the army, was the officer whose leadership won brilliant victory for the Federals on that memorable occasion. He led the One hundred and seventy-third New York Volunteers, commanded by Colonel Conrady, and so conspicuously distinguished himself that he was brevetted a captain and awarded the Medal of Honor.

WILLIAM S. BEEBE,
First Lieutenant, Ordnance Dept., U. S. A.
Highest rank attained: Major.
Born at Ithaca, New York, in 1841.

The details of the assault are told by Lieutenant Beebe himself as follows:

"I was ordered by the Chief of Staff to join the assaulting column, to urge the necessity of instant attack, as I knew our rear-guard was then engaged and we had to lay a pontoon-bridge to cross Cane River. The division was deployed for attack on Monett's Bluff; I stated the necessity of instant assault and offered to lead it. The offer was declined, but on its renewal promptly accepted. I was the first man on the bluff. The color-guard immediately behind me lost five men out of eight, and the killed and wounded in an affair of ten minutes were about two hundred."

HE KEPT HIS COLORS FLYING

ABRAM J. BUCKLES,
Sergeant, Co. E, 19th Indiana Infantry.
Born in Delaware Co., Ind., Aug. 2, 1846.

ABRAM J. BUCKLES was a sergeant in Company E, Nineteenth Indiana Volunteers, which, with the Twenty-fourth Michigan, the Second, Sixth and Seventh Wisconsin, formed the Iron Brigade, so-called, an organization composed of young farmers, lumbermen and sailors. A sturdier lot of soldiers it was impossible to find in the whole Union Army. This brigade was engaged in the battle of the Wilderness, where it sustained its enviable reputation. The Nineteenth Indiana especially gave a good account of itself, and one of its members, the aforementioned Sergeant Buckles, became a Medal of Honor hero on that memorable occasion. Though wounded in the shoulder at Gettysburg, he remained in active service. As to the fighting at the battle of the Wilderness and the incident which links his name to the struggle, Sergeant Buckles says:

"My regiment was on the first line, and, after executing some hurried movements on the morning of May 5th, was finally drawn in line of battle on the edge of the great wilderness. We were on the first line and were among the first engaged. Expecting an attack momentarily, we had thrown up a formidable line of breastworks, and the exertions thus made had started some loose bones in my shoulder. I sat down, stripped my clothes back and with a small pair of pincers I carried I pulled the fragments of bone out. Just then we got the order to advance and away we went down into the dense woods, and almost immediately striking the enemy's line of battle, we struck them hard, Iron Brigade fashion, and drove them back

---

The Wilderness.—When Grant assumed supreme command of the Federal Army his objective was Richmond, Va., and the destruction of Lee's army. His forces, consisting of about 122,000 troops and 350 guns, were confronted by Lee with a force of 62,000 men, and over 200 guns, at the Wilderness on May 5-7, 1864. This battle, which included engagements at Brock Road, Craig's Meeting House, Furnaces, Parker's Store, and Todd's Tavern, was the first of the battles of the march to Richmond.

On the 5th, Grant had fairly crossed the Rapidan River, and, having met with no opposition, pushed on through the wilderness, unconscious of the close proximity of Lee's Army. Lee, however, suspecting Grant's movement, gave him battle in the dense forest, where the fight continued throughout the day.

Early on the morning of the 6th the fight was renewed, the desperate struggle being carried on in the now burning woods. At the close of this day's battle the relative strength of the opposing armies remained about as at first; and the only decisive gain was a slight one on the Union side.

During the night of the 6th Lee's army had withdrawn, and as it showed no disposition to fight again on the 7th, Grant gave orders to move toward Spottsylvania Court House.

The losses sustained during the two days' fight were about 15,000 on each side.

until we reached a cleared place, where our line stopped to reform. Meanwhile the Johnnies crossed the clearing and posted themselves in a dense thicket. Up to this time I had been unable, because of the bushes and trees, to unfurl my colors, but on coming into the clearing I loosened its folds and shook the regiment's flag free to the breeze. From their covered position the enemy had begun to pour a withering fire into us, comrades were dropping at every hand and delay was fatal, while retreat was never dreamed of. The only possible safety lay in a charge, and believing that a short, quick rush with such a line as we had, a heavy one, would force the Confederates to fly, I ran to the front. Waving the flag above my head, I called on the boys to follow. To a man they responded, and together we dashed toward the troublesome thicket. We were going in fine style when I was struck, shot through the body. I fell, but managed to keep the flag up until little John Divelbus, one of the color-guard and as brave a man as ever lived, took it out of my hands, to be killed a few minutes later. I believed I had received my death blow, but I realize now that instead I won the Medal of Honor."

"OUR COLORS ARE DOWN!"

CHARLES E. MORSE,
Sergeant, Co. I, 62d New York Infantry.
Born in France, May 5, 1841.

AT the battle of the Wilderness Company I of the Sixty-second New York Infantry, known as the Anderson Zouaves, held a position on the left center of the regiment next to the color-guard. In the absence of a commissioned officer, Sergeant Charles E. Morse was in command of the company, which consisted of but fifteen men. The regiment was ordered to advance and charge the enemy, and carried out the order so successfully that the Confederates were driven back to their first line of defense. They were given no chance to rally and had to retreat to their second line. Then they stopped, made a stand, and by desperate fighting prevented the regiment's further advance. All efforts to dislodge the rebels were futile ; they were posted too strongly on the ridge. At the same time their fire became so destructive that the regiment was ordered to fall back to the rifle pits. Though this movement was carried out in perfect order, the Confederates concluded that the men were in full retreat and at once started in hot pursuit. They failed to bring the lines of the New York regiment into disorder, however, and the men continued to fall back, all the time loading, facing about and firing. Presently the color-sergeant was struck by a ball. He staggered, reeled and dropped, covering the colors with his body. Then someone shouted: "The colors are down!" Consternation followed the outcry. Two men at once broke out of the ranks and started toward the spot where the dying color-sergeant lay. The rebels, too, were rapidly approaching the coveted spot. Who would be the first to reach it, the enemy or the daring New Yorkers? The latter were Corporal Deitzel and Sergeant Morse. Morse was first at the side of his almost lifeless comrade and in an instant secured the precious colors. He was soon joined by Deitzel and both then retreated to their lines, holding the enemy at a safe distance by keeping up a well-directed fire. In the retreat Sergeant Morse was shot in the knee, but notwithstanding the painful wound he pluckily remained with his company all during the subsequent fighting, carrying aloft the banner he had so heroically saved.

THEIR HEROISM WAS INFECTIOUS

LEOPOLD KARPELES,
Sergeant, Co. E, 57th Mass. Infantry.
Born at Prague, Bohemia, Sept. 9, 1838.

Heroism is a virtue under any circumstance, but to be heroic in the hour of reverse and disaster is the noblest kind of valor. During the battle of the Wilderness, May 6, 1864, two Union soldiers furnished examples of bravery which belongs to this latter category. They are First Sergeant Edmund English, of Company C, Second New Jersey Infantry, and Sergeant Leopold Karpeles, of Company E, Fifty-seventh Massachusetts Infantry. Both accomplished the most unexpected and truly extraordinary results at the most critical time of the battle, when the disintegration of the Union forces had set in, demoralization prevailed and the Federals were fleeing in wild disorder. During this mad rush for the rear the Second New Jersey, along with other regiments, had been ordered to fall back. The command aroused Sergeant English's indignation. "Is there nobody to make a stand?" he exclaimed. "This is disgraceful!"

He decided to act on his own responsibility, even though it be insubordination. Quickly he seized the colors of his regiment, placed himself in front of the men, waved the colors high in the air and shouted: "Here, boys! Stand here! At least a few of us should stem the tide!"

His bravery was infectious; the men caught his spirit and one by one rallied around the flag, till at last quite a little band was gathered about the sergeant. They did not only "stem the tide," but repulsed and drove the Confederates back in wild confusion.

While this was taking place at one point of the line of battle, Sergeant Karpeles' similar conduct brought about a similar result in another place. He was the color-sergeant of his regiment and keenly felt the humiliation of soldiers deserting their colors.

"Our troops were rushing wildly to the rear," the brave sergeant narrates. "In vain did our colonel take a stand and call the boys to rally. I joined our colonel, waved the flag and likewise called on my comrades to halt and form on us. We held our position until we had gathered a sufficient force to make a charge. Presently the colonel commanded: 'Forward,' and he and I dashed ahead, I waving our flag high in the air. Our advance was entirely unexpected. It completely dazed the Confederates and brought their advance to an end. We held our position till nightfall, when we fell back in good order and reorganized our forces."

EDMUND ENGLISH,
1st Sergeant, Co. C, 2d N. J. Inf.
Highest rank attained: Captain.
Born at Cappanhite, Ireland,
Nov. 16, 1841.

DETERMINED TO FIGHT THOUGH WOUNDED

JACOB E. SWAP,
Private, Co. H, 83d Penn. Infantry.
Born at Coeymans, Albany Co., N. Y., August 12, 1846.

ON the first of May, 1864, the Eighty-third Pennsylvania Infantry broke camp at Rappahannock Station, Va., and started on the march.

Private Jacob E. Swap, a member of this regiment, had been placed on the sick list and ordered to report at the hospital, but declined to do so, whereupon the surgeon allowed him to follow the regiment on its march, in an ambulance. Upon the third day of his ride, while still convalescing, he determined to join his company. He secured a gun and a cartridge box and started to carry out his intentions, when a lieutenant of his company observed him. He immediately took the gun from Swap, who was again ordered to the rear. This time he remained there until the 5th, two days later, when he again overtook his company, just as they were unslinging their knapsacks for a charge in the Wilderness. As he stepped into the ranks, armed and ready, his lieutenant asked him where he was going.

"I'm going with the boys," replied Swap.

"Remain here and guard these knapsacks," the lieutenant ordered.

Swap, after several fruitless entreaties, reluctantly obeyed, while his comrades dashed away on the charge. They soon returned in disorder, and reformed for a second charge.

"I then saw that I had an opportunity to get into the fight," says Private Swap, "and I asked a group of my comrades whether there was one among them who would let me have his gun. One of them immediately said: 'Here, take it, I've had enough of this,' whereupon I joined in the charge.

"I was now permitted to stay in the ranks, and fought with the company on the 6th, 7th, and 8th, in the fights around the Wilderness.

"On the 8th, while we were charging on the breastworks at Spottsylvania Court House, I was wounded five times, when within a few yards of the enemy, after which I fired one more shot and then threw my gun over at the enemy.

"My wounds prevented me from gaining the rear, where I now wanted to be, and I was captured and sent to Richmond."

SHOT THE REBEL COLOR-BEARER

PATRICK De LACY,
First Sergeant, Co. A, 143d Penn. Volunteers.
Highest rank attained : Captain.
Born in Carbondale, Lackawanna Co., Pa., Nov. 25, 1834.

THE repelling of Longstreet's charge and re-taking of the Confederate lines and battery on the second day of the battle of the Wilderness were among the most thrilling episodes of the entire series of wild fights. There had been charges and repulses all forenoon and until afternoon, the Federals and Confederates moving forward and falling back alternately, until, with the ammunition entirely exhausted, the cartridge boxes of the dead soldiers were the chief resource.

At last the One hundred and forty-third Pennsylvania Infantry of Wadsworth's Division were able to halt, stack arms at the intersection of the Brock and Plank Roads and prepare their meals. Colonel Musser having been killed, Major Charles Conyngham was in command. After a rest of about an hour an order came from General Hancock directing the brigade, in command of Colonel Irwin, to save the works at the Cross-Roads, upon which Longstreet's forces were then advancing at a charge. Sergeant Patrick De Lacy, of Company A of the aforementioned regiment, in command of the company, instantly led the right of the brigade and regimental line in the advance, his men answering with a mighty yell, as they followed. As to what then happened a graphic description by one of the participants is appended:

"Away we went, double-quick, toward the woods to the left of the Plank Road, Longstreet's advance being eighty rods or so still farther to our left coming down the Brock Road. On we pushed up toward the burned clearing, under a terrific fire and with our brave comrades falling on every side. Still De Lacy kept the lead until, when right up to the works, with the Confeder-

"DASHING UP TO HIM SEIZED THE FLAG."

ates in line along the woods and keeping up their heavy fire, he made a dash to our left of fifteen or eighteen rods, right between the fires, to the edge of the works. There he found a rebel waving his colors, and, dashing up to him, seized the flag and shot the color-bearer down in plain sight of both sides. The colors dropped, and a panic followed among the Southerners for a brief period, but long enough for our regiment and brigade to reach the works and hold them. The charge had been a grand one all along the line, but it was in a very great measure inspired and encouraged by De Lacy's daring and heroism while under the concentrated fire of the enemy. His escape was a miracle, his achievement one of those incidents in the history of actual warfare which causes one to bubble over with admiration for the hero."

A RESCUE UNDER DIFFICULTIES

STEPHEN WELCH,
Sergeant, Co. C, 154th New York Volunteer Infantry.
Born at Groton, Tompkins Co., N. Y., June 14, 1824.

CHARLES W. McKAY,
Sergeant, Co. C, 154th New York Volunteer Infantry.
Born at Mansfield, N. Y., Jan. 25, 1847.

"ON the 9th of May, 1864," narrates Sergeant Stephen Welch, of Company C, One hundred and fifty-fourth New York Volunteer Infantry, "the enemy was found in a strong position at a place called Rocky Face Ridge, near Dalton, Ga. In the afternoon the brigade was got in readiness for inspection of said ridge. A few of my company were detailed to act as skirmishers. We advanced slowly and cautiously, covering ourselves as best we could till we got within four rods of a perpendicular palisade crowning the top of the ridge. I found protection behind a rock, from which point I could occasionally see three or four of the enemy on top of the hill, and had a chance to discharge my gun in that direction. Meanwhile the brigade came up, our regiment on the right. They all went up to the perpendicular palisade of rock, some going up the crevices and to death. After about half an hour the bugler sounded a recall, and the brigade went down that hill much faster than it had gone up, but soon we got into proper order again. About this time the major came along and told me that he had seen a wounded soldier of my company, between the lines, adding that I had better get someone to help me go up and get him. Taking a tent-mate, Sergeant Charles W. McKay, we started out under a heavy fire, not only from the enemy, but also from our own lines. We found George Greek, a corporal of the color-guard, badly wounded in both legs. The poor

---

Coincident with the beginning of Grant's campaign in the Wilderness began the great campaign best known as **Sherman's March to the Sea.** On the 7th of May, 1864, with a force of 100,000 men, General Sherman advanced from Chattanooga, forcing back the Confederate General, Johnston, who had an army of 60,000 men. Dalton, Resaca, Dallas, Lost Mountain, the Great and Little Kenesaw Mountains were the stands taken by the retreating Confederates, and were engagements in which they were outnumbered, outflanked and defeated. On the 22d of June, General Hood made an attack on the Union center and was repulsed with heavy loss. Five days later, General Sherman attempted to carry the Great Kenesaw Mountain, but was repulsed, losing 3,000 men. He then resumed his former tactics, outflanked the enemy and compelled him to retreat across the Chattahoochee. By the 10th of July, the whole Confederate army had retired within the defenses of Atlanta.

"THE POOR FELLOW HAD BEEN
TRYING TO DRAG HIMSELF
ALONG WITH HIS HANDS."

fellow had been trying to drag himself along with his hands, and had sunk down, overcome by faintness and exhaustion. McKay revived him with a drink from his canteen, after which the corporal, raising himself on his elbow, asked if the colors were safe. We assured him that they were, and he dropped down again, satisfied and happy. We rolled him on a blanket, picked him up, and with bullets whizzing about us, managed to get him off the field."

HE CHECKED THE PANIC

ROBERT S. ROBERTSON,
1st Lieutenant, 93d N. Y. Volunteers
Highest rank attained: Colonel,
U. S. Volunteers.
Born at Argyle, April 16, 1839.

THE engagement at Corbin's Creek was preliminary to the battle of Spottsylvania. Lieutenant Robertson gives an account of the very creditable conduct of his brigade as well as his own experience on this occasion :

"By a rapid march early in the morning of May 8, 1864, the Second Army Corps, to which I was attached as aide-de-camp, gained the road which the Fifth Corps had just passed. We reached Todd's Tavern, Va., our destination, at nine, when our Corps was aligned on the Brock Road and across the Catherpen, to prevent an expected attempt on the part of Lee to cut our marching column in two.

"Soon our brigade was pushed out through the hot pine woods to a valley, through which runs Corbin's Creek. Here on a brow of the upland we halted for a time and the picket line was posted to guard the approaches in that direction. Hardly had it been posted in a road which runs down to the valley, separated from us by a stream bordered with a dense growth of bushes and tangled vines, before it was thought necessary to extend the line further to our right, to cover another by-way there. That duty fell to me.

"The work was done, and I was riding down the road to an opening in the bushes where the stream could be crossed, when I found a line of battle moving toward me and toward our position. There was no escape except through the gap they were rapidly approaching, and no time was to be lost, for if they reached the opening before me, my march would end in Richmond as a prisoner of war.

"They evidently believed I was coming to surrender, for they invited me to join them in terms the politest of which were: 'Come in, you damned Yank, we'll take

---

Spottsylvania—On the 7th of May, 1864, after the battle of the Wilderness, the Union Army began its march toward Spottsylvania, Va. Grant, who, on his way to Richmond, had hoped to pass around Lee's right wing, found on the 8th the whole Confederate Army massing about a mile to the north and east of Spottsylvania directly in his front. Little was done by either army on this and the next day, except the strengthening of works and the posting of troops. On the 10th Grant resolved to attack Lee, and accordingly ordered attacks all along the line, the most notable of which was Upton's storming party. The armies rested on the following day, on the evening of which Grant ordered an assault for the next morning. After a difficult night march, Hancock pressed on and in a hand-to-hand fight rushed upon the enemy's breastworks and captured a whole division of Ewell's Corps. Lee hastened re-enforcements to Ewell and at this point, the "Bloody Angle," the battle raged all day and until 3 o'clock on the morning of the 13th. The Confederates tried vainly to dislodge the Union troops by massing heavily on Lee's broken line, but finally took a position in rear of his former one, and there entrenched himself.

This last twenty-four hours' fight closed the eight days' battle around Spottsylvania, the Federal Army losing 8,000 men and the Confederates about the same number.

good care of you.' But the opening was reached and I showed my horse's tail, and his speed as we galloped up the hill. Scattering volleys were fired, but the rebels were too excited to aim well, and shot wildly. At the top of the hill was a rail fence. The horse leaped it finely, but the saddle girth had become loose, the saddle turned, and I fell. To mount again was only the work of a moment, for the dread of a rebel prison almost gives one wings. The volleys meant for me had roused the brigade, which greeted me with hearty cheers as I rode into the line with my saddle under my horse instead of under me.

"The attacking column appeared, but halted to make proper dispositions for the attack, and we were ordered to a better position a little to the rear. Shortly after another rebel brigade was discovered moving on our right flank, and we had to prepare for an attack on our right and the one in our front at the same time. Re-enforcements were sent for, and we prepared to defend ourselves as best we could until they should arrive.

"The brigades in front moved steadily up the slope, their muskets at a ready. Gallant Colonel McKeen, of the Thirty-first Pennsylvania, had charge of that part of that line with his own regiment and the Twenty-sixth Michigan. He sat on his horse, calmly speaking words of encouragement to his men, many of whom were recruits who had never been under fire before.

"The 'ki-yi-yi' of the Confederates was not answered until their line was close upon us. Then a volley answered their triumphant yells, sending many to their long home, but they closed their ranks and marched steadily on. McKeen met them with another volley, which drove them down the hill. Now commenced hot work on the right. Here were the Sixty-first New York and the One hundred and fortieth and One hundred and eighty-third Pennsylvania, under General Miles in person. The Confederates charged and nearly drove in our center (the One hundred and eighty-third Pennsylvania) which broke and drifted to the rear. The staff tried to drive and coax the frightened men. I at once seized the colors from the frightened guard and rode with them in the face of the enemy to their former place. This checked the panic and inspired the men. The regiment rallied on its colors; the line was saved, and our little brigade was proud, for we had whipped two brigades of Mahone's Division before any re-enforcements reached us, and we were received with hearty cheers as we filled the trenches. We had lost nearly two hundred men, and were obliged to leave our dead upon the field."

RESCUED HIS COMRADE

MOSES A. LUCE,
Sergeant, Co. E, Fourth Michigan Infantry.
Born in Adams Co., Ill., in 1842.

"THE battle of Laurel Hill, as it is termed, was in reality a part of the battle of Spottsylvania, and is so known historically," writes Sergeant Moses A. Luce, of Company E, Fourth Michigan Infantry. "Laurel Hill was a slight elevation situated in front of the right of our army, and occupied by the Confederate army behind earthworks thrown up by them during the two previous days. Early in the morning of May 10, 1864, our regiment, containing at that time about one hundred men, and the Twenty-second Massachusetts Infantry, were designated to lead an assault on the works in front of our line. We were supported by the division drawn up in line at a short distance back of us. The morning was foggy. We were advanced close to our picket line upon a slight elevation, leaving a small valley between us and the enemy. Our muskets were unloaded, bayonets fixed, and we thus awaited the order to charge. A light wind suddenly broke the fog in front of us, when we were hastily ordered forward without any supports and were immediately observed by the enemy, who opened fire upon us from their picket line and also from their artillery. Charging rapidly toward the enemy and receiving a fire of canister and grape from their cannon, the greater portion of which, however, passed over our heads, we broke through their picket line, and paying no further attention to them pushed on to the foot of the main breastworks of the enemy. At this point the musketry of the enemy opened upon us with terrible effect. Five out of seven of my company, of which I was in command, were struck by this fire, and the assaulting column, being unsupported, fell back in disorder.

"Although not wounded, I fell prostrate into a ditch running down the hillside, where I remained possibly a minute listening to the whiz of the balls over my head and the cries of the wounded and the yells of the enemy. I was in comparative safety in the ditch, but if I remained I would be taken prisoner, and the horrors of Andersonville were then pictured in dreadful detail. I concluded to run the risk of escaping, and, rising with my musket in my hand, a ball struck the stock, which I held, and another ball cut the skin just over my eye. With all the speed I had I ran down the hillside and across the valley, under the fire of the enemy, and succeeded in reaching the first rifle pit of our pickets and leaped into it. The enemy leaped over their works, and with yells started to charge down the slope, but they were met by such a heavy fire that they soon retired. The cannonading continued at intervals on both sides with the musketry fire in broken volleys. Hearing a cry for help from some wounded soldier who lay very close to the picket rifle pits of the enemy, I asked who it was. Upon hearing that it was Sergeant La Fleur, I at once responded to his call, dropping my musket, however, and running forward toward the spot where he lay. When I reached him he was lying prostrate on the ground, with his leg broken below the knee by a grapeshot, and was bleeding profusely. He was a smaller man than I, and I tried to lift him in my arms, but finding that impossible I kneeled down and told him to get his arms about my neck and get on my back, I remaining on my hands and knees. Then rising, and in a stooping position, I carried him rapidly to the rear of our line. Here I found several men and one or two officers, and having stanched the flow of blood I returned to our rifle pits."

"LET'S SAVE OUR COMRADE!"

HOWELL B. TREAT,
Sergeant, Co. I, 52d Ohio Infantry.
Born at Painesville, Lake Co., O., in 1833.

Sergeant Howell B. Treat, of Company I, Fifty-second Ohio Infantry, won the admiration of his comrades and of his superior officers by his conduct during the engagement at Buzzard's Roost, Ga., May 11, 1864. He was on the skirmish line braving a most galling fire. Many a brave Union soldier lost his life or was wounded on that occasion. In almost every instance it was possible to bring the injured to the rear, but at one time during the charge one of Sergeant Treat's comrades was wounded and left on the field close to the rebel works.

The sergeant could not endure the sight of one of his men, covered with blood and unable to move, being made a target for further shots from the enemy.

"Boys, let us save our comrade!" he exclaimed. Immediately two men announced their willingness to accompany the sergeant.

Unheedful of the shower of bullets and terrific fire of musketry, they started for the rebel works, but had not proceeded far when the two privates were stricken down by well directed bullets, leaving Sergeant Treat alone to carry out the mission of mercy. Three times this brave soldier was struck by rebel balls, one passing through his hat above the right ear, and two going clear through the blouse, each bullet inflicting a painful though not serious wound. However he persisted in reaching his wounded comrade and succeeded in assisting him safely back to the Union lines. Cheers greeted the gallant rescuer and rescued as they returned.

WOULD HE HAVE TAKEN THE WHOLE BRIGADE?

ON the morning of May 26, 1864, Colonel Thomas C. Devin led the Second Brigade, First Division, Cavalry Corps, from Pole Cat Creek to Mangohick Church, Va., where a halt was made for several hours. The march was then taken up again and the Pamunkey River reached at a point opposite Hanover Town, Va., at daybreak the following morning. After crossing the pontoon bridge the Federals went into position on the hill to the right and in front of Hanover Town. The Seventeenth Pennsylvania thereupon was ordered to the right to support a regiment of the First Brigade, which then was advancing upon and skirmishing with the enemy. While a squadron of the Ninth New York was ordered to the extreme right to cover the flank of the Seventeenth Pennsylvania, as the Confederates showed no disposition to engage the Union forces and retired into the woods, Colonel Devin ordered part of the squadron of the Ninth New York to charge the retreating rebels. Their pickets were driven across the creek and over the opposite hill, where nearly a whole brigade of South Carolina Cavalry was attempting to get into position.

First Lieutenant John T. Rutherford, of Troop L, Ninth New York Cavalry, led the charging column. Upon finding that the bridge had been destroyed, he jumped his horse into the creek, forded it, followed by his command; and, attacking the rebels, drove them back on their reserve, where they became entangled with their train. Taking advantage of the enemy's confusion and disorder, Lieutenant Rutherford demanded the surrender of the whole brigade. This bold demand so staggered the Confederates that they were unable to gather enough energy to resist it, and were about to comply, when one of their officers with more courage than discretion called on his men not to be cowards and to form into line.

In a second Lieutenant Rutherford was at the officer's side and with one well-directed shot, which killed his horse, had him lying on the ground. The officer regained his feet, however, and Rutherford then struck at him with his now empty pistol. The Confederate's sabre parried the assault, but the next moment Rutherford landed a telling blow on his opponent's head and placed him hors de combat. The rebel surrendered and was sent to the rear.

The capture of their officer dismayed the rebels and they offered no further resistance. Then the small body of Union cavalry found itself in a peculiar position. How could they think of successfully bringing to their lines such large numbers of prisoners?

Not desiring to take chances or run any risk, they picked out some 100 prisoners and fell back upon the brigade.

Colonel Devin smiled as he received the victorious New Yorkers.

"Did you intend to take the whole brigade?" he asked Lieutenant Rutherford.

"I would, if I had enough men to guard them," was the reply.

"I believe it," the Colonel observed as he shook the brave lieutenant's hand.

HE STRUCK AT HIM WITH HIS EMPTY PISTOL.

In explanation of this unique duel it should be stated that while fording the creek Lieutenant Rutherford broke his belt and lost his sabre and that, therefore, the pistol was his only weapon.

Two weeks prior to this incident, Lieutenant Rutherford distinguished himself in a like manner, when during an engagement between General Merritt's Federal and General Stuarts Confederate Cavalry Divisions at Yellow Tavern, Va., he led his squadron in a dashing charge on the rebels, completely routing them and capturing ninety prisoners.

For both these brave acts he was awarded the Medal of Honor

HEROIC ARTILLERY WORK OF A VOLUNTEER

"ON the 12th of May, during the battle of Spott-sylvania," says Sergeant John P. Beech of Company B, Fourth New Jersey Infantry, "General Upton ordered a battery of artillery to take a position on his right to sweep the large open field in front of the 'Bloody Angle.' Lieutenant Metcalf's Section of Battery C, Fifth U. S. Artillery, immediately advanced into position, but the enemy's fire was so heavy the men and horses fell like leaves in autumn.

"Both our regiment and the rebels on our left were now advancing toward the clearing in front of the 'Angle,' the objective point for each being Met-calf's unlucky section. Upon seeing the critical position they were in and that all the men except Lieu-

JOHN P. BEECH,
Sergeant, Co. B, 4th N. J. Infantry.
Born at Derbyshire, Eng., May 1, 1844.

tenant Metcalf and Sergeant Lines had been killed or wounded, I laid down my musket and volunteered to go and help work the gun. I received permission to go, and upon reaching it proceeded to serve ammunition. We had but four charges of canister left, when a Mississippi regiment came charging down upon us, but we worked that gun as fast as it was possible for three men to work it. The rebels came to within 100 feet of us, and after giving them our four charges of canister we followed that up with spherical case and shell, until our ammunition was exhausted, when Lieutenant Metcalf ordered up the limber, but as it was coming forward the horses were shot down. A well-directed fire from the infantry behind a crest prevented the Mississippi regiment's farther advance, and for eighteen hours the fight continued at this point. In the meantime a body of our regiment finally got the piece off the field, leaving the limber there until the next day."

OBEYED AN ILL-ADVISED ORDER

LEWIS S. WISNER,
Captain, Co. K, 124th New York Infantry.
Born at Middleton, N. Y., Aug. 11, 1841.

He who stands ready to sacrifice himself rather than endanger the lives of those entrusted to his care is a most illustrious hero. The conduct of Captain Lewis S. Wisner, of Company K, One hundred and Twenty-fourth New York Infantry, engineer officer on General J. H. Hobart Ward's staff during the battle of Spottsylvania, brings him within that type of lofty military heroes.

About nine o'clock in the morning of May 12 he received written orders from the division engineer officer to lower the breastworks near the "Bloody Angle" eighteen inches in front of one of the Union batteries, which was engaged in raking the tree-tops to dislodge the rebel sharpshooters.

One side of these works was occupied by the Confederate, the other by the Union troops, and so severe was the fire at this portion of the line that a large oak tree was completely cut in two by musketry fire alone.

Captain Wisner proceeded to the breastworks, placed his men in a position of safety and reported his orders to the commanding officer of the battery. The latter received the captain with scorn.

"Lower the works?" he exclaimed. "I'll train my gun upon the man, and blow him to 'Kingdom Come,' who dares touch the works."

Captain Wisner handed him his written orders and retorted: "Here are my orders, sir. They will be obeyed, guns or no guns." And he at once proceeded to carry out his instructions.

The top of the works was capped with a heavy log raised a few inches to make a loop through which the infantry might fire. Placing two men at each end of the log, the captain ordered it to be removed. Having been wired at each end to the adjoining logs and also on the side where the Confederates were, the removal of the log could not be accomplished.

Captain Wisner was fully convinced that instant death awaited anyone who attempted to remove the obstruction, and refused to expose his men to any such danger. "I'll do it myself," he said. Provided with an ax obtained from one of his detail, he leaped to the top of the breastworks and, with one well-directed blow, severed one end of the log. He ran quickly to the other end and cut the log at that point. He escaped unhurt, but his clothes were riddled with bullets in many places. Thus the breastworks were lowered, the order obeyed, but someone had blundered!

The commander of the battery asked Captain Wisner if he would not replace the log in its former position, and the brave captain, impressed with the necessity of the request, complied. "You have accomplished the most heroic act I ever witnessed, Captain," said the battery commander as he grasped Wisner's hand.

"I'LL DO IT MYSELF," HE SAID.

WILLIAM W. NOYES,
Private, Co. F, Second Vermont Infantry.
Born at Montpelier, Vt., 1864.

AVENGED HIS COMRADE'S DEATH

ONE of the most dramatic incidents of the battle of Spottsylvania is summed up in the following words by General L. A. Grant:

"The struggle at the 'Angle' was emphatically a hand-to-hand fight. Scores were shot down within a few feet of the death-dealing muskets in the very face of the enemy. Some men clubbed their muskets, and in some instances used clubs and rails. In this way the brigade was engaged for eight hours. The slaughter of the enemy was terrible. Behind their traverses and in the pits and holes they had dug for protection, the rebel dead were found piled up on one another. Some of the wounded were almost entirely buried by the dead bodies of their companions that had fallen upon them."

Private William W. Noyes, of the Second Vermont Infantry, augments the foregoing description by the following pen-picture of the part he played in this battle:

"We had reached the 'Bloody Angle'—a pile of logs, with a slight embankment on the inner side. There the Johnnies were, just over the pile, while we lay in the slout in front. Muskets were pushed through the openings between the logs and fired right into the faces of our men. Suddenly, right near where I was lying, one of the Confederates raised a white rag or handkerchief fastened to the end of his musket. Some of our men took it for a flag of truce and one of them raised his head over the breastworks, when with a cheer the Johnnies emptied their muskets into the poor fellow, killing him instantly.

"Infuriated beyond control by such treachery and determined upon revenge, I called on the men near me to load their pieces as rapidly as possible and hand them up to me. Then I jumped to the top of the breastworks and killed the rebel nearest to me in such short order that the others became, for a moment, completely bewildered, and were unable to use their weapons. My comrades handed up their guns so rapidly that I was constantly kept busy. The enemy did not seem to regain their wits until I had fired five or six shots. They then began shooting at me, but for some reason they proved to be poor marksmen, and I continued to fire at them until a bullet knocked my hat off, when I jumped back to my former position. John Grant, one of my comrades, then mounted the embankment and fired a shot, but was immediately killed by a Confederate bullet which pierced his heart. Upon counting afterward, we found that fifteen guns had been emptied during this brief and peculiar assault."

LOST IN THE WOODS -- JOINED ANOTHER REGIMENT

"ON the night of May 11, 1864, the Army of the Potomac was encamped facing the entrenched works of the enemy at Spottsylvania, and ready for a charge at daybreak. I was detailed on the picket line and took my position on the extreme left."

The foregoing is related by Sergeant William H. Wilcox, of Company G, Ninth New Hampshire Infantry, who, recalling an interesting incident from the battlefield, continues:

"At daybreak the charge was made, the pickets being instantly converted into a skirmish line and sent in advance of the corps to ascertain the position of the enemy's picket line. We located the Confederates strongly entrenched just across a creek in the woods and at once engaged their pickets, who, in spite of a stout resistance, were soon swept away by the advancing corps.

WILLIAM H. WILCOX,
Sergeant, Co. G, 9th New Hampshire Infantry.
Born in Lempster, Sullivan Co., N. H.

"During this conflict Lieutenant Rice, the only commissioned officer with my company, my brother and several others were wounded.

"I stopped long enough to assure myself that my brother was able to walk and take care of himself, and so, bidding him good-bye, started with a corporal and a private to overtake my company, which I had seen entering the woods.

"We pressed on through the dense forest, where solid shot and exploding shells were screaming over our heads, and cutting twigs, limbs and even great tree-tops, which fell in showers about us. Thus marching for about an hour with the roar of battle as our only guide, it dawned upon us that we were lost—that we were separated from our regiment, away from our post of duty during the engagement and without leave. Here we were, three able-bodied men—idle, helpless, while our comrades were fighting a great battle!

"Naturally we were anxious to rejoin our regiment and share our comrades' fate. Presently we came upon the Sixth New Hampshire, which was brigaded with us. I asked and received permission to fight with that regiment and we three were determined to do our duty that day promptly and well.

"At night, when I asked the commanding officer to direct us to our regiment, he not only complied, but added that, if we needed assistance in accounting for ourselves, he would gladly help us out. He subsequently paid us a high compliment through the commander of our regiment."

CAPTURED A WHOLE COLOR-GUARD

JOHN H. WEEKS,
Private, Co. H, 152d N. Y. Vol.
Born at Hampton, Windom Co.,
Conn., March 15, 1845.

"ON the night of the 11th of May," says Private John H. Weeks, "we were relieved by the Fifth Corps on Laurel Ridge, where we had been lying in line of battle with the Pennsylvania Bucktails of the Fifth Corps massed in our rear, expecting to charge the enemy's works, which were in a strong position on a parallel ridge. But the woods caught fire between our line and the enemy's position, and thus caused a postponement of the charge.

"The fire had lighted up our skirmish line so brightly that we had lost six or seven men in my company by the enemy's sharpshooters. We lay in this position until about 9 o'clock P. M., when we were relieved by some of the Fifth Corps, with orders to move to the rear as silently as possible; not to allow our cups or bayonets to rattle or make any unnecessary noise. We marched all night through the mud and rain, and I don't think I ever saw it any darker.

"About break of day on the morning of the 12th, we were halted in line of battle with the orders: 'In place, rest.' The report had been in circulation during the night that we were going to relieve the Sixth Corps on the reserve, that we might have a chance to rest, as we had been under fire almost constantly since we crossed the Rapidan, six days before. We were nearly worn out for want of sleep and food. When we halted we could see the lights of camp-fires shining through the fog in our front, which I supposed belonged to the Sixth Corps.

"As soon as we were ordered to rest, I threw myself down into the mud and fell asleep. In a few minutes I was awakened by the arrival of an aide with an order for General Hancock, who happened to be near our regiment. I heard him give the order, as near as I can remember, as follows: 'General Meade sends his compliments, and directs that you move your Corps forward and occupy those works.'

"We were called to attention and ordered forward, and were in the second line of battle following close behind the first. Soon the rebel skirmishers commenced firing and then for the first time I began to realize that we had work before us. It was now getting quite light, but the fog prevented us from seeing far in advance. We soon came to an open field with a gradual ascent, on the top of which the heavy timber had been felled. The boughs were sharpened and wires were stretched through the tree-tops. Beyond this obstruction were the enemy's works, which consisted of a ditch eight feet wide and nearly as deep, with a row of long poles set into the ground in front, their sharpened points about breast-high. Immediately in rear of the ditch were the breastworks, which were formed of earth thrown up against a facing of logs, thus making the distance from the bottom of the ditch to the top of the works from twelve to fourteen feet, without the chance of a foothold.

"As soon as we came near to the top of the hill, the enemy opened upon us with canister and musketry. Their artillery had been massed at this point with about thirty guns, all double-shotted with canister. It did not seem that a line of men could possibly reach those works and pass those obstructions alive. By the time we reached the ditch there was no line of battle, but a rushing mass of yelling Yankees. We succeeded in wrenching the sharpened poles from their places, and used them in crossing the ditch and scaling the works. The point of the rebel works upon which the charge was made was an angle in the shape of the letter 'V,' projecting out of their line. Our left struck the right wing of the angle, so that when we got inside of the works we could see the rebels on the left wing opposing our men there, and, as we advanced, it brought us in the enemy's rear.

"When we had sent our prisoners to the rear, we still advanced, but very slowly, on account of our broken ranks. About this time I saw the enemy give way on the left wing, and among the rest was a color-guard surrounding its flag. These men fired their muskets at us in a volley and broke for their rear. They had to pass down our front to get out of the angle. I had discharged my gun, but, making up my mind to have those colors, I ran up to the sergeant and snatched the flag from him, threw it on the ground and put my foot on it. I cocked my empty gun and told them that the first man that moved out of his tracks would be shot, and ordered them to throw down their guns and surrender. The sergeant said to them: 'Boys, they have our colors; let us go with them.' They threw down their guns and marched to the rear as my prisoners. I recrossed the works and started for our rear, where I met General Hancock and his staff going to the front. When I saluted him, he asked: 'What colors are those you have there?' I told him. 'Are these your prisoners?' the general asked, glancing at the Confederates. I said they were. The general looked at one of his staff, smiling a little incredulously, for there were five or six lusty rebels, while I was only a lad about eighteen years old. Then he said: 'Deliver your prisoners to the provost marshal; write your name, company and regiment with the date of the action, on a slip of paper, pin it on your colors and turn them in to the adjutant of your regiment.'"

A few months later Private Weeks received his Medal of Honor.

AT THE "BLOODY ANGLE"

CHARLES H. TRACY,
Sergeant, Co. A, 37th Massachusetts Volunteers.
Born in Jewett City, Conn., Oct. 3, 1833.

S ERGEANT CHARLES H. TRACY, of Company A, Thirty-seventh Massachusetts Volunteers, relates two brave adventures, as follows:

"At the 'Bloody Angle,' Spottsylvania, May 12th, our corps, the Sixth, supported the Second in the famous charge against Johnson's Division of the Confederate Army. During the thickest of the fight, Lieutenant Wellman was badly wounded, and I was ordered to take him to the rear. It was about a mile to the hospital, and the shot and shell came so thick and fast that it was extremely hazardous to venture across with a wounded comrade, but I succeeded in carrying out the order, and after placing the lieutenant in the hospital, I came safely back through the fire. Upon reaching my company, Lieutenant Sparks congratulated me, saying: 'Tracy, I hope you will not have to cross that field on a like errand again.' Scarcely had he finished speaking, when a ball pierced his left breast and he fell into my arms. We thought he was mortally wounded, but discovering signs of life in him, decided to take him to the hospital, without waiting for orders."

"At one o'clock on the morning of April 2, 1865," continues Sergeant Tracy, "my regiment broke camp near Petersburg, Va., and moved up to the enemy's front. Brigade pioneers and sharpshooters were ordered to rush in advance of the brigade. The pioneers were to remove all obstacles in front of the enemy's works, while the sharpshooters covered the parapet. I was at that time detailed as sergeant of the Third Brigade pioneers, and was second in command in the assault. The part of the line we were expected to carry was made of enclosed works, connected by breastworks of great strength with outer obstructions in the form of two lines of chevaux de frise and two lines of abatis. It was impossible to take the works while the enemy defended them, unless the several lines of obstruction were first removed.

"As Lieutenant Shiver was wounded early in the attack the command fell on me, and in directing the removal of the first two lines of the obstructions I received a shot over my ear and one in my left side; and while removing the third line, a bullet shattered my right knee-joint, costing me, subsequently, the loss of my leg. Supporting myself on the abatis, I gave my orders to my men, and at last had the satisfaction of seeing them carry away the obstruction, thus enabling General Edwards to rout the enemy and cut the railroad and telegraph. The flag of the Thirty-seventh Massachusetts was the first to wave over the enemy's works."

BETWEEN TWO LINES OF FIRE

THE battle of Resaca, Ga., May 13 to 16, 1864, occurred during Sherman's campaign in Georgia when General Sherman had been confronted by General Johnston at Dalton, and had forced him to fall back upon Resaca.

During the engagement of the 15th an act of most conspicuous gallantry was performed by Major H. Edwin Tremain. This officer had not been assigned to duty in Sherman's army, but was attached to the personal staff of Major-General Sickles, who was visiting the command under confidential orders from the President. With his chief's permission, the major volunteered for staff duty under General Butterfield, and rendered important service in command of a brigade.

By an unfortunate accident or misunderstanding during the battle, the brigade led by General Harrison was fired upon by that of General Coburn, and was threatened with the utter confusion and disaster which are the usual and natural result of such a blunder. Major Tremain rode between the lines in front of Coburn's command, knocking down the muskets of the front rank with his sword and hands; he stopped the firing, saved the brigade from destruction, and the assault from failure.

H. EDWIN TREMAIN,
Major and A. D. C., U. A. Vols.
Highest rank attained: Bvt.
Brig-Gen.
Born in New York City.

After the battle and as Major Tremain was about to leave, General Butterfield gave expression to his appreciation of the major's services in the following letter: "As you are about to leave us this morning to resume your tour with General Sickles, with a feeling of sincere regret at losing your valuable services, it is a great pleasure to thank you for them. Your devotion and energy in camp and on the march, your gallantry at our assault of the enemy's works at Resaca, Ga., and your genial qualities have endeared you to us all."

Resaca, Ga., was one of the stands taken by the Confederates, under Johnston, who were retreating southward before Sherman's Army on its march to the sea. The battle at this place, May 13-16, 1864, was fiercely contested.

On the 13th Sherman deployed his line of battle against the town, and on the 14th he closed in, enveloping it. Skirmishing occurred all day, until late in the afternoon, when Schofield's Corps was heavily engaged and driven back some little distance. By a sharp movement, Sherman captured the town of Calhoun, Johnston's base and reserves, six miles below Resaca.

Heavy fighting continued on the 15th, in which McPherson's and Hooker's Corps were actively engaged. Meanwhile Johnston arranged to make a strong attack on the Federal left; but finding too strong opposition, he abandoned the idea and left Resaca with his army on the night of the 15th.

The losses in killed and wounded were about 3,000 on each side.

RESCUED BY A DRUMMER

WILLIAM LORD,
Drummer, Co. C, 40th Massachusetts Infantry.
Born at Bradford, England, Feb. 1, 1841.

WHEN the order, "Every man for himself!" is given and organized action has ceased, then has come the critical time for the soldier on the battlefield. Deprived of the directing hand of his superior officer the soldier finds himself thrown upon his own wit and resources to extricate himself from a generally desperate situation. An incident like that occurred during the engagement at Drewry's Bluff, Va., May 16, 1864.

Early in the morning the Union forces had carried the bluff, captured the enemy's camp and driven the Confederates into the woods. The Federal brigade then formed line in an open clearing extending from the top of the bluff to the Centralia Road, a distance of about 500 yards.

The Confederates had planted a battery to the left of the Union line, and at this point were able to greatly annoy their opponents. It became imperative to silence this rebel battery, and three companies of the Fortieth Massachusetts Infantry were sent under command of Major Jenkins to the Centralia Road to accomplish this task. Subsequently the three companies took up a position opposite the battery on this road, and from behind a hastily constructed breastwork of rails poured such effective fire into the rebels they could neither load nor discharge their pieces. Presently the Confederates changed their tactics and made a charge, and also sent a large body of troops to flank the small force behind the breastwork. The firing now became murderous. Soon the brave Massachusetts men found themselves short of ammunition and had to rifle the cartridge boxes of their dead and wounded comrades to obtain the necessary supply. The rebels charged the breastwork and engaged in a hand-to-hand fight with those on the other side. By that time the flanking rebels were approaching and the situation grew more desperate every minute, especially since the Union men's ammunition was now about completely exhausted. Realizing that further resistance would be folly, Major Jenkins gave the order: "Every man for himself!" Then confusion reigned supreme.

A description of what followed is now given in the words of Drummer William Lord, of Company C, who earned his medal on that occasion:

"It looked as if not one of us would be able to get away," he says. "Presently Sergeant Weaver ran up to me, grabbed me by the shoulder and exclaimed: 'Bill, come on or we will be captured or killed!'"

"We went. Over the fence and into the woods we ran toward our brigade, stumbling over the bodies of our wounded and dead comrades. There were the bodies of Privates Russel and Reed, friends of ours. Only the night before Reed told me that he felt as if he would be killed soon. 'If I am, Bill,' said he, 'go through my pockets and send the few belongings I have to my family.' There he was, poor fellow —dead! I stopped long enough to carry out his request. I went through his pockets and took charge of everything he carried. Weaver performed the same act for Russell. A short distance farther on we ran across Rankin, a private in my own

"LYING ON THE GROUND WITH AN UGLY WOUND IN THE JAW."

company, who was lying on the ground with an ugly wound in the jaw. A rebel had first shot and then tried to bayonet him. Though wounded, the brave fellow parried the thrust and with one blow with the butt of his rifle smashed the skull of the rebel and killed him on the spot. We took Rankin along with us. When we reached the place where we hoped to find our brigade, we discovered that it had been forced to retreat and that now we were between two lines of battle under heavy fire. We paused a second or so to decide what course to pursue, when I heard loud and agonizing cries for help. Looking about me I saw Colonel Eldridge G. Floyd, of the Third New York, shot through both legs, utterly unable to move.

The colonel complained bitterly that his men should leave and desert him in that predicament. I lifted him on my back and carried him to the field hospital about half a mile away. This place soon got within range of the rebel rifles and caught fire. I quickly got a stretcher and with the help of Private Patrick Lenahan, of my company, carried the colonel out of the blazing building over field and fences to the Richmond and Petersburg Pike, where we halted. Here we had to do some of our hardest fighting—not against the rebels—but with a disorganized mob of our own men, who, in their mad haste to retreat before the advancing enemy, came near tramping the wounded colonel to death. After many a hard struggle and more than one narrow escape, we finally were successful in carrying off our wounded officer, landing him safely at the hospital some miles in the rear."

A BRAVE COLONEL AND HIS BRAVE MARE

HENRY CAPEHART,
Colonel, 1st West Virginia Cavalry.
Highest rank attained: Brigadier-General, U. S. V.
Born at Cambria, Pa., Mar. 18, 1825.

WHILE part of Sheridan's cavalry was being thrown across the Greenbriar River, Va., May 22, 1864, Colonel Henry Capehart, of the First West Virginia Cavalry, performed a most daring rescue.

The enemy's sharpshooters were menacing the passage of the army, and, with a view to dislodging these sharpshooters, the command forded the river just above the falls.

Being an expert rider, and having a mount well-known in the army for its swimming qualities, Colonel Capehart, whenever a fording was to be made, invariably took up a station some hundred yards below the proposed crossing, his experience being that on such occasions both men and horses frequently lost their heads, thus causing the loss of life, and on more than one occasion his foresight in taking up this position enabled him to help many an unlucky rider.

A few moments after a platoon of Troop B had entered the water, one of the men, Private Watson Karr, was swept out of his saddle and down the swift stream. What followed is told by Colonel Capehart:

"When I started, I did not know that the falls were so near, until I saw Karr disappear over them. Being in the swift current, in the midst of a swollen river, I

"I REACHED OUT AND GRASPED HIM."

had only to clutch my mare by the mane with the left hand and the pommel of the saddle with my right, when we also took the plunge—and oh, such a dive! I thought I should never reach the surface again; when I did I had only time for a breath or two before the second plunge. Either this was not so great a fall as the first or I was becoming accustomed to deep diving; at any rate I did not mind it so much as the first.

"When I came up the second time I found I was close to Karr and also that Minie balls were uncomfortably numerous. I reached out and grasped him, drew him across my mare's neck, and turned her head towards the south shore. The north bank was quite near to us, but so rocky and precipitous, with a heavy current fretting against us, that I had no alternative but to swim my mare to the south side. Fortunately, I struck a bar and drew my man along until we stood upon firm ground, where we were a little under cover from the enemy's fire and could take a much needed rest. After vomiting a great quantity of water Karr regained consciousness. When I asked him some questions, however, he was not able to reply and could not speak. After a few minutes I remarked: 'Watty, you have lost your hat.' He slapped his hands down upon his trousers. 'Yes,' he said, 'and my pocketbook, too.' He had recovered his power of speech."

RESCUED HIS LIEUTENANT

ROBERT A. GRAY,
Sergeant, Company C, 21st Conn. Infantry.
Born at Philadelphia, Pa., September 21, 1834.

DURING the hotly contested battle of Drewry's Bluff, when the Union troops were compelled to fall back, a small squad of Federal soldiers — fifteen in all — were left on the field. They were members of Company C, of the Twenty-first Connecticut Infantry, under command of Lieutenant Dutton, who, having no orders to fall back, had no choice but to brave the situation. Rapidly, however, their position became more and more untenable; the enemy was fast closing in on the little band; already several of them had fallen under the increasing murderous fire from the Confederates. Lieutenant Dutton finally was forced to order a retreat, but had no sooner uttered the words, than, struck by a bullet, he sank to the ground. Sergeant Robert A. Gray was five rods away from him when he noticed the Lieutenant's absence, and, looking back, saw that the officer was disabled and sure to fall into the hands of the enemy, who were no more than twenty rods away from him. With a few leaps he was by his side and found him shot through the leg. He helped him up and managed to retreat with him. The brave sergeant assisted the wounded lieutenant to a place of comparative safety and then hurried back to his regiment.

RESCUED COMRADES FROM A STRANDED TRANSPORT

GEORGE W. BRUSH,
Lieutenant, Co. B, 34th U. S. Colored Troops.
Highest rank attained: Captain.
Born at West Hill, N. Y., Oct. 4, 1842.

COLONEL JAMES MONTGOMERY, commanding the Thirty-fourth U. S. Colored Troops, was on May 24, 1864, ordered to join an expedition under General Hatch to make a demonstration at Ashepoo River, S. C., and to burn the railroad trestle across the marsh at that point. The troop steamer Boston, detailed to carry and land the regiment at Mosquito Inlet, was of too deep draft for the steamboat wharf and so the troops were ferried to her in small boats. "When about two-thirds of our regiment were aboard the steamer," writes Lieutenant George W. Brush, "orders were given to get under way. I fastened my small boat to the stern of the vessel and soon we were steaming up stream. Mine was the only small boat taken along, the balance of the regiment and all the other small boats being left behind in the hurry to get away.

"In the fog and darkness of the night the pilot of the Boston carried us about five miles beyond Mosquito Inlet, and the first thing we knew we were hard aground on an oyster bed and at high tide.

"Soon the commander of a small Union gunboat, which we had passed about a mile below, hailed us, and suggested to our colonel that twenty-five well-armed men be sent over to his boat, where they could do good work as sharpshooters to prevent the Confederates from planting a battery and shelling us from opposite the point where we were stranded. He also promised assistance by bringing into action his heavy guns.

"The suggestion met with the approval of Colonel Montgomery and I was detailed with twenty-five men from the Fourth Massachusetts Cavalry to board the gunboat. In addition, we were joined by four volunteers, cavalry regulars, armed with Spencer carbines. Hardly had we proceeded half way to the gunboat, when the Confederates opened on the stranded Boston. The commander of the gunboat then suddenly changed his mind, and said that he did not wish to take undue risks. As the last one of my men clambered aboard his boat, I stood up in the small craft and called for volunteers to return with me to rescue our 400 companions on the grounded transport. Four cavalrymen at once answered my appeal and jumped into the small boat with me, each taking a pair of oars, They were William Downey, John Duffy, David L. Gifford and Patrick Scanlan, all privates of Troop B, Fourth Massachusetts Cavalry, all soldiers, brave and noble,

"While pulling toward the Boston, we could see some of the frightened soldiers jumping overboard to swim ashore. As we came alongside the transport, the colonel

"BEFORE WE LEFT, WE SET FIRE TO THE CRAFT."

said to me: 'Lieutenant, everything now depends on you. Yours is the only boat we have.' I thought at first that my boat would be swamped, but the men behaved well as soon as they realized that there was no need of hurry. Then we began the work of ferrying our comrades from the steamer to the south side of the river, taking about thirty men to a load. Meanwhile the enemy continued their firing, with our boat as their chief target. Now and then a shot would kill a man and several times we came near foundering; but at last we got them all safely ashore. Before we left the Boston and the large quantity of stores which she carried, besides about eighty horses, we set fire to the craft and saw her burn to the water's edge."

Lieutenant Brush and Privates Downey, Duffy, Gifford and Scanlan all received the Medal of Honor.

CHARGED TO THE MUZZLES OF THE ENEMY'S GUNS

From May 4 to June 4, 1864, the Army of the Potomac had been fighting desperately from the Rapidan to the Chickahominy, General Lee moving on defensive, parallel lines, falling back from one stronghold to another. Assault after assault upon the field-works of the enemy, by divisions and army corps, marked the line of the Federal advance, while storming columns of picket troops dashed themselves against the breastworks of the Confederate Army.

By a series of strategic movements, always in the face of the enemy, the army had moved from the North Anna to a position south of the Pamunkey River, confronting General Lee, with his army strongly entrenched on the Chickahominy, behind the outer defenses of Richmond. The field of operations during the last days of May and the first

EDWARD HILL,
Captain, Co. K, 16th Michigan Infantry.
Highest rank attained: Bvt. Col., U. S. V.

days of June covered an area of country diversified by open plains, running streams, deep ravines, morass and wooded ridges. After crossing the Pamunkey at Hanover Town, about twenty miles northeast from Richmond, the line of battle was formed with the Sixth Corps on the right, the Second Corps in the center and the Fifth Corps on the left, with Sheridan's cavalry as vanguard and rear-guard. The Ninth Corps was left on the north side of the Pamunkey, to guard the wagon-trains.

A successful assault upon the enemy's cavalry, at Hawe's Shop Cross-Roads, on May 28th, a few miles in front of Hanover Town, by the cavalry divisions of Gregg and Custer, was followed by a reconnoissance in force on the following day, to develop the position of General Lee. The right of the lines was pushed to Hanover Court House, the center towards Totopotomy Creek, and the left was advanced three miles forward on the Shady Grove Road. On May 31st, the Confederate cavalry and infantry at Cold Harbor were driven from their entrenchments by Sheridan's cavalry and the position held until re-enforced by the arrival of the Sixth Corps, which at midnight was moved from its position on the right six miles southeast from Hanover Court House, to the extreme left of the line, near Cold Harbor.

This apparent concentration of forces at Cold Harbor was detected by General Lee at daylight and General R. H. Anderson's Corps was moved from the left to the right of the Confederate line. As Anderson's troops, in the gray light of the dawn, were seen passing in front of the Fifth Corps, on the Federal center, General Warren was ordered to attack the marching columns in flank. The skirmish line of Bartlett's Third Brigade, under Captain Edward Hill, Sixteenth Michigan, which had been on picket duty through the night, occupying an advanced position on the left of the Fifth Corps, nearest the enemy, charged swiftly and steadily through the intervening timber and underbrush, up the slope to the enemy's works. As the line reached and carried the rifle pits, a destructive fire of artillery and musketry opened on front and flank, but the line pressed unfalteringly on, driving the enemy over their line of entrenchments.

This spirited reconnoissance of the skirmish line having developed the presence of the enemy in force behind his works, the attack was not pressed, but the regiments of the brigade that had advanced in close support of the skirmish line held throughout the day, against the repeated assaults of the enemy, the ground so gallantly captured by Captain Hill's line, which was composed of gallant men detailed from each regiment of the brigade. During this charge Captain Hill was severely wounded, but he remained with his men until they fell back in the evening.

TUNNELED HIS WAY TO A WOUNDED OFFICER

Two hundred and seventy Union soldiers charged a Confederate force of 15,000 men! It was at the battle of Cold Harbor, Va., June 3, 1864. Thirteen thousand brave Union lives were sacrificed on that bloody battlefield.

No fiercer struggle was there during the entire war, no more heroic deed than that desperate charge.

To give an idea of the battle a description from the pen of a Confederate officer is submitted in the following. It is the enemy who says:

"It was daylight. I had just finished a cup of coffee and was lighting my pipe when someone shouted: 'Look! Look at our pickets!'

"Our picket line was running toward us in wild confusion. I was completely taken by surprise. Not a gun had been fired; no enemy was in sight. A few seconds later I realized what was going on. The Federals were approaching. In five lines of battle they emerged from the woods at double-quick. Then the battle began. The Georgia and Alabama brigades opened with musketry and artillery.

The Federal first line wavered back upon the second and both pressed back the third line. Finally all five lines were in disorder. The Union men retreated to the woods. A second time they advanced. They had no caps on their guns and were unable to fire a single shot. On the other hand our artillery fired double-shotted canister from two rifled guns at a distance of a hundred yards and was decimating the Federals as they advanced at an awful rate, mowing them down by the dozens. At every discharge of our guns, heads, arms, legs, guns were seen flying high in the air. But we were opposing a determined and gallant foe. They closed the gaps in their lines as fast as we made them, and on they came, their lines swaying like great waves of the sea. Thus one upheaval from the rear would follow another and hurry nearer and

ORLANDO P. BOSS,

Corporal, Co. F, 25th Massachusetts Infantry, Born at Fitchburg, Mass., July 30, 1844.

nearer to the murderous fire from our works. So terrible was the slaughter of the brave Union cohorts that at some points their dead and wounded were piled upon each other five or six feet high—their blood literally drenched the field. For fully an hour and a half the Federals charged again and again—only to meet the same fate. Never before did I see such invincible resolution. Finally the Federals passed out of sight and we prepared for the next assault.

"Twenty minutes later it was reported that the battle was to be renewed. Looking out over the works I saw what I believed to be one regiment with a single flag and a single officer with drawn sword in the lead calling on his men to follow him.

"It was the Twenty-fifth Massachusetts—the only regiment which obeyed the order to return to that bloody field. And, as I subsequently learned, there were but two hundred and seventy men in that regiment at that. Not since the famous charge of the six hundred at Balaklava has a more heroic act been performed.

Cold Harbor, Va.—After the battle of Spottsylvania, General Grant placed his army across the Pamunkey River and moved to Hanover Town. On the first day of June, 1864, he began the battle of Cold Harbor, Va., a contest which he afterward acknowledged to be a mistake.

Lee's forces were strongly posted at Cold Harbor and the Federals were repulsed. On the 3d, Grant renewed the attack and was again repulsed, losing nearly 13,000 men. In all of the engagements at and around this point from June 1st to the 12th, the Union forces suffered a loss of over 14,000 men, while the Confederate loss was about 1,700.

Thereupon Grant quickly changed his base to the James River with a view to the capture of Petersburg and the conquest of Richmond from the southeast.

"With this eulogy of the glorious conduct of the regiment from the Old Bay State in mind, the writer is now acquainted with an incident which occurred during the battle and centers around a member of the same regimental organization.

"It was after the bloody repulse of one of the attacks. The brigade had fallen back to a line of earthworks about one hundred yards from the enemy's position.

"THEY USED THEIR SPOONS."

Presently a bullet whizzed through the air and struck Lieutenant Daly, of the Twenty-fifth Massachusetts, squarely in the breast. He fell, mortally wounded, to the ground about fifteen yards in front of the Union lines. Half way between the lines was a rifle pit, where Corporal Orlando P. Boss and Privates Aldrich and Battles had taken up a position.

"The former saw the lieutenant fall and heard his piteous cries for water. Unmindful of the terrific hail of bullets, Corporal Boss crawled out of his hole and approached the wounded officer near enough to be able to throw him his well-filled canteen. Returning to the pit he found that Aldrich had been wounded during his brief absence. To remain longer in the entrenchment was almost inevitable death; the plucky corporal therefore resolved to attempt to get over the breastworks.

"'Don't leave us here, if you go,' the wounded soldier moaned. It had never entered Boss' mind to desert his comrade in the hour of peril. Yet the poor fellow was so weak from loss of blood that he could not have walked a dozen paces unassisted.

"Boss quietly took his wounded comrade upon his back and with his heavy and precious burden staggered through the shower of bullets in front of three Confederate lines of battle toward the breastworks. Miraculous as it may seem, Boss accomplished his noble task and carried the wounded soldier off the field in safety. Boss now determined upon the rescue of another life—that of the wounded officer. The permission to carry out the attempt was readily granted by General Stannard and several men of the regiment volunteered to assist. It was impossible to bring the dying officer over the breastworks with any assurance of success, and it was therefore decided to first carry Lieutenant Daly to the rifle pit and thence to the Union lines through a tunnel dug through the works. Accordingly, four men were at once sent to work to do the digging, while Boss and Private William D. Blanchard started on their extremely hazardous mission of mercy. They crawled over the works and in the face of a murderous fire made a rush and a dash for the rifle pit. From here they dug a trench to the place where the officer lay, a distance, as stated before, of about fifteen yards. Having no other tools at their disposal they used their spoons and worked for four long and weary hours before they had their arduous task completed. The rebels could not fail to divine the object of their work and hurled countless shots and missiles at heroic Boss and his no less heroic companion. But a kind providence guarded their lives and crowned their efforts with success. The lieutenant was safely reached and carried back to the rifle pit on a rubber blanket. They then again called their spoons into service and excavated till they met those who were tunneling from the inside of the works. In this manner Lieutenant Daly was brought to the Union lines. The heroic deed was performed, but the officer for whom Boss and Blanchard had braved death succumbed to his injuries shortly afterward."

RESCUED THE COLONEL'S BODY

"I CANNOT order any man to such service. Is there any one in your company who will volunteer to make the search?" asked Lieutenant-Colonel Bates.

It had been a terrible day at Cold Harbor on the 2d of June, 1864, and to none more so than to the Eighth New York Heavy Artillery. Across a perfectly open field they charged through grape and canister, Colonel Porter leading on foot. In thirty minutes over 500 men were lost. In a final effort Colonel Porter fell almost under the enemy's guns. The attack was repulsed.

LEROY WILLIAMS,
Sergeant, Battery G, 8th New York H. A.
Born at Owego, N. Y., Aug. 18, 1844.

It was in discussing how to find and rescue the body of the gallant colonel that Lieutenant-Colonel Bates called for a volunteer to make the search. Sergeant LeRoy Williams, of Battery G, Eighth New York Heavy Artillery, stepped forward.

The orders were: "Go to the outposts, sweep the enemy's front with a field-glass, and locate Colonel Porter's body if possible."

Easily ordered. It was a perfectly clear day, the field open, and sharpshooters on all sides. However, fortune favored the scout. Though shot at fifteen or twenty times, he completed his errand without a scratch.

Meanwhile volunteers were called for to rescue the body. When Williams returned and reported, Colonel Bates asked him: "Would you just as soon pilot a detail to the body?"

"Certainly."

"How many men will you need?"

"The smallest number possible; four are sufficient."

"Well, Sergeant, there is your detail; take a stretcher and bring in the body of Colonel Porter at all hazards."

"I took the first four men from the right of the detail," says Sergeant Williams, "much to the disappointment of the rest of the volunteers. They were Galen S. Hicks, John Duff, Walter Harwood and Samuel Traviss.

"In passing the extreme outpost in the night, a corporal reported an officer's body directly in front, but very close to the enemy's line.

"'Why, it's worth a man's life to go out there,' he exclaimed.

"'That is the body of our colonel and we must get it,' was our answer. 'Keep watch for us as best you can, and if the ball does open, give us a little chance to get in.'

"Falling flat on my stomach, I worked my way to the body. We were right; it was the body of the colonel. Traviss soon followed. Unable to move the body without attracting attention, I sent him back for a rope, while I remained with the body to prevent its being rifled. During the hour or more I lay there I saw an officer of the enemy taking observations. He was so close I could hear the rattle of his side arms at every move. Finally the rope came. Traviss fastened it to the feet of the body, and creeping away stealthily, we gradually drew the body to the vidette post."

BRAVE AND DEVOTED TO HIS COMRADES

EUGENE M. TINKHAM,
Sergeant, Co. H, 148th N. Y. Vol. Infantry.
Born at Sprague, Conn.

AFTER the three days' fight at Cold Harbor, Companies A and H of the One hundred and forty-eighth New York Infantry, were detailed as skirmishers preceding a charge by the brigade. Sergeant Eugene M. Tinkham, who was with his company in the skirmish line, says that "the brigade advanced through the woods and charged steadily and bravely across the open field, but the odds, both as to men and position, were too great, and back over the field, which was strewn thickly with dead and wounded, we were forced to retreat into the woods from which shortly before we had emerged full of hope for victory." The sergeant continues:

"Knowing that many of our boys were on the field in a helpless condition, I asked and received permission to attempt to bring some of them back to our lines. By crouching and crawling on hands and knees I reached the side of Andrew Grainer, who lay upon the battlefield with a shattered ankle. Rolling him on a rubber blanket, I succeeded in hauling him back to his comrades. Then I made a second trip and found John Bortle who was in a critical condition and utterly helpless from a shot in the head, arms, hip and leg. He was a heavy man, and after getting him on a rubber blanket, I was forced to adopt a method of my own to drag him along. Accordingly I sat down as far from the blanket as I could reach and dug holes for my heels to get a brace to work against. Then reaching forward I pulled at the corners of the blanket and dragged the wounded man to me. This process I repeated until at last I reached the woods where the stretcher bearers were. Both wounded men belonged to my company. They died three days later at the hospital."

A REBEL GENERAL THE MUSICIAN'S PRISONER

JAMES SNEDDEN,
Principal Musician, 54th Pa. Infantry.
Born at Edinburgh, Scotland,
Sept. 19, 1844.

IN recounting his experience at the battle of Piedmont, Va., Musician James Snedden, of the Fifty-fourth Pennsylvania Infantry, says:

"On the 5th of June, 1864, after reveille and a hastily cooked breakfast, we were ordered forward on the march, which soon brought us within hearing of the enemy's firing, whereupon our lines were hastily formed and skirmishers advanced. During the formation of our line of battle we were subjected to a terrific fire from a Confederate battery of six twelve-pound guns, but on we went until our skirmish line reached a protected position, where we were ordered to lie down.

"I was principal musician of the regiment, and our colonel ordered me to take my musicians to the rear and if possible keep the command in view, in order to join them after the battle. As he spoke to me we both observed one of our men on the skirmish line, as he fell, wounded, and I at once offered to take his gun and go on the line. The colonel assented and immediately thereafter I was in the ranks with my old company.

"In a few minutes the whole line was charging the Confederate defenses, which were constructed of rails and fallen trees, and here both armies received their greatest losses. The two lines of battle were not more than seventy-five yards apart, each pouring lead into the other with good effect.

"It was during this struggle that the Confederate general, William Jones, was killed, and the loss of their gallant leader caused the Confederate line to waver and then break. Thus far we had fought for every inch we traversed, but with the break in their lines came renewed energy to our charge. Over the works we went, and in a hand-to-hand fight drove the rebels slowly back, maintaining their line formation until they reached Middle River, where we took 1,500 prisoners.

"On the banks of the river I encountered a Confederate brigadier-general and demanded his surrender, whereupon he reluctantly handed me his sword and two revolvers. I then marched my prisoner to the rear and reported to the brigade commander to whom I turned over the general and his sword."

Piedmont, Va.—General Sigel, commanding one of the two columns into which the army in the Shenandoah Valley was divided, advanced up the valley as far as Newmarket, where, after a fierce engagement, he was relieved of his command by General Hunter, who immediately took up the offensive. On the 5th of June Hunter encountered the Confederates at Piedmont, where he captured 1,500 prisoners and three pieces of artillery. After this battle he formed a junction with Crook and Averell at Staunton, from which place they moved toward Lynchburg by way of Lexington.

COURAGE, ENERGY AND MILITARY ABILITY

O N the fifth day of June, 1864, at daybreak and shortly after General Hunter's Army commenced to move on Staunton, Va., the advance force of his cavalry was attacked by the enemy and driven in. General Hunter was marching at the head of his army, and immediately ordered General Julius Stahel, who was near him, to attack the enemy with his cavalry and to check their advance. General Stahel charged the approaching enemy and broke and drove them about two miles, where, meeting a stronger force, he charged the enemy's line again with the same results as before and pursued them as far as Piedmont, where he found the enemy in great force, advantageously posted in a wood behind a line of defenses constructed of fallen timber and fence-rails. Having no infantry, General Stahel did not attempt to attack them in

JULIUS STAHEL,
Major-General, U. S. Volunteers.
Born in Hungary.

so strong a position, but kept them there with his cavalry until the arrival of General Hunter with his force. The latter at once attacked the enemy's stronghold, and ordered General Stahel, whose cavalry was somewhat exhausted, to form the reserve.

The battle raged furiously for some time, each side holding its position, until Hunter ordered a general advance all along the line and directed General Stahel to dismount that part of the cavalry which was armed with Spencer rifles — seven-shooters — and support the right wing. In compliance with this order, General Stahel rapidly moved with his dismounted force to the extreme right, attacked the enemy's entrenched position in the wood and dislodged them. During his charge General Stahel was badly wounded ; but, wishing to follow up his success, he had his wound quickly dressed to stop bleeding. As he was very weak and had the use of but one arm he was helped on his horse and, with a portion of his cavalry, which was in readiness, made a quick detour at the head of his column, charging the enemy on the flank and turning it. Just at that time General Hunter with his infantry attacked the whole line with great impetus, and Colonel Wyncoop with the balance of the cavalry charged on the right flank. The enemy was now completely demoralized and fled in great confusion, leaving over 1,000 prisoners, including a large number of officers. General W. E. Jones, the commander of the enemy's force, was killed and his body fell into the hands of the Union troops. General Hunter pursued the enemy until night set in, capturing many more prisoners, and the next morning occupied Staunton.

"HE WAS HELPED ON HIS HORSE."

The Confederate loss in this battle was estimated at nearly 3,000. General Hunter lost less than 800 men.

General Stahel's courage was highly commended by his superiors and the victories largely accredited to his gallantry, energy and military qualities. General Hunter in his report of June 9, 1864, to General Halleck, wrote: "It is but justice to Major-General Stahel to state that in the recent engagement he displayed excellent qualities of coolness and gallantry, and that for the final happy result the country is much indebted to his services."

A RIDE TO ALMOST CERTAIN DEATH

E. W. WHITAKER,
Captain, Co. E, First Connecticut Cavalry.
Highest rank attained: Bvt. Brig-Gen. U. S. V.
Born at Killingly, Conn., June 15, 1841.

A FTER its raid against the Danville and Southside Railway, the Third Cavalry Division, commanded by General James H. Wilson, on its return march to join the Army of the Potomac in front of Petersburg, found a large force of rebel infantry, cavalry and artillery in position, barring its passage at Ream's Station, Va., within five miles of army headquarters.

Captain E. W. Whitaker, who was serving on General Wilson's staff, took in the whole position at a glance. Perceiving that it would be impracticable for this column, jaded and almost worn out by a week's incessant marching, working and fighting, to force its way farther without assistance, he volunteered to take a squadron and charge through the rebel line and inform General Meade of the division's perilous straits and that help must be sent at once.

General Wilson accepted Captain Whitaker's offer and directed him to proceed immediately on his desperate mission. He was entirely ignorant of what had become of the Army of the Potomac, or where he should find it, or what perils he would encounter on the way. It looked as though he were starting on a ride to certain death.

Selecting Lieutenant Ford and forty troopers of the Third New York Cavalry, he explained to them the hazardous character of the undertaking, and instructed them that whoever should survive should make his way as rapidly as possible to army headquarters and describe the position of the cavalry column he had left behind.

Not a man faltered, but the entire detachment dashed forward after their gallant leader, who, bearing to his left and striking the rebel right, broke through their line like a tornado, and galloped on to headquarters, where he arrived at an early hour of morning with only eighteen of his gallant cavalrymen. They had cut through the enemy's line which one of General Wilson's officers, after reconnoitering, had reported as "strong as a stone wall."

Captain Whitaker gave the necessary information and at once volunteered to guide the Sixth Corps to the rescue, but its movements were so dilatory that it did not arrive until long after the cavalry column, despairing of help, had made a great detour by which it eluded the enemy, extricated itself and rejoined the army several days later.

Captain Whitaker was highly commended by General Wilson, immediately promoted to the rank of major, and received the Medal of Honor for his services in this notable charge.

A SUCCESSFUL ROUND-UP

JAMES K. STURGEON,
Private, Co. F, 46th Ohio Infantry.
Born in Perry Co., Ohio, Nov. 5, 1846.

ON the 15th of June, 1864, at the battle of Kenesaw Mountain, a large portion of Johnston's Army was in a well-defended position a few miles north of Marietta, Ga. The Forty-sixth Ohio had been ordered to make an assault on the works, supported by troops from General Morgan Smith's command, while troops of General Logan's command were to make a feint to the left to divert the attention of the enemy and draw his fire.

"The carrying out of the plan was according to orders," says Private James K. Sturgeon, "and at the outset the Forty-sixth Ohio made a charge over a hummocky field. The breastworks were ably defended and during our short plunge we were under heavy fire, but we were not to be stopped and up over the works we went. At once there was a scattering. Some of the Confederates surrendered immediately, while others, running to the rear, concealed themselves in the tall grass and underbrush of a ravine which they entered. Fortunately for us most of the Southerners threw away their guns in their flight. While our regiment was busy securing the captives, three of my comrades and I went out beyond the works and followed the fleeing Confederates. We picked up the frightened Johnnies everywhere, from behind stumps and logs, in the grass and in the bush. We continued this work until we had rounded up some thirty odd prisoners, when we marched them back to our lines."

UNDER SPECIAL PROTECTION OF PROVIDENCE

JOSEPH O. GREGG,
Private, Co. F, 133d Ohio Vol. Infantry.
Born in Circleville, O., Jan. 5, 1841.

O<small>N</small> the morning of June 16, 1864, while General Grant was crossing to the south side of the James River, and General Lee was endeavoring to reach Petersburg before Grant could occupy it in force, the First Division of the Tenth Corps, commanded by General Robert S. Foster, was pushed out to destroy as much as possible of the Richmond and Petersburg Railway, and delay the Confederate advance led by General Pickett's Division, until Grant could complete his crossing, and again get his army together.

The One hundred and thirty-third Ohio, which formed part of the division, was placed in support of a battery which fired over the men as they lay in a rifle pit lately occupied by the enemy, the division holding it against repeated assaults by Pickett's forces until about 3 o'clock P. M. Heavy re-enforcements enabled the enemy to turn the position of the Union forces, who were forced to fall back across the open, level field about one-half mile to the edge of the woods, where they formed a new line of defense. The enemy followed in close pursuit, and their skirmishers occupied the abandoned works, while their main body began to form in their immediate rear for another assault upon the Union lines.

It was then reported that Companies B, K and G, of the Ohio regiment, had not returned with the main body, and were probably in imminent danger of capture by the advancing foe. As a matter of fact, however, the companies mentioned had retreated by a different route and were safely posted in another place in the new line.

Colonel Joshua B. Howell, of the Eighty-fifth Pennsylvania, commanding the brigade, directed Colonel G. S. Innis, of the One hundred and thirty-third Ohio, to procure a volunteer to go back in the direction of the abandoned position, make a search for the missing men, and order them in. He insisted that the messenger make haste, as another assault was imminent.

Private Joseph O. Gregg of Company F, offered to go. The subsequent events are narrated by Adjutant Alanson N. Bull, who issued the call for the volunteer:

"Gregg had been quite ill the night before. The surgeon had ordered him to remain in his quarters, but when he learned that we had been ordered out to a possible fight he disregarded the surgeon's orders and took his place in the ranks.

"I hesitated about accepting his volunteer service, as he looked frail; but the exigency of the case required quick action and I directed him to discard everything which might impede his movements, and without delay go out in the direction of the abandoned breastworks a short distance and look for our missing men.

"Through a misunderstanding of my instructions Gregg walked directly across the field in full view of the Confederate lines, climbed upon the crest of the breastworks, then partly occupied by the foe, and stood looking about him as coolly as if the battle lines of the enemy did not exist at all. He apparently paid no heed to the rapidly advancing foe, whose skirmishers were already in part of the works upon which he was standing. Our anxiety for the missing companies and the imminently perilous mission of Gregg caused Colonels Howell and Innis and myself to closely watch his movements through our field glasses.

"OTHERS WERE FIRING AT CLOSE RANGE."

"We saw him mount the breastworks, look about him for a moment, then run along the crest about 100 feet to the left and suddenly spring from the embankment over which a large number of men in gray could be seen leaping in an effort to head off his retreat, while many others were firing at close range at their active young foeman, who, dodging with zig-zag rushes to avoid the blows aimed at his head, quickly gained the lead and successfully made his escape to our lines, all the while under a concentrated fire, several balls having passed through his cap and clothing, but without injury to his person other than a few bruises.

"We considered it a truly remarkable exhibition of daring. Alone, surrounded by hundreds of Pickett's best marksmen, surprised by finding himself in the midst of enemies instead of friends, and ordered to surrender, Gregg's quick decision and prompt, bold action, together with his skill in keeping a portion of his pursuers between himself and their marksmen, alone enabled him to escape with life and limb, when to us who were watching his struggle there did not seem to be a chance in his favor.

"We rode out to meet Gregg as he reached our line, and he reported to us that he had seen men behind the breastworks and imagined them to be the companies he had been sent after. He had also observed the rapidly approaching battle lines of the enemy, and, fearing they would reach the men first and capture them before he could warn them of their danger, had run along the crest of the embankment and ordered them to fall back to the woods, as we were retreating, only discovering his mistake when a voice called to him: 'Surrender, you Yankee!' He found himself surrounded and being fired at so closely that the powder almost burned his face as he leaped from the embankment, dodging others who were striking at him, and fighting himself clear of the crowd of pursuers, until he reached our lines. After hearing his report the colonel commanding said to him: 'That was bravely done; you must have been under special protection of Providence.'

"The enemy assaulted us a few minutes later, partly breaking our line, but were driven back after a sharp fight."

THREE EXAMPLES OF SOLDIERLY DEVOTION

SERGEANT JOHN BROSNAN was in command of Company E, One hundred and sixty-fourth New York Infantry, at the battle of Petersburg, Va., June 16, 1864, because so many of his superior officers had been either killed or wounded. The struggle was desperate and, after repeated charges, the Federal line began to waver.

Sergeant Brosnan sprang to the front and called on his men to renew the charge. They did, but were forced into a ravine, where they made a fierce rally. When night closed in on the worn-out soldiers and they were shielded from the enemy by the impenetrable darkness, they threw up breastworks. Early the following morning, Brosnan's attention was called to loud groans coming from a direction exposed to a very heavy fire. Investigation

JOHN BROSNAN,
Sergeant, Co. E, 164th N. Y. Inf.
Born in Ireland, July 1, 1846.

showed that a Union soldier had been wounded by concealed rebels. Sergeant Brosnan decided to rescue him, although he fully realized the danger of the task. Exposed to the fire of rebel sharpshooters, he succeeded in reaching the dying soldier, who proved to be Corporal Michael Carroll, of Company E.

"For God's sake, Sergeant, lie down or you will be killed," the moribund whispered feebly. The plucky sergeant lifted his comrade upon his arms and with great difficulty carried him out of reach of the enemy's fire and behind the breastworks. During this heroic rescue he himself was struck above the right elbow, entailing the loss of the arm. Thus the sergeant became a cripple while saving a wounded comrade.

THE same day, when the Union forces had retired from Petersburg to Bermuda Hundred, Private Francis Morrison, of Company H, Eighty-fifth Pennsylvania Infantry, performed a similar deed of heroic devotion.

The regiment was in full retreat under the murderous fire of General Pickett's advancing troops, when Private Jesse Dial, of Morrison's Company, was struck by a bullet and left behind. Private Morrison saw his comrade fall and, with utter disregard of a hail of bullets, advanced towards the enemy and was soon

FRANCIS MORRISON,
Private, Co. H, 85th Penn. Inf.
Born at Ohiopyle, Pa., Jan. 15, 1845.

at the side of his friend. As he tenderly raised him from the ground he discovered to his dismay that Dial was dead. He then carried the corpse back to his regiment.

A month later, in a charge at Deep Bottom, Va., Private Morrison himself was wounded, a musket ball passing through the breast and leaving a wound in his back which the most skillful surgery failed to heal up. The award of the Medal of Honor was the Government's graceful appreciation of such bravery and soldierly qualities.

JOHN H. HARBOURNE, of the Twenty-ninth Massachusetts Infantry, also won his medal in this action. In the heat of the conflict the entire color-guard of the

JOHN H. HARBOURNE,
Private, Co. K, 29th Mass. Inf.
Born in Birmingham, Eng., Sept. 9, 1840.

Twenty-ninth Massachusetts Infantry was killed, whereupon Private Harbourne took the colors and carried them at the head of the regiment. The Confederates could not withstand the vigorous assault and soon the charging column was on the breastworks and into the redoubt. Private Harbourne with his flag was close to the Confederate colors, lying at the side of their wounded color-bearer, and in an instant had them stripped from the staff and tucked safely under his blouse. A moment after he was wounded in the foot and fell to the ground, but upon recovering from the first shock he found that the redoubt was taken. Although he was suffering great pain from his wound, he managed to capture three rebels and brought them into the Union lines, where he turned them and the Confederate flag over to General Burnside. Next morning Private Harbourne was ordered to report at headquarters and was there thanked and commended by General Burnside, and sent to the hospital.

RECAPTURED COLORS AND TOOK TWO PRISONERS

"DURING the night of June 16th, the Forty-eighth Connecticut Infantry of the Ninth Army Corps," says Sergeant Patrick H. Monaghan, "of which I was a member, crossed a marsh in single file, and took position close to a portion of rebel ranks. While in this position every man was instructed to make no noise and be ready for a charge.

"Before daylight the order came, and we and the Thirty-sixth Massachusetts dashed forward under a heavy fire, leaped the enemy's breastworks and captured four pieces of artillery, six hundred prisoners and a thousand stand of arms. The enemy fell back in confusion toward their next line, while our troops occupied the one just taken. Other members of my company and myself followed the retreating rebels. Between the line just taken and the next the ground was undulating. A small stream flowed in the hollow. Clumps of trees and bushes lined either side of this stream and the enemy made a stand here and delivered fire. As we dashed forward, I saw an officer near the thicket and fired. He fell near the stream with his head almost in the water. Immediately a tall rebel threw down his gun and ran toward him. I rushed up swiftly and, leveling my empty gun, ordered both to surrender. The tall man cried out: 'Don't shoot the Major!'

PATRICK H. MONAGHAN,
Sergeant, Co. F, 48th Connecticut Inf.
Born at Mayo, Ireland, Nov. 4, 1843

"I told the major to get up and we would help him back. But as I was speaking, I saw another group of rapidly retreating rebels, among them a private with a gun in one hand and a flag over his shoulder. I jumped toward him and ordered him to drop his gun and surrender. He dropped the gun and I ran forward, took the flag and marched him to where my other prisoners were seated.

"By this time our troops in the line behind us had begun to fire over our heads, and the Confederates opened a heavy fire from the line in front, but I ran back to my own company with the colors. I got over the breastworks safely, and when I unfurled the flag found that it belonged to the New York Heavy Artillery, who had lost it in the fight of the previous day. My three prisoners were afterwards brought in by some of my companions."

THREE MEN CAPTURE TWENTY-SEVEN "JOHNNIES"

HENRY W. ROWE,
Private, Co. I, 11th New Hampshire
Volunteers.
Born April 1840.

Private Henry W. Rowe, of the Eleventh New Hampshire Volunteers, gives the following interesting description of how he won his Medal of Honor:

"On the night of the 15th of June, 1864, Burnside with his Ninth Corps crossed the James River, and after a twenty-four hour march arrived at the outposts of Petersburg with the advance of his corps. At 6 P. M. an advance was made in the face of a murderous fire, and the Eleventh New Hampshire Volunteers, together with the Second Maryland, succeeded in getting close under a rebel battery. After several hours of continuous firing, during which many men were killed and wounded, the assault had to be given up.

"Not discouraged by this first repulse, Burnside reconnoitered the lines and determined to make a second assault. The point chosen for the attack was a residence owned by Mr. Shand, a large two-story building shaded by buttonwood and gum trees, with a peach orchard in the rear. Fifty yards from the front door was a narrow ravine fifteen or twenty feet deep, with a brook flowing northward. West of the house about the same distance was another brook, the two joining twenty rods north of the house. A rebel brigade held this tongue of land with four guns. Their main line of breastworks was along the edge of the ravine east of the house. South, and on higher ground, was a redan with two guns, which enfiladed the ravine.

"It was Burnside's idea to take this tongue of land, break the rebel line and compel the evacuation of the redan. General Potter's Division of the Ninth Corps was selected to carry out his plan, and the attacking column was to consist of General Griffin's brigade on the right, supported by Curtis' on the left. Griffin's brigade contained, all told, only 260 men, and in the front line the Eleventh New Hampshire found its place, including Company I with its remaining five privates.

"A little past midnight General Potter led his division into the ravine in front of the house. The soldiers divested themselves of knapsacks, canteens and cups— everything which could make a noise—and moved forward stealthily. All was still and perfectly quiet. We reached the ravine, and there above us, not fifteen paces distant, were the rebel pickets. The night was warm and sultry. The sky was flecked by only a few light clouds, the moon becoming full and clear. Not a sound was heard, save the rumble of a wagon or a stray shot from the enemy's pickets.

"Finally, a little past three, as the dawn was beginning to light up in the east, the command, 'Forward!' was passed along the line in whispers.

"ONE BOUND AND THE REBEL PICKETS WERE OVERPOWERED."

"The men rose in a body from the ground; not a gunlock clicked; the bayonet was to do the work. Forward we started with steady, noiseless step. One bound and the rebel pickets were overpowered. Now toward the Shand House, and over the breastworks! At the right of the house, Comrade Batchelder, of Company I, joined me, and soon we fell in with 'Sol' Dodge, Sergeant of Company C. Passing the second corner of the house, we heard the report of a musket from a rebel pit about fifteen feet to the right. We ran around to the rear of this pit and shouted: 'Surrender, you damned rebels!' The 'Johnnies' were rather rudely awakened from their sleep, and although twenty-seven in number, dropped their guns. Guarded by our attacking force of three, they were finally turned over to the Union officers in the rear, together with a rebel flag captured by myself. The rebel line was broken and Grant's lines were drawn closer around Petersburg."

CAPTURED, BUT THEIR COLORS WERE SAVED

JAMES DRURY,
Sergeant, Co. C, 4th Vermont Infantry.
Born in Ireland in 1835.

WHILE some 600 men of the Fourth and Sixteenth Vermont Infantry were destroying the Weldon Railroad, Va., June 23, 1864, they found themselves surrounded by General Mahone's Division of 3,000 Confederates; but though they were so greatly outnumbered, they nevertheless made a brave resistance. The enemy's fire was doing terrible execution; more than half of the Union soldiers had been killed or wounded.

The commanding officer of the Vermonters, seeing they could not extricate themselves, and that capture was inevitable, stepped up to Sergeant James Drury, of the Fourth Vermont Infantry, who had the colors, and remarked that the regiment would lose its standard.

Drury replied: "They will have to kill this Irishman before they get it."

The officer pointed to a road which seemed to offer some chance as an avenue of escape.

"Go that way and perhaps you may succeed in escaping the rebels," the officer observed. Drury lost no time in following the advice. Wrapping the flag around the staff, he said to his command: "Boys, I'm going to save this flag or die in the attempt."

Privates Brown and Wilson called out: "We'll be with you, Sergeant."

And then the three started across the open fields. They had not progressed far, however, when the rebels shouted to them: "Halt, you damned Yankees!"

but the Yankees did not halt. A shower of bullets was sent after them. Poor Brown fell. To their regret they had to leave the brave fellow behind. Sergeant Drury and his remaining companion, Private Wilson, ran as fast as they could and safely reached the timber. By this time darkness had set in and the fugitives were able to conceal themselves in the woods till daybreak, when they found the Federal pickets, and thus saved the flag from falling into the enemy's hands.

RETAINED COMMAND IN SPITE OF SEVERE WOUNDS

THE battle around Saint Mary's Church, Va., June 24, 1864, brought the Second Brigade of the Second Division of Sheridan's Cavalry into a sharp and deadly struggle with superior numbers of Wade Hampton's Confederate Cavalry.

About three o'clock in the afternoon, after irregular skirmishing all morning, the enemy made an attack in great force on the Second Brigade, to which Colonel Charles H. Smith's First Maine Cavalry was attached, and from that time until dark the fight was carried on by the brigade with undaunted vigor. The enemy, over-confident because of their overwhelming numbers, charged time and again, only to be met and held in check by the gallant brigade. There were no disengaged men in the Union lines; all worked with a fury, the cavalry charging, while two batteries in the rear poured

CHARLES H. SMITH,
Colonel, 1st Maine Cavalry.
Highest rank attained: Bvt. Maj-Gen.,
U. S. A.
Born at Hollis, Me., Nov. 1, 1827.

load after load of canister into the staggering lines of the enemy. Colonel Smith, at the head of his regiment, was wounded in the thigh, but, keeping his seat, led his brave men into the thickest of the fight, where his horse was shot from under him. Mounting another, he again was in the lead. Again his horse was shot from under him, throwing him heavily to the ground. A third horse was secured, and in the retreat, after two hours of the fiercest cavalry fighting, the colonel, although again wounded, remained with his men, fighting the pursuing rebels until darkness put an end to this unequal contest.

The object of the **Trevelian Raid, Va.,** June 7-24, 1864, was to go to Lynchburg and open communication with General Hunter. That object was not accomplished and the cavalry returned via the White House Landing, where a large train of wagons was packed awaiting escort to the James River. The cavalry supplied the escort and crossed the Chickahominy at Jones' Bridge. On the morning of the 24th, Gregg's Division was sent to Saint Mary's Church as a flank guard, and, thus became separated from the main cavalry corps. Hampton discovered this fact, and, as he despaired of capturing the train, concentrated all his cavalry to capture or destroy Gregg's Division.

HE PAUSED AT THE SIDE OF HIS DEAD CAPTAIN

NELSON W. WARD,
Sergeant, Troop M, 11th Pa. Cavalry.
Born at Bellfont, Columbiana County,
Ohio, Nov. 20, 1887.

A SMALL force, part of which was the Eleventh Pennsylvania Cavalry, was sent, June 25, 1864, under command of Lieutenant-Colonel Stetzel, to destroy the railroad bridge across the Staunton River, half a mile south of Burk's Junction, Va. The enemy was strongly entrenched on the south side of the river and on both sides of the railway bridge. The approach to the bridge and the Confederates' position was flat meadow land, destitute of cover for the advancing force, excepting perhaps a slight depression caused by the dry bed of a branch of the river. The Pennsylvania Cavalry was ordered to advance on the bridge and entrenchments, led by carbineers selected from each company. A member of Troop M being suddenly stricken ill, the captain called for a volunteer to take the sick man's place, and Sergeant Nelson W. Ward, though he himself had been on sick report for a day or two, volunteered and took his place in the ranks. The story is continued by Sergeant Ward, as follows:

"Our troops moved forward in an irregular line, and, with the right resting on a small trestle between the railway station and the bridge, took a position in the dry bed of the stream. The fury of the fight was soon on, firing at short range from both artillery and infantry sending death into our ranks with terrific swiftness. With a salute to my captain, I asked: 'Isn't the colonel going to form the men in line for a charge on the bridge?' at which Captain Gerard Reynolds replied, giving the order: 'Forward, men, forward!' They were the brave officer's last words, for he fell dead, shot as he uttered the last word of his command.

"Just then, too, from under the trestle, we heard the colonel ordering the captain to move his men to the right, toward the railroad. Thus, with our company commander dead, our regimental commander skulking, it was not singular that the men wavered under the shower of shot and shell. One of the men asked me: 'What are we to do?' I replied: 'Follow me, boys,' and, swinging my carbine over my head, I led in a charge against the bridge until every man but one had been shot down."

Staunton River Bridge, Va.—While operating in Virginia in June, 1864, General James H. Wilson, commanding the Third Division of Sheridan's Cavalry Corps, ordered General Kautz's Division to attack the enemy and destroy the bridge across the Staunton River. The attack was maintained for three hours, but failed. The Federals suffered a loss of sixty in killed and wounded.

"It was an awful slaughter and a hopeless effort. With but two of us left, we started back for the dry bed depression. On the way I found the dead body of my captain, and stopping, I knelt down to secure his money, watch, revolver and spur. Although repeatedly urged by comrades across the railway and further back on the line, I remained fully twenty minutes at his side, endeavoring to procure assistance

"FINALLY HAD TO RETREAT
TO THE MAIN FORCE."

to carry the corpse off the field, but I waited and begged in vain, and finally had to retreat to the main force without the body of our brave and beloved captain."

During this truly heroic effort, a bullet struck the heel of Sergeant Ward's boot, and another bullet passed through the skirt of his blouse.

The money and other articles from Captain Reynolds were turned over to the proper authorities.

A MUSICIAN AS A SHARPSHOOTER

ALONZO P. WEBBER,
Principal Musician, 86th Illinois Vol.
Born March 16, 1828.

Alonzo P. Webber, of the Eighty-sixth Illinois Volunteers, Principal Musician of his regiment when it was engaged at the battle of Kenesaw Mountain, Ga., June 27, 1864, distinguished himself by voluntarily advancing as a sharpshooter.

Seeing the desperate situation of his regiment, with no chance to advance, he obtained permission from Colonel Fahnestock to "go in" as a sharpshooter. With a Winchester rifle and 120 rounds of ammunition, he succeeded in advancing to within twenty-seven feet of the rebel line of battle, which was formed in V shape. There he found shelter behind a tree, and although he was at the apex, with the enemy on both sides of him, he stood his ground from nine o'clock in the morning until six o'clock in the evening. Being an excellent shot he brought down a number of the enemy, while the Union forces lay behind him at the distance of a city block or more, unable to get closer to the enemy's line.

Webber's courage on that day won him the admiration of his whole regiment, none of whom had expected to see him return alive from his dangerous position.

Kenesaw Mountain, Ga.—Almost continuous fighting was engaged in from the 8th to the 27th of June, 1864, in the vicinity of Kenesaw Mountain, both sides sustaining serious losses. Sherman had moved his army to a position in front of Allatoona, occupying the railroad from Allatoona and Acworth to Big Shanty, in sight of Kenesaw Mountain, where he was joined by General Blair, with two divisions of the Seventeenth Corps, thus making his effective force 100,000 men. On the 10th he moved his army to Big Shanty, repaired the railroad and bridges, and had the cars running up to his skirmish lines.

Heavy fighting occurred on the 14th at Pine Mountain, near the Acworth and Marietta Road, in which General Polk was killed by one of Sherman's volleys from a battery fired to keep up the appearance of a bold offensive. Johnston concentrated his strength by the 20th and made his position strong, with the Kenesaw Mountain for a salient. On the 27th, Sherman, after stretching his lines to the utmost, fell upon Johnston's fortified position, the assault being made in the morning. At all points along the ten miles over which Sherman's army extended the Confederates resisted the assaults, and by noon Sherman's attempt was pronounced a failure.

Sherman's loss was about 2,500, while Johnston's was only 800. A truce was granted on the 29th of June to allow the Federals to bury their dead.

LEFT TO THEIR FATE, BUT ESCAPED

GEORGE E. DAVIS,
First Lieutenant, Co. D, 10th Vermont Inf.
Born at Dunstable, Mass., Dec. 26, 1839.
Highest rank attained: Captain.

GENERAL LEW WALLACE, who was opposing General Early's advance at the Monocacy River, Md., in July, 1864, placed a line of skirmishers on the west bank of the river to defend a railroad bridge and a wooden bridge that continued the pike from Frederick City to Washington.

On the 9th the situation was critical. Early's forces greatly outnumbered Wallace's. Ricketts was engaged with the enemy and might be driven back before the skirmishers could be retired. If the skirmishers were retired the enemy would follow on their heels, thus allowing no time to destroy the bridge.

General Wallace, seeing that it was useless to further resist the overwhelming assault, decided to destroy the bridge and sacrifice his skirmishers to save Washington.

Lieutenant George E. Davis, of Company D, Tenth Vermont Infantry, who was in command of the skirmishers, gives the following account of their brave resistance of the enemy and of their ultimate escape:

"Early in the morning on the 9th, with one second lieutenant and seventy-five men of our regiment, I was ordered to report as skirmishers to Captain Charles J. Brown, commanding Companies C and K, First Maryland Regiment, near the block-house on the west bank of the Monocacy River. He and his two hundred men had just entered the service for one hundred days, to repel this invasion of Washington, and knew nothing of actual service. The lieutenant-colonel, nominally commanding our skirmishers, was not 'present,' so that when the enemy advanced along the pike to Frederick City at about 8:30 A. M., Captain Brown insisted upon my taking command, and ordered me to hold the two bridges at all hazards, and prevent the enemy from crossing.

"I assumed command instantly, brought up my Tenth Vermonters to this point, and after a severe fight of about an hour the enemy retired. Having just assumed command, I knew nothing of the situation, or plan of battle, except as was apparent

---

After the battle of Piedmont, Va., General Hunter advanced toward Lynchburg, which he reached on the 16th of June, 1864, but for want of ammunition he sought Harper's Ferry, which left the Shenandoah Valley uncovered. General Early took prompt advantage of this opening to cross the upper Potomac into Maryland and threaten Washington. After rapid marches he crossed the Potomac on the 4th of July, but was met by General Lew Wallace at the **Monocacy River,** who, in General Hunter's absence, made an obstinate stand against the invaders. Wallace, with his small force, was unable to cope with the overwhelming force of the enemy, and retired, but not, however, until after he had held Early in check long enough to notify Grant of the situation, whereupon the latter ordered Wright's Corps to push out and to attack Early; but the Confederates retired across the Potomac with but little loss.

to the eye. The natural advantages of cover and position were in our favor. The main body of the enemy moved around to our left and crossed the river at a ford one mile southwest, compelling General Ricketts to change front to the left and advance his line to the west of the pike. This left us a part of the main line of battle, without any support in our rear, which gave the enemy the opportunity to cut us off, take us prisoners, cross the railroad bridge and turn General Ricketts' position

"WE GAINED THE RAILROAD BRIDGE AND STARTED ACROSS"

"Anticipating a flank attack, I had, on assuming command, sent pickets up and down the river, who warned me of this movement, which was entirely hidden from my view. I drew back my men to the west end of the railroad bridge, faced to the north, repelled the attack, then resumed my former position on the pike, which we held until the final retreat at about five o'clock. During all this time we were the only troops on the west side of the river.

"In the early part of this noon attack, the wooden bridge over the Monocacy River was burned, without notice to me. At the same time the Ninth New York pickets were all withdrawn, also without notice.

"The third and last attack began about 3:30 P. M. The situation was critical; the enemy came upon us in such overwhelming numbers and with such desperation that it seemed as though we should be swept into the river. The place of the Ninth New York pickets at my left had not been filled; the force of the hundred-day men was diminishing. Apprehending an advance at my left, I sent Corporal John G. Wright through a cornfield to reconnoiter. He was killed at once. Immediately the enemy were seen passing around my right, to cut us off from retreat by the railroad bridge; our division was falling back and we were obliged to do likewise at once or succumb to the merciless fire. I gave the signal to retreat to my noble Vermonters, who had stood the fire without wavering. We gained the railroad bridge and started across, stepping from tie to tie. It seemed ages before we reached the other side, though in reality it must have been only a few minutes. One poor fellow fell through the bridge to the river, forty feet below, and several were taken prisoners, for the enemy had been close at our heels all the way. Those of our number who escaped rejoined our regiment at midnight."

THE CAPTURE OF FIVE CONFEDERATE CAVALRYMEN

GEORGE W. HEALEY,
Corporal, Troop E, Fifth Iowa Cavalry.
Born in Dubuque, Iowa, Feb. 22, 1842.

CORPORAL GEORGE W. HEALEY, of Troop E, Fifth Iowa Cavalry, who participated in General McCook's Cavalry Raid during Sherman's Atlanta campaign, says: "At Newnan, Ga., July 29, 1864, our company was ordered out on the skirmish line which was on the extreme left of our main line of battle. The engagement lasted more or less all day. In moving out we struck into low ground, timber and heavy undergrowth. It was difficult to keep our alignment and intervals and consequently I soon discovered that I was alone and unobserved. Suddenly I ran into a body of Confederate soldiers. Their officer was giving a command to mount and count fours. They did not see me, so I began to retrace my steps and moved back to find my command, when, to my surprise, I came upon a Confederate who was seated on a log and ordered him to drop his gun, which he did. I picked it up and threw it into the creek. Just as I was about to move with my prisoner I heard someone approaching us. Ordering the rebel to lie down, I sought protection from behind a tree and waited. To my satisfaction I recognized in the new arrival Private Oscar Martin, of my company, who was bareheaded and coming toward me at a quick pace. He had lost his way. Looking at my prisoner and pointing to the direction whence he had come, he said: 'The woods are full of 'em.' 'Yes,' I replied, pointing to where I had been, 'and over there, too.'

"Martin scrutinized my prisoner and asked: 'What have you got in that bag?'

"The rebel answered: 'Chewing tobacco.'

"Whereupon Martin compelled him to disgorge, and, I confess, it came in handy.

"As we were about to resume our march, we heard men talking. We got behind a tree and the next minute four Confederates came, trailing in Indian fashion, toward us. Martin and I stepped from behind the trees and covered them. I ordered: 'Halt! Drop those guns!' but had to repeat the command before they obeyed. I then marched them some fifty feet, halted them, and ordered one man to advance at a time, when Martin and I relieved them of their revolvers, holsters and belts. Next, while Martin kept guard, I went back, removed the cartridges from the rifles they had dropped and returned the empty guns to them. We moved toward our lines and reached them without further interruption, where we turned our five prisoners over to General McCook, who paid us a high compliment."

Corporal Healey received a Medal of Honor; his companion died or he would doubtless have been honored in a like manner.

THE COLONEL'S WRATH WAS APPEASED

A T THE BATTLE OF PEACH TREE CREEK, Ga., before Atlanta, an act was performed by Color-Sergeant William Crosier, of the One hundred and forty-ninth New York Infantry, of which an officer of his regiment says:

"It was one of superb bravery in action and of devotion to the flag, which made him hold life as nothing beside the safety of the starry banner."

This officer continues: "The field was covered with woods, thick with undergrowth and trailing vines. The troops of the line of battle were suddenly and unexpectedly attacked by a superior force and routed. Our brigade, being in reserve in column of regiments, was ordered forward, each regiment advancing as it became

WILLIAM CROSIER,
Color Sergeant, 149th N. Y. Infantry.
Born at Skaneateles, N. Y., August 30, 1843.

During the operations before Atlanta by the Union Army, the Confederate general, Johnston, was relieved of his command by Hood, who at once engaged the Federals at **Peach Tree Creek, Ga.,** July 20, 1864. He was repulsed with a loss of 4,796. Sherman's loss was 1,710. After several engagements in which the Federals were victorious, Hood retired, September 2, to Lovejoy's Station, thirty miles away, and Sherm an took possession of the town.

deployed. This brought the regiments into action singly, and each in turn was routed by overwhelming numbers.

"Our regiment crossed the enfiladed ravine at the center, with the colors and about seventy-five officers and men, and ascended the woody acclivity thickly undergrown with brush and vines, only to recoil under a withering fire full in our faces."

Sergeant Crosier adds: "We were far ahead of the main line, trying to establish the advanced position, when the fight began. The regiments were sent in, one at a time, to check the advance of the enemy, and were literally wiped out as they were struck. Then came movements never to be forgotten. My six color-guards having all been shot down within six feet from where I stood, I found myself alone, unarmed, with Confederates storming all around me and demanding my flag. I cried to them to take it, if they could, and, swiftly tearing the flag off the staff, stuffed it under my shirt and retreated, leaving my flag-staff behind."

Out of the bushes Sergeant Crosier came staggering and covered with blood from a serious wound, and—empty handed. He met Colonel Barnum, the commander of the regiment. "Where is that flag?" he angrily demanded of the color-sergeant, drawing his sword ready to cut him down.

Sergeant Crosier smiled feebly, unbuttoned his blouse and produced the flag.

MERITED PRESIDENT LINCOLN'S ADMIRATION

M. R. WILLIAM GREBE,

Captain, Fourth Missouri Cavalry.
Born in Hildesheim, Germany, Aug. 4, 1838.
Highest rank attained: Major.

"My grateful personal acknowledgment of the almost inesteemable service you rendered the country. * * *

"Your chivalry and daring described by the above generals and so appreciated by them and by myself, which always win the admiration of the world, are acts of absolute, indomitable courage, not needing to be emblazoned by the correspondent's pen, as they are written on the annals of the American history by your sword.

"Yours very truly,

"ABRAHAM LINCOLN."

THE proud recipient of this flattering letter was Captain M. R. William Grebe of the Fourth Missouri Cavalry and aide-de-camp to Generals McPherson, O. O. Howard, and Logan.

The generals to whom the President refers are Generals Sherman, Sheridan, Logan, and Blair.

Interesting indeed must be the career of the soldier who earns the praise from these heroes of a great nation! Captain Grebe's career is highly fascinating, romantic, thrilling.

When the war broke out, Grebe, who is a native of the Province of Hanover — then the Kingdom of Hanover—was a lieutenant in the army of his country. The struggle of the Union for freedom and liberty aroused in the young officer an enthusiasm for the Federal cause which induced him to resign his rank, leave home and country and cross the ocean to espouse a cause which had appealed to him so strongly.

Upon his arrival here he at once joined the Union forces and was made a lieutenant of Troop T, Fourth Missouri Cavalry. His military training and excellent soldierly qualities at once drew the attention of his superior officers to him and ere long he found himself promoted to a captaincy in the same regiment. A little later Major-General McPherson selected him as one of his aides-de-camp.

From the very outset of his military career on this side of the Atlantic, when he first went into battle until a dramatic incident abruptly placed him back to a civilian's life, Captain Grebe's conduct was one of inspiring brilliancy—a succession of extraordinarily daring feats, so much so that Congress in awarding him the Medal of Honor found it impossible to particularize, but granted it for his general gallant behavior.

On July 22, 1864, he was sent by General McPherson to deliver a message to General Kilpatrick at Decatur, Ga. The Confederates were driving back the Union cavalry in wild confusion and had successfully turned the Federal left wing. Captain Grebe delivered his message and at once obtained permission to participate in a cavalry charge with his orderly, Henry Wagner. He himself led this charge and in a mad rush, which struck terror to the hearts of the Confederates, while it inspired his own men, broke through the ranks of the enemy, completely routing them. He caught up with the color-bearer, who had the flag fastened to his stirrup and leg, thus allowing him to handle the reins and his revolver without hindrance. The Confederate frequently fired at Grebe, two of the shots taking effect; but that did not deter the plucky captain, and when his horse was along side that of the Confederate's, he grasped the flag and cut the rebel down with a tremendous sabre blow over the head.

Captain Grebe, however, did not escape unhurt. He was bleeding profusely from two gunshot wounds in his legs, and upon his return to General McPherson was told by this commander to seek medical aid at the hospital, but the captain declined and in spite of his condition remained in the saddle all day.

During the afternoon of that same day General McPherson was shot and the captain again became a leading figure in the battle.

He was riding to the place where he had only a short time before left the general, when, to his amazement, he observed his commander's horse coming riderless from a thicket. Instantly Captain Grebe knew what had happened.

Dauntless and alone, not knowing whether he would encounter an army corps or a corporal's guard, collecting a few cavalrymen on the way, Captain Grebe charged into the thick underbrush.

General Frank P. Blair says in his official report: "The fearless captain ran up against the very rebels who had just killed General McPherson. The dead hero had been robbed of his belt, field-glasses, watch, pistol and papers. The struggle took place where the general had fallen. A rebel on horseback made a dash at Captain Grebe, who shot him down. Two men on foot raised their guns at the Captain's head. Wagner, the plucky orderly, put a bullet into one, while the captain himself split the other's head with his sabre. Then the rebels fled, leaving the general's body in the possession of Captain Grebe, who on this occasion captured a corporal and numerous other prisoners."

"HE CUT THE REBEL DOWN WITH A TREMENDOUS SABRE BLOW."

Six days later, at Ezra Church, General Logan's Corps was engaged with the enemy, who had made three furious assaults on his lines, only to be repulsed each time. After the third repulse and countercharge by the Union troops, S. Houston, of Company F, Fourth Missouri Cavalry, was missing. Some time later he was discovered midway between the lines of battle and held down by the body of his horse. Captain Grebe instantly mounted his horse and dashed out toward the enemy's line, some 700 yards distant. Reaching Houston's side he dismounted, cut him free from straps and stirrups and, getting him out from under the horse, helped him into his own saddle. Then, mounting behind, he brought him back to be received with a tremendous cheer along the whole Union lines."

At the battle of Jonesboro, August 31, 1864, Captain Grebe, at that time aide to General O. O. Howard, volunteered to cross Flint river with a message to a dismounted cavalry regiment which was needed to re-enforce the line of battle at a point which was seriously threatened. Away he started and after swimming the river and crossing an old cotton field, continuously braving a terrific fire of musketry, grape and canister, he reached the regiment and started with it in the return. As the re-enforcement took position in the line of battle, Captain Grebe dismounted and, picking up the gun of a fallen comrade, took his place in line. He was in a kneeling position, firing, with one knee for a "rest," when General Logan and his staff rode up from behind. The general, recognizing his former aide, remarked jokingly: "Captain, you're getting religious even in battle line and you will go to heaven; but this is no place for a camp meeting."

At this Captain Grebe jumped upon the earthworks and waving his gun, shouted: "To hell with camp meetings, let's go to yonder hell first. Come on boys!" General Logan's bugler sounded the call and the whole line made a most successful charge. As the Union forces met the Confederate line, which was turning to run, Captain Grebe struck a color-bearer, who fell, dragging the colors down with him. Then the captain got into a hand-to-hand fight with several Confederates and was nearly overcome, when an officer of Osterhaus' Corps came to his assistance. Captain Grebe again sprang forward to wrench the flag from the fallen color-bearer, when the sword of a hostile sergeant struck his left breast and he fell unconscious upon the body of the rebel flag-bearer. Simultaneously, Wagner again came to his captain's rescue, and with a slashing blow of his sabre cut the Confederate sergeant down.

After the battle General Logan saluted Captain Grebe with a wave of his slouch hat, saying: "Well done, Grebe; the battle is won by your intrepidity and dash."

And now follows a dramatic incident. Captain Grebe, in recognition of his unusually gallant services, was ordered to proceed to St. Louis, Mo., to be promoted Colonel of the Fourth Missouri Cavalry. While in that city he one evening escorted a lady to a theatre and was incensed at an insult to which he and the lady were subjected by Ferdinand Hansen, also a cavalry officer. A duel was the inevitable outcome. They fought with 45-calibre revolvers at a distance of twelve yards. Hansen fell, shot through the breast, but eventually recovered. Captain Grebe was cashiered from the army as well as all those who had any part in this *affaire d' honneur*.

Thirty years elapsed before Captain Grebe's case, the duel and the cause which led up to it, was investigated by Congress. Then not only was his honorable discharge ordered, but so greatly impressed were the nation's representatives with the military record of this officer that they awarded him the Medal of Honor as a just tribute of his unexcelled bravery.

INTERRUPTIONS AT A REBEL BREAKFAST

EDWIN M. TRUELL,
Private, Co. E, 12th Wisconsin Infantry.
Born at Lowell, Mass., Aug. 19, 1841.

A<small>N</small> assault was made by General Force's Brigade upon rebel works at Bald Hill, near Atlanta, Ga., July 21, 1864. The action opened early in the morning by a bayonet charge up the hill, through a cornfield and across a field of underbrush and small trees felled in all directions to obstruct the advance. The Twelfth Wisconsin formed part of the brigade, and as it swept up the hill Private Edwin M. Truell, of Company E, was severely wounded in the right foot by a Minie ball. The wound was very painful and caused the injured man to limp, but he could still travel and bravely kept up in line. The regiment took three lines of breastworks and captured many prisoners. As the Union soldiers bounded over the earthworks at the first line, the rebels in the trenches were completely taken by surprise. They were at their breakfast and left their corn and cakes and bacon in tin pans on the ground as they sprang to their feet, guns in hand. Private Truell struck three Confederates, who were so terror-stricken that they, unable to recover their wits, cried: "We surrender! We surrender! What shall we do?"

"Throw down your guns and go to the rear!" Private Truell shouted, and the rebels fairly fell over each other in their haste to comply. The advance continued. Once over the last line, Private Truell took station behind a large pine tree, where he tried to rally his comrades to his support. The order to retreat had been given, however, and the breastworks on the right, which had not been captured, were now pouring in an enfilading fire. For some few minutes Private Truell maintained his position, but, finding it impossible to bring others forward and anticipating a charge by the enemy in an effort to retake the works, he fell back across the road and rejoined his comrades. The rebels did charge and during the subsequent severe fighting the plucky private received a second shot close to the first wound and fell exhausted from loss of blood to the ground.

His comrades ran to his assistance and offered to take him to the rear, but he refused. Instead he crawled on hands and knees through a strip of woods, across the field and down the hill to a little creek, where he dressed and bandaged his own wound with a handkerchief. He returned in the same manner, and, unmindful of his own condition, directed his attention to his wounded comrades, whose thirst he quenched from his canteen, and whose sufferings he endeavored to alleviate. It was evening when he was taken off the field and conveyed to a field hospital, where, after seven weeks of intense suffering, the leg was amputated.

THE HERO OF FORT HASKELL

WHEN General Meade changed General Burnside's plan of attack at the battle of the Crater, Va., July 30, 1864, and ordered that one division of white troops should lead the assault, if fell by lot to the Fourteenth New York Artillery to lead the charge. The mine extending from the Union lines to a point under the Confederate stronghold was ready to be sprung July 29. During the night General Ledlie's Division, to which the Fourteenth New York Artillery belonged, marched out through the covered ways and formed lines just in rear of the most advanced Federal works, where it awaited the explosion with no little anxiety, and as the men had been without sleep all night many lay down for a brief rest.

"No word could be uttered aloud; orders were given in a whisper," says Captain Charles H. Houghton, of Company L, Fourteenth New York Artillery. "After hours of silent and anxious waiting we knew the time for the explosion had passed and later learned that a lieutenant and a sergeant of the Forty-eighth Pennsylvania had gone into the tunnel and found that the burning fuse had gone out where it had been spliced. It was relighted and soon after, about daylight, it reached the magazines. The effect was beyond description. The earth under us, and for some distance back of us, seemed to be the brink of a volcano, or the long roll of an ocean swell. Soldiers lying on the ground were almost lifted to a standing position; and then with a mighty power the earth opened, flames shot upward, carrying the earth, timbers, cannon, men, and everything within the fort, to a distance of seventy-five or a hundred feet. The scene was magnificently sublime, though it brought death and destruction to all within it, and to add to the reality of this inferno some two hundred pieces of artillery in our works opened fire with death-dealing missiles upon the enemy's line. Under this fire the charging columns advanced, meeting at the outset a serious obstruction, as our works at the nearest

The Battle of the Crater (Petersburg, Va.)—On the 25th of June, 1864, work was begun under the direction of Lieutenant-Colonel Henry Pleasants, of the Forty-eighth Pennsylvania Infantry, upon the structure known as the Crater. This work, approved by General Burnside, commander of the Ninth Corps, had the disapproval of General Meade, commander, and Major Duane, chief engineer of the Army of the Potomac. Accordingly Colonel Pleasants was forced to prosecute his work, under almost insurmountable disadvantage. Then, too, General Burnside's plan of attack, submitted by request of General Meade, was changed in several very material particulars. In the end, so far as the construction and explosion of the mine were concerned, the effort was a success. Otherwise, and for very many reasons, it was a great calamity to the Union Army. The Federal losses aggregated over 7,000 men, killed, wounded and missing.

point, being lower down on the sloping ground, had to be built higher than usual and had not been prepared for scaling. But ladders were quickly formed by some of our men placing their bayonets between the logs and holding the butt end of the muskets at hip and on shoulders, up which the others climbed, aided by officers standing on top of the parapet. But as rapidity of action at such time was of the greatest importance, Colonel Marshall, commanding the brigade, and standing below within the works, ordered me to go forward with what men I had. We moved without waiting for the rest of our command, at double-quick, to the Crater, and planted our flag first over its ruins, capturing many prisoners and two brass field pieces which were in the left wing of the fort not damaged by the explosion. I decided that the magazines must be near, and my men soon uncovered the entrance, which had been filled with falling earth. One gun was soon prepared for action, and silenced one of the enemy's guns which was giving us canister. Our first fire brought in a number of prisoners forced to surrender or meet death.

"On reaching the Crater, an appalling sight was witnessed. We realized something of the terrible effect which the explosion of so much powder, placed twenty-five feet directly under the fort, must cause. We found an excavation some thirty feet deep, sixty feet wide, and probably 130 feet long. One huge lump of red clay was thrown on the surface facing our own works ; broken guns, timbers, sand bags, men buried in every conceivable position, some with an arm, hand or head only uncovered ; others with feet uppermost, and still others on top of the fallen earth, with bones broken. One had fallen to the bottom of a shaft twelve feet deep, at the entrance of a countermining tunnel, toward our lines.

"We were not able to learn, nor had we time to explore its extent, but were informed by a captured lieutenant that two such shafts had been sunk, tunnels being worked at the time, and, had they gone deep enough, would have discovered our own.

"We were forced to pass through the Crater, climb the opposite slanting wall, and over the crest to traverses beyond, where our men received the fire of the Confederates from whom, in a hand-to-hand encounter, we captured a Confederate battle flag.

"But in the meantime the enemy had not been idle. A battery had been brought up from the left to a position out of range of our artillery, and opened fire with grape and canister on our troops, and sweeping the crest of the Crater, aided also by the guns in the two forts on our right, and one on the left flank, re-enforcements having been thrown into the Confederate main line on both flanks, their terrific and incessant fire concentrated upon that point rendered it impossible for us to advance and deploy.

"A brigade of General Mahone's Confederate division advanced to a charge, during which their battery had to withhold fire, giving us an opportunity to bring into action one of the captured guns, and by turning it upon this column efficient aid was rendered to our infantry in repulsing this first effort to dislodge us. The ammunition from the rebel magazine being nearly exhausted, and our gunners too exposed in working it in plain view and range of the enemy, we were compelled to discontinue its use, and soon thereafter Mahone's entire Confederate division advanced and charged our colored troops, who had done splendid fighting, and, being now compressed to a small space with no protection on front nor flank, were forced back, carrying the other troops with them to our main line.

"A SHELL EXPLODED AT HIS FEET."

"I passed through the Crater along the rear wall to the wing where I had left the two captured guns in charge of a sergeant and detachment. The entrance, a narrow passageway, was covered by rebel sharpshooters, and General Hartranft called out quickly to me to drop down and crawl in. I and my orderly, Corporal Stanford Bigelow, passed through safely.

"I found Generals Potter, Hartranft, Griffin, and one or two others; General Bartlett was in the pit of the Crater, shot through his artificial leg, and unable to walk, thus preventing his escape. The rebels were then on all sides, except that fronting our lines, and firing into the Crater. Our men still within it were placed along the rear and flank crest to keep them back; several were thus killed, shot through the head; these would fall backward, and if they did not roll to the bottom of the pit, laid with head toward it, so that the blood ran down its sloping walls in small rivulets to the bottom, where it formed pools before its absorption by the red clay.

"At this time the pit and its sides were filled with dead and wounded who could not escape capture or death. Intense suffering was being caused from want of water and surgeons; and unprotected from the sun, with not a breath of air stirring in that hell hole, many must have died under the torture, and later, many more, still living, it is believed, were buried therein by the Confederates. If the sight was appalling to iron nerves, what must it have been to those inside, awaiting death so heroically?

"Then we turned our gaze to the open field between the lines, over which we had advanced at daylight, now strewn with the bodies of hundreds of our dead and dying, white and colored, with the hot midday rays of a July sun beating mercilessly down upon them, which was still swept by the concentrated cross-fire of the enemy's artillery and infantry, over which it seemed impossible for one to pass and escape death. After remaining there for some time in the stifling heat amid such scenes of carnage and suffering, and realizing that a protracted stay would probably add to the already numerous prisoners taken by the enemy, or lengthen our long death roll, I decided to make an attempt to reach at the nearest point, our lines, over which I could see my own regimental flag floating in the slight sultry breeze, indicating its direction, which was favorable to my plan already quickly formed of releasing those general officers and all others not seriously wounded. On informing them of my decision, they protested, and endeavored to convince me of the great danger and almost certain death to go across that field under such a fire. I replied that it was sure death or starvation in rebel prisons, to remain, and I preferred to take the risk then. After watching the explosion of shell and noting the point of its striking the ground, I gave word to my orderly that on the explosion of the next I would make the start, he to follow a short distance in my rear, so we should not be in line, and we could pass beyond that point before another explosion and before the range could be changed. The rebels saw us right after the start, but passing through showers of bullets we reached, with a bound, the crest of our works and sprang from the parapet within, safe and unscathed. I immediately ordered my men, who had received ammunition and were prepared to hold these works, to open a hot fire on the enemy to the right of the Crater, who, apparently expecting another attack, replied vehemently, and very soon the field was covered with smoke, through the pall of which every general left in the angle or wing escaped in safety to our lines."

Four months after this battle Captain Charles H. Houghton was assigned to duty at Fort Haskell, Va., as commander of the post, the garrison consisting of 350 men, including several batteries of artillery. About this time printed copies of an order of amnesty issued by General Grant, providing that deserters coming into the Union lines, bringing their arms and accoutrements, would be paid a specified sum, and, on taking the oath not to again take up arms against the United States, would be furnished free transportation north, had been freely circulated along the Confederate lines. Through the operation of this very order, the Confederate general, Gordon, succeeded in entering the Union lines in his night attack on Fort Stedman on the early morning of March 25, 1865—the last general assault by Lee's army on the Federal intrenchments.

General Gordon decided to make his assault from Colquitt's Salient, a point not more than 200 yards from the Federal lines, with a force of about 12,000 infantry supported by a large cavalry force and with a heavy force in reserve. Shortly after three o'clock on the morning of the 25th when the darkness was intense, a file of 100 picked men advanced from the Confederate lines and, utilizing the tenor of the amnesty order, the first man called out: "Don't shoot; we want to come in." In this way the sentinel did not fire and was immediately killed by a noiseless bayonet thrust. Aided by the darkness, and followed by detachments to cut away the abatis, the force of the enemy grew until, having the strength of an assaulting column, they attacked that part of the unoccupied works to the right and rear of Battery Ten, next north of Fort Stedman. Here they were met by a portion of the Fourteenth New York Artillery, garrisoning the section of the line which was in position. Captain Cleary, Lieutenant Thomson and Sergeant Delack hauled one gun to the sally-port and opened on the assailants, capturing several prisoners and the flag of the Twenty-Sixth South Carolina Infantry. Lieutenant E. B. Nye, commanding the section of artillery in Battery Ten, was shot down while gallantly defending his guns.

Commandant Houghton, two days previous to Gordon's assault on Stedman, had added 60,000 rounds of ammunition for all arms to his magazine supply, and on the eve of the 25th had advised his officers to be ready to resist an attack very early the next morning. When asked for his reasons for having such an opinion, he said his premonition was strong and unexplainable and that he was advising extraordinary precautions, as he felt that they were necessary.

About three o'clock the next morning, Sylvester E. Hough, the last watch on the outer post, saw blue lights flashing along the rebel picket pits and heard the sound of chopping on the lines. He fired a signal gun, and as a more rapid fire than usual was heard along the left front of Fort Stedman the men in Fort Haskell were forming in line and answering the roll call. Captain Houghton hurried to the banquette on the right flank of his fort and at once saw that the enemy were on the left flank of Stedman, between the two forts. Word came that the Confederates were stealing along in the dark toward the front of Fort Haskell, at which the captain ordered his men to their positions on the banquette of the front parapet. There, cautioning his men to reserve their fire till he gave the command, the garrison stood silently in the darkness, with one of Captain Werner's guns loaded with case shot, and trained on the opening of the abatis through which the Union pickets passed in and out.

As Captain Houghton and his men stood there in enforced silence, the Confederate column in double rank reached the abatis and their commanders could be heard cautioning the men to move more quietly and steadily, and, "we'll have their works—steady men, steady."

"Wait," whispered Captain Houghton, "wait till you can see them ; then fire."

"Steady, men, steady," again whispered the Confederate leader as the Union soldiers waited breathless and with leveled muskets.

"Fire!" shouted Captain Houghton, and a terrific volley from cannon and muskets, heralded by a single, awful crash, swept along the ranks of the astonished band. Surprised, almost demoralized, the enemy fell back a short distance to reform and advance again up the slope. As before, they were received with a concerted volley from cannon and musketry, to once more go reeling to the rear. Then what were left quickly divided into small squads and attempted by making simultaneous attacks at different points to carry the fort, but most of them were killed for their folly.

As soon as it was light enough to see that the American flag was still flying over Fort Haskell, all the artillery of the Confederate works and the captured guns in Fort Stedman and Batteries Eleven and Twelve were turned in a concentrated fire on Captain Houghton and his gallant garrison, while the Third New Jersey Battery, in position at embrazures on the right flank and on parapet, was firing shell and case-shot into the enemy.

The rebels made three furious attacks, but were driven back in confusion each time. Up to this time the garrison had been fighting almost alone, but now they had been joined by Major Randall and a few who had escaped from Fort Stedman, and small detachments from other regiments had come in. However, on the other hand, a Union reserve artillery battery near Meade's Station began firing upon Fort Haskell, under the mistaken notion that the fort had been captured by the enemy. Color-bearer Robert Kiley with colors and a guard was sent out under fire to the rear to signal the battery to cease firing. Four of the color-guard were shot down.

During the second charge by the enemy on his right flank and rear Captain Houghton, while standing near his colors on the banquette, had his right leg shattered by a fragment from a shell which exploded at his feet, while other fragments wounded his right hand severely. He was immediately carried to a bombproof facing the parapet, where he lay, watching and directing his men. The proposed capture of Fort Haskell resulted in a complete failure.

Captain Houghton was removed to a field hospital and his leg was amputated at the thigh. He recovered and rejoined his regiment at Fort Reno, to be honorably discharged several months later.

THE GALLANT COLONEL AND HIS BRAVE ADJUTANT

DELEVAN BATES,
Colonel, 30th U. S. Colored Troops.
Highest rank attained: Bvt. Brig-Gen.
Born in Schoharie Co., N. Y., in 1840.

ABOUT two hours after the explosion of the mine, General Edward Ferrero, who had expressed the opinion that it would be inadvisable to take his division of colored troops to the Crater, was peremptorily ordered by General Burnside to lead his division at once into the "hell's hole." In compliance with this order the Thirtieth U. S. Colored Infantry immediately advanced, led by its gallant commander, Colonel Delevan Bates. The attack is described as follows:

"Under the range of a score of cannon with a perfect maelstrom of rebel lead sweeping the area, the colored men went with a dash against the line of earthworks filled with the veterans of many battle-fields. Their bravery was of the highest grade and before the charge was ended two hundred yards of breastworks, covered ways and bomb proofs were captured in a hand-to-hand combat and several hundred prisoners with a stand of colors were sent to the rear.

"At this juncture there came orders for another charge on a Confederate battery several hundred yards nearer the city of Petersburg. Again the Thirtieth, led by its commander, was under way. Subjected to a galling fire from batteries on the flanks and from infantry fire in front and partly on the flank, an attempt was made to execute the order. Colonel Bates was shot through the head, dangerously, but not fatally; Major Leeke was killed; Captain Seagraves had his leg shattered by a bullet but, refusing to surrender, killed and wounded six Confederates, and was found

ANDREW DAVIDSON,
Adjutant, 30th U. S. Colored Troops.
Highest rank attained: Captain.
Born in Scotland in 1840.

with seven deadly wounds on his person. His men fought for his body like tigers, but without success, several of them being found dead by his side. The color-guards were annihilated, one after another seizing the flag as their comrades fell dead and, finally broken up and in disorder, the rest fell back to the line from whence they started.

"After Colonel Bates was wounded and Major Leeke killed, Adjutant Andrew Davidson, assisted by the remaining company officers, made a most heroic effort to rally the broken ranks of his regiment from the desperate countercharge of the enemy and was the last officer to abandon the recaptured position and fall back to the Union line."

COLONEL DELEVAN BATES AT "THE CRATER," (PETERSBURG.)

Eight company officers were killed or wounded and two were taken prisoners; while 212 enlisted men of the regiment were killed or wounded. This was the record of a body of troops never under heavy fire before, a regiment of heroes, led by officers who knew no fear.

A BAYONET CHARGE PUT THE REBELS TO FLIGHT

ALBERT D. WRIGHT,
Captain, Co. G, 43d U. S. Colored Inf.
Born in Elkland, Tioga Co., Pa.,
Dec. 10, 1844.

ANOTHER body of colored troops, the Forty-third U. S. Colored Infantry, distinguished itself at the Mine, and one of their officers, Captain Albert D. Wright, of Company G, earned his Medal of Honor on that memorable occasion, which he himself recalls as follows:

"At the time of the explosion, our brigade was strung out in the 'covered way' leading to the fort, with the Forty-third Regiment in advance. As our troops crossed the space between our lines and the Confederates', at this point not more than one hundred yards apart, they were exposed to a scattering fire of musketry, and instead of continuing through the Crater directly to Petersburg, as planned, huddled into the Crater and stopped, while the Confederates fled from the breastworks, expecting other explosions. When the rebels found that none followed, and their lines were not occupied, except in the Crater, they rallied, and, manning their guns, began a horrible slaughter of our men, by dropping shells into the Crater from every battery within reach, and from a number of little Cohorn mortars in the vicinity.

"Not quite an hour had passed when we were hurried to the ravine immediately behind our works, massed and ordered to perform the same manoeuvre that the white troops preceding us had been ordered to execute. The narrow space between the lines was almost taken up by a line of abatis and one of chevaux-de-frise, in front of and on each side of the breastworks. These lines were impassable, unless the wires binding them together could be cut and the heavy timbers and tree-tops removed, an operation impossible to perform in the face of a line of such men as we had to meet. The break in our line was wide enough only for four men to pass out abreast, while the break in the Confederate lines was only where the abatis and chevaux-de-frise had been covered with earth from the explosion; consequently we were obliged to cross in column by fours, as if we were marching along a road.

"The balance of the regiment could not remain exposed to the awful fire which enfiladed them on both sides and for some reason they filed to the right and went between the Confederate lines and ours. In a very few moments I saw we were simply being slaughtered without a chance of defense and, seeing a little path through the Confederate lines of abatis and chevaux-de-frise, I crawled through to the Confederate breastworks, lay down on the outside and began firing my pistol alongside of every gun I could reach, as they moved them over to fire at our men. The momentary sight I got of our fellows, bravely trying to rally, drove me frantic. Six of my company had followed me through the little path, and turning to them I said: 'We cannot go back; they will kill us! If we lie here they will capture us, and they say they will take no nigger prisoners or white officers with them. Let's jump in.'

"They replied: 'All right, Cap'n.' I told them to fix bayonets, gave the word, and in we went.

"It was a surprise. We were stronger just there than they were. The colored men killed everyone within reach, instantly. This created a panic, and, thinking of our poor fellows in the field, we turned to the right, the men yelling like fiends and bayoneting everyone they could reach. We simply cleaned out the breastworks for the whole length of our regiment, the Confederates evidently mistaking our rush for a charge by the troop they knew to be in the Crater.

"While rushing down the breastwork, I saw a flag sticking out of a hole behind the works. Springing on top of the earth around the hole, and, pointing my empty revolver down, I drove out the color-sergeant and guard of six men, took the flag and sent it across to our line. This occupied only a moment, after which we continued driving the enemy out of the works until we came to an angle around the head of the ravine, the line on the opposite side of the ravine continuing straight with the line we had cleared out. There it was that the enemy could see how small our force was, and they at once opened fire on us. From where we were I could see into Petersburg, there being no other works or men between ourselves and that city.

"While throwing sand-bags across the rifle pit to protect ourselves from fire, I was wounded in the arm and went back to the hospital, and on my way back I had the satisfaction of seeing what was left of our regiment crawling through the abatis and coming into the rifle pits in safety."

TOO YOUNG FOR ENLISTMENT, BUT SERVED

NATHANIEL McL. GWYNNE,
Private, Troop H, 13th Ohio Cavalry.
Born at Urbana, Ohio, July 5, 1849.

A MERE BOY, Nathaniel McL. Gwynne, applied for enlistment at Cincinnati in the spring of 1864. The recruiting officer looked at the 15-year-old, shook his head and said: "You had better stay at home, my boy; you're too young." He was not disheartened by this refusal, but went to several officers, then about to take the field, begging for permission to go along. One officer, a captain of Company H, Thirteenth Ohio Cavalry, was so favorably impressed with the boy's desire to serve his country that he permitted him to accompany his command, and from that time on young Gwynne regularly performed the duties of a private, participating in all the engagements of the regiment, including the one at Petersburg July 30.

When the regiment was about to make a charge on a battery holding a commanding position on Fort Hill, the captain noticed young Gwynne in line, and said to him: "Young man, remember you are not mustered in. You had better stay behind."

"But that's not what I'm here for!" responded the boy.

Just then the bugler sounded the charge, and away went the troop, young Gwynne with it, across a ravine, up the hill, straight to the mouths of the cannon, where a hand-to-hand fight ensued, in which the color-sergeant of the Thirteenth was shot down and the colors captured. The enemy were the stronger; the attack failed. The colors captured, a retreat followed.

Half the distance over which the charge had been made was covered in the retreat when a horse wheeled out of line, his head toward the enemy, and charged directly toward the battery. It was young Gwynne's horse. Those who saw the dash at first wondered whether he had lost control of his horse; then, whether his reason had deserted him, for he was guiding his horse with a firm hand. On he went, heedless of the shower of bullets from the infantry, supporting the battery, riding into the midst of it, and directly to the point where his regimental colors were held, all the time urging his horse to its utmost speed. Reaching the colors, he seized them from their captor, and, turning his horse's head, started back to his regiment. Immediately every gun of the enemy was trained on him. He had not

---

Fort Hill, or "Hell," as it was familiarly known to the Union soldiers, was one of the numerous fortifications in front of Petersburg, where some of the fiercest fighting took place on the 30th of July, after the mine explosion.

"IMMEDIATELY EVERY GUN WAS TRAINED UPON HIM."

gone far, however, before the arm supporting the flag was shot away, almost tearing it from its socket, and the flag went down. He stopped his horse, took the reins in his teeth, picked up the flag and dashed away toward his regiment. Again he was shot, this time in the leg, but pluckily he rode on until he reached his comrades, whereupon he turned the flag over to them, and fell unconscious to the ground.

As a reward for his bravery, Gwynne was placed on the muster-roll of the Thirteenth Ohio Cavalry, his muster-in to date from the time of his application for enlistment.

CLEVER STRATEGY FOOLED
THE REBELS

THOMAS R. KERR,
Captain, Co. C, 14th Penn. Cavalry.
Born at Coleraine, Ireland,
April 24, 1848.

IN the extreme eastern part of West Virginia lies the little town of Moorefield. Here in the evening of August 6, 1864, the Confederate general, McCauseland, was resting his division, which was on its way back from Maryland after the burning of the village of Chambersburg, and consisted of McCauseland's Brigade, General Bradley Johnson's Brigade of Cavalry, Gilmor's Mounted Battalion and the Baltimore Battery—in all, about 3,200 men.

At dark on the same day General William W. Averell arrived with about 1,700 men of his division after a weary pursuit of 150 miles. This division had been engaged since the spring of the year in long and toilsome expeditions—twice to the Tennessee River and to Lynchburg, participating in many combats and skirmishes, so that it was in poor condition for active movements, either on the march or in battle. At the same time it was absolutely essential to a successful attack upon the Confederates that they should be surprised and fought with the utmost energy. Vigilant scouts guarded the front of Averell's force, preventing any intelligence of its coming from reaching the enemy, and at the same time ascertaining McCauseland's position.

General Averell, learning that General McCauseland was retreating toward **Moorefield, W. Va.,** pursued and overtook him at Oldfields, three miles east of Moorefield, on the 7th of August, 1864, effecting a complete surprise, routing and dispersing the whole command and capturing 420 prisoners, four guns, large quantities of small arms and 400 horses and equipments. The Federals lost twenty-eight in killed and wounded; the enemy's loss is unknown. After the engagement the enemy retreated by different roads into the Shenandoah Valley, and General Averell returned to New Creek with his prisoners and captured property, from which point he received orders to report to General Sheridan in the Shenandoah Valley, near Harper's Ferry.

McCauseland's Brigade with Gilmor's Battalion and two guns of the battery were encamped on the right bank of the Potomac, next to Moorefield, while a mile away Johnson's Brigade and two guns were encamped on the north side of the stream. After dark Averell sent 160 men by a mountain road around the east of Moorefield to blockade the highway and prevent the escape of the enemy toward Winchester—fifty miles away—to rejoin Early. Accompanied by Captain Thomas R. Kerr and a few chosen men, Averell proceeded on foot in the darkness, which was deepened by a fog, and captured the enemy's mounted videttes, from whom was learned the position of a Confederate picket and fifteen men under Lieutenant Carter. Captain Kerr with fifteen mounted men made a wide detour, striking a road beyond the picket. While returning toward them he was challenged and, answering "Relief," he drew near, dismounted and in a minute had the picket disarmed and under guard. Then General Averell sent Captain Kerr and his detachment to capture and bring back into the Union line a picket that was expected to arrive soon. About a mile away the captain was again challenged and replied: "Picket coming in." After which he and his party at once surrounded the enemy's picket and compelled its surrender. The officer in charge, however, broke away in an effort to escape, but Captain Kerr sprang after him and quickly subdued him with his sabre. Thus the road to Moorefield was clear and not a shot had been fired.

When the head of General Averell's column had reached a point within 500 yards of the enemy, it was not yet light enough to see clearly ten yards. Two Confederate troopers sent to recall patrol and pickets met General Averell in the road and informed him that their brigade was saddled and ready to move. Quickly placing one column in the road and one in the fields on each side, all following a line deployed in sets of fours, General Averell placed Captain Kerr with his company in advance of the center column. Only one squadron could be left in the rear to guard the prisoners. He then gave orders to ride over Johnson's Brigade, using only the sabre, and to continue steadily on to the river, break through it and capture General McCauseland himself.

The first part of the plan was executed, but the one squadron left behind could not hold all the prisoners taken from Johnson's Brigade, so that a large number of them escaped through the cornfields to the hills. There being but one ford at the river a slight delay ensued, giving the enemy a little time to form on the opposite side.

Captain Kerr and his company were at once across, however, closely followed by the other troops. The early morning light was not yet clear enough to distinguish individuals more than 100 yards distant so that Captain Kerr, challenged by the first troops he met, promptly answered: "Gilmor's Battalion;" but as that particular body happened to be the challenging party, a hot fire was opened on Kerr's Company as it charged. A bullet struck Captain Kerr in the face, another wounded him in the thigh; his horse was killed and fell on him, but his men went on.

CAPTAIN T. R. KERR CAPTURING REBEL COLORS NEAR MOOREFIELD, W. VA.

The captain extricated himself from the fallen horse, ran to the color-bearer of the Eighth Virginia Confederate Regiment, who was striving to get to horse, struck down the man, took his colors and horse, mounted and rejoined his company through the fleeing remnants of the enemy.

The sun was just up when all was over ; more than 150 of the enemy were killed and wounded. Three stands of colors, the battery, nearly 500 officers and men with nearly 1,000 horses and small arms were captured, and the enemy were dispersed to the mountains.

"WELL DONE, TAYLOR"

JOSEPH TAYLOR,
Private, Co. E, 7th R. I. Inf.
Born at Pascoag, R. I., Feb. 6, 1847.

ON the morning of August 18, 1864, at the Weldon Railroad, Private Joseph Taylor, of Company E, Seventh Rhode Island Infantry, was detached from his company on detail as mounted orderly at brigade headquarters and ordered to escort Adjutant-General Peleg E. Peckham through some near-by timber.

"The day was very hot and the country had been fairly flooded by rains," Private Taylor narrates. "We were riding quite rapidly and when we reached the woods I found them so dense and so filled with underbrush that it was with great difficulty I followed the general. Every now and then the limbs and branches of the brush pushed aside by my leader would spring back, striking my horse in the face so that I could not make it keep its gait. Thus, not being able to keep up with the general, I undertook to skirt the edge of the wood. In a short while I lost sight of him, but, believing that I would soon see him again, continued on, as I thought I could hear his horse going.

"Suddenly, to my entire surprise, I ran against a Confederate picket post of three infantrymen, who appeared to be as greatly surprised as myself. Immediately drawing my revolver, I commanded them to surrender and get out to the rear as quickly as possible, as a cavalry charge was to be made right over the ground where we were standing.

"I did not know whether there was any cavalry within ten miles, but the thought came to me and I simply said it.

"I EMPTIED A CHAMBER OF MY REVOLVER INTO HIS BREAST."

"The three men had stacked arms, which I ordered them to carry, when I felt a sharp pain, caused by a fourth Confederate, whom I had overlooked, lunging his bayonet through my right arm. I at once emptied a chamber of my revolver into his left breast and he dropped. Knowing that my shot would give an alarm, I ordered my three prisoners forward, and, revolver in hand, at their rear, I rode rapidly toward our line.

"As I reached headquarters with my captives, General Curtin asked with much surprise where I captured these men. 'Up in the brush, general,' I answered. 'Where is General Peckham?' asked the general, and I replied: 'I don't know, general; I lost him in the brush.'

"Just then Doctor Blackwood, of our staff, came up and asked: 'What's the matter with your arm, Joe?' 'Nothing, except it feels a little warm.' Then I saw that the blood of the bayonet wound had run to my hand and over my revolver, which I was still holding. Just then General Peckham rode up to us and, being questioned by General Curtin as to where I had captured the rebels, he said: 'I do not know—while riding through the brush with Taylor following me, as I supposed, I suddenly missed him. Two or three minutes later I heard a shot to my left and rear, and, thinking that by getting too far out of the woods Taylor had been hurt, I immediately returned to see about the matter.'

"General Curtin ordered the prisoners disarmed and said to me: 'Well done Taylor, you will get a Medal of Honor for this.'"

EQUAL TO THE EMERGENCY

INCLUDED in the operations against Petersburg was General Grant's effort to cut off the line of supplies for the Confederates by destroying the Weldon Railroad. General Warren, to whom this task was entrusted, was twice fiercely assaulted by General Lee's army, but succeeded in holding his position and carrying his mission to complete success. During one of the attacks an incident occurred of which Private Soloman J. Hottenstein, of Company C, One hundred and seventh Pennsylvania Infantry, became the hero.

The Union corps had, on August 18, 1864, made a descent on the Weldon Railroad at Yellow House, driving in the Confederate pickets. When, however, the enemy appeared in force, the One hundred and seventh Pennsylvania was thrown out and deployed as skirmishers to meet them. Then the fighting became general and very intense, and so continued until darkness had set in. Still the Federals held the road and, under cover of night, threw up breastworks.

At 2 P. M. the following day another attack was made, with partial success, and again, two hours later, the enemy made still another attack, flanking General Crawford's Division, taking many prisoners and compelling the Union forces to retreat. In this series of alternating charges and countercharges, attacks and retreats, the two forces became badly intermingled, and at times the mix-up was so bad that it would have been a difficult matter to discern the men of the two hostile armies. At one time, however, a large body of Confederates had part of the One hundred and seventh Pennsylvania surrounded and virtually captured. Still considerable confusion reigned, especially

SYLVESTER H. MARTIN,
Lieutenant, Co. K, 88th Penn. Infantry.
Highest rank attained : Captain.
Born in Chester Co., Pa., Aug. 9, 1841.

in the ranks of the Confederates, who at this particular point seemed to lack the hand of a leader, who could bring order out of the chaos and take advantage of the predicament of the Union men. On the other hand there was one soldier among the surrounded Federals who proved to be fully equal to the emergency—he was Private Soloman Hottenstein. He recognized that he was in a locality which he had passed and became thoroughly familiar with the day before while foraging. Utilizing this very opportune knowledge, he decided to resort to a ruse, which was as clever as it was desperate, to extricate himself and his comrades from their precarious position. Espying a Confederate color-bearer, he ran up to him and said: "Give me that flag!"

The rebel complied.

Then waving the Confederate colors aloft, he shouted: "Come on boys; follow me!" And for the Union lines he headed followed by his comrades and several hundred Confederates, who fairly fell over each other in their effort to fall into line and follow their flag. Bewildered by the general confusion, the hail of shot and shell from all directions, misled by the very boldness of Private Hottenstein's move, they marched right into the arms of the Federal troops, realizing their fatal mistake when it was too late and when they could do nothing but submit to capture.

During the same engagements the Eighty-eighth Pennsylvania and Ninety-seventh New York Infantry regiments found themselves in the same position as the one from which Private Hottenstein and comrades escaped.

"We were," says Lieutenant Sylvester H. Martin, of Company K, Eighty-eighth Pennsylvania Infantry, "between two lines of the enemy and entirely isolated from our corps, and after a consultation among the officers of both regiments, the colonel of the ninety-seventh being in command, decided that we should fight our way out. Having accomplished this, we reached our rear in an open field, but were immediately ordered to re-advance and recover our former position.

"The missiles were now coming from our front. Men were falling fast; among them was the commander of our regiment, pierced through the face. The colonel in command of the two regiments then called for an officer to take in a skirmish line, and send word back to him whether it would be safe to advance the line.

"I moved forward with men of my company as skirmishers, reconnoitered the position and made it possible to re-establish the line, which we held during the remainder of that action."

JOSEPH E. McCABE,
Sergeant, 17th Pennsylvania Cavalry.
Born at Bridgewater, Pa.. June 6, 1841.

TWO OF SHERIDAN'S SCOUTS

THE thrilling adventures of two of General Sheridan's scouts form an interesting chapter of the episodes of the War of the Rebellion. One of the scouts was Joseph E. McCabe, a sergeant in the Seventeenth Pennsylvania Cavalry; the other, Archibald H. Rowand, a private in Company K, First West Virginia Cavalry, the former being the general's chief scout.

Among the many achievements of these two men, the capture of the Confederate general, Harry Gilmor, and staff was the most brilliant and consequential. The occurrence dates at the time when General Sheridan had his headquarters at Winchester during the winter of 1864.

It was Rowand who first got onto the trail of the Confederate general, who in a mansion near Moorefield, W. Va., was nursing his wounds received at the battle of Winchester. He imparted his information to General Sheridan, who at once formulated plans for the capture of the wounded commander. The task was entrusted to McCabe, chief scout, Major Henry H. Young with a detachment of thirty cavalrymen, and Rowand, who acted as guide. After a ride of forty miles the party — all dressed as Confederates — reached the general's place of abode at daybreak. Approaching the house cautiously, Rowand went ahead, overpowered the sentinel and made him prisoner. McCabe and Major Young followed and demanded the surrender of the general and his staff. Resistance being out of question the order was readily complied with, and thus the two daring scouts were able to report the complete success of their mission to General Sheridan and turn over to him the Confederate commander.

McCabe was the leading scout in still another important capture—that of General Rufus Barringer.

It was on the morning of April 6, 1865, when McCabe and five companions, all attired in Confederate uniforms, were riding along on their way to Danville, Va. Presently they met a group of four Confederates, whom they halted and engaged in conversation. The Confederates said they belonged to a North Carolina brigade, and McCabe and his comrades pretended to be men of the Ninth Virginia. They rode along together till they were joined by a Confederate officer of apparent high rank. He revealed himself during the course of the conversation as General Barringer. McCabe drew from the unwary rebels much valuable information, when, without any previous warning, he presently informed the general and his men of his identity and demanded their surrender. His determined attitude completely nonplused the Confederates, who were too greatly surprised to make even a show of resistance. Only one rebel escaped. For this clever capture of General Barringer McCabe was awarded the Medal of Honor.

Rowand's other great feat was the delivery of a message from General Sheridan to General Grant in 1865.

Sheridan had been ordered to pass around to the west of Richmond and effect a junction with Sherman in North Carolina, but owing to heavy rains and swollen streams he had been delayed until the Confederates had time to throw a heavy force in his front and prevent his advance, a fact of which it was important that Grant should be notified. Rowand and his comrade, James A. Campbell, volunteered to deliver the message, and shortly thereafter, dressed as Confederates, they each received a copy of the message written on tissue paper and tightly rolled in the form of a small pellet inclosed in tin foil. Their orders were to deliver the message, but in case of capture to swallow the pellets before giving them up to the enemy.

The journey began on horseback and for forty-eight hours they were in the saddle, during which time they entered the Confederate lines and were within eight miles of Richmond. They met and conversed with a chief of Confederate scouts and were within five miles of the James River when some of the scouts of the enemy recognized them and gave chase. Rowand and Campbell put the spurs to their horses and reached the river ahead of their pursuers. Here they abandoned the horses and plunging into the river seized a floating skiff and with their hands

ARCHIBALD H. ROWAND, Jr.,

Private, Co. K, 1st W. Va. Cavalry.
Born in Allegheny City, Pa., March 6, 1845.

paddled so rapidly, going diagonally with the current, that they reached the opposite shore just as the enemy reached the south bank. The fugitives were ordered to halt and shots were sent after them, but it only stimulated Rowand and his comrade to greater exertions. And so, with the enemy coming behind, the two made a run, afoot, of about ten miles, when they reached the Union lines.

The lieutenant in charge of the picket refused to accept their statement that they were messengers from Sheridan and was inclined to treat them as spies. Finally, however, he consented to take his prisoners to the Colonel, who at once forwarded them, under escort, to Grant's headquarters. While sitting at Grant's desk waiting for the general to appear, they both fell asleep—the first time in over two days. Grant coming in, awakened Rowand by tapping him on the shoulder, and after receiving and reading the dispatches ordered that every attention be paid to the two young soldiers.

AN IMPROVISED BODYGUARD

WHEN on the 30th of July, 1864, the Confederate works at Petersburg were converted by the explosion of Lieutenant-Colonel Pleasants' mine into the horrible "Crater," Company H, of the Second New York Mounted Rifles, dismounted, was posted about 100 feet away from the enemy's works and with the crash and tumult of the explosion they received the order to charge with the remainder of the brigade across a small rise of ground and take position at the first line of the Confederate defenses. Second Lieutenant Harlan J. Swift, of Company H, a medal winner in this affair, relates:

"Of course it was hot work, but was in no way a surprise, because our entire line had been waiting long for just such an experience. We reached the objective point in short order, to see the enemy going pell-mell toward their second line of defense, a considerable distance away on the Jerusalem plank road. As we reached the top of the first line I could see several Confederates not far off, and, calling my company to halt, I sprinted on after the fugitives. I was very good on my feet and soon overhauled four of the men who, with guns loaded and bayonets fixed, had given me such a stubborn chase.

"Placing the muzzle of my revolver against the temple of one of the 'Johnnies' while still running, I ordered the four to surrender, which they did instantly, fancying, I suppose, that I had my whole company at my back. Then I formed them on either side and in front of me—as a protection against possible shots from their more speedy companions—and so marched them back to our line."

A WOMAN CAPTURED BY CHAMP FURGESON

DR. MARY E. WALKER,
Assistant Surgeon, U. S. Army.
Born at Oswego, N. Y.

Doctor Mary E. Walker is the only woman up to the present time who ever received the Medal of Honor. She was one of the very few women who at that time held a diploma from a medical college, and five years prior to the war had a general medical and surgical practice in Oswego, New York, her native city. When the war broke out, and with that self-reliance which is one of her strongest characteristics, Dr. Walker traveled alone to Washington, and at the War Department tendered her services as a physician and surgeon. There was nothing to prohibit such service and Dr. Walker, young, vigorous, unconventionally masculine in attire and demeanor, was accordingly appointed assistant surgeon without pay. After a time she was made assistant surgeon in the regular army, which carried with it the rank of first lieutenant. She was detailed for duty with Sherman's armies and, possessed of a strong constitution, a stern will and good knowledge of her profession, her services were invaluable on the march, in the field and in the hospital—particularly in the latter, where her executive ability proved of great advantage. While the division to which she was attached was operating around Gordon's Mills in the effort to flank Joseph E. Johnston's army, an epidemic of sickness prevailed among the people of that vicinity, who had no doctors, all the local physicians being with the Confederate armies. Accordingly an appeal for medical aid was made to the Union forces, and Dr. Walker volunteered her services.

The country was overrun with Wheeler's cavalry, while Champ Furgeson's infamous bushwhackers were a terror to both armies alike. Dr. Walker began making her visits to the afflicted people, accompanied by an armed escort of two officers and two orderlies; the doctor herself carrying revolvers in her holsters. Eventually, however, and in spite of repeated narrow escapes, she dispensed with her escort and arms and rode alone to her patients. Champ Furgeson had often declared that he would kill every "blue-coat" he captured, so the Union men understood that no quarter would be given by him.

One day in April, 1864, Dr. Walker was riding her horse alone and unarmed, on her way to see patients at Gordon's Mills. As she turned at a bend in the road, she suddenly found herself confronted by a group of mounted men wearing nondescript uniforms of gray, butternut and blue, and was told to surrender. Looking squarely into the eyes of the man who gave the order, she replied: "Certainly sir, as I am unarmed; but will you kindly escort me to the bedside of a dying woman, whom I am going as a physician to attend?"

The chief captor seemed puzzled by his prisoner's voice and *sang froid,* and, after scanning her face and figure closely for an instant, said : "Oh, you're the doctor takin' care of the folks over yon way. All right, pass on." Retaining her nerve entirely, Dr. Walker thanked the man and went her way unmolested. Upon her return to the Union camp she reported the episode to her brother officers and Colonel Dan McCook suggested that she had been "held up" by Champ Furgeson. The other

DR. MARY WALKER AT WORK ON THE FIELD

officers declared that impossible, because she had lived to tell the story. Later on in the war Dr. Walker was captured and was held prisoner at Castle Thunder, Richmond, for four months. Then she was exchanged for Dr. Lightfoot of Tennessee. It was not until after all this experience that she was shown a portrait of Champ Furgeson and at once recognized the features of the man who had been her captor for a few moments.

YEARNED FOR LIBERTY AND GAINED IT

Captain James Madison Drake, of Company K, Ninth New Jersey Infantry, had the honor of being the first man to unfurl the Union flag on the Confederate soil, and was the first to enter the enemy's works at Newbern, North Carolina. He commanded the Union advance from Bermuda to Point of Rocks, Virginia, May 6, 1864, and at Drewry's Bluff, May 16th, drove the enemy within his works. It was at this last engagement that he was taken prisoner. The story of his escape from captivity reads like a romance :

"I passed a fortnight in Libby Prison," Captain Drake says, "and was transferred to Macon and then to Savannah. I was constantly devising plans for regaining my liberty, and with other prisoners spent weeks of toil in constructing tunnels for escape. Though frequently baffled by treachery in promising enterprises for regaining freedom, I never ceased to cherish the hope of escape. The prospect was gloomy indeed. Confined in fetid strongholds, and surrounded by sleepless sentinels, the boldest at times were ready to despair. But even the horrors of the Charleston jail-yard did not discourage me from seeking a favorable means of escape. Our life in Charleston was not by any means without incident and excitement. Only the day after our arrival at the jail-yard shells from our batteries on Morris Island fired a dozen buildings near the jail, entirely destroying them. Frequently we were in danger from fragments of exploding shells from the Union batteries on the harbor islands.

"The Confederacy was now in danger of an overwhelming disaster. Sherman was prepared to pursue his triumphant march from the mountains to the sea, and desperate measures were adopted by the Southerners. Among other precautions taken was the transfer of several hundred Union captive officers to Columbia, where it was believed they could be securely guarded. The proposed change was hailed as an excellent opportunity for escape, and four of us, Captain Harry H. Todd, Eighth New Jersey Volunteers, Captain J. E. Lewis, Eleventh Connecticut Volunteers, Captain Albert Grant, Nineteenth Wisconsin Volunteers, and myself, resolved to take our lives in our hands and leap from the train.

"The train reached the southern end of the long, rickety bridge over the Congaree River shortly before dark. During the afternoon I had succeeded in removing the percussion caps from the rifles held by the sergeant and six privates who guarded our car, and as the box-car in which we were riding crossed the bridge my three chosen comrades and I leaped from the rapidly moving train. Fortunately none of us was injured.

"The train came to a stop a mile or so away, and men and dogs started after us. We sought refuge in a heavy cypress swamp, in order to baffle the bloodhounds which were on our trail within an hour. We remained in the swamp all through that dreary, rainy night and next day. At sunset we started on our way, and for days wandered on through the woods, living on corn from the fields, berries and grapes. We were weak and faint from hunger and exhaustion. Our only solace was the kindness of some darkies whom we came upon one day working in the fields, and who provided us with food and shelter in their cabins, treating us as their friends and benefactors.

"Crossing the Catawba River, we ran across some deserters from the Confederate Army, men who, impressed or driven into service, had escaped, and now defied the whole power of the Confederate Government. In Caldwell County we met hundreds of this class of persons. They were associated with another class called 'lyers out,' who had long lived in caves and other retreats on the mountain, resisting the conscription. Although but poorly armed with old Kentucky rifles and squirrel guns, they managed to keep at bay all forces sent against them.

"We lived with these men in their caves for several days, and persuaded a hundred or more to accompany us to Knoxville, Tenn., the nearest point to the Union lines, promising to use our influence in procuring them arms, ammunition, clothing, etc.

"We had a narrow escape from guerrillas at Crab Orchard, Tenn., and evaded them only by making a wide detour to Bull Gap, at the foot of the beautiful Cumberland Valley. The rebels, Keith and Palmer, with their bands of irregulars, got upon our trail on Higgins' Ridge, and came within an ace of gobbling us as we were climbing Big Butt Mountain, from the summit of which we beheld the valley, the promised land. 'Only fifteen miles from the foot of this hill,' said my friend Bill Estes, a refugee from North Carolina, 'and we shall be safe.' That exclamation urged me to renewed vigor.

"I had almost given up hope of reaching our lines, my feet being in terrible condition. Suddenly the unmistakable roaring of artillery and musketry in the valley halted the whole party, and looking toward the gap we saw the smoke rising from a battle in progress. The fight came to a sudden termination at nightfall, and we ascertained that Breckenridge had defeated General Gillem at Blue Lick Springs, the Union men being in full retreat upon Knoxville. Just at this moment a mountaineer, breathless with excitement, came up, declaring that the guerrillas were hot on our trail. We lost no time in seeking cover in a ravine between two mountains, where, we flattered ourselves, there would be comparative safety. Captains Todd and Grant, with a mountaineer, went down to a hamlet to obtain rations and to procure for me a pair of shoes, or some covering for my feet, for I was suffering greatly.

"During their absence we were surprised by a furious attack of guerrillas. Our camp was thrown into a state of violent confusion. For a moment my senses were bewildered, but whizzing bullets and demoniac yells speedily brought me to a realizing sense of the situation. In the darkness I could see nothing but the lurid flashes from the firearms of the guerrillas, who, having at last caught us napping, were now carrying on their awful work, firing and slashing wildly as they rode in upon us.

"I started running, sometimes falling on the frost-covered ground, intent only on widening the distance between myself and the enemy, from whom, if recaptured, I well knew I could expect no favors. On I went, my movements being of course greatly accelerated by the whizzing of bullets over my head. Faint and almost exhausted, and apparently out of immediate danger, I sat down to extricate a piece of stick which had been forced into the fleshy part of my heel.

"I sat there contemplating my condition and the manifold dangers which surrounded me, until daylight. I had no money, no knife or other weapon, no blanket, no utensil in which to cook, nothing to eat, I did not know in which direction to turn, and was ignorant of the fate and whereabouts of my companions.

"I was on the brink of despair when I heard sounds of an approaching party, and soon I recognized Major Davis, of Kirk's Third North Carolina Infantry, Captain Lewis and a score of others. Grant and Todd were missing, neither having been seen or heard from since they departed to

"WE REMAINED IN THE SWAMP - - - "

search for food. I was affectionately greeted, having been given up for dead. We hastened away, keeping under the shadows of the mountains. We managed to make between twenty and thirty miles a day, and in less than a week were safe within the Union lines at Knoxville, about seven weeks after our escape from Charleston."

CHARGED OVER A BURNING BRIDGE

LLEWELLYN G. ESTES,
Captain and A. A. Gen. Volunteers.
Highest rank attained: Brigadier-General.
Born at Oldtown, Penobscot Co., Me.,
Dec. 27, 1843.

I T was late in August, 1864, that General Sherman began a grand wheel of his armies with Schofield's force at the pivot, and Howard's Corps on the outside making a radius of twenty-five miles and aiming at Jonesboro, while General Thomas and his army moved between the two. The object was to seize both southern railways leading out from Atlanta and to destroy all stations, bridges, culverts, rails and ties, thus forcing Hood out of Atlanta. Preceded by Kilpatrick, who was handling the irrepressible annoyance from Wheeler's Cavalry, General Howard was moving with reasonable speed, and on the 30th of August his forces had been fighting all day as they advanced. At the same time Kilpatrick's Cavalry had also been kept busy.

At the request of General Kilpatrick his chief of staff and adjutant-general, Captain Llewellyn G. Estes, had taken command of the advance brigade of cavalry with instructions to keep well up with the skirmish line of the infantry and to protect their right flank. At about five o'clock in the afternoon of the 30th they had reached a point about four miles from Flint River, where General Howard had been ordered to camp for the night. Captain Estes halted his cavalry brigade and was waiting for the movement of the infantry on his left when one of General Howard's aides appeared and said that the general wished to see him. Accordingly the captain rode over and met General Howard, who remarked: "Estes, I am directed by General Sherman to halt my army here for the night. There is no water here for my troops, the enemy is harassing me all the time and I want to know if you can drive them across the Flint River." Captain Estes replied that he could do it and the general said: "Try it."

Thereupon Captain Estes rode rapidly back to the head of his command and with the Ninety-Sixth Illinois Cavalry charged the barricade of the enemy, rode over and through them before they had time to form again and pushed on to Flint River at a gallop. So surprised were the Confederates that they simply scattered in every direction, some six or eight of their companies racing along in front of the Federals down to and across the river. Within an hour from the talk with General Howard Captain Estes had forced the enemy across the river, and, General Howard following immediately behind Estes, came up and complimented him very highly for the work performed.

"ESTES, ARMED WITH A REVOLVER, WENT AHEAD WITH A RUSH."

Then Captain Estes asked: "Do you want me to take the bridge?" The general responded: "Can you do it?" And when the young cavalry leader said "Yes" the general replied: "All right, go ahead."

Estes hurriedly dismounted the Ninety-second Illinois and the Tenth Ohio, which General Kilpatrick had promptly sent forward at his request, and moved down the bank of the river, where these two regiments, armed with Spencer carbines, kept up such a constant fire on the enemy's barricades on the opposite side of the river that Estes was enabled with two companies of the Tenth Ohio Cavalry to charge across the bridge on the stringers, the planking having been removed by the enemy, and drive the Confederates back. At the time of this charge the bridge was burning in several places, but Estes, armed with a revolver, went ahead with a rush, brimful of confidence in the men at his back, as they were enthused by the valor and dash of their leader. After driving the foe from the river Estes and his men replaced the planking, thus enabling Howard's Army to cross. It was a triumph belonging jointly to the commander and his men, and probably the most pleased man in the whole of Sherman's Army that evening was General O. O. Howard, to realize that so much had been accomplished in so short a time with a loss of but six men ; four killed and two wounded.

The Union force was then within one mile of Jonesboro, through which the railroad passed on the line between Atlanta and Macon. It was a position with abundant water at hand and one which the general had not expected to reach except by virtue of a great battle involving an entire corps and at a great loss of life. In referring to Captain Estes' deed General Howard gave official expression in the following :

"* * * All the circumstances surrounding this action made it striking and impressive ; the necessity of securing water for my army and a lodgment on the eastern bank, the burning bridge and the barricades of the enemy, the charge across the burning timbers and the relief given by its success, not only impressed me but all others present at the time. * * * The action was phenomenal ; and the promptitude and gallantry of General Estes and his men under a very sharp fire were unsurpassed."

Captain Estes at the time of the above achievement was only twenty-one years old. One month after the Flint River engagement he was promoted major, a few months later lieutenant-colonel, and on September 30th, nine months after his twenty-first birthday, he received his commission as brigadier-general of volunteers.

HEROIC AND HUMANE

PRIVATE GEORGE H. MAYNARD, of Company D, Thirteenth Massachusetts Volunteers, distinguished himself through exceptional courage in several of the great battles.

At the attack on Antietam, September 17, 1862, Maynard and one of his comrades remained at the front skirmishing after their regiment had been withdrawn. He assisted two of his comrades who were wounded, off the field, and when fresh troops were pushed on to the attack he attached himself repeatedly until at the end of the day he had served with no less than six regiments.

Three months later his regiment participated in the charge at Fredericksburg, December 13, 1862, and suffered heavy loss. Maynard, who was in the skirmish line, went to the assistance of his wounded comrades and did not leave them till he had them in a place of safety. After his regiment had been

GEORGE H. MAYNARD,
Private, Co. D., 18th Massachusetts Infantry.
Highest rank attained:
Bvt-Major.
Born in Waltham, Mass., Feb. 2, 1836.

removed to another position he learned that one of his friends had been left wounded on the field. Regardless of the great danger he ran, he returned to the spot under a heavy fire, found the wounded man, and carried him safely to the rear.

One of the most interesting incidents, however, in his military career occurred in the month of September, 1864. A mounted expedition under command of General Asboth and composed of detachments from several regiments, six hundred strong, left Pensacola, Fla., to capture or destroy the Confederate military stores at Marianna, Fla., a distance of 300 miles. After five days of rapid marches the destination was reached, but the enemy, having been advised of the approach of the detachment, was found to be prepared to offer a stout resistance.

The main road entering Marianna was narrow, with houses on both sides of the street. About 300 yards from where the detachment halted a barricade of wagons and carts of all descriptions was thrown across the street.

Maynard had been promoted after the battle of Fredericksburg and assigned to duty in Florida and Louisiana and held the rank of Captain in the Eighty-second U. S. Volunteers at the time, and was acting provost-marshal of that expedition. He and Captain Young, of the Seventh Vermont Infantry, acting assistant adjutant-general, were at the head and to one side of the column. Presently General Asboth gave orders to charge and two companies of cavalry advanced about two-thirds of the way to the barricade, when the rebels opened fire and drove the charging Federals back in disorder.

General Asboth was greatly disappointed and cried "For shame! For shame!" as the retreating cavalry rushed past. The men, however, soon re-formed and another charge was ordered.

"This charge," says Maynard, "was led by the general, Captain Young and myself.

CAPTAIN MAYNARD PREVENTING A GENERAL MASSACRE.

"As our horses leaped the barricade, all three bunched together, the enemy fired, wounding General Asboth in the face and arm, and instantly killing Captain Young. I drew rein, faced a blacksmith shop full of Confederate soldiers, and fired, shooting their major through the shoulder. Our cavalry was detained by the barricade, and General Asboth's horse ran away when he was shot, so, for the time being, I was alone. When the cavalry came up I quickly directed as to the whereabouts of the general, and the location of the enemy. As soon as Colonel Zulavsky of the Eighty-second U. S. Volunteers had dismounted some of his men and they were apprised of the situation an active firing began.

"The enemy were posted behind houses on one side of the street, and behind the sheltering stones of a burial ground on the other, in the blacksmith shop, and in the church. Theirs seemed an impregnable position, but after an engagement of three-quarters of an hour they made overtures to surrender. No sooner had the Union troops ceased firing than they immediately reopened fire, killing one of our boys, which infuriated us.

"Shortly after, the rebels surrendered a second time, but our troops were so enraged at the previous treachery that they began an indiscriminate attack upon the Confederates as they were being captured.

"I at once dismounted and rushed into the graveyard, just in time to knock away a musket placed at the head of a prisoner, and threatened to blow out the brains of the first man who dared to shoot a prisoner. This course prevented a general massacre of our captured foes, numbering 108."

SEIZED HIS OPPORTUNITY

ISAAC GAUSE,
Corporal, Co. E, Second Ohio Cavalry.
Born in Trumbull Co., Ohio, Dec. 9, 1843.

"ON the morning of September 13, 1864," says Corporal Isaac Gause, of Company E, Second Ohio Cavalry, "I was sent forward with seven men to reconnoiter the enemy's position on the north side of the creek near Berryville, Va. After we had crossed the creek we captured the Confederate outposts, from whom we learned that the troops in camp were the Eighth South Carolina. Sending our prisoners to the rear in charge of two men, I rode rapidly, expecting my five remaining comrades would follow me around the woods which were at the top of the ridge half a mile beyond the creek. Presently I discovered that I was alone, my comrades having left the pike, going to the left around the south side of the woods. I also saw that our main force under General McIntosh had followed them and had attacked the enemy, who were on a hill to the west. Just at this time I reached the slope on the east and north of the woods, when I was fired at from a thicket, whereupon I rode into a ravine at the west of the pike and jumped my horse over a ditch to get under cover. As my horse landed on the other side of the ditch he went to his knees and I thought he had been hit; but he came up all right and I followed the ravine until I got back to the pike, where I met General McIntosh and his staff and reported to him that the enemy had a cavalry reserve north of the woods and that they were getting ready to come to the assistance of the troops on the hill and in the woods. 'But,' I said, 'we can get around the woods and intercept them.' Accordingly Company E of my regiment, under command of Major Nettleton, was ordered to the place directed. Our movement was quickly made, and sure enough we reached the northwest corner of the ravine which I had before visited, entering a larger one running north just in time to intercept the Confederates moving north toward their cavalry. The heads of our columns were not more than fifty yards apart. We charged at them and were met by a withering fire, but this did not stagger us, and their line began to break. 'Come on boys!' I yelled, and with wild whoops we doubled our speed. Just then the cavalry reserve began to pop at us from the rear, but at this time also our main force came up from the south and west, and the Confederates between our lines began to flee in every direction. In the mix-up that followed I captured the color-guard and a stand of colors, and this won for me the Medal of Honor."

INCIDENTS FROM WINCHESTER'S BLOODY BATTLEFIELD

THE stars and stripes and a rebel flag at the battle of Winchester, Va., September 19, 1864, made heroes of two brave Union soldiers — Color-Sergeant Alphonso M. Lunt, of Company F, Thirty-eighth Massachusetts Infantry, and of Corporal Gabriel Cole, of Company I, Fifth Michigan Cavalry. Their stories stand out prominently among the many remarkable incidents of the war.

The brigade to which Sergeant Lunt's regiment belonged was ordered to advance about 800 yards and halt. The impetus of the charge carried the troops

---

Winchester, Va.—On the 19th of September, 1864, Early, after having thrown the bulk of his army to Bunker Hill, and having reconnoitered as far as Martinsburg, was attacked by Sheridan at Winchester (or the Opequon), Va. After a most stubborn and sanguinary engagement, which lasted from early morning until 5 o'clock in the evening, the Confederates were completely defeated and driven to Winchester, closely followed by the Federal troops. Night prevented farther pursuit, and Sheridan rested with 2,500 prisoners, five pieces of artillery and nine battle-flags as his trophies of victory. The rebel General Rodes and General Godwin were killed and several other general officers unarmed. The Federal losses were severe, among them General D. A. Russell, commanding the First Division of the Sixth Corps, who was killed.

Early did not halt in his retreat southward until he reached Fisher's Hill, thirty miles from Sheridan, and which commanded the narrow Strasburg Valley, between the Shenandoah River and North Mountain.

GABRIEL COLE,
Corporal, Co. I, Fifth Michigan Cavalry.
Born at Beaver Dams, N. Y., March 22, 1831.

ALPHONSO M. LUNT,
Color-Sergeant, Co. F, 38th Mass. Infantry.
Highest rank attained: Captain.
Born at Berwick, Me., 1837.

way beyond the designated place and brought them into uncomfortable proximity with a much superior rebel force.

Because of the long, rapid advance over ploughed fields, fences, and rough broken country generally, the Union line was in no condition to face such an assault and began to waver. At this Sergeant Lunt, who carried his colors aloft thus far through the fight, seeing that a rally must be made, waved the flag and with a yell rushed ahead about 200 yards in advance of the line and shouted: "Dress on the colors!" Inspired by his bravery, the men of Company F at once responded, to be followed immediately by others, until about 100 men were supporting him, and there they stood facing a Confederate line of battle until the overwhelming numbers of the enemy forced them to retreat. No less than twenty-two bullet holes were counted in the folds of the flag which Sergeant Lunt had defended so bravely.

Corporal Cole was at another point of the battlefield participating in those fierce cavalry charges led by General Custer, which to a large extent decided the battle in favor of the Union cause. During the last great charge, which culminated in a desperate hand-to-hand fight between the opposing foes, Corporal Cole, who was in the thickest of the fray, espied a Confederate color-bearer. He dashed up to him, swung his sabre over the rebel's head and would have killed him with one blow had the man not ducked in time and dropped the flag. Corporal Cole seized the colors, but just at that instant his horse was shot in the shoulder and leg and fell. While trying to help the poor animal the brave corporal was himself wounded in the left leg. Still carrying the flag he limped along till a Union officer came to his assistance. It was not long before Corporal Cole took possession of a riderless horse and, mounting it, rejoined his regiment and stayed in the fight till the battle was ended.

Another episode from the battle of Winchester. The rebels, in full retreat before a furious cavalry attack, were being closely followed by the Federals. During this charge Andrew J. Lorish, Commissary Sergeant of the First New York Dragoons, made a dash for the colors of a Confederate regiment. He was at

ANDREW J. LORISH,
Commissary Sergeant, First N. Y. Dragoons.
Born in Dansville, N. Y., November 8, 1832.

his side just as the color-bearer, struck by a shot from his own ranks, stumbled and fell. Heedless of the Confederate color-guard of some six or seven men, the bold dragoon grabbed the standard and whirled his horse around to rejoin his comrades. At this the wounded color-bearer raised himself on his elbow and yelled: "Boys, shoot that damned Yankee! He's got our flag! He's got our flag! Shoot him!"

Already several of the color-guard were raising their muskets to fire, but Sergeant Lorish was equal to the emergency.

· "Quick as a flash," says he, "with my arm uplifted, I wheeled my horse around and, dashing directly at the five men, commanded: 'Drop those guns or I'll send every one of you to hell!' As they dropped their guns I again wheeled and putting spurs to my horse dashed down the hill, to hear, when I was fifteen or twenty rods away, the bullets singing thick and fast above my head. But I escaped with the flag and was unhurt, to be greeted with cheers from my comrades as I joined them.

"The mark of a Minie ball on the visor of my cap furnished proof of the perilousness of the situation I had encountered."

SWIMMING UNDER HEAVY FIRE

LUMAN L. CADWELL,
Sergeant, Co. B, Second New York
Cavalry.
Born in Nanticoke Springs, N. Y.,
March 22, 1836.

THE Union soldiers accomplished a brilliant achievement at Bayou Alabama, La. General Granger was pursuing a body of Confederates under General Taylor and on September 24, 1864, had forced the enemy to offer battle or surrender. The two forces were separated only by the river, which was not more than fifty yards wide. General Granger's cavalrymen dismounted and began to fight at 150 feet range. The struggle was indecisive and could only be brought to a successful close by an attack on the other side of the stream. How to cross the river, however, was a difficult problem just then, heavy autumn rains having swollen it and created a rapid current. A large flat-bottom scow was lying close in shore on the Confederate side.

A call was made for volunteers to swim the river and secure the scow. Lieutenant Westinghouse and Sergeant Luman L. Cadwell, of Company B, Second New
York Cavalry, volunteered. They started on a run for the river, plunged in
and swam directly to the enemy's line. It was an extremely dangerous undertaking, the rebels pouring a shower of bullets at them, while balls from their own comrades were flying over their heads to the other side. However, miraculous as it
may seem, the two brave swimmers reached the object of their heroic effort unhurt. After untying the scow and reaching deep water, they kept on the side more

"THEY KEPT ON THE SIDE REMOTE FROM THE HOSTILE SHORE."

remote from the hostile shore and shoved the boat successfully to the other side of
the river.

"Bullets whistled about us like hail, hitting the boat and pattering in the water
all around," Sergeant Cadwell says, in recalling the occurrence. Again, however,
he and the lieutenant remained uninjured and thus were able to furnish the much
desired means by which soon afterward the Union forces crossed the river.

Lieutenant Westinghouse was killed a few months later, while Sergeant Cadwell
lived to receive the precious medal for the heroic feat.

"LET'S GO FOR THE GUNS!"

THE capture of the Confederate artillery by the Federals at Fisher's Hill, Va., on September 22, 1864, was an achievement which was accomplished largely by the personal courage of Sergeant Sylvester D. Rhodes, of Company D, Sixty-first Pennsylvania Infantry, who during that engagement was acting as captain of his company. The rebels had been driven back to their breastworks and attempted to direct their artillery fire on the advancing Union men. Owing to the hilly nature of the country, the guns behind the breastworks could not be depressed sufficiently to strike the troops at the foot of the hill.

SYLVESTER D. RHODES,
Sergeant, Co. D, 61st Penn. Inf.
Highest rank attained : Captain.
Born in Luzerne County, Pa.,
December, 1842.

Sergeant Rhodes. with quick perception, took advantage of the situation. Stepping to the front of his company, he exclaimed, pointing to the rebel breastworks :

" Now boys, let's go for those guns !"

The men replied with a cheer and started up hill. Company F was the color company. " And," says Sergeant Rhodes in telling about the event, " when our colors moved the entire regiment followed with alacrity.

" I was the first man over the breastworks. I jumped in right between two guns, loaded and ready to fire, grabbed the hand-spike of one and turned it on the rebels, who were forming some fifty yards in the rear. By this time a number of comrades had come to my assistance and the gun which had been turned on the enemy was fired. The shell struck the top log on the works behind which the rebels were forming. They were panic-stricken and fled. Their artillery attempted to keep up with them and get way, but I shot one of the lead horses of the first piece and thus blocked the narrow road. The confusion which followed made it rather easy for us to capture the entire battery of seventeen pieces."

Fisher's Hill, Va. — Following close upon the defeat of Early at Winchester came his almost utter annihilation at Fisher's Hill, Va., on the 22nd of September, 1864. Sheridan achieved a most signal victory over Early at this place, and was prevented from totally destroying the enemy's army only by darkness, which made further operations impossible.

Early was posted in an almost impregnable position on the North Fork of the Shenandoah and extending across the Strasburg Valley. After a great deal of manoeuvreing during the day the left of the enemy's line was furiously attacked and driven from their works. In the meantime the Sixth and Nineteenth Army Corps attacked the rebel front, and the whole rebel army was forced back in utter confusion, retreating to the lower passes of the Blue Ridge, closely pursued as far as Staunton by Sheridan, who then returned and took position at Cedar Creek, Va.

The Confederates lost about 400 in killed and wounded, and 1,100 men taken prisoners, while the Union losses were about 600 in killed and wounded.

THE BONDS OF COMRADESHIP

WILLIAM G. HILLS,
Private, Co. E, Ninth New York Cavalry.
Born at Conewango, N. Y., June 26, 1841.

A N illustration of true soldierly comradeship is presented in the story of Private William G. Hills, of Company E, Ninth New York Cavalry, who saved the life of Sergeant Joel H. Lyman, of Company B, of the same regiment. How it was done the latter describes in these brief but pointed words:

"During our campaign in the Shenandoah Valley we reached Harrisburg, Va., on September 25, 1864, and on the day following we met the enemy's cavalry and drove them to the North Fork of the Shenandoah. When we arrived at the brow of the hill overlooking the river, which was quite narrow and fordable, we could see Early's Infantry drawn up in line on the opposite side. Supposing that our object was to capture the enemy's train, I galloped down the slope, but had not gone twenty rods when I was knocked from my horse by a musket ball from the rebel rifle pits, which were hidden from my view by the willow trees bordering the opposite bank.

"The regiment had been ordered back and I found myself alone and helpless, the enemy's bullets ploughing up the ground and throwing dirt all over me. Seeing my dangerous position, William Hills drove the spurs into his horse and galloped to the spot where I lay. Then coolly dismounting he lifted me to my saddle, mounted his own horse and supported me from the field, amid a veritable hail of bullets. It seemed as if the whole rebel army had concentrated its fire upon us.

"For genuine pluck and comradeship I never in my three years of active service saw anything to compare with this deed."

A SINGLE-HANDED CHARGE

T HE following account of a single-handed cavalry charge is graphically told by Captain George N. Bliss, Company C, First Rhode Island Cavalry:

"About three o'clock in the afternoon of September 28, 1864, I received an order from Major Farrington to ride to Waynesborough, Va., and give orders to the provost guards to prevent soldiers from entering the houses, as the entire cavalry force was about to pass through the town to water their horses in the Shenandoah.

"It was a perfect day of early autumn. I rode into the town, gave my orders, and was about to return when my attention was attracted by the efforts of a

Vermont cavalry regiment to destroy the railroad bridge; the woodwork had been burned, and one span of the iron work had fallen. While watching this proceeding I heard shots in the distance across the river, and looking in that direction saw the enemy about a mile away, driving in our pickets; but when the reserve was reached a charge of our men sent the rebels back again. At first I thought it was only a trifling picket line skirmish, but soon the reserve was hurled back, and I saw that it was an attack in force.

"I at once rode to Captain Willis C. Capron, of the First Rhode Island Cavalry, who had command of about a dozen men as provost guard in the little village, and ordered him to form his men in line across the main street and allow none but wounded men to pass to the rear. This was promptly done, and I was about to return to my squadron when Captain Capron said to me:

"'I wish you would take command here; you know I have never been in a fight!'

"At first I refused, but the men looked at me as though they really desired it, and I said to Captain Capron:

"'Very well, take your place in the rear of the line as junior captain,' and, drawing my sabre, I took my place in front.

"Our picket line was on the opposite side of the river fighting stoutly, but the force of the enemy was

GEORGE N. BLISS,
Captain, Co. C, First R. I. Cavalry.
Born at Eagleville, R. I., July 22. 1837.

too strong for them and the firing was rapidly approaching us, when, having rallied about thirty men, it occurred to me that a charge across the river by us, accompanied by vigorous cheering, might produce the impression on our men and upon the enemy that re-enforcements had arrived, check the advance, and give our main body more time to form for action.

"It was accordingly done, and with the effect that I had anticipated. I had nearly reached the front when a major rode up to me and said: 'Colonel Lowell wishes you to take your command to the ford of the river and stop all stragglers.'

"The order was promptly obeyed, and I was in time to stop about one hundred and fifty men. There were some lieutenants with them, who under my orders had just about succeeded in getting their men into line when a rebel battery commenced

---

Waynesborough — On the 27th of September, 1864, General Torbert moved his command to Waynesborough, Va., and on the following morning proceeded to destroy the railroad bridge across the South Fork of the Shenandoah River and burned the depot and government buildings. Late in the afternoon the enemy, under General Early, attacked the Union cavalry in strong force with infantry, cavalry and artillery. They were held in check until after dark, when General Torbert, learning that the enemy were attempting to cut him off from the main army, fell back to Spring Hill without delivering battle.

dropping shells among them, and away they went, sweeping my small force bodily across the river. In the town I again got some of my men together and endeavored to build a barricade across the main street. It was about half done when I saw that it could not be completed in time to be of any service, and we again fell back until we came to the Third New Jersey Cavalry, drawn up in column of squadrons in the western suburb of the town. Looking again towards the enemy I saw Colonel Charles Russell Lowell, who had been in command of the picket line, riding toward

"A BULLET INTENDED FOR ME, STRUCK MY MOUNT."

us with his horse on a walk, the last man to fall back before the advance of the enemy. The Confederate bullets were whistling about him, and frequent puffs of dust in the road showed where they struck right and left of this brave soldier. Putting spurs to my horse I rode forward and had the following conversation with him:

"'Colonel Lowell, I had but a few of the provost guards, and did what I could with them to help you.'

"'Well Captain, we must check their advance with a sabre charge. Isn't that the best we can do?'

"'I think so, Colonel.'

"By this time we had come up to the Third New Jersey Cavalry, known in the army as the "Butterflies," on account of their gay uniforms, and Colonel Lowell said to the officer in command: 'Major, let your first squadron sling their carbines, draw their sabres and charge.'

"The order was given, 'Forward,' but not a man moved. They were completely disheartened by having seen the other troops driven back.

"The captain in command of the squadron said: 'Corporal Jones, are you afraid?' and the corporal made no reply.

"The men wavered, and Colonel Lowell said: 'Give a cheer boys, and go at them,' and spurred his horse at a gallop toward the enemy, followed by myself, both of us waving our sabres. The squadron at once cheered and followed. After going a short distance, Colonel Lowell drew out to one side, to be ready to send other troops to the support of the squadron, and I was left to lead the charge. I was mounted on a large, strong sorrel horse, and was soon 100 yards in advance of the squadron. Reaching the partly constructed barricade, I pulled up my horse. Looking back, I saw my men coming on with a splendid squadron front; looking forward, I saw the enemy in columns of fours, turning to retreat. The ground was down hill towards the enemy; I had never seen a better opportunity for a sabre charge, and as the squadron neared me, I shouted: 'Come on boys, they are running,' and jumping my horse over the low barricade, dashed in among the rebels, only to find myself making the attack single-handed.

"I had ridden past a dozen of the enemy before I discovered my desperate situation. They were retreating in loose column of fours, and as I rode in among them there were three files on my left hand and one on my right. I felt that death was certain. Like a lightning flash my whole life seemed to pass in review before me, closing with the thought, 'and this is the end.' There was but one chance. Fifty men behind me were shouting, 'Kill that damned Yankee!'

"To turn among them and retrace my steps was impossible, but my horse was swift and I thought if I could keep on until I came to a side street I might dash into that and by making a circle again reach our lines. As I rode I kept my sabre swinging, striking six blows right and left. Two of the enemy escaped by quickly dodging their heads, but I succeeded in wounding four of them—Captain William A. Moss, Hugh S. Hamilton, color-bearer of the Fourth Virginia Cavalry, and two others unknown to me.

"The first side street reached was on the left. Keeping my head close to my horse's neck I then broke through the three files on my left and reached the side street in safety, fully twenty yards from the nearest horseman.

"For a moment I thought I was safe, when suddenly a bullet, doubtless intended for me, struck my mount and he staggered under the shock. With rein and spur I urged him on, but it was in vain; he fell with a plunge that left me lying upon the ground. Before I could rise two of the enemy reined in their horses by me and leaning over in their saddles struck at me, one with a carbine, the other with a sabre. I could parry but one, and with my sabre stopped the crushing blow from the carbine at the same instant that the sabre gave me a cut across the forehead. I at once rose to my feet and shouted to the soldier who had wounded me: 'For God's sake do not kill a prisoner!'

"'Surrender, then,' he said.

"'I do surrender,' I replied, whereupon he demanded my sword and pistol, which I gave to him, and had scarcely done so when I was struck in the back with such force as to thrust me two steps forward. Upon turning to discover the cause of this assault, I found that a soldier had ridden up on the trot and stabbed me with his sabre, which would have passed entirely through my body but for the fact that in his ignorance of the proper use of the weapon he had failed to make the half-turn of the wrist necessary to give the sabre smooth entrance between the ribs. I also saw at this moment another soldier taking aim at me with a revolver.

"My chances seemed gone, but a sudden impulse took possession of me and I called for help and protection as a Free Mason. Captain Henry C. Lee, the acting adjutant-general of the enemy's force, heard my cry and at once came to my assistance, ordering a soldier to take me to the rear and see that my wounds were dressed. The soldier in whose charge I was despoiled me of my watch and pocket-book, and with some assistance, being weak from loss of blood, I mounted behind my guard, and later in the evening I was put into an ambulance with Captain William A. Moss, at that time a lieutenant, and driven several miles to a small house in the mountains. I found Captain Moss to be a brother Mason and he did everything possible for my comfort, although he had received a severe sabre cut from me."

UNDER A MUSCADINE GRAPE-VINE

JOSEPH S. KEEN,
Sergeant, Co. D, 13th Mich. Infantry.
Born in Stanford, England, July 24, 1843.

THREE millions of rations, vast quantities of ammunition, guns and all other supplies of warfare stored at Allatoona, Ga., were the tempting objects of a bold and unexpected movement of General Hood, the Confederate Commander. Once in possession of the fort, with its costly stores, he would have robbed the Union Army of its base of supplies and forced it to retreat. He would have frustrated Sherman's march to the sea and — — But all this is mere speculation. Hood did not capture the coveted treasure ; the Union Army did not lose its base of supplies ; it did not retreat, and Sherman's march became a historical fact.

One of the reasons, and perhaps the principal one, for the failure of Hood's plan, was that Sherman was in time advised of the enemy's movements and put on his guard. That this view is shared by the great Union Army leader himself appears from his own statement. "There was great difficulty," General Sherman says, "in obtaining correct information about Hood's movements from Palmetto Station. I could not get spies to penetrate his camps, but on the 1st of October I was satisfied that the bulk of his infantry was at and across the Chattahoochee River near Campbellton. On that day I telegraphed to Grant: 'Hood is evidently across the Chattahoochee, below Sweetwater. If he tries to get on our road this side of the Etowah I shall attack him. * * *'"

Hood did try to get "on our road."

And over the heads of the Confederates Sherman signaled his celebrated message to Corse at Allatoona: "Hold the fort; I am coming."

The man who furnished General Sherman with the information in October, and upon whose report the important subsequent action was based, was Sergeant Joseph S. Keen, of Company D, Thirteenth Michigan Infantry. So valuable was his information that a Medal of Honor was awarded Sergeant Keen in appreciation of the service.

How Keen was enabled to learn the details of Hood's movements and impart them to the Federal commander forms the text of a peculiarly interesting story which he himself tells as follows:

"At the battle of Chickamauga, Ga., I was wounded, taken prisoner and sent to Richmond, where I was kept about three months. On December 12th we were shipped to Danville, Va. Five months later, on May 12, 1864, I was transferred to the prison at Andersonville, Ga., from where, on September 9, 1864, with several others, I made my escape. That day we were put into box cars and early in the afternoon reached Macon, some sixty miles north. Here we had to wait for other trains to get out of our way. Our train was standing on the outside track but one, upon which there was a long train of box cars. I noticed several prisoners were allowed to get out of the car and stand near the door conversing with the crowd that had been attracted there by our arrival. I watched my opportunity, carelessly left the car and for a while stood close beside it. A casual look at the guards in the doorway showed me at that moment that they were both looking inside. Quicker than a flash I dropped and dodged under the train and fortunately was not observed. While yet crawling across to the other side, the outer track, I heard the guard ordering all to get back inside. I put my head out the other side of the train and looked to the right and left its whole length; no one could see me. I then crawled under the train of box cars on the outside track and, gaining the other side, rolled down the embankment into the ditch.

"I worked my way along this ditch until I reached a culvert, into the darkest part of which I crawled, camping in about one foot of water. My loneliness was soon relieved by the arrival of eight others who had taken the same means of escape. We kept hiding here till darkness broke in, when, the lower part of our bodies resembling a lot of par-boiled tripe, we crawled out of the culvert. We made our way to a little grove on the outskirts of Macon and then separated; six going one way and I and two others, S. W. Ludden and John Hord, taking another direction. Our plan was to

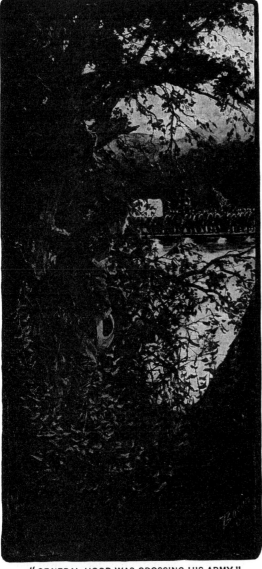

"GENERAL HOOD WAS CROSSING HIS ARMY."

march twenty-five miles west, then gradually swing around, go 100 miles due north and thence follow an easterly course which, according to our calculations, would bring us in rear of Atlanta. It was a simple plan, indeed, it looked so easy; a pleasure trip we thought as we started out. But we were soon disappointed and for twenty-one days we wandered about, aimlessly sometimes, tired and worn out always, with nothing but the moon and stars to guide us and the hope of eventually reaching our troops to keep up our strength and courage. We learned more about astronomy during these twenty-one days than we ever knew before—Jupiter, Saturn, Mars, Venus, all served us a good turn. Slowly and amidst untold hardships we worked our way to the Chattahoochee River, which we crossed and followed till we struck the Western & Atlantic Railroad.

"Our appearance at this time was anything but inviting. Our clothes were torn to shreds and partly bound up by fine bark strings from young saplings, and our shoes were tied up in the same manner. The lower parts of our legs were bound around with pieces of bark. Our best time was usually made just before and after daylight early in the morning, as fewer people were around in those hours. Thus we plodded along the river bank until one day we saw Confederate soldiers in large numbers on the opposite side of the river. The large cornfields on the hills seemed literally alive with forage teams, presenting quite an animated scene. Our position, close to the wood-skirted bank of the river, seemed safer than any other within view, so, keeping under cover, we kept working our way forward in a very cautious manner. A short distance in front, across a cornfield and on the edge of a piece of woods, could be seen column after column of rebel infantry marching from the river directly back into the country. After watching them for a time we proceeded to hide ourselves on the river bank, and after crawling around the rather thin growth of brush and grass got into a fairly good place, and when sitting up had a splendid view of the pontoon bridge on which General Hood was crossing his army. This was about ten o'clock in the morning, and from that time until night the rebel army poured across the bridge in one constant stream—infantry, artillery, cavalry, generals and staffs, all marching in regular order; no confusion, no noise, but with a military precision imposing in its magnificence that won even our admiration. Presently two rebel officers in a rowboat came floating down the stream on our side. As we did not want them to know our opinion of the grand exhibition of military splendor of their army, we thought it best not to hail them, but lay flat on the ground, expecting that they would soon drift beyond us. Now it so happened that we had selected a very poor hiding place, from the fact that a large muscadine grape-vine grew near this spot and branched out in every direction, part of its branches extending over to and hanging nearly into the river, and it was at this time loaded with grapes, and no doubt presented a tempting appearance from the river. Naturally it attracted the two officers to this particular spot, who commenced gathering grapes and hanging on to branches to prevent drifting away.

"Every time the branches were pulled the grapes would come pattering down on our heads some twenty-five feet from the officers' position, and almost in plain view, had they looked in our direction. They were looking at the top of the vine for the large grapes, completely overlooking the richer fruit at the roots. They were talking about the flank movement their army was executing and expressed the utmost confidence in its success.

"'Sherman will be obliged to evacuate Atlanta,' one said and the other assented.

"We were intensely interested in their conversation; not to that extent, however, as to forget our exposed position. What I feared most was that they would hear the beating of my heart. The suspense became dreadful. But finally the officers had their fill; they let go of the branches and the boat and its occupants drifted down the stream.

"Three minutes later we were in good hiding in a shock of cornstalks in the adjoining field, and from this time on—about four o'clock—until dark we kept very quiet. After dark we walked boldly up to the road and at the first break that occurred in their column we got over the fence, crossed the road and entered the woods on the other side. We had great difficulty in making our way in the darkness of the night and decided to halt for fear of running against some of the rebel pickets.

"At break of day we resumed our journey. Toward morning a fog commenced to gather and soon got so thick that we could not see forty feet ahead of us. That was our opportunity. We pushed ahead, and for a time were simply mixed up with the rebels. They were just getting breakfast and all seemed bustle and confusion. We lost no time in putting ourselves outside of their lines and were at least two miles away when the fog cleared up. We marched all day and night and by seven o'clock the following morning discovered our troops on the other side of the Chattahoochee River. We crossed the stream and once more we were among our own troops, our friends, our comrades.

"We were at once brought to General Kilpatrick, who questioned us sharply concerning our identity, and, having satisfied himself, discussed with us the details of the enemy's operations, of which we had been eye-witnesses. The information thus obtained was forwarded to General Sherman, who arranged his plans accordingly.

"We made our escape at Macon 103 miles south, September 10, 1864; it had taken us twenty-one days to make this apparently short distance, but I think we must have traveled 300 miles at least."

THE FALL OF FORT HARRISON

CAPTAIN CECIL CLAY, of Company K, Fifty-eighth Pennsylvania Infantry, was awarded the Medal of Honor for leading the attack on Fort Harrison, Va., bearing the flag of another regiment which he had picked up by the way. The attack was made, and the fort carried, by the first division of the Eighteenth Corps on September 29, 1864. Captain Clay writes:

CECIL CLAY
Captain, Co. K, 58th Penn. Infantry.
Highest rank attained: Bvt-Brig-General U. S. V.
Born in Philadelphia, Pa., Feb. 13, 1842.

"We were drawn up about three-quarters of a mile from Fort Harrison, and before us was a stretch of open ground. Our skirmish line advanced alternately firing and halting to reload, while before them the rebel skirmishers retired with equal deliberation. As soon as our advance

From September 28 to 30, 1864, the Army of the James was engaged in the neighborhood of New Market Road, Va. The capture of **Forts Harrison and Gilmore**, and the engagements at **Chapin's Farm** and **Laurel Hill** were included in what is generally known as the battle of **New Market Heights**. The Union Army lost 2,429 in killed and wounded and the Confederates about 2,000, but the result of the battle was in favor of the Federals.

commenced the rebel guns opened upon us all along the line. We lost a large number of men crossing the open space, but I could see no signs of wavering. When we reached a point about 100 yards from the fort, where we were protected from the fire of the enemy's guns by the steepness of the ground, we halted to get our breath and close up the gaps in our line. We lay down for a moment, and as I looked to the right I saw a few hundred yards away what appeared to be a brigade moving into the works by fours. We thought at first that it must be the Tenth Corps trying to get in ahead of us, but it occurred to me that they were rebels.

"At that moment Colonel Roberts rode up to us, his old-fashioned black stock twisted around until the big bow was at the back of his neck. Grasping a revolver by the muzzle, and, waving it as one would a war club, he shouted: 'Now men, just two minutes to take that fort! Just two minutes, men!'

"We sprang to our feet and dressed our line in an instant. 'Forward!' rang out from the officers, and away we went.

"We struck the works on the north face, where the ditch was fully ten feet deep. The rebels fired at us and threw at us anything they could lay their hands on while we were jumping into the ditch. The first Sergeant of my company was hit on the head by a fuse mallet and knocked down. He jumped to his feet, mad as a hornet, and exclaimed: 'Damn a man who will use a thing like that for a weapon.' A rebel officer mounted on an old gray horse rode out of a sally port near by, and pulling up on the bridge which spanned the ditch blazed away at us with his revolver. One of my men, named Johnson, who had been shot through the right arm, took his revolver in his left hand and emptied it at the rebel, but every shot went wide, and Johnson was left with an empty revolver.

"GAVE ME THE COLORS AND HOISTED ME UP."

"Billy Bourke, a sandy-haired Irishman, had picked up the blue State flag of the One hundred and eighty-eighth Pennsylvania, the bearer of which had been shot at the edge of the ditch. Side by side we two climbed the parapet, until we could look over into the fort. No sooner had we raised our heads than a ball struck Bourke, cutting a gash across his forehead. He knocked against me, and we rolled back into the ditch together. Bourke was unable to see, as the blood was running into his eyes, so he gave me the colors and with the aid of a sword which I had plunged into the embankment as a footstep he hoisted me up on the parapet once more. Meantime Johnston had also climbed up, and was shot through the left arm below the elbow as soon as he appeared on the parapet. Disregarding his wounds he jumped on the banquette, leveled his empty revolver at two wounded officers who were crouching there and made them surrender to him. Just then a little fellow fired at Johnson with a revolver and knocked him over. In the meantime the division was stubbornly fighting its way into the fort and the rebels were beginning to retreat when one of them turned and fired two shots at me, drilling a couple of holes in my right arm. Shifting the colors to my left hand, I continued to lead the advance until that hand was shot through also, and I had to stop and lay the colors up against the parapet. Some of the One hundred and eighty-eighth came up at this moment and I handed them their flag, which I had carried throughout the entire charge."

Captain Clay's wound proved to be so serious that it shortly afterward entailed the loss of the entire arm.

A MESSAGE DELIVERED UNDER DIFFICULTY

SAMUEL B. HORNE,
Lieutenant, Co. H, 11th Conn.
Infantry.
Born in Tullamore, Ireland.
March 3, 1843.

WITH two dangerous wounds in his body Lieutenant Samuel B. Horne, of Company H, Eleventh Connecticut Infantry, was carried off the field at Cold Harbor, Va., June 3, 1864, and sent to a hospital. Though his recovery proceeded slowly, he could not bear to be confined to his bed and three months later returned to his regiment, though still an invalid. Ten days later, at Chapin's Farm, Va., September 29, 1864, he won his medal by a display of courage almost superhuman. It happened thus: Upon his return to the regiment he was attached to the staff of General Ord as aide-de-camp, and during the attack on Fort Harrison was sent to deliver a verbal message to the colonel of one of the advancing regiments.

"Though my injuries still pained me very much I obeyed the order cheerfully," Lieutenant Horne goes on to tell. "I spurred my horse forward and soon came within range of the enemy's guns. While going at full gallop my horse was killed by grape shot and fell upon me with crushing weight, cracking some of my ribs, injuring me internally and pinioning me to the ground. Here I lay perfectly helpless and suffering intense pain, until Colonel Wells rode up and relieved me from my precarious position. Still the message had to be delivered and although lacerated, in great pain and partly denuded, I proceeded on foot to carry out my mission. I could only advance slowly and with difficulty and had to pass under the very guns of the fort before I reached the colonel of the advancing regiment. I reported to General Ord and was with him when he was wounded on the parapet and with him was taken to the rear."

THOUGHT ONLY OF SAVING THE FLAG

CHRISTIAN A. FLEETWOOD,
Sergeant-Major, 4th U. S. Colored Troops.

THE attack upon the rebel works at New Market Heights, Va., September 29, 1864, one of the most stubborn in the history of the war, was delivered by the Fourth and Sixth U. S. Colored Troops, who lost more than half their men in that bloody charge. An account of the occurrence is given by Sergeant-Major Christian A. Fleetwood of the Fourth U. S. Colored Troops, as follows:

"Our regiment lined up for the charge with eleven officers and 350 enlisted men. There was but one field officer with us, Major A. S. Boernstein, who was in command. Our adjutant, George Allen, supervised the right, and I, as sergeant-major, the left. When the charge was started our color-guard was complete. Only one of the twelve came off that field on his own feet. Most of the others are there still. Early in the rush one of the sergeants went down, a bullet cutting his flag-staff in two and passing through his body. The other sergeant, Alfred B. Hilton, of Company H, a magnificent specimen of manhood, over six feet tall and splendidly proportioned, caught up the other flag and pressed forward with them both.

"It was a deadly hailstorm of bullets, sweeping men down as hailstones sweep the leaves from the trees, and it was not long before he also went down, shot through the leg. As he fell he held up the flags and shouted: 'Boys, save the colors!'

"Before they could touch the ground, Corporal Charles Veal, of Company D, had seized the blue flag, and I the American flag, which had been presented to us by the patriotic women of our home in Baltimore.

"It was very evident that there was too much work cut out for our regiments. Strong earthworks, protected in front by two lines of abatis and one line of palisades, and in

ALEXANDER KELLY.

First Sergeant, Co. F, Sixth U. S.
Colored Troops.

Born in Indiana Co., Pa., April
7, 1846.

the rear by a lot of men who proved that they knew how to shoot and largely outnumbered us. We struggled through the two lines of abatis, a few getting through the palisades, but it was sheer madness, and those of us who were able had to get out as best we could. Reaching the line of our reserves and no commissioned officer being in sight, I rallied the survivors around the flag, rounding up at first eighty-five men and three commissioned officers. During the day about thirty more men came along—all that was left.

"I have never been able to understand how Veal and I lived under such a hail of bullets, unless it was because we were both such little fellows. I think I weighed then about 125 pounds and Veal about the same. We did not get a scratch. A bullet passed between my legs, cutting my boot-leg, trousers and even my stocking, without breaking the skin."

The brave sergeant-major and his no less brave comrades, Sergeant Alfred B. Hilton, of Company H, and Corporal Charles Veal, of Company D, were awarded the Medal of Honor.

At the same battle First Sergeant Alexander Kelly, of Company F, Sixth U. S. Colored Troops, also distinguished himself and was awarded with the medal for saving the flag of his regiment after the color-bearer and most of the company had been either killed or wounded.

THE STORY OF A YOUTHFUL HERO

WILLIAM L. GRAUL,

Corporal, Co. I, 188th Pa. Infantry

Born at Reading, Pa., July 27,
1846.

THE narrator of the following story, Corporal William L. Graul, of Company I, One hundred and eighty-eighth Pennsylvania Infantry, was a mere boy of eighteen when he earned his medal for an act of distinguished bravery and dash at the storming of Fort Harrison, Va., September 29, 1864. He writes:

"On the night of the 28th of September we were ordered to cross the James River on a muffled pontoon bridge at Akren's Landing. Just at the break of the next day we commenced a cautious advance upon the enemy, whose pickets were soon encountered and driven back, and pushing on at quick time through a wood with tangled undergrowth we at last emerged upon open ground in front of the rebel works, which were only a few yards away. Fort Harrison, strongly built and bristling with cannon, was in our immediate front, and we were ordered to charge. A long stretch of open ground was passed at a run, and though the enemy brought all their guns and small arms to bear they failed to get a good range on our advancing troops, firing for the most part too high.

"At a point within fifty yards of the fort was a slight ravine, stretching along in its front, and affording some protection. Here the line was re-formed and the men took breath. We were now under a desperate fire and an advance was sure to entail heavy slaughter, but pausing only for a moment the word was again given to charge, and without flinching the line sprang forward. A terrible volley swept our ranks and many a brave man fell. For an instant we seemed to waver, but only for an instant, and recovering we dashed on and up the hill.

"I was on the color-guard, and when about half way up the color-bearer, William Sipes, was killed and the regimental flag fell on me. I at once threw my gun away and seizing the colors ran up the hill, jumped into the ditch of the foe, then climbed up on the flag-staff and placed the colors of the One hundred and eighty-eighth Pennsylvania alongside of the rebel flag.

"I saw that the enemy were weakening, and cheered our men on. We captured Fort Harrison and then advanced on Fort Gilmore under the fire of the rebel gun-boats. We were compelled to fall back in the evening, however, and in our retreat, the color-bearer of the Fourth New Hampshire being hit, I brought their colors back with me."

A SERGEANT WHO WISELY DIS-BELIEVED

GEORGE P. DOW,
Sergeant, Co. C, 7th N. H. Infantry.
Born at Atkinson, N. H., Aug. 7, 1840.

DURING the operations before Richmond, Va., in October, 1864, the Seventh New Hampshire Infantry was stretched out in a single line in order to ascertain accurately the strength of the enemy's defenses. Company C was at the extreme left and had a rather peculiar experience, which Sergeant George P. Dow, who was in command, describes as follows:

"Advancing we came to a large stream and a bridge over which I led my company. We marched on, but the cannonading was so terrific that we could not hear the bugle from which we were to take orders. Still we advanced till we came to a clearing and presently found ourselves in front of the rebel breastworks mounted with guns and large bodies of infantry lying behind them. For some reason or other the enemy did not open on us. We halted and it was then that I made the startling discovery that my company had been separated from the regiment, which, as I afterward learned, had stopped at the stream. There was but one way out of our dangerous situation; we had to retreat. I gave the order, but in the roar of cannons and the smoke of firing we became confused and we missed the bridge and had to swim the stream. After thus crossing the water we marched for some distance and finally arrived at a farm-house, where we found a woman apparently only too willing to help us find our way.

"'Which direction has our line of battle taken?' I asked her.

"She pointed toward Richmond. I knew she was not telling the truth and took my company in an opposite direction. A little later we met one of our aides, who warned us that we were in danger of being gobbled up by the enemy's cavalry, so we started at a double-quick and found the regiment drawn up in the woods.

"My company in this advance had got nearer to Richmond than any Union troops had yet done, and the information we brought back was of great importance to the Army of the James."

REACHED THE CAPTAIN JUST IN TIME

JOHN S. DARROUGH,
Sergeant, Co. F, 113th Illinois
Infantry.
Born at Maysville, Ky., April 6, 1841.

THE deed of Sergeant John S. Darrough, of Company F, One hundred and thirteenth Illinois Infantry, was a truly noble one.

In a bad plight himself and in want of help, he forgot his own serious predicament when he saw an officer in danger and hastened to his rescue. The story is told by the sergeant in these simple words:

"Our regiment had dwindled down to 300 men, when it was dispatched from Memphis, Tenn., to cut the communications at Eastport, by tearing up the tracks and destroying the bridge. The transports, convoyed by small wooden gunboats, proceeded up the Mississippi and Tennessee Rivers, and landed us about three miles below Eastport, on the south side of the river.

"Our force was partly landed when a masked battery in a clump of trees opened fire on us at close range, doing great execution. Steam-pipes were cut and many of the men scalded. The boats backed out from the bank without waiting to haul in their gang-planks. Most of our men made their way to a point down stream where they were partly out of range, and one of the gunboats dashed in and took them off, while the other engaged the battery.

"Those of us who were unable to get to the point in time to be taken off were left to shift for ourselves. A deep bayou prevented us from going farther down the bank, and our only means of escape seemed to be by swimming the Tennessee, which was a mile wide at this point.

"I HASTENED ASHORE AND DISCOVERED THE COMRADE TO BE CAPTAIN A. W. BECKET."

"I made up my mind at once that the Tennessee was by far preferable to either being shot to death or made a prisoner, and concluded to swim across the stream. How to carry my gun and clothes was the next perplexing question, and I commenced to look for a log or limb to float them on, when, to my great joy, I presently discovered a canoe hidden in a canebrake. I quickly launched and boarded the boat and, making vigorous use of the one oar it contained, paddled out into the river, where I could see the bend. Our boats were quite a distance away and under headway, though the gunboat and battery were still carrying on their cannonading. I felt satisfied that I would either overtake the boats or cross to the opposite side of the river and have a chance at least to join the Union forces some fifty or a hundred miles away.

"Then something occurred which, for the time being, changed my entire plan. Looking ashore in the direction of the rebels, I noticed one of our men in a helpless condition. He had crossed the bayou and advanced quite a way down the river, when his strength had apparently given out. There remained but one thing to do: to get to the rescue of my comrade.

"I confess, it was not a pleasant task to paddle back toward the rebels, but I hastened ashore and then discovered the comrade to be Captain A. W. Becket, of Company B. He was faint and exhausted and about to give out completely. I placed him in the canoe and succeeded in reaching the other shore safely."

THOMAS GILBERT,

Private, 18th Ind. Battery, N. Y.
Born in Scotland, 1835.

A DISPLAY OF COOLNESS AND NERVE

AMONG the Union forces at Baton Rouge, La., in October, 1864, was Captain Mack's Black Horse Battery of Rochester, N. Y., officially known as the Eighteenth Independent Battery of New York. On the 11th of October the officer in command of the battery directed Corporal Champany to repack the limber chest belonging to his gun. It contained sixteen cartridges, each one holding two pounds of powder and thirty-two twenty-pound shell and shot. About twenty of the shells were what are known as fuse shells, filled to the nozzle with powder and iron bullets, tow being put in to keep the powder from spilling out. The remainder of the missiles were solid shot, percussion shells and canister.

Having completed the repacking, Corporal Champany found that he could not close the lid without help and called to Private Charles White to assist him. The violent pressure they together put upon the lid in some way caused a terrific explosion, killing Champany almost instantly, throwing White seventy feet away, where he landed in a mud puddle, and blowing the chest to atoms. The first man to reach the scene of the tragedy was Private Thomas Gilbert, who narrates what happened as follows:

"I ran to poor Champany, who, horribly burned and mangled, was still breathing, but just as I reached him I noticed that the tow of some of the unexploded shells was burning. Seizing a pail of water from a gunner near by and calling loudly for more water, I dashed the contents of the pail on the burning shells. Then, another pail of water having been brought, I picked up the twenty shells and dipped the burning end of each into the water. By this action the caissons of the entire battery and the lives of many men who had quickly gathered about, to say nothing of my own life, were saved. The explosion was heard miles away and it became necessary to surround the battery with guards to keep the curious away."

ROUNDED UP FORTY REBELS

FRANKLIN JOHNDRO,
Private, Co. A, 118th New York Vols.
Born at Highgate Falls, Vt.

ANOTHER interesting incident at the battle of Chapin's Farm, Va., September, 30, 1864, was Private Franklin Johndro's gathering in of forty rebels. The battle had raged for some time. The second charge of Longstreet's Army had been repulsed by the Union forces and the Confederates were falling back. The One hundred and eighteenth New York Volunteers held a position about twenty rods from the foot of a slight hill, which was occupied by the enemy. Every charge thus far made had been immediately repulsed by this regiment countercharging as soon as the enemy appeared in force on the hill This manoeuvre checked every assault at the foot of the hill. Many of the rebels found temporary protection there, but could not retreat. The captain of Company A saw quite a number of these unfortunates. He pointed out to Private Johndro the danger these fellows were putting his men in, and then induced this brave soldier to at once fix his bayonet and charge all alone on these skulkers. A heavy fire was concentrated upon him by the enemy's sharpshooters, but he succeeded in driving in no less than forty rebels as his prisoners.

A few months later when the Medal of Honor was pinned to his breast for this deed, his colonel remarked: "Johndro, if I owned this Medal of Honor and had won it in the way you did, I should think more of it than I do of the eagles that I carry on my shoulders."

TWO RIDERS ON ONE HORSE

HENRY H. CROCKER,
Captain, Co. F, 2d Mass. Cavalry.
Born at Colchester, Conn., Jan.
20, 1840.

WHEN Longstreet and Early planned to annihilate Sheridan's Army in the Shenandoah Valley, the Federal forces were at the little village of Middletown, Va., and around the immediate neighborhood, between the village and Cedar Creek. The Confederate attack made at early dawn, October 19, 1864, was a complete surprise, and came so unexpectedly that many of the Union soldiers had no time to put on their clothes. About ten o'clock in the forenoon General Sheridan reached the scene of action, and the battle of Cedar Creek — which continued throughout the day — was transformed from defeat, rout and confusion to order and victory.

The Second Massachusetts Cavalry, Lieutenant-Colonel Caspar Crowninshield commanding, was attached to Lowell's Brigade and was stationed near the village of Middletown. Captain Henry H. Crocker, of Company F, a part of the so-called California Battalion attached to this regiment, refers to the battle as follows:

"We were aroused early in the morning by the attack of the enemy. As the enemy came upon us with force we were compelled to fall back slightly, but as we did so we inclined toward the pike at our right, thus keeping our line of communication open. It was a bitter contest, the enemy coming at us in several distinct charges, in each of which they were repulsed. Colonel Lowell, our brigade commander, who was killed later in the day, rode up and down our line encouraging the men to stand together, and assuring them that General Sheridan would soon be on the field with re-enforcements.

"About this time a body of the enemy was seen to emerge form the woods and advance upon our front. My mind was immediately set upon checking those fellows, so I rode up to Colonel Crowninshield and asked permission to charge them. The colonel gave his consent, but cautioned me not to advance too far, and 'if possible,' he added, 'come back with a few prisoners.'

Cedar Creek, Va.—After his victory at Fisher's Hill, Sheridan proceeded to lay waste to the Shenandoah Valley. Frequent cavalry combats took place between Sheridan's and Early's forces at Cedar Creek, but no decisive movement occurred until the 19th of October, 1864. Soon after midnight of the 18th Early surprised General Wright, who in Sheridan's absence was in command of the Union Cavalry. The Federal troops were completely demoralized and were falling back toward Winchester. Sheridan had returned to the latter place from Washington the night before, and upon hearing the artillery firing he started in the morning on a dashing twenty-mile ride, and arrived on the field of battle in time to check the retreat and turn it into one of the most brilliant victories of the war. The Federal loss was 5,995, while the Confederate loss was 4,200.

"I hurried back to my company and told the boys, very much to their satisfaction, of the work before us. We waited until we knew that the advancing force could give us but one volley before we could reach them, then I gave the command: 'Forward! Trot! Gallop! Charge!' and away we went with sabres flashing in the sunlight. The expected volley was received, saddles were emptied and horses went down, but on we went. In less time than it takes to tell it we were among them, their line was broken and we demanded their surrender. Many ran back into the woods where we could plainly see the enemy in force, but they did not fire upon us for fear of hitting their own men. We brought back fourteen prisoners on the run.

"In the heat of our charge I had felt a dull, throbbing pain in my left leg and knew that I had been wounded, but that did not prevent me from stopping, on

"AS GENERAL SHERIDAN CAME DASHING ALONG."

our return, to pick up Lieutenant McIntosh, whose horse had been killed and who was loosening the cinch from his saddle. When he had completed his task he mounted my horse behind me and thus we rode back to our lines just as General Sheridan came dashing along the road on his famous ride from Winchester."

The prisoners captured by Captain Croker in this charge were, according to the statement of Colonel Crowninshield, the first rebels captured that day, and therefore of great importance to General Sheridan, who had them questioned closely as to the strength and formation of the opposing army. They also gave the valuable and assuring information that General Longstreet had not united forces with General Early, as had been believed by the leaders of the Union forces. This was information of such importance that it naturally changed arrangements of manoeuvres and the expected defeat of the morning was changed into a grand victory by evening.

"FORWARD!" HIS VOICE RANG OUT

THE loss of some guns was one of the most unfortunate incidents to the Union forces during the early part of the battle of Cedar Creek. The circumstances of the occurrence are referred to by General Warren J. Keifer, of the Tenth Ohio Infantry, who commanded the Third Division, as follows:

"A number of guns belonging to the Sixth Corps were posted on the hills on my left. The guns under the command of Captains McKnight and Adams and under the direction of Colonel Tompkins, Chief of Artillery of the Sixth Corps, were admirably handled and rapidly fired, although under a heavy and close musketry fire of the enemy. After over 100 artillery horses had been shot, the enemy succeeded in capturing a portion of the guns, having approached under cover of the smoke and fog from the left, which was unprotected. A charge was ordered and the guns were retaken, three of which were drawn off by hand; others were left in consequence of being disabled, but were subsequently recaptured. Great gallantry was displayed in this charge by officers and men. The rebels were fought hand-to-hand and driven from the guns."

The saving of the guns was the proud achievement of Colonel W. W. Henry, of the Tenth Vermont Infantry. He undertook the task when no one else would, and at a time when courage and heroism were most needed.

When Captain McKnight, pressed by the enemy, was forced to abandon his guns, great confusion followed within the Union lines and the entire brigade fell back some 300 yards. General Ricketts, the division commander, succeeded in stopping a further retreat, re-established the lines and ordered the capture of the abandoned guns. But in spite of the order not a regiment stirred. Vexed and annoyed, General Ricketts exclaimed: "Is there not some officer of the First Brigade who will lead the charge?"

Instead of an answer Colonel Henry stepped in front of his regiment.

"Forward!" his voice rang out.

And at the head of the color-guard he marched his men against the rebels. A wild rush for the guns was made, and while some of the Vermonters engaged the Confederates in a hand-to-hand fight others busied themselves about the guns and hauled them off. The arrival of the balance of the brigade prevented the rebels from pursuing the daring colonel and his brave regiment, and Captain McKnight's captured guns were brought back unmolested to General Ricketts.

"HALT! I WANT YOUR FLAG!"

HARRY J. PARKS,
Private, Troop A, Ninth New York
Cavalry.
Highest rank attained: Captain.
Born at Warsaw, N. Y., Feb. 24, 1848,

WHEN General Sheridan's forces, late in the afternoon of the battle of Cedar Creek, made their last charge and completely routed the enemy, it was followed by some confusion within the Union ranks themselves. Many companies became separated from their regiments, regiments from their divisions. This happened, among other troops, to the Ninth New York Cavalry, which, at the end of the battle, when nightfall came, was completely broken up.

Troop A of that regiment had charged the enemy through Strasburg, and while following the fleeing Confederates to Fisher's Hill had been separated from the main body, and, dissolved into small squads, was gathering prisoners, capturing wagons, ammunition, etc. One member of that troop, Private Harry J. Parks, in his ardor to head off the Confederate supply train, had galloped far in advance of his comrades and was, before he realized it himself, in the very midst of a large body of rebel soldiers. However, darkness shielded him from being recognized, and the plucky private's own story shows how he preserved his presence of mind and extricated himself from the dangerous situation in a manner which reflects great credit upon him. He says:

"I pushed on rapidly and presently came upon a Confederate who was carrying a stand of colors and an overcoat on his arm.

"'Halt!' I exclaimed, 'I want your flag!'

"The rebel made a quick jump behind my horse, drew his revolver and made a dash for the river.

"I wheeled my horse, pulled my own gun and fired at him. I must have scared him badly, for he threw up his hands in despair and shouted:

"'I surrender! Don't shoot again!'

"And now prisoner and flag were mine. I marched the Johnny at the side of my horse till some time later, when I met one of our men, to whom I turned over my prisoner. I advanced still farther, and at the foot of Fisher's Hill encountered two teamsters in charge of three wagons. I stopped and ordered them to 'Turn around, quick! Drive the other way! Follow me!'

"In the darkness they mistook me for one of their own men and obeyed my directions without hesitation. I led them to our own lines and within safe distance disarmed them and brought them in as prisoners. The wagons contained loads of choice eatables, cigars and tobacco, and for several days following our boys lived high and in luxury."

HOW GENERAL RAMSEUR WAS MADE A PRISONER

FREDERICK A. LYON,
Corporal. Co. A, 1st Vt.
Cavalry.
Born at Williamsburg
Mass., June 25, 1843.

WHILE it may be true that, as Corporal Frederick Lyon, of Company A, First Vermont Cavalry, states, the "luck" or "opportunity" of distinguishing oneself in the cavalry, in a measure, depends on the mount, the corporal's own achievement—as brilliant as any during the war—cannot be cited in proof of the assertion. Presence of mind, quick decision and boldness rather than the mount were the elements of this cavalryman's "luck," which is shown by Corporal Lyon's own story:

"It was at the battle of Cedar Creek, October 19, 1864. On account of being surprised the left of our line fell back during the day nearly four miles. About four or five o'clock in the afternoon General Merritt's Division of cavalry charged that branch of the rebel force on the 'Dirt Road' which ran parallel to the Pike nearly four miles distant, and we saw nothing more of them during the engagement. It was nearly night when General Custer's Division was ordered forward. Upon reaching Cedar Creek we found that the enemy had all crossed the stream. Sergeant Haskell, of Company H, of my regiment, and myself were the first to cross at some distance above the bridge, but we were not long without company, the whole command coming in a body. The ground was level for some distance after leaving the creek and many prisoners were taken and sent to the rear under their own escort. At the top of a sharp hill we halted for a moment and made some pretense of forming a line. This delay, however, was of short duration. It was getting so dark now that we could not distinguish our own men. Knowing that General Merritt had routed the enemy's entire cavalry force, and as we had no infantry on that side of Cedar Creek, it was obvious that every dismounted man we met belonged to General Early's command.

"We had only charged a short distance around the curve in the pike when we came upon the whole retreating army, infantry, artillery, ambulance, baggage wagons, etc. The charge as a command was at an end. It was every one for himself, and the longest pale knocked off the largest persimmons. All was excitement. The fun for us at least was unlimited. I never saw such a stampede. Whole companies surrendered to half a dozen mounted men. Some of us galloped forward seeking diversion nearer the front. The only way was to call your horse out on one side of the pike, ride past half a dozen wagons, or pieces of artillery, command the leading rider to halt, shooting down a horse if necessary to force obedience, and order all to the rear.

"I was getting well to the front of the retreating column. Even a rebel bugler who had been near me continually sounding the charge was ordered to the rear. It was dark ; I began to feel as if I was away from home, among a strange people. Jumping my horse upon a bank to the right, I rode past a number of wagons, and halted an ambulance that was about to cross the bridge at Strasburg. A voice from out the darkness replied : 'General Ramseur is inside and he ordered us to 'move on,'

"Now I had seen considerable of generals, but to order one to 'halt,' and a major-general at that, after he had given the order to 'move on,' was considerably out of my line. It was reversing things. I fortunately maintained my presence of mind and a second time requested their delay, informing them that I was a member in good standing of the Federal Army. 'What'—from the ambulance—'are you a

"GENERAL RAMSEUR IS INSIDE."

Yank ?' I replied that I belonged to the First Cavalry, and my questioner, a major on General Ramseur's staff, appreciated the situation at once.

"The conference was brief and ended in the ambulance turning around and starting back toward Cedar Creek and Winchester. On the return I met General William Wells, commanding our brigade, who advised me to take my prisoners to General Custer's headquarters. The ambulance contained the general, a major, driver and a battle-flag. Generals Custer and Ramseur knew each other well, having been classmates at West Point."

Within a week after this incident, Corporal Lyon received orders to report to Washington, and was there presented with a Medal of Honor by President Lincoln **in presence** of his cabinet.

STORIES OF THE FLAG AT CEDAR CREEK

JOHN WALSH,

Corporal, Co. D, 5th New York Cavalry.
Born in Co. Tipperary, Ireland, Dec. 4, 1841.

ERI D. WOODBURY,

Sergeant, Co. E, 1st Vt. Cav.
Born at Francetown, N. H.,
May 30, 1889.

THE following tell of interesting episodes centering around the colors, Federal and Confederate, at the long-drawn-out and bloody battle of Cedar Creek.

Early in the engagement the standard of the Fifteenth New Jersey Infantry had been captured by the enemy. The loss became quickly known among the Union troops and several unsuccessful attempts to recapture the flag were made. Corporal John Walsh, of Company D, Fifth New York Cavalry, during one of the subsequent fierce charges, had the good fortune to succeed where so many others had failed. During the heat of a hand-to-hand struggle he noticed a Confederate color-bearer carrying a flag which he at once recognized as the one taken from the New Jersey boys. With a sudden rush he made for the rebel guard, overpowered him and wrenched the trophy from him. All of this was done on the spur of the moment and so quickly that the Confederate color-guard and his comrades hardly realized what had happened until it was all over and the daring corporal with his precious prize was back within the Union lines.

It was an impressive scene when, after the battle, the New Jersey regiment was called out on parade, and in presence of General Sherman received back its colors at the hands of Corporal Walsh.

The last decisive charge was made in the afternoon between three and four o'clock. It was by far the bloodiest of the entire battle and put the individual bravery of the Union soldier to its highest test. The conduct of Private Martin Wambsgan, of Company D, Ninetieth New York Infantry, furnishes a good illustration. While on the advance the color-bearer of his regiment was killed, shot through the head. He fell forward on his face and landed squarely on the flag, which was riddled with bullet holes, while the staff had been shot in two.

When this occurred Private Wambsgan was only a few feet away from the unfortunate flag-bearer. With one leap he was at his side, pulled the colors from under him, and, yelling as loudly as he possibly could, waved the flag over his head. Then he ran to the front of his regiment, where he took post during the remainder of the fight, holding the colors aloft, the piece of pole and his arm serving as a flag-staff. At the time the color-bearer was killed

MARTIN WAMBSGAN,

Private, Co. D. 90th N. Y. Inf.
Born in Bavaria, Germany,
August 9, 1839.

and the colors went down the regiment showed signs of wavering, but Private Wambsgan's quick action renewed the energy and courage of the men and contributed materially to the success of the charge.

During the same charge, when the enemy were already in full retreat, Sergeant Eri D. Woodbury, of Company E, First Vermont Cavalry, encountered four Confederate infantrymen retreating toward a small knoll. He drew his sabre and ordered them to surrender. The rebels hesitated, but did not raise their rifles. The actions of one made Woodbury suspicious, and scanning him more closely he perceived that he was trailing behind him a flag rolled on his staff.

"Give up that flag!" Woodbury demanded.

Naturally, the Confederate objected, but the determination of the Union cavalryman soon convinced him that resistance would be folly and reluctantly he handed over his colors. The brave sergeant then rode proudly back to his regiment, where he handed over his prisoners and captured colors and received the commendation of his superior officers.

CAPTURE OF GENERAL MARMADUKE

THE capture of a general officer in battle is a noteworthy event, but when the officer is one of prominence the act becomes of great interest, and especially when the capture is made single-handed by a private soldier; thus the capture of Confederate General Marmaduke by Private James Dunlavy, Company D, Third Iowa Cavalry, necessarily takes a high place in the annals of history.

Amid the heavy roar of cannon, on the open plains of Kansas, the two contending forces met to do battle for supremacy at Little Osage Crossing on the morning of the 25th of October, 1864. The Confederate artillery was playing on the Federal forces with fearful effect, but notwithstanding this incessant and terrific fire the Federal infantry never wavered. The safety of the Federals lay in a charge by which the enemy's guns could be captured. The

JAMES DUNLAVY.
Private, Co. D, Third Iowa Cav.
Born in Decatur County, Ind.,
Feb. 4, 1844.

Early in the spring of 1864 it became known to General Rosecrans, commanding the department of Missouri, that the Confederate General Price intended a great invasion of Missouri, which is historically known as Price's Missouri Expedition (Aug. 29-Dec. 2, 1864), and included skirmishes, engagements and battles in Missouri, Kansas and Arkansas. At **Little Osage Crossing, Kansas**, on the 25th of October, the Federals under General Pleasanton routed the Confederates, capturing 1,000 prisoners, military arms, ammunition, and Generals Marmaduke and Cabell.

movement was begun slowly at first, but increased in velocity until it swept on resistless as an avalanche. The crash of musketry, the scream of shell, the buzzing of canister and ball enthused the dashing cavalry. The charge was successful, the rebels being routed. At this juncture Private James Dunlavy was severely wounded, his arm being shattered by a piece of shell, which also struck his horse, making him wheel suddenly to the rear. Undaunted, the plucky rider headed him in the direction of a brigade which he thought was his own, but which proved to be the enemy.

He noticed a Confederate officer riding among the excited soldiers and exhorting them to make a stand. Dunlavy raised his carbine, aimed at him and fired. The shot missed its mark, but had served to attract the officer's attention to the doughty soldier, and dashing up to him he asked in an angry tone:

"What do you mean, shooting at your own officer? Give me that revolver."

"Surrender, or I'll fire!"

To say that the Confederate officer was paralyzed with surprise at finding himself at the mercy of a Union soldier is expressing it mildly. But he offered no resistance and handed over his revolver. Just then a comrade ran up to

"HE ASKED FOR A SLOWER TEMPO."

Dunlavy. "My horse has been shot. Give me that of your prisoner," he said.

Dunlavy made the officer dismount and accommodated his comrade. Then the two started for the rear, Dunlavy on horseback, the prisoner trotting along at double-quick.

The latter was far from relishing the hurried march and soon asked for a slower tempo. "I am very tired and worn out. Have been up all night," he said.

Good naturedly the cavalryman slowed down. The Confederate made still another request.

"Can't you get me a horse? I'd like to ride."

But Dunlavy was not inclined to make further concessions. Why should I give him a horse? he thought. And his reply to the question was a curt "No."

Again the silence was broken by the prisoner.

"Will you take me to General Pleasanton?" he said. "I am personally acquainted with him." Becoming more confidential, he added: "Young man, I'll tell you who I am."

He had not quite finished the sentence when Colonel C. W. Blair, of General Curtis' staff, rode up and approached the prisoner.

"I am General Marmaduke," the officer said, addressing the new-comer.

It was now Private Dunlavy's turn to be surprised. He apologized to his distinguished prisoner and with all the politeness at his disposal turned him over to Colonel Blair, who procured a horse for General Marmaduke and brought both prisoner and captor before General Curtis, who complimented Dunlavy and ordered him to the hospital.

SCENES FROM HATCHER'S RUN

ALONZO SMITH,
Private, Co. C, 7th Michigan Infantry,
Born at Hartland, N. Y., August 9, 1842.

Some of the most thrilling and inspiring incidents occurred at the battle of Hatcher's Run, Va., October 27, 1864. It was here that Private Alonzo Smith, of Company C, Seventh Michigan Infantry, performed an act of extraordinary daring.

His regiment, in position on the edge of the woods, had not yet taken an active part in the great fight. Presently Private Smith's attention was drawn to a body of soldiers a short distance from him in the woods. Not knowing whether they were friend or foe he decided to investigate for himself and started out to ascertain their identity. When about thirty or forty rods from his own regimental line he satisfied himself that the soldiers were "Johnnies." They were approaching him so

---

Hatcher's Run, Va. — The siege of Petersburg was in progress nearly four months, when, on the 27th of October, 1864, the Army of the Potomac began a movement to extend its lines to Hatcher's Run, Va., and to still further destroy the Weldon Railroad. The Second Army Corps and the Second Division of the Fifth Corps, with cavalry in advance and on the left flank, forced a passage at Hatcher's Run and moved along the railroad until the force of cavalry and the Second Corps had reached the Boydton Plank Road where it crosses the Run. At this point a bloody combat ensued between Hancock's and Warren's Corps and the Confederate forces, resulting in driving the enemy back into their works, after which the Union forces withdrew to their fortified lines. The Federal losses were about 1,200 in killed and wounded; the Confederate losses about 1,700.

fast that he could not attempt to return to his regiment without risking detection. He therefore stepped behind a large elm tree, and with his gun loaded and bayonet fixed awaited their arrival. When they had come up to within a distance of about twenty feet from him Smith stepped from his place of hiding, faced the rebel squad and boldly demanded their surrender. The Confederates were completely taken by surprise by the sudden and wholly unexpected appearance of a Union soldier, but, nevertheless, showed little inclination to comply with the order. As Smith with increased determination repeated his order, an officer, the leader of the squad, inquired whether there were any Federal troops in the vicinity and whether he was able to enforce his demand for surrender.

CHARLES A. ORR,
Private, Co. G, 187th N. Y. Infantry.
Born at Holland, N. Y., June 28, 1848.

Pointing to the direction of his regiment, Smith replied: "There is a whole division of Union troops." At the same time he called to his comrades nearest to him to come to his assistance. The rebels now realized that they had imprudently strayed too close to the Union lines, and surrendered. Smith marched his prisoners out of the woods to his regiment, on the way relieving the rebel color-bearer of the Confederate flag. "I think," he observed facetiously, "I'll be the color-bearer for a while."

His captain, George W. LaPoint, received him as he was marching his prisoners into camp, with a broad smile. "What have you been doing, Lon?" he asked.

"Oh," Smith answered, "capturing a few prisoners and a flag."

ALONZO WOODRUFF.
Sergeant, Co. I, 1st U. S. S. S.
Born at Farmington, Mich.,
March 21, 1839.

The regiment remained in position, which was far in advance of the brigade to which it belonged, all day. In the evening the brigade was withdrawn and an orderly was sent out to notify Captain LaPoint to follow the brigade.

The orderly lost his way and failed to find the regiment, which subsequently was cut off from the main body by the advancing Confederates. Captain LaPoint and his brave men, however, maintained their perilous position all night, and starting out on their retreat early in the morning had to fight every inch of the ground on their way. Their retreat consumed over forty-eight hours, and had it not been for an old negro who piloted them through along a circuitous route, they would never have reached their destination. As it was the regiment had many a narrow escape from annihilation and more than once its capture seemed almost inevitable. At one time, when the situation looked almost hopeless and Confederates were crowding about the regiment from all sides, the men resolved to sell their lives as dearly as possible, and above all save the colors from falling into the hands of the enemy. Color-Sergeant James Donaldson took the State flag from the staff and wrapped it around his body under his clothing, while the national flag was cut into pieces and a star given to each man, the remaining pieces being distributed likewise. Thus the enemy could have only captured the colors after the death of the whole command and the search of the body of every soldier.

The rebels were not equal to such heroic determination and in the final charge, although in overwhelming numbers, were repulsed and the brave Seventh Michigan regained the Federal lines. With Captain LaPoint on his retreat was a detachment of the First Minnesota Infantry under command of Captain J. C. Farwell.

Another incident of this battle centers about a hand-to-hand fight between Sergeant Alonzo Woodruff and Corporal John M. Howard, of Company I, First United States Sharpshooters, and a body of rebels.

General B. R. Pierce, who led the Second Brigade, Third Division, Second Army Corps, gives the following version of the occurrence, of which he was an eyewitness: "I wish to call attention to the bravery displayed by Sergeant Alonzo Woodruff and Corporal John M. Howard. They were posted on the extreme left of the line as the enemy passed our left flank.

"After discharging their rifles and being unable to reload, Corporal Howard ran and caught one of the enemy who seemed to be leading that part of the line. When he was overpowered and had received a severe wound through both legs, Sergeant Woodruff went to his assistance. Clubbing his rifle, he had a desperate hand-to-hand struggle, but finally succeeded in freeing Corporal Howard and both made their escape."

A few minutes later Woodruff noticed a rebel marching a private of his company, N. J. Standard, who was wounded, away as a prisoner.

"What?" the gritty sergeant exclaimed, "The gall of those rebels!"

And he jumped right among the rebels, rushed after his comrade and not only released Standard, but even turned the tables on his captor, making him a prisoner instead. However, the brave sergeant did not escape injury, and during the last encounter was severely wounded himself and forced to seek medical assistance as soon as he reached his lines.

Mention also must be made of the deeds of Lieutenant Shannon and Private Charles A. Orr and John Williams, of Company G, One hundred and Eighty-seventh New York Infantry, who, when during this battle volunteers were asked for to rescue wounded men from between the lines, carried out their mission at the risk of their own lives. Originally thirty men had responded to the call for volunteers, but when it came to the execution of the task and the rebel fire was concentrated upon them twenty-seven abandoned the work, leaving only Orr and his two companions to bring help and aid to the wounded soldiers.

They rescued a number of men and were universally praised for their heroic efforts.

A THRILLING RIDE

I<small>N</small> November, 1864, on the field where the famous battle of Cedar Creek was fought the preceding month, occurred a most remarkable race for life and liberty, one that speaks volumes for the hero and the endurance of the man he rescued in this wild chase. A squadron of the Ninth New York Cavalry, in command of Lieutenant Edwin Goodrich, was ordered to proceed up the Shenandoah Valley on a reconnoissance to ascertain the whereabouts of the enemy. Soon after receiving his orders Lieutenant Goodrich had all in readiness, his eighty men comprising the squadron eagerly awaiting the command to march. Diligent search failed to reveal any hostile forces until they had reached a place

EDWIN GOODRICH,

1st Lieutenant, Co. D, 9th N. Y. Cav.
Highest rank attained: Brevet-Major.
Born in New York City March 22, 1843.

not far from Strasburg, Va., where a large force was suddenly encountered. As soon as Lieutenant Gooderich discovered the enemy's pickets he dispatched Sergeant Joseph N. Foster with a few men to drive them in, he and the remainder of his squadron following up in their support. The enemy observed this move and immediately sent a force of 2,000 cavalry to the support of the pickets.

Goodrich had ordered the charge to learn the strength of the rebels, and, having accomplished this, he sounded the retreat just in time to get a good start on the approaching enemy. Foster, who was among the last to fall back, felt his horse stagger under him, from the effects of a wound, so he slipped out of the saddle and started on the retreat afoot. The horse, however, gathered himself together and overtook the fleeing men, whereupon Foster again mounted him. The wounded animal carried his man but a short distance at a rapid gait; then he began to lose ground and finally brought up the rear of the column, where, exhausted, he fell, pinning his rider to the ground.

Goodrich saw Foster's plight and wheeling about he went to his assistance and hastily pulled him from under the wounded horse, leaving a boot behind. Having freed Foster, he immediately remounted; none too soon, however, for the enemy were upon them, and spurring his charger on he dashed away with Foster clinging to the horse's tail. Goodrich reached back, took Foster by the hand and brought him alongside where he could get a good hold on his collar, and in this way almost carried him by main strength, running him and encouraging him to keep up. For six miles he carried and dragged him, with the enemy in close pursuit, firing, cursing and ordering him to surrender. The 2,000 pursuing cavalrymen and their rain of bullets, their shouting and their commands to surrender could not induce Goodrich to loose his hold on his comrade's collar. Awkward as the additional

"FOR SIX MILES HE CARRIED AND DRAGGED HIM."

weight was, the gallant charger fled along the pike so swiftly that his rider felt secure in their ultimate safety. But this gait could not be maintained, and shortly after the enemy were fast closing in. At last one of Goodrich's men slowed down his horse and dropped back to the assistance of the heroic lieutenant.

This young trooper rode alongside of Goodrich, bringing Foster, who by this time was completely exhausted, between the two horses, and while still in full flight they managed with much difficulty to swing him on the trooper's horse.

Twelve miles were covered by these brave horsemen before the rebels gave up their chase, and so completely was Foster exhausted that when Winchester was reached he had to be taken to the hospital.

During this exciting retreat, when exhaustion overcame Foster, he had begged Goodrich to leave him to his fate, as he could no longer keep up. But Goodrich could not be induced to loose his iron grasp on him. After all were safely within the Union lines Goodrich remarked : " Had the pursuers overtaken us while I was extricating Foster, there would have been little danger of our being taken prisoners, for the enemy were bunched so closely together in the narrow pike, and were coming on with such impetus, that we would have been trampled to death."

A REBEL CHARGE THAT FAILED

THE following vivid description by Sergeant Henry F. W. Little, of Company D, Seventh New Hampshire Infantry. shows how much depends on the personal bravery of the individual soldier in repulsing a charge of the enemy, and also illustrates the futility of a bayonet charge against a body of men well entrenched and armed with repeating rifles.

"It was early on the morning of October 7, 1864," the sergeant says, "that our troops on the north side of the James River, Va., were aroused. We were quickly ordered into line to repel an attack. We found the cavalry under General Kautz coming toward us pell-mell, hotly pursued by the Confederates. We were at once advanced, the lines formed and thus we waited the onslaught.

HENRY F. W. LITTLE,
Sergeant, Company D, 7th New Hampshire Infantry.
Born at Manchester, N. H., June 27, 1842.

"Our line was without breastworks or protection of any kind and the Confederates pushed up to within a few rods of us. Our force was not large and our lines extended so far that we were without support, and a wavering brigade or even the falling back of a single regiment on that line would probably have given the enemy an opportunity of taking everything before them on the north side of the James River.

"Much depended on the individual bravery and the courage of the officers. As the rebels came rushing on I advised our men to keep cool and not fall back an inch, and had the gratification to see that during the subsequent events our boys above all others distinguished themselves for their calmness and the deadly accuracy of their fire.

"The charge was desperately and handsomely made and energetically repulsed. Our brigade, which seemed to have been the objective point of the Confederate attack and had borne the brunt of the assault, was armed with Spencer repeating carbines, seven-shooters, and delivered so destructive a fire that it was impossible for the enemy to withstand its effect. The Confederate dead in our front, after the charge, lay in long lines only a few feet away, showing where their battalions had stood at the time of the clash, when they found it impossible to break through our ranks.

"Many of the Confederates found it as much impossible to retreat as it was to advance, and preferred capture to almost inevitable death. The fight, although it lasted but a half hour, was extremely fierce and ended in a complete defeat of the rebels."

Sergeant Little's gallant conduct on the skirmish line was such that it commended itself to his superior officers and, later, was fittingly recognized by the award of the Medal of Honor.

A CLEVER TACTICIAN'S CLEVER ACHIEVEMENT

ORSON W. BENNETT,

First Lieutenant, Co. A, 102d
U. S. C. T.

Highest rank attained:
Captain.

Born Nov. 17, 1841, at Union
City, Branch Co., Mich.

ON the 30th day of November, 1864, at Honey Hill, S. C., First Lieutenant Orson W. Bennett, Company A, One hundred and second U. S. Colored Troops, received an order from his brother, General W. T. Bennett, chief of staff to General Hatch, in the following words:

"Lieutenant, about 100 yards in advance of our lines, on an elevation near the road, and within 150 yards of the enemy's guns, there are three pieces of artillery which have been abandoned. You are ordered to bring them in. Fix bayonets and impress upon your men that they must not pay any attention to the enemy, but bring in the guns."

Lieutenant Bennett at once selected thirty men to go with him to carry out the order, leaving the remainder of his company on the skirmish line. Then he gave the order, "Fix bayonets! Trail arms! Forward, double-quick—march!"

The little squad moved forward with great precision. The slight elevation of the land helped considerable in preventing the enemy from seeing the advance until the men were directly opposite the abandoned guns, partly screened by a fringe of low bushes. The guns were surrounded by dead and mangled men and horses, who had fallen in their defense. Lieutenant Bennett urged on his brave men to quick and concentrated action. Delay meant death. The men fully appreciated the situation and obeyed like machines. At the "rally" they sprang forward and seized the nearest gun. Lieutenant Bennett kept a watchful eye upon the Confederates, less than 200 yards distant. When he saw by their movements that they were about to fire their own guns he shouted to his men, "Down!" and they all dropped to the ground. A second later a shower of grape and canister went whizzing and shrieking over their heads. Instantly they sprang to their feet again, seized the trailer of one of the guns and dragged it safely to the Union lines. To secure the second was a more dangerous operation, for the enemy was aware of the movement and prepared to give Bennett's detachment a warm greeting.

After resting his men a few moments Bennett again ordered an advance. Just before the Confederates fired he commanded his men to drop, which they did as promptly and neatly as before. Before the smoke cleared away the gallant colored soldiers were dragging the gun out of danger.

Then Lieutenant Bennett and his men made a dash for the third gun, repeating the same tactics of dropping as the Confederates fired, and succeeded in landing it safely within the Union lines amid yells of disappointment from the enemy and cheers of enthusiastic approval from the Union troops.

In performing this daring deed, only one of Lieutenant Bennett's men was wounded and none killed, and the achievement was the more brilliant by reason of the fact that a previous attack to save the guns had ended in a failure and cost a heavy loss to the command which made the attempt.

"WE CAN GO WHEREVER THE GENERAL CAN!"

DAVID S STANLEY,
Major-General U. S. Volunteers.
Born in Cedar Valley, Wayne
Co., Ohio, June 1, 1828.

M AJOR-GENERAL DAVID S. STANLEY, commanding the Fourth Army Corps, sent by General Sherman to guard Nashville and Tennessee against an unexpected move of General Hood with a large Confederate army, reached Pulaski, Tenn., November 1, 1864. Then followed a series of manoeuvres on the part of 18,000 Union soldiers against an overwhelming rebel force, numbering fully 40,000. The clash came November 30th, when the battle of Franklin was fought.

A description of this battle is given in the general's own words, as follows :

"Early on the morning of the 29th General Wilson sent word to me that the enemy had laid a pontoon bridge at Huey's Mills. At 8 A. M. I started to Spring Hill with the First and Second Divisions, all the artillery that could be spared, and all the trains and ambulances to follow; at the same time a reconnoissance was sent up the river and soon sent word back that the enemy was crossing infantry and wagons and moving off rapidly to the north and parallel to the turnpike. It being apprehended that the enemy might make a flank attack upon the position of our force between Duck River and Rutherford's Creek, the First Division was halted and took up position to cover the crossing of the creek. At 11:30 o'clock the head of the Second Division was within two miles of Spring Hill. A cavalry soldier, who seemed badly scared, was met here and stated that a scout had come in from the direction of Raleigh Hill and reported that Buford's Division of rebel cavalry was half way between Raleigh Hill and Spring Hill and on the march to the latter place. The Second Division was pushed on, and, attracted by the firing east of the village, double-quicked into the place and deployed the leading brigade as they advanced, drove off a force of the enemy's cavalry which was driving our small force of cavalry and infantry, and would very soon have occupied the town.

"Up to this time it was thought that we had only cavalry to contend with, but a general officer and his staff, at whom we sent some complimentary shells, were seen reconnoitering our position and very soon afterward General Bradley was assailed by a force which the men said fought too well to be any dismounted cavalry.

"I received General Schofield's dispatch about the same time, telling me that the rebels had been crossing the river, and leaving no doubt but that we now confronted a superior force of rebel infantry. About the same time an attack was made upon a small wagon train by rebel cavalry at Reynolds' Station, three miles toward Franklin, and simultaneously the rebel cavalry appeared west of us and threatened the railroad station of Spring Hill. Thus we were threatened and attacked from every direction. As night closed we could see the enemy rapidly extending his line and by eight o'clock it was evident that at least a Corps of Hood's Army was formed in line of battle, facing the turnpike, and at a near distance of but little more than half a mile from it. It was determined to push our way to Franklin. At one o'clock in the morning of the 30th the train commenced to pull out. The number of wagons, including artillery and ambulances, was about 800. At the very starting point they had to pass singly over a bridge, and it was exceedingly doubtful whether the train could be put on the road by daylight. Unless this could be done, and the corps put in motion, we were sure of being attacked by daylight and compelled to fight under every disadvantage. I was strongly advised to burn the train and move on with the troops and such wagons as could be saved, but I determined to make an effort to save the train. My staff officers were busily engaged hurrying up teamsters and everything promised well when we were again thrown into despair by the report that the train had been attacked north of Thompson's Station and its progress had been stopped altogether. It was now three o'clock in the morning. General Kimball was directed to push on with the First Division and clear the road. General Wood's Division had covered the road and was directed to move on, keeping off the road and on the right flank of the train, and General Wagner's Division, although wearied by the fighting of the day before, was detailed to bring up the rear. Before Kimball's Division could reach the point at which the train was attacked Major Steele, of my staff, had gotten up a squad of our stragglers and driven off the rebels, who had succeeded in burning about ten wagons.

"The trains moved on again, and at about five o'clock I had the satisfaction of seeing the last wagon pass the small bridge. The entire corps was on the road before daylight. The rebel cavalry was in possession of all the hills to our right, and made numerous demonstrations upon our flank, but were easily driven off.

"From one o'clock until four in the afternoon the enemy's entire force was in sight and forming for attack; yet, in view of our own strong positions and reasoning from the former course of the rebels during this campaign, nothing appeared so improbable as that they would assault. I felt so confident in this belief that I did not leave General Schofield's headquarters until the firing commenced. About four o'clock the enemy advanced with his whole force, at least two corps, making a bold and persistent assault. When Wagner's Division fell back from the heights south of Franklin, Opdycke's Brigade was placed in reserve in rear and Lane's and Conrad's Brigades were deployed in the front of our main line. Here the men, as our men always do, threw up a barricade of rails. By whose mistake I cannot tell, these brigades had orders not to retire to the main line until forced to do so by the fighting of the enemy. The consequence was that the brigades stood their ground until the charging rebels were almost crossing bayonets with them, but the line then broke and men and officers made the quickest time they could to our main lines. The old soldiers all escaped, but many of the conscripts, being afraid to run under fire, were captured. A large proportion of the men came back with loaded muskets, and turning at the breastworks fired a volley into the pressing rebels, not ten steps from them. The part of the Twenty-third Corps stationed in the works broke and ran to the rear with the fugitives from Conrad's Brigade. To add to this disorder, the caissons of the two batteries in the works galloped rapidly to the rear and the enemy appeared on the breastworks and in possession of the two batteries, which they commenced to turn upon us.

"It was at this moment that I arrived on the scene of disorder. The moment was critical beyond any I have known in any battle. Colonel Opdycke's Brigade was lying down about 100 yards in the rear of the works. I rode quickly to the left of the brigade and called to them to charge; at the same time I saw Colonel Opdycke near the centre of his line urging his men forward. I gave the Colonel no order, as I saw him engaged in doing the very thing to save us, viz., to get possession of our line again. The retreating men commenced to rally. I heard old soldiers call out: 'Come on, men; we can go wherever the general can!'

"Making a rush our men immediately retook all our line, excepting a small portion just in front of a brick house on the pike. Here a rebel force held out and for fifteen or twenty minutes poured in a severe fire upon our men. So deadly was the fire that it was only by the most strenuous exertions of the officers that our men could be kept to the line. Our exertions, however, succeeded, and in twenty minutes our front was comparatively clear of rebels, who fell back. Just after the retaking of the lines by our troops, as I was passing toward the left to General Cox's position, my horse was killed, and no sooner had I regained my feet than I received a musket ball through the back of my neck. My wound, however, did not prevent my keeping the field, and General Cox kindly furnished me a remount. One hundred wagon loads of ammunition, artillery and musket cartridges were expended in this short battle.

"In the evening it was determined to withdraw to Nashville and the troops were directed to leave the line at midnight. Some villain came very near frustrating this plan by firing a house in Franklin; the flames soon spread, and the prospect was that a large fire would occur, which, lighting up objects, would make it impossible to move the troops without being seen. My own and General Wood's staff officers found an old fire engine, and getting it at work soon had the flames subdued, the darkness now being intensified by the smoke. At midnight the withdrawal was made successfully and the march to Nashville continued without interruption. Our men were more exhausted, however, than I have ever seen them on any occasion; many of them were overtaxed, broke down on the march and fell into the hands of the enemy, and altogether we were glad when our destination—Nashville—was finally reached."

OVER FIVE BARRICADES

DAVID L. COCKLEY.
First Lieutenant, Co. L, 10th
Ohio Cavalry.
Highest rank attained :
Captain.
Born in Lexington, O., June
8, 1843.

GENERAL WHEELER'S position at Waynesboro, Ga., at the beginning of December, 1864, was chosen with the utmost caution in the roughest and most inaccessible locality with a special view of affording protection against a sabre charge. General Kilpatrick was ordered to pursue Wheeler and engage him wherever he would meet him. In compliance with this order the Federal cavalry leader moved on to Waynesboro Road, and on December 4 engaged General Wheeler's rebel forces. The Confederates had dismounted and were behind heavy rail barricades.

The Federal troops were preparing for the attack and were anxiously waiting for the charge to be sounded. The commanding officer of one of the cavalry regiments had just been wounded when First Lieutenant David L. Cockley, acting aide-de-camp to General S. D. Atkins, brought the instruction to make the charge. Noting the hesitation of the troops, Lieutenant Cockley asked for permission to lead this regiment. The request was at first refused, General Atkins preferring to have the young lieutenant at his side so as to be able to use his valuable services. Cockley felt chagrined. Again, and still more urgently, he made the request. "I need your services," Colonel Atkins repeated and again refused. For a third time Cockley repeated his request and so earnestly pleaded to be allowed to participate in the fight that the colonel could no longer resist and yielded to the wishes of his brave aide-de-camp. The charge was sounded. The whole line moved forward in splendid order and never halted for one moment until, in less than twenty minutes, five lines of barricades were taken and the enemy were completely routed and driven back into the town of Waynesboro. Here a countercharge stopped, for a short time, the advance of the Federals, but soon another attack was made and the rebels were driven in wild confusion through and out of the town. A most notable victory had been gained by the Federal cavalry against a much stronger force.

Lieutenant Cockley was at the head of the regiment. When during the height of the attack and after having passed the second barricade Captain S. E. Norton, who commanded the first battalion, fell, mortally wounded, Cockley took his place and gallantly led the men to victory. No more than five of his brave followers were left with him when he finally stopped his dash. His conduct earned for him the Medal of Honor, especially since only two weeks prior to this battle he had achieved a feat in a battle episode which attracted the attention of his superior officers.

The Second Brigade, Third Cavalry Division, to which the Tenth Ohio Cavalry belonged, had left Marietta and was on the road to Bear Creek Station, Ga., pursuing

"THE REBELS WERE DRIVEN THROUGH AND OUT OF THE TOWN."

Wheeler's cavalrymen. On November 15th, while near East Point, the brigade commander, Colonel Atkins, sent Lieutenant Cockley ahead to select a locality suitable for camp purposes. This had been done by Cockley, who was returning to his lines when he suddenly found the road blocked by four rebels. With quick determination the lieutenant gave the command to charge to his orderly, his only companion, and made a dash for the Confederates, who were so completely surprised that they threw up their hands in token of surrender when ordered to do so. Cockley marched them to headquarters to receive the expressions of appreciation and congratulations from the colonel.

"I WAS MAD AS A HORNET"

MICHAEL SOWERS,
Private, Company L, Fourth Pennsylvania Cavalry.
Born in Pittsburg, Pa., Sept. 14, 1844.

INCITED by the loss of his horse Private Michael Sowers, of Company L, Fourth Pennsylvania Cavalry, fought at Stony Creek Station, Va., December 1, 1864, with such fury and rage that he attracted general attention, and, being one of the first to storm the enemy's stronghold, became the hero of the day.

"It was like this," Private Sowers says in telling of the incident; "my regiment and the Sixteenth Pennsylvania Cavalry were marched down the public road to a distance of about 500 yards from the fort, which was built of mud and logs. Then we separated, the Sixteenth going to the right, we to the left, to make a simultaneous attack. We charged. All of a sudden my horse dropped forward on his knees to rise no more. That was the third horse killed under me within a short time, I was mad as a hornet and, resolving to make some rebels pay for this last loss, slipped off the back of the gallant little animal, took my Spencer and, running ahead of the encircling cavalry, made for the fort. Of course, I had no right to do that; but I was enraged and had but one object in view, to get even with those infernal Johnnies who were killing my horses. A lot of grape and canister came my way, but not close enough to injure me, so on I went right into the fort. I do not claim that I was the first one to enter upon rebel ground—I was too excited to look about me. I do know, however, that I was one of the first, and that as soon as I was inside of the fort I emptied my gun into the rebels with telling effect. The Sixteenth Pennsylvania stormed the fort from the other side, and together we made ourselves masters of the rebel stronghold."

On the 1st of December, 1864, Grant sent General Gregg's cavalry on a reconnoissance to discover whether the enemy were moving troops south. Gregg captured **Stony Creek Station, Va.**, that day, burning 3,000 sacks of corn, 500 bales of hay, a train of cars, and a large amount of ammunition, and brought off 190 prisoners, while his own loss was very small.

WHERE OTHERS SKULKED, HE STOOD HIS GROUND

SAMUEL J. CHURCHILL,
Corporal, Co. G, Second Illinois
L. A.
Born in Rutland County, Vermont,
Nov. 1, 1842.

"He stood manfully at his post." This splendid tribute is quoted from the records relating to the award of the Medal of Honor to Corporal Samuel J. Churchill, of Company G, Second Illinois Light Artillery.

He won it December 15, 1864, when General Thomas made an attack upon the rebel army under General Hood, near Nashville, Tenn.

The battery to which Churchill belonged was in position on high ground, 200 yards from and directly in front of the rebel battery. Churchill himself commanded a twelve-pound Napoleon gun served by eight men. The Confederates worked their pieces with deadly accuracy, several men and horses being killed before Churchill's Battery succeeded in taking the desired position—a few feet to the right of a large brick house.

The firing continued and seemed to increase both in frequency and certainty of aim. But now the Union Batteries opened and replied as effectively as that of the enemy.

At Churchill's gun a cannoneer at the command of "Load!" took the sponge-staff, sponged the gun and waited for his comrade to come up with the cartridge. Just then a volley from the rebel battery enshrouded the gun and the waiting cannoneer became panic-stricken. He dropped his sponge-staff and ran behind the brick house. His terror spread to the other cannoneers and they likewise fled, leaving the corporal alone at his post. Neither entreaty nor command could induce the men to return. But Churchill never wavered. Regardless of the rain of shot and shell he stuck to his place and assumed the duties and functions of his skulking command. He loaded and fired his gun eleven times without any assistance whatever, thereby helping to silence the Confederate Battery and contributing his share to the glorious achievements of the Union Army of that day.

WHEN THE REBELS WERE ROUTED AT NASHVILLE

MARION T. ANDERSON,

Captain, Company D, Fifty-First Indiana Infantry.
Highest rank attained :
Major.
Born at Clarksburg, Indiana.
Nov. 13, 1839.

THE second day of the battle of Nashville, Tenn., December 16, 1864, which resulted in the complete victory of the Federal armies, began with a concerted attack in the afternoon all along the lines upon the fortified position of the enemy. Colonel P. Sidney Post, commanding the Second Brigade, Third Division, was ordered to charge the Confederate right at Overton Hill, and upon receipt of the order at once led his troops to the assault. When within about 100 yards of the enemy's works the gallant colonel was shot, and his men, thinking their leader killed, became terror-stricken and dropped to the ground. Two advanced lines of Colonel Abel D. Straight's Brigade came up and reaching the prostrate troops followed their example, likewise dropping to the ground. Next came the Fifty-first Indiana Infantry, led by Captain Marion T. Anderson. As he came upon the preceding troops he asked some of the officers why their men were lying down. The reply was: "Because those in our front did the same thing."

"Why don't you order them up and forward?" Captain Anderson inquired.

"We have; but they won't go," was the answer.

"Well," Captain Anderson observed, "I won't lie down here. I will take my men forward and obey orders."

He gave the order: "Charge bayonets; double-quick." And away he led his men over the bodies of the prostrate troops, up the hill and against the enemy's last line of works on the crest, forcing the rebels to abandon half of their guns and retreat in utter confusion.

While riding at the head of his regiment the brave captain was struck by a sharpshooter's bullet, and severely wounded, fell almost into the abandoned and captured trenches.

The attack on the Confederate left was made by the troops commanded by Generals A. J. Smith and John M. Schofield, and resulted in gaining possession of the Granny White Pike and cutting off the enemy's retreat.

WILLIAM T. SIMMONS,

First Lieutenant Co. C, 11th Missouri Infantry.
Born in Green County, Ill., January 29, 1843.

This assault, too, was met by the Confederates with a tremendous fire of grape and canister and musketry, and put the bravery of the Union men to hard test. Several incidents occurred which attracted general attention and won praise for the heroes of the entire Federal Army.

One of these incidents is related by First Lieutenant William . T. Simmons, of Company C, Eleventh Missouri Infantry: "Our division was massed to the right of Granny White Pike—the direct route from Nashville to Franklin—about 400 yards in front of Hood's center. My regiment was in our second line about four o'clock in the afternoon. Just before the assault all the boys in my company as well as

"THE BRAVE CAPTAIN WAS STRUCK."

myself were commenting upon a Confederate flag (the stars and bars) planted on the enemy's entrenchment directly in our front. Several of us had remarked, banteringly, that we would have the flag before dark, when the order came to assault. From the beginning we had been under a heavy fire of musketry and artillery, but as we started forward the regiment in our immediate front wavered and became somewhat broken up under the murderous fire, so that my regiment pressed forward and, passing them, dashed on about 200 yards. A moment later my captain fell. I was left in command of the company, and leaving my place as file closer I sprang to the front and led the way, making straight for the flag. Being an exceptionally speedy runner at the time, I was first to reach the breastworks, and demanded the surrender of the colors. The Confederate sergeant attempted to run away with the prize and I was compelled to shoot, wounding him and thereby securing the flag."

UNDER THE EYES OF HIS COMMANDER

No LESS a personage than Major-General James H. Wilson was the sponsor for the distinction bestowed upon First Lieutenant Joseph S. Hedges, of whom he says: "He was as good a soldier as I ever knew and would never ask his men to go where he did not actually lead them."

Lieutenant Hedges was a member of the Fourth U. S. Cavalry, and at Little Harpeth River, Tenn., on the evening of December 17, 1864, under the direction and personal observation of General Wilson, made a charge upon a rebel force which elicited the admiration of the Union commander, who after the battle "took great pleasure" in commending the lieutenant and personally secured for him the Medal of Honor.

The general himself gives this version of the noted charge:

"It was directed straight against a field battery in action at the center of the line of infantry in line of battle and was one of the best and most successful charges of cavalry it was ever my fortune to witness. Lieutenant Hedges, serving as my escort, rode along, leading his gallant regiment down the turnpike head-on against the battery, broke through it, sabred the gunners, captured or caused the abandonment of three guns, and continued his pursuit, spreading terror and confusion among the enemy until stopped by darkness. It is the only case I know of in which a cavalry regiment charged and broke through a Confederate line of battle composed of infantry and artillery in action and captured the guns."

"WE WILL, LIEUTENANT; WE WILL"

EYE-WITNESSES pronounce the feat of First Lieutenant William H. Walling at Fort Fisher, N. C., December 25, 1865, as among the most daring achievements of the entire campaign. The lieutenant's superiors and generals commanding were especially profuse in their commendation of his bravery, from Major-General Benjamin F. Butler, Brigadier-General A. Ames, Brevet Brigadier-General N. W. Curtis, Major-General Godfrey Weitzel to Lieutenant-Colonel Albert M. Barney, of the One hundred and forty-second New York Infantry, of which organization Lieutenant Walling was a member. General Curtis even went so far as to say that it was "one of the most gallant

WILLIAM H. WALLING,

First Lieutenant, Co. C, 142d
New York Infantry.
Highest rank attained: Lt-Col.
Born at Hartford, N. Y.,
Sept. 8, 1880.

exploits of the war." In fact, in view of the universal praise, Lieutenant Walling's deed stands out boldly as the one redeeming feature in an otherwise unfortunate undertaking, as the first attempt to take Fort Fisher has been characterized.

"Fort Fisher," says General Weitzel, "was a square bastioned work; it had a high relief, a wide and deep ditch, excepting on the sea front, a glacis, casements

"SECURED THE FLAG AND RETURNED UNINJURED."

and bomb-proofs sufficiently large to hold its garrison. I counted seventeen guns in position bearing up the beach and between each pair of guns there was a traverse so thick and so high above the parapet that I had no doubt they were all bomb-proofs. A stockade ran from the northeast angle of the counterscarps of the works to the water's edge on the sea-side.

"The expedition, led by General Butler, with a force of 6,500, embarked at Bermuda Hundred, Va., for Fortress Monroe, December 8th. In order to mislead the Confederate scouts and signal men as to the real object of the movement, the fleet carrying the troops took up one direction during the day and a different one at night, and on December 24th came in sight of Fort Fisher, where the naval fleet under Admiral Porter was already engaged in bombarding it. About noon the following day the troops, under cover of the gunboats, effected a landing. General Curtis at once pushed up his brigade to within a few hundred yards of the fort, captured a rebel work, called Half-Moon Fort, containing a 20-pounder gun, and captured about 100 prisoners.

"The onward movement was continued till the brigade's main line of skirmishers was within 150 paces of the fort, capturing in the advance another important outwork, which also contained a large gun. During all the time that this advance was made the navy kept up a very heavy and well directed assault, which, however, did little material damage to the fortification. The rebels were nowhere in sight, but kept in their casements as long as the shells were being thrown from the Union vessels. At the same time the fire prevented the troops from further advancing and attempting to storm the works. The minute, however, the navy would cease throwing shells, the rebels would emerge from their places of safety, mount the parapets, work their guns and pour such withering fire upon the Federals that all further progress was stopped and the help and aid of the naval fleet had to be called in again, when the Confederates would immediately withdraw to their bomb-proofs."

Three companies of the One hundred and forty-second New York Infantry were in this most advanced line of skirmishers, and the leading company, C, was commanded by the aforementioned Lieutenant Walling.

"I was just stationing my men," he says in describing the most interesting incident of the attack, "being ordered to protect them from the fire of the fleet, and had them scoop out the sand and make gopher holes to lie in, when a large shell from one of the monitors struck the ground near us, ploughing a trench so deep that some of our men took refuge therein, the shell ricochetting into the river beyond. Another shot from the fleet cut down the Confederate flag on the fort.

"I said to my men: 'I'll go and get the flag; you keep a sharp lookout for the riflemen on the works. Let every man have his gun in position to fire.'

"'We will, Lieutenant; we will!' came the response from my men as with one voice. I started off. I had gone but a few steps when one of the great monitor shells passed in front of me and exploded before reaching the river. I confess I was frightened, and for an instant halted involuntarily, stunned by the fearful crash. But, quickly recovering my wits, I proceeded and came to a place where a shell had cut a hole in the palisade a little to the left of the flag. Through this opening I entered, passed along toward the river, gained the parapet, secured the flag and returned, uninjured as I had gone, to the picket line."

And thus was Lieutenant Walling the only Union man who in that expedition had set his foot upon the rebel stronghold.

First Assault on Fort Fisher, N. C.—During the latter part of December, 1864, an expedition composed of naval and military forces sailed from Hampton Roads to gain the harbor of Wilmington, N. C., and reduce its chief defense, Fort Fisher.

Admiral Porter was in command of the naval forces, with General Butler in command of the land forces. The latter conceived the idea of blowing up an old vessel loaded with 235 pounds of powder, directly in front of the fort, with a view of throwing the enemy into confusion and then attacking the fort. The powder boat was towed to its position, and on the night of the 23d the fuse ignited; but the result, instead of being a gigantic explosion, was only a blaze lighting the heavens. Very little concussion was felt, and all that could be heard was a dull detonation.

On the 25th the troops were landed and pushed close to the fort, but Butler failed to move with energy, feeling that the works could not be carried by assault, and deliberately abandoned the enterprise and returned to Fortress Monroe with his troops the following day.

HISTORIC INCIDENTS FROM THE FALL OF FORT FISHER

JOHN WAINWRIGHT,

First Lieutenant. Co. F, 97th
Pennsylvania Infantry.
Highest rank attained: Colonel.

ZACHARIAH C. NEAHR,

Private. Co. K, 142nd New York
Infantry.
Born at Palatine Bridge, N. Y.,
Dec. 9, 1880.

AFTER General Butler's failure to capture Fort Fisher, N. C., a second expedition was decided upon and entrusted to General Alfred H. Terry, with orders to take the Confederate stronghold by storm if he could, by a siege if he must. This expedition left Bermuda Landing, Va., January 5, 1865. General Terry had with him an army of 8,457 men picked from the several army corps, the flower of the Union forces. As on the former occasion, Admiral Porter was instructed to co-operate with his ships. After some difficulty, due mainly to rough weather and a heavy surf, a landing was effected January 13th. The 8,000 men with three days' rations in their haversacks and forty rounds of ammunition in their boxes, six days' supply of hard bread in bulk, ten pieces of artillery, 300,000 additional rounds of small arm ammunition and the necessary number of entrenching tools and implements, were safely brought on shore.

Picket lines were immediately thrown out and shots exchanged with the enemy's outposts, but no serious damage was done to either side in these preliminary skirmishes.

General Terry's first object after landing was to throw a strong defensive line across the peninsula from the Cape Fear River to the sea, so as to have the rear protected. This was accomplished, though it consumed the entire day and was not completed late at night.

Second Assault on Fort Fisher, N. C.—After the dismal attack on Fort Fisher, December 23-25, 1864, both Grant and Porter were anxious to renew the assault. A plan was arranged whereby Porter was to continue to hold his position in front of the fort while General Terry was to attack with his land forces under the fire of Porter's ships.

The attack was made on the 15th of January with a vigorous fire from Porter's whole fleet, and in a short time Terry's troops gained the inside of the fort, which consisted of a system of bomb-proofs surrounded by a large fortification. Here the fighting was very severe; but being compelled to yield one traverse after another the rebels were driven out and a complete victory won. The losses of the Federals, however, were quite heavy, numbering nearly 1,000 killed and wounded. The Confederates lost 2,500 in killed, wounded and missing.

On the 14th entrenchments were dug, breastworks reaching from the river to the sea constructed and covered by abatis and a firm foothold on the peninsula secured. The assault was planned for the following day at 3 o'clock in the afternoon. In the meantime Admiral Porter was to pour a steady and destructive fire into the fort and demolish the palisades as much as possible, and furnish an opening for the advancing troops. Accordingly the admiral's guns began to roar at sundown and continued all night. Early the following morning, January 15th, all of the vessels, except a division left to aid in the defense of the northern line, moved into position and a fire, magnificent alike for its power and accuracy, was opened upon the fort. Under the protection of this fire General Terry manoeuvred and moved his troops in preparation for the great final assault so skillfully that toward the afternoon he had a body of 100 daring sharpshooters, sheltered in pits, within 175 yards of the enemy's works, firing at the parapets of the fort. Another and much larger body of troops was brought up to within 475 yards of the fort.

Shortly after 3 o'clock, all arrangements having been completed, the signal for the attack was given. Admiral Porter, as agreed, at once changed the direction of his fire and thus diverted the enemy's attention from the main points of attack. The troops sprang from their trenches and, exposed to a severe fire from the fort, dashed forward at double-quick. The ground over which they passed was marshy and difficult, but they soon reached the palisades, passed through them and effected a lodgment on the parapet. At the same time a column of sailors and marines advanced up the beach and attacked the northeastern bastion, but was met with such a murderous fire that it was unable to get up the parapet and after a severe struggle and heavy loss was compelled to withdraw.

A foothold having been secured on the parapet troops were sent to re-enforce the advanced lines, and slowly but irresistibly the rebels were driven from one position after the other. Hand-to-hand fighting of the most desperate character took place, the huge traverses of the land face being used successively by the enemy as breast-works, over the tops of which the contending parties fired in each others' faces. Nine of these traverses were carried by the attacking force. The fire of the navy upon that portion of the works not captured by the Federals continued until about dusk, when the two remaining traverses were carried and—the fort was captured; captured with all its surviving defenders, about 2,000 officers and men, including Major-General Whiting and Colonel Lamb, the commandant of the fort. In addition large quantities of ammunition and commissary stores fell into the victors' hands.

The scenes toward the close of the battle were indescribably horrible. Great cannon lay in ruins, surrounded by the bodies of their defenders; men were found partly buried in graves dug by the shells which had slain them. The outlines of the works could now and then be seen by the flash of an exploding shell or the blaze of musketry, but indistinct as the creation of some hideous dream. Soldiers were falling everywhere, shot in the head by rifle-balls. There was no outcry; simply a spurt of blood and all was over. But death does not always come in this way. There arose now and then an agonizing clamor of wounded men, writhing in the sand, beseeching those near them to end their suffering. A color-bearer had fallen, and though choked by blood and sand, he murmured: "I am gone. Take the flag." An officer who had been shot through the heart retained a nearly erect position, leaning against a gun-carriage. Some lay face downward in the sand, and others who had been close together when struck by an exploding shell had fallen in a confused mass, forming a mingled heap of broken limbs and mangled bodies. At times a grim and uncanny humor seizes a wounded man. Captain A. G. Lawrence, of General Ames' staff, lay on his back; one arm had been amputated, and the other arm as well as his neck was pierced by rifle-balls. He had told the chaplain to write his father that he could not live, and then, calling another officer to him, whispered, as he held up the stump of his amputated arm: "Isn't this a devil of a bob-tail flush?"

That there were many deeds of extraordinary merit and valor performed by the men who won one of the most brilliant successes of the war goes without saying. However, the conduct of First Lieutenant John Wainwright of Company F, Ninety-seventh Pennsylvania Infantry, in command of the three hundred men of his regiment who participated in the expedition, Private Zachariah C. Neahr of Company K, One hundred and forty-second New York Infantry, General N. M. Curtis and Colonel Galusha Pennypacker, of the Ninety-seventh Pennsylvania Infantry, was so conspicuous as to earn for them the Medal of Honor.

Brevet Brigadier-General Curtis, though in command of the First Brigade, Second Division, Twenty-fourth Army Corps, took up a musket, and, stepping into the ranks, led his men in each of the assaults, braving the storm of rebel shot and shell. The uniform of a brigadier-general in the ranks made him a conspicuous object and the rebels concentrated their fire upon him, wounding him three times. These wounds, however, did not deter the general, and he fought throughout the remainder of the day, until shortly before dark, when he fell, wounded a fourth time, and so severely that he had to be carried to the rear.

Colonel Pennypacker, commanding the second brigade of the same division, like-wise encouraged his men by personally leading them. He had gallantly led them to the third traverse and with the colors of one of his regiments in hand was the first to mount it. Amidst a hail of the enemy's bullets he bravely planted the colors on their works, but while doing this he was severely wounded. Lieutenant Wainwright, commanding the Ninety-seventh Pennsylvania Infantry, also displayed wonderful courage in leading his regiment, even after he was severely wounded in the assault. He pluckily concealed from his men the pain he was suffering and with renewed energy he led them on to victory, retiring to the hospital only after the day's fighting was done.

Private Neahr, who had volunteered with a number of others of his regiment to cut the palisading, rushed up ahead of the column and with the fire of the enemy concentrated upon him, cut it down, thus enabling the assaulting column to pass through.

RISKED BEING BLOWN TO ATOMS AT DUTCH GAP CANAL

WALTER THORN,
First Lieut., U. S. Colored Inf.
Highest rank attained:
Brev. Major Vols.
Born in Brooklyn, N. Y.,
Nov. 18, 1844.

IT WAS at the beginning of January, 1865. General Butler, commanding the Army of the James, was expected to reach and capture Richmond by operating on the south side of the James River. His movements were blocked by the sinking of obstructions which rendered it impossible for him to navigate the stream, and by a powerful Confederate battery at French Beach.

To overcome these difficulties the resourceful Butler had caused a canal to be cut through the Dutch Gap peninsula, so that the enemy's batteries could be flanked and the obstructions in the river passed by the navy.

Nothing remained to be done but remove the great earthen bulkhead that separated the two bodies of water. This had been sapped and galleried, and more powder was packed away in it than was used in blowing up the famous "Crater" at Petersburg. The main body of troops had been drawn off from the neighborhood of the vast mine for safety, and it was supposed that none had been left behind but the few whose duty it was to light the fuse and then escape.

The supreme moment had arrived. The fuse had been lighted, and the officers were standing in a group at a safe distance discussing the question whether the work was to be crowned with success.

A member of General Butler's staff galloped up and shouted excitedly:

"Has the guard opposite the bulkhead been withdrawn?"

Somebody answered, hardly articulately, rather with a sort of gasp:

"No!"

There was a score of men in the guard. There were tons of powder beside them. Fire was eating its way up the fuse and might at any second set loose the terrific force of the mine.

The bravery of the officers before whose minds those thoughts flashed could not be doubted—it had been proved too often for that—but to go and warn the squad seemed so utterly beyond reason, so surely a useless throwing away of another life, that they stood there rigid and pale, with one exception—Walter Thorn, first lieutenant of the U. S. Colored Infantry, who hesitated, but only long enough to form a resolve. Then he dashed off in the direction of the bulkhead.

Perceiving his intention, his fellow officers called to him to return—warned him, pleaded with him. Paying no heed, he ran on, reached the bulkhead, climbed to its summit, faced the storm of bullets that the rebels directed at him, and stood there until he had ordered the picket guard to flee to a place of safety.

He leaped from the top of the mine; the explosion took place; the earth was scattered in all directions and a great abyss remained, but the young lieutenant was unharmed.

"It was as deliberate an act of self-sacrifice and valor as was ever performed in our country or any other," said one of his superior officers.

ONLY ONE MAN LOST IN A GALLANT RAID

WILLIAM J. PALMER,

Colonel, 15th Penn'a Cavalry.
Highest rank attained : Brevet
Brig.-General.
Born, Kinsdale Farm, Kent Co., Del.,
Sept. 18, 1836.

HAVING driven Hood from Nashville, General Thomas lost no time in sending detachments of cavalry after the fleeing Confederates, who, scattering in different directions, were trying to find their respective ways back to Selma, Mobile or the Carolinas. Because of continuous rains and subsequent bad roads, the pursuit undertaken by the bodies of infantry, as accessory to the cavalry operations, was stopped early in January, 1865, at Eastport, Miss.

Among the forces of Union cavalry thus sent to the south was the Fifteenth Pennsylvania Cavalry, in command of Colonel William J. Palmer, he having been directed on the 13th to march in pursuit of the rebel General Lyon, who was thought to have crossed the Paint Rock River. As most of his horses were much fagged from a previous expedition, Colonel Palmer took with him only 180 men. At 4 A. M. on the 24th, after having learned that Lyon had passed through Warrenton and would probably bivouac the same night at Red Hill, Colonel Palmer started for that place and surprised his camp of 350 men. One battalion of fifty men, in command of Lieutenant-Colonel Lamborn, had first been detached to take one of Lyon's regiments, which was encamped with its artillery near Red Hill, a second battalion to take a camp of 150 men one mile from there, while Palmer and the remaining battalion pushed on to capture Lyon, who was quartered with his staff and escort at the house of Tom Noble, half a mile beyond. The advance guard reached Lyon's headquarters and captured him at the door of Noble's house, in his night clothes. The general surrendered to Sergeant Arthur P. Lyon while the advance guard was charging the escort, but begged permission to put on his pantaloons, coat and boots, which Sergeant Lyon granted, accompanying him into the bedroom for that purpose. At that moment the escort fired a volley at the advance guard, when the sergeant said : "Come, General, I can't allow you much more time." The general then suddenly seized a pistol and shot the sergeant, killing him instantly, and made his escape through the back door in the dark. Colonel Palmer pushed on in the direction of other camp fires which could be seen ahead. These proved to be at the artillery camp, where one regiment of the enemy had already become alarmed by the firing and had saddled up and moved out, only to be met by the battalion under Lieutenant-Colonel Lamborn, who at once attacked them.

Colonel Palmer thus surprised General Lyon's superior force, routed him and took over one hundred prisoners, a piece of artillery and munitions of war with the loss of only one man, Sergeant Lyon.

SWAM THE RIVER UNDER DIFFICULTIES

S. RODMOND SMITH,
Captain, Co. C, 4th Del. Inf.
Highest rank attained:
Brevet Major, U. S. Vols.
Born at Wilmington, Del.,
April 20, 1841.

DAVID E. BUCKINGHAM,
1st Lieut., Co. E, 4th Del. Inf.
Highest rank attained:
Captain, U. S. V.
Born at Pleasant Hill, Del.,
Feb. 3, 1840.

DURING the siege of Petersburg, Va., which commenced with the investment of that city by the Federal forces during the early part of June, 1864, it became the aim of General Grant to flank the position of the enemy by swinging to the left. In the execution of this movement on Feb. 5, 1865, occurred the action at Monk's Neck crossing of the Rowanty River, Va., and the engagement at Hatcher's Run on the following day.

Captain S. Rodmond Smith, of Company C, Fourth Delaware Infantry, relates the following about this affair:

"To the Fifth Army Corps was assigned the duty of initiating this movement, and the third brigade of the second division of this corps was under arms, with tents struck and three days' rations in their haversacks, all the preceding night, and about sunrise on the morning of the 5th was marching by the Halifax Road to the west for Monk's Neck Crossing. About eight o'clock A. M. the brigade was halted in the road about a quarter of a mile east of our objective point. It was ascertained that the bridge over the crossing had been burned to prevent the passage of our troops, and that substantial entrenchments had been erected on the bluff bordering the margin of the stream on the opposite side. A regiment of Pennsylvania "Bucktails," out of our brigade, was detailed to cross the stream and carry the works. After some heavy firing the Bucktails were compelled to retire.

"Our regiment, with Major D. H. Kent in command, was then detailed for the service, and immediately moved down the road toward the crossing. The ground was slightly rolling and open farm-land, except near the bank of the stream, where a thin skirt of trees bordered the river, affording some cover. Major Kent, finding that the bridge was destroyed, filed the regiment to the right, under heavy fire, but somewhat protected by the trees. He then endeavored to lead the regiment across the river, but was shot while swimming his horse and was carried to the rear.

"THE WATER PROVED TO BE OVER SIX FEET DEEP."

"There was considerable floating ice in the stream, and the regiment, seeing the depth of the water, did not cross, but continued to move slowly to the right, keeping up a brisk fire on the enemy. At a point some two or three hundred feet farther to the right I observed some bushes projecting from the water, and, thinking this an indication that the water was shallow enough to wade, called on my command to follow me, and sprang into the stream. The water proved to be over six feet deep within that distance from the shore, but I was a strong swimmer, and although encumbered by a haversack belt and cape overcoat, succeeded in reaching a small island in mid-stream, under a heavy plunging fire which splashed the water around me. In the meantime the regiment moved cautiously forward among the scattered trees to the right, and shortly after crossed the stream to the island upon the ice which had formed during the preceding two days and nights and the fallen logs frozen to the surface. From thence all hands slid and waded to the opposite shore and we carried the enemy's entrenchments with a rush, capturing some fifty or sixty rebels. The remainder of their forces had retired before we reached their works. After a short time spent in re-forming the regiment we pushed ahead in quick time until the evening and on the following day participated in the action at Hatcher's Run, Virginia."

Lieutenant David E. Buckingham, also of the Fourth Delaware Regiment, had an experience similar to that of Captain Smith, and describes it as follows:

"I was in command of Company E, on the extreme right of the regiment, and the movement by the right flank threw me at the head of my command. As we passed General Ayres, our Division Commander, I heard him say to Major Kent: 'You are expected to carry the bridge, if you lose every man!' I knew that such an order meant business, and as we broke into a double-quick and came under fire the men gave a lusty cheer, and down the road we went with Major Kent riding at my side. We reached the bridge only to discover that it had been effectually destroyed, filed to the right, and as soon as we had cleared the road and were fairly in the meadow filed to the left, and in a moment were at the water's edge.

"The general's command was ringing in my ears: 'Carry the bridge if you lose every man.' It was no time to hesitate or turn back. Three thousand men, our entire brigade, lined the meadow lands, protected by the trees, and a terrible fusillade was going on. I stepped on the ice, which extended only six feet from the shore. It broke under my weight and I struck out for the rebel side and was soon beyond my depth, but I swam to the south side, the Minie balls skimming the water all around me.

"Reaching the bank, I clutched a projecting stump root and took a view of the situation from the water. Harvey Durnall, John Bradford and Holton Yarnall, of my command, waded in up to their waists, but, discovering the depth of the stream, fell back. In the meantime Major Kent had been dangerously wounded while urging his horse into the water. The water was icy cold and I did not care to scale the bank, as I was the only man of the command who crossed the river at the bridge, having carried the ford, and the freezing question—not the burning one—was, could I hold it?

"There I remained, waiting for reinforcements, for at least fifteen minutes. But our boys were not idle; far up the stream they had been crossing on felled trees and on the ice, and soon I heard them charging down the Confederate side. When the enemy discovered they were flanked they beat a retreat and the bridge was ours.

"I reswam the river and dried my clothes beside a roaring fire which the boys had made while the engineers rebuilt the bridge."

VALOROUS DEEDS AT HATCHER'S RUN

JAMES COEY,

Major, 147th New York Vol. Inf.
Highest rank attained :
Major-General Cal. N. G.
Born in New York City, Feb. 12,
1841.

THE FIERCE fighting of Hatcher's Run and Dabney's Mills, Va., February 5 and 6, 1865, brought to light numerous examples of individual bravery among officers and men. Valorous deeds are narrated of several men who were rewarded with the Medal of Honor, as follows:

The Third Brigade, Third Division of the Fifth Army Corps, to which Major James Coey's command, the One hundred and forty-seventh New York Infantry, was attached, advanced over an open field, under a heavy fire from the enemy, who were entrenched in a wood. The brigade line of battle reached to the edge of this wood, but owing to the fierce fire it refused to advance farther, and lay down, seeking shelter on the ground. The brigade commander, General Henry A. Morrow, placed himself in front of his command and implored the line to move forward, but the effect of the enemy's fire had been so appalling that the men hesitated. The situation was most critical, because the brigade adjoining Morrow on his right was also sorely pressed and its line in danger; General Crawford, the division commander, was urging Morrow's advance, hoping to draw the fire from the right front and relieve the pressure there, but the lines had become terror-stricken. It was at this moment that Major Coey, who had, by word and action, been seconding General Morrow's efforts to advance the line and hold it to its duty, seized the colors of his regiment and advanced with them. The effect was magical! Color after color was taken until the entire brigade line was on its feet and with a cheer advanced into the woods to within a few rods of the enemy's works. Here its farther advance was stopped by a wide and deep ditch filled with water.

Major Coey communicated the situation to General Morrow, now in the rear of the line, who, seeing the fast thinning ranks of his command, and the hopelessness of advancing, ordered the line back to the edge of the wood, there to entrench. The major then called the attention of the brigade commander to the lack of ammunition, hardly five rounds to a man being left, whereupon General Morrow ordered the brigade to meet any advance of the enemy with the bayonet and go on entrenching. Coey immediately ordered the men to obtain cartridges from the dead and wounded

---

Hatcher's Run and Dabney's Mills.—Early in February, 1865, a second attempt was made to gain possession of the South Side Railroad, near Hatcher's Run, which resulted in the battle of that name and included the actions at Dabney's Mills, Rowanty Creek, and Gravelly Run. The battle began February 5th and lasted until the 7th, when the Confederates were forced to retire with a loss of 1,000 and their commander, General John Pegram. The Union loss was 2,000, the greater portion of which belonged to Crawford's Division, which was driven back by the Confederates in great confusion.

"BEING LIFTED INTO THE SADDLE AND HELD THERE BY TWO OF HIS MEN."

lying along his front, and to make obstructions to retard the enemy's advance by bending and intertwining young saplings. In this work he was setting his men an example, when the Confederates, now reinforced by artillery, opened a fierce and destructive fire, and made a spirited advance on the front and flank, driving the Union line back.

At this juncture Major Coey was severely wounded—a bullet entering below the left eye and passing out behind the right ear—and was being borne from the field in the arms of two comrades when consciousness returned. Immediately he procured a horse from an ambulance sergeant, and being lifted into the saddle and held there by two of his men he turned to the line and, rallying it, for the second time made a heroic attempt to check the advance of the enemy.

Four times on this day the One hundred and seventh Pennsylvania Infantry, to which 2nd Lieut. John C. Delaney belonged, had charged on the enemy's works, and each time had been beaten back. In each of these charges many brave men fell close to the enemy, who were thoroughly protected behind impregnable fortifications, Lieutenant Delaney had the wounded of Company I, his own company, and Company D, which was also under his command, carried back, so that none were left between the lines. It was when his regiment had been forced back for the fourth time that Lieutenant Delaney found himself up against the line of entrenchments that had been hastily thrown up by the Federal troops. The momentum of the backward movement had been so great that he could not check himself until the wall of earth stopped his run.

There he stood, surrounded by wounded men belonging to Company D, and heard his name called on all sides by its members begging to be helped off the field. The whole regiment had reached the safe side of their line of works, while he alone stood outside facing the enemy, with the pitiful appeals of the wounded ringing in his ears, and the bullets falling like hail around him. To add to the horror of the situation he now noticed that the dry leaves and underbrush had caught fire and that it was only a question of a few minutes before the wounded men would be burned alive. Rushing to the surviving members of Company D, he appealed to them to assist in saving their wounded comrades; but to his surprise and dismay they refused, several saying that it would be certain death to make the attempt. They begged him to get over the works, convinced that he would be riddled with bullets, or worse, burned alive. The sergeant then appealed to his own men, but not one of them would venture in that shower of lead. Alone he rushed out, picked up a wounded soldier much heavier than himself and started back, reaching the line of works, where many willing hands were stretched out to help lift the wounded man over. The sergeant's splendid example made such an impression on his comrades that several were now willing to join him in the perilous work, and in a short time all the wounded had been brought in ; but scarcely were the rescuers over the line when every foot of ground was in flames. Several of the men were wounded while struggling with their burdens, and they in turn had to be rescued from the fire, each unfortunate thus saved adding to the glory of his comrades.

The Thirteenth Pennsylvania Cavalry, which was stationed at Hatcher's Run, accomplished one of the most gallant charges of the day. With drawn sabres the line swept down upon the Thirty-third North Carolina Infantry, and a severe hand-to-hand fight followed. Sergeant Daniel Caldwell, of Company H, charged upon the color-guard, and knocking aside the bayonets ready to receive him, he seized the colors. Upon turning about to rejoin his regiment he espied a rebel officer and his staff coming toward him. Not waiting for them to charge him he put spurs to his horse and dashed at them. The next moment he was seen slashing and parrying with his sabre in his right hand, while with his left he managed his horse and retained the captured flag. A few severe strokes and he had cut a path through the enemy and safely regained his regiment.

While the battle was raging on the 5th the Two hundred and tenth Pennsylvania Infantry was close to the scene of action, but did not reach the battle-field until noon of the 6th. Shortly after noon it reached a position on the extreme left of the line of battle and at once pressed forward, driving the enemy quite a distance through the woods until they reached their reserve line, stationed on a low ridge. Here the rebels fought with renewed energy and, with the additional hail of lead from their reserve poured into the Union

(1) JOHN M. VANDERSLICE,
Private, Co. D, 8th Pa. Cav.
Highest rank attained :
Brig.-Gen. Pa. N. G.
Born at Valley Forge, Pa.,
1842.

(2) WILLIAM SANDS,
1st Sergt., Co. G, 88th Pa. Inf.
Born Oct. 14, 1837.

(4) CHARLES DAY,
Private, Co. K, 210th Pa. Inf.
Born at West Laurens,
N. Y., May 20, 1844.

(3) DANIEL CALDWELL,
Sergeant, Co. H, 13th Pa. Cav.
Born in Montgomery
Co., Pa.

(5) JOHN C. DELANEY,
Sergeant, Co. D, 107th Pa. Inf.
Born in Ireland,
April 22, 1848.

troops, the Federal line began to waver, then gradually fall back. One of the regiments of the brigade was thrown into utter confusion and its color-bearer killed.

Private Charles Day, of Company K, Two hundred and tenth Regiment, ran to the fallen colors and, picking them up, carried them throughout the remainder of the battle.

After having engaged the enemy's cavalry and also capturing a wagon train, on the 5th, Gregg's Cavalry Division, without rest of any kind, confronted the enemy again on the 6th. Although the men had now been in the saddle for nearly twenty-four hours there was no hesitation when the charge was sounded to repulse a sudden heavy assault of the enemy on an infantry division. Having accomplished their task, they held the line, dismounted, until the infantry had returned, when the rebel skirmish line was driven to the edge of the clearing, where within two hundred yards was a line of rebel works. The fire from these was very heavy, particularly from a party of sharpshooters in a house within the works. Orders were given for a general charge, and at the sound of the bugle the line dashed forward, carrying the works, which were first entered by Private John M. Vanderslice, of Company D, Eighth Pennsylvania Cavalry, whose speedy horse carried him far in advance and made him the leader of the line, in which position he received the undivided attention of the rebels.

Assistant Surgeon Jacob F. Raub, of the Two hundred and tenth Pennsylvania Infantry, was one of the board of operating surgeons of the field hospital of the Fifth Army Corps, established in the rear and beyond the reach of rebel shot and shell, but when he learned that his regiment was without a surgeon he volunteered to accompany it in the fight and obtained permission from the surgeon in charge of the field hospital to do so.

While attending to the wounded under a severe fire, he discovered a strong column of the enemy stealing by the left flank to the rear of the Federals. The whole division was heavily engaged at this time, and no enemy was expected or supposed to be in that direction. Raub, realizing the imminent danger of an attack on flank and rear, ran forward under a severe fire and apprised General Ayres and General Gwyn of the threatened danger. This prompt and intelligent action gave time to change the direction of part of Gwyn's brigade to meet the flank attack, and severely repulse the enemy. During the excitement of the repulse Surgeon Raub, though a non-combatant, took the musket and ammunition from a wounded soldier and fought gallantly in the ranks until the end of the engagement.

Other brave deeds performed on this eventful day are chronicled as follows:

During one of the charges of the Eighty-eighth Pennsylvania Infantry, First Sergeant William Sands, of Company G, was in advance of his company and in the face of a deadly fire he grasped the enemy's colors and brought them into the Union lines.

First Lieutenant Francis M. Smith, adjutant of the First Maryland Infantry, voluntarily remained behind with the body of his regimental commander under a heavy fire after the whole brigade had retired, and brought the body off the field. Corporal John Thompson, of Company C, and Corporal Abel G. Cadwallader, of Company M, of the same regiment, planted the national and state flags on the enemy's works in advance of the regiment's arrival.

BRILLIANT CONDUCT IN A FIERCE BATTLE

HARTWELL B. COMPSON,

Major, 8th N. Y. Cavalry.
Highest rank attained:
Brigadier-General, Ore. N. G.
Born at Tyre, Seneca Co., N. Y.,
May 4, 1845.

LEAVING Winchester, Va., on February 27, 1865, General Sheridan began his march to Petersburg, Va., with the intention of destroying the Central Railroad and James River Canal. General Early with a large Confederate force stood ready to oppose and frustrate, if possible, the expedition, and upon learning of the approach of the Federals went into position at Waynesboro, Va. The two armies clashed March 2d. The rain had been pouring in torrents for two days and the roads were bad beyond description; nevertheless the Union men seemed tireless, although neither they nor their horses could be recognized for the mud which covered them. General Early had at his disposal two brigades of infantry and some cavalry under General Rosser, the infantry occupying breastworks. General Custer was ordered to attack the enemy and, not wanting the Confederates to get up their courage during the delay that a careful reconnoissance necessitated, made his dispositions for attack at once, sending three regiments around the left flank of the enemy, which was somewhat exposed by being advanced from, instead of resting upon, the bank of the river in his immediate rear. "Our general committed an unpardonable error in posting so small a force with a swollen river in its rear and with its flanks wholly exposed," says a Confederate report of General Early's position. General Custer with two brigades, partly mounted and partly dismounted, at a given signal boldly attacked and impetuously carried the enemy's works, while the Eighth New York and the Twenty-second New York Cavalry formed in columns of fours, dashed over the breastworks and continued the charge through the little town of Waynesboro, the Twenty-second supporting the Eighth New York. The Eighth crossed the South Fork of the Shenandoah River—General Early's rear—where they formed with drawn sabres and held the east bank of the stream. The enemy being now pressed by Custer found their retreat cut off, and, completely disorganized, confused, bewildered, threw down their arms. Amidst cheers and hurrahs the victorious Federals surrounded their brave opponents.

The substantial result of this magnificent victory was the capture of the Confederate General Wharton and some 1,800 officers and men, fourteen pieces of artillery, seventeen battle-flags and a train of nearly two hundred wagons and ambulances,

---

Waynesboro, Va.—General Custer advanced, on March 2, 1865, from Staunton to Waynesboro, Va., where he found the enemy, under General Early, and engaged him. The result of the battle was the capture of a large number of prisoners, the enemy's artillery and wagon train, by the Union forces; and the opening of the roads for unresisted advance along the James River and all the roads and means of supply north of Richmond.

including General Early's headquarters wagon, containing all his official papers and records, 1,500 stands of small arms and 800 team horses and mules.

It was a battle where the Eighth New York Cavalry, under the gallant leadership of Major Hartwell B. Compson, earned undying fame. The major himself performed wonderful feats of bravery and set an example which electrified his men and inspired them to deeds of splendid heroism. At the head of his troops who were selected to

"WITH A COLOR-BEARER ON ONE SIDE AND A BUGLER ON THE OTHER."

make the attack, he charged down the highway into Waynesboro. The enemy had five pieces of artillery in the roadway and had thrown up earthworks on each side of the road; behind these breastworks infantry was posted. He was at the head of his command with a color-bearer on one side and a bugler on the other, when they struck the Confederate forces and a hand-to-hand fight took place. Just then General Early and his staff moved down their front to direct the movement of the Confederate forces.

Coming upon Early's headquarters battle-flag he ordered the bearer to surrender. A fierce fight at close quarters ensued and finally a heavy blow with the sabre knocked his opponent from his horse and the flag was captured.

Breaking through the Confederates, he moved his forces down towards South River and kept up the charge until he reached the bank. Seeing that the enemy were closing in on his rear and that his support did not come up, he crossed the river and found earthworks thrown up on the opposite side from which the enemy could have prevented their crossing had they occupied them. He at once dismounted his men and placed them in the Confederate earthworks. Then when Custer pressed down upon the rebels they were forced to cross the river, where they were ordered to surrender. The result was that when the battle was over Colonel Compson's command alone had taken 800 prisoners five pieces of artillery, 1,500 stands of small arms and eight battle-flags.

Being needed no longer at the ford, Compson, who had noticed the enemy moving their wagon-trains over the mountains by way of Rock Fish Gap, followed with his regiment, overhauled it and captured everything in sight.

It was in this action where Second Lieutenant Robert Niven, of Company H, of the same regiment, had a hot encounter with a body of rebels. "I was ordered to pick out five men from my company," says the lieutenant, "to go ahead as an advance guard and we pressed along the narrow, hilly road, densely lined with woods. By this time the atmosphere was quite foggy. I had gotten far in advance of my comrades when suddenly I found myself right in the midst of a wagon-train composed of about ten wagons and a dozen Confederates, commanded by a lieutenant. With a great show of bravery I ordered them to surrender and promised that every one who attempted to escape would be shot on the spot. But they saw that a one-man order to twelve scattered men was practically worthless, when the bushes around there offered such a good opportunity to get away. Consequently, when the regiment came up I had captured not only three or four prisoners, but also two rebel flags, ten army wagons with mules attached, the lieutenant's horse, and all of General Early's official papers."

Second Lieutenant Andrew Kuder, First Sergeant Charles A. Goheen and Sergeant Daniel Kelly of Company G, and also Corporal Henry H. Bickford and Sergeant James Congdon as well as Private John Miller of this same regiment, the Eighth New York Cavalry, were fortunate enough to capture rebel colors in this grand melee.

Rebel flags were also captured in this battle by Privates Peter O'Brien and Warren Carman, of the First New York Cavalry (Lincoln), and Harry Harvey, George Ladd and Michael Crowley of the Twenty-second New York Cavalry. All of above mentioned were awarded the Medal of Honor.

ROBERT NIVEN,
Second Lieut., Co. H, 8th
N. Y. Cavalry.
Highest rank attained:
Captain.
Born at Harlem, N. Y.,
December 18, 1833.

ANDREW KUDER,
Second Lieut., Co. G, 8th
N. Y. Cavalry.
Highest rank attained:
Captain.
Born in South Livonia,
New York, 1838.

GALLANT RESCUE OF A DROWNING COMRADE

HENRY I. SMITH,
First Lieutenant, Co.
B, 7th Iowa Inf.
Highest rank att'ned:
Captain.
Born in Nottingham,
Eng., May 4, 1840.

AFTER the defeat of Hardee at Averysboro, and just before Johnston made his futile attack at Bentonville, the Fifteenth Corps, General John A. Logan commander, found its advance contested by the Confederates at Black River, some fifteen or eighteen miles south of Bentonville. The enemy having possession of the opposite side of the river, General Rice ordered one regiment to proceed about three-quarters of a mile above and effect a crossing, and three companies from another regiment a half mile down the river to make a demonstration. At that time Lieutenant Henry I. Smith, of Company B, Seventh Iowa Infantry, was aide-de-camp on the staff of Brigadier-General Elliott W. Rice, in command of the First Brigade of the Fourth Division of Logan's Corps. Lieutenant Smith gives the details of service he rendered on this occasion as follows:

"Our progress being retarded by the presence of the enemy at Black River, N. C., on the 15th of March, 1865, I was directed to proceed with a regiment and pontoons, while our corps was engaging the Confederates at the bridge, which had been partly destroyed, farther up the stream and effect a crossing. Normally the river is only a narrow stream, but because of the spring freshets it was at this time swollen to a torrent, very rapid, and away beyond its banks until it was at least a quarter of a mile wide. Proceeding up stream a considerable distance, we began laying our pontoon bridge, when a detachment of the enemy with one piece of artillery located in the woods on the opposite shore opened on us. However, the men of the regiment put down the bridge under a hot fire of musketry across the stream proper—about one hundred feet wide at this point—and by wading waist deep in the ice-cold water and stumbling and crawling over entanglements of underbrush and cypress trees for about a quarter of a mile, they at last effected a crossing and drove the enemy back. During the progress of this crossing one of my command in stepping from the pontoon bridge into the water was caught by the torrent and swept down stream. Seeing the mishap, I threw off my sword and coat and jumped after the man. Presently I reached him, and getting a good grip upon his almost lifeless form I at last succeeded in swimming with him near enough to shore for others to come to our assistance and drag us both out of the flood more dead than alive. Of course, the entire incident occurred under fire, but luckily neither one of us was hit and we recovered sufficiently to take part in the holding of the position gained by the regiment, wearing our wet, icy clothes throughout, until morning, when the entire army began to make the crossing."

WHERE THE REBELS WERE BADLY BEATEN

GEORGE W. CLUTE.
Corporal, Co. I, 14th Michigan Inf.
Born in Marathon, Mich.,
June 11, 1842.

I<small>F</small> General Johnston had succeeded at Bentonville, N. C., March 19, 1865, he would to-day be mentioned among the greatest generals of all nations and ages. Early in the morning he addressed his troops. What he said was something like this: "I have about me here 40,000 brave and gallant troops. Shall we permit the Yankees to make further progress? No. Their army must and shall be stopped here. They are marching upon us by four different roads. We shall fall upon one column after the other and annihilate each separately."

This plan failed. The Confederate generals had forgotten to reckon with the bravery of the Union soldiers.

The first column attacked by Johnston was the Fourteenth Army Corps. At first he gained a temporary success, forcing the Federals to fall back and capturing three guns. Then the Twentieth Army Corps and General Kilpatrick were hurried upon the field, and not only was the further advance of the rebels checked, but the Union lines were re-established in their original position. All day long Johnston made a most stubborn effort to break the Union center. Six charges, one after the other in rapid succession, were made at the same point, and on the same men, and six times the enemy were beaten off with equal determination.

HENRY E. PLANT,
Private, Co. F, 14th Michigan Inf.
Born in Oswego, New York,
October 11, 1841.

General Kilpatrick was full of admiration for the pluck and gallantry of his men when darkness ended further fighting. General Johnston, discouraged, disappointed, disheartened, withdrew. His fondest hopes had come to naught.

In this battle two of Michigan's soldiers, Corporal George W. Clute of Company I, and Private Henry E. Plant of Company F, both of the Fourteenth Michigan Infantry, distinguished themselves as heroes.

The regiment had been ordered to the front on a double-quick and upon its arrival found the cavalry fighting the rebels in a large pine swamp. It was here that the six successive charges were made by the enemy. The last charge was an especially severe one. It came to a hand-to-hand fight. "In the midst of the struggle," says Clute in describing it, "I saw a Confederate

From Savannah to Bentonville.—As General Sherman and his army marched north from Savannah to Goldsboro, his opposition consisted of 27,000 infantry and 8,000 cavalry under General Johnston, and General Hood with 10,000 infantry and a division of cavalry. At Averysboro, Hardee's army was repulsed with a loss of 500 men. At Bentonville Johnston's army attacked General Slocum's wing of the Federal forces and a three days' fight ensued, resulting in the falling back of the Confederate force, after a loss of 2,825 killed and wounded and 1,641 taken prisoners. The Federal loss was 1,646 killed and wounded.

flag and made a rush for it. It was in the hands of their lieutenant. He and I were out of ammunition. Nothing but a trial of strength could determine which one of us was entitled to those colors. We had a desperate fight, but I proved to be the stronger and dragged color-bearer and flag along for over 100 feet before he let go of the staff and ran back to his lines. Carrying the captured colors aloft I ran to my company, the men of which were fighting with clubbed muskets.

"When my captain caught sight of me and my trophy he said:

"'Why didn't you kill that rebel?'

"'Because I had no ammunition,' I replied.

"While I was still talking with the captain, our own men, whose attention was attracted by the Confederate flag which I held in a raised position, began firing at us, and I was ordered to quickly drop the flag. I dragged it behind me along the ground and was just about to join my fighting comrades a few feet in front of me when I once more caught sight of the Confederate lieutenant from whom I had wrenched the colors. As his eyes fell upon me he quick as a flash took aim with his revolver and fired at me, the ball entering my right arm. Then he, with like suddenness, disappeared."

Private Plant was no less plucky. The sergeant and color-guard had been shot down in the same charge and a yawning gap was left on either side of the colors. Plant took in the situation at a glance. He ran toward the colors, seized the flag from the hand of the wounded standard-bearer and waved it, cheering on his comrades to more determined resistance. When the rebels were at last repulsed Plant was promoted sergeant and color-bearer and carried the flag he had so gallantly defended to the end of the war.

OVERWHELMED BY SHERMAN'S KINDNESS

PETER T. ANDERSON,
Private, Co. B. 31st Wis. Inf.
Highest rank att'ned: Capt.
Born in Lafayette Co., Wis.,
Sept. 4, 1847.

AN ORDERLY appeared in the bivouac of the Thirty-first Wisconsin Infantry, after the battle of Bentonville, N. C., had been fought, March 19, 1865.

"Is Private Peter T. Anderson of Company B present?" he inquired. Private Anderson stepped forward. "You're wanted at General Sherman's headquarters," the orderly stated and started back followed by the private, who trembled in anticipation of his fate. What could the general possibly want of him? Had somebody told that he had left for the rear the day before? Was he to be punished, reprimanded, rebuked? He reviewed his whole army life, scrutinized every act; he knew of no wrong that demanded punishment. He inquired of the orderly, begged him to tell what the general wanted, but this individual was annoyingly short of speech and would not or could not give the slightest hint. Finally headquarters was reached. As Anderson saluted General Sherman rose from his camp stool and with that genial manner so characteristic of the great American leader offered it to the humble soldier.

This unexpected reception bewildered and embarrassed the private to such an extent that he completely lost his composure. He mechanically followed the general's polite invitation and sat down on the camp stool—allowing the commander to stand up before him. The ludicrousness of the situation never dawned upon the good Wisconsinite at the time.

"Well, Anderson," said the general, "I am proud of you!"

He said a great many more things equally as flattering and pleasing, and ended by grasping the soldier's hand and assuring him that his services would be rewarded soon in a more substantial manner. And thus was the private, highly honored and highly elated, dismissed by the general.

What were these services?

Private Anderson's own modest version is as follows:

"It was at Waynesboro, N. C., March 16, 1865. The Confederates held a strong position. My company, with others, was deployed to oppose and divert them from our lines.

"Owing to heavy rains the day before the ground was muddy. As we advanced we came to a deep depression, filled with water four or five inches deep. Across this pond and about 200 feet from us were a lot of logs piled up. Suddenly and without a warning, as we reached the water, a volley was fired on us by a number of rebels lying in ambush behind the logs. It wrought havoc in our ranks. Our situation was critical. If we remained where we were we would all be mowed down by the next volley. Yet there was no time to retreat. Our men and officers were badly scattered. There was no officer to command us, and but one way out of the difficulty. I shouted to the boys: 'Forward!' The order was obeyed. Before the rebels had time to reload we were pointing our guns at them over the logs and demanded their surrender. They complied. Their number was about seventy-five, while we were not more than thirty. This action was witnessed from the rear by several of our officers, General Sherman among them. We brought the prisoners to our camp.

"Three days later, at the battle of Bentonville, I took sick and was told to get into an ambulance. I preferred the ranks. Our brigade, composed of three regiments, took position in the edge of the timber, to the left of the pike and to the left of the Fourteenth Corps, leaving quite a gap between us. We had just begun felling trees and making a breastwork of them when the rebels attacked us across an open field. They swung around on both flanks, practically surrounding us. We were forced to retreat.

"I was provoked at our retreat, because I could not see the rebels advancing on the sides, but noticed only their line in front. It did not take long, however, before

I fully comprehended the situation. As we fell back to the turnpike we left the Nineteenth Indiana battery behind. Someone shouted: 'For God's sake, bring out that battery!' I turned to a comrade and asked him to come with me and attempt to save the battery. He refused. I went back to the battery without any assistance. It was all limbered up, the horses hitched and ready to be moved. Turning the horses of one gun into the road, using my ramrod for a whip, I started them after our retreating ranks. I tried to mount one of the horses, but the stirrup was shot off just as I put my foot in it and I was obliged to follow along behind. The distance to our lines was from one-third to half a mile, and all this way I was under a hot rebel fire from both sides. At one time the rebels were on all sides of me and demanding my surrender. I had previously fired my gun and was now trying to reload. I had nearly succeeded when a shot struck the barrel and broke it in the middle. The same shot knocked off the tip of my right forefinger. I raised my musket and blazed away, sending ramrod and all into the rebels. An officer rode up close to me, pointed his revolver at my head and shouted: 'Surrender, you damned Yankee!' A shot from some quarter killed him outright the next moment. I finally reached my regiment which, observing my predicament, had taken a stand waiting for me to come up. Passing our rallied line I transferred the rescued field-piece to the care of a chief of artillery who came to meet me and then went to the rear, secured another gun and returned to take a hand in the next charge of the rebels."

The reward promised by General Sherman came within less than three months: Anderson received a captain's commission and the Medal of Honor.

"DON'T LET THEM GET ME"

H. S. FINKENBEINER.
Private, Co. D, 107th Ohio Inf.
Born at North Industry,
Ohio, July 29, 1849.

A PICTURESQUE feature of General Sherman's army during the grand tour from Savannah to Richmond was the rear guard with its foraging detachments and refugee train. So great were the additions of refugee negroes that at times the marching columns in the rear had the appearance of a huge army, which they were, except that a large majority of the refugees were unarmed. Whole families of negroes, afoot, riding mules, horses and cattle, trundling barrows and drawing carts and wagons, followed the Union troops. To protect this large train from the almost continuous petty assaults made by small bodies of Confederate cavalry and occasional detachments of bushwhackers was the hazardous duty of the rear guard commanded by General Porter and to which was attached the One hundred and seventh Ohio Infantry. The work required was done, very largely, in small detachments in advance, on either flank and to the rear of its own main column, so that individual actions involving these smaller bodies were almost everyday happenings. On the 23d of March, however, while Sherman's main army was bitterly engaged at Bentonville, N. C., General Porter's troops encountered a force of Confederates at Dingley's Mill, near Sumterville, S. C. The Confederates had fired the wooden bridge across the

"WE PICKED BROBST UP AND PLACED HIM ON MY RIFLE BETWEEN US."

mill race to prevent or check his attack, and evidently had good and commanding positions on their side of the race.

General Porter, thinking that the Confederates had evacuated, ordered Colonel Houghton, of the Twenty-fifth Ohio, to come down from the road, which was high and acted as a dam to the mill pond on one side. Colonel John S. Cooper, of the One hundred and seventh Ohio Volunteers, feeling sure that the enemy were still in hiding across the race, called for volunteers to cross the burning bridge and reconnoiter the enemy's position. Private H. S. Finkenbeiner, of Company D, who, accompanied by Jacob James and Jacob Brobst, volunteered for this service, tells of the affair as follows :

"We received orders to accomplish the mission and report as soon as possible. The enemy's battery was masked on a little knoll that commanded the entire road, and as we crossed at a point about ninety yards from the bridge they could plainly see every move we made, while they were hidden from our view. The support of this masked battery lay still nearer the bridge in a thicket on the right side of our advance.

"We cautiously went forward, passed the burning mill, and, reaching a place where the road makes a turn towards Sumterville, we saw the enemy for the first time. Instead of creeping back and reporting, we took a shot at them and then ran for the bridge.

"To our great surprise, we then found ourselves between the enemy's battery and their reserve. A shot of grape and canister but twenty yards from this turn was sent to intercept our run, but we were too near and it flew wide of its mark. The next instant the support just in front and to our right opened fire on us. Their second aim was better, or worse for us, for Brobst fell. His cry, 'Don't for God's sake let the rebels get me,' brought us to a stop in our headlong rush for safety, and we returned to our fallen comrade.

"By this time they had our range and were shooting uncomfortably close to us. We picked Brobst up and placed him on my rifle between us, thus carrying him in safety over the burning bridge to an ambulance corps in the woods, in the rear of our army.

"Just then we saw General Houghton come down the narrow road and file out. Knowing the terrible situation he would get into, I hurried to report our discovery to General Porter, and an orderly was sent forward at once to recall the Twenty-fifth Ohio, which would certainly have fared badly had they advanced."

"LIEUTENANT, WHAT SAY YOU?"

JOSEPH F. CARTER,
Captain, Co. D, Third Maryland Infantry.
Highest rank attained : Major.
Born in Baltimore, Maryland,
Sept. 11, 1842.

Fort Stedman, Va., had fallen into the hands of the enemy, who cunningly had taken advantage of the order allowing deserters to bring in their arms. In the disguise of such deserters they had approached the Union picket lines in small squads, overpowered and captured the pickets and gained access to the works without any alarm being given. General N. B. McLaughlin and nearly the entire garrison, sixteen officers and 480 men, were captured just before daybreak March 25, 1865, the darkness materially aiding the Confederates in their bold and tricky move.

With the break of day the occurrence revealed itself to the Federal commanders operating in the vicinity and determined efforts to recapture the fort were made immediately. The Third Maryland Infantry met large detachments of the enemy, sent to capture the adjoining Fort Haskell (see page 388), and drove them back into Fort Stedman, passing the gate and forcing the Confederates to retreat into the camp, from which they themselves had only shortly before driven the One hundredth Pennsylvania. The entrance to the fort, however, had been gained and the Pennsylvania boys now hurried to the support of their gallant comrades from Maryland. It was decided to follow up the enemy and charge the fort. This was done so successfully by an attack from two sides that within a short time the Federals were once more masters of the stronghold, capturing nearly the entire Confederate force. An occurrence that followed is the subject of an interesting story told by Captain Joseph F. Carter of Company D, Third Maryland Infantry. The captain was in command of his regiment on the expedition to recapture the fort, while the One hundredth Pennsylvania was led by Major N. J. Maxwell:

"Seeing that Major Maxwell was in control of the fort," says Carter, "I moved out to intercept the retreat of the rebels, who had advanced to our newly built railroad leading to City Point and were thus between our lines. Somehow or other my men, who were busy in gathering up prisoners outside the fort, became separated from me. I did not notice their absence, but kept right on, until I came to a cut in the road

---

Fort Stedman.—Early on the morning of March 25, 1865, the Confederate forces under General Gordon assaulted the Federal lines in front of Parke's Ninth Corps, which held the Appomattox River toward the Union left, and carried Fort Stedman and a part of the line to the right and left of it, turning the guns of the fort against the Federals. But the Union troops on either flank held their ground until reserves were brought up, when the Confederates were driven back to their lines.

The losses sustained by the Ninth Corps were 68 killed, 337 wounded and 506 missing, while those sustained by the Confederates were 2,681, among whom were 1,900 prisoners.

leading into Petersburg, with banks about ten feet high. Here, to my surprise, I found a rebel regiment which had selected this place for shelter from the heavy fire of our artillery stationed in the rear of our main line. They had been sent to the rear of Fort Stedman to seize the railroad and there received orders to retire, but were confused and waited for further orders. The recapture of Fort Stedman by our troops had cut off the retreat to their own lines. There were about three hundred of them just filing into the road getting ready to stay the advance of our skirmishers who were following up their retreat, when I appeared on the bank and shouted to the greatly surprised Confederates on the road below to surrender. A captain in command retorted:

"'Who in hell are you?'

"'A Yank,' I answered, adding quickly that we had recaptured Fort Stedman, were complete masters of the situation and that he could not possibly get back with his men to his lines. The rebel captain, however, who evidently had no knowledge of this fact, did not propose to give in so easily. 'Well,' he remarked, 'where are your men?'

"Then came a surprise on my side. Looking back of me I made the embarrassing discovery that I was alone. Surely this was a tight fix to be in, but there was no other way out of it except by strong argument and explanation. While conversing with the captain, who seemed to realize the situation, I caught sight of one of our staff officers, about 200 yards away, signaling to our batteries to cease firing on Fort Stedman, which was now occupied by our troops.

"Pointing at him I continued:

"'Captain, see that staff officer? He is ordering the firing to be stopped. The whole country around here is in our possession. It's no use, you can't get away.'

"That satisfied him and he surrendered. He asked me what he should do and I told him to march his men off by the right flank down the road to our rear, intending to bring the whole regiment to our camp alone, but when the rebel column emerged from the cut and thus became exposed, our troops renewed their fire and threatened death and destruction to my so willing and obedient prisoners. I therefore directed the captain and his men to throw down their guns and remain in the cut until our men would come up and take them.

"Again they followed out my instructions. I then signaled to our men to cease their fire and come up, but was not understood, and, being the only one exposed, became the target for a lot of General Hartranft's raw recruits. I cannot say that I enjoyed that part very much, and not experiencing any desire to be shot down by our own troops, I descended into the cut and joined the rebels. The captain was an agreeable person to chat with, and we conversed about his future prospects as a prisoner, when my attention was drawn to a rebel flag a short distance away. A lieutenant and color-guard of six men were moving along the bank trying to make their escape. I broke off my conversation abruptly and started after them, picking up a loaded gun on the way.

"Before the lieutenant realized what was happening he had the rifle placed against his breast and was commanded to surrender the flag he was carrying.

"The lieutenant was game and promptly replied : 'I'll be damned if I'll give you that flag ! And furthermore I want to tell you that you are my prisoner. Give me your gun,' and at the same time the color-guard raised their guns and made a most expressive show of resistance.

"Here I was in a pretty mess. The rebel guns were raised at my head. If I pulled my trigger I would sound my own death-knell. Surrounded by rebels, beyond the help of my own troops, it would have been folly to carry the bluff farther, so I made a virtue out of necessity and handed the lieutenant my gun.

"And thus I, who only a few minutes ago had captured a whole regiment, was made a prisoner myself. All my arguing as to him and his men being cut off brought only the curt reply, 'Come along, we'll see.'

"Taking me in their midst the lieutenant and guard moved across the open field in the direction of our works, thinking them their own lines. Immediately our batteries opened on us with at least twenty guns with spherical case shell, which tore up the ground all around us. There was a great chance of me losing my game if the lieutenant saw fit to change his course and pass around our works, as it almost seemed he would. Visions of Libby prison with all its horrors looming up before my eye determined me to make a break and at least give the rebels a run. But the guard was on to my intention and one of them yelled at me : 'You damned Yank, you try to run and we'll blow you to hell.' So I gave up the attempt to escape. Presently I noticed three soldiers in blue about sixty yards away from us. I recognized them to be men of the One hundredth Pennsylvania and yelled as loud as I could : 'Boys, I am a prisoner here !' They came toward us on a run. 'All right, Captain,' one of them spoke up, 'we'll save you.' Turning to the lieutenant he continued : 'Lieutenant, what say you now ? I guess the tables are turned. You are our prisoner.'

"The rebel officer made no long reply, but merely said : 'I surrender.'

"I now quickly seized the colors and turned my attention to the rebel regiment in the ravine. Waving the flag to signal our men to cease firing, however, had the result of increasing it, so much so that the rebel color-guard advised me to drop the flag. I tried another method. Throwing down the flag, I trampled upon it and waved my sword over my head. This had the desired effect. Our men rested their guns, but on the other hand my action had been watched by the Confederates from their works about 200 yards away. Incensed at the indignity to their colors they poured a most terrific fire in our direction, rendering our position as critical as before. I finally picked up the colors from the ground and started on a dead run with my prisoners for our works, being forced to go for sixty yards towards the enemy, and expose myself to their concentrated fire, before I reached the cover of our own works. The rebel regiment was shortly afterward brought in as prisoners by Hartranft's men."

HEROISM IN THE HOUR OF REVERSE

WILLIAM H. HOWE,
Sergeant, Co. K, 29th Mass. Inf.
Born at Haverhill, Mass.,
April 10, 1837.

CHARLES H. PINKHAM,
Sergeant-Major, 57th Mass. Inf.
Highest rank attained:
Brev.-Capt., U.S.V.
Born at Grafton, Mass.,
August 18, 1844.

THE fighting at Fort Stedman brought out many examples of great individual bravery and furnished numerous incidents which prove the pluck and indomitable courage of the Union soldier, no matter whether he was in a victorious battle or facing defeat. At Fort Stedman particularly, where the Federals were treated to a surprise by the enemy, their conduct was such as to force even the foe to admire it.

It is recorded, for instance, that one private of the Twenty-ninth Massachusetts Infantry was surrounded by a group of rebels, seized by the throat and ordered to surrender. His reply was: "Never." Whereupon he was clubbed over the back with a musket and shot in the head, but in spite of his injuries fought with his opponent, and escaped.

Other brave deeds were those of Sergeant-Major Charles H. Pinkham, of the Fifty-seventh Massachusetts Infantry, and Sergeant William H. Howe, of Company K, Twenty-ninth Massachusetts Infantry. Howe's regiment was in camp within the works when the Confederates entered and surprised them. No shots were fired, the Confederates using only the butts of their muskets. The regiment was forced to retreat, leaving a great number of its men in the hands of the victorious rebels. When the Federals were already driven out of their works and the rebels in full possession of the camp Sergeant-Major Pinkham rushed back into the very midst of the enemy, entered a tent, seized the regimental colors, and dashed back with his precious treasure to his own lines. During the subsequent fighting for the recapture of the camp, which ended in an utter rout of the rebels, Sergeant-Major Pinkham had a chance to seize the colors of the Fifty-seventh North Carolina Infantry and carried them triumphantly into the Union lines.

Sergeant Howe was one of the Union soldiers who was captured when the rebels took possession of the fort. He managed to escape his guard, however, and rejoined his comrades in front of Fort Haskell. When volunteers were called for to serve an abandoned gun, he with five others undertook to perform the work. They were exposed to a most galling fire, but he worked the gun with such telling effect after all but two of the battery men belonging to the piece were killed that the Confederates were forced to retreat before its withering fire, allowing the Federals to come up to the support of the brave volunteer gunner.

DUTY AND DEATH RATHER THAN DISHONOR

ALLEN THOMPSON,

Private, Co. K, 4th New York
Heavy Artillery.
Born at Sandy Creek, Oswego
Co., N. Y., Oct. 1, 1847.

JAMES THOMPSON,

Private, Co. K, 4th New York
Heavy Artillery.
Born at Sandy Creek, Oswego
Co., N. Y., Dec. 25, 1849.

A T THE time Grant was bending every energy and all resources to hold Lee's army in check and all military operations centered around the Appomattox campaign, the Fourth New York Heavy Artillery was serving as infantry, being attached to what was called the "Irish" Brigade, First Division Second Corps, the division commander being General Nelson A. Miles. Corps organizations were broken up, and all around Petersburg to the west and south, over a radius of thirty miles, the Federal troops were fighting by brigades in separate actions. Yet, so able were regimental, brigade, division and corps commanders, so thoroughly did the rank and file understand the situation, that together these individual actions revolved around and were practically parts of the great combat of the Appomattox, the Battle of Five Forks.

On the morning of April 2d, Miles, in pursuit of the enemy, arrived at White Oak Road. With the determination to bring the rebels to a standstill he pushed his brigade in line of battle towards their works, resolved to carry them. The works were in plain view, but not a man was in sight, not a rifle cracked to break the silence of the early morning. The brigade halted, suspicious of a trap or an ambush. The deserted look of the works appeared unnatural, the very silence seemed to call for caution. All eyes were turned towards the works, every man in the brigade was full of anxiety to know the secret they concealed.

General Miles observed that it would be necessary to call for volunteers to take the lead, advance through the woods and ascertain the situation. This call was

---

Final Operations Around Petersburg, Va. — When Grant went into winter quarters before Petersburg he had determined to resume his campaign against Lee on the 29th of March, 1865.

The heavy rains, however, prevented active operations until the 2d of April, when the general assault commenced and was pursued along Grant's whole line, which extended from Appomattox to Dinwiddie Court House. The day preceding Lee was defeated at **Five Forks,** where Sheridan gained a signal victory. This defeat seemed to bewilder Lee, and as he could not withstand the vigorous assault of the 2d—his lines having been broken in numerous places—he noiselessly withdrew his army toward the Danville Road at nightfall.

Before sunrise on the 3d Parke had gone through the enemy's lines and taken Petersburg. Grant now ordered Sheridan to push toward the Danville Road, while Meade was in close pursuit up the Appomattox.

In the afternoon Grant received word from Weitzel that Richmond had been taken early in the morning and was securely held. Notwithstanding these victories Grant was apprehensive of Lee's escape, and consequently set out in pursuit of him.

The Federal losses at Five Forks were about 800 killed and wounded ; the Confederate losses 8,500.

At the assault and fall of Petersburg the Federals lost 3,300 and the Confederates 3,000.

responded to and Private James Thompson, of Company K, Fourth New York Heavy Artillery, one of the little squad that volunteered, lived to tell the following of what happened :

"Five other comrades, my brother and myself, stepped to the front following the call of General Miles for volunteers, and received our instructions directly from the general. We were to advance about fifty feet apart, with our rifles at a ready, and to fire the instant we discovered the first sign of an enemy concealed in ambush. When we had reached a certain tree he pointed out to us one of our number was to climb it and swing his cap as a signal for the brigade to come on if we found that all was well. We started, my brother first, I next, and the other five in their regular order from right to left. After advancing perhaps one-fourth of the way, through the slashing, we had all bunched together, and proceeded in this manner perhaps fifty yards farther, when we were surprised to see an outpost of the enemy of about fifty men rise out of the slashing a little to the left of the road and within fifty feet of us. They ordered us to throw down our guns and 'come in.'

"What could we do? We had the secret of a signal that would have drawn that brigade of brave boys in our rear into this death-trap, where the enemy could have shot them down at their leisure. We knew very well that if we surrendered without giving the alarm we would be compelled to give up the signal or die, so we decided our only course was to give the alarm and die where we were. We fired, and received their volley of fifty pieces at a distance of scarcely 100 feet.

"Six of our number were stretched on the ground, five dead, one desperately wounded, and one with several holes through his clothes but without a scratch on his body, who made his way back to the rear and to his company as soon as possible. Our troops heard the alarm shots and the volley that followed, and knew at once what had happened to our little squad. The enemy's position was uncovered. The battle commenced at once. Our brigade held the position where they were, while our Second Division swung around and took them on the flank, taking a great many prisoners and compelling them to evacuate their works and hunt another position to the rear. After the battle was over our little squad was not forgotten. A detail was sent to bury them, which found me still in the land of the living, lying with my dead comrades all this time between the contending lines, praying for a ball to come and end my misery. My brother, Allan Thompson, was the one who got back to the lines in safety and made this report. He also received a Medal of Honor."

The charge upon the Confederate works at White Oak Road brought out another brave deed, of which First Lieutenant Stephen P. Corliss, of Company F, Fourth New York Heavy Artillery, was the hero. The enemy had a battery posted on an elevation near the South Side Railroad where it intersected with the White Oak Road leading into Petersburg, and was able to do great damage to the advancing Federals from that position. The order came to capture the battery, which was

"WE RECEIVED THEIR VOLLEY OF FIFTY PIECES."

protected by infantry. The brigade to which the Fourth New York Artillery were attached as infantry started to carry out the command. The enemy's fire was at once concentrated upon the advancing brigade with such telling effect that the advance was. for a time at least, checked. Again the forward movement was ordered and taken up, to be checked a second time. For a third time the advance was resumed. At this juncture the color-sergeant of one of the regiments was shot and the colors fell to the ground. Lieutenant Corliss, who witnessed the fall of the flag, at once dismounted, picked up the colors and remounted. With flag in hand he rode at the head of the brigade into the enemy's works and placed them there. The colors were closely

STEPHEN P. CORLISS,
1st Lieut., Co. F, 4th N. Y. H. A.
Highest rank attained :
Brev.-Col., U. S. V.
Born at Albany, N. Y.,
July 26, 1842.

followed by the enthused men, the works were carried and the rebels routed in utter defeat. Lieutenant Corliss' action contributed greatly in the achievement of a splendid victory.

THRILLING EPISODES AROUND PETERSBURG

GENERAL GRANT's eagerness to destroy or capture Lee's army rather than his desire to take Petersburg led to the battle of Five Forks, Va., on April 1, 1865. Lee was striving to join Johnston and free himself from the net into which he and his army had been so skillfully driven by Grant. To hold him there and catch him was the Federal commander's sole aim and purpose. To break through the meshes and escape was Lee's sole object. On the Union side was General Warren, with the Fifth Corps, and General Sheridan, commanding the Cavalry Corps.

The Confederates had a line of strong works for their support, while the nature of the country made it impossible for the Federals to intrench, and they were thus presented with the alternative of fighting or falling back. The battle began late in the afternoon, the dismounted cavalry making an attack on the works, the Fifth Corps striking the enemy's left flank. Both sides fought with great. valor and stubbornness, and the battle was handsomely contested; but before nightfall the enemy were driven from their strong line of works and completely routed. Nearly 6,000 Confederates were captured, and the remainder of the demoralized army was driven toward Petersburg, pursued for miles by the victorious cavalry.

The loss on the Union side was not severe, numerically, but some of the bravest officers lost their lives on that battlefield; for example, Colonel Winthrop, who led the First Brigade of the Second Division of the Fifth Corps. He fell at the head of his soldiers, shortly after the charge was ordered. Colonel James Grindlay, of the One hundred and forty-sixth New York Infantry, at once assumed command, was the first to enter the enemy's works and in the ensuing struggle captured two rebel battle-flags.

The contests on this battle-field abound with incidents of similar inspiring bravery.

First Lieutenant Albert E. Fernald, of Company F, Twentieth Maine Infantry, was with his regiment in the last line when the battle opened, but was in the first line when the works were reached. The left of the regiment struck the works first, he being somewhat in advance, and as he cleared the breastworks ran toward a body of Confederates with a rebel color-bearer. He rushed among the crowd and secured the flag before even his regiment had gotten into the works.

Lieutenant Henry G. Bonebrake, of Company G, Seventh Pennsylvania Cavalry, in his ardor to secure a Confederate flag ran after a Confederate color-bearer as soon as he had entered the works as one of the first of Devin's Division. He caught up to the Confederate, and in a hand-to-hand struggle dispossessed his antagonist of the flag by superior physical strength.

(1) **WILLIAM W. WINEGAR,**
Lieut., Co. B, 1st N. Y. Drag.
Born at Union Springs,
N. Y., October 20, 1844.

(2) **JOHN C. MATTHEWS,**
Pvt., Co. A, 61st Pa. Inf.
Born in Westmoreland
Co., Pa., March 29, 1846.

(3) **JOSEPH FISHER,**
Corp., Co. C, 61st Pa. Inf.
Born at Philadelphia,
Pa., Aug. 24, 1843.

(4) **J. WALLACE SCOTT,**
Capt., Co. D, 157th Pa. Inf.
Highest rank attained:
Brevet-Major.
Born, Chester Co., Pa., 1838

(5) **ROBERT L. ORR,**
Colonel, 61st Pa. Inf.
Born at Philadelphia,
Pa., March 28, 1836.

(6) **ROBERT F. SHIPLEY,**
Sergeant, Co. A, 140th N. Y.
Infantry.
Born at Williamson, N. Y.,
May 8, 1838.

(7) **ALBERT E. FERNALD,**
1st Lieut., Co. F, 20th Me. Inf.
Highest rank attain'd: Capt.
Born at Hampden, Me., May
13, 1838.

(8) **JOHN C. EWING,**
Co. E, 211th Pa. Inf.

(9) **LESTER G. HACK,**
Sergeant, Co. F, 5th Vt. Inf.
Born, Coldmill, Pa., Jan. 18, 1844.

(10) **FRANK FESQ,**
Private, Co. A, 40th N. J. Inf.
Born in Brunswick, Germany, April 4, 1840.

(11) **CHARLES A HUNTER,**
Sergt., Co. E, 34th Mass. Inf.

It was a rather critical situation in which Lieutenant William W. Winegar, of Company B, First New York Dragoons, had to exert all his wit and summon all the presence of mind at his command. In the excitement of the battle he had become separated from his company and was still advancing when his comrades were quite a distance from him. Presently he found himself surrounded by rebels. It was then he discovered that he was alone. Retreat was impossible. He had to rely on his nerve. He ran up to a Confederate color-bearer who was standing only a few feet away and, grasping the staff of his flag, demanded the surrender of the whole crowd. The rebel was not quite willing to yield. On the contrary he quickly drew his revolver and shouted: "Never! You'll not get this flag!" At this instant Lieutenant Winegar fired, and so effectively that the whole company was demoralized. Then, at his command, they surrendered and were marched to the rear.

Sergeant Robert F. Shipley, of Company A, One hundred and fortieth New York Infantry, ran across a flag-bearer of the Ninth Virginia Infantry, who had his back turned toward him. A gentle poke with the butt of the rifle reminded the Virginian that a Union soldier wanted his flag. "Pass those colors over to me," Shipley shouted. The Confederate whirled around and with the flagstaff for a club was about to let it down on the head of the sergeant, but the latter, considering this the wrong answer to his command, made good use of his bayonet, which rendered further parley superfluous, and thus secured the flag.

Simultaneously with the battle at Five Forks a bombardment was opened upon the enemy's lines of fortifications around and about Petersburg, Va., followed by a general assault on the next day, April 2d. Again the fighting was of the most determined character and the losses, even to the Union forces, correspondingly severe. The works were an extraordinarily strong line of rifle pits with deep ditches and high relief preceded by one or two lines of abatis, unusually well constructed and with a line of very strong fraise between them. At every few hundred yards were forts or batteries well supplied with artillery. They looked well-nigh impregnable, and nothing but the most resolute bravery could result in penetrating them.

The general assault was ordered shortly before five o'clock in the morning, but owing to some misapprehension the Federal pickets began to fire while the columns were still forming. This drew the enemy's fire, not only upon the pickets but also on the dense masses in the rear, causing some loss of life, considerable confusion and threatening to break the whole plan of attack. However, by the exertions of the officers the pickets soon ceased to use their rifles and quiet was restored, the Confederates apparently not being over-anxious to exchange shots in the darkness. As soon as day began to dawn the looked-for signal was given and the assault was made. The advancing columns broke over the enemy's picket line and, under a heavy fire of artillery and a more deadly yet less noisy fire of musketry from the parapets, moved over the main defenses. Abatis was cut away and through the openings thus made, and through those made by the enemy for their own convenience in permitting access to the front, their works were gained. After a sharp but brief conflict the Confederates yielded along the whole line to the superior valor of the Federals, whose prisoners they became after an unsuccessful attempt to escape. The entire rebel artillery fell into the hands of the victors.

In this assault the Sixty-first Pennsylvania Infantry played an important part and conducted itself so valiantly that no less than five of its members were honored with a Medal of Honor for distinguished gallantry.

Lieutenant-Colonel Robert L. Orr took charge of the regiment at a critical moment when the regimental commander, Colonel Crosby, fell, mortally wounded. His gallant leadership inspired the men and restored their confidence. Two color-bearers having been shot down, the colonel himself grasped one of the flags and carried it throughout the entire charge at the head of his regiment, which formed the apex of the famous wedge-shaped assault. One of these color-bearers was Corporal Joseph Fisher, of Company C. A bursting shell had shattered his arm and torn a wide gash in his side. He at first held on to the colors and with wonderful pluck and nerve attempted to crawl to the works and there plant his flag, but his strength failed and he fainted on the way.

The death of Colonel Crosby, the fall of the color-bearers, coupled with the temporary disappearance of the colors, caused some commotion, if not confusion, in the ranks, which, as stated, ceased when Lieutenant-Colonel Orr assumed command. However, much credit is due to Private John C. Mathews, of Company A, who rushed to the side of one of the fallen color-bearers and, holding the flag aloft, greatly aided in restoring order and confidence. For this fine display of quick action and presence of mind Colonel Orr promoted him a color-sergeant then and there.

Privates Milton Mathews and Theodore Mitchell, both of Company C, distinguished themselves by each capturing a Confederate battle-flag.

An idea of the fierce fighting near Petersburg, which commenced as early as March 31st, is given by the narrative of Corporal Franklin W. Lutes, of Company D, One hundred and eleventh New York Infantry, who won his medal on that day.

"When the order came to fix bayonets and charge," says Corporal Lutes, "I was left guide of my regiment. Upon jumping from behind our breastworks we were met by an awful volley from the enemy, who understood our move and determined to drive us back to our fortifications. Many fell before this storm of lead, but the remainder pushed on. Suddenly I saw, in front of their lines, the rebel color-guard, proudly waving the flag of the Forty-first Alabama Infantry.

"I yelled to my comrades that we should capture those colors, and, dashing forward about ten rods in advance of our line, dropped down behind some rails that formed a small shelter between two trees. Here I watched my opportunity, and when our line got a little closer jumped over and captured color-bearer and flag and also one of the color-guard."

Sergeant Lester G. Hack, of Company F, Fifth Vermont Infantry, adds another chapter to the many phases of the contest on the 2d of April.

"When we had driven the rebels from their works," he says, "every man began to shift for himself, pursuing the enemy, who were fleeing helter skelter in all directions.

"About one hundred yards to my right a small body of rebels were commencing to rally round their colors. I rushed at the color-sergeant and jerked the colors from his hands, at the same time ordering the rebels around me to surrender. Some of them obeyed my command, but the majority took to flight."

Private Frank Fesq, of Company A, Fortieth New Jersey Infantry, came face to face with the color-bearer of the Eighteenth North Carolina Infantry. In the ensuing struggle his hand was almost smashed and he was severely cut in the thigh with a rebel sabre, but he captured the colors.

While this fighting was going on the Twenty-fourth Army Corps, commanded by General Gibbon, carried Forts Gregg and Baldwin, which the Confederates had erected to protect their right at Petersburg. This capture practically secured possession of the place and induced the rebels, after the loss of their works, to evacuate Petersburg and retreat.

Sergeant Charles E. Hunter, of Company E, Thirty-fourth Massachusetts Infantry, whose regiment took part in this important action, says that the men fought for twenty-seven minutes outside of the parapet before the enemy surrendered. It was a herculean struggle, but ended with a brilliant victory for the attacking Federals, who would not yield until they accomplished their task. Sergeant Hunter had the honor of being the first color-bearer to enter Fort Gregg and plant his flag on the rebel stronghold. His conduct throughout the Appomattox campaign, and especially at Fort Gregg, was so exceptionally brave that two months later the Medal of Honor was pinned on his breast.

Captain J. Wallace Scott, of Company D, One hundred and fifty-seventh Pennsylvania Infantry, while leading his men at the battle of Five Forks, encountered a Confederate carrying the flag of the Sixteenth South Carolina Infantry, and in the ensuing struggle for its possession the captain wrested the flag from the Confederate and brought it safely off the field.

Private John Ewing, of Company E, Two hundred and eleventh Pennsylvania Infantry, performed a similar deed at Petersburg the following day, where he captured the standard of the Sixty-first Alabama Infantry.

The courage and daring required in the capture of a battle-flag can best be appreciated by those who have taken part in or witnessed a hand-to-hand combat for the possession of one. It is a struggle to the death. Although many, during the great war, attempted the capture of the enemy's flags, few succeeded, the majority paying for their efforts with their life-blood.

While others figured conspicuously in this battle and were rewarded with the Medal of Honor, their valorous deeds must be omitted from these pages owing to the inability of the compilers to obtain their personal reminiscences.

ATTRACTED GENERAL CUSTER'S ATTENTION

A T THE battle of Five Forks, Va., April 1, 1865, Lieutenant Wilmon W. Blackmar, of Company H, First West Virginia Cavalry was brigade provost-marshal on the staff of General Capehart, commander of the Third Brigade of General Custer's Cavalry Division. General Capehart's Brigade had been ordered to join in the general charge and follow what seemed to be the main body of the Confederates. The order was carried out. Presently Lieutenant Blackmar saw the flankers being driven in and riding to their assistance made the startling discovery that the brigade was in pursuit of a small detachment only, the main body of the enemy being posted in another direction. He also observed that the enemy were about to take advantage of the mistake and by a bold move push their troops between the cavalry and infantry in the Union line of battle. He rode rapidly after and overtook his brigade commander, hastily told what he had discovered and was ordered to ride back at once and form the brigade in line of battle (facing the enemy's position) as rapidly as it should be turned back to him. He formed a new line of battle on the edge of a deep ditch facing in the new direction. The situation was highly critical, and no one realized the danger more keenly than Lieutenant Blackmar. He had no authority to give orders to advance, nevertheless he assumed the responsibility, not waiting for the arrival of the larger portion of the brigade now moving rapidly toward the new line, and with the brigade colors and that portion of the brigade which had arrived, he ordered a charge, jumped the ditch and a most brilliant and impetuous charge was thus begun. The charge was made so irresistibly that the Confederates fled in great confusion; the brigade pursued for more than five miles, picking up prisoners, cannon, wagons and ambulances from the utterly demoralized enemy.

General George A. Custer, happened to be an eye-witness of this incident and riding to Lieutenant Blackmar's side he laid his hand on his shoulder and called him captain, at the same time joining in the charge. Recommendations from Generals Custer and Capehart promptly brought Lieutenant Blackmar commission as captain of cavalry.

WILMON W. BLACKMAR,
Lieutenant, Company H, 1st
W. V. Cav.
Highest rank att'ned: Capt.
Born in Bristol, Pa., July 1841.

O N THE 31st of March, 1865, Sheridan's Cavalry Corps developed two divisions of Confederate infantry and one of cavalry near Five Forks, Va., and Major Horatio King, chief quartermaster of the first division, feeling that he could safely leave his train in charge of the senior brigade quartermaster, tendered his services to General Devin as a volunteer aide on his staff and was granted permission to accompany him. Owing to the wooded character of the country the cavalry fought dismounted. The ground was stubbornly contested until about four P. M., when a report was brought from the Seventh Pennsylvania Cavalry that the Federal line was driven back. At this time Major King was the only staff officer remaining with General Devin, commanding the division, and he was requested to hunt up the reserve brigade under General Gibbs and hurry them to the aid of the Second Brigade. The reserve was somewhere on the extreme left of the line, so, following the direction of the firing with all possible speed for about three-quarters of a mile, the major found General Gibbs, delivered his orders, and proceeded with him at once to the critical position where the brigade was deployed. They arrived just in time to repel a charge of the Confederate infantry and save the line from serious disaster, Major King accompanying General Gibbs and participating in the charge.

HORATIO KING,

Maj. and Quartermaster, U. S. V.
Highest rank attained :
Brevet-Colonel, U. S. Volunteers.
Born in Portland, Maine,
December 22, 1837.

The fighting continued until dark, when, finding that the troops he had were unequal to the task of dislodging the Confederates from their strong works, General Devin withdrew his forces to the neighborhood of Dinwiddie Court House. On the following day, in consequence of the imminent danger of the train, General Sheridan directed Major King to return and resume charge.

ENGINEER, SURGEON AND HERO

**WILLIAM R. D. BLACKWOOD,
M. D.,**

Surg., 48th Pennsylvania Inf.
Highest rank attained :
Brevet-Lieut.-Col.
Born at Hollywood, Ireland,
May 12, 1838.

THE SIEGE of Petersburg was terminated by the action of April 2, 1865. Lee withdrew on the 3d, leaving Petersburg and Richmond in the possession of the Union generals. This scene is remarkable in the history of the Civil War for the terrible losses suffered by both armies. In this fierce assault of April 2d the number of Union killed and wounded was estimated at 3,361, the Confederate loss being somewhat less.

Among the many exhibitions of courage in the field and valuable services rendered by officers on this occasion were those of Dr. William R. D. Blackwood, of the Forty-eighth Pennsylvania. The doctor had served several times as aide-de-camp and as volunteer engineer officer. The inside work of the Petersburg Mine, the longest and most extensive on record, was largely engineered by this officer.

Early in the morning of the last assault Major Peckham, adjutant-general of the brigade, was wounded in the head during a heavy attack of the enemy. He lay for some time under the Confederate guns, the shells bursting all around him, until Dr. Blackwood rushed out at the risk of his life and conveyed him to shelter behind some low earthworks. Almost immediately this protection was destroyed by shells, which killed and wounded several who were near the spot. The doctor's efforts to save Major Peckham failed, and he died within an hour.

"AT THE RISK OF HIS LIFE CONVEYED HIM TO SHELTER.'

Dr. Blackwood performed a similar service in the case of Colonel G. W. Gowen of his regiment, who died as he was being carried from the field, and it was for his heroic efforts to save the body from destruction by the incessant shell-fire of the enemy that the doctor received the Medal of Honor.

"THEY CAN'T DRIVE YOU OUT OF HERE"

EARLY in the day on April 2, 1865, General Hartranft's Division captured a number of forts around Petersburg. In the afternoon the general detailed Captain Thomas W. Hoffman, of Company A, Two hundred and eighth Pennsylvania Infantry,

THOMAS W. HOFFMAN,
Captain, Co. A, 208th Pa. Inf.
Highest rank attained:
Brevet Lieut.-Col. U. S. Vols.
Born at Berrysburg, Pa., July
25, 1839.

who was attached to his staff as engineer, to ascertain the possibility of holding the advanced position. When he arrived at the front line he heard the order to fall back given and saw some of the officers run to the rear in undue haste. The men, too, were on the point of retreating; some of them, in fact, had already turned to the rear. The idea seemed to prevail that the Confederates, who were howling, shouting and fighting in front like demons, were flanking the advance guard. Captain Hoffman's timely arrival on the scene prevented a rout. He quickly drew his sword and yelled at the top of his voice: "Don't a man of you run! They can't drive you out of here!"

This had a reassuring effect. The men regained their confidence as soon as they saw that somebody was in command, the officers returned to their posts and the lines were re-established and presented such a solid front that the rebels did not even dare to make a serious attack, but were satisfied after several unfruitful attempts to leave the Federals masters of the field. Captain Hoffman was also brevetted lieutenant-colonel for this act.

A HERO FROM THE SOUTH

WITH an innate love for justice and the righteousness of the Union cause seventeen-year-old Charles Reeder tore away from his home in a little Virginia village and joined the Union army at the very outbreak of the war. This was the more praiseworthy as he had been reared amidst surroundings which were decidedly hostile to Northern sentiment. His father was a stanch follower of the Confederate cause and objected to his course. But young Reeder's mind was made up. In the conflict between home and parents and the Union and justice he did not hesitate in making his choice and decided for the latter. He enlisted in the Federal Army and became a private in Company G, Twelfth West Virginia Infantry.

In speaking of the action in which he won the medal, he says: "In the early dawn of the morning

CHARLES A. REEDER,
Private, Co. G, 12th West Va. Inf.
Born in Hamson Co., West
Virginia, in 1844.

of April 2, 1865, we moved out from our breastworks preparatory to making a charge upon Petersburg. Silence prevailed in the ranks. The enemy had not fired since the evening before, thinking probably that we would not attack them, fortified as they were behind strong intrenchments and a field full of mines.

"The first thing we did was to drag some heavy guns as close as we could to their works, to force an entrance into their fortifications. When within one hundred yards we were discovered by the enemy, who at once opened a heavy fire upon us with artillery. Amid this rain of shot and shell we threw up some slight fortifications for our guns and returned shot for shot. This, however, could not last long, for our defenses were slight, while those of the enemy were most formidable. Suddenly a large shell from one of our guns burst in their midst, throwing the defenders into momentary confusion. Such an opening was too good to be lost.

"We received the command to fix bayonets, and then, firing a volley, charged right up into their lines. The assault became a severe hand-to-hand fight, every man for himself. Presently I found myself in the most perilous position I had been in during the war. Being to the right of Company G, I was cut off from my comrades and lost in the wild confusion. Surrounded by the enemy I could only parry thrusts and cuts from bayonets and sabres until almost exhausted. My determination then was to sell my life as dearly as possible, and I clubbed right and left. A color-bearer was among my assailants and he, too, received the butt of my gun. Seizing the flag from his grasp was the work of but a moment, and with it I quickly ran towards my comrades, thus bringing into our lines a stand of Confederate colors."

MADE GOOD USE OF THE ENEMY'S WEAPONS

AT ABOUT ten o'clock on the night of April 1, 1865, Captain G. W. Adams, of Battery G, First Rhode Island Light Artillery, was detailed to select a detachment of twenty men from his battery to advance with the Sixth Army Corps in its intended assault on the enemy's works in front of Petersburg, Va., and with this detachment take command of all the captured guns and turn them on the enemy.

Late that night Captain Adams called his battery together and asked for volunteers for this hazardous duty, at the same time pointing out to them what it meant to go into the enemy's works with only ramrods, sponge-staffs, lanyards, friction primers and gunspikes; that, should they be unable to work the captured guns, they would have no means of defending themselves, except with these implements.

Twenty men nevertheless promptly volunteered, and at the outset of the assault, when the captain asked whether any of the twenty wished to remain with the battery, only three fell out, thus leaving seventeen to perform the duty laid out for them.

At daybreak of the 2d the assaulting column moved upon the fortifications of the enemy amid a shower of shot and shell with such resistless force that the works were carried and the enemy driven back. Here followed the little volunteer detachment of seventeen, scaling the works and at once taking possession of twelve large guns, but when they began to work them it was necessary to fire along the line of works in order to drive the enemy out of the embrasures at the end of the pits, and consequently only one gun, a twenty-four pounder Napoleon, could be used. It was in an exposed position, and the brave cannoneers received a heavy fire from the rebels in the embrasures of the forts they still retained. But the gun was kept hot by the rapid fire with which the little band poured one hundred or more shots into the enemy, causing them to become demoralized and retire. Some of the detachment were wounded, while others were under cover, but the seven who served this gun so nobly, standing up unflinchingly before the terrific fire of the enemy—Sergeant John H. Havron, Sergeant Archibald Molbone, Corporal James A. Barber, Corporal Samuel E. Lewis, Privates Charles D. Ennis, John Corcoran and George W. Potter— were rewarded for their bravery and daring with the Medal of Honor soon after this eventful day.

IN FULL VIEW OF THE ENEMY

IRA H. EVANS,
Captain, Co. 116th U.S.C.T.
Highest rank attained: Major.
Born in Piermont, N. H.,
April 11, 1844.

IN THE latter part of March, 1865, the Second Division of the Twenty-fifth Army Corps, General William Birney commanding, was detached from the Army of the James and moved to the left of the Sixth Army Corps, near Hatcher's Run, Va., to take part in the final operations against Petersburg.

On the day before the capture of the outer lines of fortifications, General Birney was instructed to have his division in readinesss for an assault on the enemy's works in front. His division lay behind a low ridge, which sheltered it from the view of the enemy. Beyond this ridge and well out toward the enemy's works, in an open field, were rifle pits in which our pickets were posted. As these rifle pits were located in open ground and within short range of the enemy's fire, the pickets could be relieved only after dark. Upon receipt of the orders stated, General Birney repeated them to the members of his staff, adding that he desired one of them to go out to the rifle pits at the front and learn all he could as to the character and extent of the enemy's defenses, so that he might know what obstructions his troops would encounter in making the proposed attack. He stated that this mission was so perilous in its character that he did not wish to order any officer of his staff to perform it, and so asked someone to volunteer for it.

A significant silence followed these remarks. Captain Ira H. Evans of Company 116th U. S. Colored Troops, was acting assistant adjutant-general of the division, thus holding the most important position on the staff, although he was the youngest officer on it, at that time lacking a few days of being twenty-one years of age. He felt that he must perform this duty and signified his willingness to do so to the general.

He dismounted, and giving his horse to an orderly went up to the top of the ridge, then ran to the line of the rifle pits as rapidly as possible. His course was through an open field, gently sloping toward the rebel works, so that he was in full view of the enemy, who at once opened a sharp musketry fire on him. He reached his goal amid a shower of bullets, and dropped in among the surprised occupants of the rifle pit without much formality. Having obtained the information he desired, he made his run back as speedily as possible, amid another shower of bullets. He was the only man in the Union lines visible to the Confederates at the time, and they gave him their undivided attention.

REWARDED TWICE

First Lieutenant Thomas W. Custer, of Company B, Sixth Michigan Cavalry, distinguished himself at Namozine Church, April 2d, and at Sailor's Creek, Va., April 6th, by the capture of a battle-flag at each place.

At Sailor's Creek Lieutenant Custer leaped his horse over the enemy's line of works and fearlessly dashed up to the rebel colors. When close to the color-bearer he received a shot in the face which knocked him backward on his horse, but in a moment he was again upright in his saddle and fired at the color-bearer, hitting him and causing him to reel. Immediately Custer reached out and grasped the flag, wrenching the standard from the color-bearer as he fell, and dashed back to his lines. Here he met his brother, General G. A. Custer, and called out to him: "The rebels have shot me, but I've got their flag." Instantly he set spurs to his horse to charge again, but the general, realizing the severity of his brother's wound, checked him, and told him to go to the rear and have it dressed. This the lieutenant refused to do, whereupon General Custer ordered him under arrest and to the rear, where it was found that the bullet had entered his cheek and passed out behind the ear.

HE REACHED HIS GOAL AMID A SHOWER OF BULLETS.

GALLANT VERMONTERS

GARDNER C. HAWKINS,
1st Lieut., Co. E, 3d Vermont Inf.
Born in Vermont,
Feb., 1846.

THE Vermont Brigade, having received orders to attack Petersburg, moved promptly on the morning of April 2d at the given signal. After passing over about half the distance, the advancing column was exposed to a well-directed musketry fire from the front and artillery fire from forts on either side, which completely enfiladed the line and caused it to waver. This was the most critical moment throughout the entire engagement; day was just beginning to dawn, and very soon the enemy would be able to discover the precise position and movements of the assaulting column. They had been apprised of the point of attack and were apparently beginning to appreciate its importance, as they were hastening to meet it with all the strength at their command. The wavering of the troops was only momentary, for there arose at the head of the column Lieutenant Gardner C. Hawkins, acting adjutant of the Third Vermont Infantry, who led his men, cheering them on, until he nearly reached the enemy's works, when he fell, pierced by a ball which passed through his head. Following the example of the brave lieutenant, the troops again pushed on with determination. The remaining ground was passed over under a most withering fire of musketry, officers and men vying with one another in the race for the works, and losing all organization in their eagerness and enthusiasm to reach them. The line of abatis was swept away like cobwebs, and the men swarmed over the works with yells and cheers that struck terror to the fleeing rebels.

Captain Charles G. Gould, of Company H, Fifth Vermont Infantry, was the first man of the Sixth Corps to mount the enemy's works. His regiment was in the first line of the brigade, and in the charge he was far in advance of his command. Upon mounting the works he received a severe bayonet wound in the face and was struck several times with clubbed muskets, but bravely stood his ground, killing with his sabre the man who bayoneted him, and retired from the works only after his comrades had come to his assistance and routed the enemy from their lines.

WILLIAM J. SPERRY,
Major, 6th Vermont Infantry.
Highest rank attained :
Brevet Lieutenant-Colonel.
Born at Cavendish, Vt., Dec. 28, 1840.

After crossing the works the brigade re-formed and again pushed forward with all the zeal of a victorious army, passing through thickets, swamps and pine woods in pursuit of the enemy, who were being pressed so closely that they had scarcely time to fire a shot. Again all organization was lost, and every man considered himself a host. Singly, or in squads of three or four, they charged upon whatever obstructions came in their paths.

Major William J. Sperry, in command of the Sixth Vermont Infantry, assisted by a few men, captured two field guns and turned them upon the scattering rebels. Being unable to procure friction primers, the pieces were discharged by firing a musket into the vent of each. In this manner twelve rounds were fired into the enemy when a section of artillery came up and the guns were turned over to its commander.

A PROFITABLE RECONNOISSANCE

CAPTAIN Augustus Merrill, of Company B, First Maine Veteran Infantry, relates in the following interesting manner how sixty-four rebels were captured by a small body of skirmishers:

"After entering the enemy's works on the morning of April 2, 1865, Lieutenant-Colonel S. C. Fletcher, commanding the First Maine Veteran Infantry, ordered me to advance with a few volunteers to ascertain the enemy's position and strength in our front.

"I took twenty men, deployed them as skirmishers, and advanced through the woods, coming upon an old camp. Here I captured a lieutenant and three men belonging to Hill's Corps, who informed me that slight resistance would be made 'this side of Hatcher's Run.'

"When our line advanced I pressed on, meeting no opposition, picking up the rebel stragglers and sending them to the rear, until I reached Hatcher's Run and found that the enemy were in position on the opposite side. Supposing that the corps was following in that direction, and not having very definite instructions, I determined to dislodge the Confederates from their position if possible. To my left was the bridge over which the telegraph road runs, defended by strong works on the other side. Near the bridge was an old wooden mill. With a small party of men who volunteered for the occasion, and who belonged to five or six different regiments of this corps, I moved along the run to the right through the woods, my left flank on the run. The eagerness of the men induced me to keep on some distance. We came to an old dam, where we discovered indications that a crossing had been made that morning, and immediately moved over by the left flank, the enemy firing a few shots as we crossed. It was a dangerous place; one man fell into the run, but came out safely, however, minus his musket, leaving me fifteen armed men. With these I advanced and captured the skirmish line, firing but a few shots. Guarding the prisoners closely, I moved on and soon came upon a rebel guard surrounding Captain John Tifft, Ninth New York Artillery. We captured the guard and released the captain, making the number of prisoners we had thus far taken sixty-four, mostly Virginia sharpshooters, who told of their various raids on our picket line during the winter, and acted as though they would like to overpower our small squad and march us off. I told them it would be useless to resist, as we had a large force in the rear, and their whole line would be taken. Two of my men then reconnoitered the woods and came to the open field, where they found a line of battle behind the enemy's works facing the Second Corps. Their left then rested on Hatcher's Run, we being directly behind them. I took the prisoners across the run and marched them to the rear without being molested by the enemy. The

"I CAPTURED A LIEUTENANT AND THREE MEN."

reconnoissance was a complete success in that the information gained proved of much value to our commander.

"Three of the men, who upon my request had volunteered to remain and watch the movements of the enemy, captured five more prisoners, making our total sixty-nine. A receipt for sixty-four was given me by the sergeant of the provost-guard, Second Division, and the three other men got credit for the capture of five."

LANGUAGE MORE FORCEFUL THAN ELEGANT

As a soldier Private John Lilley, of Company F, Two hundred and fifth Pennsylvania Infantry, was as good a fighter as he was emphatic in his speech. When there was an act of daring to be done on the field of battle, Lilley was certain to volunteer; when a bit of repartee or a cuss-word more expressive than choice passed around among the members of the regiment it could always be traced to Lilley as the original source. Both of these qualities gave him a certain standing among his comrades, and served him well in an incident at Petersburg, Va., April 2, 1865, which won for him unstinted praise.

JOHN LILLEY,
Private, Co. F, 205th Penn. Inf.
Born in Oliver Township, Mifflin County, Pa.

The signal to charge had been given and the troops, among them the Two hundred and fifth Pennsylvania, rushed forward. Three fortifications were taken with great impetuosity and in quick succession. The Two hundred and fifth charged on a fourth fortification. Presently the discovery was made that all of the commissioned officers were remaining behind and the men at once fell back, but Private Lilley who was in the lead, refused to follow suit.

"What?" he shouted, "Go back? Not by a damned sight! I don't care whether there are any officers with us or not. See that flag? I'm going to have that or croak."

The colors he referred to were those on the rebel works, and, suiting the action to his words, Lilley rushed on until he found himself at the side of the rebel color-bearer. In an instant the private had his bayonet pointed at the rebel's breast.

"You damned reb, surrender, or I'll blow you to hell!"

The suddenness of Lilley's appearance and attack amidst the smoke of the rifle fire so completely unnerved the rebel that he stammered out:

"Yank, for God's sake, don't shoot!"

Several others who were near by were also awed by Lilley's sudden appearance and emphatic command, and when he said: "Give me that flag, and the rest of you throw down your guns, or I'll make you think hell has broke loose," the color-bearer and his companions wilted and complied with his request.

Lilley then stepped to their rear, and, with the captured flag in hand, said:

"Now march, and if you all don't keep up a step that will be a credit to you and your lost cause, I'll fill you full of Yankee lead!"

By a running fire of his choicest cuss-words Lilley kept the men going at a lively gait in the direction of the fortification last captured, when presently and to his surprise he found that there was not a Union soldier to be seen. The rebels, too, noticed the absence of Union soldiers, took courage, stopped and refused to go on.

"What?" exclaimed Lilley raising his gun, "You think you can monkey with me?" Here Lilley again brought into play his whole battery of oaths, and they rolled from his mouth with such ease. and vehemence that this fire of oaths rather than his raised rifle cowed the poor rebels into submission and they again sullenly resumed the march.

"Now," said Lilley, "don't you damned rebs try to monkey with me again, or by thunder I'll shoot every one of you!"

This last speech had its effect upon the men and no further rupture occurred until they had gone about half way to the fort, when a Union officer, coming out from his shelter, commanded Lilley to hand over the flag.

"Like hell I will!" exclaimed the plucky private, suspecting that credit for capturing it was coveted by the lieutenant.

"I am your superior officer and demand that flag," repeated the lieutenant, with a supercilious air.

Flushed with anger and losing his temper, Lilley pointed his gun at him and said: "I'll be damned if you get this flag!" and without further ado he marched his prisoners past the lieutenant to the fort, where he turned the captured trophy over to his colonel. He was about to make a little speech in his characteristic fashion, but the colonel, anticipating a flow of language punctuated with choice oaths, waved his hand and smilingly said: "That's all right, Lilley, you're a brave fellow; you are relieved from duty for the day and you shall be otherwise rewarded for your brave conduct."

SAVED BY HIS HORSE

JAMES K. PEIRSOL,
Sergeant, Co. F, 13th Ohio Cav.
Born in Pennsylvania, Sept., 1843.

IN THE last race of the Army of the Potomac, ending at Appomattox, Va., Sergeant James K. Peirsol, Company F, Thirteenth Regiment Ohio Volunteer Cavalry, was acting as sergeant-major of the regiment in the absence of the officer holding that rank. After participating in the two battles of Dinwiddie Court House and Five Forks this regiment with the rest of the cavalry swung along on the left flank of Lee's retreating army until they reached Jettersville, on the Richmond & Danville Railroad, forty-five miles from Petersburg. Lee was then at Amelia Court House, a few miles up the railroad toward Richmond.

On the morning of April 5th, General Davies' Brigade of cavalry moved over to a

Jettersville, Va.—The First Brigade, Second Division of Sheridan's Cavalry Corps, under command of General Davies, in its pursuit of Lee's fleeing army, encountered the Confederates on the morning of April 6, 1865, near Jettersville, Va., where the Union forces captured a wagon train and a battery of artillery. In the afternoon this brigade again went into action to repel an attempt made by the enemy to reach Jettersville from Amelia Springs, eight miles distant, and resisted every attack made by the enemy, with but small loss.

road farther west and captured some wagons and a battery of artillery that were moving out to escape on that road. The Confederates attacked him, and the Third Brigade of the division, to which the Thirteenth Ohio belonged, was sent to his assistance. After reaching the field word came that the enemy were advancing on Jettersville by way of the railroad. The Thirteenth, with some other regiments, was hurried back to meet this attack. When the railroad was reached another Federal regiment was formed some forty rods in front. While the Thirteenth was forming its line, the Confederate cavalry charged from a woods upon the regiment in front. It scattered and disappeared. The Thirteenth was ordered to counter-charge, and was followed and supported by a Pennsylvania regiment. The charge was made with drawn sabres and at full gallop, driving the enemy into the woods and along the dirt road parallel with the railroad, where Peirsol captured a fleeing horseman and sent him under guard to the rear.

After pursuing the rebels for some distance, there was a general slacking up for the purpose of re-forming the line, when Lieutenant Hiram Platt, of the Pennsylvania regiment, dashed up, and swinging his sword, said: "Come on boys; we can drive them." "Well," said Peirsol, "I'll

"FLINGING HIMSELF ON THE HORSE'S NECK TO ESCAPE THE WHIZZING BULLETS."

go as far as you do." Platt was accompanied by two others from his regiment and Peirsol by two from the Thirteenth. Being well mounted, they soon came up with the still fleeing enemy as they passed out of the woods to some cleared ground. Here the Confederates left the road and, crossing a fence to the left, rode to a little knoll, from which they could see re-enforcements coming near at hand, which stopped their retreat. The last of them to leave the road and leap the fence was the flag-bearer of an Alabama regiment. He was immediately followed by a sergeant of the Thirteenth Ohio, who was with Peirsol in pursuit. As this sergeant went over the fence his horse became unmanageable and ran away with him. Spurring his horse, Peirsol dashed over the fence and overtook the flag-bearer just as the latter reached his comrades, who were bunched together like a flock of sheep. Peirsol dropped the reins and seized the flag-staff with his left hand, raising his sword in his right to defend himself and his prize. But his horse fortunately obviated the necessity for further strife by wheeling and plunging furiously down the hill, Peirsol flinging himself on to the horse's neck to escape the whizzing bullets that flew over him. As they went over the fence into the road he lost his stirrups. With neither rein nor stirrups and encumbered with the flag and staff, his sabre and swinging carbine, he regained the shelter of the timber.

Two days later in a charge at the crossing of the river at High Bridge, near Farmville, Va., Peirsol received a gunshot wound, but refused to leave the regiment, and was present at the surrender of Lee's Army on the 9th of April at Appomattox. He was then sent with the flag to Washington, D. C., where he delivered it to the Secretary of War, and was rewarded with a lieutenant's commission and the Medal of Honor.

"I'LL STAY WITH YOU TILL YOU ARE SAFE"

STEPHEN E. CHANDLER,
Q. M.-Sergt., Co. A, 24th N. Y. Cav.
Born in Calhoun Co., Mich.,
Nov. 20, 1841.

"I owe my life to the undaunted courage and the persistency of Sergeant Stephen E. Chandler."

This statement is made by Corporal Eugene VanBuren, of Company A, Twenty-fourth New York Cavalry, who thus pays a splendid tribute to the sergeant of his company, and narrates the circumstances of the rescue as follows:

"On the afternoon of April 5, 1865, General Sheridan, wishing to ascertain the whereabouts of the enemy, ordered a reconnoissance in the direction of Paines Cross Roads. Our brigade was selected for this duty. The route we took led us through a wooded country which was considerably cut up by hills and valleys, and near Amelia Springs, the fashionable summer resort of the south, we saw from the summit of a hill Lee's wagon-train in the distance.

"We soon found a cross-road not much wider than a bridle path, which we followed down through a valley, then across a stream and up the hill on the opposite side. Just as we neared the top of the hill we ran into a battery of five new Armstrong guns which we captured before they could fire a shot; and at the summit we found the wagon-train.

"Flankers were sent out in different directions, while the main body of the brigade 'went through' a couple of miles of the train. Judging from appearances the train was at a standstill at the time we struck it, as fires were burning all along the line with skillets and frying pans on them, in which 'hoe-cake' and other kinds of food were being cooked by the drivers and train escort; but all was abandoned in their hurry to escape. Everything in sight was captured. Orders were given to fall back to the point where we captured the battery and we started on the return march, but we were somewhat hampered by our prisoners, a few of our men who had been wounded and by being compelled to drag along the captured guns. Our progress was retarded to such an extent that the enemy's cavalry began to crowd us, and it was found necessary to form a line of battle in an open field near Amelia Springs.

"No sooner was the line of battle formed than a rebel cavalry division made its appearance, and when at a distance of forty rods opened fire. In the subsequent fighting quite a number were wounded, among them Lieutenant-Colonel Richards, who commanded our regiment, and I. Sergeant Chandler's horse was struck in the forehead by a ball, the sergeant himself narrowly escaping death. He removed his personal effects from the saddle and hastened to the assistance of the wounded colonel. I saw him and said: 'For God's sake, Chan, help me off the field. I'm wounded and can't walk.' He at once came to my aid, and after examining my wound said: 'Let's get out of this as quickly as we can and go to some place where we can get help, or you'll bleed to death.' He helped me to my feet and we started for the rear. About this time the regiment was ordered to fall back to a new position, leaving Chandler and me between the fires. The bullets flew like hail around us. 'Chan,' I said, 'you will be shot or taken prisoner. I've got my death wound anyway. You'd better lay me down and save yourself.'

"'I'll never do that,' his reply was. 'No, my boy, I'll stay with you till you are safe or we both go down.'

"A cavalry regiment of the enemy attempted to charge our men and were driven to the cover of the woods. Bullets were whistling over our heads and around us from both directions. How we ever escaped being riddled is more than I can tell. However, we struggled along slowly, I being too weak to go any faster. After much difficulty we finally reached the rear, where the regimental surgeon bandaged my wound, which stopped the flow of blood to some extent. Just then our men were compelled to fall back once more.

"Chandler took me by the arm and helped me along for a short distance, when I became so greatly exhausted that I could walk no farther. I despaired completely. 'Chan,' I said again, 'go on now; save yourself. I can't hold out any longer.' I laid down, but Chandler remained and sat down at my side. I pleaded with him to give up all further attempts to save me and think of his own safety. 'You've done enough for me. See how those bullets are flying again. Protect your own life; I can't live anyway.'

"THEY WERE HANGING ON TO THE BUGGY TO KEEP IT OFF THE HORSE'S HEELS."

"Just then a cavalryman whose horse was played out came along. Chandler asked him to let him have the animal and he complied cheerfully: 'You can have her, certainly. She's played out. I can go faster on foot. Chandler now helped me on the horse. I laid down over the pommel of the saddle, and thus we started along at a slow gait, Chandler constantly urging the horse forward. Soon after we were joined by Privates John Smith and George Back, of our company, who walked at the horse's side and held on to me, while Chandler led the horse.

"The enemy, outnumbering our forces, had by this time gotten on our flank and tried to cut us off, keeping up a terrific fire. Chandler found a stretcher, I can't remember where, and I, being then too weak to ride any farther, was placed on it and carried, Chandler keeping up the courage of his comrades by joking about the poor marksmanship of the Johnnies.

"Passing a farm barn they found an old buggy. Again I was removed and placed in the vehicle, so that I lay flat on my back with my feet dangling down at the rear.

"They were about to start off with me, hauling the buggy by hand, when Chandler, who was untiring in his efforts for my comfort, obtained a horse from a wounded cavalryman. Securing a collar and a pair of hames from the barn he hitched the animal to the wagon by means of pieces of rope used for traces.

"By this time the rebels were close upon us. They shouted 'Halt!' and fired at us, but Chandler set the improvised though none too comfortable ambulance in motion and off we started, over ditches and across fields, as fast as the horse could travel, the boys at some places where we were going down hill hanging to the buggy to keep it off the horse's heels.

"In this manner we soon reached a place of safety, where I found proper medical care and treatment. I certainly owe my life to the courage and persistency of my brave sergeant."

Lee's Surrender.—On the morning of the 3d of April, after the fall of Petersburg, the flight of the Confederate army and its pursuit began about the same time. Lee pushed toward Amelia Court House, Sheridan pushed for the Danville Road, keeping near the Appomattox River, followed by Meade with the Second and Sixth Corps, while Ord moved for Burkeville along the South Side Road; the Ninth Corps stretched along the road behind him. On the 4th Sheridan struck the Danville Road near Jettersville, where he learned that Lee was at Amelia Court House. He immediately entrenched himself and awaited the arrival of General Meade, who reached there next day. General Ord reached Burkeville on the evening of the 5th. On the morning of the 6th it was found that Lee was moving west of Jettersville toward Danville. Sheridan moved with his cavalry to strike his flank, followed by the Sixth Corps, while the Second and Fifth pressed hard after, forcing him to abandon several hundred wagons and several pieces of artillery. General Ord advanced, in the meantime from Burkeville toward Farmville, where Lee's column was detained by General Read with a small force of infantry and cavalry. In the afternoon Sheridan struck the enemy south of Sailors' Creek, and detained him until the Sixth Corps got up, when a general attack was made, which resulted in the capture of 6,000 prisoners.

Lee's chances of escape were now growing less and less, and on the 7th Grant opened communication with him, but while Grant was awaiting a reply, Lee kept up his retreat and thus gained a night's march. On the 8th Grant continued the pursuit. Sheridan gained Appomattox Station and cut off Lee's supplies, as well as his way of escape, and on the 9th General Lee requested a suspension of hostilities and an interview with Grant, which resulted in the surrender of Lee's Army of Northern Virginia.

HUMOR, PERSISTENCY, GALLANTRY

EDWARD P. TOBIE,
Sergeant-Major, 1st Me. Cav.
Born at Lewiston, Me.,
March 19, 1838.

FRANCIS M. CUNNINGHAM,
First Sergeant, Co. H, 1st W. Va.
Vet. Cav.
Born in Somerset Co., Pa.,
Dec. 21, 1837.

HARRIS S. HAWTHORN,
Private, Co. F, 121st N. Y. Inf.
Born at Salem, N. Y., 1832.

"FOR six days we had been pounding at the rebels and for six days they had been pounding at us," says Sergeant Francis Marion Cunningham of Co. H, First West Virginia Cavalry. "In fact, the pounding seemed to be one of the most popular pastimes. It was on the afternoon of April 6th that we again came up with them in a strong position on the thickly wooded banks of Sailor's Creek. They were behind rude fortifications and the thick growth of underbrush kept their numbers concealed from us. We didn't know how many rebels there were in those ditches until we charged. Then we got the information in the most convincing manner all along our line. I was one of the men lowered to terra firma swiftly, my fine black charger being killed under me. We were repulsed, and as we fell back over logs and interleaving vines, the rebel volleys continued thinning out the ranks. Men and beasts were floundering together in the dense thicket.

"I groped about with my eyes blinded with the smoke and fortunately bumped squarely into a phlegmatic mule with a Confederate saddle on. He was taking in the scenery in the most nonchalant manner and modifying the ennui of the situation by actually grazing there in that screaming pandemonium of exploding shells.

"His saddle was slippery with the life-blood of some luckless 'reb' who had fallen beneath one of our scattering volleys. There wasn't much time to talk the thing over with the mule. I mounted him and hurried back through the woods to the clearing, where our forces were rallying.

"In going back through the woods I made several observations pertinent to the disposition and qualifications of that mule. Of all his shining attainments two stood

---

Sailor's Creek.—When Richmond fell Lee's only chance lay in escape. He had ordered rations sent to Amelia Court House, but when his retreating troops arrived there on the 4th of April they found no food, and were compelled to forage through the already devastated country for nearly twenty-four hours. On the night of the 5th Lee made a new start from Amelia Court House in an endeavor to escape Grant and set out for Lynchburg. Continual fighting ensued en route on the 6th, but Lee suffered his greatest loss at Sailor's Creek, when Sheridan broke into his fugitive lines, captured Ewell's Corps and routed Gordon and his men in utter confusion. The Federal losses were 1,200 killed and wounded; the Confederate losses, 7,000 killed, wounded and taken prisoners.

out as conspicuously as his ears. He could run very fast and I think he must have broken his own record while I rode him.

"He could jump like a steeplechaser and he seemed rather to prefer taking a four-foot stump to passing around it.

"Just as I reached the rallying troops the bugle sounded 'Charge' again and back we went at those breastworks over stumps and through drooping branches. It took my mule just about four jumps to show that in an obstacle race he could outclass all others. He laid back his ears and frisked over logs and flattened out like a jackrabbit, when he had a chance to sprint. Soon I was ahead, far ahead

"SWITCHED HIS TAIL AND SAILED RIGHT OVER AMONG THE REBS."

of the rest of the boys. That mule never even stopped when he came to the breast-works. He switched his tail and sailed right over among the rebs, landing near a rebel color-bearer of the Twelfth Virginia Infantry.

"About all that I can remember of what followed was that the mule and I went after him. The color-bearer was a big brawny chap and he put up a game fight. But that mule had some new side steps and posterior upper-cuts that put the reb out of the game.

"A sabre slash across the right arm made him drop his colors and I grabbed them before they touched the ground."

The foregoing incident, humorously told by Sergeant Cunningham, was witnessed by General Custer, who was so delighted with the plucky cavalryman's valorous deed that he at once placed him on his staff, and later recommended him for the Medal of Honor. During his encounter with the color-bearer, Sergeant Cunningham was severely dealt with by rebels in the immediate vicinity, who succeeded in wounding him twice before he captured the rebel colors.

Sergeant-Major Edward P. Tobie's devotion to duty is exemplified by his conduct on the 6th of April at Sailor's Creek and on the 7th at Farmville.

Lieutenant T. Little, adjutant of the First Maine Cavalry, was wounded in the first charge of General Smith's Third Brigade on the 6th, and shortly after his successor, Lieutenant J. W. Poor, met a like fate, whereupon Colonel Cilly detailed Sergeant Tobie to assume the duties of adjutant. Just as the regiment started on the final charge that day which resulted so disastrously for the enemy a bullet pierced Tobie's foot and threw him to the ground. With great difficulty he hobbled to the rear, but upon recovering his horse, which had been caught by the colonel's orderly, he mounted it and started for the field hospital, where he had his wound bandaged. The surgeon advised him to stay in the rear, but finding his wound not to be serious he rejoined his regiment, reaching it in time to go on a scout through the woods. The regiment was on the march early next day, the plucky sergeant with it, and though his foot pained him greatly he did not hesitate and stay behind when the charge into the village of Farmville was made. He rode at the front of the second battalion with Major Hall, and dashing through the village put to rout a superior force of the enemy. In this charge Sergeant Tobie was again wounded, the bullet passing through his leg, killing his horse; but upon finding that the wound was not serious, he had it bandaged and a second time rejoined his regiment, having in the meantime procured another horse. That night found him with his regiment on its march to Appomattox, where for a third time he was, in a wounded condition, engaged with the enemy.

The One hundred and twenty-first New York Volunteer Infantry took an active part in the repulse of General Ewell's forces when they were endeavoring to recapture the wagon train Custer had taken only a few hours before, and one of its members, Private Harris S. Hawthorn, of Company F, greatly distinguished himself in the charge by capturing, single-handed, General Custis Lee. Because of the conspicuous nature of this capture Colonel Egbert Olcott, commanding the regiment, detailed Hawthorn as one of the men to conduct the noted rebel general to the headquarters of General Wheaton.

"See the Johnnies down there!" "Why doesn't the bugle sound the 'Charge'?" "You'll hear it soon enough." These were some of the remarks passed along the line as Custer's men stood 'to horse' at Sailor's Creek on the morning of April 6, 1865, and saw the enemy throw up breastworks of logs, rails and earth.

"Boys, you'll hear that bugle soon enough," said Captain Hugh P. Boon, of Company B, First West Virginia Cavalry, and soon the command came: "Mount, right dress, forward march."

CHARLES A. TAGGART,
Private, Co. B, 37th Mass. Inf.
Born at North Blanford,
Mass., Jan. 17, 1843.

LLEWELLYN P. NORTON,
Sergt., Co. L, 10th N. Y. Cav.
Highest rank attained :
Lieutenant-Colonel.
Born at Scott, N. Y., May 11,
1837.

HUGH P. BOON,
Capt., Co. B, 1st W. Va. Cav.
Born at Washington, Pa.,
July 28, 1834.

"When about 400 yards from the enemy's position," says Captain Boon, "the bugle sounded the charge, and away we went. When our line had reached the enemy's works I saw a battalion of their infantry a short distance to the right, and my command being on the extreme right I wheeled it out of line and charged the rebels. In the clash that followed I cut down the color-bearer and captured the colors of the Tenth Georgia Infantry ; but I admit I felt scared when I realized what I had done. Had I failed in checking and routing this rebel battalion I should, in all probability, have been cashiered and dishonorably dismissed the service for leaving the line of battle.

"But my action had been witnessed by one of the superior officers, who judged that I had acted correctly."

When General Davies' Brigade made a mounted charge on the enemy's breastworks, Sergeant Llewellyn P. Norton, of Company L, Tenth New York Cavalry, leaped his horse over the embankment and was one of the first to enter the Confederate works. The onslaught was terrific and many of the enemy threw down their weapons and surrendered, while others ran to the rear. Sergeant Norton pushed on in an effort to capture all the retreating rebels possible and soon came upon a detachment of six men working at a gun in a ravine about one hundred yards distant from General Ewell and his staff. Thinking that the men were attempting to spike the piece before retreating and that he might save it to the Union forces, he rode boldly toward them and ordered them to surrender. One of the men ran, but the remaining five, seizing their muskets with bayonets fixed, prepared to meet the assault of the brave cavalryman. With one upward stroke of his sabre he disarmed two of his antagonists, and before they could recover themselves he struck them to the ground.

At this juncture Corporal Andrew Bringle, of Co. F, came to his assistance and the rebels laid down their arms and surrendered. Bringle then took them to the rear, while Norton stood guard over the gun until after dark, when a team from General Davies' headquarters came after the piece and drew it off the field.

Sergeant Norton was promoted to sergeant-major and brevetted first lieutenant, and he and Bringle were awarded the Medal of Honor.

Singular in the records of the Medal of Honor is the fact that Sergeant Norton's medal could not be presented to him until May, 1888, although it had been awarded July 5, 1865. This happened because Norton's whereabouts after being mustered out could not be learned by the War Department. Only by mere chance Norton saw in Appleton's Cyclopedia that he was rewarded with a Medal of Honor, and prompt inquiry brought the much coveted decoration.

During a lull in the desperate hand-to-hand struggle of this memorable day, Private Charles A. Taggart, of Company B, Thirty-seventh Massachusetts Infantry, stepped out about twenty paces to the front of his regiment and up a slight rise of ground, from which place he saw a squad of about twenty rebels in a low, protected spot firing on the men to his right. Taking shelter behind a tree near by he fired several shots into their midst, when to his surprise he observed a rebel flag among them. Immediately he started for their color-bearer, demanding the surrender of the flag, which he grasped, and in the struggle for its possession he found himself assisted by another Union man, who had also seen the colors and who was intent upon their capture. The two wrested them from the rebel, but Taggart's comrade was shot down, while he, taking advantage of an opening, rushed back with the colors into the Union lines. Unfortunately the Federals took him for a leader of a rebel charge and it was miraculous that he escaped with but one slight wound on his right leg.

WILLIAM LUDGATE,
Capt., Co. G, 59th N. Y. Vet. Vols.
Highest rank att'd: Bvt.-Maj.
Born in London, Eng., in 1837.

A NOBLE SACRIFICE

CAPTAIN William Ludgate, of Co. G, Fifty-ninth New York Veteran Volunteers, was a prisoner of war for a period of two days. He was captured in the vicinity of Farmville, Va., April 7th, and released April 9th, when Lee surrendered his army.

The occasion on which Captain Ludgate lost his liberty was a fight near a railroad bridge, two miles from Farmville. General Barlow, commanding the First Brigade, Second Division, Second Army Corps, asked for an officer

Farmville, Va.—During the pursuit of Lee's Army General Ord advanced from Burkeville toward Farmville, sending two regiments of infantry and a squadron of cavalry, under Brevet Brigadier-General Theodore Read, to reach and destroy the bridges. This advance met the head of Lee's column near Farmville, which it heroically attacked and detained until General Read was killed and his small force overpowered. This caused a delay in the enemy's movements, and enabled General Ord to get well up with his force.

to volunteer with a small squad of men to prevent the enemy from burning the railroad bridge, as it was to serve the Union troops as a means of crossing the river.

Captain Ludgate volunteered for the duty and selected Lieutenant Bigley and twelve men from his company to go with him.

"After marching for about two miles," the captain narrates, "we came in sight of the railroad bridge. Owing to the steep bank, about twenty feet high on either side, I could not see anything of the enemy, and ordered my men to proceed to the bridge at a double-quick. Just then my attention was called to a Union soldier some distance away who was waving his flag frantically as a signal for us to return. The signal came too late, for the enemy had already opened fire from their protected position on the steep bank. Our men were completely taken by surprise, wavered and were about to retreat, when I managed to reassure and rally them.

"Some of the rebels, bolder than the others, ran down the embankment to the ravine where we were, eager to make the capture of our small squad. They met with disappointment; we captured every one of them. I then ordered my men to the top of the embankment and opened a fierce fire on the Confederates. Although we were finally surrounded on all sides by a force ten times larger than our own, my men stood their ground with heroic courage, never yielding an inch, making every shot tell and compelled to give in only when the last round of ammunition was expended. Then we surrendered, to be set free again two days later."

CAPTURE OF FORT BLAKELY

LOYD WHEATON,
Lieut.-Col., 8th Illinois Inf.
Highest rank attained:
Major-Gen., U. S. V.
Born in Calhoun Co., Mich.,
July 15, 1888.

HENRY C. MERRIAM,
Lieut.-Colonel, 73d U. S. C. T.
Highest rank attained:
Major-Gen., U. S. A.
Born in Maine, Nov. 13, 1837.

Fort Blakely, Ala., was a place inclosed by a line of works about two miles in extent, composed of redoubts constructed of earth and timber, with ditches in front, which redoubts connected by continuous rifle pits with salients and stockade work, making a continuous line from the Confederates' left, on the Tensas River, to their right, which rested on an impassable swamp and thicket. The two principal avenues of approach were known as the Stockton and Pensacola Roads. The redoubts commanded the ground in their front, and had an enfilading fire on portions of the roads and a cross-fire on almost every point of them within the range of their guns. Three

Fort Blakely.—The investment of Fort Blakely and Spanish Fort, Ala., was completed on the 5th of April, 1865, and was carried on until the afternoon of the 9th, when a concerted assault was made on Blakely by seven divisions under command of General R. S. Canby, which resulted in the capture of numerous flags, all the armament, material and supplies, and 3,700 prisoners, three of whom were generals, and 197 commissioned officers of lower grade. Prior to this assault, Spanish Fort was attacked and when it fell the Confederates, under cover of darkness, escaped to Blakely and Mobile.

marshy ravines, entering the works at different points, were obstructed by fallen timber and traversed by stockades which connected with the rifle pits on the other side. The fortifications were mounted with heavy and light guns. Three lines of abatis encircled the works, and outside of these were rifle pits for sharpshooters.

After a short siege this fort was assaulted and carried on the 9th of April, 1865. The time for the assault was set for 5:30 in the afternoon. Precisely at that hour Lieutenant-Colonel Victor Vifquain, commanding the Ninety-seventh Illinois Infantry, gave the command: "Forward, Ninety-seventh!" and with irresistible dash they advanced and sprang with him over the parapet, with loud cheers charging the line as skirmishers upon the enemy. Colonel Vifquain made for the rebel battle-flag on the works, with his color-company at his heels, and being the first man upon the works immediately cut the halyard with his sword and pulled it down, while his color-bearer planted the Union flag beside the rebel staff. For a moment Vifquain was hidden by the folds of the victorious banner mingling with those of the rebel standard and when he had freed himself from their folds he found his brave color-bearer lying by his side pierced with a bullet.

ENTERED THE EMBRASURE OF A 30-POUNDER PARROTT GUN.

The Eighth Illinois Infantry, commanded and led on the right wing by Lieutenant-Colonel Loyd Wheaton, in its assault upon the works dashed up the salient, from which a constant and fierce fire of artillery was kept up from a number of pieces, and about five minutes after the charge commenced the regiment ascended the parapet of the rebel works. Its brave colonel entered the embrasure of a thirty-pounder Parrott gun, accompanied by Sergeant Switzer of Company B, and was the first man of the regiment to enter the enemy's works. The firing of the guns was at an end as soon as he made his appearance, but the rebel infantry tried hard to maintain their ground and their fire was murderous.

HENRY C. NICHOLS,
Captain, Co. E, 73d U. S. C. T.
Born at Brandon, Vt., April 20, 1832.

"In front of my regiment, the Seventy-third U. S. Colored Infantry, Lieutenant-Colonel Merriam commanding," says Captain Henry C. Nichols, of Company C, "was the enemy's outer works—an abatis—and at the roots of the trees of which the abatis was formed was a line of rifle pits occupied by the enemy for the protection of the fort, on which were mounted six heavy guns, and two mortars in the rear. Between our pits and the abatis was a muddy ravine with a small brook at the bottom, a sharp descent from our pits to the brook, then a plain, gradually ascending to the fort. About five o'clock, Colonel Merriam ordered an assault on the outer works by four companies, which was made in fine style, driving the enemy into their main works.

"The fire from the fort was terrific, and was kept up after the assault, in an attempt to dislodge our men who were lying down on our side of the abatis, quite exposed. It was at this time that I volunteered to make a reconnoissance, the colonel wishing to know the nature of the ground he was about to charge over. I ran down into the ravine and reaching the left of the abatis stopped to get my breath. After resting about a minute I climbed into the branches of a tree and surveyed the field with my glasses. I found the ground favorable for the assault, and returning to my command on a run reported to this effect to the colonel.

SAMUEL McCONNEL,
Captain, Co. H, 119th Ill. Inf.

"Colonel Merriam then obtained permission to charge the main works—the fort—and made the assault, followed five or ten minutes later by the rest of the colored division, capturing the works on a run. The ground we traversed and which I had explored had been planted with torpedoes, but this arrangement of the enemy I was not able to detect while on my reconnoissance."

Captain Samuel McConnell, of Company H, One hundred and nineteenth Illinois Infantry, tells in the following interesting manner how he captured a Confederate flag in this battle:

"I had orders to lead the regiment with my company, our formation for the assault being in double rank, one rank about six paces behind the other, with the line of battle coming up fifty paces in the rear.

"In this order we advanced against the fort, the bullets and shells mowing down our companions with merciless precision. My clothing was cut in several places by bullets, and when I reached the breastworks I had only one man of my company, Private Wagner, with me. The others went over a little distance away from us. At the point where we reached the breastworks was an angle containing three large

THOMAS H. L. PAYNE,
1st Lieut.-Quartermaster,
37th Ill. Vols.
Highest rank attain'd: Capt.
Born at Boston, Mass. Oct.
5, 1840.

guns, which were dealing out death at an alarming rate, and making the atmosphere so smoky that we could see for only a short distance. Nevertheless we at once began to scale the breastwork, and had almost reached the top when the guns were run out for another discharge. We were so close to the muzzles of the guns that when they were discharged the air pressure thus created knocked us back into the ditch. But we immediately sprang up and managed to climb over the works before the rebels could reload.

"Seeing us come over the breastwork, the gunners turned and fled, and some surrendered, leaving us in undisputed possession.

"We started to our left and soon came in rear of what seemed to be a color-guard with a flag. When within about thirty paces they faced about and fired on us, but their shots missed. I then fired the last shot from my revolver, hitting the color-bearer, and as the rest fled, rushed up and captured the colors.

"Down at Mobile, Ala., I was decorated with the Medal of Honor in the presence of my regiment in front of General Smith's headquarters, and I enjoy the pleasant sensations of that day yet."

First Lieutenant Thomas H. L. Payne, quartermaster of the Thirty-seventh Illinois Infantry, not wishing to remain behind during the assault on the fort, asked to be assigned to the command of Company B, which was without a commissioned officer. He says:

"When the bugle sounded we rose out of our rifle pits. Having advanced our lines the preceding night, we were about five hundred yards from the fort, and before the rebels could depress their guns sufficiently to train them upon us we had pressed forward and were well across the open space, had reached the fort and were climbing as best we could upon it.

"We had to climb over lines of brush and trees piled very high and then across a wide, deep, dry moat, filled with brush, before we could get a foothold on the works. All the ground over which we charged was covered with hidden torpedoes, making it doubly dangerous. I struck out for a corner of the earthworks, shouting, 'This way, Company B!' and luckily found a place where a fallen tree formed a foot-bridge across the moat. I crossed upon this and a few of my company followed. In a minute I found myself inside the works within a few feet of a number of Confederate gunners. I ordered them to surrender as the boys came rushing along, and they actually seemed glad to do so. I think that perhaps for a couple of minutes I was the only man of our regiment upon or within the works.

"As our color-bearer, Sergeant Morrell, could not get upon the works, I took the flag from him, planted it on the side of the fort and held it until he climbed up, and thus the flag of the Thirty-seventh Illinois was the first on the fort."

BOLD CAPTURE OF THE BRIDGE

"WE LEFT Gravelly Springs, Ala., some time about the middle of March, 1865, on the Wilson Raid in pursuit of General Forrest," Private Richard H. Cosgriff, of Company L, Fourth Iowa Cavalry, narrates, "and overtook him at Selma, Ala. After a brisk engagement we drove him from there to Montgomery and thence to Columbus, Ga., on the Chattahoochee River, where he fortified himself.

"There were three bridges across the river. Forrest had burned two of them, leaving one for the use of his army, in case of retreat, as part of his force was on the Alabama side of the river, intrenched opposite Columbus.

"The remaining bridge was a wooden affair, covered with a partition running through it lengthwise. The Alabama side, on which we were posted, was protected by earthworks manned

RICHARD H. COSGRIFF,
Private, Co. L, 4th Iowa Cav.
Born at Dunkirk, N. Y.,
1845.

by infantry. At the Columbus end two pieces of artillery were planted to prevent a capture by our troops, while the structure itself was guarded by about 150 men and piled with inflammable material, ready to be fired.

"We arrived opposite Columbus on the night of April 16th, and commenced an attack on the earthworks at the left of the bridge. Our object was to cross the river to Columbus, and in order to do so it was necessary to first capture the bridge. This had to be done by surprising the sentinels who guarded it, for should we have carried the earthworks first they would have set fire to the bridge at once and thus block our game.

"About ten o'clock that night General Wilson called for two hundred volunteers to make an assault and I stepped into line with those who responded to the call.

Wilson's Raid.—In March, 1865, two well equipped cavalry expeditions were sent out from Thomas' Department in Tennessee; one under General James H. Wilson to operate in Alabama, the other under General George Stoneman to cut off Lee's last avenue of escape. Wilson's Raid, which began on the 23d of March, included engagements and skirmishes at Trion, Centreville, Bogler's Creek and Plantersville, Ala., and the battle near **Selma, Ala.,** where Wilson fought Forrest, defeating him and taking 3,000 prisoners. On the 2d of April Wilson captured Selma, destroying the arsenal for arms and military stores. From here the raid continued until the 23d, Wilson devastating everything in his course. His losses during this raid were less than 700 in killed and wounded, while the Confederates lost 1,200 killed and wounded and nearly 7,000 taken prisoners.

We were ordered to ride over the two lines of earthworks in front of the brigade at full speed and not fire a shot, but dash on and capture the guard on the bridge.

"We did as ordered and went right over the breastworks. Here we dismounted, turned our horses loose, rushed on to the bridge and captured the guards before they knew who we were.

Then taking half a dozen of the prisoners we marched them across ahead of about fifty of us and told them that if they uttered a word or gave any alarm we would shoot them down, and furthermore they were ordered to give the guard at the other end of the bridge the countersign.

"It was a very dark night and under the covered bridge it was impossible to distinguish 'Yank' from 'Johnny.' Our prisoners acted according to our instructions and when they gave the countersign we pushed them aside and rushed for the guns, and, though surprised, the rebels gave us a sharp hand-to-hand fight for about fifteen minutes. One of my opponents was the color-bearer, who fought hard to save his colors, but I succeeded in downing him and seized the flag. We drove them back and captured the two guns, which we found to be double-shotted, but they never got a chance to fire them."

A SUCCESSFUL MISSION OF DESTRUCTION

CHARLES M. BETTS,
Lieutenant-Colonel, 15th Penn. Cav.
Born in Bucks Co., Pa., Aug. 9, 1888.

"A BOUT the middle of April, 1865," says Lieutenant-Colonel Charles M. Betts, of the Fifteenth Pennsylvania Cavalry, "General William J. Palmer had arrived at Salem, N. C., with a portion of his cavalry division, among which were two battalions of our regiment under command of Major Garner and Captain Kramer, and shortly thereafter General Palmer directed me to attempt the destruction of a railroad bridge north of Greensboro, as well as a factory to the south engaged in the manufacture of fire-arms for the Confederacy. Greensboro was some seventy-five miles east of Salem, and was occupied by a rebel force estimated at 5,000, whose attention it would be necessary to divert to accomplish the work assigned to me.

"'Boots and saddles' was soon sounded and we started off in the early evening accompanied by a guide. About two o'clock A. M. I detached Major Garner with the most of his command to destroy the bridge north, and directed Captain Kramer to take his battalion and capture and burn the factory. Retaining about ninety men with me I advanced to make a demonstration against Greensboro.

"Soon after daylight, when within a few miles of the place, I learned from a negro in the field that a portion of Johnson's Third South Carolina Cavalry was

"THEY BROKE AND FLED TO A NEIGHBORING MEADOW."

encamped about half a mile to our right, the balance scouting to ascertain the whereabouts of the Yankee cavalry, of whose approach they had been apprised. The rebel camp was in an open wood on the left of a road running at right angles to the main road which led from Salem to Greensboro, and adjoining this road was a meadow separated from the woods by a sharp declivity and a fence. The command had no pickets out, depending on their scouting parties to notify them of any danger, and were then cooking breakfast. After a short conference with Adjutant Reiff and Lieutenant Beck, who, I believe, were the only officers of the party besides myself, I detailed a sergeant with ten men having good horses to take the advance and charge when in sight of the camp, making all the noise possible, the balance to follow in support. Those who had horses unfit to charge were instructed to barricade the main road where we turned to the right to reach the camp, and to protect our rear.

"We made the charge, surprised the camp, and after the exchange of some shots the enemy broke and fled to the neighboring meadow, which we reached by moving out to the main road. There they had cover from a deep ditch, but being threatened with 'no quarter without surrender,' they threw down their arms and were taken prisoners.

"After eating what they had prepared, we cut the wheels of their wagons, destroyed what arms and equipage they had, and mounted the prisoners on the poorest horses, taking their fresh ones in exchange. Upon drawing them up in line I found I had almost as many prisoners as I had men in my command. I told them that our guard had instructions to shoot without notice anyone attempting to escape, and moved my force and prisoners out to the main road. We fed our horses, and waited long enough for the rebel force at Greensboro to be informed of our presence by any that might have escaped, thereby hoping to prevent them sending any of their force to oppose our battalions north and south.

"I had been instructed to attempt the destruction of a small railroad bridge on the outskirts of Greensboro, and sent Sergeant Seldon L. Wilson and a detail of ten men with good horses on this mission. He succeeded in burning the bridge and without loss rejoined the command the same night at Salem.

"When starting back I detached Sergeant Strickler with ten men for advance guard to attack vigorously any force in front, placing a like number in our rear to drive off anything coming in that direction. This left me about fifty men to guard nearly twice that number of prisoners. We were twice threatened by small parties of rebel cavalry on the road, but drove them off without difficulty. When we reached the rendezvous where the two battalions were to meet us we found only Kramer's. He had destroyed the factory with many stands of arms in process of manufacture, and like myself was loaded down with prisoners. Major Garner rejoined the command before night, having accomplished all that was assigned to him without loss."

WAR OF THE REBELLION—SUMMARY

Volume I of Deeds of Valor would be incomplete without a summary of the War of the Rebellion, and in the following review the compass of the struggle for the preservation of the Union is given in as concise form as is consistent with a clear understanding of the struggle from its beginning to its end.

In 1850 South Carolina brought many of the southern states to the belief that a state might secede from the Union without violating the constitution, and finally, in 1860, after Lincoln's election, she led the movement of secession followed by five other states.

The slave population of the United States was at that time 4,000,000 and its money valuation something like $2,500,000,000, and the soul of the southern revolution of 1861 was historically the zeal of founding a new or reunited union of States whose corner-stone should be negro slavery—the subjugation of the colored to the white race as a normal and natural condition. The slaveholder believed in the righteousness of his system, and rather than readjust economic and industrial conditions he would break up the Union. Such was the social system of principles of the cotton-planting states that set the insurrection in motion. These states, after Lincoln's election, made no effort to conceal the fact that men were being enlisted and national forts and public property were being seized.

In February, 1861, the "Confederate States of America" were organized with Jefferson Davis as President and the first session of the provisional government levied war on the United States by acts authorizing the raising of 100,000 military volunteers and organizing the Army of the Confederate States.

After the fall of Fort Sumter, in Charleston Harbor, April 12, 1861, the first action between Northern and Southern forces, and President Lincoln's call for troops, war was recognized as existing by the Confederate government and a new bill was passed for volunteer troops in addition to those already enlisted.

From this time on until the surrender of Lee's Army of Northern Virginia, April 9, 1865, the fierce struggle for supremacy was carried on, in which, during the four years of fighting, the waning fortunes of the Confederacy became a lost cause.

Following the surrender of Lee's army that of Johnston's was expected, but not until the 14th did Johnston under a flag of truce send Sherman a proposal to suspend hostilities long enough for the civil authorities to arrange a peace. Terms of surrender of Johnston's army were agreed upon between the two generals, but the conditions given Johnston were so much better than those accorded Lee that the capitulation thus arranged was disapproved at Washington. Later, on the 25th, the terms of surrender were arranged on the same basis as Lee's, and Johnston's army, inclusive of the troops operating in Georgia and Florida, surrendered.

General Canby, who commanded the Union forces in the Gulf, had in March opened a campaign against Mobile, in co-operation with a naval fleet under Admiral Thatcher, and captured that place on the 11th of April. On the 4th of May he arranged with the Confederate, Taylor, the capitulation of all the armies east of the Mississippi River not already paroled. The Confederate forces west of the Mississippi were commanded by General E. Kirby Smith, upon whom Davis fixed his last hopes after Lee and Johnston had surrendered, and who, after one more skirmish near Brazos, Tex., surrendered his whole army to Canby at New Orleans on the 26th of May. Thus ended the military strife for the preservation of the Union, and, apropos, the capture of Davis by Union cavalry scouts on the 10th of May terminated the Southern Confederacy in its civil embodiment.

During this prolonged struggle the Northern Army was commanded successively by Major-General Winfield Scott until November 1, 1861; Major-General George B. McClellan until March 11, 1862; Major-General Henry W. Halleck until March 12, 1864; and Lieutenant-General Ulysses S. Grant, who successfully brought the war to a close by his persistent "hammering," coupled with his wonderful generalship. These commanding generals had under them, commanding the several armies and the twenty-five army corps, such men as Sherman, Sheridan, Burnside, Rosecrans, Meade, Humphreys, Warren, Wright, Parke, Ord and Weitzel.

The Confederate armies on the other hand were commanded by Generals Robert E. Lee, the two Johnstons, Joseph E. and Albert S., Early, Longstreet, "Stonewall" Jackson, Hood and Ewell.

The scope of Deeds of Valor does not include any but those heroic deeds for which the Medal of Honor was awarded, but great credit is due to all the soldiers who participated in the War of the Rebellion for their noble work in defending the Union; and to the departed heroes who laid down their lives on the battlefield, many of whom performed deeds of a most valorous and distinguished nature, and who, had they survived their heroic acts, would undoubtedly have received recognition at the hands of the Government by the award of the Medal of Honor.

The number of men enlisted in the Federal Army during the war by periods of service was as follows:

For 60 days	2,045	For 1 year	393,706
" 90 "	108,416	" 2 years	44,400
" 100 "	85,807	" 3 "	2,028,630
" 4 months	42	" 4 "	1,042
" 6 "	26,118		
" 8 "	373	Aggregate enlistments	2,780,478
" 9 "	89,899		

The strength of the Federal Army was:

January 1, 1861	16,367	January 1, 1865	959,460
" " 1862	575,917	March 31, 1865	980,086
" " 1863	918,191	May 1, 1865	100,516
" " 1864	860,737		

ILLUSTRATIONS

TITLES

MEDAL OF HONOR WINNERS MENTIONED

MEDAL OF HONOR WINNERS

The following four pages are devoted to the names and ranks of men who won their Medal of Honor during the great War of the Rebellion and whose names have not already been mentioned. The grounds of award differ in the individual cases, but they all properly come under the general head of "For distinguished gallantry in action outside the line of duty."

ADAMS, JAMES F.
Priv., Co. D., 1st W. Va. Cav.
ALBER, FREDERICK
Priv., Co. A, 17th Mich. Inf.
AMMERMAN, ROBERT W.
Corp., Co. K, 39th Ill. Inf.
ALLEN, ABNER P.
Priv., Co. B, 148th Pa. Inf.
AMES, ADELBERT
1st Lieut., 5th U. S. Art.
ANDERSON, CHARLES W.
Priv., Co. K., 1st N. Y. Cav.
ANDERSON, FREDERICK C.
Priv., Co. A, 18th Mass. Inf.
ANDERSON, THOMAS
Corp., Co. I, 1st W. Va. Cav.
APPLE, ANDREW O.
Corp., Co. I, 12th W. Va. Inf.
APPLETON, WILLIAM H.
1st Lieut., Co. H, 4th U. S. C. T
ARCHER, JAMES W.
1st Lieut., 59th Ind. Inf.
ARCHER, LESTER
Sergt., Co. E, 96th N. Y. Inf.
ARNOLD, ABRAHAM K.
Capt., 5th U. S. Cav.
AVERY, WILLIAM B.
Capt., 1st N. Y. Marine Art.
BABCOCK, WILLIAM J.
Sergt., Co E. 2d R. I. Inf.
BACON, ELIJAH W.
Priv., Co. F, 14th Conn. Inf.
BAIRD, ABSOLOM
Brig.-Gen., U. S. Vols.
BANKS, GEORGE L.
Sergt., Co. C. 15th Ind. Inf.
BARKER, NATHANIEL C.
Sergt., Co. E, 11th N. H. Inf.

BARNES, WILLIAM H.
Priv., Co. C, 38th U. S. C. T.
BARNUM, HENRY A.
Col., 149th N. Y. Inf.
BARRELL, CHARLES L.
1st Lieut., Co. C, 102d U. S. C. T
BARRY, AUGUSTUS
Sergt. Maj., 16th U. S. Inf.
BATCHELDER, RICHARD N.
Lieut.-Co. and Chief Q. M.
2d Corps.
BATES, NORMAN F.
Sergt., Co. E, 4th Iowa Cav.
BAYBUTT, PHILIP
Priv., Co. A, 2d Mass. Cav.
BEATTIE, ALEXANDER M.
Capt., Co. F, 3d Vt. Inf.
BEATY, POWHATAN
1st Sergt., Co. G, 5th U. S. C.
BEAUFORT, JEAN J.
Corp., Co. B, 8th U. S. Cav.
BEBB, EDWARD J.
Priv., Co. D, 4th Iowa Cav.
BEDDOWS, RICHARD
Priv., 34th N. Y. Battery.
BEGLEY, TERRENCE
Sergt., Co. D, 7th N.Y.H.A.
BELCHER, THOMAS
Priv., Co. I, 9th Me. Inf.
BENJAMIN, JOHN F.
Corp., Co. M, 2d N. Y. Cav.
BENJAMIN, SAMUEL N.
1st Lieut., 2d U. S. Art.
BENEDICT, GEORGE G.
2d Lieut., Co. C. 12th Vt. Inf.
BENNETT, ORREN
Priv., Co. D, 141st Pa. Inf.

BENYAURD, WILLIAM H. H.
Capt., Corps of Engs., U. S. A.
BEYER, HILLARY
1st Lieut., Co. H, 90th Pa. Inf.
BIEGER, CHARLES
Priv., Co. B, 4th Mo. Cav.
BINGHAM, HENRY H.
Capt., Co. G, 140th Pa. Inf.
BIRDSALL, HORATIO L.
Sergt., Co. D, 3d Iowa Cav.
BISHOP, FRANCIS A.
Priv., Co. C, 57th Pa. Inf.
BLACK, WILLIAM P.
Capt., Co. K, 37th Ill. Inf.
BLICKENSDERFER, MILTON
Corp., Co. E, 126th Ohio Inf.
BLODGETT, WELLS H.
1st Lieut., Co. D, 37th Ill. Inf.
BLUCHER, CHARLES
Corp., Co. H, 188th Pa. Inf.
BONNAFFON, SYLVESTER, J
1st Lieut., Co. G, 99th Pa. Inf.
BOODY, ROBERT M.
Sergt., Co. B, 40th N. Y. Inf.
BOURKE, JOHN G.
Priv., Co. E., 15th Pa. Cav.
BOWEN, CHESTER B.
Corp., Co. I, 1st N. Y. Drag.
BOWEY, RICHARD
Sergt., Co. C, 1st W. Va. Cav.
BOX, THOMAS J.
Capt., Co. D, 27th Ind. Inf.
BRADLEY, THOMAS W.
Capt., Cos. H and B, 124th N.
Inf.

BRADY, JAMES
Priv., Co. F, 10th N. H. Inf.
BRANDLE, JOSEPH E.
Priv., Co. C, 17th Mich. Inf.
BREST, LEWIS F.
Priv., Co. D, 57th Pa. Inf.
BRAS, EDGAR A.
Sergt., Co. K, 8th Iowa Inf.
BRANT, WILLIAM
Lieut., Co. B, 1st N. J. Vet. Btln.
BREWER, WILLIAM I.
Priv., Co. C, 2d N. Y. Cav.
BREYER, CHARLES
Sergt., Co. I, 90th Pa. Inf.
BRIGGS, ELIJAH A.
Corp., Co. B, 2d Conn. H. A.
BRONSON, JAMES H.
1st Sergt., Co. D, 5th U. S. C. T.
BROWN, CHARLES
Sergt., Co. C, 50th Pa. Inf.
BROWN, HENRI LE FEVRE
Sergt., Co. B, 72d N. Y. Inf.
BROWN, JEREMIAH Z.
Capt., Co. K, 148th Pa. Inf.
BROWN, JOHN H.
Capt., Co. A, 47th Ohio Inf.
BROWN, JOHN H.
Capt., Co. D, 12th Ky. Inf.
BROWN, MORRIS, JR.
Capt., Co. A, 126th N. Y. Inf.
BROWNELL, FRANCIS E.
Priv., Co. A, 11th N. Y. Inf.
BROWNER, AUGUST
Priv., Co. C, 1st N. Y. Art.
BRUTON, CHRISTOPHER C.
Capt., Co. C, 22d N. Y. Inf.
BRYAN, W. C.
Hosp. Steward, U. S. A.
BRYANT, ANDREW S.
Sergt., Co. A, 46th Mass. Inf.
BUCHANAN, GEORGE A.
Priv., Co. G, 148th N. Y. Inf.
BUCK, F. CLARENCE
Corp., Co. A, 21st Conn. Inf.
BUCKLEY, DENIS
Priv., Co. G, 136th N. Y. Inf.
BURBANK, JAMES H
Sergt., Co. K, 4th R. I. Inf.
BURK, MICHAEL
Priv., Co. D, 125th N. Y. Inf.
BURKE, THOMAS
1st Lieut. Co. H, 97th N. Y. Inf.
BURNS, JAMES M.
Sergt., Co. B, 1st W. Va. Inf.
BURRITT, WILLIAM W.
Priv., Co. G, 113th Ill. Inf.
CALKIN, IVERS S.
1st Sergt. Co. M, 2d N. Y. Cav.
CALLAHAN, JOHN H.
Priv., Co. B, 122d Ill. Inf.
CAMPBELL, JAMES A.
Priv., Co. A, 2d N. Y. Cav.
CAPRON, HORACE, JR.
Sergt., Co. G, 8th Ill. Cav.
CAREY, HUGH
Sergt., Co. E, 82d N. Y. Inf.
CARLISLE, CASPER
Priv., Co. F, Indpt. Pa. L. A.
CARPENTER, LOUIS H.
Capt., 9th U. S. Cav.
CARR, EUGENE A.
Col., 3d Ill. Cav.
CARR, FRANKLIN
Corp., Co. D. 124th Ohio Inf.
CART, JACOB
Priv., Co. A, 7th Pa. R. C.
CARTER, JOHN J.
2d Lieut., Co. B, 33d N. Y. Inf.
CARUANA, ORLANDO E.
Priv., Co. K, 51st N. Y. Inf.
CARY, JAMES L.
Corp., Co. G, 10th N. Y. Cav.
CASEY, DAVID
Priv., Co. C, 25th Mass. Inf.
CASEY, HENRY
Priv., Co. C, 20th Ohio Inf.
CAYER, OVILA
Sergt., Co. A, 14th U. S. Inf.
CHAMBERLAIN, ORVILLE T.
Capt., Co. G, 74th Ind. Inf.
CHAMBERS, JOSEPH B.
Priv., Co. F, 100th Pa. Inf.
CHANDLER, HENRY F.
Sergt., Co. E., 59th Mass. Inf.
CHAPMAN, JOHN
Priv., Co. B, 1st Me. H. A.
CHILD, BENJAMIN H.
Sergt., 1st R. I. L. A.
CILLEY, CLINTON A.
Capt., Co. C, 2d Minn. Inf.

CHRISTIANCY, JAMES I.
1st Lieut., Co. D, 9th Mich. Cav.
CLANCY, JAMES T.
Sergt., Co. C, 1st N. J. Cav.
CLAPP, ALBERT A.
1st Sergt., Co. G, 2d Ohio Cav.
CLARK, JAMES G.
Priv., Co. F, 88th Pa. Inf.
CLARK, JOHN W.
1st Lieut. and R. Q. M., 6th U. S. Inf.
CLARKE, DAYTON P.
Capt., Co. F, 2d Vt. Inf.
CLAUSEN, CHARLES H.
1st Lieut., Co. H, 61st Pa. Inf.
CLEVELAND, CHARLES F.
Priv., Co. C, 26th N. Y. Inf.
CLOPP, JOHN E.
Priv., Co. F, 71st Pa. Inf.
COATES, JEFFERSON
Sergt., Co. H, 7th Wis. Inf.
COFFEY, ROBERT J.
Sergt., Co. K, 4th Vt. Inf.
COHN, ABRAHAM
Sergt. Maj., 6th N. H. Inf.
COLLINS, HARRISON
Corp., Co. A, 1st Tenn. Cav.
COLLINS, THOMAS D.
Sergt., Co. H, 143d N. Y. Inf.
COLWELL, OLIVER
1st Lieut., Co. G, 95th Ohio Inf.
CONBOY, MARTIN
2d Lieut., Co. B, 37th N. Y. Inf.
CONNELL, FRUSTRIM
Corp., Co. I, 138th Pa. Inf.
CONNER RICHARD
Priv., Co. F, 6th N. J. Inf.
CONNERS, JAMES
Priv., Co. E, 43d N. Y. Inf.
COOKE, WALTER H.
Capt., Co. K, 4th Pa. Inf. Mil.
COPP, CHARLES D.
Capt., Co. C, 9th N. H. Inf.
CORLISS, GEORGE W.
Capt., Co. C, 5th Conn. Inf.
COUGHLIN, JOHN
Lieut.-Col., 10th N. H. Inf.
CREED, JOHN
Priv., Co. D, 23d Ill. Inf.
CROFT, JAMES E.
Priv., 12th Wis. L. A.
CROKER, ULRIC
Priv., Co. M, 6th Mich. Cav.
CULLEN, THOMAS
Corp., Co. I, 82d N. Y. Inf.
CUMPSTON, JAMES
Priv., Co. D, 91st Ohio Inf.
CURTIS, JOSIAH M.
2d Lieut., Co. I, 12th W. Va. Inf.
CUTTS, JAMES M.
Capt., 11th U. S. Inf.
DAVIDSIZER, JOHN A.
Sergt., Co. A, 1st Pa. Cav.
DAVIDSON, ANDREW
Asst. Surg., 47th Ohio Inf.
DAVIS, HARRY
Priv., Co. G, 46th Ohio Inf.
DAVIS, JOHN
Priv., Co. F, 17th Ind. Mtd. Inf.
DAVIS, JOSEPH
Corp., Co. C, 104th Ohio Inf.
DAVIS, THOMAS
Priv., Co. D, 2d N. Y. H. A.
DEANE, JOHN M.
Maj., 29th Mass. Inf.
DE COSTRO, JOSEPH H.
Corp., Co. I, 19th Mass. Inf.
DELAVIE, HIRAM H.
Sergt., Co. I, 11th Pa. Inf.
DE PUY, CHARLES H.
1st Sergt., Co. H, 1st Mich. S. S.
DICKEY, WILLIAM D.
Maj., 15th N. Y. H. A.
DILGER, HUBERT
Capt., Co. I, 1st Ohio L. A.
DOCKHAM, WARREN C.
Priv., Co. H, 121st N. Y. Inf.
DODD, ROBERT F.
Priv., Co. E, 27th Mich. Inf.
DODDS, EDWARD E.
Sergt., Co. C, 21st N. Y. Cav.
DODGE, FRANCIS S.
Capt. 9th U. S. Cav.
DOLLOFF, CHARLES W.
Corp., Co. K, 11th Vt. Inf.
DONALDSON, JOHN
Sergt., Co. L., 4th Pa. Cav.
DONOGHOE, TIMOTHY
Priv., Co. B, 69th N. Y. Inf.

DOODY, PATRICK
Priv., Co. E, 164th N. Y. Inf.
DORE, GEORGE H.
Sergt., Co. D, 126th N. Y. Inf.
DORLEY, AUGUST
Priv., Co. B, 1st La. Cav.
DORSEY, DECATUR
Sergt., Co. B, 39th U. S. C. T.
DOUGALL, ALLAN H.
1st Lieut., 88th Ind. Inf.
DOUGHERTY, MICHAEL
Priv., Co. M, 13th Pa. Cav.
DOWNS, HENRY W.
Sergt., Co. I, 8th Vt. Inf.
DU PONT, H. A.
Capt., 5th U. S. Art.
DURHAM, JOHN S.
Sergt., Co. F, 1st Wis. Inf.
EDDY, SAMUEL E.
Priv., Co. D, 37th Mass. Inf.
EDGERTON, NATHAN A.
Capt., Co. H, 6th U. S. Col. Inf.
EDWARDS, DAVID
Priv., Co. H, 146th N. Y. Inf.
ELLIOTT, ALEXANDER
Sergt., Co. A, 1st Pa. Cav.
ELLIOTT, RUSSELL C.
2d Lieut., Co. B, 3d Mass. Cav.
ELLIS, HORACE
Priv., Co. A, 7th Wis. Inf.
ELLIS, WILLIAM
1st Sergt., Co. K, 3d Wis. Cav.
ELLSWORTH, THOMAS F.
Capt., Co. B, 55th Mass. Inf.
ELSON, JAMES M.
Sergt., Co. C, 9th Iowa Inf.
EMBLER, ANDREW H.
Capt., Co. D, 59th N. Y. Inf.
EMMET, ROBERT TEMPLE
1st Lieut., 9th U. S. Cav.
ENDERLIN, RICHARD
Mus., Co. B, 73d Ohio Inf.
ENGLE, JAMES E.
Sergt., Co. I, 97th Pa. Inf.
EVANS, CORREN D.
Priv., Co. A, 3d Ind. Cav.
EVANS, JAMES R.
Priv., Co. H, 62d N. Y. Inf.
EVANS, THOMAS
Priv., Co. D, 54th Pa. Inf.
EVERSON, ADELBERT
Priv., Co. D, 185th N. Y. Inf.
FALCONER, JOHN A.
Corp., Co. A, 17th Mich. Inf.
FALLON, THOMAS T.
Priv., Co. K, 37th Ill. Inf.
FALLS, BENJAMIN F.
Color Sergt., Co. A, 19th Mass. Inf.
FANNING, NICHOLAS
Priv., Co. B, 4th Iowa Cav.
FASNACHT, CHARLES H.
Sergt., Co. A, 99th Pa. Inf.
FERRIS, EUGENE W.
1st Lieut. and Adjt., 30th Mass. Inf.
FLANAGAN, AUGUSTINE
Sergt., Co. A, 55th Pa. Inf.
FLYNN, CHRISTOPHER
Corp., Co. K, 14th Conn. Inf.
FORCE, MANNING F.
Brig. Gen., U. S. Vol.
FORD, GEORGE W.
1st Lieut., Co. E, 88th N. Y. Inf.
FORMAN, ALEXANDER A.
Corp., Co. E, 7th Mich. Inf.
FOUT, FREDERICK W.
1st Lieut., 15th Batt'y Ind. L. A.
FOX, HENRY M.
Sergt., Co. M, 5th Mich. Cav.
FOX, WILLIAM R.
Priv., Co. A, 95th Pa. Inf.
FREEMAN, ARCHIBALD
Priv., Co. E, 124th N. Y. Inf.
FREEMAN, HENRY B.
1st Lieut., 18th U. S. Inf.
FRENCH, SAMUEL S.
Priv., Co. E, 7th Mich. Inf.
FUNK, WEST
Sergt.-Maj., 121st Pa. Inf.
GALLOWAY, GEORGE N.
Priv., Co. G, 95th Pa. Inf.
GALLOWAY, JOHN
Comm'y Sergt. 8th Pa. Cav.
GARDINER, ASA B.
Capt., Co. I. 22d N. Y. S. M.
GARDINER, JAMES
Priv., Co. I, 36th U. S. C. T.

GARDNER, CHARLES N.
Priv., Co. E, 32d Mass. Inf.
GARDNER, ROBERT I.
Sergt., Co. K, 34th Mass. Inf.
GARRETT, WILLIAM
Sergt., Co. G, 41st Ohio Inf.
GASSON, RICHARD
Sergt., Co. K, 47th N. Y. Inf.
GAUNT, JOHN C.
Priv., Co. G, 104th Ohio Inf.
GAYLORD, LEVI B.
Sergt., Co. A, 29th Mass. Inf.
GERE, THOMAS P.
1st Lieut., 5th Minn. Inf.
GIBBS, WESLEY
Sergt., Co. B, 2d Conn. H. A.
GIFFORD, BENJAMIN
Priv., Co. H, 121st N. Y. Inf.
GILLESPIE, GEORGE L.
1st Lieut., Corps of Engs., U. S. A.
GILMORE, JOHN C.
Maj., 16th N. Y. Inf.
GINLEY, PATRICK
Priv. Co. G, 1st N. Y. L. A.
GODLEY, LEONIDAS M.
1st Sergt., Co. E, 22d Iowa Inf.
GOODMAN, WILLIAM E.
1st Lieut., Co. D, 147th Pa. Inf.
GOULD, CHAS. G.
Cap., Co. H, 5th Vt. Inf.
GOURAND, GEORGE E.
Capt. and A. D. C., U. S. Vols.
GRACE, PETER
Sergt., Co. G, 83d Pa. Inf.
GRAHAM, THOMAS N.
2d Lieut., Co. G. 15th Ind. Inf.
GRANT, GABRIEL
Surg., U. S. Vols.
GRAY, JOHN
Priv., Co. B, 5th Ohio Inf.
GREENE, OLIVER D.
Maj. ard A. A. G., U. S. Army
GREENWALT, ABRAHAM
Priv., Co. G, 104th Ohio Inf.
GRIBBEN, JAMES H.
Lieut., Co. C, 2d N. Y. Cav.
GRIMSHAW, SAMUEL
Priv., Co. B, 52d Ohio Inf.
GRUBE, GEORGE
Priv., Co. E, 158th N. Y. Inf.
GUERIN, FITZ W.
Priv., Battery A, 1st Mo. L. A.
HADLEY, OSGOOD T.
Corp., Co. E, 6th N. H. Vet. Inf.
HAGERTY, ASEL
Priv., Co. A, 61st N. Y. Inf.
HAIGHT, SIDNEY
Corp., Co. E, 1st Mich. S. S.
HALL, FRANCIS B.
Chaplain, 16th N. Y. Inf.
HALL, H. SEYMOUR
Capt., Co. F, 121st N. Y. Inf.
HALL, NEWTON H.
Corp., Co. I, 101th Ohio Inf.
HALLOCK, NATHAN A.
Priv., Co. K, 124th N. Y. Inf.
HAMMEL, HENRY A.
Sergt., Battery A, 1st Mo. L. A.
HANEY, MILTON L.
Chaplain, 55th Ill. Inf.
HANFORD, EDWARD R.
Priv., Co. H, 2d U. S. Cav.
HANNA, JOHN
1st Sergt., Co. B, 14th V. R. C.
HANSCOM, MOSES C.
Corp., Co. F, 19th Me. Inf.
HARDENBERGH, HENRY M.,
Priv., Co. G, 39th Ill. Inf.
HARMON AMZI D.
Corp., Co. K, 211th Pa. Inf.
HARRINGTON, EPHRAIM W.
Sergt., Co. G, 2d Vt. Inf.
HARRIS GEORGE W.
Priv., Co. B, 148th Pa. Inf.
HARRIS, JAMES H.
Sergt., Co. B, 38th U. S. C. T.
HARRIS, MOSES
1st Lieut., 1st U. S. Cav.
HART, WILLIAM E.
Priv., Co. B, 8th N. Y. Cav.
HARTRANFT, JOHN F.
Col., 4th Pa. Mil.
HASKELL, MARCUS M.
Sergt., Co. C, 35th Mass. Inf.
HATCH, JOHN P.
Brig. Gen., U. S. Vols.

HAWKEN, JAMES M.
Storekeeper, Q. M. Dept., U. S. A.
HAWKINS, THOMAS
Sergt.-Maj., 6th U. S. C. T.
HAYNES, ASBURY F.
Corp., Co. F, 17th Me. Inf.
HAYS, JOHN H.
Priv., Co. F, 4th Iowa Cav.
HEDGES, JOSEPH
1st Lieut. 4th U. S. Cav.
HENRY, GUY V.
Col., 40th Mass., Inf.
HERRON, FRANCIS J.
Lieut.-Col., 9th Iowa Inf.
HICKEY, DENNIS. W.
Sergt., Co. E, 2d N. Y. Cav.
HICKOK, NATHAN E.
Corp., Co. A, 8th Conn. Inf.
HIGBY, CHARLES
Priv., Co. F, 1st Pa. Cav.
HIGHLAND, PATRICK
Corp., Co. D, 23d Ill. Inf.
HILL, HENRY
Sergt., Co. C, 50th Pa. Inf.
HILL, JAMES
Sergt., Co. C, 14th N. Y. H. A.
HINKS, WILLIAM B.
Sergt.-Maj., 14th Conn. Inf.
HOFFMAN, HENRY
Corp., Co. M, 2d Ohio Cav.
HOGAN, FRANKLIN
Corp., Co. A, 45th Pa. Inf.
HOLCOMB, DANIEL J.
Priv., Co. A, 41st Oh.o Inf.
HOLEHOUSE, JAMES
Priv., Co. B, 7th Mass. Inf.
HOLLAND, MILTON M.
Sergt.-Maj., 5th U. S. C. T. Inf.
HOLMES, WILLIAM T.
Priv., Co. A, 3d Ind. Cav.
HOLTON, EDWARD A.
1st Sergt., Co. I, 6th Vt. Inf.
HOMAN, CONRAD
Color Sergt., Co. A, 29th Mass. Inf.
HOOKER, GEORGE W.
1st Lieut. Co. E, 4th Vt. Inf.
HOOPER, WILLIAM B.
Corp., Co. L, 1st N. J. Cav.
HOPPY, EDWARD
2d Lieut., Co. C, 12th V. R. C.
HOUGH, IRA
Priv., Co. E, 8th Ind. Inf.
HOULTON, WILLIAM
Comm'y Sergt., 1st W. Va.Cav.
HOWARD, HIRAM R.
Priv., Co. H, 11th Ohio Inf.
HOWARD, JAMES
Sergt., Co. K, 158th N. Y. Inf.
HOWE, ORION P.
Mus., Co. C, 55th Ill. Inf.
HOWE, WILLIAM H.
Sergt., Co. K, 29th Mass. Inf.
HUBBELL, WILLIAM S.
Capt., Co. A, 21st Conn. Inf.
HUDSON, AARON R.
Priv., Co. C, 17th Ind. Mtd. Inf.
HUGHEY, JOHN
Corp., Co. L, 2d Ohio Cav.
HUGHS, OLIVER
Corp., Co. C, 12th Ky. Inf.
HYMER, SAMUEL
Capt., Co. D, 115th Ill. Inf.
IMMELL, LORENZO D.
Corp., Co. F, 2d U. S. Art.
IRWIN, PATRICK
1st Lieut., Co. H, 14th Mich. Inf.
JAMES, ISAAC
Priv., Co. H, 110th Ohio Inf.
JAMES, MILES
Corp., Co. B, 36th U. S. C. T.
JENNINGS, JAMES T.
Priv., Co. K, 56th Pa. Inf.
JOHNSON, FOLLETT
Corp., Co. H, 60th N. Y. Inf.
JOHNSON, RUEL M.
Maj., 100th Ind. Inf.
JOHNSON, SAMUEL
Priv., Co. G, 9th Pa. Res.
JOHNSTON WILLIE
Mus., Co. D, 3d Vt. Inf.
JONES, WILLIAM
1st Sergt., Co. A, 73d N. Y. Inf.
JORDAN, ABSALOM
Corp., Co. A 3d Ind. Cav.

JUDGE, FRANCIS W.
1st Sergt., Co. K, 79th N. Y. Inf.
KAISER, JOHN
Sergt., Co. E, 2d U. S. Art.
KALTENBACH, LUTHER
Corp., Co. F, 12th Iowa Inf.
KANE, JOHN
Corp., Co. K, 100th N. Y. Inf.
KAUSS, AUGUSTUS
Corp., Co. H, 15th N. Y. H. A.
KARR, JOHN
1st Sergt., Co. D, 14th V. R. C.
KEELS, JOSEPH
Sergt.-Maj., 182d N. Y. Inf.
KELLEY, GEORGE V.
Capt. Co. A, 104th Ohio Inf.
KELLY, THOMAS
Priv., Co. A, 6th N. Y. Cav.
KEMP, JOSEPH
1st Sergt., Co. D, 5th Mich. Inf.
KENNEDY, JOHN
Priv., Co. M. 2d U. S. Art.
KENYON, JOHN S.,
Sergt., Co. D, 3d N. Y. Cav.
KENYON, SAMUEL P.
Priv., Co. B, 24th N. Y. Cav.
KEOUGH, JOHN
Corp., Co. E, 67th Pa. Inf.
KEPHART, JAMES
Priv., Co. C., 13th U. S. Inf.
KIMBALL, JOSEPH
Priv., Co. B, 2d W. Va. Cav.
KINDIG, JOHN M.
Corp., Co. A, 63d Pa. Inf.
KINSEY, JOHN
Corp., Co. B, 45th Pa. Inf.
KIRBY, DENNIS T.
Maj., 8th Mo. Inf.
KIRK, JONATHAN C.
Capt., Co. F, 20th Ind. Inf.
KLINE, HENRY
Priv., Co. E, 40th N. Y. Inf.
KNIGHT, CHARLES H.
Corp., Co. I, 9th N. H. Inf.
KOOGLE, JACOB
1st Lieut., Co. G, 7th Md. Inf.
KRAMER, THEODORE
Priv., Co. G, 188th Pa. Inf.
KUDER, JEREMIAH
Lieut., Co. A, 74th Ind. Inf.
LAING, WILLIAM
Sergt., Co. I, 158th N. Y. Inf.
LANDIS, JAMES P.
Chief Bugler, 1st Pa. Cav.
LANE, MORGAN D.
Priv., Signal Corps, U. S. A.
LANFARE, AARON S.
1st Lieut., Co. B. 1st Conn. Cav.
LARIMER, SMITH
Corp., Co. G, 2d Ohio Cav.
LAWSON, GAINES
1st Sergt., Co. D, 4th Tenn. Inf.
LAWTON, HENRY W.
Capt., Co. A, 30th Ind. Inf.
LEONARD, EDWIN
Sergt., Co. I, 37th Mass. Inf.
LEONARD, WILLIAM E.
Priv., Co. F, 85th Pa. Inf.
LEPORT, WILLIAM F.
Sergt., Co. K, 27th N. J. Inf.
LESLIE, FRANK
Priv., Co. B, 4th N. Y. Cav.
LITTLEFIELD, GEORGE H.
Corp., Co. G, 1st Me. Inf.
LOCKE, LEWIS
Priv., Co. A, 1st N. J. Cav.
LOHNAS, FRANCIS W.
Priv., Co. H, 1st Nebr. Vet. Cav.
LOVE, GEORGE M.
Col., 116th N. Y. Inf.
LOVERING, GEORGE M.
1st Sergt., Co. I, 4th Mass. Inf.
LOWER, CYRUS B.
Priv., Co. K, 13th Pa. Res.
LOYD, GEORGE
Priv., Co. A, 122d Ohio Inf.
LUCAS, GEORGE W.
Priv., Co. C, 3d Mo. Cav.
LUDWIG, CARL
Priv., 34th N. Y. Battery.
LUTHER, JAMES H.
Priv., Co. D, 7th Mass. Inf.
LYMAN, JOEL H.
Sergt., Troop B, 9th N. Y. Cav.

SARGENT, JACKSON
  Sergt., Co. D, 5th Vt. Inf.
SARTWELL, HENRY
  Sergt., Co. D, 123d N. Y. Inf.
SAVACOOL, EDWIN F.
  Capt., Co. K, 1st N. Y. Cav.
SCANLAN, PATRICK
  Priv., Co. A, 4th Mass. Cav.
SCHELLENBURGER, JOHN S.
  Corp., Co. B, 85th Pa. Inf.
SCHENCK, BENJAMIN W.
  Corp., Co. D, 116th Ill. Inf.
SCHILLER, JOHN
  Priv., Co. E, 158th N. Y. Inf.
SCHLACHTER, PHILIP
  Priv., Co. F, 73d N. Y. Inf.
SCHMAL, GEORGE W.
  Blacksmith, Co. M, 24th N. Y.
  Cav.
SCHMIDT, CONRAD
  1st Sergt., Co. K, 2d U. S. Cav.
SCHNEIDER, GEORGE
  Sergt., Co. A, 3d Md. Vet. Inf.
SCHOFIELD, DAVID S.
  Q. M. Sergt., Co. K, 5th N. Y.
  Cav.
SCHOFIELD, JOHN M.
  Maj., 1st Mo. Inf.
SCHORN, CHARLES
  Chief Bugler, Co. M, 1st W.
  Va. Cav.
SCHWAN, THEODORE
  Brig.-Gen., U. S. Vols.
SCHWENCK, MARTIN
  Sergt., Co. B, 6th U. S. Cav.
SCOTT, ALEXANDER
  Corp., Co. D, 10th Vt. Inf.
SCOTT, JULIAN A.
  Drummer, Co. E, 3d Vt. Inf.
SEAVER, THOMAS O.
  Col., 3d Vt. Inf.
SEDGWICK, IRVIN M.
  1st Sergt., Co. H, 18th V. R. C.
SESTON, CHARLES H.
  Sergt., Co. I, 11th Ind. Inf.
SEWELL, WILLIAM J.
  Col., 5th N. J. Inf.
SHAHAND, AMZI
  Corp., Co. A, 1st W. Va. Cav.
SHANES, JOHN
  Priv., Co. K, 14th W. Va. Inf.
SHEA, JOSEPH H.
  Priv., Co. K, 92d N. Y. Inf.
SHEPARD, IRWIN
  Corp., Co. E, 17th Mich. Inf.
SHEPHERD, WILLIAM
  Priv., Co. A, 3d Ind. Cav.
SHERMAN, MARSHALL
  Priv., Co. C, 1st Minn. Inf.
SHIEL, JOHN
  Sergt., Co. E, 90th Pa. Inf.
SHIELDS, BERNARD
  Priv., Co. E, 2d W. Va. Cav.
SHILLING, JOHN
  1st Sergt., Co. H, 3d Del. Inf.
SHOEMAKER, LEVI
  Sergt., Co. A, 1st W. Va. Cav.
SHOPP, GEORGE J.
  Priv., Co. E, 191st Pa. Inf.
SHUBERT, FRANK
  Sergt., Co. E, 43d N. Y. Inf.
SICKLES, DANIEL E.
  Maj.-Gen., U. S. Vols.
SIMMONS, JOHN
  Priv., Co. D, 2d N. Y. H. A.
SIMONS, CHARLES J.
  Sergt., Co. A, 9th N. H. Inf.
SIVEL, HENRY
  1st Sergt., Co. E, 2d Md. Vet.
  Inf.
SKELLIE, EBENEZER
  Corp., Co. D, 112th N. Y. Inf.
SLADEN. JOSEPH A.
  Priv., Co. A, 33 Mass. Inf.
SLOAN, ANDREW J.
  Priv., Co. H, 12th Iowa Inf.
SMITH, JAMES
  Priv., Co. I, 2d Ohio Inf.
SMITH, JOSEPH S.
  Lieut.-Col. and Comm'y Sub.,
  2d Army Corps.
SMITH, OTIS W.
  Priv., Co. G, 95th Ohio Inf.
SMITH, RICHARD
  Priv., Co. B, 95th N. Y. Inf.
SOUTHARD DAVID
  Sergt., Co. C, 1st N. J. Cav.

SOVA, JOSEPH E.
  Saddler, Co. H, 8th N. Y. Cav.
SPALDING, EDWARD B.
  Sergt., Co. E, 52d Ill. Inf.
SPILLANE, TIMOTHY
  Priv., Go. C, 16th Pa. Cav.
SPRAGUE, JOHN W.
  Col., 63d Ohio Inf.
SPURLING, ANDREW B.
  Lieut.-Col., 2d Me. Cav.
STARKINS, JOHN H.
  Priv., Co. D, 11th Ind. Inf.
STERLING, JOHN T.
  Priv., Co. D, 11th Ind. Inf.
STEWART, GEORGE W.
  1st Sergt., Co. E, 1st N. J. Cav.
STEWART, JOSEPH
  Priv., Co. G, 1st Md. Inf.
STICKELS, JOSEPH
  Sergt., Co. A, 83d Ohio Inf.
STOKES, GEORGE
  Priv., Co. C, 122d Ill. Inf.
STOREY, JOHN H. R.
  Sergt., Co. F, 109th Pa. Inf.
STORR, ROBERT
  Priv., Co. A, 15th N. Y. Eng.
STRASBAUGH, BERNARD A.
  1st Sergt., Co. A, 3d Md. Inf.
STREILE, CHRISTIAN
  Priv., Co. I, 1st N. J. Cav.
SWAN, CHARLES A.
  Priv., Co. K, 4th Iowa Cav.
SWAYNE, WAGER
  Lieut.-Col., 43d Ohio Inf.
SWEENEY, JAMES
  Priv., Co. A, 1st Vt. Cav.
TAYLOR, ANTHONY
  1st Lieut., Co. A, 15th Pa.
  Cav.
TAYLOR, RICHARD
  Priv., Co. E, 18th Ind. Inf.
TERRY, JOHN D.
  Sergt., Co. E, 23d Mass. Inf.
THATCHER, CHARLES M.
  Priv., Co. B, 1st Mich. S. S.
THAXTER, SIDNEY W.
  Maj., 1st Me. Cav.
THOMAS, CHARLES L.
  Sergt., Co. E, 11th Ohio Cav.
THOMAS, HAMPTON S.
  Maj., 1st Pa. Vet. Cav.
THOMAS, STEPHEN
  Col., 8th Vt. Inf.
THOMPSON, CHARLES A.
  Sergt., Co. D, 17th Mich. Inf.
THOMPSON, FREEMAN C.
  Corp., Co. F, 116th Ohio Inf.
THOMPSON, J. HARRY
  Surg., U. S. Vols.
THOMPSON, JAMES B.
  Sergt., Co. G, 1st Pa. Rifles.
THOMPSON, WILLIAM P.
  Sergt., Co. G, 20th Ind. Inf.
THOMSON, CLIFFORD
  1st Lieut., Co. A, 1st N. Y.
  Cav.
TIBBETTS, ANDREW W.
  Priv., Co. I, 3d Iowa Cav.
TILTON, WILLIAM
  Sergt., Co. C, 7th N. H. Inf.
TITUS, CHARLES
  Sergt., Co. H. 1st N. J. Cav.
TOBAN, JAMES W.
  Sergt. Co. C, 9th Mich. Cav.
TOBIN, JOHN M.
  Capt., Co. I, 9th Mass. Inf.
TOMPKINS, AARON B.
  Sergt., Co. G, 1st N. J. Cav.
TOMPKINS, CHARLES H.
  1st Lieut., 2d U. S. Art.
TOMPKINS, GEORGE W.
  Corp., Co. F, 124th N. Y. Inf.
TORGLER, ERNEST
  Sergt., Co. G, 37th Ohio Inf.
TRACY, AMASA S.
  Lieut.-Col., 2d Vt. Inf.
TRACY, BENJAMIN F.
  Col., 109th N. Y. Inf.
TRAYNOR, ANDREW
  Corp., Co. D, 1st Mich. Cav.
TRIBE, JOHN
  Priv., Co. G, 5th N. Y. Cav.
TUCKER, ALLAN
  Sergt., Co. F, 10th Conn. Inf.
TUCKER, JACOB R.
  Corp., Co. G, 4th Md. Inf.
TWEEDALE, JOHN
  Priv., Co. B, 15th Pa. Cav.

TWOMBLY, VOLTAIRE P
  Capt., Co. K, 2d Iowa Inf.
TYRRELL, GEORGE W.
  Corp., Co. H, 5th Ohio Inf.
URELL, MICHAEL
  Priv., Co. E, 82d N. Y. Inf.
VANCE, WILSON
  Priv., Co. B, 21st Ohio Inf.
VAN MATRE, JOSEPH
  Priv., Co. G, 116th Ohio Inf.
VANWINKLE, EDWARD
  Corp., Co. C, 148th N. Y. Inf.
VEAZEY, WHEELOCK G.
  Col., 16th Vt. Vols.
WAGEMAN, JOHN H.
  Priv., Co. I, 60th Ohio Inf.
WALL, JERRY
  Priv., Co. B, 126th N. Y. Inf.
WALLER, FRANCIS A.
  Corp., Co. I, 6th Wis. Inf.
WARD, WILLIAM H.
  Capt., Co. B, 47th Ohio Inf.
WARFEL, HENRY C.
  Priv., Troop A, 1st Pa. Cav.
WHEELER, HENRY W.
  Priv., Co. A, 2d Maine Inf.
WEBB., ALEXANDER S.
  Brig.-Gen., U. S. Vols.
WELCH, GEORGE
  Priv., Co. A, 11th Mo. Inf.
WELCH, RICHARD
  Corp., Co. E, 37th Mass. Inf.
WELLS, HENRY S.
  Priv. Co. C, 148th N. Y. Inf.
WESTERHOLD, JAMES
  Sergt., Co. G, 52d N. Y. Inf.
WHEELER, DANIEL D.
  1st Lieut., Co. G, 4th Vt. Inf.
WHERRY, WILLIAM M.
  1st Lieut., Co. D, 1st Mo. Res.
  Inf.
WHITE, ADAM
  Corp., Co. G, 11th W. Va. Inf.
WHITMORE, JOHN
  Priv., Co. F, 119th Ill. Inf.
WHITTIER, EDWARD N.
  1st Lieut., 5th Battery, Me.
  L. A.
WILEY, JAMES
  Sergt., Co. B, 59th N. Y. Inf.
WILKINS, LEANDER A.
  Sergt., Co. H, 9th N. H. Inf.
WILLCOX, ORLANDO B.
  Col. 1st Mich. Inf.
WILLIAMS, GEORGE C.
  Q. M. Sergt. 1st Battn., 14th
  U. S. Inf.
WILLIAMS, WILLIAM H.
  Priv., Co. C, 82d Ohio Inf.
WILLIAMSON, JAMES A.
  Col., 4th Iowa Inf.
WILLISTON, EDWARD B.
  1st Lieut., 2d U. S. Art.
WILSON, CHARLES E.
  Sergt., Co. A, 1st N. J. Cav.
WILSON, FRANCIS
  Corp., Co. B, 95th Pa. Inf.
WILSON, JOHN
  Sergt., Co. L, 1st N. J. Cav.
WILSON, JOHN M.
  1st Lieut., U. S. Engrs.
WISEMAN, WILLIAM H.
  1st Sergt., Co. E, 24th V. R. C.
WITHINGTON, WILLIAM H.
  Col. 17th Mich. Inf.
WOOD, H. CLAY
  1st Lieut., Asst U. S. Inf.
WOOD, LEONARD
  1st Lieut., Asst Surg., U. S. A.
WOODALL, WILLIAM H.
  Scout, Gen. Sheridan's Hdqrs.
WOODS, DANIEL A.
  Priv., Co. K, 1st Va. Cav.
WRAY, WILLIAM J.
  Sergt. Co K., 1st V. R. C.
WRIGHT, ROBERT
  Priv., Co. G, 14th U. S. Inf.
YEAGER, JACOB F.
  Priv., Co. H, 101st Ohio Inf.
YOUNG, ANDREW J.
  Sergt.. Co. F, 1st Pa. Cav.
YOUNG, CALVARY M.
  Sergt., Co. L, 3d Iowa Cav.
YOUNGS. BENJAMIN F.
  Corp., Co. I, 1st Mich. S. S.

BATTLES AND ENGAGEMENTS